AUDIT & ACCOUNTING GUIDE

Investment Companies

MAY 1, 2015

16369-349

ISBN 978-1-94165-183-4

Preface

(Updated as of May 1, 2015)

> This guide was prepared by the Investment Companies Special Committee.

About AICPA Audit and Accounting Guides

This AICPA Audit and Accounting Guide has been developed by the AICPA Investment Companies Guide Task Force to assist management in the preparation of their financial statements in conformity with U.S. generally accepted accounting principles (GAAP) and to assist practitioners in performing and reporting on their audit and attestation engagements.

This guide describes operating conditions and auditing procedures unique to the investment company industry and illustrates the form and content of investment company financial statements and related disclosures.

Because many investment companies are subject to regulation under the Investment Company Act of 1940, rules under that act are discussed extensively in this guide. However, the rules, regulations, practices, and procedures of the investment company industry have changed frequently and extensively in recent years. The independent practitioner should keep abreast of those changes as they occur.

The Financial Reporting Executive Committee (FinREC) is the designated senior committee of the AICPA authorized to speak for the AICPA in the areas of financial accounting and reporting. Conforming changes made to the financial accounting and reporting guidance contained in this guide are approved by the FinREC Chair (or his or her designee). Updates made to the financial accounting and reporting guidance in this guide exceeding that of conforming changes are approved by the affirmative vote of at least two-thirds of the members of FinREC.

This guide does the following:

- Identifies certain requirements set forth in the FASB *Accounting Standards Codification*® (ASC).

- Describes FinREC's understanding of prevalent or sole industry practice concerning certain issues. In addition, this guide may indicate that FinREC expresses a preference for the prevalent or sole industry practice, or it may indicate that FinREC expresses a preference for another practice that is not the prevalent or sole industry practice; alternatively, FinREC may express no view on the matter.

- Identifies certain other, but not necessarily all, industry practices concerning certain accounting issues without expressing FinREC's views on them.

- Provides guidance that has been supported by FinREC on the accounting, reporting, or disclosure treatment of transactions or events that are not set forth in FASB ASC.

Accounting guidance for nongovernmental entities included in an AICPA Audit and Accounting Guide is a source of nonauthoritative accounting guidance. As discussed later in this preface, FASB ASC is the authoritative source of U.S. accounting and reporting standards for nongovernmental entities, in addition to guidance issued by the SEC. Accounting guidance for governmental entities included in an AICPA Audit and Accounting Guide is a source of authoritative accounting guidance described in category (b) of the hierarchy of GAAP for state and local governmental entities and has been cleared by the GASB. AICPA members should be prepared to justify departures from GAAP, as discussed in the "Accounting Principles Rule" (AICPA, *Professional Standards*, ET sec. 1.320.001).

AICPA Audit and Accounting Guides also include guidance from the Technical Questions and Answers sections of AICPA *Technical Questions and Answers*. These questions and answers are not sources of established authoritative accounting principles as described in FASB ASC, the authoritative source of GAAP for nongovernmental entities. This material is based on selected practice matters identified by the staff of the AICPA's Technical Hotline and various other bodies within the AICPA and has not been approved, disapproved, or otherwise acted upon by any senior technical committee of the AICPA.

Auditing guidance included in an AICPA Audit and Accounting Guide is recognized as an interpretive publication as defined in AU-C section 200, *Overall Objectives of the Independent Auditor and the Conduct of an Audit in Accordance With Generally Accepted Auditing Standards* (AICPA, *Professional Standards*). Interpretive publications are recommendations on the application of generally accepted auditing standards (GAAS) in specific circumstances, including engagements for entities in specialized industries.

An interpretive publication is issued under the authority of the AICPA Auditing Standards Board (ASB) after all ASB members have been provided an opportunity to consider and comment on whether the proposed interpretive publication is consistent with GAAS. The members of the ASB have found the auditing guidance in this guide to be consistent with existing GAAS.

Although interpretive publications are not auditing standards, AU-C section 200 requires the auditor to consider applicable interpretive publications in planning and performing the audit because interpretive publications are relevant to the proper application of GAAS in specific circumstances. If the auditor does not apply the auditing guidance in an applicable interpretive publication, the auditor should document how the requirements of GAAS were complied with in the circumstances addressed by such auditing guidance.

An appendix to a guide or a guide chapter has no authoritative status. However, any auditing guidance in an appendix is considered other auditing guidance. In applying other auditing guidance, the auditor should, exercising professional judgment, assess the relevance and appropriateness of such guidance to the circumstances of the audit. Although the auditor determines the relevance of other auditing guidance, auditing guidance in an appendix to a guide or a guide chapter has been reviewed by the AICPA Audit and Attest Standards staff and the auditor may presume that it is appropriate.

Attestation guidance included in an AICPA Audit and Accounting Guide is recognized as an attestation interpretation as defined in AT section 50, *SSAE Hierarchy* (AICPA, *Professional Standards*). Attestation interpretations are recommendations on the application of Statements on Standards for Attestation Engagements (SSAEs) in specific circumstances, including engagements for entities in specialized industries. Attestation interpretations are issued under the authority of the ASB. The members of the ASB have found the attestation guidance in this guide to be consistent with existing SSAEs.

A practitioner should be aware of and consider attestation interpretations applicable to his or her attestation engagement. If the practitioner does not apply the guidance included in an applicable AICPA Audit and Accounting Guide, the practitioner should be prepared to explain how he or she complied with the SSAE provisions addressed by such attestation guidance.

The ASB is the designated senior committee of the AICPA authorized to speak for the AICPA on all matters related to auditing and attestation. Conforming changes made to the auditing and attestation guidance contained in this guide are approved by the ASB Chair (or his or her designee) and the Director of the AICPA Audit and Attest Standards Staff. Updates made to the auditing and attestation guidance in this guide exceeding that of conforming changes are issued after all ASB members have been provided an opportunity to consider and comment on whether the guide is consistent with the Statements on Auditing Standards (SASs) and the SSAEs.

Purpose and Applicability

Limitations

This guide does not discuss the application of all GAAP, GAAS, and PCAOB standards that are relevant to the preparation and audit of financial statements of investment companies. This guide is directed primarily to those aspects of the preparation and audit of financial statements that are unique to investment companies or those aspects that are considered particularly significant to them.

Recognition

AICPA Senior Committees

Auditing Standards Board

Marc A. Panucci, Member
Bruce P. Webb, *Chair*

Financial Reporting Executive Committee

Jay Seliber, Member
Jim Dolinar, *Chair*

The AICPA gratefully acknowledges those members of the AICPA Investment Companies Expert Panel (2014–2015) who reviewed or otherwise contributed to the development of this edition of the guide:

Brent Oswald, *Chair*
Mike Barkman
Elizabeth Bayston
James Giangrasso
Robert Kaufman
Chris May
Peggy McCaffrey
Megan Miller

Stephen Sadoski
Ari Samuel
Dale Thompson
Maryna Tully

In addition to the 2014–2015 expert panel members listed previously, the AICPA gratefully acknowledges those who reviewed and otherwise contributed to the development of this guide: Craig Brown, Christina Catalina, Rajan Chari, Colleen Crowley, Jaime Eichen, Brian Gallagher, Richard Grueter, Irina Khouade, Ryan J. Moore, John Russo, Robert Sidoti, Maryna Tully, and Christopher Van Voorhies.

AICPA Staff

Ivory Bare
Lead Technical Manager
Accounting and Auditing Content Development

Irina Portnoy
Senior Technical Manager
Accounting Standards
and
Staff Liaison
AICPA Investment Companies Expert Panel

Guidance Considered in This Edition

This edition of the guide has been modified by the AICPA staff to include certain changes necessary due to the issuance of authoritative guidance since the guide was originally issued, and other revisions as deemed appropriate. Authoritative guidance issued through May 1, 2015 has been considered in the development of this edition of the guide. However, this guide does not include all audit, accounting, reporting, and other requirements applicable to an entity or a particular engagement. This guide is intended to be used in conjunction with all applicable sources of authoritative guidance.

Authoritative guidance that is issued and effective for entities with fiscal years ending on or before May 1, 2015 is incorporated directly in the text of this guide. Authoritative guidance issued but not yet effective for fiscal years ending on or before May 1, 2015 is being presented as a guidance update. A guidance update is a shaded area that contains information on the guidance issued but not yet effective and a reference to appendix A, "Guidance Updates," where appropriate. The distinct presentation of this content is intended to aid the reader in differentiating content that may not be effective for the reader's purposes.

This includes relevant guidance issued up to and including the following:

- FASB Accounting Standards Update (ASU) No. 2015-07, *Fair Value Measurement (Topic 820): Disclosures for Investments in Certain Entities That Calculate Net Asset Value per Share (or Its Equivalent) (a consensus of the Emerging Issues Task Force)*

- SAS No. 129, *Amendment to Statement on Auditing Standards No. 122 Section 920*, Letters For Underwriters and Certain Other Requesting Parties, *as Amended* (AICPA, *Professional Standards*, AU-C sec. 920)

- AU-C section 9570, *The Auditor's Consideration of an Entity's Ability to Continue as a Going Concern: Auditing Interpretations of Section 570* (AICPA, *Professional Standards*, AU-C sec. 9570.01–.10)

- Statement of Position 13-2, *Performing Agreed-Upon Procedures Engagements That Address the Completeness, Mapping, Consistency, or Structure of XBRL-Formatted Information* (AICPA, *Professional Standards*, AUD sec. 55)

- SSAE No. 17, *Reporting on Compiled Prospective Financial Statements When the Practitioner's Independence Is Impaired* (AICPA, *Professional Standards*, AT sec. 301 par. .23)

- PCAOB Auditing Standard No. 18, *Related Parties* (AICPA, *PCAOB Standards and Related Rules*, Auditing Standards)

Users of this guide should consider guidance issued subsequent to those items listed previously to determine their effect on entities covered by this guide. In determining the applicability of recently issued guidance, its effective date should also be considered.

The changes made to this edition of the guide are identified in appendix J, "Schedule of Changes Made to the Text From the Previous Edition." The changes do not include all those that might be considered necessary if the guide were subjected to a comprehensive review and revision.

FASB ASC Pending Content

Presentation of Pending Content in FASB ASC

Amendments to FASB ASC (issued in the form of ASUs) are initially incorporated into FASB ASC in "pending content" boxes below the paragraphs being amended with links to the transition information. The pending content boxes are meant to provide users with information about how the guidance in a paragraph will change as a result of the new guidance.

Pending content applies to different entities at different times due to varying fiscal year-ends, and because certain guidance may be effective on different dates for public and nonpublic entities. As such, FASB maintains amended guidance in pending content boxes within FASB ASC until the roll-off date. Generally, the roll-off date is six months following the latest fiscal year end for which the original guidance being amended could still be applied.

Presentation of FASB ASC Pending Content in AICPA Audit and Accounting Guides

Amended FASB ASC guidance that is included in pending content boxes in FASB ASC on May 1, 2015, is referenced as "Pending Content" in this guide. Readers should be aware that "Pending Content" referenced in this guide will eventually be subjected to FASB's roll-off process and no longer be labeled as "Pending Content" in FASB ASC (as discussed in the previous paragraph).

Terms Used to Define Professional Requirements in This AICPA Audit and Accounting Guide

Any requirements described in this guide are normally referenced to the applicable standards or regulations from which they are derived. Generally the terms used in this guide describing the professional requirements of the referenced standard setter (for example, the ASB) are the same as those used in the applicable standards or regulations (for example, *must* or *should*). However, where the accounting requirements are derived from FASB ASC, this guide uses *should*, whereas FASB uses *shall*. The Notice to Constituents in FASB ASC states that FASB considers the terms *should* and *shall* to be comparable terms.

Readers should refer to the applicable standards and regulations for more information on the requirements imposed by the use of the various terms used to define professional requirements in the context of the standards and regulations in which they appear.

Certain exceptions apply to these general rules, particularly in those circumstances where the guide describes prevailing or preferred industry practices for the application of a standard or regulation. In these circumstances, the applicable senior committee responsible for reviewing the guide's content believes the guidance contained herein is appropriate for the circumstances.

Applicability of Generally Accepted Auditing Standards and PCAOB Standards

Appendix A, "*Council* Resolution Designating Bodies to Promulgate Technical Standards," to "Compliance With Standards Rule," of the AICPA Code of Professional Conduct recognizes both the ASB and the PCAOB as standard setting bodies designated to promulgate auditing, attestation, and quality control standards. Paragraph .01 of "Compliance With Standards Rule" requires an AICPA member who performs an audit to comply with the applicable standards.

Audits of the financial statements of those entities not subject to the oversight authority of the PCAOB (that is, those entities whose audits are not within the PCAOB's jurisdiction—hereinafter referred to as *nonissuers*) are to be conducted in accordance with GAAS as issued by the ASB, a senior committee of the AICPA. The ASB develops and issues standards in the form of SASs through a due process that includes deliberation in meetings open to the public, public exposure of proposed SASs, and a formal vote. The SASs and their related interpretations are codified in the AICPA's *Professional Standards*.

Audits of the financial statements of those entities subject to the oversight authority of the PCAOB (that is, those entities whose audits are within the PCAOB's jurisdiction—hereinafter referred to as *issuers*) are to be conducted in accordance with standards established by the PCAOB, a private sector, nonprofit corporation created by the Sarbanes-Oxley Act of 2002. The SEC has oversight authority over the PCAOB, including the approval of its rules, standards, and budget.

The auditing content in this guide primarily discusses GAAS issued by the ASB and is applicable to audits of nonissuers. Appendix B, "Clarified Auditing Standards and PCAOB Standards," of this guide is included to assist auditors in comparing the clarified standards, many of which are referenced throughout this guide, to the PCAOB standards. Appendix B of this guide is prepared for informational and reference purposes only. It has not been reviewed, approved, disapproved, or otherwise acted on by the PCAOB or any senior committee of the AICPA and does not represent official positions or pronouncements of the PCAOB or the AICPA.

Considerations for audits of issuers in accordance with PCAOB standards may also be discussed within this guide's chapter text. When such discussion is provided, the related paragraphs are designated with the following title: *Considerations for Audits Performed in Accordance With PCAOB Standards.*

Guidance for Issuers

Management Assessment of Internal Control

As directed by Section 404 of the Sarbanes-Oxley Act of 2002, the SEC adopted final rules requiring companies subject to the reporting requirements of the 1934 Act, other than registered investment companies and certain other entities, to include in their annual reports a report from management on the company's internal control over financial reporting. Business development companies do not fall within the scope exception contained in Section 405 and are required to include a report from management on the company's internal control over financial reporting. However, see paragraphs 1.55–.57 of this guide for discussion of the Jumpstart Our Business Startups Act of 2012, which explains that certain business development companies may be temporarily exempt from certain financial reporting disclosures and regulatory requirements, including Section 404 of the Sarbanes-Oxley Act of 2002.

The SEC rules clarify that management's assessment and report is limited to internal control over financial reporting.

As established by Rule 12b-2 of the 1934 Act, the auditor's attestation for large accelerated and accelerated filers is required. However, Section 404(c) of the Sarbanes-Oxley Act of 2002 provides that an attestation report of a registered public accounting firm on internal control over financial reporting is not required for an issuer that is neither an accelerated filer nor a large accelerated filer.

Applicability of Quality Control Standards

QC section 10, *A Firm's System of Quality Control* (AICPA, *Professional Standards*), addresses a CPA firm's responsibilities for its system of quality control for its accounting and auditing practice. A system of quality control consists of policies that a firm establishes and maintains to provide it with reasonable assurance that the firm and its personnel comply with professional standards, as well as applicable legal and regulatory requirements. The policies also provide the firm with reasonable assurance that reports issued by the firm are appropriate in the circumstances. This section applies to all CPA firms with respect to engagements in their accounting and auditing practice.

AU-C section 220, *Quality Control for an Engagement Conducted in Accordance With Generally Accepted Auditing Standards* (AICPA, *Professional Standards*), addresses the auditor's specific responsibilities regarding quality control procedures for an audit of financial statements. When applicable, it also addresses the responsibilities of the engagement quality control reviewer.

Because of the importance of audit quality, we have added a new appendix, appendix H, "Overview of Statements on Quality Control Standards," to this guide. Appendix H summarizes key aspects of the quality control standard. This summarization should be read in conjunction with QC section 10 and AU-C section 220, as applicable.

Alternatives Within U.S. Generally Accepted Accounting Principles

The Private Company Council (PCC), established by the Financial Accounting Foundation's Board of Trustees in 2012, and FASB, working jointly, will mutually agree on a set of criteria to decide whether and when alternatives within U.S. GAAP are warranted for private companies. Based on those criteria, the PCC reviews and proposes alternatives within U.S. GAAP to address the needs of users of private company financial statements. These U.S. GAAP alternatives may be applied to those entities that are not public business entities, not-for-profits, or employee benefit plans.

The FASB ASC Master Glossary defines a *public business entity* as:

> A public business entity is a business entity meeting any one of the criteria below. Neither a not-for-profit entity nor an employee benefit plan is a business entity.
>
> *a.* It is required by the U.S. Securities and Exchange Commission (SEC) to file or furnish financial statements, or does file or furnish financial statements (including voluntary filers), with the SEC (including other entities whose financial statements or financial information are required to be or are included in a filing).
>
> *b.* It is required by the Securities Exchange Act of 1934 (the Act), as amended, or rules or regulations promulgated under the Act, to file or furnish financial statements with a regulatory agency other than the SEC.
>
> *c.* It is required to file or furnish financial statements with a foreign or domestic regulatory agency in preparation for the sale of or for purposes of issuing securities that are not subject to contractual restrictions on transfer.
>
> *d.* It has issued, or is a conduit bond obligor for, securities that are traded, listed, or quoted on an exchange or an over-the-counter market.
>
> *e.* It has one or more securities that are not subject to contractual restrictions on transfer, and it is required by law, contract, or regulation to prepare U.S. GAAP financial statements (including footnotes) and make them publicly available on a periodic basis (for example, interim or annual periods). An entity must meet both of these conditions to meet this criterion.
>
> An entity may meet the definition of a *public business entity* solely because its financial statements or financial information is included in another entity's filing with the SEC. In that case, the entity is only a public business entity for purposes of financial statements that are filed or furnished with the SEC.

Considerations related to alternatives for private companies have not been discussed within this guide's chapter text as of May 1, 2015.

AICPA.org Website

The AICPA encourages you to visit the website at www.aicpa.org and the Financial Reporting Center at www.aicpa.org/FRC. The Financial Reporting Center supports members in the execution of high quality financial reporting. Whether you are a financial statement preparer or a member in public practice, this center provides exclusive member-only resources for the entire financial reporting process, and provides timely and relevant news, guidance and examples supporting the financial reporting process, including accounting, preparing financial statements and performing compilation, review, audit, attest or assurance and advisory engagements. Certain content on the AICPA's websites referenced in this guide may be restricted to AICPA members only.

Select Recent Developments Significant to This Guide

ASB's Clarity Project

To address concerns over the clarity, length, and complexity of its standards, the ASB redrafted standards for clarity and also converged the standards with the International Standards on Auditing, issued by the International Auditing and Assurance Standards Board. As part of redrafting the standards, they now specify more clearly the objectives of the auditor and the requirements with which the auditor has to comply when conducting an audit in accordance with GAAS. The clarified auditing standards are now fully effective.

As part of the clarity project the "AU-C" identifier was established to avoid confusion with references to existing "AU" sections. The AU-C identifier had been scheduled to revert back to the AU identifier at the end of 2013, by which time the previous AU sections would be superseded for all engagements. However, in response to user requests, the AU-C identifier will be retained indefinitely. The superseded AU sections were removed from *Professional Standards* at the end of 2013, as scheduled.

The ASB has completed the Clarity Project with the issuance of SAS No. 128, *Using the Work of Internal Auditors* (AICPA, *Professional Standards*), in February 2014. This guidance was effective for audits of financial statements for periods ending on or after December 15, 2014.

AICPA's Ethics Codification Project

AICPA's Professional Ethics Executive Committee (PEEC) restructured and codified the AICPA Code of Professional Conduct so that members and other users of the code can apply the rules and reach appropriate conclusions more easily and intuitively. This is referred to as the AICPA Ethics Codification Project.

Although PEEC believes it was able to maintain the substance of the existing AICPA ethics standards through this process and limited substantive changes to certain specific areas that were in need of revision, the numeric citations and titles of interpretations have all changed. In addition, the ethics rulings are no longer in a question and answer format but rather, have been drafted as interpretations, incorporated into interpretations as examples, or deleted where deemed appropriate. For example

- Rule 101, *Independence* [ET sec. 101 par. .01] is referred to as the "Independence Rule" [ET sec. 1.200.001] in the revised code.

- the content from the ethics ruling entitled "Financial Services Company Client has Custody of a Member's Assets" [ET sec. 191.081–.082] is incorporated into the "Brokerage and Other Accounts" interpretation [ET sec. 1.255.020] found under the subtopic "Depository, Brokerage, and Other Accounts" [ET sec. 1.255] of the "Independence" topic [ET sec. 1.200].

The revised code was effective December 15, 2014 and is available at http://pub.aicpa.org/codeofconduct/Ethics.aspx. References to the code have be updated in this guide. To assist users in locating in the revised code content from the prior code, PEEC created a mapping document. The mapping document is available in Excel format in appendix D, "Mapping Document," in the revised code.

TABLE OF CONTENTS

Chapter   Paragraph

Chapter 1

Overview of the Investment Company Industry

FASB Accounting Standards Update (ASU) No. 2014-09, *Revenue from Contracts with Customers (Topic 606)*

FASB ASU No. 2014-09, issued in May 2014, is effective for annual reporting periods of public entities, as defined, beginning after December 15, 2016, including interim periods within that reporting period. Early application is not permitted.

For other entities, ASU No. 2014-09 is effective for annual reporting periods beginning after December 15, 2017, and interim periods within annual periods beginning after December 15, 2018. Other entities may elect to adopt the standard earlier, however, only as of the following:

- An annual reporting period beginning after December 15, 2016, including interim periods within that reporting period (public entity, as defined, effective date), or
- An annual reporting period beginning after December 15, 2016, and interim periods within annual periods beginning after December 15, 2017, or
- An annual reporting period beginning after December 15, 2017, including interim periods within that reporting period

In April 2015, FASB issued a proposed ASU to defer the effective date of FASB ASU No. 2014-09. Readers should continue to monitor the status of this proposed ASU.

ASU No. 2014-09 provides a framework for revenue recognition and supersedes or amends several of the revenue recognition requirements in FASB *Accounting Standards Codification* (ASC) 605, *Revenue Recognition*, as well as guidance within the 900 series of industry-specific topics, including FASB ASC 946, *Financial Services—Investment Companies*. The standard applies to any entity that either enters into contracts with customers to transfer goods or services or enters into contracts for the transfer of nonfinancial assets unless those contracts are within the scope of other standards (for example, insurance or lease contracts).

Readers are encouraged to consult the full text of this ASU on FASB's website at www.fasb.org.

The AICPA has formed 16 industry task forces to assist in developing a new Accounting Guide on revenue recognition that will provide helpful hints and illustrative examples for how to apply the new standard. Revenue recognition implementation issues identified by the Asset Management Revenue Recognition Task Force will be available for informal comment, after review by the AICPA Financial Reporting Executive Committee, at www.aicpa.org/InterestAreas/FRC/AccountingFinancialReporting/RevenueRecognition/Pages/RRTF-InvestmentCo.aspx.

Readers are encouraged to submit comments to revreccomments@aicpa.org.

For more information on ASU No. 2014-09, see appendix I, "The New Revenue Recognition Standard: FASB ASU No. 2014-09," of this guide.

© Update 1-1 *Accounting and Reporting*: Fair Value Measurement

FASB ASU No. 2015-07, *Fair Value Measurement (Topic 820): Disclosures for Investments in Certain Entities That Calculate Net Asset Value per Share (or Its Equivalent) (a consensus of the Emerging Issues Task Force)*, was issued in May 2015. The amendments are effective for public business entities for fiscal years beginning after December 15, 2015, and interim periods within those fiscal years. For all other entities, the amendments are effective for fiscal years beginning after December 15, 2016, and interim periods within those fiscal years. A reporting entity should apply the amendments retrospectively to all periods presented. The retrospective approach requires that an investment for which fair value is measured using the net asset value per share practical expedient be removed from the fair value hierarchy in all periods presented in an entity's financial statements. Earlier application is permitted.

These amendments apply to reporting entities that elect to measure the fair value of an investment within the scope of paragraphs 4–5 of FASB ASC 820-10-15 using the net asset value per share (or its equivalent) practical expedient in FASB ASC 820-10-35-59.

FASB ASC 820, *Fair Value Measurement*, permits a reporting entity, as a practical expedient, to measure the fair value of certain investments using the net asset value per share of the investment. Currently, investments valued using the practical expedient are categorized within the fair value hierarchy on the basis of whether the investment is redeemable with the investee at net asset value on the measurement date, never redeemable with the investee at net asset value, or redeemable with the investee at net asset value at a future date. For investments that are redeemable with the investee at a future date, a reporting entity must consider the length of time until those investments become redeemable to determine the classification within the fair value hierarchy and whether they are near term for the assessment of the potential inclusion of a cash flow statement.

The amendments remove the requirement to categorize within the fair value hierarchy all investments for which fair value is measured using the net asset value per share practical expedient. However, the amendments require sufficient information to be provided to permit reconciliation of the fair value of assets categorized within the fair value hierarchy to the amounts presented in the statement of financial condition. The amendments also remove the requirement to make certain disclosures for all investments that are eligible to be measured at fair value using the net asset value per share practical expedient. Rather, those disclosures are limited to investments for which the entity has elected to measure the fair value using that practical expedient.

Readers are encouraged to consult the full text of this ASU on FASB's website at www.fasb.org.

Presentation of Pending Content in FASB ASC

Amendments to FASB ASC (issued in the form of ASUs) are initially incorporated into FASB ASC in "Pending Content" boxes located below the paragraphs being amended with links to the transition information. The pending content boxes are meant to provide users with information about how the guidance in a paragraph will change as a result of the new guidance.

Pending content applies to different entities at different times due to varying fiscal year-ends, and because certain guidance may be effective on different dates for public entities, as defined, and other entities. As such, FASB maintains amended guidance in pending content boxes within FASB ASC until the roll-off date. Generally, the roll-off date is six months following the latest fiscal year-end for which the original guidance being amended could still be applied.

Presentation of Pending Content in AICPA Audit and Accounting Guides

Amended FASB ASC guidance that is included in pending content boxes in FASB ASC on May 1, 2015, is referenced as "Pending Content" in this guide. Pending content referenced or discussed within this guide's chapter text is fully effective as of the date of this guide and should be considered by readers for current reporting periods. Pending content referenced or discussed within this guide's shaded "Guidance Updates" boxes or within appendix A, "Guidance Updates," is not fully effective as of the date of this guide. Readers should be aware that pending content" referenced in this guide will eventually be subjected to FASB's roll-off process and will no longer be labeled as "Pending Content" in FASB ASC (as discussed in the previous paragraph).

Introduction

1.01 The investment company industry is highly specialized; intensely competitive; and may be subject to specific governmental regulation, special tax treatment, and public scrutiny. Accordingly, before starting an engagement to audit an investment company's financial statements, an auditor should become familiar with the entity's business, its organization, and operating characteristics and the industry's terminology; legislation; and, if applicable, relevant securities and income tax laws and regulations. This chapter provides an introductory review of these topics.

Guide Application

1.02 *Auditing.* The auditing procedures discussed in this guide apply to most investment companies.[1] Fundamental considerations associated with the planning and execution of investment company financial statement audits are included in chapter 11, "General Auditing Considerations," of this guide, while auditor report considerations are provided in chapter 12, "Independent Auditor's Reports and Client Representations." When applicable, audit considerations directly associated with certain specific accounting principles are included within the respective chapters of this guide where the specific accounting principles are discussed.

---

[1] The auditing content in this guide focuses primarily on generally accepted auditing standards issued by the Auditing Standards Board and is applicable to audits of nonissuers. See the section "Applicability of Generally Accepted Auditing Standards and PCAOB Standards" of the preface to this guide for a discussion of the definitions of issuer and nonissuer as used throughout this guide. Appendix B, "Clarified Auditing Standards and PCAOB Standards," of this guide is included to assist auditors in comparing the clarified standards, many of which are referenced throughout this guide, to the PCAOB standards. Further, considerations for audits of issuers in accordance with PCAOB standards may be discussed within this guide's chapter text. When such discussion is provided, the related paragraphs are designated with the following title: *Considerations for Audits Performed in Accordance With PCAOB Standards.*

1.03 *Accounting.* The accounting principles discussed in this guide apply to all investment companies within the scope of FASB ASC 946 (as discussed in the following section of this chapter).

1.04 Consistent with "Pending Content" in FASB ASC 946-10-15-3, this guide does not apply to real estate investment trusts, which have some of the attributes of investment companies but are scoped out of FASB ASC 946.[2]

Investment Companies Defined—Scope of FASB ASC 946

1.05 "Pending Content" in FASB ASC 946-10-15-2 requires the performance of an assessment to determine whether an entity is an *investment company* for accounting purposes, and to be within the scope of industry-specific guidance in FASB ASC 946.

1.06 An entity regulated under the Investment Company Act of 1940 (1940 Act) is an investment company for accounting purposes, pursuant to "Pending Content" in FASB ASC 946-10-15-4.

1.07 "Pending Content" in paragraphs 5–9 of FASB ASC 946-10-15 states that entities that are not regulated under the 1940 Act are required to meet certain fundamental characteristics to be considered investment companies, and are also required to be assessed for other typical characteristics of investment companies. An entity's purpose and design should be considered when conducting the assessment. An entity that does not have the fundamental characteristics is not an investment company. However, failing to meet one or more of the typical characteristics does not necessarily preclude an entity from being an investment company. If an entity does not possess one or more of the typical characteristics, judgment should be applied and a determination made, considering all facts and circumstances, how the entity's activities continue to be consistent (or are not consistent) with those of an investment company.

1.08 An entity must have the following fundamental characteristics to be an investment company:

    a. It is an entity that does both of the following:

        i. Obtains funds from one or more investors and provides the investor(s) with investment management services

        ii. Commits to its investor(s) that its business purpose and only substantive activities are investing the funds solely for returns from capital appreciation, investment income, or both

    b. The entity or its affiliates do not obtain or have the objective of obtaining returns or benefits from an investee or its affiliates that are not normally attributable to ownership interests or that are other than capital appreciation or investment income.

---

[2] The summary section of FASB Accounting Standards Update No. 2013-08, *Financial Services— Investment Companies (Topic 946): Amendments to the Scope, Measurement, and Disclosure Requirements*, states that FASB does not intend for the amendments to change practice for real estate entities for which it is industry practice to issue financial statements using the measurement principles in FASB *Accounting Standards Codification* (ASC) 946, *Financial Services—Investment Companies*. Certain real estate entities for which it is industry practice to issue financial statements consistent with the measurement principles of FASB ASC 946 may continue to do so until FASB readdresses financial reporting by these entities as part of another project.

In addition, an entity should assess whether it has the following typical characteristics of an investment company:

    a. More than one investment

    b. More than one investor

    c. Investors that are not related parties of the parent entity (if there is a parent) or the investment manager

    d. Ownership interests in the form of equity or partnership interests

    e. Substantially all of its investments are managed on a fair value basis

1.09 Readers should consider and utilize the related implementation guidance in "Pending Content" in FASB ASC 946-10-55, which is an integral part of assessing investment company status and provides additional guidance for that assessment.

1.10 The aforementioned definition of an investment company has similarities to the legal definition of an investment company in the federal securities laws. Securities laws explain that typically, an investment company sells its capital shares to investors; invests the proceeds, mostly in securities, to achieve its investment objectives; and distributes to its shareholders the net income earned on its investments and net gains realized on the sale of its investments.

1.11 All existing entities were required to conduct the assessment of investment company status upon the effective date of FASB ASU No. 2013-08, *Financial Services—Investment Companies (Topic 946): Amendments to the Scope, Measurement, and Disclosure Requirements.* Entities formed after the effective date of ASU No. 2013-08 should conduct this assessment upon formation of the entity. After its adoption of ASU No. 2013-08, an entity should reassess whether it is or is not an investment company only if there is a subsequent change in the purpose and design of the entity or if the entity is no longer regulated under the 1940 Act. For information about change in status and the transition to guidance in ASU No. 2013-08, readers should review "Pending Content" in FASB ASC 946-10-25 and related implementation guidance and illustrative examples in "Pending Content" in FASB ASC 946-10-55.

Types of Investment Companies

1.12 Several types of entities may meet the aforementioned investment company scope criteria, including but not limited to

- management investment companies registered under or otherwise regulated by the 1940 Act;
- unit investment trusts (UITs);
- common (collective) trust funds;
- investment partnerships;
- special purpose funds;
- venture capital investment companies, private equity funds, hedge funds;
- certain separate accounts of life insurance companies; and
- offshore funds.

See the "Definition and Classification" section of this chapter for further discussion of these and other types of entities.

1.13 Management investment companies may include

- open-end funds, usually known as mutual funds, and
- closed-end funds, including

  — small business investment companies (SBICs) and
  — business development companies (BDCs).

1.14 Investment companies may be organized under various legal entity forms, including corporations (in the case of mutual funds, under the laws of certain states that authorize the issuance of common shares redeemable on demand of individual shareholders); common law trusts (sometimes called business trusts); limited partnerships, limited liability investment partnerships and companies; and other more specialized entities such as separate accounts of insurance companies that are not in themselves entities at all except in the technical definition of the 1940 Act.

1.15 Mutual funds and closed-end investment companies registered with the SEC under the 1940 Act are common forms of investment companies and are required to follow many rules and regulations prescribed by the SEC. These rules and regulations are discussed within the "Regulation" section of this chapter and elsewhere throughout this guide.

History

1.16 One of the first documented concepts of investment companies originated in England in 1868 with the formation of the Foreign & Colonial Government Trust. Its purpose was to provide investors of moderate means with the same advantages as those of more affluent investors (that is, to diminish risk by spreading investments over many different securities). Massachusetts Investors Trust, the first mutual fund, was organized in 1924.

1.17 The investment company industry has changed considerably since its origin and has attracted insurance companies, brokerage firms, conglomerates, banks, and others as sponsors to perform advisory or distribution services. Initially, the industry was characterized by one- or two-person managements, relatively simple investment techniques, and rudimentary sales practices. Today, investment techniques are more sophisticated, and selling practices are more creative and aggressive. For example, in the 1970s, tax-exempt and money market funds came into use; in the 1980s, funds entered foreign markets; in the 1990s, funds entered the derivative security markets, which necessitated new investment expertise and increasingly sophisticated data processing capability; and in the 2000s, funds expanded their derivative activity investing in asset-backed securities and the like, which can be difficult to value. Fund organization structures have become more complex with the introduction of multiple class funds, series funds, master-feeder funds, funds of funds, and exchange traded funds. These funds potentially provide greater flexibility to multiple markets such as retail customers (who may be charged a front-end load, level load, or contingent deferred sales load) and institutions.

Definition and Classification

1.18 The term *mutual fund* is the popular name for an open-end management investment company (open-end company) as defined in the 1940 Act. An open-end company stands ready to redeem its outstanding shares, based on net asset value, at any time. Shares of an open-end company typically are not traded. Most open-end companies offer their shares for sale to the public continuously, although they are not required to do so. The price at which the shares of mutual funds are sold is determined by dividing each fund's net assets, generally stated at fair value, by the number of its shares outstanding; the resulting net asset value per share may be increased by a sales charge, called a *load*, which provides commissions to the underwriter and dealer. Funds whose shares are sold at net asset value without a sales charge or that have a 12b-1 plan (see paragraph 8.13 of this guide) that charges not more than 0.25 percent of average net assets per year (that is, 25 basis points) are known as *no-load funds*. Some funds or classes of shares of funds may charge contingent deferred sales loads or fees when shares are redeemed.

1.19 Unlike an open-end company, a closed-end management investment company generally does not offer to redeem its outstanding capital shares on a daily basis. However, some closed-end funds do make periodic repurchase offers for their outstanding shares. Those closed-end funds that repurchase their shares on a periodic basis at stated intervals are commonly known as interval funds. The outstanding shares of closed-end funds that are not considered to be interval funds are usually exchange listed and traded on the open market at prices that generally differ from net asset value per share, although market prices are influenced by net asset value per share reported regularly in financial publications. Most closed-end companies offer their shares to the public in discrete offerings, although some closed-end funds offer their shares on a continuous basis. Closed-end investment companies may offer their shareholders a dividend reinvestment plan. Investments are valued, and net asset value per share is calculated, using the same method as mutual funds.

1.20 Investment companies are grouped according to their primary investment objectives (for example, income, growth, balanced, money market, tax exempt, or combinations of those groups). The kinds of investments made by those funds reflect their stated objectives. For example, growth funds invest almost exclusively in securities with appreciation potential, whereas money market funds invest solely in short-term debt instruments.

1.21 Investment companies registered with the SEC under the 1940 Act are classified as diversified companies or nondiversified companies.[3] According to the 1940 Act, shareholder approval is required for an investment company registered as diversified to become nondiversified but not for a company registered as nondiversified to become diversified. If a nondiversified company operates as a diversified company, it may change back to a nondiversified company

---

[3] As defined in Section 5(b) of the Investment Company Act of 1940 (1940 Act), a *diversified company* is defined as follows: at least 75 percent of the value of its total assets is represented by cash and cash items (including receivables), government securities, securities of other investment companies, and other securities for the purposes of this calculation limited in respect of any one issuer to an amount not greater in value than 5 percent of the value of the total assets of such management company and to not more than 10 percent of the outstanding voting securities of such issuer. A *nondiversified company* means any management company other than a diversified company.

within three years of the change to a diversified company without shareholder approval, provided that its registration statement has not been amended.[4]

1.22 Closed-end management investment companies include SBICs and BDCs. An *SBIC* is an entity that provides equity capital, long-term loans, or both to small businesses; is licensed by the Small Business Administration (SBA) under the Small Business Investment Act of 1958; and may also be registered under the 1940 Act or be a subsidiary of another company. It may obtain financing from the federal government in the form of subordinated debentures based on the amount of its equity capital and the amount of its funds invested in venture-type investments. A *BDC* is an entity that invests in small, upcoming businesses and often makes available significant managerial assistance to portfolio companies. Amendments to the 1940 Act, which were enacted in the 1980's, provided for the formation of BDCs under specified regulations in Sections 54–65, which allow greater flexibility and exemption from many 1940 Act provisions applicable to registered investment companies (for example, greater flexibility when dealing with their portfolio companies, issuing securities, and compensating their managers). In addition, BDCs are not required to register as investment companies under the 1940 Act. They are, however, required to register their securities under the Securities Exchange Act of 1934. BDCs are generally publically traded investment vehicles. (These closed-end companies are discussed in appendix C, "Venture Capital, Business Development Companies, and Small Business Investment Companies," of this guide.)

1.23 A UIT is an investment company organized under a trust indenture or similar instrument and registered under the 1940 Act. A UIT has no board of directors or trustees and issues only redeemable units, each representing an undivided interest in a group of securities (such as corporate debentures or municipal debt) or a unit of specified securities or securities of a single issuer (such as shares of a particular mutual fund). UITs that provide a formal method of accumulating mutual fund shares under a periodic payment plan or a single payment plan are commonly known as contractual plans.

1.24 An exchange-traded fund (ETF) is a type of open-end management investment company (or, less frequently, a UIT). Currently, ETFs are required to obtain exemptive relief from the SEC from various rules and regulations under the 1940 Act. ETF shares are listed on a stock exchange and trade throughout the day at market prices, in a manner similar to a closed-end fund. However, unlike an open-end fund, individual ETF shares are not redeemable on a daily basis directly from the fund. Rather, ETFs issue and redeem shares either in–kind or in cash in institutional lots, typically 25,000 shares or more (referred to as *creation units*) to authorized participants. The ability to issue and redeem creation units of ETF shares tends to act as an arbitrage mechanism which can help maintain the ETF's trading price at, or close to, the net asset value per share of the underlying portfolio, although there is no guarantee that the trading price will approximate net asset value at any given time. While the majority of ETFs seek to replicate various stock and bond indices, there have been increasing efforts to obtain SEC approval to launch various forms of periodically disclosed active ETF portfolios (for example, disclosing portfolios every 90 days similar to mutual funds compared to the current requirement to

---

[4] Rule 13a-1 of the 1940 Act.

provide daily portfolio disclosures), including the approval at the end of 2014 of a structure that is called an exchange-traded managed fund (ETMF).

1.25 The term *hedge fund* is a general, nonlegal term used to describe private, unregistered investment pools that are not widely available to the public and have traditionally been limited to accredited investors and large institutions. Hedge funds likely originated as private investment funds that combined long and short equity positions within a single leveraged investment portfolio. Currently, hedge funds employ a wide variety of trading strategies and techniques to generate financial returns, and may or may not utilize complex derivative instruments or leverage in the investment portfolio. Hedge funds are not mutual funds and, as such, are not subject to certain regulations that apply to mutual funds for the protection of its investors.

1.26 The term *private equity fund* is a general, nonlegal term used to describe private, unregistered investment pools that are not widely available to the public and have traditionally been limited to accredited investors and large institutions. Private equity funds typically seek to generate returns through longer term appreciation from investments in privately held and nonlisted publicly traded companies (collectively "private companies"). Private equity funds often obtain equity interests (controlling or significant minority interests) and, to a lesser extent, debt of private companies that allow for active involvement in investee operations, restructuring, and merger and acquisition activity, through board oversight positions. A private equity fund is typically a limited partnership or limited liability company with a fixed term, generally of 10 years (often with annual extensions) and at inception, investors make an unfunded commitment to the fund, which is then drawn upon over the term of the fund.

1.27 A *venture capital investment company* is a general, nonlegal term used to describe a closed-end company whose primary investment objective is capital growth and whose capital is invested at above-average risk to form or develop companies with new ideas, products, or processes. It is generally not registered under the 1940 Act.

1.28 A *commodity pool* is an investment vehicle that is organized as a limited partnership, limited liability company, trust, corporation, or similar form of enterprise, and structured so that the funds of investors are combined into a single investment vehicle for the purpose of trading in commodity interests, which include futures contracts, options on futures contracts, and swaps. Many pools also trade other financial instruments, including foreign currencies, forward contracts and securities. Generally, a commodity pool is legally structured so that an investor, other than the general partner, cannot lose more than his or her investment and so that the pool itself is not subject to U.S. tax. A commodity pool is not mutually exclusive from the types of investment companies summarized within this chapter section; rather, any type of investment company may also be considered a commodity pool. A commodity pool is organized and administered by one or more commodity pool operators (CPOs) and those CPOs may use commodity trading advisers (CTAs) to execute commodity trading strategies. See regulatory considerations associated with commodity pools in paragraphs 1.58–.59.

1.29 For descriptions and discussion regarding funds of funds, masterfeeder funds, and multiple-class structures, see chapter 5, "Complex Capital Structures," of this guide.

Organizations Providing Services to Investment Companies

1.30 Most investment companies have no employees; however, registered investment companies are required to have a chief compliance officer who may or may not be compensated wholly or partially by the investment company. Portfolio management, recording of shares, administration, recordkeeping, distribution, and custodianship are examples of significant activities that are performed for such investment companies. These activities generally are performed by organizations other than the investment company (for example, investment adviser [manager or general partner], transfer agent, administrator, recordkeeping agent, principal underwriter [distributor], and a custodian). The distributor is often a separate division or subsidiary company of the investment adviser or administrator. The use of agents to perform accounting or other administrative functions does not relieve the investment company's officers and directors or trustees (or equivalent) of the responsibility for overseeing the maintenance and reliability of accounting records and the fairness of financial reports. Management investment companies are governed by a board of directors or trustees that has certain responsibilities, as dictated by the 1940 Act. Many nonregistered investment companies have boards of directors or trustees which have similar responsibilities to those of the 1940 Act. The board's responsibilities are highlighted throughout this guide.

The Investment Adviser

1.31 The investment adviser or manager generally provides investment advice, research services, and certain administrative services under a contract, commonly referred to as the investment advisory agreement. The investment advisory agreement provides for an annual fee, which is often based on a specified percentage of net assets. The fee schedules of many contracts provide for reduced percentage rates on net assets in excess of specified amounts (break points). Other contracts may have performance fee schedules that provide for a basic fee percentage plus a bonus, or less a penalty, based on a comparison of the investment company's performance to a market index specified in the investment advisory agreement (sometimes referred to as a "fulcrum fee"). If a performance fee schedule is used for an investment company registered under the 1940 Act, the potential bonus for performance better than the index must be matched by an equivalent potential penalty for poor performance.[5] Such incentive fee arrangements need not be symmetrical if an investment company is not registered with the SEC for sale to the general public. Occasionally, the investment advisory fee may be based wholly or partly on the investment income earned by the fund. Administrative services may be provided by an entity other than the investment adviser under a separate administrative agreement.

1.32 The investment advisory agreement for a registered investment company generally should be approved by the initial shareholder (usually the investment adviser) and thereafter by a majority of the directors or trustees who are not interested persons, as defined by the 1940 Act. Continuation of the contract beyond two years requires annual approval by a vote, cast in person (usually construed to mean face to face, not by telephone), of (a) the board of directors or trustees or a majority of the outstanding shares and (b) directors

---

[5] SEC Final Rule Release No. 7484 under the 1940 Act.

or trustees who are not interested persons.[6] Significant modifications to the investment advisory agreement after a registered investment company begins its operations would be subject to approval by the board of directors or trustees and often are also subject to approval by a vote of a majority of the fund's outstanding shares.

The Distributor

1.33 The distributor, also known as an underwriter of the fund's shares, acts as an agent or a principal and sells the fund's shares as a wholesaler through independent dealers or as a retailer through its own sales network. Shares are sold at net asset value, and a sales charge may be added for the underwriter's and dealers' commissions. Other common commission structures use Rule 12b-1 fees or contingent deferred sales loads. The amount of sales charges, including asset-based sales charges such as Rule 12b-1 fees and contingent deferred sales loads, is regulated by the Financial Industry Regulatory Authority. Additionally, Rule 22d-1 of the 1940 Act permits funds to set variable sales charges. A no-load fund may or may not have a distributor.

1.34 Requirements for approval of a distributor's contract by the registered investment company's board of directors or trustees are similar to those described for the investment adviser. If the distributor's contract is approved by the board, shareholder approval is not necessary. Many registered investment companies adopt distribution plans under Rule 12b-1 permitting the use of fund assets to pay for distribution expenses. One special requirement of Rule 12b-1 is that members of the board of directors or trustees who are not interested persons, as defined, must approve the plan each year, and the plan can be terminated without penalty on 60 days' notice.

The Custodian

1.35 Custody of the fund's cash and portfolio securities is usually entrusted to a bank or, less frequently, a member of a national securities exchange that is responsible for their receipt, delivery, and safekeeping. Custody arrangements and the auditor's responsibilities are discussed in detail in chapters 2, "Investment Accounts," and 12 of this guide.

The Transfer Agent

1.36 The fund's transfer agent, which may be a bank or a private company, issues, transfers, redeems, and accounts for the fund's capital shares. Sometimes the investment adviser, distributor, or another related party performs those functions. Section 17A of the Securities Exchange Act of 1934 (the 1934 Act) requires certain transfer agents to register with the SEC and prescribes standards of performance concerning their duties.

The Administrator

1.37 The fund may engage an administrator that may or may not be independent of the investment adviser. Occasionally, if the investment adviser is engaged as the administrator, the investment adviser will engage an independent subadministrator. In all of these instances, the administrator is responsible for performing or overseeing administrative tasks such as the filing of reports with the SEC and the IRS, the registering of fund shares, corresponding

---

[6] Sections 2(a)(19), 15(a), and 15(c) of the 1940 Act.

with shareholders, and determining the fund's compliance with various restrictions. The administrator may also maintain the fund's books and records, assist with calculating the net asset value on a periodic basis, and assist with certain aspects of investment valuation, among other tasks.

Regulation

1.38 Generally, an investment company is required to register with the SEC under the 1940 Act if one of the following is true:[7]

a. Its outstanding securities, other than short-term paper, are beneficially owned by more than 100 persons (including the number of beneficial security holders of a company owning 10 percent or more of the voting securities of the investment company).[8]

b. It is offering or proposing to offer its securities to the public.

1.39 The Division of Investment Management of the SEC is responsible for reviewing such registrations. The investment company's shares are also registered under the Securities Act of 1933 (the 1933 Act) and with various state securities commissions before being offered for sale to the public. After registering with the SEC under the 1940 Act or both the 1940 Act and the 1933 Act, the company must report periodically to its shareholders and the SEC. Accordingly, auditors of investment companies should be familiar with the following acts:

a. The 1933 Act, often referred to as the disclosure act, regulates the contents of prospectuses and similar documents and is intended to assure that potential investors receive adequate information to make reasonably informed investment decisions.

b. The 1934 Act regulates securities brokers and dealers, stock exchanges, and the trading of securities in the securities markets. The distributor must register as a broker-dealer under the act. The act also governs disclosures in proxy materials used to solicit the votes of shareholders of an investment company, as does the 1940 Act. According to Section 17(A)(c) of the 1934 Act, if the fund's transfer agent is not a bank, it should be registered under the 1934 Act.

c. The 1940 Act regulates the investment company industry and provides rules and regulations that govern the fiduciary duties and other responsibilities of an investment company's management. BDCs elect to be regulated under certain sections of this act.

d. The Investment Advisers Act of 1940 requires persons paid to render investment advice to individuals or institutions, including investment companies, to register and regulates their conduct and contracts.

e. The Small Business Investment Act of 1958 authorizes the SBA to provide government funds under regulated conditions to SBICs licensed under this act.

---

[7] Otherwise, the company is exempted from registration by Section 3(c)(1) of the 1940 Act.

[8] Section 3(c)(7) of the 1940 Act allows certain companies to have more than 100 persons if those persons are qualified investors.

 f. The Small Business Investment Incentive Act of 1980 amended the 1940 Act by, among other things, allowing certain closed-end companies to elect to be regulated as BDCs under less rigorous Sections 54–65 of the 1940 Act.

Summary of Relevant SEC Registration and Reporting Forms

1.40 The federal securities laws are supplemented by formal rules and regulations; the SEC also issues a variety of other releases and statements, including its financial reporting releases and releases under the 1933 Act, the 1934 Act, the 1940 Act, and the Investment Advisers Act of 1940. Many of these rules and regulations apply to the investment company industry. The auditor should be familiar with them and the SEC registration and reporting forms. The forms illustrate the kind of information that generally should be made available to the public, the restrictions imposed on operations, the most applicable statutory provisions, and the statistics that generally should be accumulated and maintained. The forms commonly used include the following:[9]

 a. Form N-8A, the notification of registration under the 1940 Act, discloses the company's name and address and certain other general information. An investment company is registered under the act after it has filed the form, which is brief, and it is then subject to all the act's requirements and standards. The information in the form need not be audited.

 b. Form N-1A, the registration statement of open-end companies under the 1940 Act (and, if elected, the 1933 Act), describes in detail the company's objectives, policies, management, investment restrictions, and similar matters. The initial filing of Form N-1A generally requires audited financial statements, which typically are limited to a "seed capital" statement of assets and liabilities. (Form N-2 is the comparable registration statement for closed-end management investment companies.) Part A of Form N-1A includes the information required in a fund's prospectus and states that the prospectus should clearly disclose the fundamental characteristics and investment risks of the fund using concise, straightforward, and easy to understand language. When an investment company incurs organization costs that are not paid for and assumed by the fund sponsor, a "seed statement of operations" for the period from the organization date to the date of the statement of assets and liabilities for seed capital is also required (see chapter 8, "Other Accounts and Considerations," of this guide). The subsequent filing of posteffective amendments to the registration statement on Form N-1A is discussed in paragraph 1.42.[10]

---

[9] Although the commonly used forms are summarized in this listing, there are various other applicable investment company forms that are not listed here because they are less commonly used. For a complete listing of applicable forms and additional resources, readers should visit the Forms List on www.sec.gov/forms.

[10] As noted in the May 2013 Expert Panel Conference Call Highlights, the SEC staff's position is generally, if a registered investment company or business development company acquires (or knowingly will acquire shortly after the registration statement is declared effective) a significant portion of a private fund, an entire private fund, or multiple private funds, the registrant should include in its registration statement at least 2 years of audited, Regulation S-X and U.S. generally accepted accounting principles compliant financial statements of the acquired private fund(s) (or

(continued)

    c. Form N-SAR, a reporting form used for semiannual and annual reports by all investment companies (other than BDCs) registered under the 1940 Act, is divided into four sections, and only certain investment companies need to complete each section. The sections pertain to open-end and closed-end management investment companies, SBICs, or UITs. The report provides current information and demonstrates compliance with the 1940 Act. The annual report filed by a management investment company must be accompanied by a report on the company's internal control over financial reporting from a registered public accounting firm (see paragraph 12.29 of this guide for an example of that report).

    d. Form N-CSR, under which a registered investment company files its annual and semiannual shareholder reports together with the certifications of principal executive and financial officers required by Rule 30a-2 of the 1940 Act. The form also provides for disclosure of other information relating to the investment company's code of ethics, audit committee financial expert, principal accountant fees and services, internal control over financial reporting, evaluation of disclosure controls and procedures, and (for closed-end funds) proxy-voting policies. Registered investment companies that include a summary portfolio schedule of investments in reports to shareholders file complete portfolio schedules for the semi-annual and annual shareholder reports on Form N-CSR. SBICs registered on Form N-5 and UITs are not required to file Form N-CSR.

    e. Form N-Q, under which a registered investment company, other than an SBIC registered on Form N-5 and a BDC, files its complete portfolio schedules (the same schedules of investments that are required in Form N-CSR) for the first and third fiscal quarters under the 1934 Act and the 1940 Act. According to the acts, the form must be signed and certified by the principal executive and financial officers and also provides for disclosure of information relating to the investment company's evaluation of disclosure controls and procedures, and internal control over financial reporting. Per Sections 4 and 26 of the 1940 Act, UITs are not required to file Form N-Q.

    f. Form N-MFP, a reporting form which is filed by money market funds subject to Rule 2a-7 of the 1940 Act and reports pertinent information about each portfolio security held on the last business day of the prior month. Form N-MFP also requires funds to report

---

(footnote continued)

private fund(s) to be acquired shortly after the registration statement is declared effective). For example, the registrant should include in the private fund(s)' financial statements a schedule of investments listing each investment in accordance with Article 12 of Regulation S-X as opposed to a condensed schedule of investments. In certain circumstances, the SEC staff may also request registrants to include in the registration statement unaudited interim financial statements of the private fund(s), an audited special purpose schedule of investments to be acquired, pro forma financial statements, seed financial statements, and/or supplemental information that has been provided to private fund investors. Also, there may be circumstances when additional narrative information regarding the advisor's decision to select a private fund(s) or a significant portion of a private fund(s) to be acquired should be disclosed (see May 2013 Expert Panel Conference Call Highlights for examples of narrative information). In considering what information may need to be included in the registration statement, consideration should be given such that investors of the existing private fund(s) do not have more information about the private fund(s) than potential investors of the new registrant.

information about the fund, including information about the fund's risk characteristics such as the dollar-weighted average maturity of the fund's portfolio and its seven-day gross yield. Money market funds also must report on Form N-MFP the market-based values of each portfolio security and the fund's market-based net asset value per share, with separate entries for values that do and do not take into account any capital support agreements into which the fund may have entered.

g. Form N-PX, which reports the investment company's proxy voting record for each matter relating to a portfolio security considered at a shareholder meeting held during the 12-month period ending June 30.

h. Form 13F, a quarterly securities inventory of an institutional investment manager (including an investment company) that has either investment discretion or voting power over more than $100 million in securities that are admitted to trading on a national securities exchange or the automated quotation system of a registered securities association. This form is usually filed in composite for an investment adviser of multiple clients, including the combined holdings of investment companies and other clients.

i. Schedule 13G and annual amendments, each as of December 31 to be filed by the following February 14, concern possession of either investment discretion or voting power over more than 5 percent of a class of equity securities of a publicly owned company, provided that the interests were acquired in the ordinary course of business and not with the purpose or effect of influencing control; if the provision is not applicable, disclosures of changes in holdings must be made promptly on Schedule 13D. Such reports are usually filed in composite form for an investment adviser of multiple clients, including the combined holdings of investment companies and other clients.

j. Form N-3, the registration statement for variable annuity separate accounts registered as management investment companies under the 1940 Act and the 1933 Act. The form contains information and financial statements similar to the kind found in Form N-1A and information about the insurance contract and sponsoring insurance company, including financial statements of the sponsor.

k. Form N-4, the registration statement for variable annuity separate accounts registered as UITs under the 1940 Act and the 1933 Act. Information supplied in Form N-4 is similar to the information presented in Form N-1A.

l. Form N-1 is the registration statement for variable life insurance separate accounts registered as management investment companies under the 1940 Act and the 1933 Act.

m. Form N-6, the form for insurance company separate accounts that are registered as UITs and that offer variable life insurance policies.

n. Forms N-8, B-2, and S-6 are the forms for all UITs except those variable annuity and variable life separate accounts registered on Forms N-4 and N-6, respectively, under the 1940 Act and the 1933 Act.

    o. Form N-5, the registration statement for SBICs, which are also licensed under the Small Business Investment Act of 1958, is a dual-purpose form registering SBICs under both the 1933 Act and the 1940 Act. The form contains the same kind of information and audited financial statements as required by Forms N-1A and N-2 for management investment companies.

    p. Form N-14, the statement for registration of securities issued by investment companies and BDCs in business combination transactions under the 1933 Act. The form contains information about the companies involved in the transaction, historical financial statements, and, as applicable, pro forma financial statements.[11]

    q. Form PF, required to be filed by SEC-registered investment advisers that manage one or more private funds[12] with aggregate private fund regulatory assets under management of greater than or equal to $150 million as of the recently completed fiscal year. The information on this form includes information about the private funds' gross and net asset values, counterparty exposures, risk, collateral or borrowing, investor makeup, derivative exposures, investment composition by type and by geographic exposure, portfolio liquidity, portfolio turnover, strategy, performance, and clearing mechanism. SEC-registered investment advisers that are also registered as commodity pool operators with the Commodity Futures Trading Commission (CFTC) may satisfy the CFTC's requirement to file systematic information about their commodity pools by filing Form PF with the SEC instead of filing the same information on Form CPO-PQR[13] with the CFTC.

1.41 Prospectuses of mutual funds offering their shares for sale are updated at least annually. Information in a currently effective prospectus generally should be updated for significant events that have occurred since the effective date. Posteffective amendments on Form N-1A, including updated audited financial statements and a complete schedule of investments (if not included within the financial statements), must be filed and become effective under the 1933 Act and the 1940 Act within 16 months after the end of the period covered by the previous audited financial statements if the fund is to continue offering its shares.

1.42 Registration statements and reports filed by open-end and closed-end companies (other than SBICs) on various forms include financial highlights, usually for the preceding 5 years, as described in the instructions to Form N-1A, and for the preceding 10 years as described in the instructions to Form N-2 (with at least the most recent 5 years audited).

1.43 The form and content of financial statements required in registration statements are governed by Regulation S-X. Article 6, and portions of Article

---

    [11] See footnote 6 in chapter 8, "Other Accounts and Considerations" of this guide.

    [12] As defined in the Form PF Glossary of Terms, for purposes of Form PF, a private fund is any issuer that would be an investment company as defined in Section 3 of the 1940 Act, except for Sections 3(c)(1) or 3(c)(7) of the 1940 Act.

    [13] Form CPO-PQR is required to be filed quarterly with the Commodity Futures Trading Commission or National Futures Association, depending on the size of the commodity pool operator and its pools. The information included on this form, depends on the size of the commodity pools, and may include information about each commodity pool operator, its service providers, in-vestment strategies, risk exposures, leverage and derivative positions.

12, of Regulation S-X specifically addresses registered investment companies. (SBICs are covered in Article 5, but they follow the same fair value accounting model as do other investment companies.) Registration statements and Forms N-SAR and N-CSR are filed using the SEC's Electronic Data Gathering Analysis and Retrieval System.

1.44 In January 2009, the SEC issued Final Rule Release No. 33-9002, *Interactive Data to Improve Financial Reporting*, which became effective in April 2009 and requires entities to file financial statement information in an interactive data format using eXtensible Business Reporting Language (XBRL). However, the new rules did not include any investment company that is registered under the 1940 Act or any BDC (as defined in Section 2[a][48] of that act). The implementation of this rule allows registered investment companies to participate under the voluntary program of filing in XBRL.

1.45 In February 2009, the SEC issued Final Release No. IC-28617, *Interactive Data for Mutual Fund Risk/Return Summary*, which requires open-end companies (mutual funds) to provide the "Risk and Return Summary" section of their prospectuses (to the SEC and on their websites) in interactive data format using XBRL.[14,15] The existing voluntary program was modified to only allow for voluntary participation by mutual funds with respect to financial statement information. Therefore, the voluntary program continued after the compliance date for the financial statements of investment companies that are registered under the 1940 Act, BDCs, and other entities that report under the 1934 Act and prepare their financial statements under Article 6 of Regulation S-X.

Financial Reporting to Shareholders

1.46 The 1940 Act and the related rules and regulations specify the financial statements of registered investment companies and the timing of reports required to be submitted to shareholders and the SEC.[16] According to the act and the related rules, reports containing those financial statements must be submitted to shareholders and the SEC at least semiannually; annual reports must contain audited financial statements. Financial statements in such reports include

- a statement of assets and liabilities and a detailed schedule of investments or a statement of net assets. The SEC, under Regulation S-X, permits a registered investment company to include in its reports to shareholders a summary portfolio schedule of investments, provided that the complete portfolio schedule is filed with the SEC on Form N-CSR semiannually and provided to shareholders free of charge. Regulation S-X also exempts money market funds from including a portfolio schedule in reports to shareholders provided that information is filed with the SEC on Form

---

[14] SEC Regulation S-T addresses the liability for an interactive data file; however, these liability provisions are only applicable through October 31, 2014. At that point an interactive data file is subject to the same liability provisions as the related official filing.

[15] The SEC published a preparer's guide to assist in using the eXtensible Business Reporting Language (XBRL) US Mutual Fund Risk/Return Summary Taxonomy and another document that explains how the SEC's rendering engine transforms XBRL instances into HTML output for display in a web browser. Both documents can be accessed from http://xbrl.sec.gov.

[16] Rules under Section 30(d) of the 1940 Act.

N-CSR semiannually and provided to shareholders upon request free of charge. (Despite this exemption, U.S. generally accepted accounting principles does require a condensed portfolio. See paragraphs 7.27–.30 of this guide for further guidance.)

- a statement of operations.
- a statement of changes in net assets.

In addition to the basic financial statements, financial highlights (see paragraph 7.173 of this guide) should be presented either as a separate schedule or within the notes to the financial statements. Financial statements for registered and nonregistered investment companies are discussed and illustrated in chapter 7, "Financial Statements of Investment Companies," of this guide. For investment companies with complex capital structures, including those that issue multiple classes of shares, the reporting requirements and related illustrative financial statements are discussed in chapter 5 of this guide.

1.47 Registered and nonregistered investment companies also may be required to present a statement of cash flows if they do not meet the conditions specified in "Pending Content" in FASB ASC 230-10-15-4. The scope exceptions provided in "Pending Content" in FASB ASC 230-10-15-4 are discussed in paragraph 7.160 of this guide.

Accounting Rules and Policies

1.48 Rules under Section 31 of the 1940 Act prescribe the accounting records that an investment company must maintain and the periods for which they must be retained. Those rules require maintenance of journals, general and subsidiary ledgers, and memorandum records that are subject to examination by representatives of the SEC during periodic and special examinations.

1.49 The accounting policies followed by investment companies result from the companies' role as conduits for the funds of investors interested in investing as a group. Furthermore, the investment company policies are supplemented by the rules and regulations issued under the various acts administered by the SEC and the SBA. Some unique policies are described in more detail in the following chapters.

Effective Date of Transactions

1.50 FASB ASC 946-320-25 explains that when accounting for security purchases and sales, for financial reporting purposes, an investment company is to record transactions as of the trade date (the date on which the company agrees to purchase or sell the securities), so that the effects of all securities trades entered into by or for the account of the investment company to the date of a financial report are included in the financial report. Investment companies record dividend income on the ex-dividend date, not the declaration, record, or payable date, because on the ex-dividend date, the quoted market price of listed securities and other market-traded securities tends to be affected by the exclusion of the dividend declared. Also, investment companies record liabilities for dividends payable to shareholders on the ex-dividend or ex-distribution date, not the declaration date as other corporations do, because mutual fund shares are purchased and redeemed at prices equal to or based on net asset value. Investors purchasing shares between the declaration and ex-dividend dates are entitled to receive the dividend, whereas investors purchasing shares on or after the ex-dividend date are not entitled to the dividend.

1.51 However, Rule 2a-4 of the 1940 Act permits registered investment companies to record security transactions as of one day after the trade date for purposes of determining net asset value.

Other Rules and Regulations

⊙ Update 1-2 *Regulatory*: Money Market Fund Reform

On July 23, 2014, the SEC issued Final Rule Release No. 33-9616, *Money Market Fund Reform; Amendments to Form PF*. The release includes varying compliance dates for the different changes within the new rule. Compliance dates begin in 2015, and extend through 2016. Readers are encouraged to consult the full text of the release for specific compliance dates.

One of the key structural changes of the new Money Market Reform Rule is that institutional prime and municipal money market funds will be required to transact at a floating net asset value. Retail funds and government funds are not required to transact at a floating net asset value. This will require those funds that transact at a floating net asset value to transact shares, rounded to the fourth decimal place (for example, $1.0000), based on the most recently determined market value of the securities in the underlying portfolios. Separately, new tax regulations and guidance have been is-sued as a result of this change; readers are encouraged to review this new IRS guidance. The release further provides guidance on how to determine whether a fund is considered to be an institutional money market fund, a retail money market fund, or a government money market fund.

Those money market funds adopting a floating net asset value as a result of the new rules are expected to determine the values of their investments using market-based values, as opposed to using the amortized cost of such investments as an approximation of market value. In addition to this accounting change, the new rules may result in other changes to the financial reporting of all money market funds. Readers should keep abreast of future developments as they emerge.

Additionally, the amendments in Final Rule Release No. 33-9616 give the boards of directors of money market funds new tools to stem heavy redemptions. Those tools include allowing them discretion to impose liquidity fees in the event a fund's weekly liquidity level falls below the required regulatory threshold, and also provides them the discretion to suspend redemptions temporarily (that is, impose a "gate"), under similar circumstances. The new requirements dictate that all nongovernment money market funds impose a liquidity fee if the fund's weekly liquidity level falls below the rule-established threshold, unless the fund's board determines that imposing such a fee is not in the best interests of the fund.

Final Rule Release No. 33-9616 also contains additional amendments. These include enhanced disclosure requirements on fund websites, sales and marketing materials, prospectuses and SAIs; changes to Form N-MFP; an additional new Form N-CR; and various clarifying amendments under Rule 2a-7, including stress testing and diversification provisions.

(continued)

> The amendments also require investment advisers of certain large unregistered liquidity funds to provide additional information about those funds to the SEC.
>
> Readers should consult the full text of SEC Final Rule Release No. 33-9616, which can be accessed on the Final Rules page at www.sec.gov.

1.52 The 1934 Act specifies the records that must be maintained by the principal underwriter for the fund, the period for which the records must be preserved, and the reports that the principal underwriter must file with the SEC. The records are subject to examination by representatives of the SEC.[17] Once during each calendar year, each principal underwriter is required by Section 17 of the 1934 Act, and related rules, (as are other broker-dealers) to file audited financial statements, related footnotes, and supplemental information related to certain financial responsibility rules (including a report on internal control that describes any material inadequacies or material weaknesses). These requirements were amended in July 2013 to significantly expand the reporting, audit, and notification requirements for broker-dealers and their auditors.[18] The amendments include a requirement that broker-dealer audits be conducted in accordance with standards of the PCAOB in light of explicit oversight authority provided to the PCAOB by the Dodd-Frank Wall Street Reform and Consumer Protection Act (Dodd-Frank Act). The amendments further require a broker-dealer that clears transactions or carries customer accounts to agree to allow SEC representatives or the broker-dealer's designated examining authority (DEA) to review the documentation associated with certain reports of the broker-dealer's independent public accountant and to allow the accountant to discuss the findings relating to the reports of the accountant with those representatives when requested in connection with a regulatory examination of the broker-dealer. Finally, the amendments require a broker-dealer to file a new form with its DEA that elicits information about the broker-dealer's practices with respect to the custody of securities and funds of customers and noncustomers. These significant amendments are discussed in further detail within the AICPA Accounting Guide *Brokers and Dealers in Securities*.

1.53 Section 19 and Rule 19a of the 1940 Act specify the kind of notice to shareholders that should accompany distributions from sources other than accumulated undistributed income determined in accordance with good accounting practice (or net income for the current or preceding fiscal year), describing the source of such distributions. That notice must indicate clearly the portion of the payment (per share of outstanding capital stock) made from net investment income or accumulated undistributed net investment income, realized gains, accumulated undistributed net realized gains on the sales of securities, and capital. Rule 19a-1(e) further requires that "the source or sources from which a dividend is paid shall be determined (or reasonably estimated) to the close of the period as of which it is paid without giving effect to such payment."

---

[17] Rules 17a-4 and 17a-5 of the 1934 Act.

[18] Final Rule 34-70072, *Financial Responsibility Rules for Broker-Dealers,* and Final Rule 34-70073, *Broker-Dealer Reports,* were both issued on July 30, 2013.

1.54 Section 32(a) of the 1940 Act requires that the independent auditor reporting on financial statements of an investment company be selected annually by a majority of directors or trustees who are not interested persons at a meeting held no more than 30 days before or after the commencement of the investment company's fiscal year or before the annual meeting of stockholders in that year. Additionally, if the investment company is organized in a jurisdiction that does not require annual shareholder meetings and the investment company does not hold a meeting in a given year and is part of a complex of related investment companies that do not share a common fiscal year, the independent auditor may be selected by the directors or trustees at a meeting held either within 30 days before or within the first 90 days after the commencement of that company's fiscal year. The directors' or trustees' selection must be submitted to the stockholders for ratification during any year in which an annual meeting of stockholders is held, unless the appointment of the auditors is approved by an audit committee solely comprising independent directors or trustees, and the audit committee maintains a charter in an easily accessible place. The employment of the accountant is conditioned upon the right of the investment company to terminate such employment without any penalty by a vote of the outstanding shares of the investment company. If the independent auditor resigns or is unable to carry out the engagement, the disinterested directors or trustees may appoint a successor.[19]

Jumpstart Our Business Startups Act (JOBS Act)

1.55 The Jumpstart Our Business Startups Act (JOBS Act) was enacted on April 5, 2012, with the purpose of stimulating the growth of small to midsized companies by making it easier for startup and emerging growth companies to raise capital and to meet regulatory reporting requirements. The SEC's Division of Corporation Finance released frequently asked questions (FAQs) to provide guidance on the implementation and application of the JOBS Act. Questions 20–21 specifically address investment companies.

1.56 The JOBS Act creates regulatory relief for a new type of issuer—the emerging growth company. An *emerging growth company* is defined as any issuer with gross revenues of less than $1 billion during the prior fiscal year that has gone public after December 8, 2011. An issuer can maintain its emerging growth company status for five years following its initial public offering unless it has annual revenues that exceed $1 billion, becomes a large accelerated filer, or issue $1 billion or more of nonconvertible debt in a three-year period. According to questions 20–21 of the FAQs, an investment company registered under the 1940 Act would not qualify as an emerging growth company under Title I of the JOBS Act. Registered investment companies are subject to separate disclosure and reporting requirements, which were designed to address the particular structure and operations of investment companies.

1.57 However, BDCs may qualify as emerging growth companies. BDCs invest in startup and emerging growth companies for which they may provide significant managerial experience and are subject to many of the disclosure and other requirements from which Title I provides temporary exemptions, including executive compensation disclosure, say-on-pay votes, Management Discussion and Analysis, and Section 404(b) of the Sarbanes-Oxley Act.

---

[19] Section 32(a), Rule 32a-3, and Rule 32a-4 of the 1940 Act.

Regulatory Changes for Investment Companies That Invest in Commodities

1.58 Any collective investment vehicle that is operated for the purpose of trading commodity futures and options on commodity futures contracts is deemed under applicable CFTC regulations to constitute a commodity pool, subject to limited exclusions for "otherwise regulated" entities that make limited use of futures. Historically, registered investment companies that engaged in commodity futures trading activities were excluded from CFTC regulations under the CPO definition exemption criteria in Section 4.5 of the Commodity Exchange Act (CEA). However, on February 9, 2012, the CFTC issued a final rule changing Part 4 of the CEA's regulations involving registration and compliance obligations for CPOs and CTAs (see CFTC Release No. PR6176-12). The rule reinstated the trading criteria for advisers of registered investment companies claiming exclusion from the CPO definition under Section 4.5 of the CEA and added an alternative trading threshold based on net notional value of derivative positions. The rule also rescinded the exemption from CPO registration under Section 4.13(a)(4) and included new risk disclosure requirements for CPOs and CTAs regarding non securities-based swap transactions. As a result of this final rule, many registered investment companies that invest in commodities are no longer exempt from CFTC regulations and therefore are within the scope of both the SEC and CFTC.

1.59 To reduce the regulatory compliance burdens on registered investment companies affected by the changes to Section 4.5 of the CEA (see paragraph 1.28), the CFTC issued an additional final rule[20] in August 2013 that harmonizes SEC and CFTC rules for the advisers of registered investment companies that are required to register as CPOs. The rule explains that for entities that are registered with both the CFTC and SEC (dual registrants), the CFTC will accept the SEC's disclosure, reporting, and recordkeeping regime as substituted compliance for substantially all of Part 4 of the CFTC's regulations, as long as they comply with comparable requirements under the SEC's statutory and regulatory compliance regime. Essentially, the final rule allows dually registered entities to meet certain CFTC regulatory requirements for CPOs by complying with SEC rules to which they are already subject.

---

[20] CFTC Release No. PR6663-13 issued on August 13, 2013. Readers are encouraged to review the full text of the final rule available at www.cftc.gov. The related Fact Sheet and Questions and Answers were issued by the CFTC in conjunction with the final rule release and can also be accessed at www.cftc.gov.

Chapter 2

Investment Accounts

Ⓒ Update 2-1 *Accounting and Reporting*: **Fair Value Measurement**

FASB Accounting Standards Update (ASU) No. 2015-07, *Fair Value Measurement (Topic 820): Disclosures for Investments in Certain Entities That Calculate Net Asset Value per Share (or Its Equivalent) (a consensus of the Emerging Issues Task Force)*, was issued in May 2015. The amendments are effective for public business entities for fiscal years beginning after December 15, 2015, and interim periods within those fiscal years. For all other entities, the amendments are effective for fiscal years beginning after December 15, 2016, and interim periods within those fiscal years. A reporting entity should apply the amendments retrospectively to all periods presented. The retrospective approach requires that an investment for which fair value is measured using the net asset value per share practical expedient be removed from the fair value hierarchy in all periods presented in an entity's financial statements. Earlier application is permitted.

These amendments apply to reporting entities that elect to measure the fair value of an investment within the scope of paragraphs 4–15 of FASB *Accounting Standards Codification* (ASC) 820-10-15-4 using the net asset value per share (or its equivalent) practical expedient in FASB ASC 820-10-35-59.

FASB ASC 820, *Fair Value Measurement*, permits a reporting entity, as a practical expedient, to measure the fair value of certain investments using the net asset value per share of the investment. Currently, investments valued using the practical expedient are categorized within the fair value hierarchy on the basis of whether the investment is redeemable with the investee at net asset value on the measurement date, never redeemable with the investee at net asset value, or redeemable with the investee at net asset value at a future date. For investments that are redeemable with the investee at a future date, a reporting entity must consider the length of time until those investments become redeemable to determine the classification within the fair value hierarchy and whether they are near term for the assessment of the potential inclusion of a cash flow statement.

The amendments remove the requirement to categorize within the fair value hierarchy all investments for which fair value is measured using the net asset value per share practical expedient. However, the amendments require sufficient information to be provided to permit reconciliation of the fair value of assets categorized within the fair value hierarchy to the amounts presented in the statement of financial condition. The amendments also remove the requirement to make certain disclosures for all investments that are eligible to be measured at fair value using the net asset value per share practical expedient. Rather, those disclosures are limited to investments for which the entity has elected to measure the fair value using that practical expedient.

Readers are encouraged to consult the full text of this ASU on FASB's website at www.fasb.org.

Presentation of Pending Content in FASB ASC

Amendments to FASB ASC (issued in the form of ASUs) are initially incorporated into FASB ASC in "Pending Content" boxes located below the paragraphs being amended with links to the transition information. The pending content boxes are meant to provide users with information about how the guidance in a paragraph will change as a result of the new guidance.

Pending content applies to different entities at different times due to varying fiscal year-ends, and because certain guidance may be effective on different dates for public entities, as defined, and other entities. As such, FASB maintains amended guidance in pending content boxes within FASB ASC until the roll-off date. Generally, the roll-off date is six months following the latest fiscal year-end for which the original guidance being amended could still be applied.

Presentation of Pending Content in AICPA Audit and Accounting Guides

Amended FASB ASC guidance that is included in pending content boxes in FASB ASC on May 1, 2015, is referenced as "Pending Content" in this guide. Pending content referenced or discussed within this guide's chapter text is fully effective as of the date of this guide and should be considered by readers for current reporting periods. Pending content referenced or discussed within this guide's shaded "Guidance Updates" boxes or within appendix A, "Guidance Updates," is not fully effective as of the date of this guide. Readers should be aware that pending content" referenced in this guide will eventually be subjected to FASB's roll-off process and will no longer be labeled as "Pending Content" in FASB ASC (as discussed in the previous paragraph).

2.01 As stated by the FASB ASC 946-320-05-2, an investment company's securities portfolio typically comprises substantially all its net assets. Portfolio securities produce income and expense from dividends and interest, and changes in fair values of securities while they are owned or held short by the fund.

Investment Objectives and Policies

2.02 The composition of an investment company's portfolio is primarily a function of the company's investment objectives and strategies to achieve them. An investment company discloses the investment objectives adopted by its management and the strategies adopted to achieve them in its charter or partnership agreement and documents such as registration statements, prospectuses, or offering circulars. Restrictions, statutory or otherwise, are also disclosed. Those restrictions may include specific limitations or outright prohibitions of transactions in real estate, commodities or commodity contracts, and property other than securities. Other restrictions may include limitations on investing in unregistered securities; making short sales of securities; underwriting securities of other issuers; acquiring securities of other investment companies; or using leveraging techniques, such as margin accounts, bank borrowing, reverse repurchase agreements, and transactions in options, futures, and swaps.

2.03 An investment company may also specify the kinds of investments, such as bonds, preferred stocks, convertible securities, common stocks, warrants, or options, in which it may invest and the proportion of its total assets that may be invested in each kind of security. Specific limitations may relate to the following:

- The percentage of the investment company's assets that it may invest in the securities of an issuer or in issuers of a specific country, geographic region, or industry
- The percentage of voting securities of an issuer that it may acquire
- Investments in companies for the purpose of control
- The risk profile of the portfolio (for example, restrictions on the allocation of assets between domestic and foreign securities, the percentage of assets invested in illiquid or emerging market securities, or the level of investment in derivative instruments)

Operations and Controls

Recordkeeping Requirements

2.04 The Investment Company Act of 1940 (the 1940 Act) prescribes minimum accounting records for registered investment companies.[1] Section 31 of the 1940 Act and rules under that section require investment records for all registered investment companies to include the following:

- Journals or other records of original entry that show all securities purchases and sales, receipts and deliveries of securities, and collections and payments of cash for securities transactions
- A securities record or ledger showing the unit, quantity, price, and aggregate cost separately for each portfolio item and transaction as of the trade date
- A record for each portfolio item of all trading orders for purchase, sale, sell short or cover short by, or on behalf of, the investment company and the action on each order

The books and records of registered investment companies are subject to the retention and inspection requirements set forth in rules under the 1940 Act.[2]

2.05 If any records required by the rules are maintained by an agent, such as a custodian or transfer agent, the registered investment company should obtain the agent's written agreement to make the records available on request and to preserve them for the required periods.

Custody of Securities

2.06 An investment company's securities are usually held in the custody of a bank, which, for registered investment companies, must have prescribed

---

[1] Section 31 of the Investment Company Act of 1940 (the 1940 Act) and rules under that section. Section 64 of the 1940 Act states that Section 31 of the 1940 Act also applies to a business development company (BDC) to the same extent as if it were a registered closed-end investment company.

[2] Section 31(b) of the 1940 Act.

minimum aggregate capital, surplus, and undivided profits.[3] A member firm of a national securities exchange or a central securities system registered with the SEC also may serve as custodian. To use a member of a national securities exchange as custodian, a registered investment company must initially obtain the approval of a majority of its board of directors or trustees. The 1940 Act and the related rules require that securities held in custody by a member of a national securities exchange be inspected at various times by the registered investment company's auditor and that the auditor issue a report thereon to the SEC.[4] Investment companies may also enter into subcustodial agreements, usually to provide a local custody function for investment in foreign securities. The nature of these agreements can vary regarding whether the principal custodian does or does not assume responsibility for the subcustodian's actions. (See also the discussion in paragraph 2.179 relating to foreign custodian arrangements and in paragraphs 11.29–.32 and paragraphs 11.35–.39 relating to the auditor's procedures with respect to custodians.)

2.07 Registered investment companies are required to file copies of their custodial agreements with the SEC. Significant provisions of such agreements deal with the following:

- Physical and book segregation of securities in custody
- Denying custodians the power to assign, hypothecate, pledge, or otherwise encumber or dispose of any securities except in acting at the direction and for the account of the registered investment company
- Immunity of such securities to liens asserted by a custodian
- The right of the SEC and the company's independent auditor to inspect the securities at any time[5]

2.08 An investment company may retain custody of its securities by depositing them for safekeeping in a vault or other depository maintained by a bank or company whose functions and physical facilities are supervised by federal or state authorities. The 1940 Act and the related rules require all securities determined to be held in safekeeping, either by a registered investment company or an affiliated bank as a custodian, to be inspected at various times by the registered investment company's independent auditor.[6] The deposited securities are required to be physically segregated and are subject to withdrawal only by duly authorized persons under specified conditions.

Accounting for Segregated Accounts

2.09 Certain investment transactions may involve a registered investment company's issuance of a *senior security*, as defined under Section 18 of the 1940 Act.[7] Section 18 also contains restrictions on the issuance of senior

---

[3] Sections 2(a)(5), 17(f), and 26(a) of the 1940 Act. Section 58 of the 1940 Act states that Sections 2(a)(5) and 17(f) also apply to a BDC to the same extent as if it were a registered closed-end investment company.

[4] Rule 17f-1 of the 1940 Act.

[5] Rule 17f-1 of the 1940 Act.

[6] Rule 17f-2 of the 1940 Act.

[7] Section 61 of the 1940 Act provides requirements and restrictions for the issuance of senior securities by BDCs. Section 61 states that Section 18 of the 1940 Act also applies to a BDC to the same extent as if it were a registered closed-end investment company, except for certain specific requirements and restrictions. Readers should consider these requirements and restrictions in Section 61 that are unique to BDCs, when applicable.

securities. Generally, a senior security represents an indebtedness of the investment company (for example, leverage), including certain transactions under which the investment company enters into a contractual purchase or delivery obligation (for example, futures and written options on securities). The SEC does not raise the issue of compliance with Section 18 with respect to certain transactions if a registered investment company designates certain assets in a segregated account, either with the custodian or in its accounting records, as "cover" for indebtedness. Such assets consist of cash or securities, as permitted by the SEC (that is, that meet the liquidity guidelines specified by the SEC), and they may be replaced only by other similar assets.[8] According to SEC Release No. 10666 under the 1940 Act, securities maintained in such segregated accounts should be valued using an appropriate methodology for those securities. The determination of whether a senior security has been issued or adequately covered is, at times, complex and may require the involvement of legal counsel.[9]

2.10 An investment company using a bank or member of a national securities exchange as custodian of its securities may agree to have qualifying securities deposited in a clearing agency, such as a central securities system, that is registered with the SEC. Clearing agencies use the book entry shares method of accounting for securities transfers rather than methods based on the physical movement of the securities. Most investment companies' portfolio securities that qualify are now held by clearing agencies (for example, The Depository Trust Company) through arrangements with the investment companies' custodians instead of being held by the custodians in a physically issued form. Investment companies or their custodians may also use the Federal Reserve's book entry system as a depository for U.S. and federal agency securities. Special rules apply to the use of central securities systems and book entry systems.[10]

2.11 If a registered investment company uses a bank as custodian for its securities, the proceeds from sales of such securities and other cash assets, except for minor amounts in checking or petty cash accounts approved by the

---

[8] SEC Release No. 10666 under the 1940 Act, as modified by a no-action letter to Merrill Lynch Asset Management, L.P., on July 2, 1996, and a letter from the SEC Division of Investment Management Chief Accountant to Investment Company Chief Financial Officers on November 7, 1997.

[9] The SEC Division of Investment Management discussed tender option bond financings in an *Issues of Interest* release in March 2012. As discussed in the release, an open-end or closed-end investment company (fund) registered under the 1940 Act may seek to arrange a secured financing through a special purpose trust (TOB trust). In this arrangement, the fund deposits a tax-exempt or other bond into the TOB trust. The TOB trust issues two types of securities: floating rate notes (*floaters* or *TOBs*) and a residual security junior to the floaters (inverse floater). The TOB trust sells the floaters to money market funds or other investors and transfers the cash proceeds and the inverse floater to the fund. The fund typically purchases additional portfolio securities with the cash proceeds. The inverse floater entitles the fund to any value remaining after the TOB trust satisfies its obligations to the TOBs holders and allows the fund to call in the floaters and "collapse" the TOB trust. A third-party liquidity provider guarantees the TOB trust's obligations on the floaters.

This arrangement involves a borrowing by the fund and implicates Section 18 of the 1940 Act, which prohibits an open-end fund from issuing any senior security, except for a borrowing from a bank with 300 percent asset coverage, and generally requires a closed-end fund to have 300 percent asset coverage for any "senior security" that represents an indebtedness. Section 18(g) of the 1940 Act generally defines a *senior security* as "any bond, debenture, note, or similar obligation or instrument constituting a security and evidencing indebtedness," and provides that "'senior security representing indebtedness' means any senior security other than stock." The SEC staff has addressed TOB financings under Section 18 on multiple occasions in reviewing fund registration statements and in the context of other communications with various funds and their counsel.

[10] Rule 17f-4 of the 1940 Act.

board of directors or trustees, are required to be kept in the bank's custody.[11] SEC regulations also permit the maintenance of cash balances with futures commission merchants solely for the purpose of clearing daily activity in futures contracts and related options.[12]

Routine Investment Procedures

2.12 Although the overall direction of the investment activities of an investment company is the responsibility of its board of directors or trustees or general partner, the board typically delegates the routine operating and investment decisions to an investment committee; a portfolio manager; or, as occurs in most situations, an investment adviser. Investment decisions are communicated by the investment company's adviser or the adviser's employees who place orders with brokers. An investment company's registration statement or offering circular indicates its policies on selecting brokers and using affiliates to execute trades. A well-designed system of controls for investment transactions generally should include the procedures described in the following paragraphs.

2.13 A registered investment company is required by Rule 31a-1 of the 1940 Act to document, among other things, the placement of a securities order in an internal record that shows the person who authorized and placed the order, the security, the number of shares or the principal amount ordered, the price or price range, the date and time that the order was entered and executed, the commission rate or amount (or other compensation paid), the broker selected, and the reason for the selection. Executed transactions are routinely confirmed electronically or by telephone, and confirmations are followed by electronic or written advices containing all information pertinent to the trades. The advices for money market instruments ordered through a bank often consist of bank debit or credit memorandums.

2.14 An investment company generally should notify the custodian promptly of each securities transaction and issue detailed instructions to receive or deliver securities and collect or disburse cash. Those instructions ordinarily should include the name of the broker, the description and quantity of the security, the trade and settlement dates, and the net amount of cash to be collected or disbursed. New York Stock Exchange (NYSE) Rule 387 requires the electronic depository confirmation-affirmation system (also known as Broker ID System) to be used to effect securities transactions on a cash-on-delivery or delivery-versus-payment (DVP) basis. The instructions ordinarily should be signed by one or more authorized representatives of the investment company whose signatures are on file with the custodian; if instructions are given by telephone or electronically, procedures should be established to provide for proper authorization.

2.15 As advices confirming trades are received, they should be reviewed promptly for conformity of terms; clerical accuracy; and proper application of commission rates, including volume discounts or negotiated rates, as applicable, and should be compared with the internal records established when the orders were placed.

2.16 Investment companies almost always require receipt of cash for securities delivered by the custodian to settle sales of portfolio investments. Similarly, the custodian pays on a DVP basis. In certain countries, however, there

---

[11] Final Rule Release Nos. 6863 and 7164 under the 1940 Act.
[12] Rule 17f-6 under the 1940 Act.

is no DVP standard. Unless otherwise instructed, the custodian rejects a transaction if either the number of shares or settlement amount determined by the broker does not agree exactly with the written instructions previously authorized by the investment company.

2.17 The custodian notifies the investment company promptly of cash settlements and receipts or deliveries of securities. Settlement dates vary based on the kind of security traded, from same-day settlement to four weeks or more. On receipt of such notifications, the investment company ordinarily should compare them against its records to identify discrepancies. Fails to receive or fails to deliver generally should be identified on the settlement date and followed up promptly.

2.18 The custodian issues periodic statements listing all receipts and deliveries of securities and related collections and disbursements of cash. Securities on hand and the cash balance at the end of the period may also be provided. An investment company generally should reconcile promptly the custodian's statements with its books and records and ordinarily should initiate timely follow-up procedures on reconciling items. The investment company generally should be satisfied with the adequacy of the custodian's procedures and controls that relate to functions carried out on its behalf, especially procedures and controls for receipt, delivery, and safekeeping of securities.

Accounting

Net Asset Value Per Share

2.19 Virtually all open-end registered investment companies and many closed-end registered investment companies prepare daily price make-up sheets computing net asset value per share each day that the NYSE conducts trading activity. The FASB ASC glossary defines *net asset value per share* as the amount of net assets attributable to each share of capital stock (other than senior equity securities; that is, preferred stock) outstanding at the close of the period. It excludes the effects of assuming conversion of outstanding convertible securities, regardless of whether their conversion would have a diluting effect. Rule 22c-1(b) of the 1940 Act establishes customary U.S. business days as the days on which an open-end investment company, at a minimum, must price its redeemable securities, provided that customer orders have been received, and significant price changes in the fund's portfolio securities or other activities or transactions affecting the per share net asset value of the fund exist. Closed-end registered investment companies may compute net asset value per share less frequently, such as weekly or semimonthly.

2.20 Net asset values per share should reflect portfolio securities at *fair value*, as defined in FASB ASC 946-10-20 as the price that would be received to sell an asset or paid to transfer a liability in an orderly transaction between market participants at the measurement date. Securities should be valued at least as often as net asset value per share is computed or shares are issued or redeemed. Registered investment companies value their portfolios at such time of day and at such frequency as is determined by their boards of directors or trustees or the general partner.[13]

---

[13] Rule 22c-1(b) of the 1940 Act.

2.21 Rule 2a-4(a) of the 1940 Act requires that changes in security positions be reflected in the net asset value per share computations no later than the first calculation following the trade date.[14] Similarly, changes in the number of the investment company's outstanding shares from sales, distributions, and repurchases should be reflected in the computations no later than the first calculation following such changes.

2.22 Because of the importance of net asset value per share, many investment companies perform additional procedures to determine the accuracy of security valuations. The fair value assigned to each security position may be compared with the fair value used on the preceding valuation date to detect increases or decreases in specific security values that are unusual or that exceed predetermined thresholds for change in fair value amounts or percentages. In addition, unchanged security values may be reviewed to determine whether the valuation continues to be appropriate. It is advisable to review and explain unusual increases, decreases, or unchanged prices. See the "Valuing Investments" section of this chapter for further discussion of valuation controls and methodologies.

2.23 Net asset value per share should also reflect expenses, interest, dividends, and other income through the date of the calculation.[15] The 1940 Act does not require expenses, income items, or both to be accrued daily if their net cumulative amount is less than one cent per outstanding share.[16] Other aspects of accrual accounting specific to investment companies, discussed in this chapter and other chapters of the guide, could also be considered.

2.24 Mutual funds with multiple classes of stock must determine the net assets and net asset value per share for each class in accordance with the procedures enumerated by Rule 18f-3 of the 1940 Act (or in accordance with an exemptive order issued by the SEC). See chapter 5, "Complex Capital Structures," of this guide for additional information on multiple-class funds.

Basis of Recording Securities Transactions

2.25 FASB ASC 946-320-25-1 states that an investment company should record security purchases and sales as of the trade date.

2.26 Because securities transactions are recorded as of the trade date rather than the settlement date, the statement of assets and liabilities of most investment companies at the end of an accounting period includes receivables from brokers for securities sold but not delivered and payables to brokers for securities purchased but not received.

2.27 As noted in FASB ASC 946-320-25-2, a securities transaction outside conventional channels, such as through a private placement or by submitting shares in a tender offer, should be recorded as of the date that the investment company obtained a right to demand the securities purchased or to collect the proceeds of sale and incurred an obligation to pay the price of the securities purchased or to deliver the securities sold, respectively. Determining the recording date may sometimes require an interpretation by legal counsel.

---

[14] Rule 2a-4(a) of the 1940 Act permits registered investment companies to record security transactions as of one day after the trade date for purposes of determining net asset value. However, as noted by FASB *Accounting Standards Codification* (ASC) 946-320-25-1, for financial reporting purposes, security transactions should be recorded on the trade date.

[15] See footnote 14.

[16] Rule 2a-4(b) of the 1940 Act.

2.28 This topic of a securities transaction occurring outside of conventional channels is also discussed in section 404.03.a of the SEC's *Codification of Financial Reporting Policies*.

2.29 "Pending Content" in FASB ASC 946-320-30-1 states that an investment company should initially measure its investments in debt and equity securities at their transaction price. The transaction price should include commissions and other charges that are part of the purchase transaction.

2.30 FASB ASC 860, *Transfers and Servicing*, provides accounting and reporting standards that are applicable to certain investment companies' transactions, such as repurchase and reverse repurchase agreements, dollar rolls, and securities borrowed and loaned. See paragraphs 2.139–.140 for further discussion of the accounting and reporting standards associated with such transactions.

Valuing Investments

2.31 Values and changes in values of investments held by investment companies are as important to investors as the investment income earned thereon. Pursuant to FASB ASC 946-320, FASB ASC 946-323 (including related "Pending Content"), and FASB ASC 946-810 (including related "Pending Content"), investment companies are required to measure and report their investment assets (for example, debt and equity securities and derivatives) at fair value (as previously defined). As discussed in FASB ASC 820-10-35-41, a quoted price in an active market provides the most reliable evidence of the fair value and should be used without adjustment to measure fair value whenever available, except as specified in paragraph 41C of FASB ASC 820-10-35. An *active market* is defined by the FASB ASC glossary as a market in which transactions for the asset or liability take place with sufficient frequency and volume to provide pricing information on an ongoing basis.

2.32 Registered investment companies are also governed by the definition of *value* found in Section 2(a)(41) of the 1940 Act and further interpreted in section 404.03 of the SEC's *Codification of Financial Reporting Policies*. With respect to securities for which market quotations are readily available, Section 2(a)(41) states that value is defined as the market (fair) value of such securities determined by reference to market information. With respect to other securities and assets, Section 2(a)(41) states that value is defined as the fair value determined in good faith by the board of directors. This is also described in Accounting Series Release No. 118.[17]

2.33 Many financial instruments are traded publicly in active markets; therefore, end-of-day market quotations are readily available. However, if quoted market prices in active markets are not available, fair value may be estimated in a variety of ways, depending on the nature of the instrument and the manner in which it is traded.[18] Management's best estimate in good faith (under the oversight of the board of directors or trustees) of fair value should be based on the consistent application of a variety of factors, in accordance with the valuation policy followed by the fund, with the objective being to determine

---

[17] The SEC has established a bibliography of regulatory guidance relating to the valuation of investments in accordance with the 1940 Act, including references to applicable laws, regulations, releases, selected staff guidance, and enforcement actions. The bibliography is accessible in the Division of Investment Management section of the SEC website.

[18] Section 2(a)(41) of the 1940 Act.

the exit price or amount at which the investment could be exchanged in a current transaction between willing parties, other than in a forced or liquidation sale. The fair value reported for investments is not reduced by transaction costs such as estimated brokerage commissions and other costs that would be incurred in selling the investments. As noted in FASB ASC 820-10-35-2B, the fair value measurement of a particular asset or liability should consider the characteristics of the asset or liability if market participants would take those characteristics into account when pricing the asset or liability at the measurement date. Such characteristics include, for example, the following: (*a*) the condition and location of the asset, and (*b*) restrictions, if any, on the sale or use of the asset. A restriction that would transfer with the asset in an assumed sale would generally be deemed a characteristic of the asset and therefore would likely be considered by market participants in pricing the asset. Conversely, a restriction that is specific to the reporting entity holding the asset would not transfer with the asset in an assumed sale and therefore would not be considered when measuring fair value.

2.34 FASB ASC 820-10-35 establishes a fair value hierarchy that prioritizes the inputs to valuation techniques used to measure fair value into three broad levels. The fair value hierarchy gives the highest priority to quoted prices (unadjusted) in active markets for identical assets or liabilities (level 1) and the lowest priority to unobservable inputs (level 3). FASB ASC 820 also clarifies that fair value is market based, as opposed to an entity-specific measure.

2.35 An investment company's registration statement or offering circular describes the methods used to value its investments.[19] Section 404.03 of the SEC's *Codification of Financial Reporting Policies* describes various methods for estimating fair value.

2.36 As discussed in paragraphs 2–3 of FASB ASC 946-320-35, valuing securities listed and traded on one or more securities exchanges or unlisted securities traded regularly in over-the-counter (OTC) markets (for example, U.S. Treasury bonds, notes, and bills or stocks traded in the NASDAQ Stock Market) ordinarily is not difficult because quotations of completed transactions are published daily, or price quotations are readily obtainable from financial reporting services or individual broker-dealers. A security traded in an active market on the valuation date is valued at the last quoted sales price. (See also the discussion starting at paragraph 11.55.)

2.37 FASB ASC 820-10-35-6C and 820-10-30-2 provide that even when there is no observable market to provide pricing information about the sale of an asset or the transfer of a liability at the measurement date, a fair value measurement should assume that a transaction takes place at that date, considered from the perspective of a market participant that holds the asset or owes the liability. The objective of a fair value measurement focuses on the price that would be received to sell the asset or paid to transfer the liability (an *exit price*), not the price that would be paid to acquire the asset or received to assume the liability in an exchange transaction (an *entry price*). However, FASB ASC 820-10-30-3 explains that, in many cases, the transaction price will equal fair value (for example, that might be the case when, on the transaction date, the transaction to buy an asset takes place in the market in which the asset would be sold).

---

[19] Items 11 and 23 of Form N-1A.

2.38 Paragraphs 5–6 of FASB ASC 820-10-35 states that the transaction to sell the asset or transfer the liability takes place in the principal market for the asset or liability or, in the absence of a principal market, the most advantageous market for the asset or liability. As defined by the FASB ASC glossary, the *principal market* is the market with the greatest volume and level of activity for the asset or liability. Also, as defined by the FASB ASC glossary, the *most advantageous market* is the market that maximizes the amount that would be received to sell the asset or minimizes the amount that would be paid to transfer the liability, after taking into account transaction costs and transportation costs. A reporting entity need not undertake an exhaustive search of all possible markets to identify the principal market or the most advantageous market, but it should take into account all information that is reasonably available. If there is a principal market for the asset or liability, the fair value measurement should represent the price in that market (whether that price is directly observable or estimated using another valuation technique), even if the price in a different market is potentially more advantageous at the measurement date. The reporting entity must have access to the principal (or most advantageous) market at the measurement date. Because different entities (and businesses within those entities) with different activities may have access to different markets, the principal (or most advantageous) market for the same asset or liability might be different for different entities (and businesses within those entities). Therefore, the principal (or most advantageous) market (and thus, market participants) should be considered from the perspective of the reporting entity, thereby allowing for differences between and among entities with different activities.

2.39 Investment companies may find guidance in the preceding paragraphs useful when investment portfolios include securities listed on (*a*) more than one national securities exchange, or (*b*) on a national exchange and in the OTC market. When applying guidance in the preceding paragraphs to these scenarios, the exchange or market that contains the greatest volume and level of activity for that security would likely be deemed the principal market. When an investment company holds a security that is not traded in the principal market on the valuation date, the security may be valued at the last quoted sales price on the next most active market if management determines that price to be representative of fair value. If the price is determined not to be representative of fair value, the security may be valued based on quotations readily available from principal-to-principal markets, financial publications, or recognized pricing services, or a good-faith estimate of fair value should be made.

2.40 As explained in FASB ASC 820-10-35-9B, the price in the principal (or most advantageous) market used to measure the fair value of the asset or liability should not be adjusted for transaction costs, which should be accounted for in accordance with the provisions of other accounting guidance. As defined by the FASB ASC glossary, *transaction costs* are the costs to sell an asset or transfer a liability in the principal (or most advantageous) market for the asset or liability that are directly attributable to the disposal of the asset or the transfer of the liability. Transaction costs meet both of the following criteria:

a. They result directly from and are essential to that transaction.

b. They would not have been incurred by the entity had the decision to sell the asset or transfer the liability not been made (similar to costs to sell, as defined by FASB ASC 360-10-35-38).

2.41 Securities markets, financial publications, and recognized pricing services frequently provide quotations of bid price and asked price. Those quotations may be used if a principal-to-principal market is the primary market for the security on the valuation date or, in the absence of trading, on the valuation date of the security normally traded primarily on an exchange. Some investment companies use the bid price to value securities, some use the mean between the bid and asked prices, and some use a valuation within the range between the bid and asked prices that is considered to best represent fair value in the circumstances. If price quotations are obtained from individual broker-dealers making a market in the security, some investment companies will estimate fair value as the mean of the quoted prices obtained. Each of those policies is acceptable if applied consistently and in accordance with the investment company's established pricing policy. However, neither use of the asked price alone to value investments nor use of the bid price alone to value short sales or short positions is acceptable. If only a bid price or an asked price is available for a security on the valuation date, or the spread between the bid and asked price on that date is substantial, quotations for several days could be, for example, reviewed in determining whether the last quoted price is representative of fair value.

2.42 Many funds utilize pricing services to obtain security valuations. Those pricing services may provide quotations on listed securities and OTC securities, as described in the preceding paragraphs. Also, particularly for debt securities, pricing services may provide valuations determined by other pricing techniques. Methods generally recognized in the valuation of financial instruments include comparison to reliable quotations of similar financial instruments, pricing models, matrix pricing, or other formula-based pricing methods. Those methodologies incorporate factors for which published market data may be available. For instance, the mathematical technique known as matrix pricing may be used to determine fair value based on market data available with respect to the issue and similar issues without exclusive reliance on issuer-specific quoted market prices.

2.43 The incorporation of a premium or discount in the fair value measurement is discussed in FASB ASC 820-10-35-36B:

> A reporting entity shall select inputs that are consistent with the characteristics of the asset or liability that market participants would take into account in a transaction for the asset or liability (see paragraphs 2B-2C of FASB ASC 820-10-35). In some cases, those characteristics result in the application of an adjustment, such as a premium or discount (for example, a control premium or noncontrolling interest discount). However, a fair value measurement shall not incorporate a premium or discount that is inconsistent with the unit of account in the FASB ASC topic that requires or permits the fair value measurement. Premiums or discounts that reflect size as a characteristic of the reporting entity's holding (specifically, a blockage factor that adjusts the quoted price of an asset or a liability because the market's normal daily trading volume is not sufficient to absorb the quantity held by the entity, as described in FASB ASC 820-10-35-44) rather than as a characteristic of the asset or liability (for example, a control premium when measuring the fair value of a controlling interest) are not permitted in a fair value measurement. In all cases, if there is a quoted price in an active market (that is, a level 1 input) for an asset or a liability, a reporting entity shall use that quoted price without

adjustment when measuring fair value, except as specified in FASB ASC 820-10-35-41C.

2.44 To summarize, the unit of account of the asset or liability is the primary determining factor when deciding to include or exclude a premium or discount during fair value measurement. The unit of account is determined through applicable U.S. generally accepted accounting principles in the respective FASB ASC topic that permitted or required fair value measurement of the asset or liability (for example, reporting units in FASB ASC 350, *Intangibles— Goodwill and Other*).

- When a discount or premium is a characteristic of the asset or liability (the unit of account), it can be incorporated in the fair value measurement. For example, a premium associated with a controlling equity interest in an investee would be incorporated into the fair value measurement. Sale restrictions and market liquidity may be other asset or liability characteristics that generate premiums or discounts and should be incorporated into the fair value measurement.

- When a discount or premium is a characteristic of the entity's holding in an asset or liability with a unit of account, it cannot be incorporated in the fair value measurement. For example, a discount associated with a blockage factor (a factor that adjusts the quoted price of an asset or a liability because the market's normal daily trading volume is not sufficient to absorb the quantity held by the entity) would not be incorporated into the fair value measurement.

Fair Value Determination When the Volume or Level of Activity Has Significantly Decreased

2.45 Situations may arise when quoted market prices are not readily available or when market quotations are available, but it is questionable whether they represent fair value. Examples include the following instances:

- Market quotations and transactions are infrequent, and the most recent quotations and transactions occurred substantially prior to the valuation date.

- The market for the security is "thin" (that is, there are few transactions or market-makers in the security, the spread between the bid and asked prices is large, and price quotations vary substantially either over time or among individual market-makers).

- The last quoted market prices for foreign securities are as of the close of a market that precedes the fund's normal time for valuation, and certain events have taken place since the close of that foreign market that provide evidence that the market prices of those securities would be substantially different at the fund's normal time for valuation if such foreign market were open at that time. Such events are referred to by the SEC staff as significant events.[20]

---

[20] April 30, 2001, letter from the SEC Division of Investment Management to the Investment Company Institute regarding valuation issues. The letter further states that significant fluctuations in domestic markets may constitute a significant event.

- Trading in a market or for a specific security had been suspended during a trading day and had not reopened by the fund's normal time for valuation for such reasons as the declaration of a market emergency by a regulatory body, the imposition of daily price change limits or "circuit-breakers," or the intended release of information by an issuer was expected to have a material effect on a security's value.

Similar circumstances may also affect the appropriateness of valuations supplied by pricing services. Situations such as the preceding are expected to be rare but may occur. In those cases, an investment company may establish a policy to substitute a good-faith estimate of fair value for the quoted market price or pricing service valuation. Any policy adopted should be consistently applied in all situations when significant pricing differences are determined to exist.

2.46 Paragraphs 54C–54M of FASB ASC 820-10-35 clarify the application of FASB ASC 820 in determining fair value when the volume and level of activity for an asset or liability has significantly decreased. Guidance is also included in identifying transactions that are not orderly. In addition, paragraphs 90–98 of FASB ASC 820-10-55 include illustrations on the application of this guidance.

2.47 The definition of *fair value* states that it is the price obtained in an orderly transaction. The FASB ASC glossary defines an *orderly transaction* as a transaction that assumes exposure to the market for a period before the measurement date to allow for marketing activities that are usual and customary for transactions involving such assets and liabilities; it is not a forced transaction (for example, a forced liquidation or distress sale).

2.48 Consistent with FASB ASC 820-10-35-54G, even when there has been a significant decrease in the volume or level of activity for the asset or liability, the objective of a fair value measurement remains the same. A reporting entity should evaluate the significance and relevance of the factors listed in FASB ASC 820-10-35-54C to determine whether, on the basis of the evidence available, there has been a significant decrease in the volume or level of activity. According to FASB ASC 820-10-35-54D, if, after evaluating the factors, the conclusion is reached that there has been a significant decrease in the volume or level of activity for the asset or liability in relation to normal market conditions, further analysis of the transactions or quoted prices is needed. A decrease in the volume or level of activity on its own may not indicate that a transaction price or quoted price does not represent fair value or that a transaction in that market is not orderly. However, if a reporting entity determines that a transaction or quoted price does not represent fair value (for example, there may be transactions that are not orderly), an adjustment to the transactions or quoted prices will be necessary if the reporting entity uses those prices as a basis for measuring fair value and that adjustment may be significant to the fair value measurement in its entirety. Adjustments may also be necessary in other circumstances (for example, when a price for a similar asset requires significant adjustment to make it comparable to the asset being measured or when the price is stale). According to FASB ASC 820-10-35-54F, the objective is to determine the point within the range of fair value measurements that is most representative of fair value under the current market conditions. A wide range of fair value measurements may be an indication that further analysis is needed.

2.49 FASB ASC 820-10-35-54H states that estimating the price at which market participants would be willing to enter into a transaction at the measurement date under current market conditions if there has been a significant decrease in the volume or level of activity for the asset or liability depends on the facts and circumstances at the measurement date and requires judgment. A reporting entity's intention to hold the asset or to settle or otherwise fulfill the liability is not relevant, however, because fair value is a market-based measurement, not an entity-specific measurement.

2.50 According to FASB ASC 820-10-35-54I, a reporting entity should evaluate the circumstances to determine whether, based on the weight of the evidence available, the transaction is orderly. When there has been a significant decrease in the volume or level of activity for the asset or liability, it is not appropriate to conclude that all transactions are not orderly (that is, distressed or forced). Circumstances that may indicate that a transaction is not orderly include the following:

- There was not adequate exposure to the market for a period before the measurement date to allow for marketing activities that are usual and customary for transactions involving such assets or liabilities under current market conditions.
- There was a usual and customary marketing period, but the seller marketed the asset or liability to a single market participant.
- The seller is in or near bankruptcy or receivership (that is, the seller is distressed).
- The seller was required to sell to meet regulatory or legal requirements (that is, the seller was forced).
- The transaction price is an outlier when compared with other recent transactions for the same or a similar asset or liability.

The determination of whether a transaction is orderly or is not orderly is more difficult if there has been a significant decrease in the volume or level of activity for the asset or liability in relation to normal market activity for the asset or liability (or similar assets or liabilities).

2.51 FASB ASC 820-10-35-54J states that a reporting entity should consider all of the following when measuring fair value or estimating market risk premiums:

- If the evidence indicates that the transaction is not orderly, a reporting entity should place little, if any, weight (compared with other indications of fair value) on that transaction price.
- If the evidence indicates that a transaction is orderly, a reporting entity should take into account that transaction price. The amount of weight placed on that transaction price when compared with other indications of fair value will depend on the facts and circumstances, such as the volume of the transaction, the comparability of the transaction to the asset or liability being measured, and the proximity of the transaction to the measurement date.
- If a reporting entity does not have sufficient information to conclude whether a transaction is orderly, it should take into account the transaction price. However, that transaction price may not represent fair value (that is, the transaction price is not necessarily the sole or primary basis for measuring fair value or

estimating market risk premiums). When a reporting entity does not have sufficient information to conclude whether particular transactions are orderly, the reporting entity should place less weight on those transactions when compared with other transactions that are known to be orderly.

In making the determination regarding whether a transaction is orderly, a reporting entity does not need to undertake exhaustive efforts, but should not ignore information that is reasonably available. When a reporting entity is a party to a transaction, it is presumed to have sufficient information to conclude whether the transaction is orderly.

Valuation Techniques

2.52   Rule 38a-1 under the 1940 Act requires registered investment companies and business development companies (BDCs) (referred to in the adopting release as funds) to adopt policies and procedures reasonably designed to prevent the violation of federal securities laws.[21] In the adopting release, the SEC stated that Rule 38a-1

> requires funds to adopt policies and procedures that require the fund to monitor for circumstances that may necessitate the use of fair value prices; establish criteria for determining when market quotations are no longer reliable for a particular portfolio security; provide a methodology or methodologies by which the fund determines the current fair value of the portfolio security; and regularly review the appropriateness and accuracy of the method used in valuing securities, and make any necessary adjustments. [footnotes omitted][22]

Investment companies offering their shares on Forms N-1A and N-3 are also required by the SEC to provide a brief explanation in their prospectuses of the circumstances under which they will use fair value prices and the effects of using fair value pricing.[23]

2.53   The SEC's *Codification of Financial Reporting Policies* provides guidance on the factors to be considered in, and the responsibilities for and methods used for, the valuation of securities for which market quotations are not readily available.[24] The following paragraphs regarding securities valued in good faith are consistent with those SEC policies and are intended to summarize and provide guidance on this topic.

2.54   The objective of the fair value estimation process is to state the securities at the amount at which they could be exchanged in a current transaction

---

[21] Many of the operations of a fund may be carried out by entities that provide services to the fund. The service providers have their own compliance policies and procedures that may affect or be part of a fund's or investment adviser's compliance or internal control over compliance with federal securities laws. Statement of Position 07-2, *Attestation Engagements That Address Specified Compliance Control Objectives and Related Controls at Entities That Provide Services to Investment Companies, Investment Advisers, or Other Service Providers* (AICPA, *Professional Standards*, AUD sec. 40), may be a useful resource for practitioners who are engaged to report on the suitability of the design and operating effectiveness of a service provider's controls in achieving specified compliance control objectives (such as those required for compliance with Rule 38a-1 under the 1940 Act).

[22] SEC Final Rule Release No. IC-26299, *Compliance Programs of Investment Companies and Investment Advisers*, under the 1940 Act.

[23] SEC Final Rule Release No. IC-26418, *Disclosure Regarding Market Timing and Selective Disclosure of Portfolio Holdings*, under the 1940 Act.

[24] Sections 404.03–.94 of the SEC's *Codification of Financial Reporting Policies*.

between willing parties, other than in a forced or liquidation sale. The term *current transaction* means realization in an orderly disposition over a reasonable period. All relevant factors generally should be considered in selecting the method of estimating in good faith the fair value of each kind of security.

2.55 In estimating in good faith the fair value of a particular financial instrument, the board or its designee (the valuation committee) generally should, to the extent necessary, take into consideration all indications of fair value that are available. This guide does not purport to delineate all factors that may be considered; however, the following is a list of some of the factors to be considered:

- Financial standing of the issuer
- Business and financial plan of the issuer and comparison of actual results with the plan
- Cost at the date of purchase
- Size of the position held and the liquidity of the market[25]
- Security-specific contractual restrictions on the disposition
- Pending public offering with respect to the financial instrument
- Pending reorganization activity affecting the financial instrument (such as merger proposals, tender offers, debt restructurings, and conversions)
- Reported prices and the extent of public trading in similar financial instruments of the issuer or comparable entities
- Ability of the issuer to obtain the needed financing
- Changes in the economic conditions affecting the issuer
- A recent purchase or sale of a security of the entity
- Pricing by other dealers in similar securities
- Financial statements of the investees

2.56 No single method exists for estimating fair value in good faith because fair value depends on the facts and circumstances of each individual case. Valuation methods may be based on a multiple of earnings or a discount or premium from a market of a similar, freely traded security of the same issuer; on a yield to maturity with respect to debt issues; or on a combination of these and other methods. In addition, with respect to derivative products, other factors (such as volatility, interest and foreign exchange rates, and term to maturity) should be considered. The board of directors or trustees should be satisfied, however, that the method used to estimate fair value in good faith is reasonable and appropriate and that the resulting valuation is representative of fair value.

2.57 According to sections 404.03–.04 of the SEC's *Codification of Financial Reporting Policies*, the information considered and the basis for the valuation decision should be documented, and the supporting data should be retained. The board may appoint individuals to assist it in the estimation

---

[25] FASB *Accounting Standards Codification* (ASC) 820-10-35-36B explains when a discount or premium associated with the size of the position held and the liquidity of the market should be incorporated in the fair value measurement. The unit of account of the asset or liability being measured at fair value is critical in this assessment. Readers should consider this guidance, which is discussed in paragraph 2.43.

process and to make the necessary calculations. The rationale for the use of a good-faith estimate of fair value that is different from market quotations or pricing service valuations ordinarily should be documented. If material, the circumstances surrounding the substitution of good-faith estimates of fair value for market quotations or pricing service valuations should be disclosed in the notes to the financial statements.

2.58 Paragraphs 24–27 of FASB ASC 820-10-35 describe the valuation techniques that should be used to measure fair value. The objective of using a valuation technique is to estimate the price at which an orderly transaction to sell the asset or to transfer the liability would take place between market participants at the measurement date under current market conditions. Three widely used valuation techniques are the *market approach*, *cost approach*, and *income approach*. These approaches are described in paragraphs 3A–3G of FASB ASC 820-10-55, as follows:

- The *market approach* uses prices and other relevant information generated by market transactions involving identical or comparable assets, liabilities, or a group of assets and liabilities, such as a business. Valuation techniques consistent with the market approach include matrix pricing and often use market multiples derived from a set of comparables.

- The *cost approach* reflects the amount that currently would be required to replace the service capacity of an asset (often referred to as current replacement cost).

- The *income approach* converts future amounts (for example, cash flows or income and expenses) to a single current (that is, discounted) amount. When the income approach is used, the fair value measurement reflects current market expectations about those future amounts. Valuation techniques consistent with the income approach include present value techniques, option-pricing models, and the multiperiod excess earnings method.

2.59 FASB ASC 820-10-35-24 states that valuation techniques that are appropriate in the circumstances and for which sufficient data are available to measure fair value, maximizing the use of relevant observable inputs, and minimizing the use of unobservable inputs, should be used by a reporting entity. FASB ASC 820-10-35-24B explains that in some cases, a single valuation technique will be appropriate (for example, when valuing an asset or a liability using quoted prices in an active market for identical assets or liabilities). In other cases, multiple valuation techniques will be appropriate (for example, that might be the case when valuing a reporting unit). If multiple valuation techniques are used to measure fair value, the results (that is, respective indications of fair value) should be evaluated, considering the reasonableness of the range indicated by those results. FASB ASC 820-10-55-35 illustrates the use of multiple valuation techniques. A fair value measurement is the point within that range that is most representative of fair value in the circumstances.

2.60 As explained in paragraphs 25–26 of FASB ASC 820-10-35, valuation techniques used to measure fair value should be applied consistently. However, a change in a valuation technique or its application is appropriate if the change results in a measurement that is equally or more representative of fair value in the circumstances. Such a change would be accounted for as a change in accounting estimate, in accordance with the provisions of FASB

ASC 250, *Accounting Changes and Error Corrections.* However, as explained in FASB ASC 250-10-50-5, the disclosures in FASB ASC 250 for a change in accounting estimate are not required for revisions resulting from a change in a valuation technique or its application.

Present Value Techniques

2.61 Paragraphs 5–20 of FASB ASC 820-10-55 describe the use of present value techniques to measure fair value. Those paragraphs neither prescribe the use of a single specific present value technique nor limit the use of present value techniques to measure fair value to the techniques discussed therein. A fair value measurement of an asset or a liability using a present value technique captures all of the following elements from the perspective of market participants at the measurement date:

- An estimate of future cash flows
- Expectations about possible variations in the amount and timing of the cash flows
- Time value of money
- The price for bearing the uncertainty inherent in the cash flows (that is, a risk premium)
- Other factors that market participants would take into account in the circumstances
- For a liability, the nonperformance risk relating to that liability, including the reporting entity's (that is, the obligor's) own credit risk

2.62 FASB ASC 820-10-55-6 provides the general principles that govern any present value technique used to measure fair value, as follows:

- Cash flows and discount rates should reflect assumptions that market participants would use when pricing the asset or liability.
- Cash flows and discount rates should take into account only the factors attributable to the asset or liability being measured.
- To avoid double counting or omitting the effects of risk factors, discount rates should reflect assumptions that are consistent with those inherent in the cash flows. For example, a discount rate that reflects the uncertainty in expectations about future defaults is appropriate if using the contractual cash flows of a loan (that is, a discount rate adjustment technique), but is not appropriate if using expected (that is, probability-weighted) cash flows (that is, an expected present value technique) because the expected cash flows already reflect assumptions about the uncertainty in future defaults.
- Assumptions about cash flows and discount rates should be internally consistent. For example, nominal cash flows, which include the effects of inflation, should be discounted at a rate that includes the effects of inflation.
- Discount rates should be consistent with the underlying economic factors of the currency in which the cash flows are denominated.

2.63 FASB ASC 820-10-55-9 describes how present value techniques differ in how they adjust for risk and in the type of cash flows they use. For example, the discount rate adjustment technique (also called the traditional present value technique) uses a risk-adjusted discount rate and contractual, promised, or most likely cash flows. In contrast, method 1 of the expected present value technique uses risk-adjusted expected cash flows and a risk-free rate. Method 2 of the expected present value technique uses expected cash flows that are not risk adjusted and a discount rate adjusted to include the risk premium that market participants require. That rate is different from the rate used in the discount rate adjustment technique. FASB ASC 820-10-55-13 notes that, in the expected present value technique, the probability-weighted average of all possible future cash flows is referred to as the expected cash flows. The traditional present value technique and two methods of expected present value techniques are discussed more fully in FASB ASC 820-10-55.

The Fair Value Hierarchy

2.64 Because fair value is a market-based measurement, as stated in FASB ASC 820-10-35-9, fair value should be measured using the assumptions that market participants would use in pricing the asset or liability (referred to as inputs), assuming that market participants act in their economic best interest. The FASB ASC glossary defines *inputs* as assumptions that market participants would use when pricing the asset or liability, including assumptions about risk, such as the risk inherent in a particular valuation technique used to measure fair value (such as a pricing model) or the risk inherent in the inputs to the valuation technique. Inputs may be observable or unobservable (both as defined by the FASB ASC glossary):

- *Observable inputs* are developed using market data, such as publicly available information about actual events or transactions, and reflect the assumptions that market participants would use when pricing the asset or liability.

- *Unobservable inputs* are inputs for which market data are not available and are developed using the best information available about the assumptions that market participants would use when pricing the asset or liability.

2.65 Paragraphs 37–54B of FASB ASC 820-10-35 establishes a fair value hierarchy that distinguishes between observable and unobservable inputs. FASB ASC 820-10-05-1C states that when a price for an identical asset or liability is not observable, a reporting entity measures fair value using another valuation technique that maximizes the use of relevant observable inputs and minimizes the use of unobservable inputs.

2.66 The fair value hierarchy in FASB ASC 820-10-35 prioritizes the inputs to valuation techniques used to measure fair value into three broad levels. The three levels are discussed in FASB ASC 820-10-35, and are summarized as follows:

- *Level 1 inputs.* Paragraphs 40–46 of FASB ASC 820-10-35 state that level 1 inputs are quoted prices (unadjusted) in active markets for identical assets or liabilities that the reporting entity can access at the measurement date. FASB ASC 820-10-35-44 affirms the requirement that the fair value of a position in a single asset or liability (including a position comprising a large number of identical assets or liabilities, such as a holding of financial instruments) that trades in an active market should be measured within level 1 as the product of the quoted price for the individual asset or liability and the quantity held by the reporting entity. That is the case even if a market's normal daily trading volume is not sufficient to absorb the quantity held, and placing orders to sell the position in a single transaction might affect the quoted price.

- *Level 2 inputs.* Paragraphs 47–51 of FASB ASC 820-10-35 state that level 2 inputs are inputs other than quoted prices included within level 1 that are observable for the asset or liability, either directly or indirectly. If the asset or liability has a specified (contractual) term, a level 2 input must be observable for substantially the full term of the asset or liability. Adjustments to level 2 inputs will vary depending on factors specific to the asset or liability. Those factors include the condition or location of the asset, the extent to which inputs relate to items that are comparable to the asset (including those factors described in FASB ASC 820-10-35-16D), and the volume or level of activity in the markets within which the inputs are observed. An adjustment to a level 2 input that is significant to the entire measurement might result in a fair value measurement categorized within level 3 of the fair value hierarchy if the adjustment uses significant unobservable inputs. Level 2 inputs include the following:

  — Quoted prices for similar assets or liabilities in active markets

  — Quoted prices for identical or similar assets or liabilities in markets that are not active

  — Inputs other than quoted prices that are observable for the asset or liability (for example, interest rates and yield curves observable at commonly quoted intervals, implied volatilities, and credit spreads)

  — Inputs that are derived principally from, or corroborated by, observable market data by correlation or other means (market-corroborated inputs)

- *Level 3 inputs.* Paragraphs 52–54A of FASB ASC 820-10-35 state that level 3 inputs are unobservable inputs for the asset or liability. Unobservable inputs should be used to measure fair value to the extent that relevant observable inputs are not available, thereby allowing for situations in which there is little, if any, market activity for the asset or liability at the measurement date. A reporting entity should develop unobservable inputs using the best information available in the circumstances, which might include the entity's own data. In developing unobservable inputs, a reporting entity may begin with its own data, but it should adjust those data if reasonably available information indicates that other market participants would use different data or there is something particular to the reporting entity that is not available to other market participants (for example, an entity-specific synergy). A reporting entity need not undertake exhaustive efforts to obtain information about market participant assumptions. Unobservable inputs should reflect the assumptions that market participants would use when pricing the asset or liability, including assumptions about risk. Assumptions about risk include the risk inherent in a particular valuation technique and the risk inherent in the inputs to the valuation technique. A measurement that does not include an adjustment for risk would not represent a fair value measurement if market participants would include one when pricing the asset or liability. The reporting entity should take into account all information about market participant assumptions that is reasonably available.

2.67 As explained in FASB ASC 820-10-35-37A, in some cases, the inputs used to measure the fair value of an asset or a liability might be categorized within different levels of the fair value hierarchy. In those cases, the fair value measurement is categorized in its entirety in the same level of the fair value hierarchy as the lowest level input that is significant to the entire measurement. Adjustments to arrive at measurements based on fair value, such as costs to sell when measuring fair value less costs to sell, should not be taken into account when determining the level of the fair value hierarchy within which a fair value measurement is categorized.

2.68 As discussed in FASB ASC 820-10-35-38, the availability of relevant inputs and their relative subjectivity might affect the selection of appropriate valuation techniques. However, the fair value hierarchy prioritizes the inputs to valuation techniques, not the valuation techniques used to measure fair value. For example, a fair value measurement developed using a present value technique might be categorized within level 2 or level 3, depending on the inputs that are significant to the entire measurement and the level of the fair value hierarchy within which those inputs are categorized.

2.69 As stated in FASB ASC 820-10-35-2C, the effect on the measurement arising from a particular characteristic will differ depending on how that characteristic would be taken into account by market participants. FASB ASC 820-10-55-51 illustrates a restriction's effect on fair value measurement.

Application of Fair Value Measurements

2.70 FASB ASC 820-10-35-10A states that a fair value measurement of a nonfinancial asset takes into account a market participant's ability to generate economic benefits by using the asset in its highest and best use or by selling it to another market participant that would use the asset in its highest and best use. The FASB ASC glossary defines *highest and best use* as the use of a nonfinancial asset by market participants that would maximize the value of the asset or the group of assets and liabilities (for example, a business) within which the asset would be used. Further, FASB ASC 820-10-35-11A states that the fair value measurement of a nonfinancial asset assumes that the asset is sold consistent with the unit of account (which may be an individual asset). That is the case even when that fair value measurement assumes that the highest and best use of the asset is to use it in combination with other assets or with other assets and liabilities because a fair value measurement assumes that the market participant already holds the complementary assets and associate liabilities.[26]

---

[26] FASB ASC 820-10-35 limits the application of the "highest and best use" concept to nonfinancial assets. FASB Accounting Standards Update (ASU) No. 2011-04, *Fair Value Measurement*

(continued)

2.71 According to paragraphs 16–16A of FASB ASC 820-10-35, a fair value measurement assumes that a financial or nonfinancial liability or an instrument classified in a reporting entity's shareholders' equity is transferred to a market participant at the measurement date. The transfer of a liability or an instrument classified in a reporting entity's shareholders' equity assumes that (*a*) a liability would remain outstanding and the market participant transferee would be required to fulfill the obligation and (*b*) an instrument classified in a reporting entity's shareholders' equity would remain outstanding and the market participant transferee would take on the rights and responsibilities associated with the instrument. It is also assumed the liability or instrument would not be settled with the counterparty, cancelled, or otherwise extinguished on the measurement date. Even when there is no observable market to provide pricing information about the transfer of a liability or an instrument classified in a reporting entity's shareholders' equity (for example, because contractual or other legal restrictions prevent the transfer of such items), there might be an observable market for such items if they are held by other parties as assets (for example, a corporate bond or a call option on a reporting entity's shares).

2.72 Paragraphs 16B–16BB of FASB ASC 820-10-35 states that when a quoted price for the transfer of an identical or a similar liability or instrument classified in a reporting entity's shareholders' equity is not available, and the identical item is held by another party as an asset, a reporting entity should measure the fair value from the perspective of a market participant that holds the identical item as an asset at the measurement date. In such cases, a reporting entity should measure the fair value of the liability or equity instrument as follows:

a. Using the quoted price in an active market for the identical item held by another party as an asset, if that price is available

b. If that price is not available, using other observable inputs, such as the quoted price in a market that is not active for the identical item held by another party as an asset

c. If the observable prices in items *a–b* are not available, using another valuation technique, such as an income approach or a market approach

2.73 According to FASB ASC 820-10-35-16D, a reporting entity should adjust the quoted price of a liability held by another party as an asset only if there are factors specific to the asset that are not applicable to the fair value measurement of the liability or equity instrument. A reporting entity should determine that the price of the asset does not reflect the effect of a restriction preventing the sale of that asset. Some factors that may indicate that the quoted price of the asset should be adjusted include (*a*) the quoted price for the asset relates to a similar, but not identical, liability or equity instrument held by another party as an asset, or (*b*) the unit of account for the asset is not the same as for the liability or equity instrument.

2.74 According to FASB ASC 820-10-35-16H, when a quoted price for the transfer of an identical or a similar liability is not available and the identical

---

(footnote continued)

(Topic 820): Amendments to Achieve Common Fair Value Measurement and Disclosure Requirements in U.S. GAAP and IFRSs, specifies that the highest and best use and valuation premise are relevant only when measuring the fair value of nonfinancial assets and are not relevant when measuring the fair value of financial assets or liabilities.

item is not held by another party as an asset, a reporting entity should measure the fair value of the liability or equity instrument using a valuation technique from the perspective of a market participant that owes the liability or has issued the claim on equity.

2.75 When measuring the fair value of a liability, FASB ASC 820-10-35-18B states that a reporting entity should not include a separate input or an adjustment to other inputs relating to the existence of a restriction that prevents the transfer of the item because the effect of that restriction is either implicitly or explicitly included in the other inputs to the fair value measurement. Refer to FASB ASC 820-10-35-18C for an example of the fair value measurement of a liability with such a restriction.

2.76 Paragraphs 17–18 of FASB ASC 820-10-35 provide that the fair value of a liability should reflect the effect of nonperformance risk (which includes, but is not limited to, a reporting entity's own credit risk). Nonperformance risk is assumed to be the same before and after the transfer of the liability. When measuring the fair value of a liability, a reporting entity should take into account the effect of its credit risk (credit standing) and any other factors that might influence the likelihood that the obligation will or will not be fulfilled.

2.77 FASB ASC 820-10-35-18A discusses fair value measurement of a liability that has an inseparable third-party credit enhancement (for example, debt that is issued with a financial guarantee from a third party that guarantees the issuer's payment obligation). The fair value of a liability reflects the effect of nonperformance risk on the basis of its unit of account. In accordance with FASB ASC 825, *Financial Instruments*, the issuer of a liability issued with an inseparable third-party credit enhancement that is accounted for separately from the liability should not include the effect of the credit enhancement (for example, the third-party guarantee of debt) in the fair value measurement of the liability. If the credit enhancement is accounted for separately from the liability, the issuer would take into account its own credit standing and not that of the third-party guarantor when measuring the fair value of the liability.

2.78 Private equity funds or BDCs (collectively, a fund) may hold a controlling interest in an investee company and hold both equity and debt instruments issued by the investee. From a business strategy perspective, in this circumstance, the fund's management may view their investment in the debt and equity instruments as an aggregate position rather than as separate financial instruments. Technical Questions and Answers (Q&A) section 6910.34, "Application of the Notion of Value Maximization for Measuring Fair Value of Debt and Controlling Equity Positions" (AICPA, *Technical Questions and Answers*), discusses when it may be appropriate to apply the notion of value maximization (as discussed in paragraph BC49 of FASB ASU No. 2011-04, *Fair Value Measurement (Topic 820): Amendments to Achieve Common Fair Value Measurement and Disclosure Requirements in U.S. GAAP and IFRSs*) to assist management of a fund that holds a controlling interest in an investee company and hold both equity and debt instruments issued by the investee for which there are not observed trades. BC49 of ASU No. 2011-04 states

> Market participants seek to maximize the fair value of a financial or nonfinancial asset or to minimize the fair value of a financial or nonfinancial liability by acting in their economic best interest in a transaction to sell the asset or to transfer the liability in the principal (or most advantageous) market for the asset or liability. Such a transaction might involve grouping assets and liabilities in a way in which

market participants would enter into a transaction, if the unit of account specified in other Topics (of the FASB ASC) does not prohibit that grouping.

2.79 This language provides fair value measurement guidance in situations when the unit of account is not specified. Because FASB ASC 946, *Financial Services—Investment Companies*, does not specify the unit of account for measuring fair value, it might be appropriate to consider how fair value would be maximized, which may be in a transaction that involves both the debt and controlling equity position if that is how market participants would transact.[27] Consistent with the guidance in paragraph BC49 of ASU No. 2011-04, this transaction (and, thus, fair value) might be measured using an enterprise value approach measured in accordance with the guidance in FASB ASC 820 (that is, an exit price from the perspective of market participants under current conditions at the measurement date).

2.80 Because the enterprise value approach results in a fair value for the entire capital position (that is, both debt and equity), an allocation to the individual units of account would be necessary. FASB ASC 820 does not prescribe an allocation approach, but FASB ASC 820-10-35-18F discusses that a "reporting entity should perform such allocations on a reasonable and consistent basis using a methodology appropriate in the circumstances." Facts and circumstances, such as relevant characteristics of the debt and equity instruments, must be considered when making this allocation. Generally, the allocation method should be consistent with the overall valuation premise used to measure fair value.

2.81 Q&A section 6910.35, "Assessing Control When Measuring Fair Value" (AICPA, *Technical Questions and Answers*), discusses when it may be appropriate to aggregate positions across multiple reporting entities (multiple funds) to assess control[28] for purposes of whether a control premium might be appropriate in a fair value measurement. Q&A section 6910.35 explains that control of an investee company may be achieved by virtue of a single fund holding a controlling financial interest, through multiple funds in the same fund complex[29] under common control being allocated financial interests in the investee company, or through "club deals" in which a group of unrelated investment managers jointly make controlling investments in a private company on behalf of funds they manage. For example, a single adviser may decide to make a controlling financial investment in an investee and then allocate that investment across multiple legal and reporting entities. Individually, no one entity may control the investee (Q&A section 6910.35 assumes this is the case); however, the entities in aggregate may have a controlling financial interest in the investee.

2.82 It is not consistent with the fair value measurement framework in FASB ASC 820 for a reporting entity to aggregate positions across multiple reporting entities (multiple related funds or unrelated club deals) to assess

---

[27] This assessment would include a consideration of the entity's prior history in selling similar investments. Consideration of specific terms of the instruments that are considered characteristics, as discussed in FASB ASC 820, *Fair Value Measurement*, is also necessary (for example, change in control provisions).

[28] This question and answer does not address consolidation matters. Control in this question and answer refers to the ability to cause a controlling financial interest in the investee to be sold.

[29] Fund complex refers to a group of funds managed by the same investment adviser.

control[30] for purposes of whether a control premium might be appropriate in a fair value measurement. However, when determining the fair value of the position the reporting entity holds, that determination should consider whether other premiums and discounts (relative to the price of a noncontrolling interest) are appropriate. For example, observed transaction data for similar investments may indicate that market participants pay a premium multiple relative to the multiples observed for the guideline companies because some market participants place additional value on being part of the controlling group that has the right to determine the company's strategy.

2.83 A reporting entity should consider all available evidence about how a market participant would exit the investments (and the prices it would receive) in determining the principal (or most advantageous) market and whether premiums to noncontrolling interests are appropriate.

Offsetting Positions in Market Risks or Counterparty Credit Risk

2.84 FASB ASC 820-10-35-18D provides that a reporting entity that holds a group of financial assets and financial liabilities (including derivatives) is exposed to market risks (that is, interest rate risk, currency risk, or other price risk) and to the credit risk of each of the counterparties. When certain criteria are met, reporting entities are permitted to measure the fair value of the net asset or liability on the basis of the price that would be received to sell a net long position (that is, an asset) for a particular risk exposure or to transfer a net short position (that is, a liability) for a particular risk exposure in an orderly transaction between market participants at the measurement date under current market conditions. This is an exception to the general fair value measurement requirements in FASB ASC 820. This exception is intended to be utilized by entities who manage exposure to certain market or counterparty risks on a net basis, and the exception allows for valuation in a manner consistent with how market participants would price the net risk position. FASB ASC 820-10-35-18E states that

> A reporting entity is permitted to use the exception only if the reporting entity does all of the following:
>
> - Manages the group of financial assets and financial liabilities on the basis of the reporting entity's net exposure to a particular market risk (or risks) or to the credit risk of a particular counterparty in accordance with the reporting entity's documented risk management or investment strategy
> - Provides information on that basis about the group of financial statements and financial liabilities to the reporting entity's management
> - Is required or has elected to measure those financial assets and financial liabilities at fair value in the statement of financial position at the end of each reporting period.

2.85 Paragraphs 18F–18L of FASB ASC 820-10-35 provide further details on this exception, including consideration of scope, financial statement

---

[30] This is not consistent because it does not consider that, for example, kick-out rights may prevent a reporting entity from having unilateral control (even though the fund is part of a complex with the same adviser). Said another way, control is not a characteristic of the individual fund's investment in these assumed facts and circumstances.

presentation,[31] similarities between offsetting assets and liabilities (risks and duration), exposure to counterparty credit risk, and accounting policy elections.

Investments in Entities That Calculate Net Asset Value per Share

2.86 Paragraphs 54B and 59–62 of FASB ASC 820-10-35 contain guidance for permitting the use of a practical expedient, with appropriate disclosures, when measuring the fair value of an alternative investment that does not have a readily determinable fair value if certain criteria are met. A reporting entity is permitted, as a practical expedient, to estimate the fair value of an investment within the scope of paragraphs 4–5 of FASB ASC 820-10-15 using the net asset value per share (or its equivalent, such as member units or an ownership interest in partners' capital to which a proportionate share of net assets is attributed) of the investment, if the net asset value per share of the investment (or its equivalent) is calculated in a manner consistent with the measurement principles of FASB ASC 946 as of the reporting entity's measurement date. "Pending Content" in FASB ASC 820-10-15-4 explains that this guidance applies only to an investment that meets both of the following criteria as of the reporting entity's measurement date:

    a.   The investment does not have a readily determinable fair value.[32]

    b.   The investment is in an investment company within the scope of FASB ASC 946 or is an investment in a real estate fund for which it is industry practice to measure investment assets at fair value on a recurring basis and to issue financial statements that are consistent with the measurement principles in FASB ASC 946.

2.87 Certain attributes of the investment (such as restrictions on redemption) and transaction prices from principal-to-principal or brokered transactions will not be considered in measuring the fair value of the investment if the practical expedient is used. The practical expedient reduces complexity and improves consistency and comparability in the application of FASB ASC 820 while reducing the costs of applying FASB ASC 820. This guidance also improves transparency by requiring additional disclosures about investments within its scope to enable users of financial statements to understand the nature and risks of investments and whether the sale of the investments is probable at amounts different from net asset value per share.

2.88 As discussed in Q&A section 2220.18, "Applicability of Practical Expedient" (AICPA, *Technical Questions and Answers*), these investments, typically referred to as alternative investments, include interests in hedge funds,

---

[31] The ability to measure the fair value of a portfolio of financial assets and financial liabilities on the basis of net exposure does not affect the basis of financial statement presentation of those instruments. FASB ASC 820-10-35-18F explains that the basis for financial statement presentation of financial instruments in the statement of financial position may differ from the basis for the measurement of financial instruments. The reporting entity should consider other applicable FASB ASC topics, including FASB ASC 210-20, to determine the basis for financial statement presentation of financial instruments.

[32] FASB ASC 820-10-15-5 states that the definition of readily determinable fair value indicates that an equity security would have a readily determinable fair value if any one of three conditions is met. One of those conditions is that sales prices or bid-and-asked quotations are currently available on a securities exchange registered with the SEC or in the over-the-counter (OTC) market, provided that those prices or quotations for the OTC market are publicly reported by the National Association of Securities Dealers Automated Quotations System or Pink Sheets LLC. The definition notes that restricted stock meets that definition if the restriction expires within one year. If an investment otherwise would have a readily determinable fair value, except that the investment has a restriction expiring in more than one year, the reporting entity should not apply paragraphs 59–62 of FASB ASC 820-10-35 and FASB ASC 820-10-50-6A to the investment.

private equity funds, real estate funds, venture capital funds, offshore fund vehicles, commodity funds, and funds of funds. Further, Q&A section 2220.19, "Unit of Account" (AICPA, *Technical Questions and Answers*), states that, for interests in alternative investments, the appropriate unit of account is the interest in the investee fund itself, not the underlying investments within the investee fund; this is because the reporting entity owns an undivided interest in the whole of the investee fund portfolio and typically lacks the ability to dispose of individual assets and liabilities in the investee fund portfolio.

2.89 FASB ASC 820-10-35-60 states that, if the net asset value obtained from the investee is not as of the reporting entity's measurement date or is not calculated in a manner consistent with the measurement principles of FASB ASC 946, the reporting entity should consider whether an adjustment to the most recent net asset value is necessary. The objective of this adjustment would be to estimate a net asset value per share that is consistent with the aforementioned measurement principles.

2.90 Q&A section 2220.20, "Determining Whether NAV Is Calculated Consistent With FASB ASC 946, *Financial Services—Investment Companies*" (AICPA, *Technical Questions and Answers*), provides guidance to assist management of the reporting entity in determining whether net asset value is calculated consistent with FASB ASC 946. As part of this determination, a reporting entity should independently evaluate the fair value measurement process utilized by the investee fund manager to calculate the net asset value. This evaluation is a matter of professional judgment and includes determining that the investee fund manager has an effective process and related internal controls in place to estimate the fair value of its investments that are included in the net asset value calculation. The reporting entity's controls used to evaluate the process of the investee fund manager may include initial due diligence, ongoing monitoring, and financial reporting controls. Only after considering all relevant factors can the reporting entity reach a conclusion about whether the reported net asset value is calculated consistent with the measurement principles of FASB ASC 946. The reporting entity may consider the following key factors relating to the valuation received from the investee fund manager:

- The investee fund's fair value estimation processes and control environment and any changes to those processes or control environment

- The investee's fund policies and procedures for estimating fair value of the underlying investments and any changes to those policies or procedures

- The use of independent third-party valuation experts to augment and validate the investee fund's procedures for estimating fair value

- The portion of the underlying securities held by the investee fund that are traded on active markets

- The professional reputation and standing of the investee fund's auditor (this is not intended to suggest that the auditor is an element of the investee fund's internal control system but as a general risk factor in evaluating the integrity of the data obtained from the investee fund manager)

- Qualifications, if any, of the auditor's report on the investee fund's financial statements

- Whether there is a history of significant adjustments to the net asset value reported by the investee fund manager as a result of the annual financial statement audit or otherwise

- Findings in the investee fund's adviser or administrator's type 2 SOC 1® report, if any

- Whether net asset value has been appropriately adjusted for items such as carried interest and clawbacks

- Comparison of historical realizations to the last reported fair value

2.91 Q&A section 2220.20 goes on to discuss the scenario in which a reporting entity invests in a fund of funds. That reporting entity could conclude on the consistency of the net asset value calculation with FASB ASC 946 by assessing (a) whether the fund-of-funds manager has a process that considers the aforementioned key factors in the calculation of the net asset value reported by the fund of funds and (b) if the fund-of-funds manager has obtained or estimated the net asset value from underlying fund managers in a manner consistent with paragraphs 59–62 of FASB ASC 820-10-35 as of the measurement date. The reporting entity is not required to look through the fund-of-funds interest to underlying fund investments if the reporting entity has concluded that the fund-of-funds manager reports net asset value consistent with FASB ASC 946 for the fund-of-funds interest.

2.92 Q&A section 2220.22, "Adjusting NAV When It Is Not as of the Reporting Entity's Measurement Date" (AICPA, *Technical Questions and Answers*), illustrates how the reporting entity should estimate an adjustment when net asset value is calculated consistently with FASB ASC 946 but not as of the reporting entity's measurement date. One option is for the reporting entity to request the investee fund manager to provide a supplemental net asset value calculation consistent with the measurement principles of FASB ASC 946 as of the reporting entity's measurement date. Alternatively, it may be necessary to adjust or roll forward (or roll back) the reported net asset value for factors that could cause it to differ from the net asset value at the measurement date. When the reporting entity's measurement date is prior to the net asset value calculation date, it may be more appropriate to use that net asset value and perform a rollback, rather than using a reported net asset value calculated prior to the entity's measurement date. Q&A section 2220.22 lists factors that may necessitate an adjustment to the reported net asset value when it is not calculated as of the reporting entity's measurement date and contains an example rollforward net asset value calculation.

2.93 Q&A section 2220.23, "Adjusting NAV When It Is Not Calculated Consistent With FASB ASC 946" (AICPA, *Technical Questions and Answers*), illustrates how a reporting entity may estimate the adjustment when a reported net asset value is not calculated consistently with the measurement principles of FASB ASC 946. In this situation, the reporting entity should consider and understand the reasons why net asset value has not been based upon fair value, whether a fair value based net asset value can be obtained from the investee manager, and whether the specific data needed to adjust the reported net asset value can be obtained and properly utilized to estimate a fair value based net asset value. Some examples of circumstances in which the reporting entity may be able to obtain data to estimate an adjustment include, but are not limited to, the reported net asset value is on a cash basis, the reported net asset value utilizes blockage discounts taken in determining the fair value of investment securities (which is inconsistent with FASB ASC 820; see paragraph 2.43 for further consideration of premiums and discounts in fair value measurements), and the reported net asset value has not been adjusted for the impact of unrealized carried interest or incentive fees. Consequently, if the reporting entity finds that it is not practicable to calculate an adjusted net asset value, then the practical expedient is not available. The reporting entity may also elect not to utilize the practical expedient. In those cases, the reporting entity should apply the general measurement principles of FASB ASC 820 instead.

2.94 FASB ASC 820-10-35-61 states that a reporting entity should decide on an investment-by-investment basis whether to apply the practical expedient and should apply the practical expedient consistently to the fair value measurement of the reporting entity's entire position in a particular investment, unless it is probable at the measurement date that the reporting entity will sell a portion of an investment at an amount different from net asset value per share (or its equivalent), as described in FASB ASC 820-10-35-62 (see the following paragraph). In those situations, the reporting entity should account for the portion of the investment that is being sold in accordance with other provisions in FASB ASC 820 and should not apply the practical expedient discussed in FASB ASC 820-10-35-59.

2.95 According to FASB ASC 820-10-35-62, a reporting entity is not permitted to estimate the fair value of an investment within the scope of paragraphs 4–5 of FASB ASC 820-10-15 using the net asset value per share of the investment (or its equivalent) as a practical expedient if it is probable at the measurement date that a reporting entity will sell a portion of the investment at an amount different from the net asset value per share (or its equivalent). A sale is considered probable only if all of the following criteria are met as of the reporting entity's measurement date:

- Management, having the authority to approve the action, commits to a plan to sell the investment.
- An active program to locate a buyer and other actions required to complete the plan to sell the investment have been initiated.
- The investment is available for immediate sale subject only to terms that are usual and customary for sales of such investments.
- Actions required to complete the plan indicate that it is unlikely that significant changes to the plan will be made or that the plan will be withdrawn.

2.96 Q&A section 2220.27, "Determining Fair Value of Investments When the Practical Expedient Is Not Used or Is Not Available" (AICPA, *Technical Questions and Answers*), discusses what inputs or investment features should be considered in estimating fair value for entities that do not elect to use net asset value as a practical expedient or are unable to adjust the most recently reported net asset value to estimate a net asset value that is calculated in a manner consistent with the measurement principles of FASB ASC 946 as of the reporting entity's measurement date. In this situation, examples of factors that could be used when estimating fair value (depending on the valuation technique[s] and facts and circumstances) are as follows:

- Net asset value (as one valuation factor)
- Transactions in principal-to-principal or brokered markets (external markets) and overall market conditions

- Features of the alternative investment
- Expected future cash flows appropriately discounted
- Factors used to determine whether there has been a significant decrease in the volume and level of activity for the asset when compared with normal market activity for the asset (FASB ASC 820-10-35-51A)

2.97 Q&A section 2220.27 discusses several investment features of alternative investments in detail, including lockup periods and the ability of the fund to identify and make acceptable investments. A reporting entity may consider these investment features in determining fair value when the practical expedient is unavailable or not elected.

2.98 According to FASB ASC 820-10-35-54B, categorization within the fair value hierarchy of a fair value measurement of an investment that is measured at net asset value per share requires judgment. This guidance provides the following considerations:

- If a reporting entity has the ability to redeem its investment with the investee at net asset value per share (or its equivalent) at the measurement date, the fair value measurement of the investment should be categorized within level 2 of the fair value hierarchy.

- If a reporting entity will never have the ability to redeem its investment with the investee at net asset value per share (or its equivalent), the fair value measurement of the investment should be categorized within level 3 of the fair value hierarchy.

- If a reporting entity cannot redeem its investment with the investee at net asset value per share (or its equivalent) at the measurement date, but the investment may be redeemable with the investee at a future date (for example, investments subject to a lockup or gate or investments whose redemption period does not coincide with the measurement date), the reporting entity should take into account the length of time until the investment will become redeemable in determining whether the fair value measurement of the investment should be categorized within level 2 or level 3 of the fair value hierarchy. For example, if the reporting entity does not know when it will have the ability to redeem the investment, or it does not have the ability to redeem the investment in the near term at net asset value per share (or its equivalent), the fair value measurement should be categorized within level 3 of the fair value hierarchy.[33]

2.99 Q&A section 2220.24, "Disclosures—Ability to Redeem Versus Actual Redemption Request" (AICPA, *Technical Questions and Answers*), discusses

---

[33] Refer to the May 12, 2011, AICPA Expert Panel Meeting Highlights. Expert panel (EP) members discussed situations in which an investment company holds investments in multiple classes of an investee fund. For instance, a fund of funds holds $3,000,000 in class A of the investee, and $500,000 in class S (a side pocket class) of the investee. For the purposes of leveling in the FASB ASC 820 hierarchy, a question arises whether the investment should be bifurcated if the investment into class A meets the criteria for level 2, but the investment into class S is illiquid, and, therefore, a level 3 investment. The EP discussed industry practice in leveling such investments and noted that the EP members generally believe that in the situation of a unitized fund as described previously, there could be multiple units of account for an interest in an investee fund, and that a similar analogy would apply to investments in partnerships where a portion of the investment is locked up or has other varying liquidity characteristics.

redemptions from alternative funds. In most cases, redemptions at net asset value are only permitted with advance notice, ranging from 30 to 120 days. Even if the reporting entity has not submitted a redemption request effective on the measurement date, as long as the reporting entity has the ability to redeem at net asset value in the near term (for example, it has the contractual and practical ability to redeem) at the measurement date, then, consistent with FASB ASC 820-10-35-54B(a), the investment may be classified within level 2 of the fair value hierarchy. Q&A section 2220.25, "Impact of 'Near Term' on Classification Within Fair Value Hierarchy" (AICPA, *Technical Questions and Answers*), explains that what is viewed as near term is a matter of professional judgment and depends on the specific facts and circumstances. A redemption period of 90 days or less generally would be considered near term because any potential discount relative to the time value of money to the next redemption date would be unlikely to be considered a significant unobservable input, in accordance with FASB ASC 820. However, other factors, such as the likelihood or actual imposition of gates, may influence the determination of whether the investment will be redeemable in the near term.

Money Market Funds

> **⊚ Update 2-2 *Regulatory*: Money Market Fund Reform**
>
> On July 23, 2014, the SEC issued Final Rule Release No. 33-9616, *Money Market Fund Reform; Amendments to Form PF*. The release includes varying compliance dates for the different changes within the new rule. Compliance dates begin in 2015, and extend through 2016. Readers are encouraged to consult the full text of the release for specific compliance dates.
>
> One of the key structural changes of the new Money Market Reform Rule is that institutional prime and municipal money market funds will be required to transact at a floating net asset value. Retail funds and government funds are not required to transact at a floating net asset value. This will require those funds that transact at a floating net asset value to transact shares, rounded to the fourth decimal place (for example, $1.0000), based on the most recently determined market value of the securities in the underlying portfolios. Separately, new tax regulations and guidance have been issued as a result of this change; readers are encouraged to review this new IRS guidance. The release further provides guidance on how to determine whether a fund is considered to be an institutional money market fund, a retail money market fund, or a government money market fund.
>
> Those money market funds adopting a floating net asset value as a result of the new rules are expected to determine the values of their investments using market-based values, as opposed to using the amortized cost of such investments as an approximation of market value. In addition to this accounting change, the new rules may result in other changes to the financial reporting of all money market funds. Readers should keep abreast of future developments as they emerge.
>
> Additionally, the amendments in Final Rule Release No. 33-9616 give the boards of directors of money market funds new tools to stem heavy redemptions. Those tools include allowing them discretion to impose liquidity fees in the event a fund's weekly liquidity level falls below the required regulatory threshold, and also provides them the discretion to suspend redemptions temporarily (that is, impose a "gate"), under similar circumstances. The new

requirements dictate that all nongovernment money market funds impose a liquidity fee if the fund's weekly liquidity level falls below the rule-established threshold, unless the fund's board determines that imposing such a fee is not in the best interests of the fund.

Final Rule Release No. 33-9616 also contains additional amendments. These include enhanced disclosure requirements on fund websites, sales and marketing materials, prospectuses and SAIs; changes to Form N-MFP; an additional new Form N-CR; and various clarifying amendments under Rule 2a-7, including stress testing and diversification provisions.

The amendments also require investment advisers of certain large unregistered liquidity funds to provide additional information about those funds to the SEC.

Readers should consult the full text of SEC Final Rule Release No. 33-9616, which can be accessed on the Final Rules page at www.sec.gov.

2.100   As set forth in Rule 2a-7 under the 1940 Act, a money market fund may value securities using the amortized cost or penny-rounding method,[34] subject to certain determinations by its board of directors or trustees. Rule 2a-7 requires, among other things, in the case of a money market fund using the amortized cost method, that the fund's board of directors or trustees "establish written procedures reasonably designed ... to stabilize the money market fund's net asset value per share, as computed for the purpose of distribution, redemption and repurchase at a single value." Rule 2a-7 sets forth procedures that must be adopted by the board of directors or trustees when using the amortized cost or penny-rounding method of valuation. Additionally, for funds using the amortized cost method, the board of directors or trustees should perform a periodic review of both the monitoring of and the extent of any deviation from fair value and the methods used to calculate the deviations.

Determining Costs and Realized Gains and Losses

2.101   As stated in "Pending Content" in FASB ASC 946-320-40-1, the cost of investment securities held in the portfolio of an investment company and the net realized gains or losses thereon should be determined on the specific identification or average-cost methods. An investment company should use only one method for all of its investments.

2.102   Rule 2a-2 of the 1940 Act states that the cost of investment securities held in the portfolio of a registered investment company and the net realized gains or losses thereon are determined, for financial accounting purposes, on the specific certificate, first in first out, last in first out, or average-value methods. The average-value method of computing gains and losses may not presently be used for federal income tax purposes.

2.103   An investment company occasionally may be entitled to receive award proceeds from litigation relating to an investment security. Awards should be recorded in accordance with the gain contingency provisions of FASB

---

[34] A money market fund using either method (*a*) may not acquire any instrument with a remaining maturity (as the term is defined in Rule 2a-7) of greater than 397 calendar days; (*b*) must maintain a dollar-weighted average portfolio maturity of 60 days or less; or (*c*) must maintain a dollar-weighted average portfolio maturity of 120 calendar days, determined without reference to the exceptions regarding interest rate readjustments.

ASC 450, *Contingencies*, considering such factors as the enforceability of the right to settlement and the ability to determine the amount receivable.

2.104 As explained in FASB ASC 946-320-35-21, if the investment company holds the securities, the proceeds from litigation awards are accounted for as a reduction of cost. If the investment company no longer holds the securities, the proceeds should be accounted for as realized gains on security transactions.

2.105 As provided in paragraphs 2–3 of FASB ASC 946-320-30, an investment company may receive securities in a spin-off wherein the entity in which the investment company has invested spins off a portion of its operations. A portion of the cost of the securities held should be allocated to the securities received in the spin-off. That amount is based on the ratio of the fair value of the securities received to the sum of the fair value of such securities and the fair value of the original securities held by the investment company of the entity affecting the spin-off.

2.106 Spin-offs are usually tax-free reorganizations, and no gain or loss is recognized for income tax or financial reporting purposes.[35]

2.107 From time to time, tender offers may be received for securities held by an investment company. The terms of the offer may be for cash, debentures of the acquiring entity, stock of the acquiring entity, or a combination thereof.

2.108 As explained in FASB ASC 946-320-25-3, even if the investment company tenders its securities, it should continue to value the shares tendered until the number of shares accepted in the tender is known. Thereafter, the investment company should value the assets to be received for the shares tendered.

2.109 Accrued interest on bonds bought between interest dates should be accounted for as accrued interest receivable. Accrued interest on bonds sold should be accounted for as a reduction of accrued interest receivable and is not a factor in determining gain or loss on a sale.

Accounting for Investment Income[36]

2.110 An investment company's investment income consists primarily of dividends and interest.

2.111 *Dividends.* As stated in FASB ASC 946-320-35-5, dividends on investment securities should be recorded on the ex-dividend date. Distributions that represent returns of capital should be credited to investment cost rather than investment income.

---

[35] For further information related to spinoffs, see FASB ASC 845, *Nonmonetary Transactions*, and 810, *Consolidation*.

[36] FASB issued the proposed ASU *Financial Instruments—Overall (Subtopic 825-10): Recognition and Measurement of Financial Assets and Financial Liabilities* in February 2013. Entities that follow specialized industry guidance in FASB ASC 946 would continue to follow existing initial measurement and subsequent measurement guidance in FASB ASC 946-320-35 for investments in debt and equity securities. The same entities would also continue to follow existing measurement guidance on (*a*) dividends and interest, (*b*) investment securities sold, (*c*) capital stock sold, and (*d*) other accounts receivable, such as receivables from related parties, including expense reimbursement receivables from affiliates, and receivables for variation margin on open futures contracts. Finally, measurement guidance on foreign currency gains or losses in FASB ASC 946-830 would continue to be applied. Readers should remain alert for developments on this topic, which can be accessed from the Project Roster & Status page at www.fasb.org.

2.112 As provided in FASB ASC 946-320-35-6, stock splits and stock dividends in shares of the same class as the shares owned are not income to the investment company. However, dividends for which the recipient has the choice to receive cash or stock are usually recognized as investment income in the amount of the cash option because, in such cases, cash is usually the best evidence of fair value of the stock.

2.113 FASB ASC 946-320-35-7 states that other noncash dividends should be recognized as investment income at the fair value of the property received.

2.114 FASB ASC 946-320-35-8 explains that stock rights (that is, subscription rights) received should be allocated a prorated portion of the cost basis of the related investment; however, allocation is not required if the fair value of the rights is 15 percent or less of the fair value of the investment company's holdings.

2.115 Investment companies usually follow tax accounting from IRC Section 307 that, consistent with the guidance of the prior paragraph, does not require allocation if the fair value of the stock rights is 15 percent or less of the fair value of the investment company's holdings.

2.116 As stated in FASB ASC 946-320-35-9, cash dividends declared on stocks for which the securities portfolio reflects a short position as of the record date should be recognized as an expense on the ex-dividend date.

2.117 As a routine operating policy, investment companies should consult reliable published or other sources for daily dividend declarations and other corporate actions to be sure that they obtain and record relevant dividend information in a timely manner. Investment companies should have procedures that provide for follow up and disposition of dividends not collected in the regular course of business because of delays in settling securities transactions or completing transfer procedures.

2.118 *Interest.* As stated in FASB ASC 946-320-35-20, premiums and discounts should be amortized using the interest method. As explained in FASB ASC 310-20-35-18, the objective of the interest method is to arrive at periodic interest income (including recognition of fees and costs) at a constant effective yield on the net investment (that is, the principal amount of the investment adjusted by unamortized fees or costs and purchase premium or discount). FASB ASC 835-30-35-2 states that the difference between the present value and the face amount of the net investment should be treated as a discount or premium and amortized as interest expense or income over the life of the note in such a way as to result in a constant rate of interest when applied to the amount outstanding at the beginning of any given period.

2.119 The economic substance of an investment in a debt security is that the discount or premium paid is an adjustment of the stated interest rate to a current market rate. Amortizing premiums and accreting discounts, as an adjustment to interest income, is consistent with the economic substance of the transaction.

2.120 Paydown gains and losses on mortgage- and asset-backed securities should also be presented as an adjustment to interest income. Amortization of bond premiums and accretion of bond discounts for federal income tax purposes is discussed in chapter 6, "Taxes," of this guide. Original issue discount on bonds and other debt securities is required to be amortized for tax and financial reporting purposes. Discounts on the purchase of bonds that do not provide for periodic interest payments, sometimes called zero coupon bonds, should be amortized to income by the interest method.

2.121 FASB ASC 325-40-15-7 states that for income recognition purposes, beneficial interests classified as trading are included in the scope of FASB ASC 325-40 because it is practice for certain industries (such as investment companies) to report interest income as a separate item in their income statements, even though the investments are accounted for at fair value. The FASB ASC glossary defines *beneficial interests* as rights to receive all or portions of specified cash inflows received by a trust or other entity, including, but not limited to, all of the following: senior and subordinated shares of interest, principal, or other cash inflows to be passed through or paid through; premiums due to guarantors; commercial paper obligations; and residual interests, whether in the form of debt or equity.

2.122 FASB ASC 325-40-35-1 explains that the holder of a beneficial interest should recognize accretable yield as interest income over the life of the beneficial interest using the effective yield method. The holder of a beneficial interest should continue to update, over the life of the beneficial interest, the expectation of cash flows to be collected. FASB ASC 325-40-35-3 goes on to explain that after the transaction date, *cash flows expected to be collected* are defined as the holder's estimate of the amount and timing of estimated principal and interest cash flows based on the holder's best estimate of current information and events. In FASB ASC 325-40, a change in cash flows expected to be collected is considered in the context of both the timing and amount of the cash flows expected to be collected.

2.123 FASB ASC 325-40-35-4 notes that, if based on current information and events, there is a favorable (or an adverse) change in cash flows expected to be collected from the cash flows previously projected, then the investor should recalculate the amount of accretable yield for the beneficial interest on the date of evaluation as the excess of cash flows expected to be collected over the beneficial interest's reference amount. The reference amount equals the initial investment minus cash received to date plus the yield accreted to date. Based on cash flows expected to be collected, interest income may be recognized on a beneficial interest even if the net investment in the beneficial interest is accreted to an amount greater than the amount at which the beneficial interest could be settled if prepaid immediately in its entirety. The adjustment should be accounted for prospectively as a change in estimate, in conformity with FASB ASC 250, with the amount of periodic accretion adjusted over the remaining life of the beneficial interest.

2.124 Paragraphs 5–6 of FASB ASC 325-40-35 explain that determining whether there has been a favorable (or an adverse) change in cash flows expected to be collected from the cash flows previously projected (taking into consideration both the timing and amount of the cash flows expected to be collected) involves comparing the present value of the remaining cash flows expected to be collected at the initial transaction date (or at the last date previously revised) against the present value of the cash flows expected to be collected at the current financial reporting date. The cash flows should be discounted at a rate equal to the current yield used to accrete the beneficial interest.

2.125 According to Q&A section 6910.21, "Recognition of Premium/Discount on Short Positions in Fixed-Income Securities" (AICPA, *Technical*

Questions and Answers), when recognizing interest income on long positions or when recognizing interest expense on short positions on fixed-income securities, all economic elements of interest should be recognized, including premium and discount to the par value of the bond.

2.126 Interest income on debt securities, such as corporate bonds, municipal bonds, or treasury bonds, is accrued daily. An investment company should also consider collectability of interest when making accruals.

2.127 Interest received on bonds that were in default or that were delinquent in the payment of interest when acquired should be accounted for as follows: (*a*) the amount of interest earned from the date of acquisition of the bond through the current period should be recorded as interest income, and (*b*) the amount of interest in arrears at the date of acquisition of the bond should be recorded as a reduction of the cost of the investment.[37]

2.128 The accrued interest receivable account should be analyzed at regular intervals to make sure that interest payments due are received promptly and in the correct amount. Similarly, the disposition of purchased interest receivable and interest accruals on debt securities sold between interest dates should be analyzed periodically.

Defaulted Debt Securities

2.129 In accordance with the guidance provided by FASB ASC 450-20-25-2, accrued interest should be written off when it becomes probable that the interest will not be collected, and the amount of uncollectible interest can be reasonably estimated.

2.130 As explained in paragraphs 17–18 of FASB ASC 946-320-35, the portion of interest receivable on defaulted debt securities written off that was recognized as interest income should be treated as a reduction of interest income. Write-offs of purchased interest should be reported as increases to the cost basis of the security, which will result in an unrealized loss until the security is sold.

Accounting for Expenditures in Support of Defaulted Debt Securities

2.131 As noted in FASB ASC 946-320-05-9, when issuers of debt securities default, the bondholders often become active in any negotiations and the workout process. This process often results in new terms that restructure the obligations to allow the issuer to continue to meet its ongoing interest obligations and maintain some, if not all, of the principal value to the holders of the obligations.

2.132 As explained in FASB ASC 946-320-05-10, adverse economic developments often lead to increases in the default rates of debt securities. In addition to occasional capital infusions, professional fees to legally restructure the investments are frequently incurred by the bondholders.

2.133 *Capital infusions.* The nature of capital infusions is to enhance or prevent substantial diminution in the fair value of the investment. According to the FASB ASC glossary, *capital infusions* are expenditures made directly

---

[37] Section 404.02 of the SEC's *Codification of Financial Reporting Policies.*

to the issuer to ensure that operations are completed, thereby allowing the issuer to generate cash flows to service the debt. Such expenditures are usually nonrecurring. In certain cases, bondholders may receive additional promissory notes, or the original bond instrument may be amended to provide for repayment of the capital infusions. As further noted in FASB ASC 946-320-35-14, all capital infusions in support of defaulted securities should be recorded as an addition to the cost basis of the related security.

2.134 *Workout expenditures*. According to the FASB ASC glossary, *workout expenditures* consist of professional fees (legal, accounting, appraisal) paid to entities unaffiliated with the investment company's adviser or sponsor in connection with (*a*) capital infusions, (*b*) restructurings or plans of reorganization, (*c*) ongoing efforts to protect or enhance an investment, or (*d*) the pursuit of other claims or legal actions. Paragraphs 15–16 of FASB ASC 946-320-35 further explain that workout expenditures that are incurred as part of negotiations of the terms and requirements of capital infusions or that are expected to result in the restructuring of, or a plan of reorganization for, an investment should be recorded as realized losses. Ongoing expenditures to protect or enhance an investment or expenditures incurred to pursue other claims or legal actions should be treated as operating expenses.

2.135 Required disclosure information associated with credit enhancements and financial support provided, or contractually required to provide, to investees are discussed in paragraphs 7.43–.44 of this guide.

Lending of Portfolio Securities and Repurchase Financing

Ⓒ **Update 2-3** *Accounting and Reporting*: **Transfers and Servicing**

FASB ASU No. 2014-11, *Transfers and Servicing (Topic 860): Repurchase-to-Maturity Transactions, Repurchase Financings, and Disclosures*, was issued in June 2014. The accounting amendments are effective, for public business entities, for the first interim or annual period beginning after December 15, 2014. For all other entities, the accounting amendments in the ASU are effective for annual periods beginning after December 15, 2014 and interim periods beginning after December 15, 2015. Early adoption is prohibited for public business entities; however, all other entities may elect to adopt the accounting guidance for interim periods beginning after December 15, 2014. An entity is required to present changes related to adopting the new accounting guidance for transactions outstanding on the effective date as a cumulative-effect adjustment to retained earnings as of the beginning of the period of adoption.

For public business entities, the disclosure for certain transactions accounted for as a sale is required to be presented for interim and annual periods beginning after December 15, 2014. Such entities would apply the disclosure requirement related to repurchase agreements, securities lending transactions, and repurchase-to-maturity transactions accounted for as secured borrowings, in annual periods beginning after December 15, 2014, and interim periods beginning after March 15, 2015. For all other entities, both new disclosures are required to be presented for annual periods beginning after December 15, 2014, and interim periods beginning after December 15, 2015. The disclosures are not required to be presented for comparative periods before the effective date.

ASU No. 2014-11 requires two accounting changes. First, the amendments in this ASU change the accounting for repurchase-to-maturity transactions to secured borrowing accounting. Second, for repurchase financing arrangements, the amendments require the transferor and transferee to symmetrically account for the initial transfer of the financial asset as a sale (provided that derecognition conditions are met) and purchase, respectively. In addition, the ASU requires entities to evaluate and account for the repurchase component of the combined transaction in a manner similar to how they would evaluate and account for other typical repurchase agreements.

ASU No. 2014-11 also sets forth two new disclosure requirements to respond to the needs of users of financial statements for additional disclosures for repurchase agreements and similar transactions. An entity is required to disclose information about certain transactions accounted for as a sale in which the transferor retains substantially all of the exposure to the economic return on the transferred financial assets through an agreement with the same counterparty. Those disclosures are intended to provide users of financial statements with information to compare those types of transactions accounted for as sales with similar transactions accounted for as secured borrowings. An entity also will be required to disclose information about repurchase agreements, securities lending transactions, and repurchase-to-maturity transactions that are accounted for as secured borrowings. Those disclosures are intended to provide transparency about the types of collateral pledged in the agreements and the associated liability. Note that banks and broker-dealers refer to a sale of securities with an agreement to repurchase as a repurchase agreement (repo) whereas an investment company refers to this transaction as a reverse repurchase agreement (reverse repo).

Readers are encouraged to consult the full text of this ASU on FASB's website at www.fasb.org.

Refer to section A.02 in appendix A for more information on this ASU if it is applicable to your reporting period.

2.136 Investment companies may lend securities (principally to broker-dealers). Such transactions are documented as loans of securities in which the borrower of securities generally is required to provide collateral to the lender, commonly cash but sometimes other securities or standby letters of credit, with a value slightly higher than that of the securities borrowed. If the asset received as collateral is cash, the lender of securities normally earns a return by investing that cash, typically in short-term, high-quality debt instruments, at rates higher than the rate paid or rebated to the borrower. Investment of cash collateral is subject to the investment company's investment restrictions. If the asset received as collateral is other than cash, the lender of securities typically receives a fee. The investment company, as lender of securities, receives amounts from the borrower equivalent to dividends and interest on the securities loaned. As with other extensions of credit, there are risks of delay in recovery or even loss of rights in the collateral should the borrower of the securities fail financially.

2.137 FASB ASC 860-30-25-3 provides that transfers of financial assets in exchange for cash collateral cannot be distinguished from borrowing cash. Accordingly, all cash collateral should be recorded as an asset by the party receiving it (the secured party), together with a liability for the obligation to return it to the payer (obligor), whose asset is a receivable. As discussed in FASB ASC 860-30-25-7, many securities lending transactions are accompanied by an agreement that both entitles and obligates the transferor to repurchase or redeem the transferred financial assets before their maturity. "Pending Content" in FASB ASC 860-10-40-24 states that an agreement that both entitles and obligates the transferor to repurchase or redeem transferred financial assets from the transferee maintains the transferor's effective control over those assets, as described in the "Pending Content" in FASB ASC 860-10-40-5(c)(1), if all of the conditions in "Pending Content" in FASB ASC 860-10-40-24 are met (the financial assets to be repurchased or redeemed are the same or substantially the same as those transferred, the agreement is to repurchase or redeem them before maturity at a fixed or determinable price, and the agreement is entered into contemporaneously with, or in contemplation of, the transfer.). Those transactions should be accounted for as secured borrowings in which either cash or securities that the holder is permitted by contract or custom to sell or repledge received as collateral are considered the amount borrowed, the securities loaned are considered pledged as collateral against the cash borrowed and reclassified as set forth in FASB ASC 860-30-25-5(a), and any rebate paid to the transferee of securities is interest on the cash that the transferor is considered to have borrowed.

2.138 Paragraphs 4–5 of FASB ASC 860-30-25 explain that the accounting for noncash collateral by the debtor (or obligor) and the secured party depends on whether the secured party has the right to sell or repledge the collateral and whether the debtor has defaulted. Cash collateral should be derecognized by the payer and recognized by the recipient not as collateral but, rather, as proceeds of either a sale or borrowing.

2.139 Paragraphs 42–47 of FASB ASC 860-10-40 specifically discuss the accounting for a *repurchase financing*, which is defined by the FASB ASC glossary as a repurchase agreement (or reverse repurchase agreement) that relates to a previously transferred financial asset between the same counterparties (or consolidated affiliates of either counterparty) that is entered into contemporaneously with, or in contemplation of, the initial transfer. FASB ASC 860-10-05-21B explains that if a transferor transfers a financial asset and also enters into a repurchase financing with the transferee, there are typically three transfers of the financial asset:

- *Initial transfer.* The initial transferor transfers a financial asset to an initial transferee.

- *Execution of a repurchase financing.* The initial transferee (the borrower) transfers the previously transferred financial asset back to the initial transferor (the lender) as collateral for a financing between the initial transferor and initial transferee.

- *Settlement of the repurchase financing.* The initial transferor (the lender) returns the financial asset (or substantially the same asset) to the initial transferee (the borrower) upon receipt of payment from the initial transferee.

2.140 FASB ASC 860-10-40-42 states that a transferor and transferee should not separately account for a transfer of a financial asset and a related repurchase financing unless both of the following conditions are met: the two transactions have a valid and distinct business or economic purpose for being entered into separately, and the repurchase financing does not result in the initial transferor regaining control over the financial asset. Paragraphs 44–47 of FASB ASC 860-10-40 discuss the qualifications to categorize the transactions as linked and the resulting applicable accounting guidance to follow. Paragraphs 17A–17C of FASB ASC 860-10-55 provide implementation guidance related to repurchase financings.

Accounting for Derivatives

2.141 FASB ASC 815, *Derivatives and Hedging*, establishes accounting and reporting standards for derivative instruments, including certain derivative instruments embedded in other contracts (referred to collectively as *derivatives*), and hedging activities. FASB ASC 815-10-15-83 defines a *derivative instrument* as a financial instrument or other contract with all of the following characteristics:

a. It has (i) one or more underlying instruments and (ii) one or more notional amounts or payment provisions or both. Those terms determine the amount of the settlement or settlements, and, in some cases, whether or not a settlement is required.

b. It requires no initial net investment or an initial net investment that is smaller than would be required for other types of contracts that would be expected to have a similar response to changes in market factors.

c. Its terms implicitly or explicitly require or permit net settlement, it can readily be settled net by a means outside the contract, or it provides for delivery of an asset that puts the recipient in a position not substantially different from net settlement.

2.142 FASB ASC 815 requires that an entity recognize all derivatives as either assets or liabilities in the statement of financial position and measure those instruments at fair value, and recognize changes to fair value in the statement of operations for those not designated as hedging instruments.

2.143 FASB ASC 815-10-50 contains extensive disclosure requirements for derivatives. Refer to the full text of FASB ASC 815 when testing accounting and reporting issues related to derivative instruments.

2.144 The following transactions may meet the definition of a derivative, and therefore require certain additional disclosures:

- Swaps (credit default, interest rate, total return, and currency)

- Future contracts (eurodollar, treasuries, municipal bond indexes, equity indexes, commodities, individual stocks, foreign bonds)

- Forward currency contracts, interest rate caps and floors

- Purchased and written options (equities, indices, futures, currencies, treasuries, and the like)

- Swaptions (total return, credit default and interest rate swaps)

- Certain capital support arrangements (for example, money market fund support agreements to maintain a $1.00 net asset value)

- Certain warrants (refer to chapter 3, "Financial Instruments," of this guide for further discussion relating to when a warrant could be considered a derivative)

Accounting for Foreign Investments

2.145 Investments in securities of foreign issuers involve considerations not typically associated with domestic investments. Foreign securities are denominated and pay distributions in foreign currencies, exposing investment companies to changes in foreign currency exchange rates. Investments in certain foreign countries may include the risk of expropriation or confiscatory taxation, limitations on the removal of funds or other assets, political or social instability, or adverse diplomatic developments. Individual foreign economies may differ from the economy of the United States in growth of gross domestic product, rates of inflation, capital reinvestments, resource self-sufficiency, and balance of payments positions. Securities of many foreign entities may be less liquid and their prices more volatile.

2.146 Because most foreign securities are not registered with the SEC, most of the issuers of foreign securities are not subject to the SEC's reporting requirements. As a result, financial or regulatory information concerning certain foreign issuers of securities may not be as readily available. Also, foreign entities may not be subject to uniform accounting, auditing, and financial reporting standards or practices and requirements comparable to those that apply to domestic entities. Further, many foreign stock markets are not as developed or efficient as those in the United States. Fixed commissions on transactions on foreign stock exchanges usually are higher than negotiated commissions on U.S. exchanges. The time between the trade and settlement dates of securities transactions on foreign exchanges ranges from one day to four weeks or longer.

2.147 Foreign exchange transactions may be conducted on a cash basis at the prevailing spot rate for buying or selling the currency. Under normal market conditions, the spot rate differs from the published exchange rate because of the costs of converting from one currency to another. Some funds use forward foreign exchange contracts as hedges against possible changes in foreign exchange rates. These funds contract to buy or sell specified currencies at specified future dates and prices that are established when the contract is initiated. Dealings in forward foreign exchange contracts may relate to specific receivables or payables occurring in connection with the purchase or sale of portfolio securities, hedging all or a portion of a portfolio or the payment of dividends and other distributions.[38]

2.148 The cost of foreign currency transactions varies with such factors as the currency involved, the length of the contract period, and prevailing market conditions. Because exchanges in foreign currencies are usually transacted by principals, most often, there are no fees or commissions.

2.149 As an alternative to buying shares of foreign-based entities in overseas markets, investment companies can buy shares in the United States, denominated in U.S. dollars (for example, American depository receipts [ADRs]). These receipts are for shares of a foreign-based corporation that are held by a U.S. bank as trustee. The trustee bank collects dividends and makes payments to the holders of the ADR. The trustee bank may charge holders of ADRs a custody fee for the work it performs on the ADR including performing registration, compliance, dividend payment, communication and recordkeeping

---

[38] Registered investment companies investing in forward foreign exchange contracts are subject to limitations under Section 18 of the 1940 Act.

services. Trustee banks commonly subtract such fees from the gross dividends payable to ADR holders.

2.150 *Valuation of foreign securities.* FASB ASC 946-320-35-4 states that, in general, the discussion of valuation of securities in the related subtopic of FASB ASC 946-320 (and in this chapter) also applies to foreign securities. Portfolio securities that are traded primarily on foreign securities exchanges should be valued at the functional currency (usually the U.S. dollar equivalent) values for such securities on their exchanges.

2.151 *Other matters.* In addition to the foreign currency risk associated with investing in foreign securities, such investments present the following additional risks that need to be assessed continuously by management and considered for financial statement disclosure, as stated in FASB ASC 946-830-50-2:

- *Liquidity.* Because certain foreign markets are illiquid, market prices may not necessarily represent realizable value.

- *Size.* If market capitalization is low, a fund's share in the entire market (particularly if single-country funds are involved) or in specific securities may be proportionately very large, and the fair value, consistent with FASB ASC 820, may not be representative of the price that would be received if the fund sold its large proportion of the specific security ("block") at the measurement date.

- *Valuation.* Because of liquidity and size problems, as well as other factors, such as securities that are unlisted or thinly traded, funds would have to adopt specific fair valuation procedures for determining the values of such securities. Doing so may be difficult in a foreign environment; although others may perform the research and provide supporting documentation for fair values, the ultimate responsibility for determining the fair values of securities rests with the management.

2.152 FASB ASC 946-830-50-3 explains that the disclosures suggested in the prior paragraph are no different from those that could be required for domestic securities with the same attributes. The preceding risks should be disclosed in the notes to the financial statements if such factors exist in the markets in which the fund has material investments.

2.153 Management should also make sure that prices provided by local sources (such as the last sale price, bid or ask, mean of bid and ask, closing price, and so on) do represent the fair value of the securities. This is especially important for open-end funds or closed-end funds that allow limited redemption.

2.154 *Gains and losses from foreign investment holdings and transactions.*[39] As stated in paragraphs 2–4 of FASB ASC 946-830-45, the differences between originally recorded amounts and currently consummated or measured amounts in the reporting currency are a function of changes in both of the following factors: foreign exchange rates and changes in market prices. Those effects should be identified, computed, and reported other than for gains and losses on investments. The practice of not disclosing separately the portion

---

[39] See footnote 36.

of the changes in fair values of investments and realized gains and losses thereon that result from foreign currency rate changes is permitted. However, separate reporting of such gains and losses is allowable and, if adopted by the reporting entity, should conform to the guidance in FASB ASC 946-830. Refer to appendix F, "Illustrations for Separately Calculating and Disclosing the Foreign Currency Element of Realized and Unrealized Gains and Losses," of this guide for illustrations of separately calculating and disclosing the foreign currency element of realized and unrealized gains and losses.

2.155 As explained in FASB ASC 946-830-45-15, a fund investing in foreign securities generally invests in such securities to reap the potential benefits offered by the local capital market. It may also invest in such securities as a means of investing in the foreign currency market or benefiting from the foreign currency rate fluctuation. The extent to which separate information regarding foreign currency gains or losses will be meaningful will vary, depending on the circumstances, and separate information may not measure with precision foreign exchange gains or losses associated with the economic risks of foreign currency exposures. A foreign currency rate fluctuation, however, may be an important consideration in the case of foreign investments, and a reporting entity may choose to identify and report separately any resulting foreign currency gains or losses as a component of unrealized gain or loss on investments.

2.156 *Bifurcation.* As noted in FASB ASC 946-830-45-16, the fair value of securities should be determined initially in the foreign currency and translated at the spot rate on the purchase trade date. The unrealized gain or loss between the original cost (translated on the trade date) and the fair value (translated on the valuation date) comprises both of the following elements:

    a. Changes in the fair value of securities before translation

    b. Movement in foreign currency rate

2.157 FASB ASC 946-830-45-17 states that such movements may be combined as permitted by FASB ASC 946-830-45-4. If separate disclosure of the foreign currency gains and losses is chosen, the changes in the fair value of securities before translation should be measured as the difference between the fair value in foreign currency and the original cost in foreign currency translated at the spot rate on the valuation date. The effect of the movement in the foreign exchange rate shall be measured as the difference between the original cost in foreign currency translated at the current spot rate and the historical functional currency cost. These values can be computed as follows:

    a. (Fair value in foreign currency – original cost in foreign currency) × valuation date spot rate = unrealized fair value appreciation or depreciation

    b. (Cost in foreign currency × valuation date spot rate) – cost in functional currency = unrealized foreign currency gain or loss

2.158 FASB ASC 946-830-45-19 notes that, for short-term securities held by a fund that uses the amortized cost method of valuation, the amortized cost value should be substituted for fair value in the preceding formulas if separate reporting is chosen by the reporting entity.

2.159 *Sales of securities.* FASB ASC 946-830-45-20 explains that if separate reporting of foreign currency gains and losses on sales of securities is chosen by the reporting entity, the computation of the effects of market change and the foreign currency rate change is similar to that described in paragraph 2.157.

Fair value in the formula given in paragraph 2.157 should be replaced with sale proceeds, and the valuation date should be replaced with the sale trade date, as follows:

    a. (Sale proceeds in foreign currency – original cost in foreign currency) × sale trade date spot rate = realized market gain or loss on sale of security

    b. (Cost in foreign currency × sale trade date spot rate) – cost in functional currency = realized foreign currency gain or loss

2.160 As discussed in FASB ASC 946-830-45-21, the sale of a security results in a receivable for the security sold. That receivable should be recorded on the trade date at the spot rate. On the settlement date, the difference between the recorded receivable amount and the actual foreign currency received converted into the functional currency at the spot rate is recognized as a realized foreign currency gain or loss.

2.161 *Purchased interest and sale of interest.* FASB ASC 946-830-45-14 explains that purchased interest represents the interest accrued between the last coupon date and the settlement date of the purchase. It should be recorded in the functional currency as accrued interest receivable at the spot rate on the purchase trade date and marked to market using each valuation date's spot rate. After the settlement date, daily interest income should be accrued at the daily spot rate. It may be impractical to prepare the foregoing calculations daily; therefore, the use of a weekly or monthly average rate may be appropriate in many cases, especially if the exchange rate does not fluctuate significantly. However, if the exchange rate fluctuation is significant, the calculation should be made daily.

2.162 As stated by FASB ASC 946-830-45-22, interest sold represents the accrued interest receivable between the last coupon date and the settlement date of sale of the security. The difference between the recognized interest receivable amount and the actual foreign currency received (converted into the functional currency at the spot rate) should be recognized as a realized foreign currency gain or loss.

2.163 *Receivables and payables.* As explained in FASB ASC 946-830-45-23, all receivables and payables that are denominated in a foreign currency relating to income or expense or securities sold or purchased should be translated into the functional currency at each valuation date at the spot rate on that date. The difference between that amount and the functional currency amount that was recorded at various spot rates for income and expense items and at the trade date spot rate, in the case of sales and purchases of securities, is unrealized foreign currency gain or loss. Upon liquidation of the receivable or payable balance in a foreign currency, the difference should be reclassified as realized foreign currency gain or loss.

2.164 *Cash.* As explained in FASB ASC 946-830-45-7, foreign currency cash balances and movements should be accounted for in the same way that foreign currency-denominated securities are. Every receipt of a foreign currency should be treated as a purchase of a security and recorded in the functional currency at the spot rate on the cash receipt date. Similarly, every disbursement of a foreign currency should be treated as a sale of a security and the appropriate functional currency cost should be released, depending on whether a specific identified cost, first-in first-out method, or average cost method is used.

2.165 Paragraphs 8–9 of FASB ASC 946-830-45 state that the acquisition of foreign currency does not result in any foreign currency gain or loss. However, the disbursement of foreign currency results in a realized foreign currency gain or loss that is the difference between the functional currency equivalent of the foreign currency when it was acquired and the foreign currency disbursement translated at the spot rate on the disbursement date. Also, as is the case with all other assets and liabilities denominated in foreign currency, foreign currency cash balances should be translated on each valuation date at the spot rate on that date, resulting in unrealized foreign currency gain or loss.

2.166 *Dividends and interest.* As noted in FASB ASC 946-830-45-31, dividend income on securities denominated in a foreign currency should be recorded on the ex-dividend date using the spot exchange rate to translate the foreign currency amount into the functional currency on that date. The related dividend receivable should be translated into the functional currency daily at the spot rate, and the difference between the dividend accrued in the functional currency and the foreign currency receivable at the valuation date spot rate is unrealized foreign currency gain or loss. When the dividend is received, the unrealized foreign currency gain or loss should be reclassified as realized foreign currency gain or loss.

2.167 Further, FASB ASC 946-830-45-32 notes that the preceding approach to measuring investment income ensures that investment income accrued on foreign securities reflects the investment transaction without regard to the foreign currency gain or loss created in the time between the accrual and collection of the income.

2.168 FASB ASC 946-830-45-25 explains that interest on securities denominated in a foreign currency should be calculated at the stated rate of interest in the foreign currency. Interest on these securities should be accrued daily in the foreign currency at the stated interest rate and translated into the functional currency at the daily spot rate. Preparing such a calculation daily may be impractical; therefore, the use of a weekly or monthly average rate may be appropriate in many cases, especially if the exchange rate does not fluctuate significantly. However, if the exchange rate fluctuation is significant, the calculation should be made daily.

2.169 As noted in FASB ASC 946-830-45-26, the related receivable balance along with purchased interest, if any, should be accumulated in the foreign currency and translated into the functional currency daily using the spot rate for that date. The difference between the income accrued in the functional currency and the foreign currency receivable at the valuation date spot rate is unrealized foreign currency gain or loss.

2.170 As further stated in FASB ASC 946-830-45-27, when the interest is received and recorded in the functional currency at the spot rate on that date, the unrealized foreign currency gain or loss should be reclassified as realized foreign currency gain or loss.

2.171 FASB ASC 946-830-45-30 states that recording dividends on foreign securities is often difficult because, in certain countries, entities customarily declare dividends retroactively, or there is a lack of timely information. Additionally, in some countries, the sequencing of the declaration date and ex-dividend date may be different from the sequencing of these dates in the United States, thus necessitating a modification of the practice of recording dividends on the ex-dividend date (see paragraph 2.111). Also, foreign entities often declare stock dividends instead of cash dividends or take other corporate actions, such as issuing rights or warrants.

2.172 The SEC staff has stated that delayed recording of foreign corporate actions may be acceptable for registered investment companies if the investment company, exercising reasonable diligence, did not know that the corporate action had occurred; in such event, the investment company should record the action promptly after receipt of the information.[40]

2.173 *Amortization.* FASB ASC 946-830-45-28 states that amortization of premiums and accretion of discounts on bonds should be calculated daily in the foreign currency. The resulting amount of income or offset to income should be translated into the functional currency using that day's spot rate. The same foreign currency amount should be recorded as an addition to cost for accretion of discounts and a reduction to cost for amortization of premiums. Accordingly, cost consists of the original cost, translated at the spot rate in effect on the trade date that the bond was bought, adjusted for discount accretion or premium amortization at the spot rate on the date of adjustment. As stated in FASB ASC 946-830-45-25 (see paragraph 2.168), use of a weekly or monthly average rate may be appropriate in certain circumstances.

2.174 As discussed in FASB ASC 946-830-45-29, on maturity, the carrying cost (including accretion or amortization) of the security in the foreign currency equals the proceeds. However, this will not be the case in the functional currency. The original cost should be translated into the functional currency at the spot rate on the trade purchase date, and the accretion or amortization is translated at periodic spot rates. The proceeds should be translated into the functional currency at the spot rate on the maturity date. The difference between the proceeds and the accumulated cost in the functional currency is realized foreign currency gain or loss.

2.175 *Withholding tax.* As explained in FASB ASC 946-830-05-3, dividends and interest received from foreign investments may result in withholding taxes and other taxes imposed by foreign countries, usually at rates from 10 percent to 35 percent. Tax treaties between certain countries and the United States may reduce or eliminate such taxes. According to FASB ASC 946-830-45-33, many foreign countries do not tax capital gains on investments by foreign investors; however, if such gains are taxable, an accrual for capital gains taxes payable on both realized and unrealized gains should be included in the net asset value per share calculation.

2.176 The auditor should review the collectability of recorded receivables if withholding taxes have been reclaimed. FASB ASC 946-830-45-34 explains that whenever tax is to be withheld from investment income at the source, the amounts to be withheld that are not reclaimable should be accrued at the same time as the related income on each income recognition date if the tax rate is fixed and known. If a tax withheld is reclaimable from the local tax authorities, the tax should be recorded as a receivable, not an expense. When the investment income is received net of the tax withheld, a separate realized foreign currency gain or loss should be computed on the gross income receivable and the accrued tax expense. If the tax rate is not known or estimable, such expense or receivable should be recorded on the date that the net amount is

---

[40] November 1, 1996, Letter of SEC Division of Investment Management Chief Accountant to Investment Company Chief Financial Officers.

received; accordingly, there would be no foreign currency gain or loss. However, if a receivable is recorded, there may be a foreign currency gain or loss through the date such receivable is collected.

2.177 FASB ASC 946-830-45-39 states that taxes withheld that are not reclaimable on foreign source income should be deducted from the relevant income item and shown either parenthetically or as a separate contra item in the "Income" section of the statement of operations. Taxes levied on the aggregate income or capital gains of the investment company itself should be presented in a manner that is similar to that used for income taxes. The normal withholding taxes should be presented as follows.

Interest or dividend income (net of withholding taxes of $X) $XXX

Or

Interest or dividend income $XXX

Less withholding tax   (XXX)

See paragraph 7.221 of this guide for an illustrative disclosure of the first method.

2.178 *Expenses.* FASB ASC 946-830-45-35 states that the accounting for expenses payable in a foreign currency is analogous to that for investment income receivable in a foreign currency. An expense should be accrued as incurred and translated into the functional currency at the spot rate each day. The use of an average weekly or monthly foreign currency rate would be acceptable if the foreign currency rate does not fluctuate significantly. The related accrued expense balance should be accumulated in the foreign currency and translated into the functional currency daily, using the spot rate for that date. The difference between the expense accrued in the functional currency and the related foreign currency accrued expense balance translated into the functional currency at the valuation date spot rate is unrealized foreign currency gain or loss. When the expense is paid, the unrealized foreign currency gain or loss should be reclassified as realized foreign currency gain or loss.

2.179 *Safekeeping of foreign assets.* Investing in foreign securities often involves custodial or subcustodial agreements with U.S. banks and their foreign branches, as well as foreign banks and trust entities, for the safekeeping of fund assets held outside the United States. Rule 17f-5 of the 1940 Act permits registered investment companies to maintain their foreign securities with eligible foreign custodians (for example, foreign banks and trust entities that meet certain requirements, securities depositories, and clearing agencies). Rule 17f-5 sets forth the conditions that must be included in the foreign custody agreement, as well as the specific responsibilities of the investment company's board of directors or trustees in reviewing and approving the arrangements. Additionally, Rule 17f-7 establishes conditions under which an investment company may place its assets in the custody of a foreign central securities depository.

Chapter 3

Financial Instruments

3.01 This chapter provides brief descriptions of certain financial instruments of investment companies. Consideration should be given to FASB *Accounting Standards Codification* (ASC) 815, *Derivatives and Hedging*; 820, *Fair Value Measurement*; 460, *Guarantees*; and 860, *Transfers and Servicing*, in connection with accounting and financial statement presentation for these financial instruments.

Money Market Investments

3.02 Short term investments, such as short term government obligations, commercial paper, bankers' acceptances, and certificates of deposit (CDs), may be bought at their face amount or a discount or premium from their face amount.

3.03 The amortized cost of money market investments that mature within a relatively short period (for example, 60 days) usually approximates fair value. However, the impairment of the credit standing of the issuer or unusual changes in interest rates can affect their fair value significantly. In those circumstances, amortized cost may not approximate the fair value of such investments.[1]

Repurchase Agreements

> ⓞ **Update 3-1** *Accounting and Reporting*: **Transfers and Servicing**
>
> FASB Accounting Standards Update (ASU) No. 2014-11, *Transfers and Servicing (Topic 860): Repurchase-to-Maturity Transactions, Repurchase Financings, and Disclosures*, was issued in June 2014. The accounting amendments are effective, for public business entities, for the first interim or annual
>
> *(continued)*

---

[1] In SEC Release No. 33-9616, *Money Market Fund Reform; Amendments to Form PF*, the SEC the use of amortized cost for valuation. Registered investment companies and busi-ness development companies (BDCs) may use amortized cost to value debt securities with remaining maturities of 60 days or less if fund directors, in good faith, determine that the fair value of the debt securities is their amortized cost value, unless the particular circumstances warrant otherwise. The SEC generally believes that a registered investment company or BDC may only use the amortized cost method to value a portfolio security with a remaining maturity of 60 days or less when it can reason-ably conclude, at each time it makes a valuation determination, that the amortized cost value of the portfolio security is *approximately the same* as the fair value of the security as determined without the use of amortized cost valuation. Existing credit, liquidity, or interest rate conditions in the relevant markets and issuer specific circumstances at each such time should be taken into account in making such an evaluation. Accordingly, it would not be appropriate for a registered investment company or BDC to use amortized cost to value a debt security with a remaining maturity of 60 days or less and thereafter not continue to review whether amortized cost continues to be approximately fair value until, for example, there is a significant change in interest rates or credit deterioration. The SEC generally believes that a registered investment company or BDC should, at each time it makes a valuation determination, evaluate the use of amortized cost for portfolio securities, not only quarterly or each time the registered investment company or BDC produces financial statements. This guidance does not apply to stable NAV money market funds, who may use the amortized cost method of valuation to value their entire portfolio (subject to the conditions in SEC Rule 2a-7) and may not use the amortized cost method to value individual securities when they shadow price their shares pursuant to SEC Rule 2a-7(h)(10)(iii).

period beginning after December 15, 2014. For all other entities, the accounting amendments in the ASU are effective for annual periods beginning after December 15, 2014, and interim periods beginning after December 15, 2015. Early adoption is prohibited for public business entities; however, all other entities may elect to adopt the accounting guidance for interim periods beginning after December 15, 2014. An entity is required to present changes related to adopting the new accounting guidance for transactions outstanding on the effective date as a cumulative-effect adjustment to retained earnings as of the beginning of the period of adoption.

For public business entities, the disclosure for certain transactions accounted for as a sale is required to be presented for interim and annual periods beginning after December 15, 2014. Such entities would apply the disclosure requirement related to repurchase agreements, securities lending transactions, and repurchase-to-maturity transactions accounted for as secured borrowings, in annual periods beginning after December 15, 2014, and interim periods beginning after March 15, 2015. For all other entities, both new disclosures are required to be presented for annual periods beginning after December 15, 2014, and interim periods beginning after December 15, 2015. The disclosures are not required to be presented for comparative periods before the effective date.

ASU No. 2014-11 requires two accounting changes. First, the amendments in this ASU change the accounting for repurchase-to-maturity transactions to secured borrowing accounting. Second, for repurchase financing arrangements, the amendments require the transferor and transferee to symmetrically account for the initial transfer of the financial asset as a sale (provided that derecognition conditions are met) and purchase, respectively. In addition, the ASU requires entities to evaluate and account for the repurchase component of the combined transaction in a manner similar to how they would evaluate and account for other typical repurchase agreements.

ASU No. 2014-11 also sets forth two new disclosure requirements to respond to the needs of users of financial statements for additional disclosures for repurchase agreements and similar transactions. An entity is required to disclose information about certain transactions accounted for as a sale in which the transferor retains substantially all of the exposure to the economic return on the transferred financial assets through an agreement with the same counterparty. Those disclosures are intended to provide users of financial statements with information to compare those types of transactions accounted for as sales with similar transactions accounted for as secured borrowings. An entity also will be required to disclose information about repurchase agreements, securities lending transactions, and repurchase-to-maturity transactions that are accounted for as secured borrowings. Those disclosures are intended to provide transparency about the types of collateral pledged in the agreements and the associated liability. Note that banks and broker-dealers refer to a sale of securities with an agreement to repurchase as a repurchase agreement (repo) whereas an investment company refers to this transaction as a reverse repurchase agreement (reverse repo).

Readers are encouraged to consult the full text of this ASU on FASB's website at www.fasb.org.

Refer to section A.02 in appendix A, "Guidance Updates," for more information on this ASU if it is applicable to your reporting period.

3.04 A *repurchase agreement* (repo) is, in its simplest form, the purchase of a security at a specified price with an agreement to sell the same or substantially the same security to the same counterparty at a fixed or determinable price at a future date with a stipulated interest rate. A repo allows the investment company to transfer uninvested cash to a seller, usually a broker, for a security. The seller agrees to repay cash plus interest to the investment company in exchange for the return of the same or substantially the same security. Because a repo between the two specific parties involved is not transferable, a repo has no ready market. The repo's settlement date is usually specified in the agreement. When the repo's settlement date (or maturity date) is equal to the settlement date (or maturity date) of the underlying security, the repurchase agreement is commonly referred to as a *repo-to-maturity*.

3.05 Repos are usually entered into with banks, brokers, or dealers. According to SEC Release No. 10666 under the Investment Company Act of 1940 (the 1940 Act), the investment company should always be sure that the repo, including accrued interest, is fully secured by the fair value of the collateral that it has received.[2] Rule 5b-3 under the 1940 Act states that for purposes of Sections 5 and 12(d)(3) of the 1940 Act, the acquisition of a repo may be deemed to be an acquisition of the underlying securities, provided that the obligation of the seller to repurchase the securities from the investment company is fully collateralized at all times by cash items, U.S. government securities, or other securities. When the collateral is other than cash or U.S. government securities, such securities are required to consist of securities that the fund's board of directors (or its delegate) determines at the time the repurchase agreement is entered into are (*a*) issued by an issuer that has an exceptionally strong capacity to meet its financial obligations on the securities collateralizing the repurchase agreement and (*b*) sufficiently liquid that they can be sold at approximately their carrying value in the ordinary course of business within seven calendar days.

Reverse Repurchase Agreements

3.06 A *reverse repurchase agreement* (reverse repo or resale) is, in its simplest form, the sale of a security at a specified price and interest factor with an agreement to repurchase the same or substantially the same security from the same counterparty at a fixed or determinable price at a future date. A reverse repo allows the investment company to transfer possession of a security to a buyer, usually a broker, for cash. The investment company agrees to repay cash plus interest in exchange for the return of the same security.

U.S. Government Securities (Treasury Bills, Notes, and Bonds)

3.07 U.S. government negotiable debt obligations, known as Treasuries, are secured by the government's full faith and credit and issued at various maturities. These securities clear through book entry form at the Federal Reserve

---

[2] SEC Release No. 10666 under the Investment Company Act of 1940 (the 1940 Act) sets forth the SEC's position that repurchase agreements should be fully collateralized (that is, "the value of the transferred security ... is at least equal to the amount of the loan including accrued interest earned thereon").

Banks. The income from Treasury securities is exempt from state and local, but not federal, taxes. Treasuries include the following:

- *Treasury bills.* Short term securities with maturities of 1 year or less are issued at a discount from face value. Auctions of 4, 13, and 26 week bills take place weekly, and the yields are watched closely in the short-term markets for signs of interest rate trends. Many floating-rate loans and variable-rate mortgages have interest rates tied to these bills. The Treasury also auctions 52 week bills once every 4 weeks. Treasury bills are issued in minimum denominations of $100. Individual investors who submit a non-competitive bid are sold bills at the discount rate determined at auction. Treasury bills are the primary instrument used by the Federal Reserve in its regulation of the money supply through open market operations.
- *Treasury notes.* Intermediate securities with original maturities of 2 to 10 years. Denominations start at $100. The notes are sold through a bank or broker or via auction.
- *Treasury bonds.* Long term debt instruments with an original maturity of 30 years issued in minimum denominations of $100.

3.08 In addition to these basic security types, the government issues other structures, such as Separate Trading of Registered Interest and Principal of Securities also known as stripped Treasury securities and Treasury Inflation-Protected Securities.

Municipal Notes and Bonds

3.09 Municipal securities are issued by states, cities, and other local government authorities to fund public projects. The interest on these bonds is usually exempt from federal taxes and under certain conditions is exempt from state and local taxes. Municipal notes usually mature in less than three years. They are usually designated as tax, revenue, or bond anticipation notes because they are redeemable on the receipt of anticipated taxes or revenues or on financing from the proceeds of municipal bonds. They include short term tax-exempt project notes issued by public housing or urban renewal agencies of local communities with payment of principal and interest guaranteed by the U.S. government. Another common municipal note is a variable rate demand note, which is a floating rate instrument with frequent reset coupon rates and usually a put feature.

3.10 Municipal bonds are principally classified as general obligation bonds and revenue bonds. General obligation bonds represent the issuer's unqualified pledge, based on its full faith, credit, and taxing power, to pay principal and interest when due. Revenue bonds are payable from revenues derived from a particular class of facilities or other specific revenue sources. Tax-exempt industrial development bonds are usually revenue bonds and do not carry the pledge of the municipal issuer's credit, but may be supported by the credit of a private not-for-profit institution (health care or educational institution, for example) or for-profit business entity (utility or industrial company, for example). Yields on municipal bonds depend on a variety of factors, including market conditions, maturity date, ratings assigned to the issue, credit support, and tax-exempt status. Some municipal bonds may be prerefunded by the issuer whereby the bonds are collateralized by securities or U.S. Treasury obligations. Because many of these are guaranteed by Treasury obligations, they often maintain an AAA rating and may trade at a premium over other municipal bonds. Other common municipal bonds include municipal lease obligations, which represent a certificate of participation in the cash flows for certain projects or services, whose funding must be appropriated annually by the municipality.

3.11 Among investment companies, municipal notes and bonds are held primarily in the portfolios of both tax-exempt money-market and municipal bond funds and generally require special considerations for valuation. They are traded in a dealer market in which little published price information is available. New issues of municipal notes or bonds are usually sold by competitive bidding. Subsequent market quotations may be obtained from dealers in those securities.

3.12 A significant decline in the fair value of a municipal security that appears to relate to the issuer's creditworthiness may indicate the probability of default. Comparisons of the fair value of the security with the fair value of similar securities or a downgrading of the issuer's credit rating may indicate such decline.

Insured Portfolios

3.13 As stated in FASB ASC 946-20-05-12, many municipal bond funds, primarily those organized as unit investment trusts with fixed portfolios, arrange for insurance for the payment of principal and interest when due. The insurance applies to portfolio securities only while they are owned by the fund, and its coverage is not transferable to buyers of the securities. That arrangement differs from those in which the issuer of the securities (the municipality) acquires the insurance, which makes the insurance feature an element of the securities and becomes transferable on changes in ownership. According to FASB ASC 946-20-25-11, if the insurance applies only to the fund's portfolio, it does not have a measurable fair value in the absence of default of the underlying securities or of indications of the probability of default; accordingly, the cost of the policy should be treated as an operating expense.

To Be Announced Securities

3.14 The term *to be announced* (TBA) is derived from the fact that the actual security that will be delivered to fulfill a TBA transaction is not designated at the time the trade is made. The securities that will ultimately be delivered upon settlement are "announced" 48 hours prior to the established trade settlement date. The fund trading TBA securities makes a forward commitment to purchase a preset principal amount at a preset price on a preset date in the future.

3.15 TBA securities resulting from these transactions are generally included in the portfolio of investments and are considered to be a regular-way transaction. At the time a fund enters into a commitment to purchase or sell a security, the transaction is recorded and the value of the security underlying the commitment is reflected in the fund's net asset value. The price of such security and the date that the security will be delivered and paid for is fixed at the time the transaction is negotiated. No interest accrues to the fund until payment and delivery takes place. At the time that a fund enters into this type

AAG-INV 3.15

of transaction, the fund is required to have sufficient cash or liquid securities to cover its commitments.

3.16 The value of the security may vary with market fluctuations, and losses may arise due to changes in the value of the underlying securities or if the counterparty does not perform under the contract's terms, or if the issuer does not issue the securities due to political, economic or other factors. Additionally, losses may arise due to declines in the value of the securities prior to settlement date.

3.17 Funds may enter into TBA commitments with the intent to take possession of or deliver the underlying asset, but can extend the settlement or roll the transaction. TBA commitments involve a risk of loss if the value of the security to be purchased or sold declines or increases, respectively, prior to settlement date.

3.18 Pursuant to recommendations of the Treasury Market Practices Group, which is sponsored by the Federal Reserve Bank of New York, beginning January 1, 2014, a fund or its counterparty generally will be required to post collateral when entering into certain forward-settling transactions, including without limitation TBA transactions.

3.19 For long TBA positions, as with other long investments, the security name, par value, coupon rate, maturity date, cost (presented as part of the aggregate cost of investments) and value should be shown in the Schedule of Investments. The TBA security should be designated as having been purchased on a delayed delivery or when-issued basis, if the settlement extends beyond the "normal" settlement period. For short TBA positions, the security name, par value, coupon rate, maturity date proceeds and value should be presented for each position in the securities sold short section of the Schedule of Investments. The TBA security should be designated as having been sold on a delayed delivery or when-issued basis, if the settlement extends beyond the "normal" settlement period.

When-Issued Securities

3.20 Some securities, principally municipal securities, are traded on a when-issued basis. A municipal securities underwriter solicits expressions of interest in a proposed issue and sends a when-issued price confirmation against which securities are delivered later when the terms of the issue are known. The securities usually begin trading on a when-issued basis on the issuance of the confirmation as if they had been issued a few days before the closing date.

3.21 Securities offerings are rarely aborted after when-issued trading begins. A when-issued security and the obligation to pay for the security should be recorded when the commitment becomes fixed, which is the date that the priced transaction confirmation is issued. When-issued securities for which the fund has not taken delivery are required to be identified in a registered investment company's financial statements.[3] Securities may also be bought on a delayed delivery contract under which the underwriter agrees to deliver securities to buyers at later specified dates.

---

[3] SEC Release No. 10666 under the 1940 Act.

Synthetic Floaters

3.22 Many investment advisers use tax-exempt derivative securities as a way to increase the pool of creditworthy tax-exempt securities. These derivatives include synthetic floaters, under which issuers of such instruments use interest payments from long term municipal bonds, which may be coupled with an interest rate swap and a put feature, to pay the floating short term interest rates on the synthetic floater. The investor receives regular interest payments that are tied to short term municipal rates while the issuer earns the spread between the long term coupon rate and short term floating rate. The investor may either hold the trust certificate representing ownership of the underlying bond to maturity or put it back to the issuer for cash.

3.23 In some instances, these tax exempt derivative securities are created by the deposit of fixed-rate tax-exempt bonds into special purpose trusts against which synthetic floater certificates and inverse floater certificates, representing rights to principal and any interest remaining after interest payments are made on the synthetic floaters, are issued. The inverse floater certificates often allow, upon unanimous consent of the holders of the inverse floater certificates, for the liquidation of the trust, together with full repayment of the synthetic floaters and delivery of the underlying fixed rate bonds to the holders of the inverse floater certificates. If the holders of the inverse floater certificates also participated in the formation of the special purpose trust (that is, the inverse floater certificates were not acquired on the secondary market), FASB ASC 860 should be considered in evaluating the appropriate accounting and whether the initial transfer of the security into the special purpose trust and subsequent issuance of synthetic floater certificates would be considered a secured borrowing or sale.

Mortgage-Backed Securities

3.24 As defined by the FASB ASC glossary, *mortgage-backed securities* (MBSs) are securities issued and guaranteed by a governmental agency or corporation (for example, the Government National Mortgage Association [GNMA] or the Federal Home Loan Mortgage Corporation [FHLMC or Freddie Mac]) or private issuers (for example, the Federal National Mortgage Association [FNMA], banks, and mortgage banking entities). MBSs generally are referred to as mortgage participation certificates or pass-through certificates. A participation certificate represents an undivided interest in a pool of specific mortgage loans. Periodic payments on GNMA participation certificates are backed by the U.S. government. Periodic payments on FHLMC and FNMA certificates are guaranteed by those corporations but not backed by the U.S. government.

3.25 An MBS is a pass-through security created by pooling mortgages and selling interests or participations in the MBS. In some instances the mortgage originator will continue to service the underlying mortgage, or the servicing may be sold to a subsidiary or another institution. Mortgage originators will usually pool mortgage loans and sell interests in the pools created. By selling MBSs, originators can obtain funds to issue new mortgages while retaining the servicing rights on the pooled loans. The GNMA is a U.S. government owned corporation that approves the issue of MBSs whose principal and interest are then fully guaranteed by the U.S. government. The FNMA is a U.S. government sponsored entity that purchases mortgages, including mortgages backed by the Federal Housing Administration or guaranteed by the Veterans

Administration and other conventional mortgages, and resells them to investors. Freddie Mac is a government sponsored entity that issues MBSs known as participation certificates. Principal and interest payments received from mortgagors are passed on to the MBS holders 45 days later for the GNMA, 55 days later for the FNMA, and 75 days later for Freddie Mac (45 days for gold Freddie Mac).

3.26 Mortgages are not homogeneous, and as a result different pools have different prepayment experience. MBSs are considered seasoned once they have been outstanding for four to five years. Investors are typically willing to pay more for seasoned mortgages than unseasoned mortgages because seasoned mortgages have payment experience, which investors use to make estimates of future prepayments. Unseasoned MBSs possess more unknown variables and, thus, are more sensitive to market volatility.

Adjustable Rate Mortgages

3.27 An *adjustable rate mortgage* (ARM) is a mortgage loan whose interest rate is reset periodically to reflect market rate changes. In addition, ARMs usually have caps that provide borrowers with some protection from rising interest rates. ARMs' interest rates are usually calculated based on one of three indexes: (*a*) U.S. Treasury securities, (*b*) the Cost of Funds Index, or (*c*) average mortgage rates. Typically, ARM rates are reset every six months, one year, three years, or five years. ARMs are usually priced at a spread above the U.S. Treasury yield. In addition, the GNMA, the FNMA, and the FHLMC or private insurance companies guarantee many ARMs.

Collateralized Mortgage Obligations

3.28 Different kinds of collateralized mortgage obligation (CMO) structures exist, each of which has different cash flow characteristics. A security holder may invest in a CMO equity form (for example, trust interests, stock, and partnership interests) or nonequity form (for example, participating debt securities). Some of these structures include the following:

- CMO bonds are bonds collateralized by either a pool of pass-through securities or a pool of mortgage loans and may be issued in several tranches having different maturities and interest rates. The cash flow from the pool of assets is used to pay the principal and interest on the bonds. The sequence of payments is deal specific and is modeled by the issuer.

- CMO residuals represent the excess cash flows from MBSs or a pool of loans used as collateral for a CMO bond and include reinvestment income thereon after paying the debt service on the CMO and related administrative expenses. Cash flows are generated from the interest differential between the collateral for the CMOs and the CMO itself, the interest differential between the various classes of bonds, reinvestment income, and overcollateralization income. Many different kinds of CMO residuals, including floating-rate residuals; inverse floating residuals (inverse floaters [that is, interest rates vary inversely with floating rates]); and principal amortization class residuals, are available.

- Interest-only (IO) and principal-only (PO) securities are created by splitting a traditional MBS or pool of loans into an IO and a PO portion. IO securities may have fixed or variable interest rates. Both IO and PO securities are subject to prepayments and therefore prepayment risk. IO investors are at risk for faster than anticipated prepayments and PO investors for slower than anticipated prepayments. Assumptions regarding the rates of prepayment play a significant role in the price of these securities. Because they may not pay a current coupon, prices of IOs and POs are more sensitive to changing interest rates than coupon bonds. They can be stripped from fixed or adjustable-rate loans or a pool of fixed-rate loans containing a range of different mortgage rates. The individual mortgages are subject to prepayment and default risk. PO securities issued by government sponsored entities (that is, the FNMA, the FHLMC, and so on) are usually fully or partially guaranteed against credit loss.

- An IOette is an IO with a relatively low principal amount and high coupon rate. The principal and interest components of MBSs are sometimes separated and recombined in varying proportions to create synthetic coupon securities.

Real Estate Mortgage Investment Conduits

3.29 The real estate mortgage investment conduit (REMIC) is a form of CMO specially designated for federal income tax purposes so that the related income is taxed only once (to the security holder). A corporation, a partnership, an association, or a trust may elect to be a REMIC and many special purpose entities that issue CMOs, IOs, POs, and MBSs have elected to structure themselves as REMICs.

High-Yield Securities

3.30 As defined by the FASB ASC glossary, *high-yield debt securities* are corporate and municipal debt securities having a lower-than-investment-grade credit rating (BB+ or lower by Standard & Poor's or Ba1 or lower by Moody's). Because high-yield debt securities typically are used when lower-cost capital is not available, they have interest rates several percentage points higher than investment-grade debt and often have shorter maturities. These high-yielding corporate and municipal debt obligations are frequently referred to as junk bonds. As further explained in FASB ASC 946-320-05-4, they are typically unsecured and subordinate to other debt outstanding. Many issuers of high-yield debt securities are highly leveraged with limited equity capital. These inherent differences from investment grade bonds, including a market for such securities that may not always be liquid, may increase the market, liquidity, and credit risks of these securities as follows:

> **Market risk.** In contrast to investment-grade bonds (the market prices of which change primarily as a reaction to changes in interest rates), the market prices of high-yield bonds (which are also affected by changes in interest rates) are influenced much more by credit factors and financial results of the issuer and general economic factors that influence the financial markets as a whole. Such

factors often make it difficult to substantiate the market valuation of high-yield bonds.

Liquidity risk. The market risk is often heightened by liquidity risk (that is, the absence of centralized high-yield bond exchanges and relatively thin trading markets, which make it more difficult to liquidate holdings quickly and increase the volatility of the market price). There is generally no centralized or regulated procedure for pricing high-yield debt issues.

Credit risk. Issues of high-yield debt securities are more likely to default on interest or principal than are issues of investment-grade securities.

3.31 SEC yield formula calculations are required to be made using the specific guidelines presented in SEC Final Rule Release No. 33-6753. Yields calculated that way might not be the same as the interest reported in the financial statements. The ultimate realizable value and the potential for early retirement of securities should be considered when computing SEC yields. Management's best estimates of ultimate realizable value should be reasonable. If current values of high-yield debt securities decline significantly from the issue price, computed yields may be higher than rates expected to be ultimately realized. To avoid unsound yield information, consideration should be given to capping yields of individual securities at some reasonable level and examining the underlying economic viability of the issuers.

Payment-in-Kind Bonds

3.32 As defined in the FASB ASC glossary, *payment-in-kind bonds* (PIK) are bonds in which the issuer has the option at each interest payment date of making interest payments in cash or additional debt securities. Those additional debt securities are referred to as baby bonds or bunny bonds. Baby bonds usually have the same terms, including maturity dates and interest rates, as the original bonds (parent PIK bonds). Interest on baby bonds may also be paid in cash or additional like-kind debt securities at the option of the issuer.

3.33 FASB ASC 946-320-35-10 states that the interest method should be used to determine interest income on PIK bonds. The FASB ASC glossary defines the *interest method* as the method used to arrive at a periodic interest cost (including amortization) that will represent a level effective rate on the sum of the face amount of the debt and (plus or minus) the unamortized premium or discount and expense at the beginning of each period. As further explained in FASB ASC 946-320-30-4, PIK bonds typically trade flat (that is, interest receivable is included in the price quotation obtained each day). Accordingly, that portion of the quote representing interest income needs to be identified. The sum of the acquisition amount of the bond and the discount to be amortized should not exceed the undiscounted future cash collections that are both reasonably estimable and probable. Further, FASB ASC 946-320-35-11 notes that, to the extent that interest income to be received in the form of baby bonds is not expected to be realized, a reserve against income should be established .That is, it should be determined periodically that the total amount of interest income recorded as receivable, plus the initial cost of the underlying PIK bond does not exceed the current fair value of those assets.

Step Bonds

3.34 As defined by the FASB ASC glossary, *step bonds* are characterized by a combination of deferred-interest payment dates and increasing interest payment amounts over the bond lives. Thus, they bear some similarity to zero-coupon bonds and traditional debentures.

3.35 As noted in paragraphs 12–13 of FASB ASC 946-320-35, income on step bonds should be recognized using the interest method. Additionally, to the extent that interest income is not expected to be realized, a reserve against income should be established. The sum of the acquisition amount of the bond and the discount to be amortized should not exceed the undiscounted future cash collections that are both reasonably estimable and probable.

Put and Call Options

3.36 An *option* is a contract giving its owner the right, but not the obligation, to buy (call) or sell (put) a specified item at a fixed price (exercise or strike price) during a specified period (American option) or on a specified date (European option). Options may be exchange traded or over the counter. Options may be written on a variety of instruments, indexes, commodities or currencies. The buyer pays a nonrefundable fee (the premium) to the seller (the writer). An investment company may buy or write put and call options, if permitted, as disclosed in its prospectus. As consideration for an option, the buyer pays the writer a premium that is the maximum amount that the buyer could lose. That amount is influenced by such factors as the duration of the option, the difference between the exercise price and fair value of the underlying securities, price volatility, and other characteristics of the underlying securities. In return for the premium

- a covered writer of a call option (a writer who owns the underlying securities) gives up the opportunity to profit from an increase in the fair value of the underlying securities to a point higher than the exercise price of the option outstanding but retains the risk of loss if the fair value of the securities declines.

- an uncovered writer of a call option (a naked option) does not own the underlying securities but assumes the obligation to deliver the underlying securities on exercise of the option. An uncovered writer is exposed to the risk of loss if the fair value of the underlying securities increases above the strike price but has no risk of loss if the fair value of the underlying securities does not exceed the option exercise price.[4]

- a writer of a put option is exposed to the risk of loss if the fair value of the underlying securities declines but profits only to the extent of the premium received if the underlying security increases in value because the holder of the option will not exercise it if the holder can obtain a greater price elsewhere. The writer is covered

---

[4] An investment company may be exposed to additional losses resulting from the price appreciation of the underlying security. For registered investment companies, Section 18 of the 1940 Act provides additional guidance for writers of naked call options. For example, an investment company may mitigate the option's exposure to Section 18 prohibitions by segregating cash or other securities in an amount greater than or equal to the option written or by purchasing a call option on the underlying security for similar terms.

if a put option is bought on the same underlying securities with an exercise date equal to or earlier than the option that it covers and an exercise price equal to or greater than the option written.

3.37 After an option is written, the writer's obligation may be discharged in one of the following ways:

    a. The option expires on its stipulated expiration date.

    b. The writer enters into a closing transaction.

    c. The option holder exercises the right to call (buy) or put (sell) the security (not applicable for index options).

3.38 The writer or buyer of an option traded on an exchange can liquidate the position before the exercise of the option by entering into a closing transaction. Such a transaction, in effect, cancels the existing position. The cost of a liquidating purchase, however, may be higher than the premium received for the original option. Because the writer or buyer can enter into a closing transaction, the option originally written may never be exercised. An option traded on an exchange is exercised only through the Options Clearing Corporation (OCC), the obligor on every option, by the timely submission of an exercise notice by the clearing broker acting on behalf of the exercising holder. The exercise notice is assigned by the OCC to a clearing broker acting on behalf of a writer of an option of the same series as the exercised option. The clearing broker is obligated to deliver the underlying security against payment of the exercise price. The assigned broker is selected randomly from clearing members having accounts with the OCC with options outstanding of the same series as the option being exercised.

3.39 Freestanding written put options and certain contracts that function as fair value guarantees on a financial asset that is owned by the guaranteed party, even when classified as derivatives under FASB ASC 815, are within the scope of the disclosure provisions of FASB ASC 460-10-50. Under those provisions in FASB ASC 460-10-50-4, guarantors are required to disclose the following information about each guarantee or each group of similar guarantees, even if the likelihood of the guarantor's having to make payments under the guarantee is remote:

    a. The nature of the guarantee, including its approximate term; how the guarantee arose; the events or circumstances that would require the guarantor to perform under the guarantee; and the current status (that is, as of the date of the statement of financial position) of the payment or performance risk of the guarantee (for example, the current status of the payment or performance risk of a credit risk-related guarantee could be based on either recently issued external credit ratings or current internal groupings used by the guarantor to manage its risk). An entity that uses internal groupings should disclose how those groupings are determined and used for managing risk.

    b. The undiscounted maximum potential amount of future payments that the guarantor would be required to make under the guarantee, which should not be reduced by the effect of any amounts that may possibly be recovered under any recourse or collateralization provisions. If the terms of the guarantee provide for no limitation to the maximum potential future payments under the guarantee, that fact should be disclosed. If the guarantor is unable to develop an estimate of the maximum potential amount of future payments under its guarantee, the reasons why it cannot estimate the maximum potential amount should be disclosed.

c. The current carrying amount of the liability, if any, for the guarantor's obligations under the guarantee (including the amount, if any, recognized under FASB ASC 450-20-30 that deals with loss contingencies), regardless of whether the guarantee is freestanding or embedded in another contract.

d. The nature of any recourse provisions that would enable the guarantor to recover any amounts paid under the guarantee from third parties.

e. The nature of any assets held either as collateral or by third parties that, upon the occurrence of any triggering event or condition under the guarantee, the guarantor can obtain and liquidate to recover all or a portion of the amounts paid under the guarantee.

f. If estimable, the approximate extent to which the proceeds from liquidation of assets held either as collateral or by third parties would be expected to cover the maximum potential amount of future payments under the guarantee.

Warrants

3.40 A warrant is an instrument giving its owner the right, but generally not the obligation, to purchase shares in an issuer at a predefined price, within a specified time period. Unlike a call option (which may exist between two parties unrelated to the issuer of the shares), the warrant exists solely between the issuer (that is, the entity in which additional shares will be issued upon exercise of the warrant) and the owner of the warrant. Warrants can exist either as freestanding contracts or as instruments embedded in convertible debt or convertible preferred equity.

3.41 An assessment to determine if a warrant is a derivative may include consideration of the net settlement criteria in FASB ASC 815-10-15-119, in which one of the parties is required to deliver an asset of the type described in FASB ASC 815-10-15-100, but that asset should be readily convertible to cash or is itself a derivative instrument. FASB ASC 815-10-15-131 states that shares of stock in a publicly traded company to be received upon the exercise of a stock purchase warrant do not meet the characteristic of being readily convertible to cash if both of the following conditions exist: (a) the stock purchase warrant is issued by an entity for only its own stock (or stock of its consolidated subsidiaries) and (b) the sale or transfer of the issued shares is restricted (other than in connection with being pledged as collateral) for a period of 32 days or more from the date the stock purchase warrant is exercised. In contrast, FASB ASC 815-10-15-132 states that restrictions imposed by a stock purchase warrant on the sale or transfer of shares of stock that are received from the exercise of that warrant issued by an entity for other than its own stock (whether those restrictions are for more or less than 32 days) do not affect the determination of whether those shares are readily convertible to cash. The accounting for restricted stock to be received upon exercise of a stock purchase warrant should not be analogized to any other type of contract. Refer to paragraphs 133–138 of FASB ASC 815-10-15 for further guidance on when to consider a warrant a derivative and hence trigger FASB ASC 815 disclosure requirements.

Loan Commitments

3.42 Certain investment companies acquire interests in bank lending facilities, including interests in lines of credit and other commitments to lend. Loan commitments are generally defined as written agreements, signed by the borrower and lender, detailing terms and conditions under which a loan of up to a specified amount will be made. The commitment has an expiration date and typically a fee will be paid for agreeing to make the commitment. A commitment can be irrevocable or, in many instances, conditioned on the maintenance by the borrower of satisfactory financial standing and absence of default in other covenants. Lines of credit are often less detailed than a formal loan commitment, and are often letter expressions of willingness to lend up to a certain amount over a specified time frame, usually one year. Many lines of credit are cancellable if the borrower's financial condition deteriorates; others are subject to cancellation at the bank's option.

3.43 Loan commitments are typically regarded by financial institutions as off-balance-sheet financial instruments but are not within the scope of FASB ASC 815.

Standby Commitments

3.44 A *standby commitment* is an optional delivery forward placement commitment contract. On the sale of a standby commitment, an investment company is contractually bound to accept future delivery of a security at a guaranteed price or fixed yield on the exercise of an option held by the other party to the agreement. In effect, the investment company sells a put option and receives a fee for its commitment to buy the security. The investment company bears the risk of loss if interest rates rise, causing the fair value of the security at the delivery date to be less than the exercise (strike) price of the option less the fee received.[5]

Commodity and Financial Futures Contracts

3.45 Commodity and financial futures contracts are traded on various exchanges and are thus distinguished from forward contracts, which are entered into privately by the parties. A *commodity futures contract* is a firm commitment to buy or sell a specified quantity of a specified grade of a specified commodity or, for financial futures contracts (including index futures contracts), a standardized amount of a deliverable grade security (or a basket[6] for index futures) at a specified price and specified future date unless the contract is closed before the delivery date. For futures contracts, the date is a specified delivery month, and the contract is typically settled by executing an offsetting futures contract before or during the delivery month.

---

[5] The SEC indicated in Release No. 10666 under the 1940 Act that an investment company's participation in a firm commitment agreement (forward placement commitment or agreement to purchase when-issued securities), standby commitment, or reverse repo may involve the issuance of a security by the investment company. The security may be a *senior security* as defined in Section 18(g) of the 1940 Act, and the investment company entering into the agreement may be in violation of Section 18(f) (1). However, the Division of Investment Management has determined that it will not raise the issue of compliance with Section 18 with the SEC if the investment company covers the senior security by establishing and maintaining certain segregated accounts.

[6] A group of securities that compose the underlying index.

3.46 The quantity and quality provisions of futures contracts are standardized. For example, every cotton futures contract traded on ICE Futures U.S. (formerly the New York Board of Trade) is for 50,000 pounds, and every Treasury bill futures contract traded on the International Money Market of the Chicago Mercantile Exchange is for $1 million notional par value.

3.47 Although a confirmation of the trade is submitted showing the pertinent price, quantity, and commodity data, no amount is usually entered in the general ledger. The ledger reflects only the margin deposit and the daily mark to market for variation margin. Details of open contracts are in memorandum format. Variation margin normally is settled in cash with the broker each morning for the amount of the previous day's mark to market.

3.48 To initiate a futures contract, the investor is required to make an initial margin deposit in an amount established by the various exchanges. This amount varies according to the commodity or security, the prevailing price, whether the investor is speculating or hedging, and market conditions. The initial margin may often be deposited in Treasury bills. In those cases, the restriction of the ability to trade the Treasury bills should be disclosed in the fund's schedule of investments. Brokers sometimes require margins in excess of those set by the exchanges.

3.49 An investment company may deposit initial margin on futures contracts directly with futures commission merchants (FCMs) that are registered under the Commodity Exchange Act and that are not affiliated with the investment company. A registered investment company is generally not permitted to deposit initial margin deposits on futures contracts in three-party special segregated custody accounts. Cash or securities deposited to meet margin requirements should be identified as margin deposits on the investment company's records. Alternatively, the investment company may arrange to put up performance bonds with FCMs.

Forward Contracts

3.50 A *forward contract* is a legal contract between two parties to purchase and sell a specified quantity of a financial instrument or commodity at a price specified now, with delivery and settlement at a specified future date. Forward contracts are similar to futures contracts, except that they are not traded on an exchange. Their terms are not standardized, and they can be terminated only by agreement of both parties to the forward contract. If a forward contract is held until expiration, settlement by delivery is required. Most forwards are settled in cash. Typically, they do not settle on a daily basis by margin settlement as do futures contracts, although contracts may require collateral to be deposited under certain conditions.

Forward Exchange Contracts

3.51 As defined by the FASB ASC glossary, *a forward exchange contract* is an agreement between two parties to exchange different currencies at a specified exchange rate at an agreed-upon future date.

3.52 Although these contracts can be speculative in nature, a fund typically enters a forward exchange contract to hedge overall portfolio currency risk or settle foreign security transactions. If the purpose of the contract is to hedge portfolio risk, the contract is typically closed by entering into an offsetting contract before the settlement date. In this way, on the settlement date the fund is only obligated to deliver or purchase the net amount of foreign currency involved.

Interest Rate, Currency, and Equity Swaps and Swaptions

3.53 Many variations of swaps exist. Swaps can be linked to any number of underlying instruments and indexes, and swap terms can vary greatly. The *trade date* is the date of the commitment to enter into the swap. The *effective date* is the date on which the parties begin calculating accrued obligations, such as fixed and floating interest payment obligations on an interest rate swap. The *termination date* (often called *maturity date*) is the date on which obligations no longer accrue and the final payment occurs. The *term* of a transaction lasts from the effective date to the termination date.

3.54 Interest rate swaps represent an agreement between counterparties to exchange cash flows based on the difference between two interest rates applied to a notional principal amount for a specified period. The most common kind of interest rate swap involves the exchange of fixed-rate cash flows for variable-rate cash flows. Interest rate swaps do not involve the exchange of principal between the parties. Interest is paid or received periodically. Swaps range in maturities, usually 1 to 30 years. Market risk and credit risk are two important risks associated with swaps. Credit risk is often minimized by requiring the counterparty to post collateral if any indication of credit risk exists or if the fair value of the swap changes so that a party to the swap becomes significantly "in the money", or by engaging in swaps only with highly rated counterparties. See discussion of centrally cleared swaps beginning at paragraph 3.58. Market risk requires a careful understanding of the effects on the swap's fair value of changing market conditions. Both risks require close monitoring. Swaps may be structured so that the notional principal amount is adjusted up or down during the term of the swap. Floating rate reset periods vary, ranging from daily to yearly.

3.55 A *currency swap* is an agreement between two parties to exchange two different currencies with an agreement to reverse the exchange at a later date at specified exchange rates. The exchange of currencies at the inception date of the contract takes place at the current spot rate. The re-exchange at maturity may take place at the same exchange rate, a specified rate, or the then current spot rate. Interest payments, if applicable, are made between the parties based on interest rates available in the two currencies at the inception of the contract. The term of currency swap contracts may extend for many years. Currency swaps are usually negotiated with commercial and investment banks. Contracts are subject to the risk of default by the counterparty and, depending on their terms, may be subject to exchange rate risk. Some currency swaps may provide only for exchanging interest cash flows, not principal cash flows.

3.56 Some funds may enter into equity swaps to manage their exposure to the equity markets. In an equity swap, cash flows are exchanged based on a commitment by one party to pay interest in exchange for a market-linked return based on a notional amount. The market-linked return may include, among other things, the total return of a security, custom basket of securities, or an index. These agreements involve elements of credit and market risk. Risks include the possibility that no liquid market exists for these obligations, the counterparty may default on its obligation, or unfavorable changes may exist in the security or index underlying the swap.

3.57 A swaption includes any option that gives the buyer the right, but not the obligation, to enter into a swap on a future date. It also includes any option that allows an existing swap to be terminated or extended by one of the counterparties. These structures are also called cancelable, callable, or putable swaps. Swaptions can be American, exercisable at any point during the option term, or European, exercisable only on the last day of the option term. Swaptions that establish swaps when exercised may be puts or calls. In both cases, the fixed rate that will be exchanged is established when the swaption is purchased. The term of the swap is also specified. If a call interest rate swaption is exercised, the option holder will enter a swap to receive the fixed rate and pay a floating rate in exchange. The exercise of a put would entitle the option holder to pay a fixed rate and receive a floating rate. Calls become more valuable when the underlying securities' prices rise and rates fall. The option holder will exercise a call swaption when rates have fallen from the strike level. The put swaption will be exercised when market rates rise above the fixed rate that the option holder can pay (that is, prices have fallen).

Centrally Cleared Swaps

3.58 In July 2010, the Dodd-Frank Wall Street Reform and Consumer Protection Act (Dodd-Frank Act) was signed into law. Title VII of the Dodd-Frank Act established a comprehensive new regulatory framework for swaps and security-based swaps. One of Title VII's broad objectives is improved over-the-counter (OTC) derivatives market transparency, which is intended to be achieved through a variety of new requirements currently being enacted through the U.S. Commodity Futures Trading Commission (CFTC) and SEC rules.[7] These requirements include, among other items, the central clearing of eligible OTC derivatives (including most swap agreements). Central clearing requires a central clearing party (CCP, also referred to as a derivatives clearing organization) that functions as an intermediary between the buyer and seller. Two distinct contracts are formed, one between the CCP and the buyer and

---

[7] Title VII of the Dodd-Frank Wall Street Reform and Consumer Protection Act provides that the U.S. Commodity Futures Trading Commission (CFTC) will regulate "swaps," the SEC will regulate "security-based swaps," and the CFTC and SEC will jointly regulate "mixed swaps." In July 2012, the SEC and CFTC issued Final Rule No. 33-9338, Further Definition of "Swap," "Security-Based Swap," and "Security-Based Swap Agreement;" Mixed Swaps; Security-Based Swap Agreement Recordkeeping. The Final Rule provides interpretations under the Commodity Exchange Act and the Securities Exchange Act of 1934 (the 1934 Act) to further define the term swap, among other terms, in order to provide clarity of the scope of Title VII. Additionally, in June 2014, the SEC issued Final Rule No. 34-72472, Application of "Security-Based Swap Dealer" and "Major Security-Based Swap Participant" Definitions to Cross-Border Security-Based Swap Activities, which is intended to provide guidance to address the application of certain provisions of the 1934 Act that were added by Title VII to cross-border security-based swap activities. These rules and guidance in large part focus on the application of the Title VII definitions of *security-based swap dealer* and *major security-based swap participant* in the cross-border context. The SEC also adopted a procedural rule related to the submission of applications for substituted compliance, and a rule addressing the scope of our authority, with respect to enforcement proceedings, under section 929P of the Dodd-Frank Act.

one between the CCP and the seller. This method is in contrast to the bilateral trading model that has historically been used in the OTC derivatives market, whereby the buyer and seller directly enter into the OTC derivative contract with no intermediary. A multiphase implementation of the central clearing requirement occurred during 2013 for most interest rate swaps and credit default swaps regulated by the CFTC.

3.59 The central clearing mandate intends to reduce counterparty default risk by incorporating a CCP margin reserve fund that guarantees the creditworthiness of both counterparties. The buyer and seller parties contribute margin requirements, through their respective clearing members, to the CCP's guarantee fund. These margin requirements include an "initial" margin requirement and subsequent "variation" margin requirements. The initial margin requirement is paid to the CCP when the centrally cleared swap contract is executed. This initial margin, typically in the form of cash or qualifying highly liquid, high-quality short-term securities, is held by the CCP in a default fund to be used in the event of default by a counterparty. Following the initiation of the contract, on a daily basis, the CCP determines a new derivative contract "value." This value is based primarily on the derivative contract's prevailing market price and, if deemed appropriate by the CCP or a clearing member, may also include an additional component to mitigate any nonpayment or other risks. This incremental daily change in the derivative contract's "value" represents a net gain for one counterparty and a net loss for the other counterparty. The value of the daily net loss represents the "variation" margin for that given day, which is settled daily by a cash transfer from the counterparty, who incurred the net loss via the clearing member to the CCP.

3.60 The following illustration explains the differences between the bilateral model and the central clearing model:

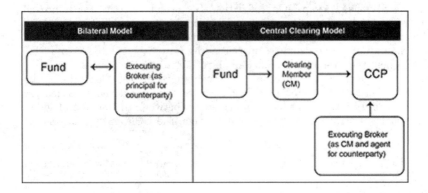

3.61 The following illustration explains the trade flow in the central clearing model:

3.62 Several accounting and reporting considerations arise in conjunction with the adoption and implementation of the central clearing requirements. Readers should consider all applicable provisions of the Dodd-Frank Act, Title VII and related final and proposed rules of the CFTC and SEC.

Credit Derivatives

3.63 Many funds enter into credit derivatives, including credit default swaps, credit spread options, and credit index products. The FASB ASC glossary defines a *credit derivative* as a derivative instrument for which (*a*) one or more underlyings are related to the credit risk of a specific entity (or group of entities) or, alternatively, an index based on the credit risk of a group of entities, and (*b*) the derivative exposes the seller to potential loss from credit-risk-related events specified in the contract.

3.64 Credit derivatives related to the credit risk of a specific entity are often referred to as *single-name* credit derivatives.

Structured Notes or Indexed Securities

3.65 A *structured note*, as defined by the FASB ASC glossary, is a debt instrument whose cash flows are linked to the movement in one or more indexes, interest rates, equities, foreign exchange rates, commodities prices, prepayment rates, or other market variables. Structured notes are issued by U.S. government sponsored enterprises, multilateral development banks, municipalities, and private entities and can be either short term or long term. The notes typically contain embedded (but not separable or detachable) forward components or option components, such as caps, calls, and floors. Contractual cash flows for principal, interest, or both can vary in amount and timing throughout the life of the note based on nontraditional indexes or nontraditional uses of traditional interest rates or indexes.

3.66 Additionally, structured notes are sometimes called *indexed securities*. These packaged securities have some similar characteristics to a plain debt instrument, such as commercial paper, medium-term notes, or CDs. Instead of paying a fixed interest rate over time and repaying par at maturity, structured notes index the coupon, principal, or both to virtually anything with a trading market. The indexing may be to currencies, interest rate spreads, stock market indexes, or the price of a security or commodity completely unrelated to the transaction. For example, from the standpoint of the holder, many convertible bonds are considered, for accounting purposes, to represent a form of structured note.

3.67 Although structured notes economically represent a debt instrument with an embedded derivative, FASB ASC 815-15-25-1 discusses that embedded derivatives are only required to be separated from their host contract and accounted for as a derivative instrument if, among other things, the instrument is not remeasured at fair value under otherwise applicable generally accepted accounting principles with changes in fair value reported in earnings as they occur.

3.68 Because investment companies report all their investments at fair value with changes in fair value reported in earnings, derivatives embedded within structured notes owned need not be separated from their host contracts and separately reported.

Short Positions

3.69 A short sale creates a senior security for registered investment companies that is subject to the limitation of Section 18 of the 1940 Act. To comply with the provisions of Section 18, a registered investment company that sells securities short must establish a segregated account, as discussed in the section on accounting for segregated accounts, to account for cash or cash equivalents equal in fair value to the securities sold short or equivalent securities already owned if the sale is against the box.

Mortgage Dollar Rolls

3.70 Mortgage dollar rolls (MDRs) involve selling mortgage securities and simultaneously agreeing to purchase mortgage securities on a later date at a set price from the same counterparty.[8] Dollar rolls differ from regular reverse repo agreements in that the securities sold and repurchased, which are usually of the same issuer, are represented by different certificates; and are collateralized by similar, but not identical, mortgage pools (for example, single-family residential mortgages with the same coupon rate and contractual term to maturity, such as 15 to 30 years). Additionally, the securities returned to close an MDR need not have identical principal amounts from the securities initially sold, but must be within the recognized standards for "good delivery"

---

[8] See SEC Final Rule Release No. IC-22389.

for trading in MBSs. The most common kinds of dollar rolls are fixed-coupon and yield-maintenance arrangements.

3.71 The investment company and the counterparty may decide to extend the contract and not return the securities involved in the roll. The contract may be extended in this manner over a number of periods with the agreement of both counterparties.

3.72 An MDR can also be executed entirely in the to-be-announced market when the investment company makes a forward commitment to purchase a security, and instead of accepting delivery, the position is offset by a sale of the security with a simultaneous agreement to repurchase in the future.

3.73 Compensation to the investment company for the risks involved in an MDR transaction is in the form of either a fee or a reduction in the repurchase price of the security, referred to as the drop.

3.74 The appropriate accounting treatment for an MDR transaction should be based on FASB ASC 860.

Chapter 4

Capital Accounts

4.01 This chapter deals primarily with operations, controls, and accounting and auditing matters affecting the capital accounts of open-end investment companies. Among the regulations and limitations that affect the accounting for capital stock transactions of open-end investment companies are the following:

- Rules 2a-4 and 12b-1 of the Investment Company Act of 1940 (the 1940 Act)
- Financial Industry Regulatory Authority (FINRA) limits on sales charges
- Load structures and arrangements for reduced sales charges as established in fund prospectuses
- Rule 18f-3 of the 1940 Act and exemptive orders in effect for individual fund complexes relating to multiple classes of shares

Most issuances and repurchases of shares of closed-end investment companies can be accounted for and audited similarly to other commercial entities.

Operations and Controls

Distributors

4.02 As stated in chapter 1, "Overview of the Investment Company Industry," of this guide, many open-end investment companies enter into agreements with a separate distributor (also called an underwriter) under which the distributor obtains the exclusive right, as either principal or agent for the fund, to deal in fund shares as a wholesaler, reselling the shares to independent dealers or through its own sales network. Commonly, the distributor is an affiliate of the fund sponsor.

4.03 Distributor compensation is dependent on the kind of arrangement that applies to the shares that they are selling. A commission or sales charge (load) may be assessed on mutual fund investments when the shares are purchased (at the front end), when the shares are redeemed (at the back end), or during the period that the shares are held by a shareholder (level load). Fund shares sold through full-service distribution channels, such as brokers or financial planners, typically include a sales charge or fee of some sort in exchange for providing additional investment advice or services.

4.04 When shares with a front-end load are distributed through independent dealers, a significant portion of the load is retained by the independent dealer for its services (including payment of a commission to the broker actually selling the shares) and the remainder is remitted to the distributor. The distributor retains the full front-end load when its own sales network is responsible for selling shares but pays commissions to its employees out of the load. When shares with a back-end load, typically known as a contingent deferred sales load (CDSL) or contingent deferred sales charge, are sold, no commission is subtracted from the proceeds received from the investor. Instead, the distributor pays the commission to the independent dealer or its employees. Other installment or noncontingent deferred sales loads may be applied that do not decline to zero, as well as loads paid after purchase during the shareholder's time in the fund.[1]

4.05 Sales commission rates on mutual funds with front-end loads typically decline as the amount of the sale increases. Some funds offer various arrangements, including letters of intent and rights of accumulation, entitling individual purchasers to reduced sales charges based on aggregate purchases of shares of either the individual fund or funds within the same mutual fund complex. Also, front-end loads may either be reduced or waived when shares are sold under employee benefit arrangements such as 401(k) plans.

4.06 Rule 12b-1 (under the 1940 Act) fees generated by the sale of level-load shares are typically used to compensate dealers and sales personnel for their selling and servicing efforts. CDSL shares are typically offered in combination with a Rule 12b-1 distribution plan under which the fund makes payments to the distributor for distribution services. The distributor typically uses 12b-1 payments and CDSL receipts to recover the initial commission that it paid for sales of CDSL shares. The amount of payments that a fund may make for this purpose is capped under FINRA rules.[2]

4.07 Some funds offer both front-end and back-end load shares, including shares with different sales charges, to retail and institutional investors by issuing multiple classes of shares, each with different load structures and distribution fees. To issue multiple classes of shares, most fund groups obtained individual exemptive orders from the SEC until Rule 18f-3, which provides standard conditions under which multiple classes of shares may be offered, was issued in 1995. Some funds with unique variations have elected not to adopt the provisions of Rule 18f-3 and continue to rely on their individual exemptive orders. Because discounts typically are not provided on sales commissions for back-end load shares, multiple class funds often limit the dollar amount that may be invested by a retail investor in back-end load shares and require those orders over a certain amount to be treated as orders for front-end load shares. Chapter 5, "Complex Capital Structures," of this guide contains a more comprehensive discussion of multiple classes of shares.

Orders to Purchase or Redeem

4.08 Investors buy at an offering price, which, for front-end load funds, consists of the net asset value received by the fund plus a sales charge received by the principal underwriter and, in some instances, may include a purchase premium, which, to the extent received by the fund, is credited to capital. Investors redeem shares at net asset value, although in some instances, a fund may charge redemption fees, which, to the extent received by the fund, are

---

[1] SEC Final Rule Release No. IC-22202, *Exemption for Certain Open-End Management Investment Companies to Impose Deferred Sales Loads.*

[2] Under the maximum sales charge rule in the Financial Industry Regulatory Authority's Rules of Fair Practice, no member may offer or sell shares of any open-end investment company registered under the 1940 Act if the public offering price includes a sales charge that is excessive. Under existing rules, the maximum front-end sales charge may not exceed 8.5 percent of the offering price of mutual fund shares. The maximum amount is scaled down in steps to 6.25 percent if investors are not offered 1 of 3 additional services or benefits: dividend reinvestment at net asset value, quantity discounts, or rights of accumulation. Further, asset-based sales charges specifically exclude service fees. *Service fees* are defined as payments by an investment company for personal service or the maintenance of shareholder accounts or both.

credited to capital.[3] Orders accepted by the fund or its agent are executed at prices based on the net asset value per share that is first computed after the order is accepted (forward pricing) and time-stamped when received to substantiate the price.[4] Most funds price their shares once per day, but some do so multiple times per day. Confirmations of share transactions are sent to investors. Funds have adopted a variety of ways for shareholders to redeem their shares, including the use of debit cards, ATMs, check writing, wire orders, and telephone redemption procedures. Most funds have established websites that permit shareholders to conduct transactions in fund shares electronically. The auditor should become acquainted with the particular redemption methods described in the fund's prospectus.

4.09 Complete and accurate recording of sales and redemptions of fund shares depends on the adequacy of the distributor's, fund's, and transfer agent's controls over order processing. The accuracy of the information on the order tickets about the investor, the number of shares, and dollar amount depends mainly on the reliability of the distributor's information. The processing of sales and redemptions depends on the integration of a variety of systems that gather and disperse information. The key element of control used when capturing such information to be recorded on the fund's books and records is the daily balancing of net dollars received or paid by the fund with net shares issued or redeemed. The daily reconciliation of cash flows, capital stock receivables and payables, and capital shares outstanding between the fund's accounts and those of the transfer agent and subtransfer agent (if applicable) helps the maintenance of accurate capital accounts.

4.10 Certain kinds of funds (such as money market funds) may sell or redeem a large volume of shares in response to market volatility. The transfer agent's controls over such activities as check writing, wire transfers, telephone redemptions, and electronic transactions via websites should be adequate to support periods of heavy volume.

4.11 The fund is responsible for establishing criteria for honoring redemptions. For redemptions made within a prescribed number of days of a purchase by personal check, funds usually do not remit redemption proceeds until they can be assured that the purchase check has cleared. This remittance delay generally does not apply to purchases made by wire transfer or federal funds. Control procedures should provide for the identification, for all accounts, of amounts and dates of purchases by personal checks.

4.12 Capital account data are recorded in sales journals, redemption journals, distribution records, and outstanding share records. Also, to meet SEC disclosure requirements and state Blue Sky laws, the sales journal may contain the source of the order by dealer (primarily load funds), sales statistics by geographic area, the size of the order, and other share data.

---

[3] This is applicable to all investment companies; however, for funds regulated under the 1940 Act, Rule 22c-2 of that act permits fund directors or trustees (including a majority of independent directors or trustees) of registered open-end investment companies to approve a redemption fee on shares redeemed within 7 or more calendar days after the shares were purchased. The redemption fee may not exceed 2 percent of the value of shares redeemed. The fund would retain the fee. The requirements of Rule 22c-2 do not apply to money market funds; funds that issue securities that are listed on a national securities exchange; and funds that affirmatively permit short term trading and prominently disclose in the prospectus that short term trading of fund shares is permitted and may result in additional costs to the fund, unless those funds elect to impose a redemption fee. See SEC Final Rule Release No. IC-26782, *Mutual Fund Redemption Fees*, for more information.

[4] Rules 2a-4 and 22c-1 under the 1940 Act.

Cancellation of Orders

4.13 A purchase or redemption may occasionally be canceled by an investor or broker-dealer before the settlement date. A change in net asset value per share between the original sales date and the date of cancellation or correction results in a gain or loss to the fund. If a distributor is involved and cancellation results in a loss, the distributor may bear the loss or collect cash from the broker-dealer in the amount of the loss. If the cancellation results in a gain, the distributor may accumulate the gain to offset losses from future cancellations and periodically settle the net losses with the fund. If no distributor is involved, the fund should consider refusing to accept sales orders not accompanied by payment, unless a responsible person has indemnified the fund for the failure to pay. Except for preauthorized expedited redemption procedures, the fund might accept orders for redemptions only if the stock certificates or written requests for book shares are properly endorsed and the signatures guaranteed by an appropriate organization, unless indemnified by a responsible person against failure to complete the transaction.

Shareholder Transactions

4.14 Because of the continuous sales and redemptions of open-end fund shares, shareholder transactions are an integral part of a mutual fund's operations and more complex than stock transfers of usual commercial entities. The records for total shares outstanding, total shares issued, and detailed shareholder accounts are kept current on a daily basis. According to federal and state regulations, specialized procedures, controls, and systems are required to maintain adequate shareholder records. Although mutual fund shares may be processed by an in-house operation (an affiliated company of the fund's investment adviser or distributor), an independent transfer agent is often employed to perform this function. The basic operations of all funds are the same; however, the methods used by funds to control stock transfers vary depending on the distribution channel, load structure, and role of the transfer agent in distributing the fund.

4.15 The transfer agent maintains a separate account for each shareholder; performs the detailed recordkeeping associated with sales, redemptions, distributions, and reinvestments within the account; and prepares and mails shareholder communications. Accounts may also be maintained on an omnibus level, in which case a separate entity (subtransfer agent, broker-dealer, or plan administrator) performs the detailed subaccounting by shareholder. A fund and its distributor depend on information provided by the transfer agent's daily statement to record sales and redemption orders sent by investors directly to a transfer agent. The transfer agent's daily statements show the day's activity both in shares and dollars and should be reconciled to the fund's records to promptly identify and satisfactorily account for differences. A significant difference in the number of shares outstanding between the transfer agent's and fund's records could affect net asset value per share.

4.16 Cash used to settle transactions received by the fund, its distributor, or its transfer agent is forwarded to the custodian bank. Cash for redemptions is usually disbursed by the transfer agent to the investor or broker-dealer. Under arrangements in which the distributor and fund do not handle cash, the fund depends on the transfer agent to provide information on paid and unpaid sales and redemptions. Sales of stock and redemptions are usually settled within three business days. The transfer agent, distributor, or fund administrator, depending on the arrangement, follows up on delinquent accounts receivable and unpaid redemption orders.

4.17 A shareholder in an investment company usually chooses to receive distributions from net investment income and net realized gains from securities transactions in cash or additional capital shares. Such payments or issuances of shares are usually made by the transfer agent. IRS regulations may require tax withholding on certain distributions. Besides distributing cash or shares, the transfer agent is responsible for preparing and mailing annual tax notices to all shareholders about the amount and character of distributions paid. Timely transmission of such information from the fund to the transfer agent permits more accurate and timely communication from the transfer agent to the shareholders.

4.18 Money market funds and some fixed income funds declare and accumulate distributions daily for each account and usually distribute them in cash or additional shares monthly. The fund or its transfer agent mails periodic confirmation statements to the shareholders showing the cash distribution or additional shares credited to the account.

4.19 Accounting for treasury stock may be significant for commercial entities and certain closed-end investment companies. It is less important to mutual funds because only the total number of shares outstanding is relevant in their financial statements. Further, the number of shares previously redeemed by a fund is important only in connection with certain requirements of regulatory authorities. The SEC and state authorities have varying requirements for the registration of shares sold in their respective jurisdictions. Sections 24e–24f of the 1940 Act permit retroactive registration, under the Securities Act of 1933 (the 1933 Act), of shares sold in excess of shares registered and permit registration of an indefinite number of shares. Therefore, the fund needs to keep adequate records of the number of shares registered and the number and dollar amounts of shares sold in various jurisdictions. The fund also needs to make the mandated filings within the time permitted under applicable regulatory statutes.

4.20 The 1940 Act and the Securities Exchange Act of 1934 (the 1934 Act) specify certain recordkeeping requirements for funds and transfer agents, respectively. The SEC staff periodically inspects the records for compliance.

4.21 The fund should determine that the number of outstanding shares shown on the fund's general ledger and the transfer agent's shareholder control ledger and master security holder file[5] agree and that the detailed shareholder accounts are posted currently. Items that require close attention include transactions in the shareholder control ledger and master security holder file not yet applied to the detailed shareholder accounts and errors in posting to individual shareholder accounts, including postings to incorrect accounts. In addition to these and other similar monitoring activities, the fund may find it necessary to periodically review the transfer agency operation on site. The review often includes an inspection of the files containing shareholders' correspondence and inquiries; these files must be maintained by the fund or its transfer agent. A significant volume of complaint letters may indicate problems in the detailed shareholder accounts. The fund should also obtain a copy of any service auditor's report on controls at the transfer agent. When a transfer agent is

---

[5] *Shareholder control ledger* and *master security holder file* are defined in Rule 17Ad-9 of the Securities Exchange Act of 1934 (the 1934 Act). These files are commonly referred to as supersheets for open-end investment companies.

used by a fund, the user auditor should refer to the guidance in AU-C section 402, *Audit Considerations Relating to an Entity Using a Service Organization*[6] (AICPA, *Professional Standards*). AU-C section 402 guidance is discussed in further detail within appendix B, "Reports on Controls at Outside Service Organizations," of chapter 11, "General Auditing Considerations."

Considerations for Audits Performed in Accordance With PCAOB Standards

Paragraphs .B17–.B27 of appendix B, "Special Topics," of PCAOB Auditing Standard No. 5, *An Audit of Internal Control Over Financial Reporting That Is Integrated with An Audit of Financial Statements* (AICPA, *PCAOB Standards and Related Rules*, Auditing Standards), provides further guidance regarding the use of service organizations when performing an integrated audit of financial statements and internal control over financial reporting. See the preface to this guide for more information about management's assessment of the effectiveness of internal control over financial reporting. As discussed in the preface, Section 405 of the Sarbanes-Oxley Act of 2002 generally exempts registered investment companies from the provisions of Section 404 that require a report of management and an attestation report of a registered public accounting firm on internal control over financial reporting. Business development companies, however, do not fall within the scope of the exception contained in Section 405 and are required, by Section 404, to include a report of management on the company's internal control over financial reporting. However, see paragraphs 1.55–.57 of this guide for discussion of the Jumpstart Our Business Startups Act of 2012, which explains that certain business development companies may be temporarily exempt from certain financial reporting disclosures and regulatory requirements, including Section 404 of the Sarbanes-Oxley Act of 2002. Additionally, Section 404(c) of the Sarbanes-Oxley Act of 2002 provides that an attestation report of a registered public accounting firm on internal control over financial reporting is not required for an issuer that is neither an accelerated filer nor a large accelerated filer.

Accounting for Capital Share Transactions and Distributions[7]

4.22 As described in paragraphs 7–8 of FASB *Accounting Standards Codification* (ASC) 946-20-25, accounting for shareholder transactions of open-end

---

[6] Paragraph .42 of AT section 801, *Reporting on Controls at a Service Organization* (AICPA, *Professional Standards*), states that a service auditor should inquire whether management is aware of any events subsequent to the period covered by management's description of the service organization's system up to the date of the service auditor's report that could have a significant effect on management's assertion.

The AICPA Guide *Service Organizations: Reporting on Controls at a Service Organization Relevant to User Entities' Internal Control Over Financial Reporting* contains information for practitioners reporting on controls at a service organization that affect user entities' internal control over financial reporting. Also, the AICPA Guide *Reporting on Controls at a Service Organization Relevant to Security, Availability, Processing Integrity, Confidentiality, or Privacy (SOC 2®)* summarizes the three new SOC engagements and provides detailed guidance on planning, performing, and reporting on SOC 2 engagements.

[7] For guidance on accounting for scenarios in which a nonregistered investment partnership reports capital by investor class and has provisions that delay the recognition of certain events in the capital accounts until certain conditions have been met, see paragraphs 7.125–.128 of this guide.

funds differs from the accounting followed by commercial entities in several key aspects. Sales of fund shares are recorded daily by crediting capital stock for the par value of the stock to be issued and additional paid-in capital for the amount paid over the par value; redemptions are recorded daily by debiting those accounts. The offsetting debit (credit), however, is made to an asset (liability) account, typically captioned "Receivable for Fund Shares Sold" ("Payable for Fund Shares Redeemed"). These entries are made on or as of the date that the order to purchase or sell fund shares is received (trade date), not the day that the payment is due (settlement date), as is typical practice for the recording of the issuance of equity shares by commercial entities. Investment partnerships should record a capital subscription as of the effective date stipulated in the partnership agreement. Cash received before this date should be recorded as an advance capital contribution liability. A receivable for the issuance of equity should be accounted for in accordance with FASB ASC 505-10-45, which generally explains that equity should not be funded by a receivable.

4.23 Capital redemptions from investment partnerships should be recorded in the manner described in FASB ASC 480-10-25. FASB ASC 480-10-65 describes the related transition guidance.

4.24 For multiple classes of shares, capital accounts are maintained by class and the transfer agent provides separate share activity that is recorded, as previously stated, on a class-specific basis. Feeder funds within a master-feeder structure account for their capital share activity like typical single-tier funds. If the master fund is a partnership, no capital share transactions are recorded at the master level. Instead, contributions and withdrawals of the various feeders are recorded by the master fund.

4.25 Net investment income and net realized gains on securities transactions and their distributions are usually accumulated in separate accounts. Proper recording of distributions depends on, among other things, proper recording of the number of outstanding shares. Multiple class funds require specialized earnings allocation and distribution practices as described in chapter 5 of this guide.

4.26 As stated in FASB ASC 946-20-25-9, both closed-end and open-end investment companies record distribution liabilities on the ex-dividend date rather than the declaration date. For closed-end companies, a purchaser typically is not entitled to a dividend for shares purchased on the ex-dividend date. Open-end companies record the liability on the ex-dividend date to properly state the net asset value at which sales and redemptions are made. When large (in excess of 15 percent of a closed-end fund's net asset value) dividends or distributions are declared, it is the policy of some exchanges to postpone the ex-dividend date until the dividend has been paid. In such circumstances, the liability for the dividend distribution would be recorded on the books of the fund on the payment date.

4.27 Shareholders of investment companies that offer the right to reinvest distributions (that is, receive distributions in additional shares) usually notify the company at the time they make their first purchase of shares of their intention to accept cash or reinvest future distributions. An investment company establishes a policy regarding the date for the reinvestment of distributions (the reinvestment date), which is typically the same as, or the day after, the ex-dividend date. For both closed-end and open-end investment companies issuing shares on reinvestment, the reinvestment date is the date at which the issuance of additional shares must be recognized in the accounts. Although the payment date is significant to those receiving the distribution in cash, the reinvestment date is important to those electing to reinvest the distribution in additional shares. At the reinvestment date, the actual or, if necessary, estimated number of shares to be issued and the price per share for reinvestment are set using the ex-dividend date's net asset value per share. The total net assets reflect the total dollars reinvested and additional shares outstanding resulting from the distribution reinvestment. At the reinvestment date, both shares and dollars show the effect of the reinvested dividends. Pursuant to a dividend reinvestment plan, a closed-end investment company may be required to purchase shares in the open market when the fund's market price per share is less than the net asset value per share.

Equalization

4.28 Certain open-end investment companies use the accounting practice of equalization, which is unique to their industry. The practice was adopted in the 1930s in an attempt to keep the continuing shareholders' interest in undistributed income from being affected by changes in the number of shares outstanding by applying a portion of the proceeds from sales and costs of repurchases of capital shares to undistributed income.

4.29 The equalization theory states that the net asset value of each share of capital stock sold or repurchased comprises the par value of the stock, undistributed income, and paid-in and other surplus. When shares are sold or repurchased, the investment company calculates the amount of undistributed income available for distribution to its shareholders and, based on the number of shares outstanding, determines the amount associated with each share. The per share amount so determined is credited to the equalization account when shares are sold and charged to the equalization account when shares are repurchased.

4.30 Registered investment companies using equalization accounting should disclose net equalization debits or credits in the statement of changes in net assets as stated by Rule 6.09.2 of Regulation S-X.

Auditing Procedures[8]

Principal Audit Objectives

4.31 The tests of the capital accounts (shareholder accounting) of a mutual fund cover a broad area encompassing various aspects of transactions with shareholders. The principal audit objectives are to make sure that

- the number of outstanding shares of capital stock at the audit date is stated properly.

---

[8] The auditing content in this guide focuses primarily on generally accepted auditing standards issued by the Auditing Standards Board and is applicable to audits of nonissuers. See the section "Applicability of Generally Accepted Auditing Standards and PCAOB Standards" of the preface to this guide for a discussion of the definitions of issuer and nonissuer as used throughout this guide. Appendix B, "Clarified Auditing Standards and PCAOB Standards," of this guide is included to assist auditors in comparing the clarified standards, many of which are referenced throughout this guide, to the PCAOB standards. Further, considerations for audits of issuers in accordance with PCAOB standards may be discussed within this guide's chapter text. When such discussion is provided, the related paragraphs are designated with the following title: *Considerations for Audits Performed in Accordance With PCAOB Standards.*

- procedures are satisfactory for determining the number of outstanding shares used to compute daily net asset value per share.

- procedures are satisfactory for determining the number of shares required to be registered under the 1933 Act.

- the receivable for capital stock sold and the payable for capital stock redeemed are stated properly.

- distributions from net investment income, net realized gains from securities transactions and capital, and their reinvestments, if any, are computed and accounted for properly.

- procedures are satisfactory for maintaining control over the recordkeeping for individual shareholder accounts.

- the capital stock purchased and sold throughout the period is accounted for properly.

- the components of net assets, including paid-in-capital, accumulated undistributed (distributions in excess of) net investment income, accumulated undistributed net realized gains (losses) on investment transactions and net unrealized appreciation (depreciation) in value of investments, are accurately stated at the balance sheet date.

Obtaining an Understanding of the Entity and Its Environment, Including Internal Control

4.32 AU-C section 315, *Understanding the Entity and Its Environment and Assessing the Risks of Material Misstatement* (AICPA, *Professional Standards*), addresses the auditor's responsibility to identify and assess the risks of material misstatement in the financial statements through understanding the entity and its environment, including its internal control.[9] Specific to an audit of an investment company, the auditor should obtain an understanding of the following:

- The rules and regulations under the 1940 Act, the 1933 Act, and Section 17 of the 1934 Act that encompass shareholder accounting, including pricing of fund shares, recordkeeping requirements, and applicable exemptive orders

- The fund's current prospectus, or other legal agreements, which states the fund's policies for accepting sales orders and redemption of fund shares

The auditor may also obtain an understanding of the following:

- The agreement among the fund, its distributor, and those responsible for the stock transfer function as well as agreements with intermediaries for the acceptance and processing of transactions in fund shares

- State Blue Sky laws, FINRA rules, and the fund's procedures for monitoring compliance

---

[9] For additional nonauthoritative guidance pertaining to internal control and risk assessment, refer to Technical Questions and Answers (Q&A) sections 8200.05–.16 (AICPA, *Technical Questions and Answers*).

4.33 The auditor also should obtain an understanding of the shareholder accounting and transfer function, whether performed by the fund or outside agents. (See the discussion of reports on controls at outside service organizations in appendix B of chapter 11.) To obtain an understanding of this function, the auditor may obtain an understanding of the relevant controls over the processing of, among other things, the following:

- Sales
- Redemptions
- Reinvestments
- Cash distributions
- Correspondence
- Stock issuance and stock dividends
- Letters of intent
- Transactions subject to rights of accumulation
- Collections on sales and repayments for redemptions
- Cancellation of sales and redemptions
- Check writing, telephone redemptions, and website transactions
- Account maintenance (address, name, dividend option, and so on) changes
- Inactive accounts (for example, dormant or undeliverable accounts)
- Fees imposed on or other restrictions placed on frequent trading of fund shares

4.34 If the preceding procedures are implemented properly, the fund or its agent would be furnished promptly with the information required to process properly process its shareholder records.

4.35 Administrative arrangements providing for such services as sub-transfer agency and recordkeeping may exist among the fund, its custodian, its transfer agent, or its underwriter. The auditor should obtain an understanding of the contractual responsibilities of the various parties to those arrangements to determine whether to

- obtain information about the controls of those parties that may affect the investment company's IT.[10]
- obtain a service auditor's report on controls at service organizations that may affect the investment company's IT.
- perform other procedures.

4.36 Based on the understanding of the entity and its environment, including its internal control, the assessed risk of material misstatement, and controls at service organizations, if applicable, the auditor may decide to test the operating effectiveness of controls. In accordance with paragraph .08 of AU-C section 330, *Performing Audit Procedures in Response to Assessed Risks and Evaluating the Audit Evidence Obtained* (AICPA, *Professional Standards*), the

---

[10] AU-C section 315, *Understanding the Entity and Its Environment and Assessing the Risks of Material Misstatement* (AICPA, *Professional Standards*), describes the aspects of an entity's IT that are relevant to an audit of financial statements.

auditor should design and perform tests of controls to obtain sufficient appropriate audit evidence about the operating effectiveness of relevant controls if (a) the auditor's assessment of risks of material misstatement at the relevant assertion level includes an expectation that the controls are operating effectively (that is, the auditor intends to rely on the operating effectiveness of controls in determining the nature, timing, and extent of substantive procedures) or (b) when substantive procedures alone cannot provide sufficient appropriate audit evidence at the relevant assertion level. As further explained in paragraph .A21 of AU-C section 330, tests of controls are performed only on those controls that the auditor has determined are suitably designed to prevent, or detect and correct, a material misstatement in a relevant assertion. If substantially different controls were used at different times during the period under audit, each is considered separately. Paragraphs .A122–.A124 of AU-C section 315 provide further guidance on relating controls to specific assertions.

4.37 The auditor may select transactions throughout the audit period to test controls in some of the following areas:

- Pricing shares at net asset values next computed
- Review and approval of daily transaction totals
- As-of transactions
- Reprocessed transactions

If the auditor obtains audit evidence about the operating effectiveness of controls during an interim period, paragraph .12 of AU-C section 330 states that the auditor should (a) obtain audit evidence about significant changes to those controls subsequent to the interim period and (b) determine the additional audit evidence to be obtained for the remaining period.

4.38 The auditor may wish to review schedules maintained by the fund of sales of shares in each state concerning Blue Sky laws and federal regulations to test compliance with regulatory requirements or determine that management is monitoring such compliance.

Examination of Transactions and Detail Records [11]

4.39 The auditor performs substantive tests of activity and balances in the capital accounts based on many factors, including the assessment of the risk of material misstatement.

4.40 *Sales and redemptions of fund shares.* The auditor may wish to test whether details on the order form or other customer evidence used in processing a sale or redemption agree with the copy of the form ultimately sent to the shareholder to confirm the sale or redemption. Such tests should determine whether the transactions conform with the fund's prospectus (including sales charges) and the reinvestment and redemption options selected by the shareholder in his or her account application.

---

[11] Paragraphs .05–.06 of AU-C section 330, *Performing Audit Procedures in Response to Assessed Risks and Evaluating the Audit Evidence Obtained* (AICPA, *Professional Standards*), state that the auditor should (a) design and implement overall responses to address the assessed risks of material misstatement at the financial statement level and (b) design and perform further audit procedures whose nature, timing, and extent are based on, and responsive to, the assessed risks of material misstatement at the relevant assertion level. Paragraph .A8 of AU-C section 330 explains that the auditor requirements regarding the nature, timing, and extent of further audit procedures provide a clear linkage between the auditor's further audit procedures and the risk assessment. Refer to AU-C section 330 for additional guidance.

4.41 Depending on the method used to redeem shares, the auditor may examine shareholder requests (electronic via website, or manual), wire order forms, telephone tape recordings, telephone order forms, and copies of checks remitted to shareholders.

4.42 The auditor may test totals of daily sales and redemptions of capital shares by comparing them with postings in the related journals. Capital stock outstanding for the days tested may be compared against the applicable daily net asset valuation worksheets used as the basis for computing the net asset value per share.

4.43 *Settlement of sales and redemption transactions.* The auditor should obtain an understanding of the internal controls in place to ensure that receivables for shares sold and payables for shares redeemed are priced and settled promptly. Subsidiary trial balances of receivables and payables may be reconciled with general ledger control accounts as of the balance sheet date. Such tests might determine the timely cancellation of sales and redemptions not settled within a specified time and the disposition of losses that may result.

4.44 *Reconciliation of shares outstanding.* The auditor should determine that the fund has reconciled its general ledger account for outstanding shares with reports of the transfer agent throughout the audit period and satisfactorily resolved all reconciling items. The auditor should examine the underlying support for the reconciling items to the extent considered necessary.

4.45 At the balance sheet date, the auditor should confirm shares outstanding directly with the transfer agent as well as determine whether the shares have been reconciled with the shares shown as outstanding in the fund's records. If the auditor concludes that audit risk has not been reduced to an acceptably low level by the combination of obtaining an understanding of the internal controls (including consideration of any related service auditor's report) and confirming shares outstanding in total with the transfer agent, the auditor may confirm outstanding shares directly with shareholders.[12]

4.46 *Dividends and distributions to shareholders and reinvestments.* Payments of dividends on capital stock may be tested to determine that payments in cash or additional capital stock have been computed properly. Distributions based on long term realized gains from securities transactions, except for a supplemental distribution of up to 10 percent of the aggregate amount distributed for a taxable year, may not be paid more than once per year by a registered investment company (as defined by the IRC), except that an additional distribution of long term gains may be made solely to comply with IRC distribution

---

[12] Paragraph .A32 of AU-C section 500, *Audit Evidence* (AICPA, *Professional Standards*), indicates that even when information to be used as audit evidence is obtained from sources external to the entity, circumstances may exist that affect its reliability. For example, regardless of whether a response is obtained in paper form or by electronic or other medium, paragraphs .A12–.A13 of AU-C section 505, *External Confirmations* (AICPA, *Professional Standards*), explain that all responses carry some risk of interception, alteration, or fraud. The auditor's consideration of the reliability of information obtained through the confirmation process to be used as audit evidence includes consideration of the risks that (a) the information obtained may not be from an authentic source, (b) a respondent may not be knowledgeable about the information to be confirmed, and (c) the integrity of the information may have been compromised. When the auditor utilizes an electronic confirmation process or system, the auditor's consideration of the risks described in the preceding sentence includes the consideration of risks that the electronic confirmation process is not secure or is improperly controlled. Refer to AU-C section 330 for requirements and application guidance on when to use external confirmations and refer to AU-C section 505 for further requirements and application guidance on the auditor's use of external confirmation procedures to obtain audit evidence.

requirements under excise tax regulations. However, pursuant to Rule 19b-1(e) of the 1940 Act, a fund may file a request with the SEC for authorization to make an additional distribution or distributions of long term capital gains.[13]

4.47 The auditor should inspect the board of directors' or trustees' minutes for relevant dates and amounts of dividend declarations and may test whether shares outstanding on that date (ex-dividend date for open-end companies), according to the fund's records, have been reconciled to information reported by the transfer agent. The total dividend may be recomputed (outstanding shares times rate) and compared against a notification from the dividend-paying agent, who is usually also the transfer agent. To test that the liability for a dividend was recorded on the proper date, the dividend may be compared with the general ledger and the applicable daily net asset valuation worksheet. The computation of the number of shares to be reinvested, as reported by the dividend-paying agent, may be tested, and the portion of the dividend taken in shares may be compared against the capital stock accounts for agreement of both number of shares and dollar amounts.

4.48 The computations of daily dividend rates for funds that declare dividends daily may be tested for selected dates throughout the period.

4.49 *Recordkeeping for individual shareholder accounts.* Based on the assessed level of control risk for assertions that relate to the activities of the transfer agent or shareholder servicing agent, the auditor may wish to select some accounts to test the validity and proper documentation of transactions for name and address changes, share transfers to or from individual accounts, and transactions that are not routine. The auditor may find it desirable to confirm some shareholder accounts, such as for a transfer agent that is not independent of the investment company or situations in which the auditor cannot rely on the transfer agent's controls.

Other Auditing Matters

4.50 If equalization accounting is used, the auditor may test the calculation of equalization amounts.

4.51 Auditors may review, on a test basis, correspondence from shareholders received by the fund or transfer agent. A significant volume of complaints relating to pricing or incorrect calculations of shares issued may suggest to the auditor that additional testing may be necessary.

4.52 The auditor may evaluate the volumes of gross fund share sales and redemptions in relation to total shares outstanding for unusual relationships, in particular considering prospectus restrictions on frequent trading of fund shares or requirements to impose redemption fees on such trading.

---

[13] Rule 19b-1(e) under the 1940 Act indicates that such request should be deemed granted unless the SEC denies such request within 15 days after the receipt. As noted in the March 2014 Expert Panel Conference Call Highlights, the SEC staff asks registrants to include in the request all relevant facts and explain the circumstances that would justify such distribution, which the SEC staff will use to consider whether relief under Rule 19b-1(e) is warranted. The SEC staff also noted that given the 15 day clock, a registrant should submit a draft of the request via email to the SEC staff in advance of an official filing with the SEC, so the draft request can be promptly reviewed by the Chief Accountant's Office and the Chief Counsel's Office in the Division of Investment Management, who then can contact the registrant with questions or comments. Draft requests can be submitted via email. When filing the official request for relief, the SEC staff has not objected to registrants filing the request on EDGAR electronically as a 40-APP.

4.53 The auditor may wish to confirm balances receivable for capital stock and balances payable for capital shares to be redeemed by the fund directly with the investor or dealers who sell the fund's shares. Details of specific capital stock transactions may also be confirmed. Alternative auditing procedures may also be used to satisfy the auditor concerning receivables and payables for fund shares sold and redeemed.

4.54 Management's representation letter should state that fund shares were sold and redeemed in accordance with the fund's prospectus, the SEC's rules and regulations (see paragraph 12.48 of this guide), and state securities regulations.

4.55 For funds with multiple classes of shares, the auditor should determine that the fund has allocated its daily activities among each respective class of shares, based upon the method chosen (see chapter 5 of this guide), and properly calculated its net asset values throughout the period. The auditor should examine the allocations and their underlying support, including records of shares outstanding. In addition, the auditor should obtain evidence that class-level fee waivers and reimbursements were not in violation of Rule 18f-3 under the 1940 Act or any related SEC exemptive orders. The auditor should also consider the possible implications of any waivers on the fund's distributions under the IRC (see chapter 6, "Taxes," of this guide).

Chapter 5

Complex Capital Structures

© **Update 5-1** *Regulatory*: **Money Market Fund Reform**

On July 23, 2014, the SEC issued Final Rule Release No. 33-9616, *Money Market Fund Reform; Amendments to Form PF*. The release includes varying compliance dates for the different changes within the new rule. Compliance dates begin in 2015, and extend through 2016. Readers are encouraged to consult the full text of the release for specific compliance dates.

One of the key structural changes of the new Money Market Reform Rule is that institutional prime and municipal money market funds will be required to transact at a floating net asset value. Retail funds and government funds are not required to transact at a floating net asset value. This will require those funds that transact at a floating net asset value to transact shares, rounded to the fourth decimal place (for example, $1.0000), based on the most recently determined market value of the securities in the underlying portfolios. Separately, new tax regulations and guidance have been issued as a result of this change; readers are encouraged to review this new IRS guidance. The release further provides guidance on how to determine whether a fund is considered to be an institutional money market fund, a retail money market fund, or a government money market fund.

Those money market funds adopting a floating net asset value as a result of the new rules are expected to determine the values of their investments using market-based values, as opposed to using the amortized cost of such investments as an approximation of market value. In addition to this accounting change, the new rules may result in other changes to the financial reporting of all money market funds. Readers should keep abreast of future developments as they emerge.

Additionally, the amendments in Final Rule Release No. 33-9616 give the boards of directors of money market funds new tools to stem heavy redemptions. Those tools include allowing them discretion to impose liquidity fees in the event a fund's weekly liquidity level falls below the required regulatory threshold, and also provides them the discretion to suspend redemptions temporarily (that is, impose a "gate"), under similar circumstances. The new requirements dictate that all nongovernment money market funds impose a liquidity fee if the fund's weekly liquidity level falls below the rule-established threshold, unless the fund's board determines that imposing such a fee is not in the best interests of the fund.

Final Rule Release No. 33-9616 also contains additional amendments. These include enhanced disclosure requirements on fund websites, sales and marketing materials, prospectuses and SAIs; changes to Form N-MFP; an additional new Form N-CR; and various clarifying amendments under Rule 2a-7, including stress testing and diversification provisions.

The amendments also require investment advisers of certain large unregistered liquidity funds to provide additional information about those funds to the SEC.

Readers should consult the full text of SEC Final Rule Release No. 33-9616, which can be accessed on the Final Rules page at www.sec.gov.

> ***Presentation of Pending Content in FASB ASC***
>
> Amendments to FASB *Accounting Standards Codification* (ASC) (issued in the form of Accounting Standards Updates [ASUs]) are initially incorporated into FASB ASC in "Pending Content" boxes located below the paragraphs being amended with links to the transition information. The pending content boxes are meant to provide users with information about how the guidance in a paragraph will change as a result of the new guidance.
>
> Pending content applies to different entities at different times due to varying fiscal year-ends, and because certain guidance may be effective on different dates for public entities, as defined, and other entities. As such, FASB maintains amended guidance in pending content boxes within FASB ASC until the roll-off date. Generally, the roll-off date is six months following the latest fiscal year-end for which the original guidance being amended could still be applied.
>
> ***Presentation of Pending Content in AICPA Audit and Accounting Guides***
>
> Amended FASB ASC guidance that is included in pending content boxes in FASB ASC on May 1, 2015, is referenced as "Pending Content" in this guide. Pending content referenced or discussed within this guide's chapter text is fully effective as of the date of this guide and should be considered by readers for current reporting periods. Pending content referenced or discussed within this guide's shaded "Guidance Updates" boxes or within appendix A, "Guidance Updates," is not fully effective as of the date of this guide. Readers should be aware that pending content" referenced in this guide will eventually be subjected to FASB's roll-off process and will no longer be labeled as "Pending Content" in FASB ASC (as discussed in the previous paragraph).

5.01 Many investment companies adopt complex capital structures to increase flexibility in pricing and access to alternative distribution channels for their shares. Such structures are principally of two kinds: multiple-class funds and master-feeder funds. In addition, many organizations are offering funds of funds. Funds of funds either permit a fund complex to provide asset allocation products using funds in the complex or allow an investment adviser to allocate assets among many unaffiliated investment advisers. Master-feeder and multiple-class structures permit a common investment vehicle to be distributed through different channels or with different distribution charges to the shareholder, or both.

Operational and Accounting Issues

Multiple-Class Funds

5.02 As stated in the "Pending Content" in FASB ASC 946-20-05-1D, multiple-class funds issue more than one class of shares. Each class of shares may have different types of sales charges, such as a front-end load, contingent deferred sales load, 12b-1 fee, or combinations thereof. Multiple-class funds may charge different classes of shares for specific or incremental expenses, such as transfer-agent, registration, and printing expenses related to each class.

5.03 An example of a (commonly used) multiple-class structure for registered investment companies includes (but is not limited to) the following classes of shares:

- *Class A*. Class A shares are primarily charged a front-end sales load. (The shares might also be assessed a low 12b-1 or service fee.)

- *Class B*. Class B shares bear a contingent deferred sales load (CDSL) coupled with a 12b-1 distribution or service fee. Class B shares often convert to class A shares at a specified future date to avoid being assessed a higher 12b-1 fee for an extended period.

- *Class C*. Class C shares bear a level sales load, typically a 12b-1 distribution or service fee similar to the level charged in class B. Class C shares usually have a 1 percent CDSL assessed for 1 year. There is usually no conversion to another class.

- *Institutional shares*. Shares typically bear no sales load and usually do not have 12b-1 distribution charges. There may be a service fee depending upon the source of the shares, whether they are sold through wrap programs or trust departments. Such selling agents often have their own structures that charge the fee directly to the investor.

5.04 Although no legal requirements exist regarding specific class designations, many in the industry have voluntarily adopted the previously mentioned nomenclature to avoid shareholder and sales force confusion.

5.05 Multiple-class funds have unique operational and accounting issues. These issues include the methods and procedures to (*a*) allocate income, expenses, and gains or losses to the various classes to determine the net asset value per share for each class; (*b*) calculate dividends and distributions to shareholders for each class; and (*c*) calculate investment performance for each class (such as total return and SEC yield).

5.06 Rule 18f-3 under the Investment Company Act of 1940 (the 1940 Act) establishes a framework for an open-end fund's issuance of multiple classes of shares representing interests in the same portfolio. The rule permits certain differences in expenses between classes and prescribes how income, expenses, and realized and unrealized gains and losses may be allocated among the classes.

5.07 To calculate the net asset value per share of each class for multiple-class funds, income, expenses, and realized and unrealized gains or losses must be allocated to each class. Fees and expenses of the fund need to be classified as either fund or class-level expenses. Fund-level expenses, such as investment management fees, apply to all classes. Rule 18f-3 identifies certain expenses, such as distribution and servicing fees, as being class-level expenses and requires that they be generally charged directly to the individual classes to which they relate. Under the rule, other expenses, such as transfer-agent and registration fees attributable to individual classes, may be designated as class-level expenses at the discretion of the fund's board of directors or trustees or remain fund-level expenses. All other expenses are allocated among the classes based on a methodology discussed in paragraph 5.10. Rule 18f-3 provides for the exercise of judgment by the fund and its directors or trustees concerning the appropriateness and fairness of the expense allocation methodology. Because certain expenses are charged to the classes of shares differently, net asset value per share and dividends per share must be calculated separately for each class of shares and may differ. Class B and class C shareholders will normally receive a smaller dividend per share from net investment income than class A shareholders because of higher distribution and servicing fees.

5.08 Each class of shares bears all its identified class-specific expenses. The IRS currently takes the position that funds with multiple classes have only one class of shares for tax purposes. Revenue Procedure 96-47 essentially provides that if a fund pays dividends of differing amounts (differential dividends) to its various classes of shares pursuant to a capital structure allowed by (or similar to that allowed by) Rule 18f-3, the IRS will not consider such dividends to be preferential. This revenue procedure allows differential dividends due to divergent charges for items such as 12b-1 fees, shareholder servicing fees, and any other class-specific expenses. Fund-level expenses, such as management fees, custodian fees, and other expenses related to the management of the company's assets, must be allocated proportionally among all classes using an allocation methodology discussed in paragraph 5.10. For distributions in taxable years beginning after December 22, 2010, the preferential dividend rule in IRC Section 562(c) has been repealed for publicly offered regulated investment companies (RICs) by the RIC Modernization Act of 2010. Full details of changes from the RIC Modernization Act of 2010 are discussed in chapter 6, "Taxes," of this guide.

5.09 Class-specific expenses may be waived or reimbursed at different amounts for individual classes. However, Rule 18f-3 requires a fund's board of directors or trustees to monitor waivers or reimbursements to guard against cross-subsidization among the classes. For nonpublicly offered RICs, fund management must also ensure that such waivers or reimbursements do not create a preferential dividend to a particular class of shares from a tax perspective. Revenue Procedure 99-40 covers circumstances under which such expenses may be reimbursed for tax purposes. To protect themselves from an inadvertent preferential dividend, a rigorous approach to the documentation of class expense differences (including waivers or reimbursements) and also compliance with any private letter rulings should be followed carefully by multiple-class funds. See paragraphs 6.68–.69 of this guide for more specific guidance regarding preferential dividends, including details of the repeal of this rule for publicly offered RICs.

5.10 The methods for allocating income, fund-level expenses, and realized and unrealized gains or losses set forth in Rule 18f-3 are as follows:

- *Fair value of shares outstanding—relative net assets.* Under this method, each class of shares participates based on the total net asset value of its shares in proportion to the total net assets of the fund. Under Rule 18f-3, it is expected that this method will be the primary method used to allocate income, fund-level expenses, and realized and unrealized gains and losses for calculating the net asset value of nondaily dividend funds.

- *Fair value of settled shares outstanding.* Under this method, earnings are allocated based on the fair value of settled shares. It is typically used to achieve consistency between the allocation method and a fund's dividend policy with respect to the shares eligible to receive dividends. For example, most daily dividend funds pay dividends only to settled shares and; therefore, in a fund that requires settlement of its shares on a trade-date-plus-three basis, the appropriate basis of allocation of income and nonclass-specific expenses would be the fair value of settled shares. Rule 18f-3 permits daily dividend funds to use the settled-shares method for allocating income and expenses and the relative-net-assets method for allocating realized and unrealized gains and losses.

- *Shares outstanding.* This method provides for each share outstanding to participate equally in the nonclass-specific items of income, expense, gains, and losses. Under Rule 18f-3, this method may be used by funds, provided that (*a*) the fund is a daily dividend fund that maintains the same net asset value per share in each class, (*b*) the fund has agreements in place for waivers or reimbursements of expenses to ensure that all classes maintain the same per share net asset value, and (*c*) payments waived or reimbursed under such agreements may not be carried forward or recouped at a future date.

- *Simultaneous equations.* This method ensures that the annualized rate of return of each class will differ from that of the other classes only by the expense differential among the classes.

- *Any appropriate method.* A fund may use any appropriate allocation method so long as a majority of the fund's directors or trustees, including a majority of the directors or trustees who are not interested persons of the fund, determines that the method is fair to the shareholders of each class and that the annualized rate of return of each class will generally differ from that of the other classes only by the expense differentials among the classes.

Whichever method is selected, Rule 18f-3 requires the fund to use that method consistently. Rule 18f-3 does not specify any requirements regarding the distribution calculation methods that a multiple-class fund generally should use. Illustrations using the allocation methods discussed previously are presented in exhibit 5-1.

5.11 The methods, as they are each defined by the FASB ASC master glossary, generally used to calculate distributions to shareholders from net investment income are as follows:

- *Record-share method.* The sum of net investment income available for all classes after deducting allocated expenses but before consideration of class-specific expenses is divided by the total outstanding shares on the dividend record date for all classes to arrive at a gross dividend rate for all shares. From this gross rate, an amount per share for each class (the amount of incremental class specific expenses accrued during the period divided by the record date shares outstanding for the class) is subtracted. The result is the per share dividend available for each class.

- *Actual-income-available method.* Actual net investment income that has been allocated to each class (as recorded on the books) is divided by the record date shares for each class to derive the dividend payable per share.

- *Simultaneous-equations method.* This method seeks to ensure, by using simultaneous equations, that the distribution rates will differ among the classes by the anticipated differential in expense ratios.

Illustrations of the distribution calculation methods are presented in exhibit 5-2.

5.12 The record-share method is most commonly used by funds that do not pay dividends daily (nondaily dividend funds). It is also used by daily dividend funds that employ policies to manage their dividend payout levels (such as to distribute stable dividend amounts or to compensate for book-tax differences). The dividend payout level may be managed for only one share class; the dividend rates for the other classes will vary because class-level expenses differ between classes. The record-share method is simple to apply, provides assurance that the annualized distribution rate for the class with higher expenses will be lower than that for the class with lower expenses, and minimizes the likelihood of a preferential dividend being paid. The disadvantage of this method is that the annualized distribution rates of the various classes usually will not reflect the precise expense ratio difference between the classes because the directly related expenses accrued over time on a varying number of shares are reduced to a per share amount on the record date shares. The larger the fluctuation in shares over time, the greater the potential difference.

5.13 The actual-income-available method is used for funds that declare daily dividends per share equal to the amount of net investment income allocated to each class. This results in the same per share net asset value for all classes (except for differences that may result from rounding). The actual-income-available method is not typically used for funds that pay dividends on a periodic basis.

5.14 The simultaneous-equations method is used for periodic dividend funds and is more complex than other methods. This method ensures that the annualized distribution rates will differ among classes by the approximate amount of the expense ratio difference. Per share net asset value will usually converge after the dividend has been recorded.

5.15 Because distribution amounts under both the record-share and simultaneous-equations methods are determined independently of the amount of net investment income allocated to each class, situations can result whereby, after recording the dividends, one class has positive undistributed income whereas the other class is negative.

5.16 As stated in FASB ASC 946-505-50-4, for financial reporting purposes of multiple-class funds, a return of capital is not determined at the class level, and distributable earnings are disclosed only at the fund level.

5.17 Regardless of the frequency of income dividends or the distribution calculation method selected, to avoid paying a preferential dividend for tax purposes (see paragraph 5.08 and chapter 6 for a discussion on the repeal of the preferential dividend rule for publicly traded RICs by the RIC Modernization Act of 2010), multiple-class funds ordinarily should declare long term capital gain distributions at the fund level, rather than at the class level, so that all shares receive the same per share gain distribution.

Master-Feeder Funds

5.18 In master-feeder structures, separate investment companies often perform the investment management and distribution functions. Feeder investment companies, each having similar investment objectives but different distribution channels for their shares, such as retail or institutional customers or for jurisdictional purposes, generally invest their assets solely in another investment company known as the master fund. Generally, most investment management functions are conducted by a master fund whereas distribution, shareholder-servicing, and transfer agent functions are conducted by the feeders.

5.19 The master fund is generally organized as a trust, with attributes that qualify it as a partnership for tax purposes, and may be registered under the 1940 Act. For nonregistered investment companies, master funds are generally organized as a partnership or offshore corporation. If the master fund is organized outside the United States, it may serve as an investment vehicle for both offshore feeder funds sold solely to foreign investors (or, in certain circumstances, U.S. tax-exempt investors) and domestic feeder funds sold solely to U.S. investors. Feeder funds are generally organized as corporations or trusts, may be taxed under the IRC as RICs, and may be registered as investment companies under the 1940 Act and the Securities Act of 1933 (the 1933 Act) (and the Securities Exchange Act of 1934, as appropriate). Feeder funds may also be organized under a different legal structure if they are not registered products and are being used as vehicles for nonpublic investing. Feeder funds may be organized with a multiple-class structure.

5.20 Master-feeder sponsors sometimes apply to the IRS for a private letter ruling to ensure that the master will be treated as a partnership for federal income tax purposes and that each feeder will be treated as an owner of its proportionate share of the earnings and profits and net assets of the master. This is to make sure that the feeders maintain their status as RICs and can afford their shareholders the pass-through tax benefits that result from that status.

5.21 Master-feeder accounting involves allocating the master portfolio's income, expenses, and realized and unrealized gains and losses among its feeder funds. Because most master funds are typically structured as partnerships for tax purposes, the allocation of income, expenses, gains, and losses follows partnership tax allocation rules (partner's distributive share rules, as provided for in IRC Section 704[b]). According to the IRC, each feeder must be allocated its share of gain or loss realized by the master when the master disposes of a particular security lot. The tax allocation process is complicated because the relative interest of the feeder funds in the master portfolio changes, sometimes as often as daily, as feeder fund shares are sold or redeemed. Two allocation methodologies are permitted under the IRC. The first allocation method follows the literal partnership allocation methodology that implies a property-by-property (lot-by-lot) method for investment partnerships. Performing tax allocations under the property-by-property method requires evaluating each feeder's share of the realized gain or loss on the security lot sold. The second method allows allocation based on an aggregate method. Performing tax allocation under the aggregate method requires evaluating each feeder's share of the unrealized gains or losses on its entire (that is, aggregate) interest in the master, rather than each feeder's share of the realized gain or loss on the sold security lot alone. In the absence of a ruling from the IRS, the regulation allowing an aggregate method for allocating gains and losses does not apply to built-in gains and losses from securities contributed by a feeder to a master in a nontaxable event. However, certain qualified master-feeders that meet the requirements of Revenue Procedure 2001-36 are permitted to use the aggregate method for contributed property, although other fund groups would still require a private letter ruling from the IRS.

Funds of Funds

5.22 Funds of funds are investment companies that invest in other investment companies. A typical fund-of-funds structure involves investments in more than one investee fund. A master-feeder structure can also be viewed as a fund-of-funds, but the feeder usually invests substantially all of its assets into one investee fund (the master fund). Historically, a registered investment company's ability to invest in other investment companies was limited by Section 12(d) of the 1940 Act. Under Section 12(d), an open-end investment company is limited, among other restrictions, to aggregate investments in other investment companies of 10 percent of the acquiring company's total assets. Master-feeder structures, however, are specifically permitted by Section 12(d)-(1)(E)(ii) of the 1940 Act. As a result, except for a limited number of registered funds that received exemptive orders from the SEC, fund-of-funds structures had been limited to unregistered investment companies. In 1996, Section 12(d) was amended to permit registered investment companies to invest in other investment companies provided that both the investor and investee funds were part of the same group of investment companies (affiliated funds). Investments in nonaffiliated funds would continue to be subject to the historical limitations under Section 12(d) unless an exemptive order is obtained from the SEC.

5.23 In 2006, the SEC adopted Rules 12d1-1 through 12d1-3 under the 1940 Act to broaden the ability of a fund to invest in shares of another fund consistent with the public interest and protection of investors. Rule 12d1-1 allows funds to invest in shares of money market funds in excess of the limits of Section 12(d)(1) and is intended to allow funds to utilize money market funds in "cash sweep" arrangements in which available cash is invested in a money market fund in lieu of short term investments. Rule 12d1-2 permits funds structured as funds of affiliated funds to also purchase shares of unaffiliated funds up to the statutory limits of Section 12(d)(1) and to make direct investments in stocks, bonds, and other types of securities. Rule 12d1-3 provides greater flexibility in operating funds of unaffiliated funds.

5.24 Many multitiered structures are U.S. domiciled, but recent trends include the creation of offshore, domestic, and blended structures. A blended structure might include a fund with significant investments in other investment companies and also investments in individual securities. Participants in such structures include both foreign and domestic investors, individually and through funds, commodity pools, retirement accounts, and other sources.

5.25 For many investee funds, fair value is usually readily determinable through observable market quotes (or, for investments in mutual funds, published net asset values that are used as the basis for current transactions). Refer to the "Investments in Entities That Calculate Net Asset Value per Share" section in chapter 2, "Investment Accounts," of this guide for guidance on the use of net asset value per share (or its equivalent) as a practical expedient to value an investment in an investee fund that does not have a readily determinable fair value. The valuation of an investee fund by the investor generally should reflect any incentive or performance fee or incentive allocation of earnings to the general partner based on the current performance of the investee fund.

Other Considerations for Investments in Nonpublicly Traded Investees

5.26 Proper execution of the fund-of-funds strategy ordinarily requires management of the investor fund to exercise significant judgment in selecting and monitoring the performance of the investee funds. Occasionally, management may engage an outside consultant to assist in the performance monitoring and selection process. This process may include many procedures, and a review of prior audited financial results should be included.

5.27 Monitoring the performance is an essential control in the operation of the fund. Fund management ordinarily should review regular (for example quarterly) investment results and periodically review the trading strategy being followed by the investee fund to make sure that it is consistent with the strategy approved at the time of the initial investment. The results of daily monitoring functions established by management of the investee fund generally should also be reviewed periodically. Discussions with each investee fund to identify any significant changes or problems with systems, illiquid securities, personnel, or trading strategies generally should be held periodically and documented. At times, such as when there are significant changes in market conditions or a particularly risky strategy, monthly or more frequent discussions may be advisable. Another essential control that management of the investor fund normally should exercise is the comparison of preliminary annual results reported by the investee fund with the investee fund's audited financial statements. The audited financial statements should substantiate the reliability of the investee fund's reporting processes.

5.28 In addition, management of the investor fund may wait for the receipt of audited financial statements and individual capital account statements from investee funds to make sure that no significant changes in previously reported results have occurred before the investor fund issues its audited financial statements. This approach provides key audit evidence related to the valuation assertion and instills discipline into the investor fund's financial reporting system.

5.29 Refer to the "Investments in Entities That Calculate Net Asset Value per Share" section in chapter 2 of this guide for further discussion of controls over investments in nonpublicly traded investees, including a discussion of Technical Questions and Answers (Q&A) sections 2220.18–.27 (AICPA, *Technical Questions and Answers*).

5.30 From time to time, mutual funds have opportunities to invest in operating companies. Typically, these types of investments generate "bad income" for the mutual fund under the IRC of 1986, as amended. A mutual fund can potentially avoid generating this bad income by making its investment in the underlying entity indirectly through a wholly (or jointly) owned investment that has elected to be treated as a corporation for tax purposes (a blocker). The blocker converts operating income from the underlying entity into either dividend income to the mutual fund or gains recognized in connection with the sale of blocker stock, both of which are "good income" under the IRC. The blocker would generally be subject to a corporate tax on the income and gains from the investment in the underlying entity, with after-tax amounts available for distribution to the mutual fund as a dividend. Through Investment Management Guidance Update 2014-11, *Guidance Regarding Investment Company Consolidation*, the SEC expressed that wholly owned blocker investments should be consolidated by the reporting mutual fund.

Financial Statement Presentation

5.31 As discussed in FASB ASC 946-210-45, management investment companies that have multiple classes of shares or master-feeder structures follow reporting guidelines discussed in the following paragraphs when preparing financial statements, including financial highlights. Illustrations are presented at the end of this chapter.

Multiple-Class Funds

5.32 *Example financial statements.* Exhibit 5-3 contains illustrations of multiple-class fund financial statements. Items to follow correspond to this exhibit.

5.33 *Statement of assets and liabilities.* As noted in FASB ASC 946-210-45-4, the composition of net assets is reported in total, but net asset value per share and shares outstanding should be reported for each class. Consideration may be given to presenting this information for outstanding subseries' of each class, either directly on this statement, on a supplemental schedule, or within the footnotes of the financial statements.

5.34 The maximum public offering price per share is often reported for each class.

5.35 *Statement of operations.* FASB ASC 946-225-45-9 explains that class-specific expenses are reported for each class (or disclosed in the notes to the financial statements). Reporting the amount of fund-level expenses allocated to each class is not required, but disclosure of fund-level expenses by class in the statement of operations or notes to the financial statements is permitted.

5.36 *Statement of changes in net assets.* FASB ASC 946-205-45-4 notes that dividends and distributions paid to shareholders and capital share transactions for each class are required to be presented (or disclosed in the notes to the financial statements).

5.37 *Notes to financial statements.* As FASB ASC 946-235-50-2 states, the notes should

- describe each class of shares, including sales charges, shareholder servicing fees, and distribution fees.
- disclose the method used to allocate income and expenses and realized and unrealized capital gains and losses to each class.
- describe fee arrangements for class-specific distribution plans and any other class-level expenses paid to affiliates.
- disclose capital share transactions (if not disclosed separately in the statement of changes in net assets) for each class.
- disclose total sales charges paid to any affiliates for each class.

5.38 *Financial highlights.* As explained in FASB ASC 946-205-50-27, financial highlights, including total return, should be presented by class except for portfolio turnover, which is calculated at the fund level. As stated in paragraph 7.182 of this guide, portfolio turnover is only required for registered investment companies. The financial highlights for any class for which the shareholders are precluded from investing may be omitted.

5.39 Because the financial highlights table is considered to be a financial statement disclosure, not a financial statement, the SEC has accepted the presentation of a financial highlights table only for a specific class or classes of shareholders for whom the financial statements are intended. In such situations, the auditor's report should be addressed to the fund board and the shareholders in the specific class or classes, not all shareholders taken as a whole. If a class terminates during the year, the financial highlights are not required to be presented in the financial statements for that class.

Master-Feeder Funds

5.40 *Example financial statements.* Exhibits 5-4 and 5-5 contain illustrations of relevant feeder fund and master fund financial statements. Items to follow correspond to these exhibits.[1]

5.41 Under current SEC policies, the annual and semiannual reports for feeder funds should contain two sets of financial statements: one for the master fund and the other for the specific feeder fund. When the master and feeder funds have different year-ends, the SEC has indicated[2] that it would not object if, at each feeder investment company year-end, the audited shareholder report of the feeder is accompanied by the latest audited shareholder report of the master as well as an unaudited balance sheet and schedule of investments of the master as of the date of the feeder's financial statements.

5.42 *Statement of assets and liabilities.* As stated in FASB ASC 946-210-45-6, each feeder fund's statement of assets and liabilities should show an investment in the master fund, which is the sole or principal investment of the feeder fund. The total of all feeder funds' investments in the master fund should equal the total net assets of the master fund. A schedule of portfolio investments is not presented at the feeder level, unless the feeder fund also holds direct investments in addition to its investment in the master fund. The net asset value per share, total shares outstanding, and the components of net assets should be reported. Should the feeder fund have a multiple-class structure, it would report the multiple-class information specified in FASB ASC 946-210.

5.43 As explained in paragraph 5.19, master funds are usually organized as trusts, or in the case of nonregistered investment companies, as a partnership or offshore corporation. In accordance with FASB ASC 946-210-45-5, the statement of assets and liabilities of the master fund usually does not report the components of net assets, shares outstanding, or net asset value per share. The portfolio of investments should be included only in the master fund's financial statements.

5.44 *Statement of operations.*[3] As described in paragraphs 11–12 of FASB ASC 946-225-45, the statement of operations reports details of the feeder fund's allocated share of net investment income from the master fund (that is, separate disclosure of allocated interest, dividends, and expenses). The statement also reports separately the feeder's allocated share of the master fund's realized

---

[1] As noted in the SEC's Investment Management Guidance Update No. 2014-11, *Investment Company Consolidation*, in the circumstances of a feeder fund, generally, the SEC staff has taken the position that the financial presentation that is most meaningful is unconsolidated, provided that other conditions are satisfied. However, if the design and purpose of the master-feeder structure is for the master fund to be wholly owned by a sole feeder fund, the SEC staff encourages registrants to consult with the staff on whether consolidated financial presentation would be the most meaningful. Readers are encouraged to read the full text of the SEC's Investment Management Guidance Update No. 2014-11, available at www.sec.gov/investment/im-guidance-2014-11.pdf.

[2] See the December 30, 1998, "Dear CFO Letter" issued by the Chief Accountant of the SEC Division of Investment Management.

[3] As noted in the SEC's Investment Management Guidance Update No. 2014-11, it is the SEC staff's position that if the master fund is organized as a corporation, classification of the master fund's income in the feeder fund's financial statements depends upon the distribution policies of the master fund. Until it is distributed, income received by the master fund is recorded by a feeder fund as unrealized appreciation. See SEC Staff Generic Comment Letter for Investment Company CFOs (Nov. 2, 1995), available at www.sec.gov/divisions/investment/noaction/1995/accountingcomment110295.pdf.

and unrealized gains and losses. The total of all feeders' income, expense, and realized and unrealized gain or loss components should agree to the corresponding totals of the master fund. Feeder funds should disclose their fund-specific expenses, such as transfer agent, distribution, legal and audit expenses, and registration and directors' or trustees' fees. Additionally, any fee waivers or reimbursements at the feeder-fund level should be reported.

5.45 If the feeder fund has its own separate trading activity besides what is allocated directly from the master fund, the realized and unrealized gains or losses are generally separately reported.

5.46 As stated in FASB ASC 946-225-45-10, for master funds, the standard reporting format for investment companies with simple capital structures should be used.

5.47 *Statement of changes in net assets.* FASB ASC 946-205-45-4 states that, for feeder funds, the standard reporting format for investment companies with simple capital structures is used. If the feeder fund is a multiple-class fund, the guidance for multiple-class funds in FASB ASC 946-205-45-4 applies, which states that dividends and distributions paid to shareholders and capital share transactions for each class are required to be presented or disclosed in the notes to financial statements.

5.48 FASB ASC 946-205-45-4 also explains that the statement of changes in net assets of a master fund should report capital transactions from or to feeder funds as contributions and withdrawals, respectively. Dividend distributions are normally not made by the master fund when the master fund is treated as a partnership for tax purposes. In those situations when the master fund is treated as a RIC and taxed either as a corporation or trust, there may be distributions to the feeder funds to eliminate any accumulated taxable income at the master fund level.

5.49 *Notes to financial statements.* FASB ASC 946-235-50-3 explains that notes to the financial statements of each feeder fund should include the following:

- A general description of the master and feeder structure
- The feeder's percentage ownership share of the particular master fund at the reporting date
- A statement that the feeder invests all its investable assets in a corresponding open-end management investment company having the same investment objectives as the feeder and a reference to the financial statements of the master fund, including the portfolio of investments
- Disclosure of or reference to the accounting policies of the master fund that affect the feeders (such as valuation of investments of the master fund)

5.50 FASB ASC 946-235-50-3 further explains that information concerning the purchases and sales of investments and gross unrealized appreciation or depreciation of investments on a tax basis (required by Regulation S-X) is not applicable to the feeder's financial statements.

5.51 *Financial highlights.* As FASB ASC 946-205-50-28 notes, the feeder fund's ratios of expenses and net investment income to average net assets should include the expenses of both the feeder and master fund. Balance credits earned by the master fund should be reflected in the feeder fund ratios as if they had been earned by the feeder fund directly.

5.52 Feeder funds need not disclose a portfolio turnover rate because feeders invest substantially all their assets in the master fund. However, to the extent that the financial highlights table conforms to the instructions of Form N-1A, it should report the portfolio turnover rate experienced by the master. The financial highlights of feeder funds that are registered investment companies generally should comply with the same requirements as for registered investment companies not organized in a master-feeder structure (see the "Financial Highlights" section in chapter 7, "Financial Statements of Investment Companies," of this guide).

5.53 FASB ASC 946-205-50-29 states that the financial highlights section of the master fund organized as a partnership is substantially modified because per share information is not applicable. The master fund financial highlights section should include the total return, ratios of expenses and net investment income to average net assets, and portfolio turnover rate. Master funds not organized as partnerships should report normal per share data in the financial highlights section.

5.54 *Auditor's report.* The auditor's report for the feeder fund is modified to exclude the phrase "including the portfolio of investments" because the portfolio of investments is not part of the feeder fund's financial statements, unless the feeder fund also holds direct investments in addition to its investment in the master fund (see paragraph 5.42 for further information).

Funds of Funds [4]

5.55 *Example financial statements.* Exhibit 5-6 contains illustrations of relevant fund-of-funds financial statements. Items to follow correspond to this exhibit.

5.56 *Statement of assets and liabilities.* [5] FASB ASC 946-210-45-7 explains that the reporting fund may list the investee (portfolio) funds directly on the

---

[4] As noted in the SEC's Investment Management Guidance Update No. 2014-11, in the circumstances of a fund of funds, generally, the SEC staff has taken the position that the financial presentation is most meaningful also is unconsolidated. A fund of funds typically invests in multiple underlying funds, may hold controlling financial interests in some underlying funds and noncontrolling interests in other underlying funds, and the level of its interest in any particular underlying fund might fluctuate between controlling and noncontrolling. In such circumstances, in the SEC staff's view, if the fund of funds were to consolidate the financial statements of certain of its underlying funds for certain periods, the resulting financial presentation may not be meaningful and may be confusing to the fund of funds' investors. The SEC staff notes, a fund of funds also should consider whether its investment in a single underlying fund is so significant to the fund of funds that its presentation of financial statements should be made in a manner similar to a master-feeder fund. (See generally, FASB ASC 946-210-45-7, and SEC Staff Generic Comment Letter for Investment Company CFOs [Nov. 7, 1997] available at www.sec.gov/divisions/investment/noaction/1997/cfo110797.pdf). The SEC staff notes that this consideration should be made regardless of whether the fund of funds has a controlling financial interest or a noncontrolling interest in the underlying fund.)

[5] Rule 3-09 of Regulation S-X describes the circumstances under which separate financial statements of an unconsolidated majority-owned subsidiary (for example, unconsolidated nonregistered investment company) must be filed with the SEC and the circumstances under which those separate financial statements must be audited. It also explains that, insofar as practicable, the subsidiary's separate financial statements must be as of the same dates and for the same periods as the audited financial statements of the registrant. In accordance with Rule 4-01(a)(1) of Regulation S-X, the subsidiary's financial statements that are filed with the SEC must be prepared in accordance with U.S. generally accepted accounting principles and must comply with Regulation S-X.

(continued)

statement of assets and liabilities. Additional disclosures may be required for those funds that hold a mixture of investments in other investment companies and direct investments in securities. However, there is usually no need for a separate schedule of investments. Fund management should consider whether an investment in a single underlying fund is so significant to the fund of funds to make the presentation of financial statements in a manner similar to a master-feeder fund (exhibits 5-4–5-5) more appropriate.

5.57 For registered investment companies, investments in affiliated funds are considered investments in affiliates subject to Rule 12-14 of Regulation S-X. Such investments may not be reported using the summary portfolio schedules permitted under Rule 12-12C of Regulation S-X. (Refer to chapter 7 of this guide for further discussion of U.S. generally accepted accounting principles applicable for the preparation of financial statements of investment companies.)

5.58 *Statement of operations.* Paragraphs 13–14 of FASB ASC 946-225-45 describe how income reflected on the statement of operations should represent the net earnings received from investee funds. For example, if the investee funds are all registered investment companies (as in the example in the exhibit), then the income would represent the dividends received from such investee funds. The investor fund should not reflect any operating expenses if the investee funds have agreed to assume certain of the investor fund expenses. To the extent that the investor fund has such agreements, they should be disclosed in the notes.

5.59 FASB ASC 946-225-45-15 notes that when investing in registered investment companies, distributions received from capital gains should be reported as realized gains together with gains realized on the disposition of shares of investee entities.

5.60 A registered investment company will be considered a qualified fund of funds if, at the close of each quarters of its taxable year, at least 50 percent of the value of its total assets is represented by interests in other RICs. A qualified fund of funds will be entitled to pass through to its shareholders the tax-exempt interest character of dividends received from municipal bond funds, other individual investments held (if direct securities are held), and foreign tax credits received as a result of its investment in funds investing in non-U.S. securities.

5.61 FASB ASC 946-225-45-16 notes that expenses are those incurred only at the reporting fund level. Expenses of the investee funds are embedded in the net earnings from such funds.

(footnote continued)

Rule 4-08(g) of Regulation S-X states that summarized financial information must be presented, in the notes to the financial statements, for unconsolidated subsidiaries. It explains that, insofar as practicable, the summarized financial information must be as of the same dates and for the same periods as the audited financial statements of the registrant. Rule 4-08(g) also explains that the summarized financial information must include the disclosures prescribed by Rule 1-02(bb) of Regulation S-X. Rule 1-02(bb) of Regulation S-X permits registrants in specialized industries to provide summarized balance sheet information as to the nature and amount of the majority components of assets and liabilities. Rule 1-02(bb) of Regulation S-X permits registrants in specialized industries to provide in their summarized income statement other information necessary for a more meaningful presentation in lieu of providing the required disclosures specified by the rule.

5.62 *Notes to financial statements.* Paragraphs 4–5 of FASB ASC 946-235-50 illustrate that fund management should consider whether, and to what extent, disclosure of the investee funds' investment policies is appropriate. Notes to the financial statements of the reporting fund should include the following:

- A general description of the fund-of-funds structure
- Disclosure of the valuation policy; values are generally based on information reported by investee funds.[6]

5.63 *Financial highlights.* FASB ASC 946-205-50-30 explains that the financial highlights for the reporting fund in a fund-of-funds structure are usually similar to a standalone feeder fund in a master-feeder structure. Net investment income and expense ratios should be computed based upon the amounts reported in the statement of operations, and portfolio turnover should be measured based on the turnover of investments made by the reporting fund in the investee funds, not looking through the investee funds to their portfolio activity.

Audit Considerations[7]

5.64 In some cases, master-feeder structures are capitalized by transferring the investments and related assets and liabilities of an existing fund to a newly organized master fund. In exchange for the assets transferred, the original fund becomes a feeder fund and receives a proportional ownership interest in the master fund. The auditor should be aware that management may obtain a private letter ruling from the IRS or tax opinions from counsel, in certain instances, to ensure treatment as a tax-free contribution. The auditor should also be familiar with the tax rules that may require subsequent tracking and special allocation of the contributed unrealized gain or loss on the investments transferred to the master fund.

5.65 *Multiple-class funds.* In connection with the audit of multiple-class funds, the auditor should consider whether

- class-level and fund-level expenses have been determined, as required by Rule 18f-3.
- income, expenses, and realized and unrealized gains or losses have been allocated among the classes of shares, in accordance with the allocation methods in Rule 18f-3.

---

[6] For those investee funds that do not have readily determinable fair values, refer to the "Investments in Entities That Calculate Net Asset Value per Share" section in chapter 2, "Investment Accounts," of this guide for further guidance on the use of net asset value per share (or its equivalent) as a practical expedient to value an investment in an investee fund that does not have a readily determinable fair value.

[7] The auditing content in this guide focuses primarily on GAAS issued by the Auditing Standards Board and is applicable to audits of nonissuers. See the section "Applicability of Generally Accepted Auditing Standards and PCAOB Standards" of the preface to this guide for a discussion of the definitions of issuer and nonissuer as used throughout this guide. Appendix B, "Clarified Auditing Standards and PCAOB Standards," of this guide is included to assist auditors in comparing the clarified standards, many of which are referenced throughout this guide, to the PCAOB standards. Further, considerations for audits of issuers in accordance with PCAOB standards may be discussed within this guide's chapter text. When such discussion is provided, the related paragraphs are designated with the following title: *Considerations for Audits Performed in Accordance With PCAOB Standards.*

- IRS regulations have been considered regarding the maintenance of class-level expense differentials necessary to avoid preferential dividends for income tax purposes (see paragraphs 5.09 and 6.68– .69 for additional information).

- differences between expense and net investment income ratios of various share classes appear reasonable when compared with the amount or percentage differences in class-level expenses.

5.66 *Master-feeder funds.* In connection with the audit of master-feeder funds, the auditor should consider whether

- fees and expenses incurred by the master fund or feeder funds are in accordance with contractual agreements, as disclosed in the registration statement. Advisory and custodian fees are normally incurred only at the master fund; fees and expenses relating to distribution and shareholder servicing are normally incurred at the feeder level.

- controls and procedures are adequate for investment valuation and for proper allocation of related income components to feeder funds.

- systems and controls are adequate to record accurately and timely contributions and withdrawals between the feeder funds and master fund, which could be as often as daily. This is important to determine properly each feeder fund's proportionate ownership interest for purposes of computing daily allocations. All shareholder purchases and redemptions are recorded at the feeder level. Assuming that cash is transferred on the same day, after the total daily net sales or redemptions are known for each feeder, contributions and withdrawals in the master fund are recorded to reflect changes in the feeders' ownership interests (that is, a net redemption at the feeder level will result in a withdrawal from the master fund). All such transactions at the feeder level generally will affect the investment in the master fund. At the master-fund level, the cash movements flow through the partnership equity or net assets account.

- satisfaction has been obtained concerning the accuracy of master fund tax adjustments allocated to the feeder funds.

5.67 A master-feeder structure, or a fund of funds structure, could consist of a master fund and feeder funds that are not related to each other, except that they are each feeders of the same master fund. Each feeder could have a different auditor who may also differ from the auditor of the master fund. Considering that the portfolio of investments is held by the master fund and the feeder fund audit would typically consist of auditing the internal profit and loss and owner allocations, it is ordinarily more efficient and preferable to have a single audit firm represent the entire master-feeder group. It is also possible that the master and feeder funds could have different year-ends (see paragraph 5.41). See the following sections for audit considerations when the audit of feeder funds have different auditors or year-ends from those of the master fund.

Planning

5.68 The feeder fund auditor may discuss with the master fund's auditor the results of the most recent audit of the master fund.

5.69 The feeder fund auditor should inquire of feeder fund management and may inquire of master fund management about any changes in the operation of the fund. Examples of such changes may include fee structures, affiliated transactions, significant contingencies, results of regulatory reviews, or proposed transactions since the previous feeder fund and master fund audits. Consideration should be given to the implications of fund operation changes on the nature, scope, and timing of audit testing and feeder fund financial statement presentation and disclosure.

5.70 Timing and logistics considerations will make planning and coordination among management and the auditors of the master and feeder funds necessary.

Control Environment

5.71 In accordance with paragraph .15 of AU-C section 315, *Understanding the Entity and Its Environment and Assessing the Risks of Material Misstatement* (AICPA, *Professional Standards*), feeder fund auditors should obtain an understanding of the control environment by evaluating whether (*a*) management, with the oversight of those charged with governance, has created and maintained a culture of honesty and ethical behavior and (*b*) the strengths in the control environment elements collectively provide an appropriate foundation for the other components of internal control and whether those other components are not undermined by deficiencies in the control environment. Paragraph .A71 of AU-C section 315 explains that the control environment includes the governance and management functions and the attitudes, awareness, and actions of those charged with governance and management concerning the entity's internal control and its importance in the entity. The feeder fund auditor may also consider the control and monitoring procedures performed by the feeder fund's management over its investment in the master fund. AU-C section 240, *Consideration of Fraud in a Financial Statement Audit* (AICPA, *Professional Standards*), should also be considered.

5.72 Much of the information obtained by the auditor's inquiries is obtained from management and those responsible for financial reporting. However, paragraph .A6 of AU-C section 315 explains that the auditor also may obtain information through inquiries with the internal audit function, if the entity has such a function, and others within the entity. The feeder fund auditor also may review the master fund auditor's audit documentation related to the evaluation and testing of the master fund's control environment.

5.73 Inquiries may be made of the master fund's management and auditors with respect to changes or issues in the control environment since the last fiscal year-end of the master fund or since the performance of the most recent tests of controls.

5.74 Based upon the results of the feeder fund auditor's evaluation of the control environment at the master fund, the feeder fund auditor may directly perform or consider requesting the master fund auditor to perform additional tests of controls.

Investment in Master Fund and Income-Gain Allocations

5.75 The auditor should obtain, as of the date of the feeder fund's financial statements, an understanding of the nature of the securities held by the master fund and the procedures used to value these securities. Consideration may be given to directly performing or requesting the master fund auditor to perform additional procedures, particularly related to fair valued,[8] illiquid, or difficult-to-price securities. This may be particularly relevant if the feeder fund has a different year-end from the master fund.

5.76 The feeder fund auditor may consider requesting the master fund auditor to review the master fund's reconciliation of portfolio securities with the custodian bank and brokers as of the date of the feeder fund's financial statements. Based upon the results of these procedures, the feeder fund auditor might request the master fund auditor to test the existence of the master fund's investments in securities with the custodian and brokers as of the date of the feeder fund's financial statements.[9]

5.77 The feeder fund auditor might review the master fund auditor's audit documentation related to valuation testing, existence testing, or both types of testing as of the most recent master fund audit.

5.78 The auditor may obtain confirmation from master fund management, as of the date of the feeder fund financial statements, of the value of the feeder fund's investment in the master fund, the feeder fund's percentage ownership in the master fund, allocations of income or gain from the master fund to the feeder fund during the period under audit, and capital contributions and withdrawals during the period under audit.

Other Transactions

5.79 Through procedures such as discussions with feeder fund and master fund management and inspection of the master fund's financial statements accounting records, the auditor should consider whether significant transactions of the master fund have been accounted for and disclosed properly in the feeder fund's financial statements.

Prospectus Restrictions and Compliance

5.80 The auditor may consider making inquiries of master fund management with respect to the results of investment restrictions compliance monitoring, including any detected compliance violations and related resolutions during the period of the feeder fund financial statements.

5.81 The auditor may consider directly reviewing or requesting the master fund auditor to review the analyses and documentation with respect to the master fund's investment restrictions compliance.

5.82 The feeder fund auditor may review the master fund auditor's related audit documentation. The feeder fund auditor might directly perform or

---

[8] AU-C section 540, *Auditing Accounting Estimates, Including Fair Value Accounting Estimates, and Related Disclosures* (AICPA, *Professional Standards*), addresses the auditor's responsibilities relating to accounting estimates, including fair value accounting estimates and related disclosures, in an audit of financial statements. Portions of AU-C section 540 have been incorporated into the guidance contained in paragraphs 11.60–.76 of this guide.

[9] When the feeder fund has a different year-end from the master fund, another consideration is for the master fund auditor to perform an agreed-upon-procedures engagement for the period between the master fund year-end and the feeder fund year-end.

request the master fund auditor to perform additional tests based upon the results and timing of such inquiries.

5.83 AU-C section 580, *Written Representations* (AICPA, *Professional Standards*), addresses the auditor's responsibility to obtain written representations from management, and, when appropriate, those charged with governance in an audit of financial statements. Consideration may be given to obtaining analyses and schedules related to investment compliance from master fund management or obtaining direct representation of investment compliance from master fund management.

Tax Qualifications and Compliance

5.84 The auditor may review analyses and documentation with respect to the master fund's tax compliance. Any tests of compliance with diversification requirements need to be met for both the master's and feeder's fiscal periods.

5.85 The auditor should obtain sufficient appropriate audit evidence of feeder fund tax compliance (for example, sufficiency of distributions) for the period of the financial statements, consistent with the requirements of Interpretation No. 1, "The Effect of an Inability to Obtain Audit Evidence Relating to Income Tax Accruals," of AU-C section 500, *Audit Evidence* (AICPA, *Professional Standards*, AU-C sec. 9500 par. .01–.22).

5.86 The auditor might review the related master fund auditor's audit documentation.

5.87 The auditor may consider obtaining direct representations of relevant tax compliance aspects from master fund management.

Financial Statements

5.88 As noted in paragraph 5.83, the auditor should obtain a management representation letter. In addition to the written representations required by paragraphs .10–.18 of AU-C section 580, paragraph .A18 of AU-C section 580 notes that the auditor may consider it necessary to request other written representations about the financial statements. For example, representations may be included in regard to the appropriateness of the measurement methods and significant assumptions used to determine fair value for financial statement measurement and disclosure purposes.

5.89 The feeder fund auditor should read the most recent financial statements of the master fund.

5.90 Generally, when master and feeder funds share common reporting periods, the feeder fund's auditor's report should not be dated prior to the master fund's auditor's report.

Funds of Funds

5.91 Significant audit risks[10] may exist if management does not use strong procedural controls in selecting and monitoring a fund's investments in

---

[10] Refer to paragraphs .28–.30 and .A125–.A132 of AU-C section 315, *Understanding the Entity and Its Environment and Assessing the Risks of Material Misstatement* (AICPA, *Professional Standards*), for audit requirements and application guidance, respectively, pertaining to risks that require special audit consideration (significant risks).

investee companies and determining the investments' fair value. The audit approach to an investor fund's investments in investee funds might focus on the following three areas:

  a. Evaluating the investor and investee funds' control environments

  b. Substantiating the existence of and fair value attributed to investments in investee funds[11]

  c. Review of periodic performance reported by each investee that is recorded by the investor fund

5.92 An investor fund's auditors may receive audited financial statements of an investee and corroborate that the investor's carrying value matches its proportionate ownership based on the year-end audited financial statements of the investee. It is possible, however, that all or most of the adjustment to the investor's accounting records occurred during the last interim period of the reporting period, which could mask misstatements in the earlier periods. Although the year-end net asset value of the investee would be correct, the interim period misstatements could cause an error in periodic allocations of performance among investors. The auditor may consider reviewing the periodic performance reported by each investee that is recorded by the investor fund.

Control Environment

5.93 The primary concern in the control environment relates to the procedures that management of the investor fund uses to monitor its investments in investee funds. Investments in public investee funds may be valued based on reported daily net asset values, and the auditor may rely upon the structure established by the 1940 Act and the 1933 Act to gain comfort that such reported fair values are accurate.

5.94 For investments in nonpublic investee companies for which the practical expedient discussed in paragraph 2.86 of this guide has been adopted, the auditor might consider the process and controls adopted by the investor fund to evaluate whether net asset value has been calculated consistent with FASB ASC 946, *Financial Services—Investment Companies* (including the controls discussed in paragraphs 2.90–.91 of this guide). Audit tests may include observation of management site visits or telephone calls to investee funds, or inspection of documentation of such visits or calls. Prior experience with the investee funds' management, results of prior-year audits, or the history of adjustments to unaudited results reported by the investee funds, if any, are considered in determining the extent to which such participation is necessary. For example, observation of management site visits would be more appropriate if the investee funds represented a significant investment by the investor fund or if serious concerns about the management controls at the investee fund existed. The auditor should also test the investor fund's reconciliation of the unaudited financial results received from the investee funds to their audited financial statements for the prior year if the current year's audited financial statements are not available. Any significant variations, their causes, and their effect on the investor fund's financial statements should be identified.

5.95 If significant variations are discovered in the comparison of prior-year audited financial statements with financial information obtained from

---

[11] See the guidance regarding auditing investments in securities where a readily determinable fair value does not exist in paragraph 11.58 of this guide.

the investee funds, the auditor should perform additional procedures, such as observing the management site visit; reviewing the investee fund's audited financial statements; or vouching withdrawals, if any, made from the investee fund after year-end, as part of the annual audit tests.

5.96 If the investor fund elects not to or is not permitted to utilize the practical expedient, the auditor might consider evaluating the determination of fair value in a manner similar to its evaluation of the fair value of other investments determined by management, including the inputs discussed in paragraph 2.96 of this guide.

Exhibit 5-1

Methods of Allocating Income, Fund-Level Expenses, and Realized and Unrealized Gains (Losses)

	Total	Class A	Class B
Assumptions:			
Total shares outstanding		2,000,000	3,000,000
Settled shares outstanding		1,990,000	2,900,000
Net asset value per share		$10.52	$10.49
Fair Value of Shares Outstanding—Relative Net Assets:			
Total shares outstanding	5,000,000	2,000,000	3,000,000
Net asset value per share		$10.52	$10.49
Net asset value	$52,510,000	$21,040,000	$31,470,000
Allocation percentage		40.0686%	59.9314%
Fair Value of Settled Shares Outstanding:			
Settled shares outstanding	4,890,000	1,990,000	2,900,000
Net asset value per share		$10.52	$10.49
	$51,355,800	$20,934,800	$30,421,000
Allocation percentage		40.7642%	59.2358%
Shares Outstanding:			
Total shares outstanding	5,000,000	2,000,000	3,000,000
Allocation percentage		40.0%	60.0%

Exhibit 5-2

Methods of Computing Income Distributions Per Share

	Total	Class A	Class B
Assumptions:			
Net investment income before class-specific expenses	$1,000,000		
Class-specific expenses:			
Class A		$13,000	
Class B			$59,000
Record date shares outstanding	5,000,000	2,000,000	3,000,000
Record-Share Method			
Net investment income before class-specific expenses	$1,000,000		
Total record date shares outstanding	5,000,000		
Gross dividend rate for all shares	$.2000	$.2000	$.2000
Per share class-specific expenses:			
Class A ($13,000/2,000,000)		(.0065)	
Class B ($59,000/3,000,000)			(.0197)
Per share dividend for each class		$.1935	$.1803
Actual-Income-Available Method			
Actual net investment income recorded on books of each class	$928,000	$417,600	$510,400
Record date shares outstanding for each class		2,000,000	3,000,000
Per share dividend for each class		$.2088	$.1701

(continued)

Exhibit 5-2—continued

Methods of Computing Income Distributions Per Share

	Total	Class A	Class B
Simultaneous-Equations Method			

EQUATION #1: A + B = $928,000

When—A and B represent the total dividend amounts to be paid to each class.

EQUATION #2: A/2,000,000
B/3,000,000 = (0.5% × $10.50)/4

When

2,000,000 and 3,000,000 represent the record date shares of each class
0.5% represents the expense differential between class A and class B
$10.50 represents the average daily net asset value of the Fund
4 refers to the fact that the dividend period is a quarter

Solving the previous simultaneous equations produces the following results:

	Total	Class A	Class B
Total dividends to be paid	$928,000	$386,961	$541,039
Record date shares outstanding for each class		2,000,000	3,000,000
Per share dividend for each class		$.1935	$.1803
Annualized distribution rates to average daily net asset value		7.37%	6.87%
Difference in distribution rates		0.50%	

Note: The illustrative financial statements and note disclosures included in this guide have been updated to reflect FASB ASC. However, FASB's notice to constituents suggests the use of plain English in financial statement note disclosures to describe broad FASB ASC topic references. FASB suggests a reference similar to "as required by the Derivatives and Hedging Topic of the FASB *Accounting Standards Codification*." Entities might consider revising their financial statement references to reflect this plain English referencing, rather than the use of specific FASB ASC references. The AICPA has provided these detailed references as a resource for its users.

Exhibit 5-3

XYZ Multiple-Class Fund
Statement of Assets and Liabilities
December 31, 20X8

Assets

Investments in securities at fair value (cost $18,674,000)	$ 21,101,000
Cash	199,000
Deposits with brokers for securities sold short	1,555,000
Collateral for securities loaned at fair value	620,000
Receivables:	
Dividends and interest	46,000
Investment securities sold	24,000
Capital shares sold	54,000
Other assets	26,000
Total assets	23,625,000

Liabilities

Options written at fair value (premiums received $110,000)	230,000
Securities sold short at fair value (proceeds $1,555,000)	1,673,000
Demand loan payable to bank	2,000,000
Payable upon return of securities loaned	620,000
Due to broker—variation margin	10,000
Payables:	
Investment securities purchased	52,000
Capital shares reacquired	8,000
Other	4,000
Accrued expenses	8,000
Distribution payable	158,000
Total liabilities	4,763,000
Net assets	$18,862,000

Net assets consist of:[12]

Paid-in capital	$ 15,184,000
Undistributed ordinary income	912,000
Accumulated undistributed net realized gain	339,000
Net unrealized appreciation	2,427,000
Total net assets	$18,862,000

Net asset value per share:

Class A—based on net assets of $15,089,600 and 3,375,750 shares outstanding	$4.47
Class A public offering price ($4.47 net asset value divided by 0.95)	$4.71
Class B—based on net assets of $3,772,400 and 845,830 shares outstanding	$4.46

Redemption price per class B share is equal to net asset value less any applicable contingent deferred sales charge

The accompanying notes are an integral part of these financial statements.

---

[12] This breakout presentation of net assets in this illustration is required by rules 6-04.16-.18 of Regulation S-X and is typically not relevant for nonregistered investment companies.

Exhibit 5-3—continued

XYZ Multiple-Class Fund
Statement of Operations
Year Ended December 31, 20X8

Investment income:	
Dividends (net of foreign withholding taxes of $20,000)	$ 742,000
Interest	209,000
Income from loaned securities—net	50,000
Total income	1,001,000
Expenses:	
Investment advisory fee	137,400
Service fees—class A	36,600
Distribution and service fees—class B	37,000
Interest	10,000
Professional fees	18,000
Custodian	5,000
Transfer agent fees—class A	10,000
Transfer agent fees—class B	12,000
Directors' fees	10,000
Dividends on securities sold short	3,000
Total gross expenses	279,000
Less waivers:	
Distribution and service fees—class B	(18,500)
Investment advisory fee	(34,500)
Total net expenses	226,000
Investment income—net	775,000
Realized and unrealized gain (loss) on investments:	
Net realized gain (loss) on investments	1,089,000
Net change in unrealized appreciation (depreciation) on investments	(1,649,000)
Net loss on investments	(560,000)
Net increase in net assets resulting from operations	$215,000

The accompanying notes are an integral part of these financial statements.

Exhibit 5-3—continued

XYZ Multiple-Class Fund
Statements of Changes in Net Assets
Years Ended December 31, 20X8 and 20X7

	20X8	*20X7*
Increase (decrease) in net assets from operations:		
Investment income—net	$ 775,000	$ 724,000
Net realized gain on investments	1,089,000	1,000,000
Net change in unrealized appreciation or depreciation on investments	(1,649,000)	1,319,000
Net increase in net assets resulting from operations	215,000	3,043,000
Distributions to shareholders:		
Class A	(1,505,250)	(1,104,500)
Class B	(360,750)	(239,500)
Tax return of capital:		
Class A	—	(52,800)
Class B	—	(13,200)
Total distributions	(1,866,000)	(1,410,000)
Net increase from capital share transactions	2,721,000	4,700,000
Total increase in net assets	1,070,000	6,333,000
Net assets:		
Beginning of year	17,792,000	11,459,000
End of year	$18,862,000	$17,792,000

The accompanying notes are an integral part of these financial statements.

Exhibit 5-3—continued

XYZ Multiple-Class Fund
Notes to Financial Statements

> *The following notes are limited to illustrations of disclosures unique to a multiple-class fund structure. In addition to the disclosures provided, notes for a multiple-class fund would include all standard disclosures presented as part of the illustrative financial statements in chapter 7.*

1. Significant Accounting Policies

XYZ Multiple-Class Fund (the Fund) is registered under the Investment Company Act of 1940 as a diversified, open-end management investment company. The Fund follows accounting and reporting guidance in the *Accounting Standards Codifications* 946, *Financial Services—Investment Companies*. The Fund offers 2 classes of shares (class A and class B). Each class of shares has equal rights concerning earnings and assets, except that each class bears different distribution, shareholder service, and transfer agent expenses. Each class of shares has exclusive voting rights with respect to matters that affect just that class. Income, expenses (other than expenses attributable to a specific class), and realized and unrealized gains or losses on investments are allocated to each class of shares based on its relative net assets. Class B shares are subject to a maximum contingent deferred sales charge of 5 percent upon redemption, decreasing to zero over a period of 6 years. Class B shares automatically convert to class A shares at the end of the month following the second anniversary of issuance.

2. Capital Share Transactions

The Fund is authorized to issue an unlimited number of shares in an unlimited number of classes.

Transactions in the capital shares of the Fund were as follows:

	20X8		20X7	
	Shares	Amount	Shares	Amount
Class A:				
Shares sold	309,000	$1,444,500	690,500	$3,176,000
Shares issued from reinvestments	195,000	1,040,000	171,000	770,000
Shares redeemed	(57,000)	(253,500)	(40,000)	(186,000)
Shares converted from class B to class A	4,790	22,800		
Net increase from capital share transactions	451,790	$2,253,800	821,500	$3,760,000
Class B:				
Shares sold	61,925	$290,100	185,000	$848,000
Shares issued from reinvestments	57,875	270,000	35,000	160,000
Shares redeemed	(15,000)	(70,100)	(15,000)	(68,000)
Shares converted from class B to class A	4,800	22,800		
Net increase from capital share transactions	100,000	$467,200	205,000	$940,000

Exhibit 5-3—continued

3. Investment Advisory Fees and Other Transactions With Affiliates

The Fund has entered into a distribution plan, pursuant to Rule 12b-1 under the Investment Company Act of 1940, with XYZ Distributors (distributors). Under the plan, class A shares pay a monthly shareholder servicing fee at an annual rate of 0.25 percent of class A average daily net assets. Class B shares pay monthly shareholder servicing and distribution fees at the annual rate of 0.25 percent and 0.75 percent, respectively, of class B average daily net assets. These fees compensate distributors for the services they provide and expenses borne by distributors under the agreement. During the year ended December 31, 20X8, distributors waived $18,500 of their distribution fees related to class B shares.

For the year ended December 31, 20X8, distributors received $70,000 in sales commissions from the sale of class A shares. Distributors also received $6,500 of contingent deferred sales charges relating to redemptions of class B shares.

XYZ Service Company provides transfer agent services to the Fund. Under the transfer agent agreement with XYZ Service Company, the Fund pays a monthly fee equal, on an annual basis, to $15 and $18 per shareholder account for class A and class B shares, respectively.

Exhibit 5-3—continued

XYZ Multiple-Class Fund
Financial Highlights[13]

	Class A			Class B		
	20X8	20X7	20X6[14]	20X8	20X7	20X6[15]
Per share operating performance:[16]						
Net asset value, beginning of year	$4.88	$4.46	$4.00	$4.88	$4.45	$4.00
Income from investment operations:						
Net investment income	0.21	0.20	0.12	0.19	0.20	0.11
Net realized and unrealized gain (loss) on investment transactions	(0.12)	0.71	0.50	(0.12)	0.71	0.49
Total from investment operations	0.09	0.91	0.62	0.07	0.91	0.60
Less distributions:						
Dividends and distributions	(0.50)	(0.44)	(0.16)	(0.49)	(0.43)	(0.15)
Tax return of capital distributions	0	(0.05)	0	0	(0.05)	0
Total distributions	(0.50)	(0.49)	(0.16)	(0.49)	(0.48)	(0.15)
Net asset value, end of year	$4.47	$4.88	$4.46	$4.46	$4.88	$4.45
Total return[17]	1.84%	20.40%	15.50%	1.43%	19.90%	15.00%
Percentages and supplemental data:						
Net assets, end of year (000s)	$15,090	$14,167	$9,167	$3,772	$3,625	$2,292
Ratios to average net assets:						
Expenses[18]	1.23%	1.30%	1.35%[19]	1.48%	2.05%	2.10%[20]
Net investment income[21]	4.15%	2.82%	4.00%[22]	3.90%	2.07%	3.25%[23]
Portfolio turnover rate	92%	80%	75%	92%	80%	75%

The accompanying notes are an integral part of these financial statements.

---

[13] Item 13(a) of Form N-1A requires financial highlights to be presented for the latest 5 years; however, in this exhibit, the fund commenced operations 3 years ago, thus only 3 years are presented.

[14] For the period from June 1, 20X6 (commencement of operations), to December 31, 20X6.

[15] See footnote 14.

[16] Selected data for a share of capital stock outstanding throughout the year.

[17] Total return excludes the effect of sales charges.

[18] During 20X8, 20X7, and 20X6, the adviser and distributor voluntarily waived a portion of their advisory fees and a portion of the class B distribution and service fee (0.50 percent). Absent these waivers, the expense percentages would have been approximately 1.48 percent, 1.55 percent, 1.60 percent, 2.23 percent, 2.80 percent, and 2.85 percent, respectively.

[19] Annualized.

[20] Annualized.

[21] See footnote 18.

[22] Annualized.

[23] Annualized.

Exhibit 5-4

ABC Feeder Fund, Inc.
Statement of Assets and Liabilities
December 31, 20X8

Assets

Investment in ABC Master Portfolio	$15,089,600
Receivable for capital shares sold	110,000
Prepaid expenses and other assets	35,000
Total assets	15,234,600

Liabilities

Administrative fee payable	20,000
Payable for capital shares redeemed	30,000
Dividends payable	40,000
Other accrued liabilities	25,000
Total liabilities	115,000
Net assets	$15,119,600

Net assets consist of:[24]

Paid-in capital, 1,250,000 shares outstanding	$12,258,600
Undistributed ordinary income	957,000
Accumulated undistributed net realized gain	785,000
Net unrealized appreciation	1,119,000
Total net assets	$15,119,600
Net asset value per share	$12.10
Public offering price ($12.10 net asset value divided by 0.95)	$12.74

The accompanying notes are an integral part of these financial statements.

[24] This breakout presentation of net assets in this illustration is required by rules 6-04.16–.18 of Regulation S-X and is typically not relevant for nonregistered investment companies.

Exhibit 5-4—continued

ABC Feeder Fund, Inc.
Statement of Operations[25,26]
Year Ended December 31, 20X8

Net investment income allocated from ABC Master Portfolio:	
Dividends	$ 579,000
Interest	168,200
Income from loaned securities—net	40,000
Expenses[27]	(179,000)
Net investment income from ABC Master Portfolio	608,200
Fund expenses:	
Administrative fees	15,000
Distribution and servicing fees	37,500
Professional fees	12,000
Transfer agent fees	35,000
Directors' fees	10,000
Registration fees	26,000
Other expenses	12,000
Total expenses	147,500
Investment income—net	460,700
Realized and unrealized gain (loss) on investments allocated from ABC Master Portfolio:	
Net realized gain on investments	865,000
Net change in unrealized appreciation (depreciation) on investments	(1,320,000)
Net loss on investments	(455,000)
Net increase in net assets resulting from operations	$5,700

The accompanying notes are an integral part of these financial statements.

---

[25] In the initial year of adopting a master-feeder structure, the feeder's statement of operations may be a combination of (a) direct income, expenses, and realized gains and losses for the period prior to adoption of the master-feeder structure and (b) the allocated amounts from the master portfolio for the period from adoption to fiscal year-end.

[26] In this example, ABC Master Portfolio is a pass-through entity for tax purposes. If the master portfolio was not a pass-through entity, allocations may not be presented but, rather, distributions may be presented, similar to the fund-of-funds example included within exhibit 5-6.

[27] Any expense waivers should be reported in a note to the statement of operations.

Exhibit 5-4—continued

ABC Feeder Fund, Inc.
Statements of Changes in Net Assets
Years Ended December 31, 20X8 and 20X7

	20X8	20X7
Increase (decrease) in net assets from operations:		
Investment income—net	$ 460,700	$ 369,000
Net realized gain on investments	865,000	750,000
Net change in unrealized appreciation or depreciation	(1,320,000)	1,178,000
Net increase in net assets resulting from operations	5,700	2,297,000
Distributions to shareholders	(1,178,700)	(1,071,000)
Net increase from capital share transactions:		
Sold 147,000 and 207,000 shares	1,782,600	2,359,000
Distributions reinvested of 72,000 and 73,000 shares	880,000	820,000
Redeemed 20,700 and 13,000 shares	(250,000)	(150,000)
Net increase from capital share transactions	2,412,600	3,029,000
Net increase in net assets	1,239,600	4,255,000
Net assets: Beginning of year	13,880,000	9,625,000
End of year	$15,119,600	$13,880,000

The accompanying notes are an integral part of these financial statements.

Exhibit 5-4—continued

ABC Feeder Fund, Inc.
Notes to Financial Statements[28]

> *The following notes are limited to illustrations of disclosures unique to feeder fund financial statements. Besides the following disclosures, notes for a feeder fund would include all standard disclosures presented as part of the illustrative financial statements in chapter 7. Exceptions to the standard chapter 7 disclosures would be the omission of notes relating to the master fund portfolio activity and expenses, such as the advisory fee incurred, that are disclosed in the master fund financial statements.*

1. Significant Accounting Policies

ABC Feeder Fund, Inc. (the Fund) is registered under the Investment Company Act of 1940 as a diversified, open-end management investment company. The Fund invests substantially all of its assets in the ABC Master Portfolio, an open-end investment company that has the same investment objectives as the Fund. The Fund follows the accounting and reporting guidance in FASB *Accounting Standards Codification* 946. The financial statements of the ABC Master Portfolio, including the schedule of investments, are included elsewhere in this report and should be read with the Fund's financial statements. The percentage of ABC Master Portfolio owned by the Fund at December 31, 20X8, was 80 percent.

Valuation of investments. The Fund records its investment in ABC Master Portfolio at fair value. The notes to the ABC Master Portfolio financial statements included elsewhere in this report provide information about ABC Master Portfolio's valuation policy and its period-end security valuations.

Investment income and expenses. The Fund records daily its proportionate share of the ABC Master Portfolio's income, expenses, and realized and unrealized gains and losses. In addition, the Fund accrues its own expenses.

---

[28] Item 13(a) of Form N-1A requires financial highlights to be presented for the latest 5 years; however, in this exhibit, the fund commenced operations 3 years ago, thus only 3 years are presented.

     ©2015, AICPA

Exhibit 5-4—continued

ABC Feeder Fund, Inc.
Financial Highlights

	20X8	20X7	20X6[29]
Per share operating performance:[30, 31]			
Net asset value, beginning of year	$13.11	$11.75	$10.00
Income from investment operations:			
Net investment income	0.40	0.41	0.38
Net realized and unrealized gain (loss) on investment transactions	(0.39)	2.12	2.47
Total from investment operations	0.01	2.53	2.85
Less distributions	(1.02)	(1.17)	(1.10)
Net asset value, end of year	$12.10	$13.11	$11.75
Total return	0.08%	21.53%	28.50%
Percentages and supplemental data:			
Net assets, end of year (000s)	$15,119	$13,880	$9,625
Ratios to average net assets:[32]			
Expenses	2.25%	2.30%	2.32%[33]
Net investment income	3.21%	2.48%	2.58%[34]

The accompanying notes are an integral part of these financial statements.

---

[29] For the period from March 1, 20X6 (the date of commencement of operations), to December 31, 20X6.

[30] Selected data for a share of capital stock outstanding throughout the year.

[31] The per share amounts and percentages reflect income and expenses assuming inclusion of the fund's proportionate share of the income and expenses of ABC Master Portfolio.

[32] See footnote 30.

[33] Annualized.

[34] Annualized.

Exhibit 5-5

ABC Master Portfolio
Statement of Assets and Liabilities
December 31, 20X8

Assets

Investments in securities at fair value (cost $18,674,000)	$ 21,101,000
Cash	199,000
Deposits with brokers for securities sold short	1,555,000
Collateral for securities loaned at fair value	620,000
Receivables:	
Dividends and interest	100,000
Investment securities sold	24,000
Other assets	26,000
Total assets	23,625,000

Liabilities

Options written at fair value (premiums received $110,000)	230,000
Securities sold short at fair value (proceeds $1,555,000)	1,673,000
Demand loan payable to bank	2,000,000
Payable upon return of securities loaned	620,000
Due to broker—variation margin	10,000
Payables:	
Investment securities purchased	210,000
Other	12,000
Accrued expenses	8,000
Total liabilities	4,763,000
Net assets	$18,862,000

The accompanying notes are an integral part of these financial statements.

Exhibit 5-5—continued

ABC Master Portfolio
Statement of Operations
Year Ended December 31, 20X8

Investment income:	
Dividends (net of foreign withholding taxes of $20,000)	$ 742,000
Interest	209,000
Income from loaned securities—net	50,000
Total income	1,001,000
Expenses:	
Investment advisory fee	171,900
Interest	10,000
Professional fees	18,000
Custodian	13,100
Directors' fees	10,000
Dividends on securities sold short	3,000
Total expenses	226,000
Investment income—net	775,000
Realized and unrealized gain (loss) on investments:	
Net realized gain on investments	1,089,000
Net change in unrealized appreciation on investments	(1,649,000)
Net loss on investments	(560,000)
Net increase in net assets resulting from operations	$215,000

The accompanying notes are an integral part of these financial statements.

Exhibit 5-5—continued

ABC Master Portfolio
Statements of Changes in Net Assets
Year Ended December 31, 20X8 and 20X7

	20X8	20X7
Increase (decrease) in net assets from operations:		
Investment income—net	$ 775,000	$ 492,000
Net realized gain on investments	1,089,000	1,000,000
Net change in unrealized appreciation or (depreciation)	(1,649,000)	1,551,000
Net increase in net assets resulting from operations	215,000	3,043,000
Proceeds from contributions	3,000,000	5,000,000
Withdrawals	(2,145,000)	(2,751,000)
	855,000	2,249,000
Net increase in net assets	1,070,000	5,292,000
Net assets:		
Beginning of year	17,792,000	12,500,000
End of year	$18,862,000	$17,792,000

The accompanying notes are an integral part of these financial statements.

Exhibit 5-5—continued

ABC Master Portfolio
Notes to Financial Statements

The following notes are limited to illustrations of disclosures unique to master-fund financial statements. Besides the following disclosures, notes for a master fund would include all standard disclosures presented as part of the illustrative financial statements in chapter 7. Exceptions to the standard chapter 7 disclosures would be the omission of notes regarding dividend distributions, capital share transactions, and distribution fees, each of which is disclosed in the financial statements of the feeder fund.

1. Significant Accounting Policies

ABC Master Portfolio (the portfolio) is organized as a trust and registered under the Investment Company Act of 1940 as a diversified, open-end management investment company. The Declaration of Trust permits the trustees to issue nontransferable interests in the portfolio. The portfolio follows the accounting and reporting guidance in FASB *Accounting Standards Codification* 946. For federal income tax purposes, the portfolio qualifies as a partnership, and each investor in the portfolio is treated as the owner of its proportionate share of the net assets, income, expenses, and realized and unrealized gains and losses of the portfolio. Accordingly, as a pass-through entity, the portfolio pays no income dividends or capital gain distributions.

2. Federal Income Taxes

The portfolio will be treated as a partnership for federal income tax purposes. As such, each investor in the portfolio will be subject to taxation on its share of the portfolio's ordinary income and capital gains. It is intended that the portfolio's assets will be managed so an investor in the portfolio can satisfy the requirements of Internal Revenue Code Subchapter M.

3. Financial Highlights[35]

Financial highlights for the portfolio for each period were as follows:

	20X8	20X7	20X6 [36]
Total return	1.21%	24.34%	31.20%
Ratios to average net assets:			
Expenses	1.23%	1.25%	1.27%[37]
Net investment income	4.23%	3.25%	3.34%[38]
Portfolio turnover rate	92%	80%	102%

---

[35] Item 13(a) of Form N-1A requires financial highlights to be presented for the latest 5 years; however, in this exhibit, the fund commenced operations 3 years ago, thus only 3 years are presented.

[36] For the period from March 1, 20X6 (the date of commencement of operations), to December 31, 20X6.

[37] Annualized.

[38] Annualized.

Exhibit 5-6

FOF Fund, Inc.
Statement of Net Assets
September 30, 20X8

> *The following sample financial statements are limited to matters directly related to funds of funds. The sample financial statements in this chapter and chapter 7 should be referred to for relevant disclosures.*

Assets:

204,100 shares of FOF Growth Fund, Inc.	$2,046,762
182,633 shares of FOF International Fund, Inc.	2,224,470
96,152 shares of FOF Income Fund, Inc.	1,046,134
602,908 shares FOF Money Market Fund, Inc.	602,908
Total investments (cost $5,617,279)[39]	5,920,274
Cash	9,000
Receivable for fund shares sold	23,652
Other assets	2,710
Total assets	5,955,636

Liabilities:

Payable for fund shares repurchased	37,123
Accrued expenses	8,327
Total liabilities	45,450

Net assets (equivalent to $10.73 per share based on 550,810 shares of capital stock issued and outstanding; unlimited shares authorized)	$5,910,186

Components of net assets:

Paid-in capital	$5,569,426
Distributable earnings	340,760
	$5,910,186

The accompanying notes are an integral part of these financial statements.

---

[39] Investments in investee funds may be presented in a separate schedule of investments rather than on the statement of net assets.

Exhibit 5-6–continued

FOF Fund, Inc.
Statement of Operations
Year Ended September 30, 20X8

Investment income:

Dividends from investment company shares		$201,942
Expenses:		
Custodian and transfer agent fees	$22,560	
Professional fees	8,318	
Registration fees	1,040	
Directors' fees	1,982	
Total expenses		33,900
Net investment income		168,042
Realized and unrealized gain on investments:		
Realized gain on sales of investment company shares	$12,067	
Realized gain distributions from investment company shares	321,939	
Net realized gain		334,006
Net change in unrealized appreciation (depreciation) on investments during the year		219,837
Net realized and unrealized gain		553,843
Net increase in net assets resulting from operations		$721,885

The accompanying notes are an integral part of these financial statements.

Exhibit 5-6–continued

FOF Fund, Inc.
Statements of Changes in Net Assets
Years Ended September 30, 20X8 and 20X7[40]

	20X8	20X7
Increase (decrease) in net assets from:		
Net investment income	$168,042	$32,177
Net realized gain on investments	334,006	16,090
Net change in unrealized appreciation	219,837	83,158
	721,885	131,425
Distributions to shareholders	(484,617)	(27,933)
Capital share transactions—net	2,172,589	3,396,837
Net increase in net assets	2,409,857	3,500,329
Net assets:		
Beginning of year	3,500,329	—
End of year	$5,910,186	$3,500,329

The accompanying notes are an integral part of these financial statements.

---

[40] The fund commenced operations on October 1, 20X6.

Exhibit 5-6–continued

FOF Fund, Inc.
Notes to Financial Statements

1. Significant Accounting Policies

FOF Fund, Inc. (the fund) is registered under the Investment Company Act of 1940, as amended, as a diversified, open-end management investment company. The fund invests solely in shares of other funds within the FOF Group of Mutual Funds with the objective of seeking high total return through investments allocated to diverse equity and fixed-income markets. The Fund follows the accounting and reporting guidance in FASB *Accounting Standards Codification* 946.

Security valuation. Investments in funds within the FOF Group of Mutual Funds are valued at fair value based on the net asset values reported by the underlying funds.

Transaction dates. Share transactions are recorded on the trade date. Dividend income and realized gain distributions from other funds are recognized on the ex-dividend date. Distributions to shareholders, which are determined in accordance with income tax regulations, are similarly recorded on the ex-dividend date. In determining the net gain or loss on securities sold, the cost of securities is determined on the identified cost basis.

Federal income taxes. The fund's policy is to comply with the requirements of the Internal Revenue Code applicable to regulated investment companies and to distribute all of its taxable income to its shareholders. Thus, no federal income tax provision is required.

2. Investment Transactions and Valuation

Cost of purchases and proceeds of sales of shares of funds within the FOF Group of Mutual Funds (excluding FOF Money Market Fund, Inc.) for the year ended September 30, 20X8, were $2,482,315 and $336,232, respectively. At September 30, 20X8, the cost of investments for federal income tax purposes was $5,617,279 and gross unrealized appreciation was $302,995; there was no gross unrealized depreciation.

The fund utilizes various methods to measure the fair value of most of its investments on a recurring basis. U.S. GAAP establishes a hierarchy that prioritizes inputs to valuation methods. The three levels of inputs are as follows:

- *Level 1.* Unadjusted quoted prices in active markets for identical assets or liabilities that the fund has the ability to access.

- *Level 2.* Observable inputs other than quoted prices included in level 1 that are observable for the asset or liability, either directly or indirectly. These inputs may include quoted prices for the identical instrument on an inactive market, prices for similar instruments, interest rates, prepayment speeds, credit risk yield curves, default rates, and similar data. For investments in funds, investments that are redeemable at net asset value per share (or its equivalent) in the near-term are included in level 2.

- *Level 3.* Unobservable inputs for the asset or liability to the extent that observable inputs are not available, representing the fund's own assumptions about the assumptions that a market participant would use in valuing the asset or liability; they would be based on the best information available.

The following table summarizes the inputs used to value the fund's assets measured at fair value as of September 30, 20X8.[41]

Valuation Inputs	Investments in Mutual Funds
Level 1	$5,920,274
Level 2	—
Level 3	—
Total	$5,920,274

There were no transfers between level 1 and level 2 during the year.[42]

3. Financial Support to Investees

The fund provides financial support to its investees as part of its investment strategy. The tables below summarize financial support provided during the year ended September 30, 20X8:

Financial support the fund was contractually required to provide:

Type	Amount	Reasons for Providing Support
XX	$XX	XX

Financial support the fund was not contractually required to provide:

Type	Amount	Reasons for Providing Support
XX	$XX	XX

The following table summarizes financial support the fund will be contractually required to provide subsequent to September 30, 20X8:

Type	Amount	Reasons for Providing Support
XX	$XX	XX

4. Investment Advisory Services and Other Transactions With Affiliates

The fund receives investment management and advisory services, consisting principally of determining the allocation of the assets of the fund among designated underlying funds, under a management agreement with FOF Investment Management, Inc. (the manager). The manager receives no compensation under this agreement; however, the fund pays management fees and expenses to the manager indirectly as a shareholder in funds of the FOF Group of Mutual Funds. Additionally, each fund in which the fund invests (except FOF Money

---

[41] The classification of various financial instruments in this table is for illustrative purposes only and should not be construed as recommended practice for any particular financial instrument or class of financial instruments.

[42] In accordance with FASB ASC 820-10-50, public entities should disclose transfers during the year between level 1 and level 2 of the fair value hierarchy; however, nonpublic entities are only required to disclose transfers into and out of level 3 of the fair value hierarchy.

Market Fund, Inc.) pays a distribution fee to FOF Distributors, Inc., the distributor of the fund, in the amount of 0.25 percent of average annual net assets. The fund pays no sales loads or similar compensation to FOF Distributors, Inc., to acquire shares of each fund in which it invests.

Because the underlying funds have varied expense and fee levels and the fund may own different proportions of underlying funds at different times, the amount of fees and expenses incurred indirectly by the fund will vary.

5. Capital Share Transactions

Transactions in capital shares were as follows:

| | *Years Ended September 30,* | | | |
| | *20X8* | | *20X7* | |
	Shares	*Amount*	*Shares*	*Amount*
Shares sold	204,017	$2,077,520	354,695	$3,590,241
Shares issued in reinvestment of dividends	41,817	425,255	2,615	27,013
Shares redeemed	(30,948)	(330,186)	(21,386)	(220,417)
Net increase	214,886	$2,172,589	335,924	$3,396,837

6. Components of Capital

Components of capital on a federal income tax basis at September 30, 20X8, were as follows:

Paid-in capital	$ 5,569,426
Undistributed ordinary income	11,460
Undistributed net realized gain	26,305
Unrealized appreciation	302,995
	$ 5,910,186

The tax character of distributions paid during the years ended September 30, 20X8, and 20X7, was as follows:

	20X8	20X7
Ordinary income	$160,826	$27,933
Long term capital gain	323,791	—
	$484,617	$27,933

Exhibit 5-6–continued

Financial Highlights[43]

	Year Ended September 30,	
	20X8	*20X7*
Per share data (for a share outstanding throughout the period):		
Net investment income[44]	$ .38	$ .20
Net realized and unrealized (gain) loss on investments	1.04	.38
Total from investment operations	1.42	.58
Less: Distributions to shareholders	(1.11)	(.16)
Net increase (decrease)	.31	.42
Net asset value:		
Beginning of year[45]	10.42	10.00
End of year	$10.73	$10.42
Total return	13.59%	5.86%
Net assets, end of year (000s)	$5,910	$3,500
Ratio of expenses to average net assets[46]	0.72%	0.89%[47]
Net investment income as a percentage of average net assets[48]	3.59%	1.96%[49]
Portfolio turnover rate	21%	5%

---

[43] Item 13(a) of Form N-1A requires financial highlights to be presented for the latest 5 years; however, in this exhibit, the fund commenced operations 2 years ago, thus only 2 years are presented.

[44] Recognition of net investment income by the fund is affected by the timing of the declaration of dividends by the underlying investment companies in which the fund invests. The ratio does not include net investment income of the investment companies in which the fund invests.

[45] Investment operations commenced on October 1, 20X6.

[46] Does not include expenses of the investment companies in which the fund invests.

[47] Annualized.

[48] See footnote 44.

[49] Annualized.

Chapter 6

Taxes

Presentation of Pending Content in FASB ASC

Amendments to FASB *Accounting Standards Codification* (ASC) (issued in the form of Accounting Standards Updates) are initially incorporated into FASB ASC in "Pending Content" boxes located below the paragraphs being amended with links to the transition information. The pending content boxes are meant to provide users with information about how the guidance in a paragraph will change as a result of the new guidance.

Pending content applies to different entities at different times due to varying fiscal year-ends, and because certain guidance may be effective on different dates for public entities, as defined, and other entities. As such, FASB maintains amended guidance in pending content boxes within FASB ASC until the roll-off date. Generally, the roll-off date is six months following the latest fiscal year-end for which the original guidance being amended could still be applied.

Presentation of Pending Content in AICPA Audit and Accounting Guides

Amended FASB ASC guidance that is included in pending content boxes in FASB ASC on May 1, 2015, is referenced as "Pending Content" in this guide. Pending content referenced or discussed within this guide's chapter text is fully effective as of the date of this guide and should be considered by readers for current reporting periods. Pending content referenced or discussed within this guide's shaded "Guidance Updates" boxes or within appendix A, "Guidance Updates," is not fully effective as of the date of this guide. Readers should be aware that pending content" referenced in this guide will eventually be subjected to FASB's roll-off process and will no longer be labeled as "Pending Content" in FASB ASC (as discussed in the previous paragraph).

Overview

6.01 This chapter provides information on the Internal Revenue Code of 1986, as amended. Its intended purpose is to provide auditors with background information, not as a detailed explanation of the IRC. Thus, the auditor should consult a tax adviser with respect to tax issues that arise in the course of an audit. Auditors may not be able to resolve tax issues that arise in the course of an audit based solely on the background information provided in this chapter.

6.02 This chapter has been divided into two sections to focus on distinct aspects of taxes for investment companies: "Financial Statements and Other Matters" and "RICs." Due to the extensive interrelationships between taxes and the underlying accounts or products, certain tax matters also appear in other chapters, as follows.

Topic	Paragraph Reference
Dividends to shareholders and reinvestments	4.46
Characterization of dividends for financial statement purposes	7.112–.113
Financial statement disclosures:	
• Status under IRC Subchapter M	7.189
• Capital loss carryforwards and post-October capital and currency loss deferrals	7.188
Multiple classes of shares	5.08–.09, 5.16–.17
Master-feeder funds	5.18–.21
Tax-free business combinations	8.44–.54
Unit investment trusts	9.14–.15
Variable contracts	10.39–.56

Financial Statements and Other Matters

Income Tax Expense

6.03   Federal income tax expense normally is not paid by investment companies that qualify under IRC Subchapter M,[1] and distribute all their investment company taxable income and taxable realized gains from securities transactions. For investment companies that qualify as regulated investment companies (RICs) under Subchapter M of the IRC (see the "Qualification Tests" section beginning at paragraph 6.45 for qualification criteria), federal income taxes payable on security gains that the investment company elects to retain (see paragraph 6.40) are accrued only on the last day of the tax year.[2] Only shareholders of record on the last day of the fiscal year are entitled to the credit for income taxes paid by the fund. Information regarding retained gains and taxes paid is sent to those shareholders to enable them to report their proportionate share of the gains and taxes paid on their individual returns. Also, no expense for federal excise taxes is required if a fund timely distributes substantially all of its taxable ordinary income, calculated on a calendar-year basis, and substantially all of its taxable capital gains, calculated generally on the basis of a 12 month period ending October 31 (see paragraph 6.84). Excise taxes imposed on underdistributed income should be recorded when determinable.

6.04   Income tax expense related to net investment income and net realized gains on investments should be recorded when it is probable that an investment company subject to IRC Subchapter M will not qualify under that

---

[1] Subchapter M consists of IRC Sections 851–860G and provides special tax rules for regulated investment companies (RICs), real estate investment trusts, real estate mortgage investment conduits, and financial asset securitization investment trusts. The rules affecting RICs are found in IRC Sections 851–855 and 860.

[2] Section 404.06b of the SEC's *Codification of Financial Reporting Policies.*

subchapter. Management should consider the need for recording a deferred tax expense if management concludes that it is probable that the investment company will not meet its qualification requirements for a period longer than one year. The auditor might consider assessing the assumptions used by an entity in determining its income tax status under IRC Subchapter M.

6.05 Some investment companies may be subject to state, local, or foreign taxes on net investment income and realized gains on a recurring basis. State, local, and foreign taxes, if payable, are reported on the accrual basis, including deferred taxes on the unrealized appreciation or depreciation of investments. A valuation allowance should be established for any deferred tax asset resulting from temporary differences related to unrealized depreciation that could result in deductible amounts in future years when the probability of realization of the tax benefit does not meet the more likely than not criterion of FASB ASC 740-10-25-6.

6.06 FASB ASC 740, *Income Taxes*, clarifies the accounting for uncertainty in income taxes recognized in an enterprise's financial statements and prescribes a recognition threshold and measurement attribute for the financial statement recognition and measurement of a tax position taken or expected to be taken in a tax return. FASB ASC 740 also provides guidance on derecognition, classification, interest and penalties, accounting for interim periods, disclosure, and implementation. The scope of FASB ASC 740 includes domestic and foreign entities preparing financial statements in accordance with U.S. generally accepted accounting principles. FASB ASC 740 also provides guidance on how an entity should determine whether a tax position is effectively settled for the purpose of recognizing previously unrecognized tax benefits. It uses the terms *effectively settled* and *settlement* in the context of income taxes.

6.07 FASB ASC 740-10-15-2AA clarifies that the sections of FASB ASC 740-10 relating to accounting for uncertain tax positions are applicable to all entities, including tax-exempt not-for-profit entities, pass-through entities, and entities that are taxed in a manner similar to pass-through entities such as real estate investment trusts and registered investment companies. *Tax position*, as defined by the FASB ASC glossary, is a position in a previously filed tax return or a position expected to be taken in a future tax return that is reflected in measuring current or deferred income tax assets and liabilities for interim or annual periods. A tax position can result in a permanent reduction of income taxes payable, a deferral of income taxes otherwise currently payable to future years, or a change in the expected realizability of deferred tax assets. The term tax position also encompasses, but is not limited to, the following:

- A decision not to file a tax return
- An allocation or a shift of income between jurisdictions
- The characterization of income or a decision to exclude reporting taxable income in a tax return
- A decision to classify a transaction, an entity, or other position in a tax return as tax exempt
- An entity's status, including its status as a pass-through entity or a tax-exempt not-for-profit entity

6.08 FASB ASC 740-10-50-15(c)–(e) discusses required disclosures by all entities related to unrecognized tax benefits. At the end of each annual reporting period, an entity is required to disclose the total amounts of interest and penalties recognized in both the statement of operations and statement of financial position; for positions for which it is reasonably possible that the total amounts of unrecognized tax benefits will significantly increase or decrease within 12 months of the reporting date, the nature of the uncertainty, the nature of the event that could occur in the next 12 months that would cause the change, and an estimate of the range of the reasonably possible change or a statement that an estimate of the range cannot be made; and a description of tax years that remain subject to examination by major tax jurisdictions.

6.09   "Pending Content" in FASB ASC 740-10-45 discusses presentation requirements for all entities related to unrecognized tax benefits. With the exception certain specific circumstances, an unrecognized tax benefit, or a portion of an unrecognized tax benefit, should be presented in the financial statements as a reduction to a deferred tax asset for a net operating loss carryforward, a similar tax loss, or a tax credit carryforward. An exception to this presentation is described in "Pending Content" in FASB ASC 740-10-45-10B, which states

> to the extent a net operating loss carryforward, a similar tax loss, or a tax credit carryforward is not available at the reporting date under the tax law of the applicable jurisdiction to settle any additional income taxes that would result from the disallowance of a tax position or the tax law of the applicable jurisdiction does not require the entity to use, and the entity does not intend to use, the deferred tax asset for such purpose, the unrecognized tax benefit shall be presented in the financial statements as a liability and shall not be combined with deferred tax assets.

6.10   As explained in FASB ASC 740-10-50-15A, in addition to the nonpublic entities' disclosure requirements discussed in FASB ASC 740-10-50, public entities should disclose a tabular reconciliation of the total amounts of unrecognized tax benefits at the beginning and end of each period and the total amount of unrecognized tax benefits that, if recognized, would affect the effective tax rate.

6.11   Example 30 in FASB ASC 740-10-55-217 gives sample disclosures relating to uncertainty in income taxes. Further, paragraphs 223–229 of FASB ASC 740-10-55 include examples of defining a tax position, attributing income taxes to the entity or its owners, and reporting tax positions for a group of related entities. Per FASB ASC 740-10-50-16, a public entity that is not subject to income taxes because its income is taxed directly to its owners should disclose that fact and the net difference between the tax bases and the reported amounts of the entity's assets and liabilities.

6.12   On December 22, 2006, the staff of the SEC's Division of Investment Management issued a letter to the Investment Company Institute on the implementation of accounting for uncertainty in income taxes by registered investment companies. In that letter, the staff

- expressed its belief that the guidance "places [no] limits on the type of evidence that an enterprise can look to in making its determination of the technical merits of a tax position" and that a registered investment company may consider "less formal forms of guidance from [a] taxing authority," weighing "all available forms of evidence based on their persuasiveness."
- observed that "the administrative practices and precedents of [a] taxing authority should be considered in fund's analysis"

regarding whether a tax position meets the recognition threshold, including any practice, to the extent that such exists, of addressing industry taxation issues on a prospective basis.

Federal Income Tax Provisions Affecting Investment Accounts

6.13   In establishing investment policies, companies intending to qualify as RICs under IRC Subchapter M must comply with the requirements of Subchapter M relating to diversification of assets, sources of income and realized gains, and similar matters. Those requirements are described later in this chapter.

Foreign Withholding Taxes

6.14   As stated in FASB ASC 946-830-45-34, whenever tax is withheld from investment income at the source, the amounts withheld that are not reclaimable should be accrued, along with the related income on each income recognition date if the tax rate is fixed and known. If the tax withheld is reclaimable from the local tax authorities, it should be recorded as a receivable, not an expense. When the investment income is received net of the tax withheld, a separate realized foreign currency gain or loss should be computed on the gross income receivable and accrued tax expense. If the tax rate is not known or estimable, such expense or receivable should be recorded on the date that the net amount is received; accordingly, there would be no foreign currency gain or loss. However, if a receivable is recorded, there may be a foreign currency gain or loss through the date that such receivable is collected.

Financial Statement Presentation

6.15   FASB ASC 946-225-45-4 explains that income tax expense should be presented by investment companies under the separate income categories (such as investment income or realized and unrealized gains) to which it applies. In addition, taxes in certain foreign jurisdictions may be based on the net investment income and realized gains of the fund within that jurisdiction; the guidance in FASB ASC 740 is applicable to such taxes. According to FASB ASC 946-225-45-3(h), other taxes, such as foreign withholding taxes, should be deducted from the relevant income item and disclosed parenthetically or shown as a separate contraitem in the "Income" section. FASB ASC 946-225-45-6(b)(1) states that any provision for deferred taxes should be presented separately.

Diversification of Assets

6.16   As noted in paragraph 8.55–.56 of this guide, the diversification requirements appearing in an investment company's prospectus and specified in various SEC rules and interpretations may differ from those in IRC Subchapter M, discussed later in this chapter.

RICs

General Discussion of the Taxation of RICs

6.17   This chapter discusses, in general terms, the requirements for qualification and taxation as a RIC under IRC Subchapter M, as well as the excise tax on certain undistributed taxable income and certain other federal tax matters affecting investment companies. (Although many states and municipalities have adopted provisions similar to Subchapter M, a discussion of state and local taxes is beyond the scope of this chapter, as is discussion of the tax aspects of investment companies formed as partnerships.) In designing the detailed audit plan, the auditor should refer to the latest IRC, Treasury regulations, and IRS rulings and applicable state laws to be certain that all requirements for qualification have been covered and to determine the need for accruing income, excise, or other taxes.

Taxation of a RIC's Taxable Income and Net Capital Gains

6.18　An investment company organized as a corporation or as a business trust is taxable as a corporation and, as such, subject to federal income taxes and certain state and local taxes the same as any other domestic corporation. However, if the investment company is registered under the Investment Company Act of 1940 (the 1940 Act), it may elect to qualify under the IRC for special federal income tax treatment as a RIC, which allows it to deduct dividends paid to shareholders and pass through tax-favored income, such as capital gains and tax-exempt income (see the "Taxation of Shareholder Distributions" section beginning at paragraph 6.25). A *dividend*, for this purpose, is defined as a distribution of current or accumulated earnings and profits (E&P). Thus, an investment company distributing all its taxable income to its shareholders would have no taxable income and, therefore, no tax liability. If an investment company fails to qualify as a RIC, it will be taxed as a regular corporation. The deduction for dividends paid by the investment company will not be available, and all distributions out of E&P will be taxed as ordinary income to shareholders. The effects of the failure to qualify may extend beyond the income tax consequences because net asset values may be improperly stated in such situations.

6.19　Certain investment companies are organized as series funds. Additionally, shareholders of each respective portfolio may have separate rights with respect to each portfolio's net assets. A series fund includes several portfolios, each of which may have a different investment objective. Series funds are required to treat each portfolio as a separate corporation for tax purposes (IRC Section 851(g)).

6.20　To determine if a RIC has a federal income tax liability, the RIC's investment company taxable income and net capital gain must be computed separately. Investment company taxable income is regular taxable income modified by certain adjustments. The following are among those adjustments:

- Net capital gain (that is, net long term capital gain for the taxable year in excess of any net short term capital loss for such year) is excluded (IRC Section 852(b)(2)(A)).
- Net operating losses are not allowed as a deduction (IRC Section 852(b)(2)(B)).
- The corporate deduction for dividends received is not allowed (IRC Section 852(b)(2)(C)).
- The deduction for dividends paid is allowed (as computed without regard to capital gain dividends and exempt-interest dividends) (IRC Section 852(b)(2)(D)).
- The tax imposed by subsections (d)(2) and (i) of IRC Section 851 for failures to satisfy the gross income or assets tests, or both, for the taxable year is deducted (IRC Section 852(b)(2)(G)).

6.21   Note that although investment company taxable income excludes net capital gain, it includes net short term capital gain in excess of net long term capital loss. Subsequent to the enactment of the Regulated Investment Company Act of 2010, a capital loss (called a postenactment capital loss), incurred by a RIC in taxable years beginning after December 22, 2010, retains its character as short term or long term, and can be carried forward without expiration (IRC Section 1212(a)(3)). Net capital losses incurred by a RIC in taxable years beginning before December 23, 2010 (preenactment capital losses), continue to be treated as short term and, to the extent not used, expire eight taxable years after the taxable year of their origination. Preenactment capital losses may not be used to offset capital gains until all postenactment capital losses have been utilized. As a result, some capital loss carryovers incurred by a RIC in preenactment years that would have been utilized under prior law may expire unused. A RIC is prohibited from claiming a net operating loss deduction (IRC Section 852(b)(2)(B)). Because net short term capital gains are considered ordinary income for IRC purposes, a net investment loss incurred in the same taxable year may be offset against any net short term capital gains. However, if the net investment loss exceeds net short term gains, such net in-vestment loss may not be carried forward and deducted as a net operating loss if the investment company elects to be a RIC in succeeding taxable years.

6.22   In order for a RIC to eliminate the imposition of any entity-level federal income tax liability, it must distribute ordinary dividends to shareholders sufficient to offset investment company taxable income and capital gain dividends sufficient to offset net capital gain.

6.23   The RIC's investment company taxable income may be reduced to zero by dividends other than capital gain dividends and exempt-interest dividends paid to shareholders from a RIC's E&P. The RIC's net capital gain may be offset by a capital gain dividend paid by the RIC to its shareholders and reported as a capital gain dividend in written statements furnished to its shareholders (IRC Section 852(b)(3)(C)). The computation of a RIC's required annual distributions to shareholders is discussed in further detail in the "Distribution Test" section beginning at paragraph 6.64.

6.24   An investment company that does not meet all the RIC qualification requirements in a taxable year will be taxed as a regular corporation for that year and must comply with provisions in a subsequent year if it elects to be taxed as a RIC, as follows:

  a. When a regular corporation makes a qualified election to be subject to tax as a RIC, the RIC generally will be subject to entity-level tax on the net built-in gain in the corporation's assets if the RIC recognizes such gain within 10 years.[3] Gain recognition applies even if the RIC distributes the recognized, built-in gain to investors. These consequences to the RIC can be avoided, however, if the regular corporation makes a "deemed sale election" with respect to its assets which become property of the RIC. Under the deemed sale election, the regular corporation recognizes gain or loss as if its assets were sold to an unrelated party at fair market value at the end of the last day of the corporation's last taxable year before the

---

[3] Treasury Regulations 1.337(d)-7. These regulations govern any "conversion transaction," which means the qualification of a C corporation as a RIC or REIT or the transfer of property owned by a C corporation to a RIC or REIT. The regulations generally apply to conversion transactions that occur on or after January 2, 2002.

first taxable year in which it qualifies to be taxed as a RIC (Treasury Regulations 1.337(d)-7(c)). This general rule is designed to prevent regular corporations with appreciated assets from qualifying as a RIC, selling the assets at a gain, and eliminating corporate-level tax by distributing all income to the shareholders of the RIC.

b. From the general rule discussed previously, it might appear that a RIC disqualified in one taxable year but qualifying the next year would owe a corporate-level tax on the net built-in gain of its assets, if they were recognized within 10 years. However, an exception to the general rule is provided stating that a previously qualifying RIC that fails to meet the requirements of the RIC tax provisions for a period not exceeding two taxable years and then requalifies as a RIC will not be subject to the otherwise applicable gain recognition rules (Treasury Regulations 1.337(d)-7(d)(2)).

c. A corporation that accumulates E&P in a year in which it is not taxed as a RIC is required to distribute such E&P before the end of its RIC year if it wishes to be taxed as a RIC in such year (IRC Section 852(a)(2) and Treasury Regulation 1.852-12).

Taxation of Shareholder Distributions

6.25 A *dividend* is a distribution from current year E&P or E&P accumulated in prior taxable years. E&P is generally determined by adjusting taxable income for items that constitute economic income or deductions (Treasury Regulation 1.312-6). Under Subchapter M, the amount of a RIC's E&P is generally adjusted so that the full amount of a RIC's income otherwise subject to corporate taxation is taxable to shareholders if currently distributed (IRC Sections 561 and 852(c)). Examples of these adjustments include tax-exempt income, amortization of organization costs, and federal income taxes. Expenses and premium amortization allocated to tax-exempt income and net capital losses reduce current E&P, to the extent they offset capital gains. E&P are not reduced for any capital loss carryforwards (IRC Section 852(c), as amended by Section205, *Amendments relating to Regulated Investment Company Modernization Act of 2010*, of the Tax Increase and Prevention Act of 2014).

6.26 Distributions from a RIC are reported to shareholders on Form 1099-DIV as

a. ordinary dividends, to the extent of the RIC's current or accumulated E&P (IRC Sections 301(c)(1) and 316);

b. nontaxable distributions (that is, return of capital), to the extent that distributions paid within a RIC's taxable year exceed the RIC's current and accumulated E&P (IRC Section 301(c)(2));

c. long term capital gains (IRC Section 301(c)(3));

d. qualified dividends;

e. IRC Section 1202 gains on certain small business stock;

f. IRC Section 1250 depreciation recapture, generally from dividends received by the RIC from real estate investment trusts;

g. collectibles gains, generally from derivatives based on precious metals;

h. foreign tax credits; and

i. exempt-interest dividends.

6.27 If a RIC has made distributions during a taxable year in excess of its current and accumulated E&P, it is required to file Form 5452 with its Form 1120-RIC and report the taxable and nontaxable components of such distributions to its shareholders on Form 1099-DIV. A RIC is also required to file a Form 8937 reporting any return of capital occurring during or after 2012 as an "organizational action" affecting shareholder basis (IRC Section 6045B). For taxable years beginning after December 22, 2010, E&P is allocated first to distributions paid during the portion of the taxable year prior to December 31 (IRC Section 316(b)(4)). For prior years, IRC and Treasury regulations require the pro rata allocation of E&P among all distributions during the taxable year.

6.28 A dividend from investment company taxable income may qualify in whole or part for the dividends-received deduction available to corporate shareholders (IRC Sections 854(b) and 243).

6.29 A dividend does not qualify for the dividends-received deduction if the stock on which the dividend was paid is held for less than 46 days during a 91-day period that begins 45 days before the stock becomes ex-dividend with respect to the dividend (or, for certain preferred stock, less than 91 days during a 181-day period that begins 90 days before the stock becomes ex-dividend). The holding period generally is suspended for this purpose during any time that the RIC has diminished its risk of loss (for example, through hedging) (IRC Section 246(c)).

6.30 The portion of the dividend qualifying for the dividends-received deduction must be reported in a written statement furnished to its shareholders for the RIC's tax year in which the dividend was paid (IRC Sections 854(b)(1)).

6.31 If greater than 50 percent of the fair market value of the RIC's gross assets comprises, at the end of the taxable year, stock or securities of foreign corporations or, at the close of each quarter of a taxable year, at least 50 percent of the fair market value of the RIC's gross assets comprises shares of other RICs, the RIC may elect to pass through to its shareholders the foreign source character of certain investment income earned, as well as foreign income taxes that the RIC paid during such taxable year in respect to such foreign source income (IRC Sections 853(a)-(b) and 852(g)). A RIC that makes this election is not entitled to a tax deduction for the expense or a foreign tax credit in respect to such foreign taxes. However, the RIC is entitled to treat such foreign income taxes passed through to its shareholders as part of the RIC's dividends paid deduction. Qualified funds of funds can also pass through foreign tax credits reported to them from underlying funds (IRC Section 852(g)).

6.32 Shareholders must report as taxable income the gross income received from the RIC (increased by any foreign income taxes deemed passed through by the RIC) and are entitled to either a foreign tax credit (subject to certain limitations) or a deduction (subject to other limitations) for their allowable share of foreign taxes paid by the RIC and passed through to them (IRC Section 853(b)(2)). To claim or pass through a foreign tax credit, a RIC must hold the stock for 16 days within the 31-day period beginning 15 days before the ex-dividend date (45 days within the 91-day period for certain preferred stock) (IRC Section 901(k)). The holding period generally is suspended for this purpose during any time that the RIC has diminished its risk of loss (for example, through hedging). Foreign taxes paid by a RIC that do not qualify for the foreign tax credit do not increase the taxable income reported to the shareholders (that is, the RIC is allowed to deduct such taxes in computing its investment company taxable income) (IRC Section 853(e)).

6.33 The amount of foreign source income and foreign taxes must be reported by a RIC in a written statement furnished to shareholders for the RIC's tax year in which the dividend was paid (IRC Section 853(c)).

6.34 A RIC that, at the end of each quarter of its taxable year, has at least 50 percent of its assets comprising federally tax-exempt obligations or shares of other RICs is eligible to distribute exempt-interest dividends to its shareholders. Exempt-interest dividends received by a shareholder are treated as federally tax-exempt income (IRC Sections 852(b)(5) and 852(g)).

6.35 The maximum amount reported as exempt-interest dividends may not exceed the net tax-exempt interest earned by a RIC eligible to distribute exempt-interest dividends. *Net tax-exempt interest* is defined as tax-exempt interest income reduced for the amortization of premium on tax-exempt bonds and also for expenses attributable to the production of its tax-exempt interest income.

6.36 Generally, an acceptable basis for allocation of a RIC's expenses allocable to tax-exempt income is the ratio of gross tax-exempt income to gross investment income (tax exempt plus taxable), excluding capital gain net income (IRC Sections 265(a)(3) and 1222(9)). The required amortization of premium on tax-exempt bonds must be allocated to the tax-exempt income (IRC Section 171(a)(2)).

6.37 Net gain or loss realized on the sale of tax-exempt securities is treated as capital gain or loss, except to the extent of any gain treated as market discount, which is taxable as ordinary income.

6.38 An exempt-interest dividend must be reported by a RIC in a written statement furnished to a shareholder for the RIC's tax year in which the dividend was paid (IRC Section 852(b)(5)(A)). However, if the aggregate reported amount of a RIC's exempt-interest dividends in respect of the RIC's taxable year exceeds the RIC's net tax-exempt income for such taxable year, the RIC would be eligible to treat as an exempt-interest dividend for such taxable year only an amount equal to the RIC's net tax-exempt income for such taxable year (IRC Section 852(b)(5)(A)(ii)).

6.39 A capital gain dividend is any dividend reported as such by a RIC in a written statement furnished to shareholders (IRC Section 852(b)(3)(C)). A capital gain dividend distributed by a RIC to a shareholder is generally characterized as long term capital gain by the shareholder, regardless of the actual holding period of the shareholder's shares in such RIC (IRC Section 852(b)(3)(B)).

6.40 A RIC may retain all or any portion of its net capital gain and elect to have shareholders include the gain in their taxable income as though a capital gain dividend had been paid. In such a case, the RIC will pay corporate income tax (currently 35 percent) on the undistributed net capital gain within 30 days of its year-end and notify shareholders within 60 days of the RIC's tax year-end of the allocable retained capital gain and related income tax paid (IRC Sections 852(b)(3)(D)(i) and (iv)). The gain is treated as long term capital gain, and the tax is treated as a tax payment by the shareholders (IRC Section 852(b)(3)(D)(ii)). Each shareholder is entitled to increase the basis of his or her shares by a percentage (currently 65 percent) of the deemed distribution

(IRC Section 852(b)(3)(D)(iii)). Notification must be provided to shareholders on Form 2439 (Treasury Regulation 1.852-9).

6.41 A RIC may also retain all or any portion of the net capital gain and pay the income tax thereon without notifying shareholders. In this situation, the shareholders will not include the capital gain as income nor will they receive a credit for the taxes paid by the RIC or an adjustment to the basis of their shares held.

6.42 A noncorporate taxpayer may generally exclude from taxable income 50 percent of capital gains resulting from the sale of certain qualified small business stock held for more than 5 years (IRC Section 1202). Such gains, however, are taxed (before exclusion) at a rate of 28 percent. To qualify for this exclusion, the stock must be acquired directly by the taxpayer (or indirectly, for example, through a RIC) at its original issuance after August 10, 1993; must be held by the RIC for more than 5 years; and the noncorporate taxpayer must hold shares of the RIC on the date that the RIC acquired the qualified small business stock and at all times thereafter until disposition of the stock by the RIC (IRC Section 1202(g)). For stock acquired after February 17, 2009, and on or before September 27, 2010, the exclusion is increased to 75 percent (IRC Section 1202(a)(3)). For stock acquired after September 27, 2010, and before January 1, 2015, the exclusion is 100 percent (IRC Section 1202(a)(4)).

6.43 Certain types of ordinary dividends received by a RIC may be reported as *qualified dividend income* (QDI) and are eligible for individual taxation at capital gains rates (IRC Section 1(h)(11)). The American Taxpayer Relief Act of 2012 made the treatment permanent. In order for dividends received by a RIC to be considered QDI, a RIC must hold the stock for 61 days within a 121 day period beginning 60 days before the ex-dividend date (91 days within a 181 day period for certain preferred stock). The holding period generally is suspended for this purpose during any time that the RIC has diminished its risk of loss (for example, through hedging) (IRC Section 1(h)(11)(B)).

Excess Reported Amounts

6.44 For RICs with taxable years other than the calendar year, the RIC's net capital gain is allocated first to distributions reported to shareholders as capital gain dividends during the portion of the taxable year ending on December 31, so that any excess reported amounts are allocated first to amounts reported as capital gain distributions after December 31 (IRC Section 852(b)(3)(C)(iii)(II)). Similar rules apply to other pass-through items, such as tax-exempt interest (IRC Section 852(b)(5)(A)(iii)(II)), and qualified interest income[4] and short term capital gains distributed to non-U.S. shareholders.[5] For taxable years of a RIC beginning on or before December 22, 2010, any excess was allocated pro rata among all distributions designated as capital gain during the taxable year.

Qualification Tests

6.45 *Requirements for qualification.* To qualify as a RIC for tax purposes, an investment company must meet all of the following requirements:

---

[4] IRC Section 871(k)(1)(C)(iii)(II). A qualified interest dividend may not be paid with respect to any taxable year of a RIC beginning after December 31, 2014.

[5] IRC Section 871(k)(2)(C)(iii)(II). A short-term capital gain dividend may not be paid with respect to any taxable years of a RIC beginning after December 31, 2014.

 a. Be a domestic corporation (or a business trust taxable as a corporation) registered for the entire taxable year under the 1940 Act (IRC Section 851(a)). An investment company is registered upon filing its notification of registration on Form N-8A.[6] An issuer must first file a notification of registration with the SEC on Form N-8A in order to register as an investment company. After filing the notification of registration, a registration statement must be filed on the appropriate form within 3 months. Common forms used are Form N-1A (Registration form for mutual funds) and Form N-2 (Registration for closed end funds). A comprehensive list of forms can be obtained on the SEC's website.

 b. Elect, if it has not previously done so, to be taxed as a RIC (IRC Section 851(b)(1)). To elect RIC status, an investment company prepares and timely files a federal income tax return computing taxable income in accordance with the provisions of Subchapter M. Once elected, the company's status is unchanged as long as the company continues to qualify as a RIC under the IRC.

 c. Meet the 90 percent gross income test (see paragraphs 6.48–.52).

 d. Meet certain requirements concerning diversification of its total assets at the end of each quarter of the taxable year (see paragraphs 6.53–.57).

6.46 In order for its distributions to be used to offset taxable income, the RIC must distribute at least 90 percent of its investment company taxable income (which includes net short term capital gains, if any) and net tax-exempt income for the taxable year (see the "Distribution Test" section beginning at paragraph 6.64).

6.47 A RIC should keep a record of the computations supporting qualification under the foregoing tests.

6.48 *90 percent gross income test.* A RIC must derive at least 90 percent of its gross income from (*a*) dividends; interest (including tax-exempt interest income); payments with respect to securities loans; and gains (without including losses) from the sale or other disposition of stocks, securities, or foreign currencies or (*b*) other income (including but not limited to gains from options, futures, or forward contracts) derived with respect to the RIC's investing in such stock, securities, or currencies and net income from an interest in a qualified publicly traded partnership (PTP) (IRC Section 851(b)(2)).

6.49 Although the IRS may issue regulations that would exclude from qualifying income foreign currency gains that are not directly related to the RIC's principal business of investing in stock or securities (or options and futures with respect to stock or securities), no such guidance has been issued.

6.50 For a partnership that is not a qualified publicly traded partnership, gross income (distinguished from what is generally reported on the partner's Form K-1 as taxable income or from cash distributions received by the partner during the year) is treated by the RIC in the same manner as if it were realized directly by the RIC for purposes of the 90 percent gross income test (IRC Section 851(b)). Thus, gross income earned by a partnership other than

---

[6] Each series of a series fund will be considered a registrant for this purpose.

income described in paragraph 6.48 would be treated by a RIC partner of such partnership as nonqualifying income.

6.51   Other items of gross income, such as redemption fees, expense reimbursements, and lawsuit settlements, may require individual consideration to determine their tax status and effect on the 90 percent gross income test. The IRS has ruled that if in the normal course of its business a RIC receives a reimbursement of investment advisory fees that was not the result of a transaction entered into to artificially inflate the RIC's qualifying gross income, such reimbursement may be considered qualifying income for purposes of the 90 percent test (Revenue Ruling 92-56).

6.52   An investment company that fails to meet the 90 percent gross income test would not lose its RIC status if such failure is due to reasonable cause, not willful neglect, and if the investment company pays a deductible tax equal to the excess of its nonqualifying gross income over 1/9 of the qualifying gross income (IRC Sections 851(i) and 852(b)(2)(G)).

6.53   *50 percent test.* At the end of each quarter of a RIC's taxable year, at least 50 percent of the fair market value of the RIC's total assets must be represented by cash and cash items (including receivables), U.S. government securities, securities of other RICs, and other securities. For this purpose, other securities do not include investments in the securities of any 1 issuer if they represent more than 5 percent of the fair market value of the investment company's total assets or more than 10 percent of the issuer's outstanding voting securities (except as provided in IRC Section 851[e]) (IRC Section 851(b)(3)(A)).

6.54   *25 percent test.* At the end of each quarter of a RIC's taxable year, not more than 25 percent of the RIC's total assets may comprise the securities of any 1 issuer, except for the securities of the U.S. government or other RICs. This requirement also prohibits investing more than 25 percent of the RIC's total assets in 2 or more issuers that are controlled by the RIC and engaged in the same (or similar) or related trades or businesses (IRC Section 851(b)(3)(B)). For that purpose, the RIC controls the issuers if it has 20 percent or more of the combined voting power of each corporation (IRC Section 851(c)(2)). This requirement also prohibits investing more than 25 percent of the RIC's total assets in 1 or more qualified PTPs, as defined in IRC Section 851(h) (IRC Section 851(b)(3)(B)).

6.55   For purposes of the diversification tests, the issuer of an option or futures contract is the corporation or government that issued the underlying security (Revenue Ruling 83-69, 1983-1 C.B. 126). For index instruments, the IRS has concluded in Private Letter Rulings and General Counsel Memoranda that the issuers of an option on a stock index are the issuers of the stocks or securities underlying the index, in proportion to the weighting of the stocks or securities in the computation of the index, regardless of whether the index is broad based or narrow based. The IRS has not issued "published" or "binding" guidance on the valuation of derivative instruments for purposes of this test.

6.56   A RIC that meets the asset diversification requirements at the end of the first taxable quarter of its existence will not lose its status as a RIC if it fails to satisfy those requirements in a later taxable quarter, provided that the noncompliance is due neither in whole nor in part to the acquisition of a security or other property. If a RIC fails to meet the diversification requirements because of an acquisition, it may reestablish its status for such taxable quarter end by eliminating the discrepancy between the diversification requirements and its holdings within 30 days after the end of the quarter using the securities' values as of the end of the quarter (IRC Section 851(d)(1)). A RIC that fails to meet the diversification requirements will not be disqualified

    a. if the failure is due to the ownership of assets with a value less than $10 million and less than 1 percent of total assets of the RIC at the end of the quarter, and the RIC disposes of assets or otherwise meets the diversification requirements within 6 months after the quarter in which the failure is identified; or

    b. if the failure is due to reasonable cause, not willful neglect, and the RIC notifies the IRS; files a list of the assets that caused the failure; pays a deductible tax equal to the greater of $50,000 or the highest corporate tax rate times the taxable income attributable to the identified assets during the period of failure; and disposes of the identified assets or otherwise complies with the diversification requirements within 6 months after the quarter in which the failure is identified or such other time period as specified in regulations (IRC Sections 851(d)(2) and 852(b)(2)(G)).

6.57   Special rules apply to an investment company that qualifies as a venture capital investment company (IRC Section 851(e)).

Variable Contracts

6.58   In addition to the diversification requirements applicable to all RICs (discussed in the previous paragraphs), special quarterly asset diversification tests are to be met by RICs used as investment vehicles for variable annuity, endowment, and life insurance contracts. The fund must meet these diversification requirements on a calendar-year basis without regard to the fund's fiscal year (Treasury Regulation 1.817-5(c)(1)). In general, a segregated asset account will be considered adequately diversified if all of the following criteria from Treasury Regulation 1.817-5(b) are met:

    a. No more than 55 percent of total assets are represented by any 1 investment

    b. No more than 70 percent of total assets are represented by any 2 investments

    c. No more than 80 percent of total assets are represented by any 3 investments

    d. No more than 90 percent of total assets are represented by any 4 investments

In general, for a separate account to be permitted to look through to the assets of a RIC, all the interests in the RIC must be held by one or more insurance company separate accounts or other permissible entities identified in the Treasury regulations and other administrative guidance promulgated under IRC Section 817 (Treasury Regulation 1.817-5(f)(3) and Revenue Ruling 2007-58, 2007-2 C.B. 562).

6.59   All securities of the same issuer, all interests in the same real property project, and all interests in the same commodity are each treated as a single investment. Each governmental agency or instrumentality is treated as a separate issuer (Treasury Regulation 1.817-5(b)(1)(ii)).

6.60   The IRS regulations provide a safe harbor for segregated asset accounts. If the segregated asset account meets the safe harbor test, it will be deemed as being diversified. The safe harbor test is met if a segregated asset account meets the RIC diversification tests, and the segregated asset account has no more than 55 percent of the value of its total assets invested in cash, cash items, government securities, and securities of other RICs (IRC Section 817(h)(2)).

6.61 Special rules apply to a segregated asset account with respect to variable life insurance contracts (Treasury Regulation 1.817-5(b)(3)).

6.62 If the diversification test is not met on the last day of a particular quarter, the separate account is allowed a 30 day grace period after such quarter-end to meet the diversification requirements (Treasury Regulation 1.817-5(d)). An exception is also available for certain separate accounts that are in the start-up mode, whereby accounts are considered diversified for the first year of their existence (Treasury Regulation 1.817-5(c)(2)).

6.63 Failure of the underlying segregated asset accounts (separate accounts) to qualify will adversely affect the tax treatment of the variable annuity, endowment, or life insurance contracts (Treasury Regulation 1.817-5(a)(2)). It will not directly affect the tax status of the RIC. However, the auditor should consider the account's compliance with the asset diversification requirements and, if the diversification test is not passed, the effect on financial statement disclosure.

Distribution Test

6.64 *90 percent distribution test.* A RIC must annually pay dividends (exclusive of capital gain dividends) equal to the sum of 90 percent of investment company taxable income and 90 percent of net tax-exempt income for the year. In addition, a corporation that has E&P from non-RIC years must distribute such E&P by the end of its first RIC year (IRC Section 852(a)(12)).

6.65 For purposes of this distribution test, a RIC may elect to treat as paid on the last day of the fiscal year all or part of any dividends declared after the end of its taxable year. Such dividends must be declared on or before the later of the 15th day of the 9th month following the close of the taxable year or the extended due date of the return for the taxable year. The dividends must be paid within 12 months after the end of the taxable year and not later than the first dividend payment of the same type of dividend after such declaration (IRC Section 855(a)).

6.66 If a RIC meets all the qualification tests and the 90 percent distribution test but does not distribute all its investment company taxable income, it must pay corporate income taxes on the undistributed portion (IRC Sections 852(b)(1) and 852(b)(3)(A)). Similarly, if the company fails to distribute its net capital gains it is subject to tax on any such undistributed gains.

6.67 A nondeductible excise tax on undistributed income is imposed on a RIC to the extent that the RIC does not satisfy certain distribution requirements for a calendar year (see the "Excise Tax on Undistributed Income" section beginning at paragraph 6.83).

6.68 *Preferential dividends.* For nonpublicly offered RICs, a dividends paid deduction is allowed only for distributions that are pro rata, with no preference regarding any share of stock compared with any other share of the same class of stock (IRC Section 562(c)). This rule has been repealed for RICs that are treated as publicly offered. A publicly offered RIC is any RIC, the shares of which are continuously offered pursuant to a public offering within the meaning of the Securities Act of 1933, regularly traded on an established securities market, or held by or for no fewer than 500 persons at all times during the taxable year (IRC Section 67(c)(2)(B)). For distributions subject to the preferential dividend rule, a RIC is considered to have only 1 class of stock if the only differences among the classes are expense allocations. However, certain class-specific expenses may be allocated to a particular class if the requirements of IRC Revenue Procedure 96-47 are met. Other expenses, such as advisory fees, must be allocated among all shares pro rata. IRC Revenue Procedure 99-40 provides guidance on waivers or reimbursements of expenses in a multiclass context.

6.69   A RIC must allocate the various kinds of dividends it pays (such as tax-exempt interest, net capital gains, or the dividends-received deduction) proportionately among the classes of stock outstanding if more than one class of stock exists (Revenue Ruling 89-81, 1989-1 C.B. 226).

6.70   *Distributions made after December 31.* For purposes of a dividend paid deduction for the RIC and income recognition for the shareholder, distributions declared in October, November, or December payable to shareholders of record in such months and actually paid during January of the following year must be treated as having been paid on December 31 of the previous year to the extent of E&P (IRC Section 852(b)(7)). This rule applies for both income and excise tax purposes.

6.71   A RIC may elect to treat as having been paid in the prior fiscal year (spillback or throwback) all or part of any dividends declared after the end of such taxable year (see paragraph 6.65). This election applies to regular dividends, capital gain dividends, and exempt-interest dividends. It affects only the RIC and does not change the year in which distributions are reported by the shareholders.

6.72   *Deficiency dividends.* A RIC may pay a deficiency dividend as a result of an increase in investment company taxable income, net capital gain, or a decrease in the deduction for dividends paid to protect its special status or avoid the imposition of entity-level federal income taxation (IRC Section 860(a)).

6.73   For taxable years beginning after December 22, 2010, a deficiency dividend is subject to an interest charge for the period from the due date of the return for the year of the deficiency dividend deduction to the filing of a claim for the deduction. For prior taxable years, a deficiency dividend is subject to both the interest charge and a penalty equal to the less of 100 percent of the interest charge or 50 percent of the deficiency dividend amount (IRC Section 860(c)).

6.74   *Equalization distributions.* An open-end investment company may use equalization accounting to prevent changes in the per share equity in its undistributed net income that may be caused by the continuous issuance and redemption of shares. Equalization for tax purposes differs substantially from book equalization because the calculation ignores the impact of share subscriptions by purchasing shareholders (for example, gross equalization credits). See also paragraph 4.30 of this guide.

6.75   If a RIC is not considered a personal holding company, the RIC would be permitted to claim a dividends-paid deduction for the E&P associated with the redemption of shares (gross equalization debits) (Revenue Ruling 55-416, 1955-1 C.B. 416). Shareholders generally treat the entire redemption distribution as sales proceeds (IRC Section 302(b)(5)).

6.76 The treatment of equalization debits as a component of a RIC's dividends-paid deduction is well established in the income tax rules (Treasury Regulation 1.562-1(b)(1)). However, the precise method of calculating the E&P attributable to the redeemed shares is not particularly clear. Management generally should consider the most recent IRS pronouncements if equalization debits are to be used.

6.77 Equalization debits used as dividends paid by a RIC may be used to satisfy the RIC's regular distribution requirements and, also, the excise tax distribution requirements.

6.78 *Capital gain dividends.* A RIC may defer all or a portion of any post-October capital loss or late-year ordinary loss in determining the amount of the RIC's capital gain dividends subject to reporting (IRC Sections 852(b)(3)(C) and (b)(8)).

6.79 *Elective deferral of late year losses.* A RIC may elect to defer any portion of a qualified late-year ordinary loss to the first day of the following taxable year (IRC Section 852(b)(8)). A qualified late year-loss is defined as any post-October capital loss, and any late-year ordinary loss.

6.80 A *post-October capital loss* is

a. any net capital loss attributable to the portion of the taxable year after October 31, or

b. if there is no such loss—

   i. any net long-term capital loss attributable to such portion of the taxable year, or

   ii. any net short-term capital loss attributable to such portion of the taxable year.

6.81 A *late-year ordinary loss* is the net ordinary loss from the sale or other disposition of capital assets for the portion of the taxable year after October 31 (that is, a "specified loss" under IRC Section 4982(e)(5)) and other ordinary income or loss for the portion of the taxable year after December 31 (IRC Sections 4982(e)(5)).

6.82 The elective deferral of late year losses does not apply if a RIC's taxable year-ends in December (IRC Section 852(b)(8)(G)(ii)). RICs with November and December year-ends who have made an election under 4982(e)(4) to use its fiscal year-end for computing capital gains and losses for excise tax purposes may not consider post-October capital losses or post-October specified losses in its calculation of its late year losses (IRC Section 852(b)(8)(G)(i)).

Excise Tax on Undistributed Income

6.83 *Introduction.* A nondeductible 4 percent entity-level excise tax on undistributed income is imposed on a RIC to the extent that the RIC does not satisfy certain distribution requirements for a calendar year (IRC Section 4982(a)) (as shown in the following paragraphs).

6.84 *Measurement periods.* To determine the excise tax, a RIC's ordinary income and capital gain net income are measured separately.

6.85   Ordinary income generally equals the RIC's investment company taxable income before the dividends paid deduction, determined using a calendar-year measurement period, excluding any gains or losses from the sale of capital assets. Ordinary gains or losses from the sale of capital assets after October 31 are generally treated as arising on January 1 of the following year (IRC Sections 4982(e)(1) and (e)(5)).

6.86   A RIC with a taxable year other than the calendar year may elect to treat a net ordinary loss for the portion of a taxable year ending on December 31 as arising on January 1 of the following calendar year for excise tax purposes (IRC Section 4982(e)(7)).

6.87   *Capital gain net income* is generally defined as the excess of gains over losses from sales or exchanges of capital assets measured using a one year period ending on October 31. This amount is reduced by net ordinary loss for the calendar year but not below net long term capital gain (IRC Section 4982(e)(2)).

6.88   RICs with fiscal years ending in November or December may elect to determine their capital gain net income as of the end of that fiscal year (IRC Section 4982(e)(4)).

6.89   *Calculation and elections.* No excise tax is imposed if the RIC makes sufficient distributions during each calendar year at least equal to the sum of the following:

     a.   98 percent of the ordinary income for the calendar year

     b.   98.2 percent of the capital gain net income for the one year period ending on October 31

     c.   100 percent of the ordinary income or capital gain net income of the prior year that was not previously distributed (IRC Section 4982(b))

6.90   Provided that a RIC distributes in the aggregate an amount at least equal to the sum of the amounts listed previously, the excise distribution requirement will be satisfied.

6.91   Any overdistribution (other than that attributable to a return of capital) from the prior year may be applied to the required distribution of the current year (IRC Section 4982(c)(2)).

6.92   If a RIC retains a portion of its taxable income or gains and pays income tax on that amount, the amount will be treated as distributed for excise tax purposes. A RIC may treat payments of estimated income tax as distributed for excise tax purposes. If a RIC distributes less than the minimum excise requirement, the RIC will be subject to a 4 percent excise tax on the difference between the RIC's minimum annual distribution requirement and the amount actually distributed by the RIC and include 100 percent of such amount on which the excise tax was imposed in the calculation of required distributions in the subsequent year (IRC Section 4982(c)(1)).

6.93   RIC feeder funds include their ratable amounts of all items of income, gain, and loss earned by a master fund organized as a partnership in which it invests for the excise tax periods described in paragraphs 6.87–.88.[7]

---

[7]   Revenue Ruling 94-40, 1994-1 C.B. 274 and Revenue Ruling 94-40A, 1994-1 C.B. 276,

This contrasts with a RIC maintaining an equity interest in a partnership outside the master-feeder structure. In the latter case, partnership income is generally included in the measurement period that includes the year-end of the partnership (Revenue Procedure 94-71, 1992-2 C.B. 810.

6.94 In determining a RIC's required excise tax distribution, foreign currency gains or losses from Section 988 transactions, the mark-to-market rules for Section 1256 contracts and Section 1296 passive foreign investment company (PFIC) stock, and other provisions which treat property as disposed of or by reference to a value on the last day of the taxable year are applied using October 31 as a year-end (or November 30 or December 31 if a fiscal year election is made).[8] Capital loss carryovers computed using the excise tax measuring period may be used to reduce capital gain net income for purposes of the excise tax.[9] Capital gain net income may be reduced (but not below net long term capital gain) by the RIC's ordinary loss for the calendar year (IRC Section 4982(e)(2)(B)).

6.95 *Exemption for certain RICs.* Excise tax rules do not apply to a RIC if, at all times during a calendar year, each shareholder was a qualified pension trust or segregated asset account of a life insurance company held in connection with variable contracts. Shares owned by the investment adviser attributable to the seed money it contributed (up to $250,000) are not counted for this purpose (IRC Section 4982(f)). RICs that are wholly owned by other exempt entities or other RICs that qualify for this exemption are also exempt from the excise tax rules.

Computation of Taxable Income and Gains

6.96 *Dividends and interest.* RICs record dividend income on the ex-dividend date for tax and accounting purposes (IRC Section 852(b)(9)).

6.97 If a dividend or other distribution received by a RIC represents a return of capital, the basis of the security from which such distribution is made is reduced for tax purposes. If the distribution exceeds the RIC's tax basis in the security, the excess is treated as capital gain (IRC Section 301(c)).

6.98 Interest and original issue discount (OID) are accrued on a daily basis for tax and accounting purposes. However, differences in book and tax accounting for interest and OID related to complex securities and troubled debt securities may exist.

6.99 *Sales of securities.* The basis of securities sold or otherwise disposed of may be either identified specifically or determined following a first in first out convention; average cost may not be used for tax purposes. Identification procedures are prescribed in regulations (Treasury Regulation 1.1012-1(c)(1)).

6.100 Under the IRC, a wash sale occurs on a sale of securities (including options) if the seller acquires or enters a contract or an option to acquire substantially identical securities within a period beginning 30 days before the date of a sale at a loss and ending 30 days after such date (61-day period) (IRC Section 1091). A loss resulting from such a transaction is deferred for tax purposes; the amount of the loss increases the tax basis of the new security purchased, and the holding period of the new position includes the holding

---

[8] Tax Reform Act of 1986; IRC Sections 4982(e)(5) and (6).

[9] Tax Reform Act of 1986.

period of the original position (IRC Sections 1091(b),(c), and (d) and 1223(3)). However, a gain on the same type of transaction is taxable, and the tax basis of the new security is not affected by the sale of the old security. Wash sale rules also apply to short-sale transactions such that the date that a short sale is made, rather than the date of close, is considered in determining whether a wash sale has occurred (Treasury Regulation 1.1091-1(g)).

6.101   *Commissions.* Commissions related to purchases or sales of securities are not deductible but are added to the basis of the securities or offset against the selling price (Treasury Regulation 1.263(a)-2(e)).

6.102   *Bond discount and premium.* Special, detailed rules prescribe the calculation and treatment of discount and premium on taxable and tax-exempt securities. Although a discussion of these rules is beyond the scope of this guide, the auditor should consider the application of these rules and how they affect the recognition and characterization of income and the deductibility of interest expense for tax purposes.

6.103   *Section 1256 contracts.* Certain financial instruments (Section 1256 contracts) held by a RIC may be subject to mark-to-market rules. Section 1256 contracts include any regulated futures contracts, foreign currency contract, nonequity option, dealer equity option, and dealer securities futures contract. Under these detailed rules, a RIC is treated for tax purposes as selling any Section 1256 contract held on the last day of its taxable year for its fair market value. Gain or loss on an actual or deemed disposition of a Section 1256 contract is treated as 40 percent short term capital gain or loss and 60 percent long term capital gain or loss, regardless of the holding period for the Section 1256 contract (IRC Section 1256). A detailed discussion of these rules is beyond the scope of this guide.

6.104   *Tax straddles.* The term *straddle* describes offsetting positions in personal property in which the fair market value of each position is expected to fluctuate inversely to that of the other. The term *position* means an interest (including a futures or forward contract or option) in personal property. An offsetting position occurs whenever risk of loss has been substantially diminished by holding one or more other positions (IRC Section 1092(c)).

6.105   The straddle rules provide that a loss from any position should be recognized only to the extent that such loss exceeds the unrecognized gain with respect to one or more offsetting positions or successor positions or positions that are offsetting to successor positions. Although a detailed discussion of the straddle rules is beyond the scope of this guide, it is important to note that funds that engage in hedging may have significant book versus tax differences in capital gains or losses as a result of the straddle rules.

6.106   *Stock issuance costs.* Stock issuance costs paid by an open-end investment company are deductible for tax purposes, except costs incurred during the initial stock offering period. This also applies to 12b-1 fees (Revenue Rulings 73-463 and 94-70). Stock distribution costs of a closed-end investment company that redeems shares quarterly (an "interval fund") are also deductible. Registration fees and expenses, including accounting procedures, are discussed in further detail in chapter 8, "Other Accounts and Considerations," of this guide.

6.107 *Stock redemption costs.* Only stock redemption costs of an open-end investment company, not a closed-end investment company, are deductible in computing investment company taxable income (IRC Section 162(k)(2)(B)).

6.108 *Limitations on tax benefits of losses.* A 50 percent change of ownership, taking into account only 5 percent shareholders, within a 3-year period, whether through a reorganization or in the ordinary course of business, may limit the tax benefits of losses realized or unrealized before the ownership change in periods after the ownership change. The annual limit on such losses is generally the net fair market value of the assets of the RIC that has experienced the ownership change, multiplied by a long term tax-exempt interest rate on the date of the ownership change (IRC Sections 381–384).

6.109 *Section 988 transactions.* Special rules apply to the treatment of foreign currency gains and losses attributable to Section 988 transactions. Foreign currency gains and losses from such transactions are characterized as U.S.-source ordinary income or loss (IRC Section 988(a)).

6.110 A foreign currency gain or loss will result from a Section 988 transaction, described as follows, denominated in a currency other than the RIC's functional currency (nonfunctional currency) or the fair value of which is determined by reference to nonfunctional currency:

a. Acquiring a debt instrument or becoming the obligor under a debt instrument

b. Accruing any item of expense or gross income or receipt that is to be paid or received at a later date

c. Entering or acquiring any forward contract, futures contract, option, or similar financial instrument

d. Disposing of any nonfunctional currency (IRC Section 988(c)(1))

6.111 The *functional currency* of a RIC is the currency of the economic environment in which the RIC's operations are predominantly conducted and the currency used in keeping its books and records. The functional currency of a RIC is generally the U.S. dollar. Certain single-country funds may have a functional currency other than the dollar (IRC Section 985(b) and example 2 of Treasury Regulation 1.985-1(f)).

6.112 Interest income or expense (including OID and discounts on certain short term obligations) on a nonfunctional currency debt instrument is determined in units of nonfunctional currency and translated into functional currency at the average exchange rate for the accrual period for accrual-basis RICs (Treasury Regulation 1.988-2(b)(1)).

6.113 Foreign currency gain realized on the disposition of a Section 988 debt security will be recognized for tax purposes and treated as U.S.-source ordinary income to the extent of the lesser of the foreign currency gain or the overall gain realized. Similarly, if a foreign currency loss is realized in a Section 988 transaction, it will be recognized for tax purposes and treated as a U.S.-source ordinary loss to the extent of the lesser of foreign currency loss or the overall loss realized (IRC Section 988(b)).

6.114 The acquisition of nonfunctional currency is treated as an acquisition of property (Treasury Regulation 1.988-1(a)) with a functional currency tax basis determined with reference to the spot contract exchange rate (spot rate). A spot contract is a contract to buy or sell nonfunctional currency on or before two business days following the date of the execution of the contract (Treasury Regulation 1.988-1(b)). The disposition or other use of nonfunctional currency will result in a Section 988 transaction if it is exchanged for another nonfunctional currency or functional currency (Treasury Regulation 1.988-2(a)).

6.115   Although Section 988 does not apply to transactions involving equity securities, any fluctuation in the exchange rate between the trade date and settlement date of either a purchase or sale of an equity security will result in a foreign currency gain or loss because the payment of the settlement liability constitutes a Section 988 transaction (Treasury Regulation 1.988-2(a)(2)).

6.116   The sale, closing, or settlement (including by taking or making delivery of currency) of any forward contract, futures contract, option, or other similar financial instrument denominated in (or the fair market value of which is determined by reference to) a nonfunctional currency results in ordinary income or loss, unless the contract is a futures or listed option contract traded on a qualified board or exchange (Treasury Regulation 1.988-2(a)). However, certain elections are available for these kinds of financial instruments that permit income or gain to be characterized differently. A detailed discussion of these rules is beyond the scope of this guide.

6.117   The IRS has provided special rules for certain Section 988(d) hedging transactions. Current regulations cover certain debt instruments, the currency risk (or a portion thereof) of which is entirely eliminated through a qualified hedge; executory contracts that are hedged; and hedges of trade to settlement date receivables and payables arising due to the sale or purchase of stocks or securities traded on an established securities market. These regulations provide integrated treatment for Section 988(d) hedging transactions. The IRS may also issue rulings to taxpayers regarding net hedging and anticipatory hedging methods (Treasury Regulation 1.988-5).

6.118   The timing of the recognition of gain or loss from contracts subject to both Sections 988 and 1256 is governed by the rules of Section 1256 (Treasury Regulation 1.988-2(d)). Such contracts, therefore, are marked to market at fiscal year-end. The character of such gain or loss may be either ordinary or capital, depending upon the kind of contract and whether certain elections are made.

6.119   *Passive foreign investment companies.* If a RIC owns equity securities of a corporation that is determined to be a PFIC for U.S. tax purposes, the RIC may be subject to an entity-level interest charge on excess distributions received from the PFIC, including gains realized on the sale or other disposition of such PFIC's shares. This is true even if the RIC has met its distribution requirements for the taxable year in which such excess distribution is deemed to have occurred.

6.120   The intent of the PFIC legislation was to prevent U.S. taxpayers from deferring taxes by acquiring equity securities of foreign investment companies, which are not subject to U.S. income tax and do not pay dividends currently. The PFIC rules effectively result in the recognition of taxable income by U.S. taxpayers that would be consistent with a situation as if the foreign company made a taxable distribution of all its income and appreciation each year.

6.121   A foreign corporation is a PFIC for a taxable year if 75 percent or more of the corporation's gross income is passive income or if 50 percent or more of the foreign corporation's assets produce (or are held for the production of) passive income (IRC Section 1297(a)). Passive income includes dividends, interest, royalties, rents, annuities, and net gains from the sale of securities; foreign currency; and certain commodity transactions that are not realized from an active trade or business engaged in by the PFIC (IRC Section 1297(b)). Examples of passive assets include cash (even if maintained for working capital requirements), stocks, bonds, and other securities held by the PFIC.

6.122 A RIC that owns a PFIC's equity securities may be able to avoid the imposition of a RIC-level interest charge if the RIC elects to treat the PFIC as a qualified electing fund (QEF) (IRC Section 1295). The RIC's share of the PFIC's ordinary income and capital gain each year are included as taxable income if the election is made (IRC Section 1293(a)). The earnings of the QEF must be determined based on U.S. tax principles making it difficult for many foreign corporations to provide the necessary information.

6.123 A RIC may alternatively elect to mark its PFIC shares to market at the close of the RIC's taxable year, as well as on October 31, and treat increases in unrealized appreciation (and decreases to the extent that increases have been included previously in taxable income) as part of the RIC's taxable income and required excise tax distribution (IRC Sections 1296 and 4982(e)(6)).

6.124 Both the QEF and mark-to-market elections may result in the RIC having to make distributions of income that it has not yet received.

6.125 A failure to make either of these elections may subject the RIC to an entity-level interest charge, in which case the recording of a tax liability generally should be considered.[10] Thus, it is important to determine that RICs holding foreign securities have policies and procedures to identify PFICs timely.

Offshore Funds

6.126 In recent years, the number of funds that are organized outside the United States (offshore funds) has increased substantially. This has occurred as U.S. fund advisers sought to globalize their customer base and as foreign institutions increased their investments in U.S. securities.

6.127 A myriad of U.S. and foreign tax issues are associated with offshore funds. These funds are typically organized in the form that is most suitable for the expected owners. Further, they are located in the jurisdiction that provides the most beneficial taxation and regulation of the entity, taxation of owners, and withholding tax treatment for income earned and distributions made.

6.128 Offshore funds are usually not subject to income taxes imposed by the country in which they are domiciled. However, they are generally subject to U.S. withholding tax on dividends from U.S. stock holdings. They are not generally subject to entity-level U.S. income taxation, provided that they are structured in such a way that they are not considered engaged in a U.S. trade or business for U.S. tax purposes (Treasury Regulation 1.864-2).

6.129 Consideration of both U.S. and local country tax and regulatory regimes is necessary for each offshore fund due to those regimes' often complex nature. Because an investment company must be organized in the United

[10] FASB *Accounting Standards Codification* 740-10-45-25 discusses income statement classification of interest and penalties.

States in order to qualify as a RIC, an offshore fund subject to U.S. tax cannot elect to be treated as a RIC.

6.130   Management of offshore funds generally should have tax policies and procedures addressing the taxation of the fund in the offshore country in which the fund is domiciled, the taxation of the fund's portfolio securities in the country in which the securities are taxed, and the taxation of fund shareholders in the countries in which they reside.

Small Business Investment Companies

6.131   Small business investment companies (SBICs) formed as corporations are generally subject to the corporate tax rules, unless they qualify and elect to be treated as RICs. SBICs also may be structured either as partnerships or disregarded as entities separate from their owners.

6.132   An SBIC organized as a corporation and operating under the Small Business Investment Act of 1958 (SBIA), receives special tax treatment. It is allowed a 100 percent deduction for dividends received that qualify for the dividend received deduction, unless it elects to be taxed as a RIC (IRC Section 243(a)(2)). In addition, the SBIC may be excluded from the definition of a *personal holding company* (IRC Section 542(c)(7)).

6.133   A shareholder in an SBIC operating under the SBIA may characterize a loss on its stock as an ordinary loss. In computing the net operating loss deduction, such a loss is treated as a loss from a trade or business (IRC Section 1242).

6.134   The tax rules permit special treatment for investors, including investment companies, in SBICs other than those licensed under the SBIA. Investors in small business corporations may qualify for ordinary loss treatment on the sale of their shares (IRC Section 1244). Investors in qualified small business stock may qualify for a 50 percent exclusion from gross income on the sale of small business stock (IRC Section 1202). Investors may also defer recognition of gain on sales of publicly traded securities by rolling over the proceeds into a specialized SBIC (IRC Section 1044).

Chapter 7

Financial Statements of Investment Companies

FASB Accounting Standards Update (ASU) No. 2015-07, *Fair Value Measurement (Topic 820): Disclosures for Investments in Certain Entities That Calculate Net Asset Value per Share (or Its Equivalent) (a consensus of the Emerging Issues Task Force)*, was issued in May 2015. The amendments are effective for public business entities for fiscal years beginning after December 15, 2015, and interim periods within those fiscal years. For all other entities, the amendments are effective for fiscal years beginning after December 15, 2016, and interim periods within those fiscal years. A reporting entity should apply the amendments retrospectively to all periods presented. The retrospective approach requires that an investment for which fair value is measured using the net asset value per share practical expedient be removed from the fair value hierarchy in all periods presented in an entity's financial statements. Earlier application is permitted.

These amendments apply to reporting entities that elect to measure the fair value of an investment within the scope of paragraphs 4–5 of FASB *Accounting Standards Codification* (ASC) 820-10-15 using the net asset value per share (or its equivalent) practical expedient in FASB ASC 820-10-35-59.

FASB ASC 820, *Fair Value Measurement*, permits a reporting entity, as a practical expedient, to measure the fair value of certain investments using the net asset value per share of the investment. Currently, investments valued using the practical expedient are categorized within the fair value hierarchy on the basis of whether the investment is redeemable with the investee at net asset value on the measurement date, never redeemable with the investee at net asset value, or redeemable with the investee at net asset value at a future date. For investments that are redeemable with the investee at a future date, a reporting entity must consider the length of time until those investments become redeemable to determine the classification within the fair value hierarchy and whether they are near term for the assessment of the potential inclusion of a cash flow statement.

The amendments remove the requirement to categorize within the fair value hierarchy all investments for which fair value is measured using the net asset value per share practical expedient. However, the amendments require sufficient information to be provided to permit reconciliation of the fair value of assets categorized within the fair value hierarchy to the amounts presented in the statement of financial condition. The amendments also remove the requirement to make certain disclosures for all investments that are eligible to be measured at fair value using the net asset value per share practical expedient. Rather, those disclosures are limited to investments for which the entity has elected to measure the fair value using that practical expedient.

Readers are encouraged to consult the full text of this ASU on FASB's website at www.fasb.org.

Presentation of Pending Content in FASB ASC

Amendments to FASB ASC (issued in the form of ASUs) are initially incorporated into FASB ASC in "Pending Content" boxes located below the paragraphs being amended with links to the transition information. The pending content boxes are meant to provide users with information about how the guidance in a paragraph will change as a result of the new guidance.

Pending content applies to different entities at different times due to varying fiscal year-ends, and because certain guidance may be effective on different dates for public entities, as defined, and other entities. As such, FASB maintains amended guidance in pending content boxes within FASB ASC until the roll-off date. Generally, the roll-off date is six months following the latest fiscal year-end for which the original guidance being amended could still be applied.

Presentation of Pending Content in AICPA Audit and Accounting Guides

Amended FASB ASC guidance that is included in pending content boxes in FASB ASC on May 1, 2015, is referenced as "Pending Content" in this guide. Pending content referenced or discussed within this guide's chapter text is fully effective as of the date of this guide and should be considered by readers for current reporting periods. Pending content referenced or discussed within this guide's shaded "Guidance Updates" boxes or within appendix A, "Guidance Updates," is not fully effective as of the date of this guide. Readers should be aware that pending content" referenced in this guide will eventually be subjected to FASB's roll-off process and will no longer be labeled as "Pending Content" in FASB ASC (as discussed in the previous paragraph).

7.01 As illustrated in FASB ASC 946-205-45-1, the overall objective of financial statements, including financial highlights, of investment companies is to present net assets, results of operations, changes in net assets, and financial highlights resulting from investment activities and, if applicable, capital share transactions. In reporting to shareholders, nonregistered investment companies and investment companies registered with the SEC should present financial statements and financial highlights as follows.

Nonregistered Investment Companies	Registered Investment Companies
A statement of assets and liabilities with a schedule of investments or statement of net assets, which includes a schedule of investments therein, as of the close of the latest period. At a minimum, a condensed schedule of investments (as discussed in paragraphs 4–10 of FASB *Accounting Standards Codification*	A statement of assets and liabilities with a schedule of investments or statement of net assets, which includes a schedule of investments therein (that is, a detailed list of investments in securities, options written, securities sold short, and other investments) as of the close of the latest period.[1] A schedule of

---

[1] If the most current statement of assets and liabilities included in a registration statement is as of a date more than 245 days prior to the date that the filing is expected to become effective, then the financial statements, which may be unaudited, included in such filing are to be updated to a date

(continued)

Nonregistered Investment Companies	Registered Investment Companies
[ASC] 946-210-50) should be provided for each statement of assets and liabilities.	investments should be provided for each statement of assets and liabilities in conformity with Rule 12-12 or 12-12C of Regulation S-X.[2]
A statement of operations for the latest period.	A statement of operations for the latest year.[3,4]
A statement of cash flows for the latest period (if not exempted by FASB ASC 230-10).[5]	A statement of cash flows for the latest year (if not exempted by FASB ASC 230-10).[6,7,8]
A statement of changes in net assets for the latest period.	A statement of changes in net assets for the latest two years (for semiannual reports, the most recent semiannual period and preceding fiscal year).[9,10]

(continued)

(footnote continued)

within 245 days of the expected effective date. A statement of assets and liabilities as of such date must be provided as well as a statement of operations and cash flows (if applicable) and statement of changes in net assets for the interim period from the end of the most recent fiscal year for which a statement of assets and liabilities is presented and the date of the most recent interim statement of assets and liabilities.

[2] In 2004, the SEC adopted rule and form amendments that, among other matters, amended Articles 6 and 12 of Regulation S-X to permit a registered investment company to include, under Rule 12-12C, a summary schedule of investments in securities of unaffiliated issuers in its reports to shareholders, provided that the complete portfolio schedule required by Rule 12-12 is filed with the SEC semiannually and provided to shareholders upon request free of charge. All other complete portfolio schedules required by Regulation S-X (Rule 12-12A, *Investments—Securities Sold Short*; Rule 12-12B, *Open Option Contracts Written*; Rule 12-13, *Investments Other than Securities*; and Rule 12-14, *Investments In and Advances To Affiliates*) continue to be required in both shareholder reports and Form N-CSR. The amendments also exempt money market funds (which utilize the exemptive requirements of Rule 2a-7 under the Investment Company Act of 1940 [the 1940 Act]) from including a portfolio schedule in reports to shareholders, provided that this information is filed with the SEC on Form N-CSR semiannually and provided to shareholders upon request free of charge. See SEC Release No. IC-26372 under the 1940 Act for additional information.

Although the SEC rule allows a money market fund to exclude its portfolio of investments from its shareholder reports, the U.S. generally accepted accounting principles (GAAP) requirement discussed in this guide that a money market fund present, at a minimum, a condensed schedule of investments for each statement of assets and liabilities (see paragraphs 1–3 of FASB *Accounting Standards Codification* [ASC] 946-210-50) has not been modified.

[3] See footnote 1.

[4] The SEC staff currently requires that sufficient fiscal periods be presented to cover at least 12 calendar months' results of operations ending on the most recent fiscal year-end date (24 calendar months' changes in net assets and 60 months' financial highlights).

[5] Investment companies which meet certain conditions described in paragraph 7.160 are exempted from providing a statement of cash flows.

[6] See footnote 5.

[7] See footnote 1.

[8] See footnote 4.

[9] See footnote 1.

[10] See footnote 4.

Nonregistered Investment Companies	Registered Investment Companies
Financial highlights for the latest period consisting of per share operating performance, net investment income, and expense ratios and total return for all investment companies organized in a manner using unitized net asset value.[11]	Financial highlights for the latest five fiscal years[12,13,14] (for semiannual reports, the semiannual period and generally the preceding five fiscal years).

7.02 In addition to complying with U.S. generally accepted accounting principles (GAAP), the financial statements of investment companies registered with the SEC should comply with applicable SEC requirements.

7.03 The financial statements illustrated in this chapter are for typical open-end management investment companies and may need to be modified to fit the requirements of other types of investment companies. Financial reporting requirements with respect to unit investment trusts and variable annuity separate accounts are discussed in chapters 9, "Unit Investment Trusts," and 10, "Variable Contracts—Insurance Entities," of this guide. For guidance on financial statement presentation and disclosure of venture capital and small business investment companies, including additional regulatory requirements, refer to appendix C, "Venture Capital, Business Development Companies, and Small Business Investment Companies," of this guide. Aspects of reporting on interim financial information are discussed in paragraphs 7.206–.212.

7.04 Financial statements and related disclosures should be presented for each series in a series fund although one or more series may be presented in a separate document.[15] For funds with multiple classes of shares, certain information relating to each class is required to be disclosed as discussed in chapter 5, "Complex Capital Structures," of this guide.

Comparative Financial Statements

7.05 FASB ASC 946, *Financial Services—Investment Companies*, does not require comparative financial statements for nonregistered investment partnerships. If an entity elects to prepare comparative financial statements, the general guidance for the presentation of comparative financial statements, as found in paragraphs 2 and 4 of FASB ASC 205-10-45, indicate that (*a*) in any one year it is ordinarily desirable that the statement of financial position, the income statement, and the statement of changes in equity be presented for one or more preceding years, as well as for the current year, and (*b*) notes to financial statements, explanations, and accountants' reports containing qualifications that appeared on the statements for the preceding years should be

---

[11] For investment companies not using unitized net asset value, financial highlights should be presented and consist of net investment income and expense ratios and total return, or the internal rate of return since inception, if applicable.

[12] See footnote 1.

[13] See footnote 4.

[14] Item 13(a) of Form N-1A requires financial highlights to be presented for the latest 5 years in the fund's prospectus. Item 4 of Form N-2 requires financial highlights to be presented for the latest 10 years in the fund's prospectus.

[15] Rule 6.03(j) of Regulation S-X.

repeated, or at least referred to, in the comparative statements to the extent that they continue to be of significance.

7.06 According to Technical Questions and Answers (Q&A) section 6910.19, "Information Required to Be Disclosed in Financial Statements When Comparative Financial Statements of Nonregistered Investment Partnerships Are Presented" (AICPA, *Technical Questions and Answers*), when comparative financial statements of a nonregistered investment partnership are presented, comparative schedules of investments should be presented as of the end of each period presented. Because the schedule of investments would continue to be considered of significance relative to the statement of assets and liabilities for the prior year, the schedule of investments for the prior year should be included as part of the comparative statements.

7.07 Q&A section 6910.19 also notes that when comparative financial statements of a nonregistered investment partnership are provided, comparative financial highlights should be presented for each period provided. Consistent with the requirements of FASB ASC 205-10-45, discussed in paragraph 7.05, comparative financial highlights should be presented when comparative statements of operations are provided because they would be considered a significant disclosure for the prior periods of operation included in the financial statements.

Consolidation [16, 17]

> ⊚ **Update 7-2 *Accounting and Reporting*: Consolidation**
>
> FASB ASU No. 2014-13, *Consolidation (Topic 810): Measuring the Financial Assets and the Financial Liabilities of a Consolidated Collateralized Financing Entity (a consensus of the FASB Emerging Issues Task Force)*, was issued in August 2014. The amendments in ASU No. 2014-13 are effective for public business entities for annual periods, and interim periods within those annual periods, beginning after December 15, 2015. For entities other than public business entities, the amendments in this Update are effective for annual periods ending after December 15, 2016, and interim periods beginning after December 15, 2016. Early adoption is permitted as of the beginning of an annual period.
>
> A reporting entity may apply the amendments in ASU No. 2014-13 using a modified retrospective approach by recording a cumulative-effect adjustment to equity as of the beginning of the annual period of adoption. A reporting entity also may apply the amendments retrospectively to all relevant prior periods beginning with the annual period in which the amendments in ASU No.

---

[16] In June 2013, FASB issued Accounting Standards Update (ASU) No. 2013-08, *Financial Services—Investment Companies (Topic 946): Amendments to the Scope, Measurement, and Disclosure Requirements*. FASB decided not to make changes to existing consolidation and equity method investment guidance in FASB ASC 946-810 and 946-323, as discussed in the "Consolidation" section of this chapter, through the issuance of ASU No. 2013-08. However, FASB has an active project titled *Investment Companies: Disclosures about Investments in Another Investment Company*. The project intends to require disclosures in an investment company's financial statements that will provide transparency into the risks, returns, and expenses of an investee that is also an investment company. Readers should remain alert for updates on this project, which can be accessed from the Project Roster and Status page at www.fasb.org.

[17] In October 2014, the SEC released Investment Management Guidance Update No. 2014-11, *Investment Company Consolidation*. Readers are encouraged to read the full text, available at www.sec.gov/investment/im-guidance-2014-11.pdf.

2009-17, *Consolidations (Topic 810): Improvements to Financial Reporting by Enterprises Involved with Variable Interest Entities*, were initially adopted.

A reporting entity is required to consolidate in its financial statements a collateralized financing entity, such as a collateralized debt obligation or collateralized loan obligation entity, when the reporting entity determines that it is the primary beneficiary of the collateralized financing entity in accordance with the guidance in FASB ASC 810, *Consolidation*. A collateralized financing entity is a variable interest entity with no more than nominal equity that holds financial assets and issues beneficial interests in those financial assets; the beneficial interests have contractual recourse only to the related assets of the collateralized financing entity and are classified as financial liabilities.

Many reporting entities currently elect or are required to account for the financial assets and the financial liabilities of a consolidated collateralized financing entity at fair value. The fair value, as determined under GAAP, of a collateralized financing entity's financial assets may differ from the fair value of its financial liabilities even when the financial liabilities have recourse only to the financial assets.

The ASU provides entities that consolidate a collateralized financing entity with an optional practicability exception to applying the fair value measurement guidance when all of the financial assets and financial liabilities of the consolidated collateralized financing entity are measured at fair value through net income (for example, when the entity had elected the fair value option for all of the collateralized financing entity's financial assets and financial liabilities). If elected, the practicability exception allows a reporting entity to measure both the financial assets and the financial liabilities of the collateralized financing entity by using the more observable of the fair value of the financial assets and the fair value of the financial liabilities, effectively eliminating any measurement difference. The practicability exception is

- available on an entity-by-entity basis,
- required to be elected at initial consolidation of the collateralized financing entity (or upon transition in connection with a reporting entity's adoption of the ASU),
- no longer applicable if, after initial consolidation, all of the collateralized financing entity's financial assets are no longer measured at fair value through net income (for example, the reporting entity subsequently transfers to the collateralized financing entity financial assets measured at fair value through other comprehensive income or amortized cost).

Readers are encouraged to consult the full text of this ASU on FASB's website at www.fasb.org.

7.08   As explained in "Pending Content" in FASB ASC 946-810-45-2, except as discussed in paragraph 7.10, it is not appropriate for an investment company to consolidate an investee that is not an investment company. Rather, an investment company's controlling ownership interests in noninvestment company investees should be measured in accordance with guidance in FASB ASC 946-320, which requires investments in debt and equity securities to be initially measured at their transaction price and subsequently measured at fair value (for measurement guidance, see the section titled "Valuing Investments" in chapter 2, "Investment Accounts," of this guide). Rule 6-03(c)(1) of Regulation S-X also precludes consolidation by a registered investment company of any entity other than another investment company.

7.09   As explained in "Pending Content" in FASB ASC 946-323-45-1, except as discussed in paragraph 7.10, use of the equity method of accounting by an investment company is not appropriate. Rather, all noncontrolling ownership interests held by an investment company should be measured in accordance with guidance in FASB ASC 946-320, which requires investments in debt and equity securities to be initially measured at their transaction price and subsequently measured at fair value (for measurement guidance, see the section titled "Valuing Investments" in chapter 2 of this guide).

7.10 "Pending Content" in FASB ASC 946-323-45-2 and 946-810-45-3 note that an exception to the general consolidation and equity method requirements occurs if the investment company has an investment in an operating entity that provides services to the investment company (for example, an investment adviser or transfer agent). In those cases, the purpose of the investment is to provide services to the investment company, rather than realize a gain on the sale of the investment. If an individual investment company holds a controlling financial interest in such an operating entity, the investment company should consolidate that investee, rather than measuring that interest at fair value. If an investment company holds a noncontrolling ownership interest in such an operating entity that otherwise qualifies for use of the equity method of accounting, the investment company should use the equity method of accounting for that investment.

7.11   The guidance discussed in previous paragraphs is consistent with long-standing industry practice. That practice results in investment company financial statements that focus on a net asset value that reflects the fair value of the underlying investments. The purpose and nature of investment companies makes fair value for their investments the most relevant measure to report to their investors, the principal users of their financial statements who typically evaluate the performance of the investment company based on changes in net asset value. Exchanges of open-end investment company shares are at, or based on, net asset value. Purchasers and sellers of other investment company shares (for example, closed-end investment company shares) often consider the premium or discount to net asset value that is present in the exchange price.

Other Consolidation Considerations

7.12   Public investment companies organized pursuant to master-feeder arrangements, as defined by the SEC,[18] must provide master financial statements with each feeder financial statement, pursuant to SEC requirements.[19] Nonpublic investment companies should follow the applicable provisions of subtopics 205, 210, 225, 230, and 235 of FASB ASC 946. (See also footnote 5 to paragraph 5.54 of this guide discussing the SEC's regulations which require public investment companies that are regulated under the 1940 Act meeting certain criteria to file financial statements or include summarized financial

---

[18] The SEC defines a *master-feeder arrangement* as a registered investment company that invests in a single investment vehicle. Also see paragraphs 5.18–.21 of this guide.

[19] From the SEC's Annual Industry Comment Letter From the Division of Investment Management dated December 30, 1998. The full text of the letter can be accessed under the "Division of Investment Management" section of the SEC's website.

information in the notes to the financial statements, as appropriate, for investments in unconsolidated majority-owned subsidiaries or other unconsolidated subsidiaries.)

7.13 FASB ASC 946-205-45-6 states that nonpublic investment companies may also present a complete set of master financial statements with each feeder financial statement in a manner that is consistent with the requirements for public investment companies.

7.14 FASB ASC 810-10-40 discusses when deconsolidation of a subsidiary or derecognition of a group of assets is appropriate and the applicable accounting guidance. FASB ASC 810-10-45 provides accounting and reporting guidance related to the consolidated financial statement presentation of parent and subsidiary financial statements and combined financial statements.

7.15 FASB ASC 810-10-45-15 states that the ownership interests in the subsidiary that are held by owners other than the parent are noncontrolling interests. The noncontrolling interest in a subsidiary is part of the equity of the consolidated group. Further, FASB ASC 810-10-45-16 explains that the noncontrolling interest should be reported in the consolidated statement of financial position within equity and separately from the parent's equity. That amount should be clearly identified and labeled (for example, as noncontrolling interest in subsidiaries). An entity with noncontrolling interests in more than one subsidiary may present those interests in aggregate in the consolidated financial statements. FASB ASC 810-10-55-4I illustrates the application of this guidance.

7.16 According to paragraphs 18–21 of FASB ASC 810-10-45, the amount of intraentity income or loss eliminated in the preparation of consolidated financial statements is not affected by the existence of a noncontrolling interest. The complete elimination of the intraentity income or loss is consistent with the underlying assumption that consolidated financial statements represent the financial position and operating results of a single economic entity. The elimination of the intraentity income or loss may be allocated between the parent and noncontrolling interests. Revenues, expenses, gains, losses, and net income or loss should be reported in the consolidated financial statements at the consolidated amounts, which include amounts attributable to the owners of the parent and noncontrolling interest. Net income or loss should be attributed to the parent and noncontrolling interest. Losses attributable to the parent and noncontrolling interest in a subsidiary may exceed their interests in the subsidiary's equity. The excess and any further losses attributable to the parent and noncontrolling interest should be attributed to those interests. That is, the noncontrolling interest should continue to be attributed its share of losses even if that attribution results in a deficit noncontrolling interest balance.

7.17 Commodity pool operators (CPOs) of registered investment companies (registered funds) that trade in commodity interests through wholly-owned subsidiaries (known as controlled foreign corporations or CFCs) that are consolidated with such registered funds for financial reporting purposes may rely on no-action relief to permit CPOs of registered funds that consolidate their CFCs for financial reporting purposes to file with the National Futures Association an annual report for the CFC, to the extent required by Commodities Futures Trading Commission (CFTC) Regulation 4.22(c), that contains audited consolidated financial statements of the registered fund, in lieu of a separate annual report for the CFC. In instances where the CPO prepares an annual report of the registered fund that contains consolidated audited financial statements for the registered fund, such financial statements must include, and also separately indicate, the holdings, gains and losses, and other financial statement amounts attributable to the CFC. Paragraph 7.236 provides an illustrative example of this disclosure.

Reporting Financial Position [20]

7.18   As stated in FASB ASC 946-210-45-1, investment companies report financial position by presenting either a statement of assets and liabilities or statement of net assets.

7.19   Rule 6.05 of Regulation S-X provides that a statement of net assets may be presented if the amount of investments in securities of unaffiliated issuers is at least 95 percent of total assets.

7.20   The statement of assets and liabilities presents a list of assets and liabilities and an amount for net assets equal to the difference between the totals. A separate schedule of investments is required, as described in paragraphs 7.27–.47.

7.21   FASB ASC 946-210-45-2 notes that the statement of net assets includes a schedule of investments (disclosure requirements for a schedule of investments can be found in FASB ASC 946-210-50, and are also discussed in paragraphs 7.27–.47). Details of related-party balances and other assets and liabilities should be presented in the statement of net assets or notes to the financial statements.

7.22   Rule 6.05 of Regulation S-X includes additional disclosures for registered investment companies. According to regulations, net asset value per share for each class of shares of capital stock outstanding should be presented as noted in chapter 5.

Reporting of Fully Benefit-Responsive Investment Contracts

7.23   FASB ASC 946-210 describes the limited circumstances in which the net assets of investment companies should reflect their net asset value using the contract value of investments attributable to fully benefit-responsive investment contracts (as defined by the FASB ASC glossary). Specifically, FASB ASC 946-210-45-11 states that contract value is the relevant measurement attribute for the portion of net assets attributable to fully benefit-responsive investment contracts, provided that the investment company is established under a trust whereby the trust itself is adopted as part of one or more qualified employer-sponsored defined contribution plans (including both health and welfare and pension plans). A qualified plan refers to a plan that qualifies under the IRC by allowing full or partial tax-deferred contributions and tax-deferred investment gains on those contributions. Further, FASB ASC 946-210-50-14 requires disclosure (among other disclosures) of a reconciliation between the

---

[20] Staff Accounting Bulletin (SAB) No. 108, *Considering the Effects of Prior Year Misstatements when Quantifying Misstatements in Current Year Financial Statements,* points out that some registrants do not consider the effects of prior year errors on current year financial statements. This allows the entity to report unadjusted (and improper) assets and liabilities. SAB No. 108 also notes that an immaterial error on the balance sheet could be material on the income statement. The purpose of SAB No. 108 is to address diversity in practice in quantifying financial statement misstatements and the potential build-up of improper accounts on the balance sheet and to provide illustrative examples. See the SEC's website for the full text of this SAB.

beginning and ending balance of the amount presented on the statement of assets and liabilities that represents the difference between net assets reflecting all investments at fair value and net assets for each period in which a statement of changes in net assets is presented.

7.24 FASB ASC 946-210-45-15 requires that the following line items be separately reported on the statement of assets and liabilities, with a parenthetical reference that such amounts are being reported at fair value:

    a. Investments (including traditional guaranteed investment contracts)

    b. Wrapper contracts

7.25 As further stated in FASB ASC 946-210-45-16, the statement of assets and liabilities should present the following:

    a. Total assets

    b. Total liabilities

    c. Net assets reflecting all investments at fair value

    d. Net assets

The net assets amount represents the amount at which participants can transact with the fund and should be used for purposes of preparing per share disclosures required by FASB ASC 946-205-50 and as the beginning and ending balance in the statement of changes in net assets of the fund. The difference between net assets reflecting all investments at fair value and net assets should be presented as a single amount on the face of the statement of assets and liabilities, calculated as the sum of the amounts necessary to adjust the portion of net assets attributable to each fully benefit-responsive investment contract from fair value to contract value. Additional financial statement presentation and disclosure requirements for fully benefit-responsive investment contracts are discussed in paragraphs 17–18 of FASB ASC 946-210-45 and FASB ASC 946-210-50-14 (see paragraphs 7.32, 7.146, and 7.190).

7.26 FASB ASC 946-210-45-18A explains that to be considered within the scope of paragraphs 15–18 of FASB ASC 946-210-45 (as previously discussed), any portion of the net assets of the investment company attributable to a particular plan investee that is not held in trust for the benefit of participants in a qualified employer-sponsored defined contribution plan is not permitted to increase, except for reinvestment of income earned.

Schedule of Investments

Investment Companies Other Than Nonregistered Investment Partnerships

7.27 As explained in FASB ASC 946-210-50-1, in the absence of regulatory requirements, investment companies other than nonregistered investment partnerships (see the "Investment Companies That Are Nonregistered Investment Partnerships" section of this chapter) should

    a. disclose the name, share, or principal amount of all of the following:

        i. Each investment (including short sales, written options, futures contracts, forward contracts, and other investment-related liabilities) whose fair value constitutes more than 1 percent of net assets. In applying the 1-percent test, total long and total short positions in any one issuer should be considered separately.

ii. All investments in any one issuer whose fair values aggregate more than 1 percent of net assets. In applying the 1-percent test, total long and total short positions in any one issuer should be considered separately.

iii. At a minimum, the 50 largest investments.

b. categorize investments by both of the following characteristics:

i. The type of investment (such as common stocks, preferred stocks, convertible securities, fixed income securities, government securities, options purchased, options written, warrants, futures contracts, loan participations and assignments, short term securities, repurchase agreements, short sales, forward contracts, other investment companies, and so forth).

ii. The related industry, country, or geographic region of the investment.[21]

c. disclose the aggregate other investments (each of which is not required to be disclosed by item a) without specifically identifying the issuers of such investments and categorize them as required by item b. The disclosure should include both of the following:

i. The percent of net assets that each such category represents.

ii. The total value for each category in items b(i)–b(ii).

7.28 As required by paragraphs 20–21 of FASB ASC 825-10-50, in addition to the categorization chosen from the preceding, any other significant concentration of credit risk should be reported. For example, an international fund that categorizes its investments by industry or geographic region should also report a summary of its investments by country, if such concentration is significant.

7.29 Additionally, as contemplated by the requirement to disclose certain significant estimates in paragraphs 6–15 of FASB ASC 275-10-50, the use of estimates by directors or trustees, general partners, or others in an equivalent capacity to value securities should be reported. (See also the "Fair Value Disclosures," section of this chapter for further consideration of disclosures associated with valuation of investments.)

7.30 Rules 6.03, 6.04, 6.05, 12-12, 12-12A, 12-12B, 12-12C, 12-13, and 12-14 of Regulation S-X apply to registered investment companies. In 2004, the SEC adopted rule and form amendments that among other matters amended Articles 6 and 12 of Regulation S-X to permit a registered investment company to include, under Rule 12-12C, a summary schedule of investments in securities of unaffiliated issuers in its reports to shareholders. See footnote 2 for more information. That SEC rule also allows a money market fund to exclude its portfolio of investments from its shareholder reports. The GAAP requirement

---

[21] Refer to the March 1, 2012, AICPA Investment Companies Expert Panel Conference Call Highlights. The Expert Panel members shared that generally geographic classification is based on the concentration of the risk and economic exposure (where the principal business actually takes place).

discussed in paragraph 7.27 stating that a money market fund present, at a minimum, a condensed schedule of investments for each statement of assets and liabilities has not been modified.

7.31   For public registrants, disclosure relating to repurchase agreements should include the parties to the agreement, the date of the agreement, the total amount to be received upon repurchase, the repurchase date, and a brief description of the nature and terms of the collateral.[22] For public registrants that prepare a summary schedule of investments, fully collateralized repurchase agreements are aggregated and treated as a single issue, with a footnote that indicates the range of dates of the repurchase agreements, the total purchase price of the securities, the total amount to be received upon repurchase, the range of repurchase dates, and a description of securities subject to the repurchase agreements, without regard to the percentage of net assets or issuer.[23] Public registrants are also required to disclose investments in restricted securities, affiliated companies, securities subject to call options, and when-issued securities in the schedule of investments; disclosure of specific information in the notes to the financial statements may also be required by other authoritative FASB guidance.[24] The SEC also requires that each security that is nonincome-producing should be identified as such.[25] Securities pledged as collateral should be identified.[26] When a detailed list of short term investments is presented, such investments may be summarized by issuer, disclosing their ranges of interest rates and maturity dates. For public registrants that prepare a summary schedule of investments, short term debt instruments of the same issuer are aggregated and treated as a single issue, with disclosure indicating the range of interest rates and maturity dates.[27]

7.32   FASB ASC 946-210-45-18 requires the following information be disclosed as part of the schedule of investments related to the portion of net assets of an investment company attributable to fully benefit-responsive investment contracts, to the extent that schedule is already required under FASB ASC 946-210-50-1 (in the absence of regulatory requirements, for investment companies other than nonregistered investment partnerships), and reconciled to the corresponding line items on the statement of assets and liabilities:

 a. The fair value of each investment contract (including separate disclosure of the fair value of the wrapper contract and the fair value of each of the corresponding underlying investments, if held by the fund, included in that investment contract)

 b. Adjustment from fair value to contract value for each investment contract (if the investment contract is fully benefit responsive)

 c. Major credit ratings of the issuer or wrapper provider for each investment contract

FASB ASC 946-210-55-2, illustrates the application of this guidance, see paragraph 7.231.

---

[22] Rule 12.12 of Regulation S-X requires that each issue shall be listed separately.

[23] Rules 12.12 and 12.12C of Regulation S-X.

[24] For specific requirements concerning disclosures of information relating to restricted securities and affiliated companies, see Sections 404.03 and 404.04 of the SEC's *Codification of Financial Reporting Policies* and Rule 12-14 of Regulation S-X.

[25] See footnote 23.

[26] Rule 4.08(b) of Regulation S-X.

[27] See Rule 12.12C of Regulation S-X.

Investment Companies That Are Nonregistered Investment Partnerships

7.33 As noted in paragraphs 4–6 of FASB ASC 946-210-50, investment partnerships that are exempt from SEC registration under the 1940 Act include hedge funds, limited liability companies, limited liability partnerships, limited duration companies, offshore investment companies with similar characteristics, and commodity pools subject to regulation under the Commodity Exchange Act of 1974. Except for investment partnerships regulated as brokers and dealers in securities under the Securities Exchange Act of 1934 (the 1934 Act) (registered broker-dealers) that manage funds only for those who are officers, directors or trustees, or employees of the general partner, investment partnerships that are exempt from SEC registration under the 1940 Act should, at a minimum, include a condensed schedule of investments in securities owned (sold short) by the partnership at the close of the most recent period. Such a schedule should

- *a.* categorize investments by all of the following:
    - i. Type (such as common stocks, preferred stocks, convertible securities, fixed-income securities, government securities, options purchased, options written, warrants, futures, loan participations, short sales, other investment companies, and so forth).
    - ii. Country or geographic region, except for derivative instruments for which the underlying is not a security (see item *a*[iv]).[28]
    - iii. Industry, except for derivative instruments for which the underlying is not a security (see item *a*[iv]).
    - iv. Derivatives for which the underlying is not a security, by broad category of underlying (for example, grains and feeds, fibers and textiles, foreign currency, or equity indexes) in place of categories *a*(ii)–*a*(iii).
- *b.* report the percentage of net assets that each such category represents and the total value and cost (proceeds of sale) for each category in *a*(i)–*a*(ii).
- *c.* disclose the name, shares or principal amount, value, and type of both of the following:
    - i. Each investment (including short sales), constituting more than 5 percent of net assets, except for derivative instruments, as discussed in items *e–f*. In applying the 5 percent test, total long and total short positions in any one issuer should be considered separately.
    - ii. All investments in any one issuer aggregating more than 5 percent of net assets, except for derivative instruments as discussed in items *e–f*. In applying the 5 percent test, total long and total short positions in any one issuer should be considered separately.
- *d.* aggregate other investments (each of which is 5 percent or less of net assets) without specifically identifying the issuers of such investments and categorize them in accordance with the guidance in

---

[28] See footnote 21.

a. In applying the 5 percent test, total long and total short positions in any one issuer should be considered separately.

e. disclose the number of contracts, range of expiration dates, and cumulative appreciation (depreciation) for open futures contracts of a particular underlying (such as wheat, cotton, specified equity index, or U.S. Treasury bonds), regardless of exchange, delivery location, or delivery date, if cumulative appreciation (depreciation) on the open contracts exceeds 5 percent of net assets. In applying the 5 percent test, total long and total short positions in any one issuer should be considered separately.

f. disclose the range of expiration dates and fair value for all other derivatives (such as forwards, swaps [such as interest rate and currency swaps], and options) of a particular underlying (such as foreign currency, wheat, a specified equity index, or U.S. Treasury bonds), regardless of the counterparty, exchange, or delivery date, if fair value exceeds 5 percent of net assets. In applying the 5 percent test, total long and total short positions in any one issuer should be considered separately.

g. provide the following additional qualitative description for each investment in another nonregistered investment partnership whose fair value constitutes more than 5 percent of net assets:

  i. The investment objective

  ii. Restrictions on redemption (that is, liquidity provisions)

7.34 As explained in chapter 12, "Independent Auditor's Reports and Client Representations," of this guide, if financial statements of an investment partnership that is exempt from SEC registration do not include the required schedule of investments disclosures that are listed in the previous paragraph, and it is practicable for the auditor to determine them or any portion thereof, the auditor should include the information in his or her report expressing the qualified or adverse opinion.

7.35 According to Q&A section 6910.16, "Presentation of Boxed Investment Positions in the Condensed Schedule of Investments of Nonregistered Investment Partnerships" (AICPA, *Technical Questions and Answers*), long and short positions in the same security (*boxed positions*) should be disclosed on a gross basis in the schedule of investments. Although there may be a perfect economic hedge in boxed positions, the determination of which components of the boxed position would be required to be presented in the schedule of investments should be evaluated separately on a gross basis for the purposes of the 5 percent of net assets test. To the extent that one (or both) of the components is required to be disclosed, such component should be disclosed on the schedule of investments because there may be market risk if one position is removed before the other or experiences settlement costs or losses upon disposition. In the event that only one of the positions is required to be disclosed, a nonregistered investment partnership is not precluded from disclosing both positions.

7.36 Q&A section 6910.17, "Disclosure of Long and Short Positions" (AICPA, *Technical Questions and Answers*), further explains that if a nonregistered investment partnership has a long position that exceeds 5 percent of net assets and a short position in the same issuer that is less than 5 percent of net assets, the investment partnership is not required to disclose both the long and short position in the condensed schedule of investments. In applying the

5 percent test to determine the investments to be disclosed in the condensed schedule of investments, total long and total short positions in any one issuer should be considered separately. Because the value of the long position exceeds 5 percent of net assets, disclosure of the long position is required; however, disclosure of the short position is not required because the short position does not exceed 5 percent of net assets.

7.37 According to Q&A section 6910.18, "Disclosure of an Investment in an Issuer When One or More Securities or One or More Derivative Contracts Are Held—Nonregistered Investment Partnerships" (AICPA, *Technical Questions and Answers*), if a nonregistered investment partnership holds one or more securities of the same issuer and one or more derivative contracts for which the underlying is a security of the same issuer, the disclosure on the condensed schedule of investments should be consistent with the classification of the securities on the statement of assets and liabilities. However, derivative contracts may be netted for statement of assets and liabilities presentation when the right of offset exists under FASB ASC 210-20 and 815-10, although the disclosures in the condensed schedule of investments should reflect all open contracts by their economic exposure (that is, long exposure derivative versus short exposure derivative). The netting concepts allowed by FASB ASC 210-20 and 815-10 are not considered for purposes of presentation in the condensed schedule of investments. Those securities (fair value) and derivative contracts (appreciation or fair value) that are classified as period-end assets on a gross basis (for derivative contracts, regardless of whether they represent long or short exposures) should be aggregated. To the extent that the sum constitutes more than 5 percent of net assets, the positions should be disclosed in accordance with FASB ASC 946-210-50-6 (discussed in paragraph 7.33). The investment company should similarly sum all the positions classified as liabilities on a gross basis and determine whether they exceed 5 percent of net assets. Separate computations should be performed for assets and liabilities. Illustrative examples of how to apply the disclosure guidelines can be found in Q&A section 6910.18 and paragraph 7.230.

7.38 According to Q&A section 6910.30, "Disclosure Requirements of Investments for Nonregistered Investment Partnerships When Their Interest in an Investee Fund Constitutes Less Than 5 Percent of the Nonregistered Investment Partnership's Net Assets" (AICPA, *Technical Questions and Answers*), if a nonregistered investment partnership owns an interest in another investment partnership[29] (investee fund) that constitutes less than 5 percent of the nonregistered investment partnership's net assets, the reporting investment partnership must still apply the guidance discussed in paragraph 7.42. Even though the amount of the investment in the investee fund does not exceed 5 percent of the reporting investment partnership's net assets, the reporting investment partnership's proportional share of the investee fund's investments in an individual issuer may nonetheless exceed 5 percent of the reporting investment partnership's net assets because an investee fund may have issued debt (recourse or nonrecourse) to purchase investments or may have significant short positions or other liabilities.

7.39 Q&A section 6910.31, "The Nonregistered Investment Partnership's Method for Calculating Its Proportional Share of Any Investments Owned by

---

[29] Such investment partnerships include, but are not limited to, investment partnerships, funds of funds, special purpose vehicles, disregarded entities, and limited liability companies.

an Investee Fund in Applying the '5 Percent Test' Described in Section 6910.30" (AICPA, *Technical Questions and Answers*), further explains that the reporting investment partnership should calculate its proportional share of any investments owned by the investee fund as its percentage ownership of the investee fund. Additionally, consistent with the provisions related to direct investments, indirect long and short positions of the same issuer held by the investee fund should not be netted. The disclosure of investments in issuers exceeding 5 percent of the reporting investment partnership's net assets should be made either on the face of the (condensed) schedule of investments or within the financial statement footnotes.

7.40 Q&A section 6910.32, "Additional Financial Statement Disclosures for Nonregistered Investment Partnerships When the Partnership Has Provided Guarantees Related to the Investee Fund's Debt" (AICPA, *Technical Questions and Answers*), further explains that in addition to considering the recognition provisions described in FASB ASC 460-10-50, the reporting investment partnership should further disclose any guarantees that it has provided on investee fund debt even though the risk of loss may be remote.

7.41 These disclosure requirements are described in FASB ASC 460-10-50 and FASB ASC 946-20-50 and include the following:

    a. Loss contingencies, such as guarantees of indebtedness of others, including indirect guarantees of indebtedness of others and the nature and amount of the guarantee

    b. Guarantor's obligation, including the nature of the guarantee, the approximate term of the guarantee, how the guarantee arose, and the events or circumstances that would require the guarantor to perform under the guarantee

Investments in Other Investment Companies

7.42 Paragraphs 8–10 of FASB ASC 946-210-50 explain that investments in other investment companies (investees), such as investment partnerships, limited liability companies, and funds of funds, should be considered investments for purposes of applying FASB ASC 946-210-50-1(a) and (b) and 946-210-50-6. If the reporting investment company's proportional share of any investment owned by any individual investee exceeds 5 percent of the reporting company's net assets at the reporting date, each such investment should be named and categorized as discussed in FASB ASC 946-210-50-6. These investee disclosures should be made either in the condensed schedule of investments (as components of the investment in the investee) or a note to that schedule. If information about the investee's portfolio is not available, that fact should be disclosed.

Credit Enhancements

7.43 FASB ASC 946-210-45-8 states that credit enhancements should be shown as a component of the security description in the schedule of investments. As illustrated in paragraphs 11–13 of FASB ASC 946-210-50, the terms, conditions, and other arrangements relating to the enhancement should be disclosed in the notes to the financial statements. In addition, for a put option provided by an affiliate, the schedule of investments should describe the put as from an affiliate, and the notes to the financial statements should include the name and relationship of the affiliate. For a letter of credit, the name of the entity issuing the letter of credit should be disclosed separately.

7.44 Separate disclosure of a credit enhancement should be provided on the face of the schedule of investments and should comply with Rules 6.04.1 and 6.04.3 of Regulation S-X, when applicable.

Financial Support to Investees[30]

7.45 "Pending Content" in paragraphs 15–16 of FASB ASC 946-20-50 require certain disclosures by an investment company that has provided, or is contractually required to provide but has not yet provided, financial support to an investee during periods presented.

7.46 If, during the periods presented, an investment company provides financial support to an investee, it should disclose information about both of the following items, disaggregated by (*a*) financial support that it was contractually required to provide, and (*b*) financial support that it was not previously contractually required to provide:

- The type and amount of financial support provided, including situations in which the investment company assisted the investee in obtaining financial support.
- The primary reasons for providing financial support.

7.47 An investment company also should separately disclose both of the following items about financial support that it is contractually required to provide to any of its investees but has not yet provided:

- The type and amount of financial support to be provided, including situations in which the investment company must assist the investee in obtaining financial support.
- The primary reasons for the contractual requirement to provide the financial support.

Assets

7.48 Following are the major asset categories reported in a statement of assets and liabilities and statement of net assets.

7.49 *Investments in securities.* The general practice in the investment company industry is to report investments in securities as the first asset because of their relative importance to total assets. *Securities*, as used in this guide, include but are not limited to stocks, bonds, debentures, notes, rights, warrants, certificates of interest or participation in equity or debt instruments, U.S. government securities, bank certificates of deposit, banker's acceptances, commercial paper, repurchase agreements, purchased options, and tranches of fixed income securities (such as interest-only and principal-only investments). Rule 6.04 of Regulation S-X contains guidance for balance sheets of registered investment companies regarding how to present different types of investments, including those of unaffiliated issuers, investments in and advances to affiliates, and investments other than in securities.

7.50 As discussed in FASB ASC 946-320, investment companies should report their investments in debt and equity securities at fair value. Investments in foreign securities should be reported at fair value by converting their

---

[30] In June 2013, FASB issued ASU No. 2013-08. The amendments in this ASU are effective for an entity's interim and annual reporting periods in fiscal years that begin after December 15, 2013. Earlier application is prohibited.

foreign currency-denominated value into the functional currency using current exchange rates.

7.51 *Cash.* As described in paragraphs 1–2 of FASB ASC 946-305-45, cash on hand and demand deposits are included under the general caption "Cash." Amounts held in foreign currencies should be disclosed separately at value, with acquisition cost shown parenthetically.

7.52 Time deposits and other funds subject to withdrawal or usage restrictions should be presented separately from other cash amounts.[31] Applicable interest rates and maturity dates should be disclosed.

7.53 Q&A section 1100.15, "Liquidity Restrictions" (AICPA, *Technical Questions and Answers*), addresses the potential accounting and auditing implications when a fund or its trustee imposes restrictions on a nongovernmental entity's ability to withdraw its balance in a money market fund or other short term investment vehicle. The question and answer section discusses some considerations for when these restriction events occur, such as determining (*a*) whether any assets subject to these restrictions qualify as cash equivalents or current assets; (*b*) whether disclosures about the risks and uncertainties resulting from such restrictions should be made; (*c*) whether these restrictions may trigger violations of debt covenants and consequently if that liability should be classified as current; (*d*) if the occurrence of such restriction occurs between the balance sheet date and issuance date and whether the financial statements need to be adjusted; and (*e*) if the restriction events call into question the entity's ability to continue as a going concern.

7.54 *Receivables.* As paragraphs 1–2 of FASB ASC 946-310-45 explain, receivables are listed separately at net realizable value for each of the following categories, among others:

- Dividends and interest
- Investment securities sold
- Capital stock sold
- Other accounts receivable, such as receivables from related parties, including expense reimbursement receivables from affiliates, and variation margin on open futures contracts

7.55 Receivables denominated in foreign currencies should be converted into the functional currency at current exchange rates and may be categorized with the corresponding functional currency receivables.

7.56 Rule 6.04 of Regulation S-X also contains guidance related to receivables of investment companies which is consistent with the guidance described in the previous paragraph.

7.57 Deferred offering costs, prepaid taxes, and prepaid insurance are normally included under the "Other Assets" caption. Separate amounts are usually not reported unless significant. For public registrants, amounts held by others in connection with short sales, open option contracts, and collateral received for securities loaned[32] should be stated separately.

---

[31] Rule 5.02.1 of Regulation S-X.
[32] Rule 6.04.7 and 6.04.11 of Regulation S-X.

7.58 *Derivatives.*[33] As explained in FASB ASC 815-10-25-1, an entity should recognize all its derivative instruments in its statement of financial position as either assets or liabilities, depending on the rights or obligations under the contracts. In accordance with FASB ASC 815-10-50-1, an entity with derivative instruments should disclose information to enable users of the financial statements to understand all of the following:

- How and why an entity uses derivative instruments
- How derivative instruments and related hedged items are accounted for under FASB ASC 815, *Derivatives and Hedging*
- How derivative instruments and related hedged items affect an entity's financial position, financial performance, and cash flows

7.59 Further, as discussed in paragraphs 1A–1B of FASB ASC 815-10-50, an entity with derivative instruments should disclose its objective for holding or issuing those instruments, the context needed to understand those objectives, its strategies for achieving those objectives, and information that would enable users of its financial statements to understand the volume of its activity in those instruments for every annual and interim reporting period for which a statement of financial position and statement of financial performance are presented. Regarding the disclosure that would enable users to understand the volume of the entity's activity in those instruments, an entity should select the format and specifics of disclosures relating to its volume of such activity that are the most relevant and practicable for its individual facts and circumstances. Regarding the disclosures of the entity's objectives, context, and strategies, they should be disclosed in the context of each instrument's primary underlying risk exposure (that is, interest rate, credit, foreign exchange rate, interest rate and foreign exchange rate, or overall price). Moreover, those instruments should be distinguished between those used for risk management purposes and those used for other purposes. FASB ASC 815-10-50-4 adds that for derivative instruments not designated as hedging instruments, the description should indicate the purpose of the derivative activity.

7.60 FASB ASC 815-10-50-4A states that an entity that holds or issues derivative instruments should disclose all of the following for every annual and interim reporting period for which a statement of financial position and statement of financial performance are presented:

- The location and fair value amounts of derivative instruments reported in the statement of financial position
- The location and amount of the gains and losses on derivative instruments reported in either the statement of financial performance or statement of financial position (note that investment companies generally report all gains and losses in the statement of operations)

---

[33] In May 2010, FASB issued the proposed ASU *Accounting for Financial Instruments and Revisions to the Accounting for Derivative Instruments and Hedging Activities—Financial Instruments (Topic 825) and Derivatives and Hedging (Topic 815).* This was followed up with a discussion paper in February 2011 intended to solicit input on how to improve, simplify, and converge the financial reporting requirements for hedging activities. Specifically, it requested stakeholders to comment on whether the IASB's exposure draft, *Hedge Accounting* (issued in December 2010), is a better starting point for any changes to GAAP as it relates to derivatives and hedging activities. The topic is currently classified as a FASB research project on the Project Roster & Status page at www.fasb.org. Readers should remain alert for developments on this topic.

7.61   Paragraphs 4D–4E of FASB ASC 815-10-50 add that this information should be presented separately by type of contract (for example, interest rate contracts, foreign exchange contracts, equity contracts, commodity contracts, credit contracts, and other contracts). The line item(s) in the statement of financial performance in which the gains and losses for these categories of derivative instruments are included should also be disclosed. Further, these disclosures should be presented in tabular format. Additional related disclosure requirements for derivative instruments are provided in paragraphs 4B–4C of FASB ASC 815-10-50. More specific information related to the disclosure of derivatives in prospectuses and shareholder reports is available in the July 2010 SEC letter to the Investment Company Institute. This letter can be accessed from the SEC's website at www.sec.gov under "Division of Investment Management," "Staff Guidance and Studies."

7.62   FASB ASC 815-10-50-4F discusses the disclosure requirements when the entity's policy is to include derivative instruments not designated or qualifying as hedging instruments under FASB ASC 815-20 in its trading activities (for example, as part of its trading portfolio that includes both derivative instruments and nonderivative or cash instruments). For those derivative instruments, the entity can elect to not separately disclose gains and losses, as required by FASB ASC 815-10-50-4C(e), provided that the entity discloses all of the following:

   a.   The gains and losses on its trading activities (including both derivative instruments and nonderivative instruments) recognized in the statement of financial performance separately by major types of items (for example, fixed income interest rates, foreign exchange, equity, commodity, and credit)

   b.   The line items in the statement of financial performance in which trading activities gains and losses are included

   c.   A description of the nature of its trading activities and related risks and how the entity manages those risks

If this disclosure option is elected, the entity should include a footnote in the required tables referencing the use of alternative disclosures for trading activities. FASB ASC 815-10-55-184 and 815-10-55-182 illustrate a footnote referencing the use of alternative disclosures for trading activities and the disclosure of information required in items *a* and *b*, respectively.

7.63   According to FASB ASC 815-10-50-4H, an entity that holds or issues derivative instruments should make the following disclosures for every annual and interim reporting period for which a statement of financial position is presented:

   a.   The existence and nature of credit-risk-related contingent features

   b.   The circumstances in which credit-risk-related contingent features could be triggered in derivative instruments (or such nonderivative instruments) that are in a net liability position at the end of the reporting period

   c.   The aggregate fair value amounts of derivative instruments (or such nonderivative instruments) that contain credit-risk-related contingent features that are in a net liability position at the end of the reporting period

   d.   The aggregate fair value of assets that are already posted as collateral at the end of the reporting period *e.* The aggregate fair value of additional assets that would be required to be posted as collateral if the credit-risk-related contingent features were triggered at the end of the reporting period

    f. The aggregate fair value of assets needed to settle the instrument immediately if the credit-risk-related contingent features were triggered at the end of the reporting period

FASB ASC 815-10-55-185 illustrates a credit-risk-related contingent feature disclosure.

7.64 FASB ASC 815-10-50-4I states that if information on derivative instruments is disclosed in more than a single footnote, an entity should cross-reference from the derivative instruments footnote to other footnotes in which derivative-instrument-related information is disclosed. FASB ASC 815-10-55-182 illustrates the disclosure of fair value amounts of derivative instruments and gains and losses on derivative instruments in tabular format.

7.65 The FASB ASC glossary defines a *credit derivative* as a derivative instrument that has both of the following characteristics: one or more of its underlyings are related to the credit risk of a specified entity (or a group of entities) or an index based on the credit risk of a group of entities; and it exposes the seller to potential loss from credit-risk-related events specified in the contract. Examples of credit derivatives include, but are not limited to, credit default swaps, credit spread options, and credit index products.

7.66 Paragraphs 4J–4K of FASB ASC 815-10-50 specify that the use of the term *seller* refers to the party that assumes the credit risk, which could be either a guarantor in a guarantee-type contract or any party that provides the credit protection in an option-type contract, a credit default swap, or any other credit derivative contract. A seller of credit derivatives should disclose information about its credit derivatives and hybrid instruments (for example, a credit-linked note) that have embedded credit derivatives to enable users of financial statements to assess their potential effect on the seller's financial position, financial performance, and cash flows. Paragraphs 4K–4L of FASB ASC 815-10-50 discuss the specific required disclosures and a method of presentation.

7.67 FASB ASC 815-10-45-4 states that, with respect to derivative instruments, unless the specified conditions in FASB ASC 210-20-45-1 for a right to offset are met, the fair value of derivatives in loss positions should not be offset against the fair value of derivatives in gain positions. Similarly, amounts recognized as accrued receivables shall not be offset against amounts recognized as accrued payables unless a right of setoff exists.

7.68 As further discussed in FASB ASC 815-10-45-5, without regard to the condition in FASB ASC 210-20-45-1(c) (when the reporting party intends to set off), a reporting entity may offset fair value amounts recognized for derivative instruments and fair value amounts recognized for the right to reclaim cash collateral (a receivable) or the obligation to return cash collateral (a payable) arising from a derivative instrument or instruments recognized at fair value executed with the same counterparty under a master netting arrangement. Solely as they relate to the right to reclaim cash collateral or the obligation to return cash collateral, fair value amounts include amounts that approximate fair value. The preceding sentence shall not be analogized to for any other asset or liability. The fair value recognized for some contracts may include an accrual component for the periodic unconditional receivables and payables that result from the contract; the accrual component included therein may also be offset for contracts executed with the same counterparty under a master netting arrangement. A master netting arrangement exists if the reporting entity has multiple contracts, whether for the same type of derivative instrument or different types of derivative instruments, with a single counterparty that are subject to a contractual agreement that provides for the net settlement of all contracts through a single payment in a single currency in the event of default on, or termination of, any one contract.

7.69   FASB ASC 815-10-45-6 notes that a reporting entity should make an accounting policy decision to offset fair value amounts, pursuant to the preceding paragraph. The reporting entity's choice to offset must be applied consistently. A reporting entity should not offset fair value amounts recognized for derivative instruments without offsetting fair value amounts recognized for the right to reclaim cash collateral or the obligation to return cash collateral. A reporting entity that makes an accounting policy decision to offset fair value amounts recognized for derivative instruments, pursuant to the preceding paragraph but determines that the amount recognized for the right to reclaim cash collateral or the obligation to return cash collateral is not a fair value amount should continue to offset the derivative instruments.

7.70   FASB ASC 815-10-45-7 explains that a reporting entity that has made an accounting policy decision to offset fair value amounts is not permitted to offset amounts recognized for the right to reclaim cash collateral or the obligation to return cash collateral against net derivative instrument positions if those amounts either were not fair value amounts or arose from instruments in a master netting arrangement that are not eligible to be offset.

Liabilities

> © **Update 7-3 *Accounting and Reporting*: Transfers and Servicing**
>
> FASB ASU No. 2014-11, *Transfers and Servicing (Topic 860): Repurchase-to-Maturity Transactions, Repurchase Financings, and Disclosures*, was issued in June 2014. The accounting amendments are effective, for public business entities, for the first interim or annual period beginning after December 15, 2014. For all other entities, the accounting amendments in the ASU are effective for annual periods beginning after December 15, 2014, and interim periods beginning after December 15, 2015. Early adoption is prohibited for public business entities; however, all other entities may elect to adopt the accounting guidance for interim periods beginning after December 15, 2014. An entity is required to present changes related to adopting the new accounting guidance for transactions outstanding on the effective date as a cumulative-effect adjustment to retained earnings as of the beginning of the period of adoption.
>
> For public business entities, the disclosure for certain transactions accounted for as a sale is required to be presented for interim and annual periods beginning after December 15, 2014. Such entities would apply the disclosure requirement related to repurchase agreements, securities lending transactions, and repurchase-to-maturity transactions accounted for as secured borrowings, in annual periods beginning after December 15, 2014, and interim periods beginning after March 15, 2015. For all other entities, both new disclosures are required to be presented for annual periods beginning after December 15, 2014, and interim periods beginning after December 15, 2015. The disclosures are not required to be presented for comparative periods before the effective date.

ASU No. 2014-11 requires two accounting changes. First, the amendments in this ASU change the accounting for repurchase-to-maturity transactions to secured borrowing accounting. Second, for repurchase financing arrangements, the amendments require the transferor and transferee to symmetrically account for the initial transfer of the financial asset as a sale (provided that derecognition conditions are met) and purchase, respectively. In addition, the ASU requires entities to evaluate and account for the repurchase component of the combined transaction in a manner similar to how they would evaluate and account for other typical repurchase agreements.

ASU No. 2014-11 also sets forth two new disclosure requirements to respond to the needs of users of financial statements for additional disclosures for repurchase agreements and similar transactions. An entity is required to disclose information about certain transactions accounted for as a sale in which the transferor retains substantially all of the exposure to the economic return on the transferred financial assets through an agreement with the same counterparty. Those disclosures are intended to provide users of financial statements with information to compare those types of transactions accounted for as sales with similar transactions accounted for as secured borrowings. An entity also will be required to disclose information about repurchase agreements, securities lending transactions, and repurchase-to-maturity transactions that are accounted for as secured borrowings. Those disclosures are intended to provide transparency about the types of collateral pledged in the agreements and the associated liability. Note that banks and broker-dealers refer to a sale of securities with an agreement to repurchase as a repurchase agreement (repo) whereas an investment company refers to this transaction as a reverse repurchase agreement (reverse repo).

Readers are encouraged to consult the full text of this ASU on FASB's website at www.fasb.org. Refer to section A.02 in appendix A for more information on this ASU if it is applicable to your reporting period.

7.71 The following categories of liabilities are reported in the statement of assets and liabilities.

7.72 *Accounts payable.* FASB ASC 946-405-45-1 states that accounts payable should be listed separately for investment securities purchased and capital stock reacquired. As noted in FASB ASC 850-10-50-1, separate disclosure is required for material related-party transactions other than compensation arrangements, expense allowances, and other similar items in the normal course of business. However, disclosure of transactions that are eliminated in the preparation of consolidated or combined financial statements is not required in those statements.

7.73 *Call or put options written, futures contracts, and securities sold short.* Call or put options written and securities sold short at the close of the period should be presented separately at fair value in the statement of assets and liabilities, with premiums received on written options and proceeds from short sales disclosed parenthetically. Variation margin due to a broker on futures contracts should be disclosed separately, if significant. Details of the securities sold short, options written, and futures contracts should include information about quantities, fair values, and proceeds and should be presented within the schedule of investments, as discussed in paragraphs 7.27–.47. Information presented for options written should include the number of shares or principal amount, the fair value of each option, the strike price, and the exercise date.

7.74 *Accrued liabilities.* Accrued liabilities include liabilities for management fees, performance fees, distribution fees, interest, compensation, taxes, and other expenses incurred in the normal course of operations.

7.75 *Notes payable and other debt.* Notes payable to banks, including bank overdrafts, and other debt should be stated at amounts payable, net of unamortized premium or discount, and reported separately, unless the fair value option that is permitted under FASB ASC 825, *Financial Instruments*, is elected. Information relating to unused lines of credit, conditions of credit agreements, and long term debt maturities should be disclosed in the notes to the financial statements. If the fair value option is not elected, the investment company should also disclose the fair value of liabilities, in accordance with the disclosure requirements of FASB ASC 825-10-50. The fair value option is discussed further in paragraphs 7.99–.102.

7.76 On November 5, 2007, the SEC released Staff Accounting Bulletin (SAB) No. 109, *Written Loan Commitments Recorded at Fair Value Through Earnings*, which expresses the views of the staff regarding written loan commitments that are accounted for at fair value through earnings under GAAP. Previously, SAB No. 105, *Application of Accounting Principles to Loan Commitments*, stated that in measuring the fair value of a derivative loan commitment, it would be inappropriate to incorporate the expected net future cash flows related to the associated servicing of the loan. SAB No. 109 supersedes SAB No. 105 and expresses the current view of the SEC staff that is consistent with the guidance in FASB ASC 860-50 and 825. Both topics express the view that the expected net future cash flows related to the associated servicing of the loan should be included in the measurement of all written loan commitments that are accounted for at fair value through earnings.

7.77 *Reverse repurchase agreements.* According to Q&A section 6910.22, "Presentation of Reverse Repurchase Agreements" (AICPA, *Technical Questions and Answers*), *reverse repurchases agreements* are defined as the sale of a security at a specified price with an agreement to purchase the same or substantially the same security from the same counterparty at a fixed or determinable price at a future date.[34] Because reverse repurchase agreements represent a fixed, determinable obligation of the investment company, such agreements should also be presented at amounts payable, unless the fair value option that is permitted under FASB ASC 825 is elected. A reverse repurchase agreement denominated in a currency that differs from the reporting currency should be translated at the current exchange rate.

7.78 *Deferred fees.* According to Q&A section 6910.27, "Treatment of Deferred Fees" (AICPA, *Technical Questions and Answers*), the governing documents of some offshore funds may provide that the investment adviser may elect to defer payment of its management fee, incentive fee, or both. Based on the documents, the deferred fees that are payable to the investment adviser

---

[34] The FASB ASC glossary definition of a *repurchase agreement* notes that in certain industries, the terminology is reversed (that is, entities in those industries refer to this type of agreement as a *reverse repurchase agreement*). Investment companies may fall into this category of reverse terminology. See also appendix A, "Guidance Updates," of this guide for changes to this definition resulting from the issuance of FASB ASU No. 2014-11, *Transfers and Servicing (Topic 860): Repurchase-to-Maturity Transactions, Repurchase Financings, and Disclosures.*

do not take the form of a legal capital account and are settled exclusively in cash. Under this arrangement, the fund retains the fee amount and is obligated to pay the investment adviser the deferred fees at a later date, adjusted for the fund's rate of return (whether positive or negative). In accordance with guidance from paragraph 35 of FASB Concept Statement No. 6, *Elements of Financial Statements—a replacement of FASB Concepts Statement No. 3 (incorporating an amendment of FASB Concepts Statement No. 2)*, the fund should record the cumulative deferred fees as a liability. The indexing of this liability to the fund's rate of return represents a hybrid instrument that has a host debt instrument with an embedded derivative, which has attributes of a total return contract. Although FASB ASC 815-15-25-1 and 815-15-55-190 require the embedded total return contract to be bifurcated from the host debt instrument, the SEC staff has previously indicated[35] that the bifurcation requirements of FASB ASC 815 do not extend beyond measurement to financial statement presentation if the embedded derivative and host debt instrument, together, represent the principal and interest obligations of a debt instrument. Although the fund should fair value the embedded return component of the deferral arrangement, according to the guidance from FASB ASC 815-10-25-1, 815-10-30-1, and 815-10-35-1, generally, the fair value of such return component would be the same as the appreciated or depreciated return of the fund because (*a*) the fund fair values all its investments, whether assets or liabilities, which generally represent substantially all its net assets, and (*b*) if the deferred fee liability was transferred, the transfer would likely be transacted at the current net asset value.[36] The deferred fees and embedded total return contracts associated with deferred fees that are at an appreciated or depreciated position as of the reporting date may be presented as one amount titled "Deferred incentive fees payable" on the statement of assets and liabilities.

7.79 *Other liabilities.* As stated by FASB ASC 946-405-45-2, other liabilities include amounts due to counterparties for collateral on the return of securities loaned, deferred income, and dividends and distributions payable. Payables denominated in foreign currencies should be converted into the functional currency at current exchange rates and may be categorized within the corresponding functional currency payables.

7.80 Rule 6.04 of Regulation S-X contains guidance for balance sheets of registered investment companies regarding how to present other liabilities. It requires the following items to be stated separately on the balance sheet: amounts payable for investment advisory, management, and service fees and the total amount payable to officers and directors or trustees, controlled companies, and other affiliates, excluding any amounts owing to noncontrolled affiliates that arose in the ordinary course of business and that are subject to usual trade terms.

7.81 FASB ASC 860-30-25-5 describes the accounting for noncash collateral by the debtor (obligor) and secured party, which depends on whether the secured party has the right to sell or repledge the collateral and whether the debtor has defaulted. FASB ASC 860-30-25-4 explains that cash collateral used in securities lending transactions should be derecognized by the debtor and recognized by the secured party, not as collateral, but, rather, as proceeds

---

[35] Remarks by E. Michael Pierce at the Twenty-Eighth Annual National Conference on Current SEC Developments held December 4–6, 2000.

[36] All concepts of FASB ASC 820, *Fair Value Measurement*, should be considered.

of either a sale or borrowing. FASB ASC 860-30-25-7 explains that many securities lending transactions (including those of many investment companies) often both entitle and obligate the transferor to repurchase or redeem the transferred financial assets before their maturity. In such a transaction, the transferor maintains effective control over those assets when all the following conditions in FASB ASC 860-10-40-24 are met:

- The financial assets to be repurchased or redeemed are the same or substantially the same as those transferred. (To be substantially the same, the financial asset that was transferred and the financial asset that is to be repurchased or redeemed need to have certain characteristics. See FASB ASC 860-10-40-24 for a detailed listing of all such characteristics, and see FASB ASC 860-10-55-35 for related implementation guidance).
- The agreement is to repurchase or redeem them before maturity at a fixed or determinable price.
- The agreement is entered into contemporaneously with, or in contemplation of, the transfer.

  [Note that neither the transferor's ability to repurchase or redeem the financial assets at substantially the same agreed terms, nor the transferor's maintenance of sufficient collateral, are considered during the assessment of effective control.]

FASB ASC 860-30-25-7 continues to explain that those transactions should be accounted for as secured borrowings, in which (a) cash (or other securities that the holder is permitted by contract or custom to sell or repledge) received as collateral is considered the amount borrowed, (b) the securities loaned are considered pledged as collateral against the cash borrowed and reclassified as set forth in FASB ASC 860-30-25-5(a), and (c) any rebate paid to the transferee of securities is interest on the cash that the transferor is considered to have borrowed.

7.82 FASB ASC 860-10-50 discusses required disclosures for transfers and servicing for all entities. FASB ASC 860-10-50-3 explains that the principal objectives of these disclosures are to provide financial statement users with an understanding of the following:

- A transferor's continuing involvement, if any, with transferred financial assets
- The nature of any restrictions on assets reported by an entity in its statement of financial position that relate to a transferred financial asset, including the carrying amounts of those assets
- How servicing assets and servicing liabilities are reported under FASB ASC 860-50
- For transfers accounted for as sales, if a transferor has continuing involvement with the transferred financial assets, how the transfer of financial assets affects an entity's financial position, financial performance, and cash flows
- For transfers of financial assets accounted for as secured borrowings, how the transfer of financial assets affects an entity's financial position, financial performance, and cash flows

7.83 Under "Pending Content" in FASB ASC 480-10-25-4, mandatorily redeemable financial instruments, such as mandatorily redeemable preferred stock, should be classified as a liability, unless the redemption is required to occur upon liquidation or termination of the reporting entity. Although mutual fund shares are not mandatorily redeemable, other types of equity instruments should be considered under FASB ASC 480, *Distinguishing Liabilities from Equity*. Paragraphs 7.108–.109 provide further discussion regarding the various effective dates and deferrals related to "Pending Content" in FASB ASC 480-10-25-4.

Fair Value Disclosures

7.84 FASB ASC 820-10-50 discusses the disclosures required for assets and liabilities measured at fair value. FASB ASC 820-10-50-1 explains that for assets and liabilities that are measured at fair value on a recurring or nonrecurring basis in the statement of financial position after initial recognition, the reporting entity is required to disclose certain information that enables users of its financial statements to assess the valuation techniques and inputs used to develop those measurements. For recurring fair value measurements using significant unobservable inputs (level 3), the reporting entity is required to disclose certain information to help users assess the effect of the measurements on earnings (or changes in net assets) for the period.

7.85 Professional judgment may need to be applied as reporting entities implement and address the broad disclosure objectives summarized in the preceding paragraph. FASB ASC 820-10-50-1A lists the following items that are required to be considered when addressing disclosure objectives in FASB ASC 820-10-50-1:

    a. The level of detail necessary to satisfy the disclosure requirements

    b. How much emphasis to place on each of the various requirements

    c. How much aggregation or disaggregation to undertake

    d. Whether users of financial statements need additional information to evaluate the quantitative information disclosed

7.86 FASB ASC 820-10-55-104 builds on this guidance, adding that a reporting entity might disclose some or all of the following:

    a. The nature of the item being measured at fair value, including the characteristics of the item being measured that are taken into account in the determination of relevant inputs

    b. How third-party information such as broker quotes, pricing services, net asset values, and relevant market data was taken into account when measuring fair value

7.87 FASB ASC 820-10-50-2 requires a reporting entity to disclose, at a minimum, the following information for each class of assets and liabilities measured at fair value in the statement of financial position after initial recognition:

    a. For recurring and nonrecurring fair value measurements, the fair value measurement at the end of the reporting period, and for nonrecurring fair value measurements, the reasons for the measurement. Recurring fair value measurements of assets or liabilities are those that other FASB ASC topics require or permit in the statement of financial position at the end of each reporting period. Nonrecurring fair value measurements of assets or liabilities are those that other FASB ASC topics require or permit in the statement of financial position in particular circumstances (for example, when a reporting entity measures a long-lived asset or disposal group classified as held for sale at fair value less costs to sell in accordance with FASB ASC 360, *Property, Plant and Equipment*, because the asset's fair value less costs to sell is lower than its carrying value).

b. For recurring and nonrecurring fair value measurements, the level within the fair value hierarchy in which the fair value measurements are categorized in their entirety (level 1, 2, or 3).

c. For assets and liabilities held at the end of the reporting period that are measured at fair value on a recurring basis, the amounts of any transfers between level 1 and level 2 of the fair value hierarchy, the reasons for the transfers, and the reporting entity's policy for determining when transfers between levels are deemed to have occurred. Transfers into each level should be disclosed separately from transfers out of each level. FASB ASC 820-10-50-2C explains that a reporting entity should disclose and consistently follow its policy for determining when transfers between levels of the fair value hierarchy are deemed to have occurred. The policy about the timing of recognizing transfers should be the same for transfers into the levels as that for transfers out of the levels. Examples of policies for determining the timing of transfers include the following: the date of the event or change in circumstances that caused the transfer, the beginning of the reporting period, and the end of the reporting period.

d. For recurring and nonrecurring fair value measurements categorized within level 2 and level 3 of the fair value hierarchy, a description of the valuation technique(s) and the inputs used in the fair value measurement. If there has been a change in valuation technique (for example, changing from a market approach to an income approach or the use of an additional valuation technique), the reporting entity should disclose that change and the reason(s) for making it.

e. For fair value measurements categorized within level 3 of the fair value hierarchy, a reporting entity should provide quantitative information about the significant unobservable inputs used in the fair value measurement. A reporting entity is not required to create quantitative information to comply with this disclosure requirement if quantitative unobservable inputs are not developed by the reporting entity when measuring fair value (for example, when a reporting entity uses prices from prior transactions or third-party pricing information without adjustment). However, when providing this disclosure, a reporting entity cannot ignore quantitative unobservable inputs that are significant to the fair value measurement and are reasonably available to the reporting entity.

f. For recurring fair value measurements categorized within level 3 of the fair value hierarchy, a reconciliation from the opening balances to the closing balances, disclosing separately changes during the period attributable to any of the following:

     i. Total gains or losses for the period recognized in earnings (or changes in net assets), and the line items(s) in the statement of income (or activities) in which those gains or losses are recognized.

ii. Total gains or losses recognized in other comprehensive income, and the line item(s) in other comprehensive income in which those gains or losses are recognized.

iii. Purchases, sales, issuances, and settlements (each of those types of changes disclosed separately).

iv. The amounts of any transfers into or out of level 3 of the fair value hierarchy, the reasons for those transfers, and the reporting entity's policy for determining when transfers between levels are deemed to have occurred. Transfers into level 3 should be disclosed and discussed separately from transfers out of level 3.

g. For recurring fair value measurements categorized within level 3 of the fair value hierarchy, the amount of the total gains or losses for the period in item f(i) included in earnings (or changes in net assets) that is attributable to the change in unrealized gains or losses relating to those assets and liabilities still held at the end of the reporting period, and the line item(s) in the statement of income (or activities) in which those unrealized gains or losses are recognized.

h. For recurring and nonrecurring fair value measurements categorized within level 3 of the fair value hierarchy, a description of the valuation processes used by the reporting entity (including, for example, how an entity determines its valuation policies and procedures and analyzes changes in fair value measurements from period to period).

i. For recurring fair value measurements categorized within level 3 of the fair value hierarchy, a narrative description of the sensitivity of the fair value measurement to changes in unobservable inputs if a change in those inputs to a different amount might result in a significantly higher or lower fair value measurement. If there are interrelationships between those inputs and other unobservable inputs used in the fair value measurement, a reporting entity should also provide a description of those interrelationships and how they magnify or mitigate the effect of changes in the unobservable inputs of the fair value measurement. To comply with that disclosure requirement, the narrative description of the sensitivity to changes in unobservable inputs should include, at a minimum, the unobservable inputs disclosed when complying with items d–e.

j. For recurring and nonrecurring fair value measurements, if the highest and best use of a nonfinancial asset differs from its current use, a reporting entity should disclose that fact and why the nonfinancial asset is being used in a manner that differs from its highest and best use.

Paragraph 7.224 provides an illustrative example of the disclosures required by FASB ASC 820-10-50-2.

7.88 FASB ASC 820-10-50-2F states that a nonpublic entity is not required to disclose the information required by FASB ASC 820-10-50-2(bb) and (g) and FASB ASC 820-10-50-2E (discussed in paragraphs 7.87c, 7.87i, and

7.97 of this guide) unless required by another FASB ASC topic. A *nonpublic entity* is defined by the FASB ASC glossary as an entity that does not meet any of the following conditions:

  a. Its debt or equity securities trade in a public market either on a stock exchange (domestic or foreign) or in an over-the-counter market, including securities quoted only locally or regionally.

  b. It is a conduit bond obligor for conduit debt securities that are traded in a public market (a domestic or foreign stock exchange or an over-the-counter market, including local or regional markets).

  c. It files with a regulatory agency in preparation for the sale of any class of debt or equity securities in a public market.

  d. It is required to file or furnish financial statements with the SEC.

  e. It is controlled by an entity covered by items *a–d.*

FASB ASC 820-10-50-2F includes the phrase "unless required by another FASB ASC Topic." This phrase requires nonregistered investment companies to consider whether other applicable FASB ASC topics (for example, FASB ASC 825, which is discussed in further detail in paragraph 7.102) require any of the disclosures referenced in FASB ASC 820-10-50-2F.

7.89 When implementing the quantitative information disclosure requirement in paragraph 7.87*e*, investment companies may consider the following:

  • *Disaggregation.* Determining the appropriate level of disaggregation may require professional judgment. FASB ASC 820 does not specify what level of disaggregation is required for quantitative disclosures, but the illustrative disclosure example in FASB ASC 820-10-55-103 indicates that at least each class of asset or liability may be listed. However, some reporting entities may find that further disaggregation is necessary, in order to provide financial statement users with the ability to evaluate and sufficiently understand the quantitative information (see considerations listed in paragraphs 7.85–.86). When determining whether further disaggregation is necessary, an entity may consider the results of its fair value hierarchy classification analysis, and the inputs evaluated during such analysis. The same inputs that were identified as relevant during the fair value hierarchy classification analysis may also be considered significant enough to warrant disclosure in the quantitative disclosure about significant unobservable inputs. Further, when multiple types of fair value measurement techniques are used to value individual assets (or liabilities) or groups of assets (or liabilities) within an individual class of assets (or liabilities), disaggregation below the asset class level may be necessary in order to sufficiently address the objectives in paragraphs 7.85–.86. If a wide range of quantitative data occurs at a certain disaggregation level, it may be an indicator that the level of disaggregation is not appropriate. Generally, the disaggregation level depends on the nature and risks of the investment.

  • *Quantitative information types.* Professional judgment may be required when determining what quantitative information is relevant and should be disclosed. Reporting entities may consider the overall objectives of paragraphs 7.84–.86 when applying such judgment in this area, including determining what type of information is most meaningful to the users of the financial statements. FASB ASC 820 does not specify what type of quantitative information is required to be disclosed. However, the illustrative disclosure example in FASB ASC 820-10-55-103 indicates that the high and low end range values and the weighted average of the range may be disclosed.[37]

The following comments provided in paragraph BC86 of ASU No. 2011-04, *Fair Value (Topic 820)—Amendments to Achieve Common Fair Value Measurement and Disclosure Requirements in U.S. GAAP and IFRS*, may also be helpful in understanding the objective of the quantitative information disclosure:

> The Boards concluded that the information required by the disclosure will facilitate comparisons of the inputs used over time, providing users with information about changes in management's views about particular unobservable inputs and about changes in the market for the assets and liabilities within a particular class. In addition, that disclosure might facilitate comparison between reporting entities with similar assets and liabilities categorized within level 3 of the fair value hierarchy.

> The Boards noted that the objective of the disclosure is not to enable users of the financial statements to replicate the reporting entity's pricing models but to provide enough information for users to assess whether the reporting entity's views about individual inputs differed from their own and, if so, to decide how to incorporate the reporting entity's fair value measurement in their decisions.

- *Exceptions to the disclosure requirement in paragraph 7.87e*:

  — As discussed in paragraph 7.87e, the reporting entity does not have to disclose quantitative information if inputs are not developed by the entity when measuring fair value. However, the same paragraph states that a company cannot ignore quantitative information that is significant and is reasonably available to the entity. Investment companies may consider whether they have obtained and evaluated the third party's price (or inputs to the price) during due diligence required by FASB ASC 820-10-35-54K, which allows reporting entities to use quoted prices from third parties to determine fair value measurements, but requires reporting entities to perform due diligence to ensure those prices were developed in accordance with FASB ASC 820. When performing such due diligence, an investment company may consider the

---

[37] As noted in the November 2012 Expert Panel Conference Call Highlights (available at the Expert Panel – Investment Companies page of www.aicpa.org), the SEC staff was requested to provide feedback on ASU No. 2011-04, *Fair Value Measurement (Topic 820): Amendments to Achieve Common Fair Value Measurement and Disclosure Requirements in U.S. GAAP and IFRSs*, disclosures identified in its financial statement reviews. The SEC staff commented on the use of wide ranges of unobservable inputs in tabular disclosures in accordance with ASU No. 2011-04. In one situation in which the valuation technique used was discounted cash flow model and disclosure had a wide range of discount rates being used, the registrant was asked to provide a weighted average range of the discount rate, consistent with illustrative disclosures included in FASB ASC 820-10-55.

following procedures: gain an understanding of the techniques and models used by the third party, compare valuations received to market information and information received from other vendors, if available, and perform back testing. Also, FASB Staff Position No. 157-3, *Determining the Fair Value of a Financial Asset When the Market for That Asset Is Not Active* (codified in FASB ASC 820-10-35), provides guidance on how vendor prices and broker quotes should be considered in assessing observable and unobservable inputs for the fair value measurement.

— The reporting entity does not have to disclose quantitative information if the net asset value is used as a practical expedient to determine fair value of the investment (see paragraph 7.94 for discussion of disclosure requirements for investments in companies that calculate net asset value per share, regardless of whether the practical expedient has been applied). Paragraph BC89 of ASU No. 2011-04 supports this by stating "...disclosures about the fair value of those assets and liabilities that are subject to the practical expedient and categorized within level 3 of the fair value hierarchy would not be meaningful for such instruments because the determination of the level in the hierarchy is made on the basis of the reporting entity's ability to redeem its investment, rather than on the basis of whether the inputs used in the measurement are observable or unobservable." However, when an adjustment to the practical expedient value is necessary, the adjustment may need to be considered for the level 3 input table disclosure.

- *Presentation of disclosed quantitative information.* FASB ASC 820-10-50-8 requires quantitative information to be disclosed in a tabular format.

7.90   When implementing the disclosure requirement related to valuation processes in paragraph 7.87*h*, investment companies may consider disclosing the following items listed in FASB ASC 820-10-55-105:

- For the group within the reporting entity that decides the reporting entity's valuation policies and procedures, (*a*) its description, (*b*) to whom that group reports, and (*c*) the internal reporting procedures in place (for example, whether and, if so, how pricing, risk management, or audit committees discuss and assess the fair value measurements)
- The frequency and methods for calibration, back testing, and other testing procedures of pricing models
- The process for analyzing changes in fair value measurements from period to period
- How the reporting entity determined that third-party information, such as broker quotes or pricing services, used in the fair value measurement was developed in accordance with FASB ASC 820

- The methods used to develop and substantiate the unobservable inputs used in a fair value measurement

7.91 When implementing the narrative description of sensitivity disclosure requirement in paragraph 7.87*i*, investment companies may consider paragraph BC96 of ASU No. 2011-04, which explains that "the Boards expect that the narrative description will focus on the unobservable inputs for which quantitative information is disclosed because those are the unobservable inputs that the entity has determined are most significant to the fair value measurement." Further, investment companies may consider the example provided in FASB ASC 820-10-55-106:

> The significant unobservable inputs used in the fair value measurement of the reporting entity's residential mortgage-backed securities are prepayment rates, probability of default, and loss severity in the event of default. Significant increases (decreases) in any of those inputs in isolation would result in a significantly lower (higher) fair value measurement. Generally, a change in the assumption used for the probability of default is accompanied by a directionally similar change in the assumption used for the loss severity and a directionally opposite change in the assumption used for prepayment rates.

7.92 FASB ASC 820-10-50-2B explains that a reporting entity should determine appropriate classes of assets and liabilities on the basis of the nature, characteristics, and risks of the asset or liability, and the level of the fair value hierarchy within which the fair value measurement is categorized. Further, the number of classes may need to be greater for fair value measurements within level 3 of the fair value hierarchy because those measurements have a greater degree of uncertainty and subjectivity. A class of assets and liabilities will often require greater disaggregation than the line items presented in the statement of financial position.

7.93 FASB ASC 820-10-50-3 states that, for derivative assets and liabilities, the reporting entity should present both the fair value disclosures discussed in paragraph 7.87*a–c* on a gross basis (which is consistent with the requirements in FASB ASC 815-10-50-4B[a]) and the reconciliation disclosures discussed in paragraph 7.87*f–g* on either a gross or net basis.

7.94 FASB ASC 820-10-50-6A states that for investments in certain entities that calculate net asset value per share (investments that are within the scope of paragraphs 4–5 of FASB ASC 820-10-15) and measured at fair value on a recurring or nonrecurring basis during the period, a reporting entity should disclose information that help users of financial statements to understand the nature and risks of the investments and whether the investments are probable of being sold at amounts different from net asset value per share (or its equivalent).

7.95 These disclosures are required, regardless of whether the practical expedient, as discussed in chapter 2, has been applied. These disclosures, according to FASB ASC 820-10-50-6A, to the extent applicable, are required for each class of investment. The required disclosures, according to FASB ASC 820-10-50-6A, at a minimum, are as follows:

> *a.* The fair value measurement (as determined by applying paragraphs 59–62 of FASB ASC 820-10-35) of the investments in the class at the reporting date and a description of the significant investment strategies of the investee(s) in the class.

b. For each class of investment that includes investments that can never be redeemed with the investees, but the reporting entity receives distributions through the liquidation of the underlying assets of the investees, the reporting entity's estimate of the period of time over which the underlying assets are expected to be liquidated by the investees.

c. The amount of the reporting entity's unfunded commitments related to investments in the class.

d. A general description of the terms and conditions upon which the investor may redeem investments in the class (for example, quarterly redemption with 60 days' notice).

e. The circumstances in which an otherwise redeemable investment in the class (or a portion thereof) might not be redeemable (for example, investments subject to a lockup or gate). Also, for those otherwise redeemable investments that are restricted from redemption as of the reporting entity's measurement date, the reporting entity should disclose its estimate of when the restriction from redemption might lapse. If an estimate cannot be made, the reporting entity should disclose that fact and how long the restriction has been in effect.

f. Any other significant restriction on the ability to sell investments in the class at the measurement date.

g. If a reporting entity determines that it is probable that it will sell an investment or investments for an amount different from net asset value per share (or its equivalent), as described in FASB ASC 820-10-35-62, the reporting entity should disclose the total fair value of all investments that meet the criteria in FASB ASC 820-10-35-62 and any remaining actions required to complete the sale.

h. If a group of investments would otherwise meet the criteria in FASB ASC 820-10-35-62, but the individual investments to be sold have not been identified (for example, if a reporting entity decides to sell 20 percent of its investments in private equity funds, but the individual investments to be sold have not been identified), so the investments continue to qualify for the practical expedient in FASB ASC 820-10-35-59, the reporting entity should disclose its plans to sell and any remaining actions required to complete the sale(s).

7.96   Paragraph 7.233, from FASB ASC 820-10-55-107, provides an example of the disclosures required by FASB ASC 820-10-50-6A.

7.97   FASB ASC 820-10-50-2E provides disclosure requirements for those classes of assets and liabilities not measured at fair value in the statement of financial position but for which the fair value is disclosed. Specifically, for those classes of assets and liabilities, a reporting entity should disclose the information required by paragraph 7.87b, d, and h. No other disclosures in FASB ASC 820-10-50 (summarized in paragraphs 7.84–.96) are required for those classes of assets and liabilities. Paragraphs 3–4 of FASB ASC 825-10-55 list examples of financial instruments that a financial entity and nonfinancial entity, respectively, would include in their disclosures about the fair value of financial instruments, including the following:

- Cash and short-term investments

- Investment securities and trading account assets
- Long-term investments
- Loan receivables
- Deposit liabilities
- Long-term debt
- Commitments to extend credit
- Standby letters of credit
- Written financial guarantees

Other examples may include, but would not be limited to, the following: tender option bonds, reverse repurchase agreements, lines of credit, and variable-rate demand preferred shares.

7.98   Q&A section 2220.26, "Categorization of Investments for Disclosure Purposes" (AICPA, *Technical Questions and Answers*), explains that certain entities that specialize in one particular investment category or have a significant investment in one such category should categorize investments and tailor disclosures to address the concentrations of risk that are specifically attributable to the investments. For example, a private equity fund of funds should not simply categorize its investments as "private equity" because this categorization is not specific enough to address the nature and risks of the investee funds. More specific categorization, perhaps relating to industry; geography; vintage year; or the strategy of the investees (venture, buyout, mezzanine), may be more appropriate and useful to the reader.

Fair Value Option

7.99   FASB ASC 825 creates a fair value option under which an entity may irrevocably elect fair value as the initial and subsequent measure for many financial instruments and certain other items, with changes in fair value recognized in earnings as those changes occur. FASB ASC 825-10-35-4 explains that a business entity should report unrealized gains and losses on items for which the fair value option has been elected in earnings at each subsequent reporting date. An election is made on an instrument-by-instrument basis (with certain exceptions), generally when an instrument is initially recognized in the financial statements. The fair value option need not be applied to all identical items, except as required by FASB ASC 825-10-25-7. Most financial assets and liabilities are eligible to be recognized using the fair value option, as are firm commitments for financial instruments and certain nonfinancial contracts.

7.100   As explained by FASB ASC 825-10-15-5, specifically excluded from eligibility of the fair value option are

- an investment in a subsidiary that the entity is required to consolidate.
- an interest in a VIE that the entity is required to consolidate.
- an employer's and a plan's obligations for pension benefits, other postretirement benefits (including health care and life insurance benefits), postemployment benefits, employee stock option and stock purchase plans, and other deferred compensation arrangements (or assets representing net overfunded positions in those plans).

- financial assets and liabilities recognized under leases (this does not apply to a guarantee of a third-party lease obligation or contingent obligation arising from a cancelled lease).

- deposit liabilities of depository institutions.

- financial instruments that are, in whole or in part, classified by the issuer as a component of shareholder's equity (including temporary equity) (for example, a convertible debt security with a noncontingent beneficial conversion feature).

7.101 FASB ASC 825-10-45 and 825-10-50 also include presentation and disclosure requirements designed to facilitate comparisons between entities that choose different measurement attributes for similar types of assets and liabilities. Paragraphs 1–2 of FASB ASC 825-10-45 state that entities should report assets and liabilities that are measured using the fair value option in a manner that separates those reported fair values from the carrying amounts of similar assets and liabilities measured using another measurement attribute. To accomplish that, an entity should either (*a*) report the aggregate of both fair value and nonfair-value items on a single line, with the fair value amount parenthetically disclosed or (*b*) present separate lines for the fair value carrying amounts and the nonfair-value carrying amounts. As discussed in FASB ASC 825-10-25-3, upfront costs and fees related to items for which the fair value option is elected should be recognized in earnings as incurred and not deferred.

7.102 Nonregistered investment companies may consider the provisions in "Pending Content" in FASB ASC 825-10-50-3, which provides an exception from the disclosure requirements in paragraphs 10–19 of FASB ASC 825-10-50 for entities that meet all of the following criteria:

a. The entity is a nonpublic entity (see paragraph 7.88 for definition of *nonpublic entity*).

b. The entity's total assets are less than $100 million on the date of the financial statements.

c. The entity has no instrument that, in whole or in part, is accounted for as a derivative instrument under FASB ASC 815 other than commitments related to the origination of mortgage loans to be held for sale during the reporting period. For purposes of this disclosure guidance, a receive-variable, pay-fixed interest rate swap for which the simplified hedge accounting approach (see FASB ASC 815-20) is applied should not be considered an instrument that is accounted for as a derivative instrument under FASB ASC 815.

Further, pursuant to FASB ASC 825-10-50-3A, a reporting entity that is a nonpublic entity (see paragraph 7.88) is not required to disclose the level of the fair value hierarchy within which the fair value measurements are categorized in their entirety (level 1, 2, or 3) (disclosure requirement in FASB ASC 825-10-50-10(d)) for items disclosed at fair value but not measured at fair value in the statement of financial position.

Net Assets

7.103 FASB ASC 946-20-50-11 requires all investment companies to disclose only two components of capital on the balance sheet: shareholder capital and distributable earnings. The components of distributable earnings, on a tax basis, should be disclosed in a note to the financial statements. This information enables investors to determine the amount of accumulated and undistributed earnings that they potentially could receive in the future and on which they could be taxed. Additionally, as stated by FASB 946-20-50-12, the notes should disclose the tax-basis components of distributable earnings as of the most recent tax year-end, including undistributed ordinary income, undistributed long term capital gains, capital loss carryforwards, and unrealized appreciation (depreciation).

7.104　The statement or the notes should also disclose information about the following:[38]

    a.　Units of capital, including the title of each class of capital shares or other capital units, the number authorized, the number outstanding, and the dollar amount.

    b.　Paid-in capital, which includes the net proceeds received on the sale of capital shares less the cost of reacquired shares and the return of capital distributions (that is, the tax return of capital distributions [see paragraphs 7.147–.148]). In addition, certain differences between GAAP-basis income or gain amounts and tax-basis amounts distributed from income or gain are reclassified to paid-in capital in the period in which such differences become permanent differences (see paragraphs 7.147–.148).

7.105　As further explained by FASB ASC 946-20-50-13, if a provision for deferred income taxes on unrealized appreciation exists, it should be charged against the unrealized gains account and disclosed as such in the statement of operations. Explanations should be provided for the differences between the total of these amounts and distributable earnings (accumulated losses). FASB ASC 946-20-50-14 notes that investment partnerships and other pass-through entities should aggregate all elements of equity into partners' capital because the results from operations are deemed distributed to each partner.

7.106　Net asset value per share should be disclosed for each class of shares, as explained by FASB ASC 946-505-50-1. *Net asset value per share* is defined by the FASB ASC glossary as the amount of net assets attributable to each share of capital stock (other than senior equity securities [that is, preferred stock]) outstanding at the close of the period. It excludes the effects of assuming conversion of outstanding convertible securities, regardless of whether their conversion would have a diluting effect.

7.107　Consistent with FASB Emerging Issues Task Force (EITF) Topic No. D-98, SEC Staff Announcement "Classification and Measurement of Redeemable Securities," a registered investment company should not include preferred stock under the caption "Net Assets" if the investment company may be required to redeem all or part of the preferred stock upon failure to satisfy statistical coverage requirements imposed by its governing documents or a rating agency. The Chief Accountant's Office of the Division of Investment Management released more guidance specific to the application of the "Pending

---

[38] Rules 6.04.16 and 604.17 of Regulation S-X require such information to be included on the face of the statement of assets and liabilities, if such statement is presented. In addition, components of distributable earnings are required to be presented separately.

The requirements of SEC Regulation S-X to disclose individual components of distributable earnings (undistributed income, accumulated gains [losses], and unrealized appreciation [depreciation]) under Rules 6.04.16 and 604.17 and distributions (income, gain, and return of capital) under Rule 6-09.3 continue to apply for SEC registrants, and preparers should continue to accumulate and disclose the necessary additional information.

Content" guidance in FASB ASC 480-10 to closed-end funds. Of most significance, the staff indicated that distributions to preferred stockholders should be presented below net investment income on the statement of operations, the statement of changes in net assets, and financial highlights as a component of the net increase (decrease) in net assets resulting from investment operations. The staff indicated that the "Pending Content" in FASB ASC 480-10 provides guidance on preferred stock arrangements that are redeemable on a fixed or determinable date.

7.108   FASB ASC 480-10-65-1 describes the effective date and transition information for all "Pending Content" guidance in FASB ASC 480-10 that is linked to that paragraph. For instruments issued by nonpublic entities that are not SEC registrants and that are mandatorily redeemable on fixed dates for amounts that are either fixed or determined by reference to an interest rate index, a currency index, or another external index, the classification, measurement, and disclosure provisions of FASB ASC 480-10 were effective for fiscal years beginning after December 15, 2004. The guidance in FASB ASC 480-10 is indefinitely deferred pending further FASB action for mandatorily redeemable financial instruments issued by nonpublic entities that are not SEC registrants, other than those mandatorily redeemable instruments described previously. During the indefinite deferral, FASB plans to reconsider implementation issues and, perhaps, classification or measurement guidance for those instruments in conjunction with FASB's ongoing project on liabilities and equity. Mandatorily redeemable financial instruments issued by SEC registrants are not eligible for that deferral, even if the entity meets the definition of a nonpublic entity in FASB ASC 480-10. Those entities should follow the effective dates required by FASB ASC 480-10 and related guidance, including the deferral for certain mandatorily redeemable noncontrolling interests, as appropriate. If an entity is a nonpublic entity that is not an SEC registrant and (*a*) has issued shares that are required to be redeemed under related agreements, and (*b*) if the shares are issued with the redemption agreement and the required redemption relates to those specific underlying shares, then the shares are mandatorily redeemable and fall under the deferral stated previously.

7.109   FASB ASC 480-10-65-1 also explains that the effective date of FASB ASC 480-10 is deferred for certain mandatorily redeemable noncontrolling interests (of all entities, public and nonpublic) as follows:

a. For mandatorily redeemable noncontrolling interests that would not have to be classified as liabilities by the subsidiary under the liquidation exception in paragraphs 4 and 6 of FASB ASC 480-10-25 but would be classified as liabilities by the parent in consolidated financial statements, the classification and measurement provisions of FASB ASC 480-10 are deferred indefinitely pending further FASB action.

b. For other mandatorily redeemable noncontrolling interests that were issued before November 5, 2003, the measurement provisions of FASB ASC 480-10 are deferred indefinitely, both for the parent in consolidated financial statements and for the subsidiary that issued the instruments that result in the mandatorily redeemable noncontrolling interest, pending further FASB action. For those instruments, the measurement guidance for redeemable shares and noncontrolling interests in other predecessor literature (for example, in EITF Topic No. D-98) continues to apply during the deferral period. However, the classification provisions of FASB ASC 480-10 are not deferred.

FASB plans to reconsider implementation issues and, perhaps, classification or measurement guidance for those noncontrolling interests during the deferral period, in conjunction with FASB's ongoing projects. During the deferral period for certain mandatorily redeemable noncontrolling interests, all public entities as well as nonpublic entities that are SEC registrants are required to follow the disclosure requirements in paragraphs 1–3 of FASB ASC 480-10-50, as well as disclosures required by other applicable guidance. Further, this project is a joint project between FASB and the International Accounting Standards Board.

7.110 Under "Pending Content" in FASB ASC 480-10-25, financial instruments that are mandatorily redeemable on a fixed date or upon the occurrence of an event certain to occur should be classified initially as liabilities. Contingently redeemable securities, such as those described in paragraph 7.107, are not within the scope of FASB ASC 480-10-25 unless and until the contingency occurs, at which time the instruments should be reclassified as liabilities. "Pending Content" in FASB ASC 480-10-25-7 explains that a financial instrument that will be redeemed only upon the occurrence of a conditional event would be assessed at each reporting period to determine whether circumstances have changed such that the instrument now meets the definition of a mandatorily redeemable instrument (that is, the event is no longer conditional). If the event has occurred, the condition is resolved, or the event has become certain to occur, the financial instrument is reclassified as a liability. Therefore, with respect to contingently redeemable securities for which the contingency has not occurred, the guidance discussed in paragraph 7.107 should continue to be followed by registered investment companies.

Statement of Operations

7.111 As described by FASB ASC 946-225-45-1, the objective of the statement of operations is to present the increase or decrease in net assets resulting from all the company's investment activities by reporting investment income from dividends, interest, and other income less expenses, the amounts of realized gains or losses from investment and foreign currency transactions, and changes in unrealized appreciation or depreciation of investments and foreign currency-denominated assets and liabilities for the period. That format helps the user understand the contribution of each aspect of investment activity to the company's overall operations.

Investment Income

7.112 *Dividend income.* FASB ASC 946-320-25-4 states that dividend income is recorded on the ex-dividend date, not the declaration, record, or payable date, because on the ex-dividend date, the quoted market price of listed securities and other market-traded securities tends to be affected by the exclusion of the dividend declared. As noted by FASB ASC 946-20-50-9, dividends from affiliates and controlled companies should be disclosed.

7.113 Rule 6.07.1 of Regulation S-X for SEC registrants also requires that income from affiliates and controlled companies be disclosed. Investment companies are also required to comply with FASB ASC 850, *Related Party Disclosures*. (Chapter 2, "Investment Accounts," of this guide discusses noncash dividends, dividends in arrears on preferred stocks, and dividends from other than distributable earnings.)

7.114 *Interest income.* Interest income (including amortization of premiums and accretion of discounts) is generally accrued on all debt securities. However, chapter 2 discusses special reporting requirements for interest on high-yield debt securities, bonds in default, and other kinds of securities such as payment-in-kind bonds and step bonds. Interest earned on securities of affiliates and controlled companies should be disclosed separately.

7.115 *Other income.* Other income includes fee income from securities loaned and miscellaneous sources. Individual items, if material, should be disclosed separately. Rule 6.07 of Regulation S-X requires the separate disclosure of any category of income that exceeds 5 percent of the total investment income.

Expenses

7.116 As stated in FASB ASC 946-225-45-3, all of the following expenses are commonly reported separately:

- *a.* Investment advisory (management) fees (or compensation).
- *b.* Administration fees payable to an affiliate (if accrued under a separate agreement).
- *c.* Shareholder service costs, including fees and expenses for the transfer agent and dividend disbursing agent.
- *d.* Distribution (12b-1) expenses (discussed in chapter 8, "Other Accounts and Considerations," of this guide).
- *e.* Custodian fees.
- *f.* Cost of reports to shareholders.
- *g.* Federal and state income taxes. These expenses should be shown separately after the income category to which they apply, such as investment income and realized or unrealized gains. (Chapter 6, "Taxes," of this guide discusses the provision for taxes for entities that do not meet the requirements necessary to qualify as a regulated investment company [RIC].)
- *h.* Other taxes. (Foreign withholding taxes should be deducted from the relevant income item and disclosed parenthetically or shown as a separate contra-item in the "Income" section.)
- *i.* Interest (including interest on debt, bank borrowings, and reverse repurchase agreements).
- *j.* Dividends on securities sold short.
- *k.* Professional fees.
- *l.* Directors' or trustees' fees.
- *m.* Registration fees and expenses (discussed in chapter 8).

7.117 Regulation S-X requires separate disclosure of each expense exceeding 5 percent of total expenses. Additionally, the notes to the financial statements should include the total amounts by which expenses are increased and list each category that is increased by at least 5 percent of total expenses.[39]

---

[39] Rule 6.07(g) of Regulation S-X.

7.118   Amounts paid to affiliates or related parties (such as advisory fees, administration fees, distribution fees, brokerage commissions, and sales charges) should be disclosed, in accordance with FASB ASC 850. Significant provisions of related-party agreements, including the basis for determining management, advisory, administration, or distribution fees, and, also, other amounts paid to affiliates or related parties should be described in a note to the financial statements.

7.119   As explained in FASB ASC 946-20-05-11, an adviser or a third party may voluntarily or involuntarily waive its fee and reimburse expenses (waivers). An example of an involuntary waiver is when the advisory agreement (or other regulation or agreements that are either outside the adviser's control or require shareholder approval) provides that the adviser should reimburse the investment company for expenses in excess of a specified percentage of average net assets. As further described in FASB ASC 946-20-50-7, all voluntary and involuntary waivers should be disclosed on the face of the statement of operations as a reduction of total expenses. The expense ratio in the financial highlights should be shown net of voluntary and involuntary waivers. The effect of only voluntary waivers on the expense ratio should be disclosed (either as the basis point effect on the ratio or as the gross expense ratio) in a note to, or as part of, the financial highlights. In addition, the terms of all voluntary and involuntary waivers should be disclosed in the notes to the financial statements.

7.120   As noted in FASB ASC 946-20-50-4, if a 12b-1 distribution reimbursement plan[40] provides for the carryover of unreimbursed costs to subsequent periods, the terms of reimbursement and the unreimbursed amount should be disclosed.

7.121   The disclosure requirements in Section 30(e)(5) of the 1940 Act address aggregate remuneration to directors or trustees and each company of which any officer or director is an affiliated person. The auditor may conclude that the investment company has complied with the requirements by disclosure in the notes to the financial statements or in another manner that the investment company's management or legal counsel determines to be appropriate.

7.122   As noted in FASB ASC 946-20-05-9, an investment company may have a brokerage service arrangement with a broker-dealer or an affiliate of a broker-dealer under which the broker-dealer (or its affiliate), in connection with the investment company's brokerage transactions directed to the broker-dealer, provides or pays for services to the investment company (other than brokerage and research services as those terms are used in Section 28(e) of the 1934 Act). As further explained in FASB ASC 946-20-45-3, the relevant expense caption on the statement of operations and the expense ratio in the financial highlights should include the amount that would have been incurred by the investment company for such services had it paid for the services directly in an arm's length transaction. Such amounts should also be shown as a corresponding reduction in total expenses, captioned as "Fees paid indirectly."

---

[40] The FASB ASC glossary defines a *reimbursement plan* as a plan that provides for a 12b-1 fee, payable by the fund that may not exceed the lesser of an annual percentage of the fund's average net assets or actual costs incurred by the distributor net of contingent deferred sales load received by the distributor.

7.123 As stated in FASB ASC 946-20-45-5, expense offset arrangements under which a third party explicitly reduces its fees by a specified or readily ascertainable amount for services provided to the investment company in exchange for use of the investment company's assets should be presented in the statement of operations, the expense ratio in the financial highlights, and the notes to the financial statements in the same manner as brokerage service arrangements.

7.124 As discussed in FASB ASC 946-20-05-10, investment companies organized as limited partnerships typically receive advisory services from the general partner. Many partnerships pay fees for such services, chargeable as expenses to the partnership; others allocate net income from the limited partners' capital accounts to the general partner's capital account; and still others employ a combination of the two methods. Further, FASB ASC 946-20-45-4 notes that the amounts of any such payments or allocations for advisory services from the general partner should be presented in either the statement of operations or the statement of changes in partners' capital. FASB ASC 946-20-50-5 states that the method of computing such payments or allocations should be described in the notes to the financial statements.

7.125 According to Q&A section 6910.29, "Allocation of Unrealized Gain (Loss), Recognition of Carried Interest, and Clawback Obligations" (AICPA, *Technical Questions and Answers*), the governing documents of some nonregistered investment partnerships may contain provisions that do not allow allocations of unrealized gains or losses or do not require the recognition of carried interest (also referred to as *carry, incentive,* or *performance fees and allocations*) and clawback obligations (also referred to as *lookback, negative carried interest,* or *general partner*[41] *giveback*) until a specified date or time (for example, at the time of the partnership's liquidation or termination) or the occurrence of a specific event (such as the actual disposition of an investment). Often, in these cases, the partnership's investments are either not marketable or of such limited liquidity that interim valuations are highly subjective, and the intent of the provision is to delay the general partner's receipt of incentive allocations in cash until the gains can be measured objectively.

7.126 Q&A section 6910.29 also explains that if a nonregistered investment partnership reports capital by investor class, cumulative unrealized gains (losses), carried interest, and clawback provisions should be reflected in the equity balances of each class of shareholder or partner at the balance sheet date as if the investment company had realized all assets and settled all liabilities at the fair values reported in the financial statements and allocated all gains and losses and distributed the net assets to each class of shareholder or partner at the reporting date consistent with the provisions of the partnership's governing documents. Further discussion of each of these items follows:

> a. *Cumulative unrealized gains (losses).* Cumulative unrealized gains (losses) should be included in the ending balances of each class of shareholders' or partners' interest in the reporting entity at the reporting date, and the changes in such amounts should be reported

---

[41] Various terms may be used by different legal structures as the equivalents of *general partner* and *limited partner* (for example, *managing member* and *member* for limited liability companies). For convenience, the terms *partnership, general partner,* and *limited partner* are used throughout the Q&A section 6910.29, "Allocation of Unrealized Gain (Loss), Recognition of Carried Interest, and Clawback Obligations" (AICPA, *Technical Questions and Answers*), discussion but are intended to refer to any equivalent structure.

in the changes in net asset value and partners' capital for the reporting period.

b. *Carried interest.* The carried interest generally is due to the investment manager, an affiliated entity, or both and is either in the form of a fee (usually for offshore funds) or as an allocation from the limited partners' capital accounts, pro rata, to the general partner's capital account (usually for domestic funds). Although many variations exist, the investment manager is often entitled to receive its carry on a deal-by-deal basis. On this basis, as individual investments are sold, the investment proceeds are allocated based on a specific methodology defined in the governing documents to determine the amount of carry, if any, to which the investment manager is entitled. In presenting each class of shareholders' or partners' interest in the net assets as of the reporting date, the financial statements should consider the carry formula as if the investment company had realized all assets and settled all liabilities at their reported fair value and allocated all gains and losses and distributed the net assets to each class of shareholder or partner at the reporting date.

c. *Clawback.* Although all classes of shareholder or partner may be subject to clawback provisions in the governing documents, a clawback most frequently involves an obligation on the part of the investment manager to return previously received incentive allocations to the investment fund due to subsequent losses. Such clawback amounts, when paid, are typically distributed to other investors. The impact of a clawback should be calculated as of each reporting date under the methodology specified in the fund's governing documents.

7.127 Q&A section 6910.29 notes that, consistent with FASB ASC 310-10-45-14, such an obligation should not be recognized as an asset (receivable) in the entity's financial statements unless substantial evidence exists of the ability and intent to pay within a reasonably short period of time. Rather, in most instances, the obligation should be reflected as a deduction from the general partner's capital account. The specific circumstances, including whether the clawback represents a legal obligation to return or contribute funds to the reporting entity, require consideration before determining whether a clawback, resulting in a negative general partner capital balance (that is, contra-equity), is recognized in the financial statements. Additionally, it may not be appropriate to reflect a negative general partner capital balance (and a corresponding increase to limited partner capital balances) if the general partner does not have the financial resources to make good on its obligation.

7.128 Even if not recognized within the capital accounts, at a minimum, it would be appropriate to disclose the existence of a clawback in the footnotes to the financial statements because in almost all cases, the existence of the clawback would modify the manner in which future distributions are made.

7.129 *Deferred fees.*[42] According to Q&A section 6910.27, because the fund directly earns or incurs the income, expenses, net realized gains or losses, and unrealized appreciation or depreciation on the deferred fee retained in the fund,

---

[42] For further discussion of deferred fee arrangements, see paragraph 7.78.

such amounts should be presented within their respective line items in the investment company's statement of operations. The net change in unrealized appreciation or depreciation on the total return contracts associated with the deferred fees should be reported in earnings (that is, reflected as an expense [appreciation of deferred fees] or a negative expense [depreciation of deferred fees] of the fund, rather than an allocation of earnings or losses) and, following the guidance from FASB ASC 850, should be presented separately from the current period management or incentive fee.

Net Investment Income

7.130 As noted in FASB ASC 946-225-45-5, the excess of investment income over total expenses should be shown as net investment income (or loss). Further, as explained in FASB ASC 946-225-50-1, any income tax provision relating to net investment income should be disclosed separately.

Net Realized Gain or Loss From Investments and Foreign Currency Transactions

7.131 *Net realized gain or loss from investments.* As explained in FASB ASC 946-225-45-6 and 946-225-50-2, the statement of operations should disclose net realized gains or losses. Net realized gains or losses resulting from sales or other disposals should be reported net of brokerage commissions. Gains or losses arising from in-kind redemptions should be disclosed. The net realized gains or losses from investments and net realized gains or losses from foreign currency transactions may be reported separately or combined.

7.132 Registered investment companies should disclose in the statement of operations net realized gains or losses by major kinds of investment transactions as required by Rule 6.07.7 of Regulation S-X. An income tax provision charged against realized gains should also be disclosed separately.

7.133 *Net realized gains or losses from foreign currency transactions.* As explained in FASB ASC 946-225-45-6 and 946-225-50-2, net gains or losses from assets or liabilities denominated in foreign currencies during the period should be reported separately. If separate reporting of foreign currency effects on realized gains or losses from investments is elected, those effects should be included in this caption. Guidance for computing such amounts appears in chapter 2. The net realized gains or losses on investments resulting from foreign currency changes may be reported separately or combined with net realized gains or losses from investments. Notes to the financial statements should state an entity's practice of either including or excluding that portion of realized and unrealized gains and losses from investments that result from foreign currency changes with or from other foreign currency gains and losses.

7.134 The 1940 Act requires the disclosure of proceeds from sales of securities and the cost of securities purchased.[43] The SEC staff permits exclusion of short term securities (those securities with a maturity of one year or less) from this disclosure. Information about common stocks, bonds, and preferred stocks may be combined or disclosed separately.

---

[43] Section 30(e)(6) of the 1940 Act.

Net Increase (Decrease) in Unrealized Appreciation or Depreciation on Investments and Translation of Assets and Liabilities in Foreign Currencies

7.135 *Net increase (decrease) in unrealized appreciation or depreciation on investments.* As discussed in FASB ASC 946-225-45-6, changes in net unrealized appreciation or depreciation during the period should be reported in the statement of operations. The major components of unrealized appreciation or depreciation should be disclosed in a manner that is consistent with the guidance discussed in paragraph 7.131. Either combining the net unrealized gains or losses from investments with net unrealized gains or losses from foreign currency transactions or reporting them separately is permissible. Any provision for deferred taxes should be reported separately.

7.136 *Net increase (decrease) in unrealized appreciation or depreciation on translation of assets and liabilities in foreign currencies.* As noted in FASB ASC 946-225-45-6, the net change during the period from translating assets and liabilities denominated in foreign currencies should be reported under this caption. Guidance for computing such amounts appears in chapter 2.

Net Increase From Payments by Affiliates and Net Gains (Losses) Realized on the Disposal of Investments in Violation of Restrictions

7.137 As illustrated in FASB ASC 946-20-05-2, affiliates may make payments to a fund related to investment losses for either of the following reasons:

a. *Payments by affiliates.* To reimburse the effect of a loss (realized or unrealized) on a portfolio investment, often caused by a situation outside the fund's or its affiliates' direct control, such as an issuer default or a decline in fair value.

b. *Investment restriction violations (investments not meeting investment guidelines).* Occasionally, a fund adviser may purchase an investment for a fund that violates the fund's investment restrictions (investment restrictions are described in the prospectus or statement of additional information for registered funds and in partnership agreements or offering memorandums for nonregistered funds). The investment held in violation of the fund's investment restrictions may appreciate or depreciate in value. In the case in which the investment has depreciated in value and the fund has consequently incurred a loss, the fund adviser may make a payment to the fund in lieu of settlement of a potential claim resulting from the violation of the fund's investment restrictions. This payment, in effect, makes the fund whole relative to the loss that it has incurred. This type of transaction is, in essence, a payment to put the fund's shareholders in the position they would have been in had the violation not occurred.

7.138 As explained in FASB ASC 946-20-45-1, payments made by affiliates for those two reasons should be combined and reported as a separate line item entitled "Net increase from payments by affiliates and net gains (losses) realized on the disposal of investments in violation of restrictions" in the statement of operations as part of net realized and unrealized gains (losses) from investments and foreign currency. That separate line item would comprise amounts related to the following:

  a. Voluntary reimbursements by the affiliate for investment transaction losses

  b. Realized and unrealized losses on investments not meeting the investment guidelines of the fund

  c. Reimbursements from the affiliate for losses on investments not meeting the investment guidelines of the fund

  d. Realized and unrealized gains on investments not meeting the investment guidelines of the fund

As further discussed in FASB ASC 946-20-50-2, the amounts and circumstances of payments by affiliates to reimburse the fund for losses on investment transactions should be described in the notes to the financial statements. The gains and losses on investments not meeting investment guidelines of the fund should also be disclosed in the notes to the financial statements. In addition, the effect on total return, which is presented in the financial highlights, of the payments, as well as any gains or losses on investments not meeting investment guidelines of the fund, should be quantified and disclosed in the financial highlights in a manner similar to disclosure of the effect of voluntary waivers of fees and expenses on expense ratios. This is disclosed in accordance with FASB ASC 850-10. Total return should be presented in the financial highlights. The following is an example of total return being presented in a footnote to the financial highlights, as shown in FASB ASC 946-20-55-1:

> In 20XX, a.aa% of the fund's total return consists of a voluntary reimbursement by the adviser for a realized investment loss, and another b.bb% consists of a gain on an investment not meeting the fund's investment restrictions. Excluding these items, total return would have been c.cc%. Additionally, the adviser fully reimbursed the fund for a loss on a transaction not meeting the fund's investment guidelines, which otherwise would have reduced total return by d.dd%.

7.139   The Financial Reporting Executive Committee (FinREC) believes that due to the underlying reasons for such payments, the inclusion of the payments in the statement of operations should not be changed if the person making the payment is also a shareholder in the fund. FinREC was able to distinguish these payments from transactions undertaken by an entity's principal shareholder for the benefit of the entity (see SEC Topic 5T, "Accounting for Expenses or Liabilities Paid by Principal Stockholder[s]" of the SEC's *Codification of Staff Accounting Bulletins*), as arising from the person's service relationship to the fund, not its shareholder relationship. FinREC observed that the payments typically do not enhance the value of the person's equity investment in the fund beyond a pro rata interest in the payment itself, because the value of investment company shares either equals or is directly related to net asset value per share. Thus, FinREC believes that the payments ordinarily are intended to maintain a person's service relationship with the fund, rather than enhance or maintain the value of the person's investment in the fund.

7.140   In considering the presentation of the payments within the statement of operations, FinREC considered the guidance in FASB ASC 225-20-45-16. FinREC recognizes that payments of the type specified in paragraph 7.137*a* historically have been infrequent, typically occurring when an investment-grade issuer suddenly and unexpectedly defaulted, and that transactions in violation of investment restrictions, whether resulting in gains or losses, and payments of the type described in paragraph 7.137*b* are inherently infrequent. Thus, FinREC recommends the presentation of such items within a separate component of the statement of operations, as described in paragraph 7.138. Fin-REC also believes that the inconsistency between these transactions and the operating practices stated in the fund's governing documents provides further support for such presentation.

7.141   As explained in FASB ASC 946-20-05-3, payments by affiliates may take several forms, such as the following:

- A direct cash contribution to the fund to offset the effect of a realized loss on a portfolio investment

- Purchase of securities from the fund at prices in excess of the securities' current fair value

- Provision of a credit enhancement to maintain the investment's value

7.142   Further, FASB ASC 946-20-25-2 notes that a credit enhancement provided by an affiliate to maintain an investment's value should be recognized when the enhancement becomes available to the fund. FASB ASC 946-20-30-1 adds that the amount of the payment is initially measured by the cost of obtaining a similar enhancement in an arm's length transaction. Lastly, FASB ASC 946-20-35-1 states that any subsequent change in the value of the enhancement should be accounted for as unrealized appreciation or depreciation.

7.143   A fund may receive other payments from affiliates for reasons other than those described in FASB ASC 946-20-05-2. An evaluation must be made to determine whether to disclose the payments on the statement of operations or statement of changes in net assets. Regardless of the type of payment received, the fund should separately disclose the payments received in the respective financial statement, show the impact on the total return relating to such items in the financial highlights, and provide a narrative disclosure of the reasons why such payments were made.

Net Realized and Unrealized Gain or Loss From Investments and Foreign Currency

7.144   FASB ASC 946-225-45-6(c) states that the sum of the net realized gain or loss and change in unrealized gain or loss on investments and foreign currency-denominated assets and liabilities should be presented in the statement of operations as a net gain or loss on investments and foreign currency.

Net Increase or Decrease in Net Assets From Operations

7.145   As noted in FASB ASC 946-225-45-7, the sum of net investment income or loss and net realized and unrealized gain or loss on investments and foreign currency should be shown as a net increase or decrease in net assets resulting from operations.

Reporting of Fully Benefit-Responsive Investment Contracts

7.146   FASB ASC 946-210-45-17 requires that the statements of operations and changes in net assets be prepared on a basis that reflects income credited to participants in the fund and realized and unrealized gains and losses only on those investment contracts that are not deemed fully benefit-responsive.

Statement of Changes in Net Assets

7.147   FASB ASC 946-205-45-3 states that the statement of changes in net assets summarizes results from operations, net equalization credits or debits, dividends and distributions to shareholders, capital share transactions, and capital contributions.

7.148   The increase or decrease in net assets of a registered investment company comprises the following categories:

a. *Operations.* Net investment income or loss, net realized gains or losses from investments and foreign currency transactions, and changes in unrealized appreciation or depreciation on investments and translation of assets and liabilities in foreign currencies, as shown in the statement of operations, should be presented separately to arrive at the net change in net assets resulting from operations.

b. *Net equalization debits or credits.* If equalization accounting is used, undistributed investment income included in the price of capital shares issued or reacquired should be shown as a separate line item.

c. *Distributions to shareholders.* Distributions should be disclosed as a single line item, except for the tax return of capital distributions, which should be disclosed separately.

FASB ASC 946-505-50-5 states that the tax-basis components of dividends paid (ordinary income distributions, long term capital gains distributions, and return of capital distributions) should be disclosed in the notes to the financial statements.

FASB ASC 946-20-50-8 requires consistent treatment of dividends. Disclosing dividends on a tax basis is consistent with how dividends are reported to shareholders during, and at the end of, the calendar year. The financial highlights table would disclose per share information that is consistent with the statement of changes in net assets.

FASB ASC 946-205-45-3(c) notes that distributions made by RICs often differ from aggregate GAAP-basis undistributed net investment income (including net equalization credits or debits and undistributed net investment income) and accumulated net realized gains (total GAAP-basis net realized gains). The principal cause is that required minimum fund distributions are based on income and gain amounts determined in accordance with federal income tax regulations, rather than GAAP. The differences created can be temporary, meaning that they will reverse in the future, or they can be permanent. FASB ASC 946-505-50-6 explains that the primary reasons for any significant difference between total GAAP-basis net investment income and net realized gain and actual distributions should be disclosed in the notes to the financial statements. FASB ASC 946-205-45-3(c) notes that if in a subsequent period all or a portion of a temporary difference becomes a permanent difference, the amount of the permanent difference should be reclassified to paid-in capital.

d. *Capital share transactions.* FASB ASC 946-505-50-2 states the net change in net assets (excluding amounts shown separately if equalization accounting is used) arising from capital share transactions that should be disclosed for each class of shares. The components of the change should be disclosed on the face of the statement or in the notes to the financial statements for each class of shares, as follows:

    i. The number and value of shares sold

    ii. The number and value of shares issued in the reinvestment of distributions

    iii. The number and cost of shares reacquired

    iv. The net change

    e. *Capital contributions—net assets.* FASB ASC 946-505-50-3 states that net assets at the beginning and end of the year should be disclosed. The balance of net assets at the end of the year should agree with the comparable amount shown in the statement of assets and liabilities or statement of net assets.

7.149 As explained in FASB ASC 946-205-45-5, for investment partnerships, the statement of changes in net assets may be combined with the statement of changes in partners' capital if a statement of changes in net assets is presented.

7.150 According to Q&A section 6910.28, "Reporting Financial Highlights, Net Asset Value (NAV) Per Share, Shares Outstanding, and Share Transactions When Investors in Unitized Nonregistered Funds Are Issued Individual Classes or Series of Shares" (AICPA, *Technical Questions and Answers*), when a unitized nonregistered fund issues a separate series of shares to each individual investor in the fund, which remains outstanding so long as the investor maintains its investment in the fund and is not closed until the investor fully redeems, the fund should present disclosures of each series of shares outstanding at period-end and share transactions during the period on an aggregate share basis. These series may be issued within multiple classes of shares, with each series within a class bearing the same economic characteristics. The shares are legally issued and outstanding until redemption (that is, they are not notional interests) but will not be converted or otherwise consolidated into an identifiable permanent series of shares in a series roll-up.[44] Essentially, these unitized funds apply partnership accounting. The issuance of a separate series of shares to each individual investor is done for operational purposes because this enables a fund to allocate profit and loss to each investor in the same manner as a limited partnership allocates profit and loss to an individual partner's capital account.

7.151 FASB ASC 946-210-45-4 indicates that net asset value per share and shares outstanding should be reported for each class. FASB ASC 946-505-50-2 requires disclosure of the number and value of shares sold, the number and value of shares issued in reinvestment of distributions, the number and cost of shares reacquired, and the net change in shares.

7.152 Q&A section 6910.28 explains that for funds that issue a separate series of shares to each investor, such funds should satisfy the disclosure

---

[44] A series roll-up typically occurs at the end of the year when a temporary series of shares has increased above its high watermark (for example, the highest level in value that a series has achieved, adjusted for subscriptions and redemptions), at which time the outstanding shares of a temporary series of shares are converted (or rolled up) into the permanent series of shares.

requirements in FASB ASC 946-210-45-4 and 946-505-50-2 by presenting such disclosures on an aggregate share basis. For funds that issue multiple classes of shares that contain multiple series of shares, such disclosure requirements should be presented at the aggregate level for each permanent class of shares from which the individual series of shares have been issued.

Subsequent Events

7.153   Investment companies often distribute, after year-end, a portion of undistributed investment income and security gains realized in the preceding year. If declared before the audit opinion date, per share amounts relating to those distributions are frequently disclosed in the notes to the financial statements.

7.154   FASB ASC 855-10-25-1 explains that an entity should recognize in the financial statements the effects of all subsequent events that provide additional evidence about conditions that existed at the date of the balance sheet, including the estimates inherent in the process of preparing financial statements. The FASB ASC glossary defines *subsequent events* as events or transactions that occur after the balance sheet date but before financial statements are issued or available to be issued. There are two types of subsequent events:

- The first type consists of events or transactions that provide additional evidence about conditions that existed at the date of the balance sheet, including the estimates inherent in the process of preparing financial statements (that is, recognized subsequent events).
- The second type consists of events that provide evidence about conditions that did not exist at the date of the balance sheet but arose subsequent to that date (that is, nonrecognized subsequent events).

The FASB ASC glossary defines *financial statements are issued* as when they are widely distributed to shareholders and other financial statements users for general use and reliance in a form and format that complies with GAAP (U.S. SEC registrants are also required to consider applicable SEC guidance). *Financial statements are available to be issued* is defined by the FASB ASC glossary as when they are complete in a form and format that complies with GAAP, and all approvals necessary for issuance have been obtained (for example, from management, the board of directors or trustees, or significant shareholders). The process involved in creating and distributing the financial statements will vary depending on entity's management and corporate governance structure, as well as statutory and regulatory requirements. FASB ASC 855-10-55-1 contains examples of recognized subsequent events.

7.155   As stated in FASB ASC 855-10-25-1A, an entity that is an SEC filer or a conduit bond obligor for conduit debt securities that are traded in a public market should evaluate subsequent events through the date that the financial statements are issued. The FASB ASC glossary defines an *SEC filer* as an entity that is required to file or furnish its financial statements with either of the following:

- The SEC
- With respect to an entity subject to Section 12(i) of the 1934 Act, the appropriate agency under that section

Financial statements for other entities that are not otherwise SEC filers whose financial statements are included in a submission by another SEC filer are not included within this definition. FASB ASC 855-10-25-2 states that an entity that does not meet the criterion in FASB ASC 855-10-25-1A should evaluate subsequent events through the date that the financial statements are available to be issued.

7.156 In accordance with FASB ASC 855-10-25-3, an entity should not recognize subsequent events that provide evidence about conditions that did not exist at the date of the balance sheet but arose after the balance sheet date but before financial statements are issued or available to be issued. FASB ASC 855-10-55-2 contains examples of nonrecognized subsequent events, including changes in the fair value of assets or liabilities (financial or nonfinancial) after the balance sheet date but before financial statements are issued or available to be issued.[45] Further, paragraphs 2–3 of FASB ASC 855-10-50 explain that some nonrecognized subsequent events may be of such a nature that they must be disclosed to keep the financial statements from being misleading. For such events, an entity should disclose the nature of the event and the estimate of its financial effect or a statement that such an estimate cannot be made. Occasionally, a nonrecognized subsequent event may be so significant that disclosure can best be made by means of pro forma financial data.

7.157 The FASB ASC glossary defines *revised financial statements* as financial statements revised only for either correction of an error or retrospective application of GAAP. According to paragraphs 4–5 of FASB ASC 855-10-50, unless the entity is an SEC filer, an entity should disclose in the revised financial statements the dates through which subsequent events have been evaluated in both the issued or available-to-be-issued financial statements and the revised financial statements. Further, revised financial statements are considered reissued financial statements. FASB ASC 855-10-25-4 notes that an entity may need to reissue financial statements (for example, in reports filed with the SEC or other regulatory agencies). After the original issuance of the financial statements, events or transactions may have occurred that require disclosure in the reissued financial statements to keep them from being misleading. An entity should not recognize events occurring between the time that the financial statements were issued or available to be issued and the time that the financial statements were reissued, unless the adjustment is required by GAAP or regulatory requirements.

7.158 FASB ASC 855-10-50-1 explains that if an entity is not an SEC filer, then the entity should disclose the date through which subsequent events have been evaluated and whether that date is either the date that the financial statements were issued or the date that the financial statements were available to be issued.

Statement of Cash Flows

7.159 FASB ASC 230-10-15-3 requires entities providing financial statements that report both financial position and results of operations to also provide a statement of cash flows for each period for which results of operations

---

[45] Q&A section 9070.06, "Decline in Market Value of Assets Subsequent to the Balance Sheet Date" (AICPA, *Technical Questions and Answers*), addresses whether a decline in fair value of an asset subsequent to the balance sheet date should result in the adjustment of the financial statements.

are provided. However, "Pending Content" in FASB ASC 230-10-15-4 exempts investment companies meeting certain conditions from the requirements of FASB ASC 230, *Statement of Cash Flows.*

7.160 "Pending Content" in FASB ASC 230-10-15-4 exempts from the requirement to provide a statement of cash flows investment companies within the scope of FASB ASC 946, provided that all the following conditions are met:

a. During the period, substantially all the entity's investments were carried at fair value and classified as level 1 or level 2 measurements in accordance with FASB ASC 820.

b. The entity had little or no debt, based on average debt outstanding during the period in relation to average total assets. For this purpose, obligations resulting from redemptions of shares by the entity from unsettled purchases of securities or similar assets or from covered options written generally may be excluded from average debt outstanding. However, any extension of credit by the seller that is not in accordance with standard industry practice for redeeming shares or settling purchases of investments should be included in average debt outstanding.

c. The entity provides a statement of changes in net assets.

7.161 According to Q&A section 6910.25, "Considerations in Evaluating Whether Certain Liabilities Constitute 'Debt' for Purposes of Assessing Whether an Investment Company Must Present a Statement of Cash Flows" (AICPA, *Technical Questions and Answers*), although presented in the "Liabilities" section of the statement of assets and liabilities, options sold or written (whether covered or uncovered), short sales of securities, and other liabilities recorded as a result of investment practices are not necessarily debt; rather, their classification depends on the nature of the activity. Certain transactions (for example, securities lending, mortgage dollar rolls, or short sale transactions) may have a practice of being entered into solely for operating purposes (similarly to unsettled purchases of securities) or as an investing strategy (similarly to covered options written), and the investment company either retains the proceeds in cash accounts or uses them to invest in securities that are cash equivalents under FASB ASC 230. In such cases, the proceeds from the transaction should not be considered debt for purposes of assessing whether the conditions in the previous paragraph are met.

7.162 FASB ASC 230-10-45 states that a statement of cash flows should explain the change during the period in cash and cash equivalents. The statement classifies cash receipts and cash payments as resulting from operating, investing, and financing activities and includes a reconciliation of net cash provided by, and used for, operating activities to net increase or decrease in net assets from operating activities.

7.163 When it is necessary to provide a statement of cash flows, the following information should be disclosed for a presentation using the direct method. (The indirect method is more commonly used. This method adjusts net increase or decrease in net assets from operations to arrive at net cash flows from operating activities.) Cash flows from operating activities should include the fund's investing activities, which may include the following:

a. Interest and dividends received

b. Operating expenses paid

  c. Purchases of long term investments (at cost)

  d. Sales of long term investments (proceeds)

  e. Net sales or purchases of short term investments

  f. Cash flows for other types of investing activities related to changes in margin accounts and collateral status, such as written options, financial futures contracts, securities lending, and so forth

7.164 According to Q&A section 6910.20, "Presentation of Purchases and Sales/Maturities of Investments in the Statement of Cash Flows" (AICPA, *Technical Questions and Answers*), a nonregistered investment partnership should present purchases and sales and maturities of long term investments (securities purchased with no stated maturity or with a stated maturity of greater than one year at the date of acquisition) on a gross basis in the statement of cash flows, pursuant to FASB ASC 230, although the nonregistered investment partnership may consider the provisions in FASB ASC 230-10-45-9 in determining whether or not certain purchases and sales/maturities qualify for net reporting. However, purchases and sales and maturities of short term investments (securities purchased with a stated remaining maturity of one year or less at the date of acquisition) may be presented on a net basis, as described in FASB ASC 230-10-45-18. Additionally, proceeds and costs reported for transactions in short positions are reflected separately from proceeds and costs associated with long positions.

7.165 Q&A section 6910.26, "Additional Guidance on Determinants of Net Versus Gross Presentation of Security Purchases and Sales/Maturities in the Statement of Cash Flows of a Nonregistered Investment Company" (AICPA, *Technical Questions and Answers*), further explains that one of the requirements of FASB ASC 230-10-45-9 is that the original maturity of assets and liabilities qualifying for net reporting is three months or less. However, FASB ASC 230-10-45-18 permits banks, brokers and dealers in securities, and other entities that carry securities and other assets in a trading account to classify cash receipts and cash payments from such activities as operating cash flows, and cash flows from transactions in available-for-sale securities are reported gross as investing activities. Refer to paragraphs 11 and 18–20 of FASB ASC 230-10-45 and FASB ASC 310-10-45-11 for additional guidance.

7.166 In other industries, operating cash flows relating to trading account securities typically are reported on a net basis. If a nonregistered investment company presents a statement of cash flows, the investment company's trading style, investment objectives stated in its offering memorandum, and portfolio turnover should be the primary determinants of net versus gross reporting. Where the investment company's overall activities comport with *trading*, as discussed in FASB ASC 230 and 320, *Investments—Debt and Equity Securities*, netting is permissible; otherwise, gross reporting of purchases and sales and maturities is required. Regardless of whether net or gross reporting is appropriate based on the stated criteria, an entity should separately report its activity related to long positions from activity related to short positions (that is, changes and activity in account balances reported as assets should not be netted against changes and activity in account balances reported as liabilities).

7.167 The FASB ASC glossary defines *trading securities* as securities that are bought and held principally for the purpose of selling them in the near term and, therefore, held for only a short period of time. Trading generally reflects active and frequent buying and selling, and trading securities are generally used with the objective of generating profits on short term differences in price.

7.168 Although investment companies do not apply FASB ASC 320 and, therefore, do not normally categorize securities as trading, available for sale, or held to maturity, the concepts of whether the securities are held for trading purposes and whether the related cash flows would be classified as operating cash flows under paragraphs 11 and 18–20 of FASB ASC 230-10-45 and FASB ASC 310-10-45-11 are relevant in determining whether cash flows from purchases and sales of securities should be presented gross or net by investment companies.

7.169 Cash flows from financing activities include the following:

    a. Issuance and redemption of fund shares, including both common and preferred shares (excluding reinvestment of dividends and distributions)

    b. Proceeds from and repayments of debt

    c. Dividends and distributions to shareholders (not including stock or reinvested dividends and distributions)

    d. Bank overdrafts

7.170 The reconciliation of net cash provided by, or used for, operating activities to net increase or decrease in net assets from operating activities includes the following:

    a. Changes in noninvestment asset and liability accounts (such as interest receivable, accrued expenses, and other liabilities)

    b. Noncash income and expense items (such as amortization of deferred charges, accretion of discount, and amortization of premium)

    c. Realized and unrealized gains and losses on investment and foreign currency transactions

7.171 FASB ASC 830-230-45-1 states that the effect of any foreign exchange fluctuations on cash balances should be disclosed as a separate part of the reconciliation of the change in cash and cash equivalents during the period. FASB ASC 830-230-55-1 provides an illustration of this guidance.

7.172 FASB ASC 946-230-55-1 states that information about noncash investing and financing activities, such as reinvestments of dividends and distributions, should be disclosed.

Financial Highlights

7.173 Paragraphs 1–3 and 7 of FASB ASC 946-205-50 state that financial highlights (see paragraph 7.01) should be presented either as a separate schedule or within the notes to the financial statements for each class of common shares outstanding. Per share amounts presented are based on a share outstanding throughout each period presented. Investment companies with multiple classes of shares may present financial highlights only for those classes of shares that are included in reports to such shareholders. In such cases, the investment company should include appropriate disclosures related to all classes to ensure that the financial statements are complete (for example, detail of capital share activity in the statement of changes in net assets or notes to the financial statements). Nonregistered investment partnerships should disclose all classes of ownership interests in general purpose financial statements.

7.174 Further, FASB ASC 946-205-50-4 notes that only the classes related to the nonmanaging investors (that is, classes of investors that do not consist exclusively of managing investor interests) are considered to be the common interests requiring financial highlight disclosure.

7.175 According to the FASB ASC glossary term *nonregistered investment partnerships—financial highlights*, nonregistered investment partnerships, when disclosing financial highlights, should interpret the terms classes, units, and theoretical investments as follows:

a. *Classes*. Nonregistered investment funds typically have one of the following two classes of ownership interest: management interest and investment interest:

  i. For unitized funds (that is, funds with units specifically called for in the governing underlying legal or offering documents), the management interest usually is a voting class, and the investment interest is a nonvoting class. Temporary series of shares (that is, shares that are intended at the time of issuance to be consolidated at a later date with another specified series of shares that remains outstanding indefinitely) are not considered separate classes. Permanent series of a class of share should be the basis for which that share's financial highlights are determined and presented.

  ii. For nonunitized funds, the management interest usually is the general partner class, and the investment interest usually is the limited partner class. Generally, a class has certain rights, as governed by underlying legal documents or offering documents and local law. Rights to certain investments that do not otherwise affect the rights available under the underlying legal documents and local law do not ordinarily represent a separate share class. For example, rights to income and gains from a specific investment attributed solely to investors at the date that the investment is made (side-pocket investments) are not considered to give rise to a share class. Similarly, a temporary series of shares is not considered a share class.

b. *Units*. Only funds with units specifically called for in the governing underlying legal or offering documents should be considered unitized. Some funds may employ units for convenience in making allocations to investors for internal accounting or bookkeeping purposes, but the units are not required or specified by legal or offering documents and, for all other purposes, operate like nonunitized investment partnerships. For per share operating performance, those funds are not considered unitized.

c. *Theoretical investment*. The term *theoretical investment* in FASB ASC 946-205-50-20 should be considered as the actual aggregate amount of capital invested by each reporting class of investor as of the beginning of the fiscal reporting period, adjusted for cash flows related to capital contributions or withdrawals during the period.

7.176   As stated in FASB ASC 946-205-50-5, if a fund is not unitized, only investment returns (either total return or internal rate of return) and net investment income and expense ratios are required to be disclosed as indicated in paragraphs 10–25 of FASB ASC 946-205-50.

7.177   As explained in paragraphs 7–8 of FASB ASC 946-205-50, the following per share information should be presented for registered investment companies and investment companies that compute unitized net asset value. Nonregistered investment partnerships that compute unitized net asset value should disclose information for each reporting share class related to nonmanaging investors. The information should be disclosed for each major category affecting net asset value per share (as shown in the statement of operations and statement of changes in net assets of the fund). The caption descriptions in the per share data should be the same captions used in the statement of operations and statement of changes in net assets to allow the reader to determine which components of operations are included in, or excluded from, various per share data:

 a.   Net asset value at the beginning of the period.

 b.   Per share net investment income or loss. Methods other than as described in paragraph 7.178, such as dividing net investment income by the average or weighted average number of shares outstanding during the period, are acceptable.

 c.   Realized and unrealized gains and losses per share, which are balancing amounts necessary to reconcile the change in net asset value per share with the other per share information presented. The amount shown in this caption might not agree with the change in aggregate gains and losses for the period. If such is the case, the reasons should be disclosed.

 d.   Total from investment operations, which represents the sum of net investment income or loss and realized and unrealized gain or loss.

 e.   Distributions to shareholders should be disclosed as a single line item, except the tax return of capital distributions should be disclosed separately. Details of distributions should conform to those shown in the statement of changes in net assets.

 f.   Purchase premiums, redemption fees, or other capital items.

 g.   Payments by affiliates (paragraphs 2–3 of FASB ASC 946-20-05).

 h.   Net asset value at the end of the period.

The information required in items *b–g* is not required for separate accounts that represent an ownership interest in the underlying separate account portfolios or mutual funds. Refer to paragraphs 10.57–.64 of this guide for information regarding financial highlights for separate accounts and illustrative financial statements.

7.178   Per share net investment income or loss for registered investment companies is calculated in accordance with the requirements of Forms N-1A or N-2. A more detailed discussion of per share calculation methods for registered investment companies may be found in the instructions for the preparation of registration statements on Forms N-1A and N-2. If an alternative method is used by a registered investment company, the method employed must be disclosed in a note to the table in conformity with SEC requirements. For Form N-2 registrants only, the quoted market price for the fund's common shares value at the end of the period should also be presented.

7.179 As explained in paragraphs 10–17 and 25 of FASB ASC 946-205-50, ratios of expenses and net investment income to average net assets are generally annualized for periods less than one year. The ratio of expenses to average net assets should be increased by brokerage service and expense offset arrangements (see paragraphs 3 and 5 of FASB ASC 946-20-45), as follows:

a. When determining expense and net investment income ratios, non-registered investment partnerships should calculate average net assets by using the fund's (or class's) weighted-average net assets as measured at each accounting period or periodic valuation (for example, daily, weekly, monthly, quarterly), adjusting for capital contributions or withdrawals from the fund occurring between accounting periods or valuations. (This provision is not intended to require any additional interim accounting period or periodic valuation date beyond that which may be provided in offering or organizational documents of the partnership.)

The expense and net investment income ratios should be calculated by nonregistered investment partnerships based on the expenses allocated to each common or investor class (for example, the limited partner class) prior to the effects of any incentive allocation. Adequate disclosure should be made to indicate that the net investment income ratio does not reflect the effects of any incentive allocation. Expenses directly related to the total return of the fund, such as incentive fees, and nonrecurring expenses, such as organizational costs, should not be annualized when determining the expense ratio. Disclosure should be made of the expenses that have not been annualized.

Generally, the determination of expenses for computing those ratios should follow the presentation of expenses in the fund's statement of operations. Accordingly, if the investment adviser's or general partner's incentive is structured as a fee, rather than an allocation of profits, the incentive fee would be factored into the computation of an expense ratio. Because an incentive allocation of profits is not presented as an expense, it should not be considered part of the expense ratio. However, to avoid potentially significant inconsistencies in ratio presentations based solely on the structuring of incentives as fees or allocations, all incentives should be reflected in the disclosure of financial highlights. See paragraph 7.226 for an example of that disclosure.

Additionally, for the expense ratio, disclosure should be made of the effect of any agreement to waive or reimburse fees and expenses to each reporting class as a whole, as described in FASB ASC 946-20-50-7, and of expense offsets, as described in paragraphs 3 and 5 of FASB ASC 946-20-45. FASB ASC 946-205-50-15 states that agreements to waive a portion or all of certain fees to a specific investor, which do not relate to the share class as a whole, do not require disclosure in the financial highlights. However, as ratios are calculated for each common class taken as a whole, the financial statements should disclose that an individual investor's ratio may vary from those ratios.

b. Investment companies that obtain capital commitments from investors and periodically call capital under those commitments to make investments (principally limited-life nonregistered investment partnerships) should disclose in the financial highlights or a note to the financial statements the total committed capital of the partnership (including general partner), the year of formation of the entity, and the ratio of total contributed capital to total committed capital.

c. Funds of funds should compute the expense and net investment income ratios using the expenses presented in the fund's statement of operations. Therefore, funds of funds typically should compute these ratios based on the net investment income and expense items at the fund-of-funds level only. Adequate disclosure should be made so that it is clear to users that the ratios do not reflect the funds-of-funds' proportionate share of income and expenses of the underlying investee funds. In a master-feeder structure, the feeder should include its proportionate share of the income and expenses of the master when computing the ratios at the feeder level. If, in a master-feeder structure, an incentive is levied as an allocation at the master level, the feeder should present its share of the incentive allocation as a separate line item in the statement of operations.

7.180   As discussed in paragraphs 18–24 of FASB ASC 946-205-50, total return is required to be presented for all investment companies (for interim periods, the disclosure should include that total return has not been annualized) and should be computed as follows:

a. For nonregistered investment companies organized in a manner utilizing unitized net asset value, based on the change in the net asset value per share during the period and assuming that all dividends are reinvested.

b. For investment companies not utilizing unitized net asset value, including investment partnerships, based on the change in value during the period of a theoretical investment made at the beginning of the period. The change in value of a theoretical investment is measured by comparing the aggregate ending value of each class of investor with the aggregate beginning value of each such class, adjusted for cash flows related to capital contributions or withdrawals during the period.

If capital cash flows occur during the reporting period, returns are geometrically linked based on capital cash flow dates. In general, geometrically linking requires the computation of performance for each discrete period within a year in which invested capital is constant (that is, for each period between investor cash flow dates) then multiplying those performance computations together to obtain the total return for a constant investment outstanding for the entire year.

Because incentive allocations or fees may vary among investors within a class, total return for reporting classes subject to an incentive allocation or fee should report total return before and after the incentive allocation or fee for each reporting class taken as a whole. The effect of incentive allocations on total return is computed on a weighted-average aggregate capital basis. This results in an incentive computation less than the maximum if, for example, certain partners had loss carryovers at the beginning of the period. See paragraph 7.228 for an example of that total return calculation and related disclosures.

    c. Investment companies that, by the terms of their offering documents, (i) have limited lives; (ii) do not continuously raise capital and are not required to redeem their interests upon investor request (obtaining initial capital commitments from investors at the time of organization and subsequently drawing on those commitments to make investments is not considered continuous for this purpose); (iii) have as a predominant operating strategy the return of the proceeds from disposition of investments to investors; (iv) have limited opportunities, if any, for investors to withdraw prior to termination of the entity; and (v) do not routinely acquire (directly or indirectly) as part of their investment strategy market-traded securities and derivatives should, instead of disclosing annual total returns before and after incentive allocations and fees, disclose the internal rate of return since inception (IRR) of the investment company's cash flows and ending net assets at the end of the period (residual values), as presented in the financial statements, net of all incentive allocations or fees, to each investor class, as of the beginning and end of the period. A footnote to the financial highlights should disclose that the IRR is net of all incentives. The IRR should be based on a consistent assumption, no less frequently than quarterly, about the timing of cash inflows and outflows (for example, on actual cash-flow dates or cash inflows at the beginning of each month or quarter and cash outflows at the end of each month or quarter). All significant assumptions should be disclosed in the footnotes to the financial highlights. See paragraph 7.227 for an example of an IRR calculation and related disclosures.

7.181 For Form N-1A registrants, total return should be calculated based on the change in the net asset value per share during the period and the assumption that all dividends are reinvested. For Form N-2 registrants, total investment return should be calculated based on the change in the quoted market price of the fund's shares taking into account dividends reinvested in accordance with the terms of the dividend reinvestment plan or, lacking such a plan, at the lesser of net asset value or market price on the dividend distribution date (total return computed based on net asset value per share may also be presented if the difference in results between the two calculations is explained).

7.182 Additional information for investment companies filing on Forms N-1A and N-2 includes the following ratios and supplemental data:

    a. Net assets, end of period.

    b. Portfolio turnover rate.

    c. If an investment company filing on Form N-2 has senior securities, Item 4.3 requires, as of the end of the last 10 fiscal years, the total amount outstanding (exclusive of treasury securities), the asset coverage per unit, involuntary liquidating preference per unit, and the average market value per unit (excluding bank loans) for each class of senior securities (including bank loans).[46]

---

[46] The Item 4 instructions in Form N-2 note that business development companies may be omitted from providing financial highlights but do explain that they are required to furnish the financial information required by Items 301, 302, and 303 of Regulation S-K.

7.183   The method of computing the portfolio turnover rate is described in the instructions to Forms N-SAR, N-1A, and N-2.

7.184   *Deferred fees.*[47] According to Q&A section 6910.27, the per share information, net investment income ratio, and net expense ratio included in the financial highlights should reflect the amounts presented on the statement of operations including the adjustment associated with the deferred fee amount. In order to reflect the effect of the adjustment on the fund's expense ratio, the fund may also present an expense ratio that excludes the amount of deferred fee expense or negative expense reported in the statement of operations. Consistent with guidance in FASB ASC 946, the fund should disclose the nature of the deferred fee arrangement, including the priority of claim in the event of liquidation; the current period and cumulative amounts deferred; the cumulative earnings or losses on the deferral; the terms of payment; the date that the deferral payments commence (or the next payment date); and the manner in which the deferral will be invested.

7.185   According to Q&A section 6910.28, when a unitized nonregistered fund issues a separate series of shares to each individual investor in the fund, which remains outstanding so long as the investor maintains its investment in the fund and is not closed until the investor fully redeems, the fund should present financial highlights (per share data, ratios, and total return) similar to that of a partnership (that is, a nonunitized fund). These series may be issued within multiple classes of shares with each series within a class bearing the same economic characteristics. The shares are legally issued and outstanding until redemption (that is, they are not notional interests) but will not be converted or otherwise consolidated into an identifiable permanent series of shares in a series roll-up.[48] Essentially, these unitized funds apply partnership accounting. The issuance of a separate series of shares to each individual investor is done for operational purposes because this enables a fund to allocate profit and loss to each investor in the same manner as a limited partnership allocates profit and loss to an individual partner's capital account.

7.186   Q&A section 6910.28 also states that the financial highlights should be presented at the aggregate level for the entire permanent series of shares from which the individual series of shares has been issued. Because the fund operates like a partnership, the financial highlights should include only those financial highlights applicable to a partnership, which are the ratios to average net assets and total return, but not per share data. When a separate series of shares is issued to each individual investor and remains outstanding until the investor fully redeems, the permanent series of shares will be the fund as a whole, excluding managing investor interests, if the shares otherwise have substantially similar terms. There are situations when a fund will issue multiple classes of shares, which contain multiple series of shares, due to differing fee arrangements or restrictions affecting an investor's ability to participate in the profits and losses generated by new-issue securities. When a fund issues multiple classes of shares, and in each class of shares, a series of shares is issued to each individual investor and remains outstanding until the investor fully redeems, financial highlights should be presented at the aggregate level

---

[47] For further discussion of deferred fee arrangements, see paragraph 7.78.

[48] A series roll-up typically occurs at the end of the year when a temporary series of shares has increased above its high water-mark (for example, the highest level in value that a series has achieved, adjusted for subscriptions and redemptions), at which time the outstanding shares of a temporary series of shares are converted (or rolled up) into the permanent series of shares.

for each permanent class of shares from which the individual series of shares have been issued. For example, if a fund has outstanding, at year-end, class A shares series 1–40, which have a 1 percent management fee; class B shares series 1–300, which have a 2 percent management fee; and class C shares, which are only held by the managing investor, the fund should present financial highlights information for class A as a whole and class B as a whole. There is no requirement to present financial highlights for class C because FASB ASC 946-205-50-4 requires financial highlights to be presented only for nonmanaging investors.

7.187 Q&A section 6910.28 explains that it would be acceptable for a fund to present supplemental financial highlights data for a single series of shares that the fund determines to be representative. Such financial highlights may be labeled as representing supplemental information and may only be presented in addition to those financial highlights that are required. Factors to consider when determining the representative series of shares include the following:

    a. The series of shares was outstanding for the entire fiscal period (or, if all units of a series of shares outstanding at the beginning of the fiscal period were redeemed during the period, the series of shares at period-end outstanding for the longest period of time).

    b. The fees and other offering terms of the series of shares most closely conform to those that may be described in the fund's offering documents.

    c. The series of shares represent the largest ownership interest in the fund.

The basis of presentation of the financial highlights and the criteria used to determine the most representative series of shares should be disclosed in a note to those highlights and consistently applied. If appropriate, a fund may present other supplemental information if determined to be informative and not misleading.

Other Disclosure Requirements

> ⊗ **Update 7-4 *Accounting and Reporting*: Going Concern**
>
> FASB ASU No. 2014-15, *Presentation of Financial Statements—Going Concern (Subtopic 205-40): Disclosure of Uncertainties about an Entity's Ability to Continue as a Going Concern*, was issued in August 2014. The amendments in this ASU are effective for the annual period ending after December 15, 2016, and for annual periods and interim periods thereafter. Early application is permitted.
>
> The amendments in ASU No. 2014-15 provide guidance in GAAP about management's responsibility to evaluate whether there is substantial doubt about an entity's ability to continue as a going concern and to provide related footnote disclosures. In doing so, the amendments should reduce diversity in the timing and content of footnote disclosures.
>
> Readers are encouraged to consult the full text of this ASU on FASB's website at www.fasb.org.

7.188 FASB ASC guidance that usually affects disclosures by investment companies under GAAP includes the following topics in FASB ASC:

- FASB ASC 740, *Income Taxes*. In particular, as explained in FASB ASC 946-740-55, the amounts and expiration dates of capital loss carryforwards and the amounts of any post-October capital and currency loss deferrals should be considered when an entity discloses the approximate tax effect of each type of temporary difference and carryforward that gives rise to a significant portion of deferred tax liabilities and deferred tax assets (before allocation of valuation allowances). RICs may have realized net capital and foreign currency gains during the period from the beginning of their current taxable year to October 31, which they are required to distribute to avoid federal excise tax. If those RICs then incur net capital or currency losses from November 1 to the close of their taxable year, their Form 1120-RIC tax returns would indicate that they had made distributions during the taxable year in excess of taxable gains (that is, returns of capital), even though the distributions were properly paid from gains at the time of the excise-tax distribution. To avoid this result, federal income tax regulations permit such post-October losses to be deferred and recognized on the Form 1120-RIC tax return of the next succeeding taxable year.

- FASB ASC 825. In particular, as noted in FASB ASC 825-10-05-5(b), the fair value option guidance in FASB ASC 825 establishes presentation and disclosure requirements designed to facilitate comparisons between entities that choose different measurement attributes for similar types of assets and liabilities. Paragraphs 1–2 of FASB ASC 825-10-45 explain that entities should report assets and liabilities that are measured using the fair value option in a manner that separates those reported fair values from the carrying amounts of similar assets and liabilities measured using another measurement attribute. To accomplish that, an entity should either (*a*) present the aggregate of fair value and nonfair-value amounts in the same line item in the statement of financial position and parenthetically disclose the amount measured at fair value included in the aggregate amount or (*b*) present two separate line items to display the fair value and nonfair-value carrying amounts.

- FASB ASC 815.

- FASB ASC 860, *Transfers and Servicing*.

- FASB ASC 275, *Risks and Uncertainties*.

- FASB ASC 820.

7.189 When applicable, investment companies should also disclose the fact that the fund is not subject to income taxes. For registered investment companies, disclosing the fact that they are not subject to income taxes is typically addressed by describing the company's status as a registered investment company under IRC Subchapter M and, also, the principal assumptions on which the company relied in making or not making income tax provisions and deferred tax calculations. Additionally, if the fund is not subject to income taxes, the net difference between the tax bases and the reported amounts of the fund's assets and liabilities should be disclosed. See chapter 6 for further discussion on taxes.

Fully Benefit-Responsive Investment Contract Disclosures

7.190 As discussed in FASB ASC 946-210-50-14, investment companies identified in FASB ASC 946-210-45-11 should disclose the following in the aggregate in connection with fully benefit-responsive investment contracts:

a. A description of the nature of those investment contracts, how they operate, and the methodology for calculating the interest crediting rate, including the key factors that could influence future average interest crediting rates, the basis for and frequency of determining interest crediting rate resets, and any minimum interest crediting rate under the terms of the contracts. This disclosure should explain the relationship between future interest crediting rates and the amount reported on the statement of assets and liabilities representing the adjustment for the portion of net assets attributable to fully benefit-responsive investment contracts from fair value to contract value.

b. A reconciliation between the beginning and ending balance of the amount presented on the statement of assets and liabilities that represents the difference between net assets reflecting all investments at fair value and net assets for each period in which a statement of changes in net assets is presented. This reconciliation should include

   i. the change in the difference between the fair value and contract value of all fully benefit-responsive investment contracts and

   ii. the increase or decrease due to changes in the fully benefit-responsive status of the fund's investment contracts.

c. The average yield earned by the entire fund (which may differ from the interest rate credited to participants in the fund) for each period for which a statement of assets and liabilities is presented. This average yield should be calculated by dividing the annualized earnings of all investments in the fund (irrespective of the interest rate credited to participants in the fund) by the fair value of all investments in the fund.

d. The average yield earned by the entire fund with an adjustment to reflect the actual interest rate credited to participants in the fund for each period for which a statement of assets and liabilities is presented. This average yield should be calculated by dividing the annualized earnings credited to participants in the fund (irrespective of the actual earnings of the investments in the fund) by the fair value of all investments in the fund.

e. The following two sensitivity analyses:

   i. The weighted average interest crediting rate (that is, the contract value yield) as of the date of the latest statement of assets and liabilities and the effect on this weighted average interest crediting rate, calculated as of the date of the latest statement of assets and liabilities and the end of the next four quarterly periods, under two or more scenarios in which there is an immediate hypothetical increase or decrease in market yields, with no change to the duration of the underlying investment portfolio and no contributions or withdrawals. Those scenarios should include, at a minimum, immediate hypothetical increases and decreases in market yields equal to one-quarter and one-half of the current yield.

   ii. The effect on the weighted average interest crediting rate calculated as of the date of the latest statement of assets and liabilities and the next four quarterly reset dates, under two or more scenarios in which there are the same immediate hypothetical changes in market yields in the first analysis, combined with an immediate, one-time, hypothetical 10 percent decrease in the net assets of the fund due to participant transfers, with no change to the duration of the portfolio.

   f. A description of the events that limit the ability of the fund to transact at contract value with the issuer (for example, premature termination of the contracts by the fund, plant closings, layoffs, plan termination, bankruptcy, mergers, and early retirement incentives), including a statement about whether the occurrence of those events that would limit the fund's ability to transact at contract value with the participants in the fund is probable or not probable.

   g. A description of the events and circumstances that would allow issuers to terminate fully benefit-responsive investment contracts with the fund and settle at an amount different from contract value.

Paragraph 7.231, from FASB ASC 946-210-55-2, illustrates the application of this guidance.

Offsetting Assets and Liabilities[49]

7.191 FASB ASC 210-20-50 discusses disclosures about certain financial instruments and derivative instruments that are either (*a*) offset in accordance with either FASB ASC 210-20-45 or FASB ASC 815-10-45 or (*b*) are subject to an enforceable master netting arrangement or similar agreement, irrespective of whether they are offset in accordance with either FASB ASC 210-20-45 or FASB ASC 815-10-45.

Scope

7.192 FASB ASC 210-20-50-1 establishes the scope of the disclosure requirements in paragraphs 2–5 of FASB ASC 210-20-50. To summarize paragraph 1, the scope of the offsetting disclosures is limited to recognized derivative instruments accounted for in accordance with FASB ASC 815, including bifurcated embedded derivatives, repurchase agreements and reverse repurchase agreements, and securities borrowing and securities lending transactions, that are either offset in accordance with FASB ASC 210-20-45 or FASB

---

[49] The offsetting disclosure discussion within in this section reflects the amendments in ASU No. 2011-11, *Balance Sheet (Topic 210): Disclosures about Offsetting Assets and Liabilities*, and ASU No. 2013-01, *Balance Sheet (Topic 210): Clarifying the Scope of Disclosures about Offsetting Assets and Liabilities*. The amendments in ASU Nos. 2011-11 and 2013-01 became effective for fiscal years beginning on or after January 1, 2013, and related interim periods within that year. An entity should provide the disclosures required by those amendments retrospectively for all comparative periods presented.

ASC 815-10-45 or subject to an enforceable master netting arrangement or similar agreement.

7.193 Although the scope is limited to specified instruments and transactions, management may find it challenging to identify all such instruments and transactions that are under legally enforceable master netting arrangements or similar agreements. Master netting arrangements exist in a myriad of contracts and agreements. Management may consider evaluating existing arrangements, with the assistance of legal counsel, to ensure all master netting or similar arrangements have been identified. As a common example within the investment company industry, an investment company may have an open total return swap in an asset position and a forward contract in a liability position with the same counterparty. Under the related agreement (an International Swaps and Derivatives Association, Inc. Master Agreement and Credit Support Annex [ISDA Agreement], for example) between the investment company and the counterparty, the investment company may be able to legally settle the two positions on a net basis. The investment company's legal counsel determined that this master netting agreement is legally enforceable in the case of counterparty default. In this example, the instruments would likely be within the scope of the offsetting disclosure requirements, even if the investment company does not net the positions on its balance sheet or intend to settle the positions net.

7.194 The consideration of legal enforcement is critical when determining which instruments and transactions under master netting arrangements are within the scope of the FASB ASC 210-20-50 disclosure requirements. Each arrangement should be evaluated to determine when the entity can legally enforce a netting provision. The expertise of legal personnel likely will be necessary in order to determine which netting arrangements are enforceable in a court of law and which are not, as well as which are enforceable only upon a default versus those which are unconditional. Further, readers are reminded that the "legal enforcement" threshold for netting of positions may differ from the criteria in FASB ASC 210-20-45 or FASB ASC 815-10-45. It would be inappropriate for management to conclude that the disclosure requirements are not applicable because all positions are presented gross on the balance sheet. Finally, readers are reminded that agreements should be evaluated for both conditional and unconditional rights of setoff. Whereas unconditional rights of setoff provide for general payment netting, conditional rights of setoff provide for the net settlement of cash flows only under certain defined conditions; for example, a provision in a master netting arrangement that permits close-out netting in the event of bankruptcy.

7.195 Special consideration may be required when evaluating contracts that provide for "one-side master netting." For example, one-side master netting may exist in a relationship between a hedge fund and a broker-dealer, whereby one party may be able to legally net positions under the arrangement, but the other party may not be able to legally net positions based on the terms of the arrangement. If the reporting entity does not, from its perspective, have a master netting arrangement, instruments subject to that arrangement would not be within the scope of the offsetting disclosure requirements for the reporting entity (unless the instruments were actually offset in the statement of financial position and therefore met the scope criterion in FASB ASC 210-20-50-1(c)). The arrangement would be within the scope of the offsetting disclosure requirements under FASB ASC 210-20-50 for the counterparty (the party that does possess a right of offset).

Disclosure Requirements

7.196 FASB ASC 210-20-50-3 requires an entity to disclose at the end of the reporting period the following quantitative information separately for assets and liabilities that are within the scope of FASB ASC 210-20-50-1:

a. The gross amounts of those recognized assets and those recognized liabilities

b. The amounts offset in the statement of financial position (pursuant to FASB ASC 210-20-45 and FASB ASC 815-10-45)

c. The net amounts presented in the statement of financial position

d. The amounts subject to an enforceable master netting arrangement or similar agreement not otherwise included in item (*b*)

    i. The amounts related to recognized financial instruments and other derivative instruments that either

        (1) management makes an accounting policy election not to offset or

        (2) do not meet some or all of the guidance in either FASB ASC 210-20-45 or FASB ASC 815-10-45

    ii. The amounts related to financial collateral (including cash collateral)

e. The net amount after deducting the amounts in item (*d*) from the amounts in item (*c*)

[*Note*: Pursuant to FASB ASC 210-20-50-4, the total amount disclosed in accordance with item (*d*) for an instrument should not exceed the amount disclosed in accordance with item (*c*) for that instrument. An entity may choose to footnote or otherwise disclose the amount of overcollateralization.]

Refer to illustrative note 3 in paragraph 7.224 for an example disclosure table.

7.197 FASB ASC 210-20-50-4 explains that presentation of this information in tabular format, separately for assets and liabilities, is required unless another format is more appropriate. FASB ASC 210-20-50-5 also requires reporting entities to provide a description of the rights (including the nature of those rights) of setoff associated with an entity's recognized assets and recognized liabilities subject to an enforceable master netting arrangement or similar agreement. In addition, the standard requires disclosure of collateral received and posted in connection with master netting agreements or similar arrangements. FASB ASC 210-20-50-6 explains that cross-referencing is required when the required disclosures exist in more than a single note to the financial statements.

7.198 As discussed in the previous paragraph, presentation in tabular format is required, unless another format is more appropriate. As an example of an alternative format that may be more appropriate for some investment companies, the existing footnote disclosure for a certain instrument type (repurchase agreements, for example) may be enhanced in narrative format to meet the disclosure requirements. This alternative format is illustrated in note 1 to the financial statements in paragraph 7.224.

7.199 The standard allows for flexibility with respect to how the required information can be presented in a disclosure table. As summarized from paragraphs 15–16 of FASB ASC 210-20-55, an entity may choose to present the information by type of instrument or transaction (for quantitative information items a–e) or may choose to present a portion of the information by counterparty (allowable only for quantitative information items c–e). When making this determination, an entity may consider aligning the disclosure table presentation with the related master netting arrangements (that is, if the master netting arrangement allows for netting by type, the disclosure table may follow the same format). Further, there is no requirement in FASB ASC 210-20 to list the name of counterparties in the disclosure table. However, if general designators are used (for example, use of "Counterparty A" and "Counterparty B") instead of legal names, the same general designator must be used for the same counterparty in all future years. (Note: although FASB ASC 210-20 does not require the use of counterparty legal names, the SEC requires registrants to name the counterparties as part of the descriptions of various positions in portfolio schedules. Therefore, in practice, registered investment companies typically disclose the names of the counterparties consistently throughout the financial statements).

7.200 Additional implementation guidance is provided in paragraphs 1–19 of FASB ASC 210-20-55, and illustrative example disclosure tables are provided in paragraphs 20–22 of FASB ASC 210-20-55.

7.201 *Collateral.* Some collateral received from a counterparty may be recorded on the reporting entity's balance sheet (cash, for example) whereas other securities received from a counterparty may be held separately by the custodian and are not recorded on the reporting entity's balance sheet. The collateral types that are not recorded on the balance sheet require disclosure pursuant to requirement (d) of FASB ASC 210-20-50-3 (as described in paragraph 7.196). Moreover, FASB ASC 210-20-50 explains that the collateral amounts included in the table cannot exceed the related net amount of the position recorded in the statement of financial position. For example, assume that an entity's overall exposure to counterparty A is $10, and it is an asset position. If collateral received is $100, the entity would only disclose $10 instead of the full amount of $100.

7.202 Many organizations have uniform pricing policies for their financial reporting. However, a valuation determination made by using a company's collateral management systems may not incorporate those uniform pricing policies. The amended guidance requires disclosure of amounts related to financial collateral (including cash collateral). Therefore, when financial statements are produced, investment companies should ensure that the collateral is appropriately valued.

7.203 Understanding, monitoring, and reporting collateral information may be challenging for a variety of reasons. For example, complexity may increase when an investment company has multiple subsidiaries or may utilize multiple sub-advisers that each have their own collateral agreements. Although investment companies generally monitor collateral at a granular level, because the gathering of this information does not typically reside within the financial reporting function, such information may be difficult to compile. Investment companies need to ensure not only that their disclosures comply with the requirements but also that adequate internal controls are established for gathering the information. Entity management should consider enhancing or implementing processes, systems (for example, collateral management systems), and controls designed to achieve the following:

- Identify and understand all existing master netting arrangements

- Link collateral to master netting arrangements
- Track and monitor changes to master netting arrangements over time
- Involve all necessary parties within the organization who may hold information or who may be needed to interpret contracts
- Ensure necessary information is provided to the financial reporting personnel on a timely basis

Other Disclosure Requirements for Business Development Companies[50]

7.204 Investment Management Guidance Update No. 2013-07, *Business Development Companies—Separate Financial Statements or Summarized Financial Information of Certain Subsidiaries*, as issued by the SEC, reminds registrants that Rules 3-09 and 4-08(g) of Regulation S-X (Rule 3-09 and Rule 4-08(g), respectively) apply to Business Development Companies (BDCs) and indicates that if a BDC believes the application of Rule 3-09 or Rule 4-08(g) results in the presentation of either financial statements or summarized financial information of an unconsolidated subsidiary that is not necessary to reasonably inform investors, the BDC should contact the Division of Investment Management's Chief Accountant's Office. In addition, if a BDC is required to present summarized financial information pursuant to Rule 4-08(g), the Division of Investment Management generally would not object if the BDC presents summarized financial information in the notes to the financial statements individually for each unconsolidated subsidiary which individually meets the definition of a "significant subsidiary" in Rule 1-02(w) but does not present summarized financial information in the notes to the financial statements for all unconsolidated subsidiaries. Readers are encouraged to consult the full text of Guidance Update No. 2013-07, available at www.sec.gov/divisions/investment/guidance/im-guidance-2013-07.pdf.

7.205 As noted in the October 2013 Expert Panel Conference Call Highlights, in response to some questions the SEC staff received subsequent to issuing Guidance Update No. 2013-07, the SEC staff highlighted the following:

- This guidance applies regardless of whether a BDC's subsidiary is an investment company, an entity that functions similarly to an investment company, or a noninvestment company (for example, a portfolio company);

---

[50] Rule 3-09 of Regulation S-X describes the circumstances under which separate financial statements of an unconsolidated majority-owned subsidiary (for example, an unconsolidated nonregistered investment company) must be filed with the SEC and the circumstances under which those separate financial statements must be audited. It also explains that, insofar as practicable, the subsidiary's separate financial statements must be as of the same dates and for the same periods as the audited financial statements of the registrant. In accordance with Rule 4-01(a)(1) of Regulation S-X, the subsidiary's financial statements that are filed with the SEC must be prepared in accordance with GAAP and must comply with Regulation S-X.

Rule 4-08(g) of Regulation S-X states that summarized financial information must be presented, in the notes to the financial statements, for unconsolidated subsidiaries. It explains that, insofar as practicable, the summarized financial information must be as of the same dates and for the same periods as the audited financial statements of the registrant. Rule 4-08(g) also explains that the summarized financial information must include the disclosures prescribed by Rule 1-02(bb) of Regulation S-X. Rule 1-02(bb) of Regulation S-X permits registrants in specialized industries to provide summarized balance sheet information as to the nature and amount of the majority components of assets and liabilities. Rule 1-02(bb) of Regulation S-X permits registrants in specialized industries to provide in their summarized income statement other information necessary for a more meaningful presentation in lieu of providing the required disclosures specified by the rule.

- All three tests under Rule 1-02(w) must be performed to determine whether the BDC must either file separate financial statements or present summarized financial information in the notes to its financial statements as required by Rules 3-09 or 4-08(g), respectively;

- For purposes of Rules 3-09 and 4-08(g), the definition of *control* which is used in the Regulation S-X Rule 1-02(x) definition of *subsidiary* is based on the 1940 Act definition, which includes the presumption that a person who owns more than 25 percent of the voting securities of the company has control. The SEC staff cautioned that structuring transactions to avoid presenting summarized financial information for the subsidiaries might raise issues under Section 48(a) of the1940 Act.

Interim Financial Statements

7.206   Rule 30d-1 of the 1940 Act requires that registered investment companies send semiannual reports to shareholders that should be complete, based on GAAP, and conform to the principles used in preparing annual financial statements. The statement of changes in net assets for registered investment companies should present information on the latest interim period (from the preceding fiscal year-end to the end of the interim period) and the preceding fiscal year. For semiannual reports, financial highlights should be presented for the semiannual period and generally the preceding five fiscal years. Many nonregistered investment companies also prepare semiannual reports and distribute those reports to shareholders.

7.207   FASB ASC 946-20-50-10 states that if management of a fund determines that a tax return of capital is likely to occur for the fund's fiscal year, although the exact amount may not be estimable, that fact should be disclosed in a note to the interim financial statements.

7.208   Unaudited interim financial data should be marked accordingly. Data summarized in condensed form should be labeled. If the auditor is named or identified in interim reports on which no audit or review procedures have been performed, the auditor should insist that the reference be deleted or that a notation be included that the auditor does not express an opinion.

7.209   AU-C section 930, *Interim Financial Information* (AICPA, *Professional Standards*), addresses the auditor's responsibilities when engaged to review interim financial information of nonissuers, including nonregistered investment companies, under conditions specified therein (see the section "Applicability of Generally Accepted Auditing Standards and PCAOB Standards" of the preface to this guide for a discussion of the definitions of *issuer* and *nonissuer* as used throughout this guide). The term *auditor* is used throughout AU-C section 930, not because the auditor is performing an audit, but because the scope of AU-C section 930 is limited to a review of interim financial information performed by an auditor of the financial statements of the entity. AU-C section 930 applies to a review of interim financial information when

a. the entity's latest annual financial statements have been audited by the auditor or a predecessor auditor;

b. the auditor either

    i.   has been engaged to audit the entity's current year financial statements, or

    ii.   audited the entity's latest annual financial statements, and in situations in which it is expected that the current year financial statements will be audited, the engagement of another auditor to audit the current year financial statements is not effective prior to the beginning of the period covered by the review;

c.   the entity prepares its interim financial information in accordance with the same financial reporting framework as that used to prepare the annual financial statements; and

d.   all of the following conditions are met if the interim financial information is condensed:

    i.   The condensed interim financial information purports to be prepared in accordance with an appropriate financial reporting framework, which includes appropriate form and content of interim financial information.

    ii.   The condensed interim financial information includes a note that the financial information does not represent complete financial statements and is to be read in conjunction with the entity's latest audited annual financial statements.

    iii.   The condensed interim financial information accompanies the entity's latest audited annual financial statements or such audited annual financial statements are made readily available by the entity.

7.210   Paragraphs .A1–.A3 of AU-C section 930 provide application and other explanatory guidance associated with items *a–d* preceding, as follows:

- The ability to apply the provisions of AU-C section 930 even when the auditor does not expect to be engaged to audit the current year financial statements provides for appropriate transitions between the predecessor auditor and the auditor of the current year financial statements.

- Appropriate financial reporting frameworks for condensed interim financial information may include, for example, FASB ASC 270, *Interim Reporting*, and Article 10 of SEC Regulation S-X with respect to accounting principles generally accepted in the United States of America or International Accounting Standard 34, *Interim Financial Reporting*, with respect to International Financial Reporting Standards issued by the International Accounting Standards Board. FASB ASC 270 outlines the application of U.S. generally accepted accounting principles (GAAP) to the determination of income when interim financial information is presented, provides for the use of estimated effective income tax rates, and specifies certain disclosure requirements for condensed interim financial information issued by public companies, and may be adapted by nonissuers as a fair presentation framework for condensed interim financial information. In addition to FASB ASC 270, other FASB ASC topics also include disclosure requirements for interim financial information.

- The meaning of *readily available* in item *d*(iii) is provided in paragraph .A3 of AU-C section 930, which states that audited financial statements are deemed to be readily available if a third-party user can obtain the financial statements without any further action by the entity (for example, financial statements on an entity's website may be considered readily available, but being available upon request is not considered readily available).

7.211 AU-C section 930 defines *interim financial information* as financial information prepared and presented in accordance with an applicable financial reporting framework that comprises either a complete or condensed set of financial statements covering a period or periods less than 1 full year or covering a 12-month period ending on a date other than the entity's fiscal year-end.

Considerations for Audits Performed in Accordance With PCAOB Standards

Registered public accounting firms must comply with the standards of the PCAOB in connection with the preparation or issuance of any report on reviews of interim financial information of an issuer (see the section "Applicability of Generally Accepted Auditing Standards and PCAOB Standards" of the preface to this guide for a discussion of the definitions of issuer and nonissuer as used throughout this guide). AU section 722, *Interim Financial Information* (AICPA, *PCAOB Standards and Related Rules*, Interim Standards), is the relevant standard for performing reviews of interim financial statements of issuers. Paragraphs .07 and .18*g* of AU section 722 also provide guidance to auditors with respect to evaluating management's quarterly certifications about internal control over financial reporting, where applicable. (See the preface of this guide for more information about management's assessment of the effectiveness of internal control.)

7.212 Q&A section 9170.02, "Supplementary Information That Accompanies Interim Financial Information" (AICPA, *Technical Questions and Answers*), explains that an auditor is not required to report on supplementary information when an entity presents supplemental information along with interim financial statements (when the auditor is performing an interim review in accordance with AU-C section 930). However, the auditor can report on supplementary information if he or she chooses to do so. If the auditor decides to report on the supplementary information, the auditor may disclaim on the supplementary information or issue a report based on the limited procedures performed as part of the interim review. Q&A section 9170.02 provides an example of a report based on the limited procedures applied in the review.

Illustrative Financial Statements of Investment Companies

7.213 This section contains illustrative financial statements, disclosures, and calculations that may be of interest to preparers and auditors of investment companies. The following table functions as a topical overview of the illustrative content in this section, and provides related paragraph numbers for quick reference.

Illustration Description	Paragraph(s) Reference
Comprehensive Financial Statements, Footnotes, and Financial Highlights of a Registered Investment Company:	
Statement of Assets and Liabilities	7.216
Schedule (or Portfolio) of Investments in Securities	7.217
Schedule of Call Options Written	7.218
Schedule of Securities Sold Short	7.219
Statement of Net Assets	7.220
Statement of Operations	7.221
Statements of Changes in Net Assets	7.222
Statement of Cash Flows	7.223
Notes to Financial Statements	7.224
Financial Highlights	7.225
Other Financial Reporting Considerations for Non Registered Funds (Private Investment Entities):	
Calculations and Disclosures When Reporting Expense and Net Investment Income Ratios	7.226
Calculation and Disclosure When Reporting the Internal Rate of Return	7.227
Calculation and Disclosure When Reporting the Total Return Ratio	7.228
Condensed Schedule of Investments	7.229
Nonregistered Investment Partnerships Schedule of Investments	7.230
Presentation of Fully Benefit-Responsive Investment Contracts	7.231
Deferred Fees	7.232
Disclosure—Fair Value Measurements of Investments in Certain Entities That Calculate Net Asset Value per Share (or its Equivalent)	7.233
Reporting Financial Highlights, Net Asset Value Per Share, Shares Outstanding, and Share Transactions When Investors in Unitized Nonregistered Funds Are Issued Individual Classes or Series of Shares	7.234
Statement of Changes in Net Assets (Changes in Partners' Capital) of a Nonregistered Investment Partnership That Includes a General Partner and One or More Limited Partners	7.235
Disclosure for a Registered Fund Issuing Consolidated Financial Statements and Relying on CFTC Letter No. 13-51	7.236

7.214 The amounts in the accompanying financial statements, including the financial highlights, are illustrative[51] only and may not indicate relationships among accounts. The financial statements illustrate the presentation of various items, if material. In addition, in some circumstances, information presented in the notes to the financial statements may be better presented within the financial statements.

7.215 To comply with SEC rules and regulations, registered investment companies must make certain disclosures in addition to those required by GAAP. The illustrative financial statements and related footnote disclosures presented in paragraphs 7.216–.225 are those of a registered investment company. They include certain, but not all, disclosures required by SEC regulation in addition to requirements under GAAP. From time to time, the SEC may administratively require additional disclosures in the financial statements. At the time of this guide's publication, SEC compliance disclosures in the illustrative financial statements that are not required under GAAP include, but are not limited to, the following:[52]

- A requirement to present a statement of assets and liabilities instead of a statement of net assets if the amount of investments in securities of unaffiliated issuers represents less than 95 percent of total assets

- Additional disclosures required by Rules 12-12 and 12-12C (note 1) of Regulation S-X pertaining to collateral for repurchase agreements

- Details with respect to written options activity as required by Rule 6.07.7(c) (note 3) of Regulation S-X

- Gross unrealized appreciation and depreciation, as well as net unrealized appreciation or depreciation, all on a tax basis, in accordance with Rules 12-12 and 12-12C (note 4) of Regulation S-X

- Disclosure of nonincome producing securities as required by Rules 12-12 and 12-12C of Regulation S-X

- Additional disclosures required by Rules 6.04.2(b), 6.07.1, and 6.07.7 of Regulation S-X pertaining to investments in and income from affiliates and controlled companies, as defined by Section 2 of the 1940 Act to include any investment in which more than 5 percent of the outstanding voting securities is owned by the fund

- The weighted average interest rate and the maximum amount of debt outstanding during the period, in accordance with Rule 6.04.13(b), referring to Rules 5.02.19(b) and 5.02.22(b), of Regulation S-X (note 5)

Significant disclosures for a registered investment company that are required by SEC regulation, in addition to those required by GAAP, but not presented in the illustrative financial statements include the following:

---

[51] The statement of net assets in the illustrative financial statements that follow presents investments in unaffiliated issuers (not excluding securities loaned) that represent only 90 percent of total assets. An investment company registered with the SEC would be required to present a statement of assets and liabilities, including a separate schedule of investments, rather than a statement of net assets.

[52] See footnote 1.

- Additional disclosures required by Rule 4-08(m) of Regulation S-X if the carrying amounts of repurchase or reverse repurchase agreements exceed 10 percent of total assets, or the amount at risk (as defined) under such agreements exceeds 10 percent of net asset value.

- Additional disclosures about restricted securities (acquisition date, unit carrying value, and cost, among others), in accordance with section 404 of the SEC's Codification of Financial Reporting Policies and Rules 12-12 and 12-12C of Regulation S-X.

- Additional disclosures about investments in affiliates, as required by Rules 6-04.2 and 12-14 of Regulation S-X.

Disclosures included in the illustrative financial statements presented in the remainder of this chapter are not intended to be comprehensive and are not intended to establish preferences among alternative disclosures.

Note: The illustrative financial statements and note disclosures included in this guide have been updated to reflect FASB ASC. However, in FASB's notice to constituents, it suggests the use of plain English in financial statement note disclosures to describe broad FASB ASC topic references. FASB suggests a reference similar to "as required by the Derivatives and Hedging Topic of the FASB *Accounting Standards Codification*." Entities might consider revising their financial statement references to reflect this plain English referencing, rather than the use of specific FASB ASC references. We have provided these detailed references as a resource for our users.

7.216

XYZ Investment Company
Statement of Assets and Liabilities
December 31, 20X8

Assets

Investments in securities, at fair value (cost $19,292,000)—including $570,000 of securities loaned (note 8)[53]	$21,721,000
Cash denominated in foreign currencies (cost $141,000)	139,000
Cash	60,000
Deposits with brokers for securities sold short	1,555,000
OTC swap premiums paid (note 3)	5,000
Unrealized gain on OTC swap contract (note 3)	1,000
Receivables	
Variation margin on derivative instruments (note 3)	3,000
Dividends and interest	46,000
Investment securities sold	24,000
Capital shares sold	54,000
Unrealized gain on foreign currency forward exchange contract (note 3)	419,000
Other assets	26,000
Total assets	24,053,000

Liabilities

Call options written at fair value (premiums received: $110,000)	230,000
Securities sold short at fair value (proceeds: $1,555,000)	1,673,000
Demand loan payable to bank (note 5)	2,000,000
Payable upon return of securities loaned (note 8)	620,000
Unrealized loss on foreign currency exchange contract (note 3)	108,000
Unrealized loss on swap contract (note 3)	21,000
OTC swap premiums received (note 3)	2,000
Payables	
Investment securities purchased	52,000
Variation margin on derivative instruments (note 3)	10,000
Capital shares reacquired	8,000
Other	4,000
Accrued expenses	8,000
Distribution payable	137,000
Total liabilities	4,873,000
Net assets	**$19,180,000**

Analysis of Net Assets:[54]

Net capital paid in on shares of capital stock	$15,184,000
Undistributed ordinary income	1,304,000
Accumulated undistributed net realized gain	1,152,000
Net unrealized appreciation	1,540,000
Net assets (equivalent to $4.55 per share based on 4,216,000 shares of capital stock outstanding) (note 6)	$19,180,000

The accompanying notes are an integral part of these financial statements.

---

[53] Investments in securities include securities purchased with cash proceeds from securities loans.

As discussed in FASB ASC 860-30-25-3, when cash is received as collateral in secured borrowings, the cash received should be recognized as the investment company's asset along with the obligation to return the cash. Consistent with FASB ASC 860-30-25-8, if the investment company makes investments with the cash, even if made by agents or in pools with other securities lenders, the investment company should reflect the investments as part of its holdings in the schedule of investments and footnote any restrictions associated with the investment because of the collateral arrangements.

With regard to collateral received in the form of securities in secured borrowings, if the securities received may be sold or repledged, the investment company should account for those securities in the same way as it would account for cash received. That is, the investment company should record the securities received as the investment company's asset along with the obligation to return the securities. However, if the investment company does not have the right to sell or repledge the securities received as collateral, then the investment company should not record the securities or related liability on its books.

[54] This breakout of paid in capital and distributable earnings is typically not relevant for nonregistered investment companies.

7.217

XYZ Investment Company
Schedule (or Portfolio) of Investments in Securities
December 31, 20X8

> **Note**: Securities may be arranged by industry groupings or other groupings (showing percentage of total portfolio or net assets invested in each grouping) that the company believes are most meaningful to users. The basis of the computation of percentages shown (which in this illustration is the ratio of the specific category of securities to the total portfolio owned) should be disclosed.

	Shares	Fair Value
Common stocks—29%		
Consumer durable goods—5%		
Allied Manufacturing Corporation[55]	25,000	$620,000
Baker Industries, Inc.[56]	15,000	150,000
Consumer Goods Company	8,000	300,000
Other		16,000
		1,086,000
Consumer nondurable goods—16%		
Amalgamated Buggy Whips, Inc.	10,000	3,280,000
American Company	4,000	100,000
Other		55,000
		3,435,000
Service industries—4%		
Service Company, Inc.[57]	10,000	465,000
Cannon Sales[58]	13,000	396,000
Other		4,000
		865,000
Other industry groupings—4%		921,000
[*Additional industry groupings and details of the 50 largest holdings are not included in this illustration.*]		
Total common stocks		6,307,000

[55] A portion of the security is pledged as collateral for call options written.
[56] Nonincome-producing security.
[57] A portion of the security is on loan.
[58] See footnote 57.

Convertible bonds—25%	Principal	Fair Value
American Retailing Inc.—5.5% debenture due 20XX	$500,000	525,000
Paper Airplane Corporation—6.25% debenture due 20XX	4,500,000	4,875,000
Total convertible securities		5,400,000
Indexed securities—10%		
American Trust Co. (principal linked to Euro yield curve)—10% due 20XX	2,000,000	2,100,000
Mortgage-backed securities—12%		
FNMA 8% due 20XX	2,000,000	1,950,000
FNMA strip, principal only, zero coupon, due 20XX	1,000,000	760,000
Total mortgage-backed securities		2,710,000
Warrants—0.02%		
Banking Corp. (Expires 1/16/X9)	100	1,000
Car Motor Co. (Expires 1/01/Y3)	200	3,000
Total warrants[59]		4,000
U.S. government obligations—16%		
U.S. Treasury 6% notes due 20XX	500,000	490,000
U.S. Treasury 8% notes due 20XX	3,000,000	2,985,000
Total U.S. government obligations		3,475,000
Short term notes—6%		
Commercial Paper, Inc., 5.5% due 2/5/X9	505,000	506,000
U.S. Treasury bills, 5.2% due 1/20/X9[60][61]	720,000	719,000
Total short term notes		1,225,000
Repurchase agreements—2%		
Money Center Bank of Large City, 4%, dated 12/29/X8, due 1/3/X9, repurchase price $500,274; collateralized by U.S. Treasury 4% bonds due 20XX, par $500,000 and value $510,000	500,000	500,000
Total—100% (cost $19,292,000)		$21,721,000

Note—Aggregate value of segregated securities—$372,000.

The accompanying notes are an integral part of these financial statements.

---

[59] Warrants entitle the company to purchase a predetermined number of shares of common stock, and are nonincome producing. The purchase price and number of shares are subject to adjustment under certain conditions until the expiration date, if any. In this example, warrants presented are considered to be derivatives as defined in FASB ASC 815, *Derivatives and Hedging*, and as such, would require derivative disclosures required in FASB ASC 815.

[60] A portion of the security is purchased with the cash proceeds from securities loans. (The investment company should also footnote any restrictions associated with the investment because of the collateral arrangements.)

[61] A portion of the security is pledged as collateral margin for centrally cleared swaps.

7.218

XYZ Investment Company
Schedule of Call Options Written
December 31, 20X8

Common Stocks	Counter-party	Number of Contracts	Exercise Price	Expiration Date	Fair Value
Allied Manufacturing Corporation	AMR	10,000	25	7/20/20XX	$50,000
Allied Manufacturing Corporation	AMR	5,000	30	10/20/20XX	2,500
Consumer Goods Company	AMR	7,000	45	9/20/20XX	177,500
Total (premiums received: $110,000) (note 3)					$230,000

The accompanying notes are an integral part of these financial statements.

7.219

XYZ Investment Company
Schedule of Securities Sold Short
December 31, 20X8

Name of Issuer	Common Shares	Fair Value
International Widgets, Inc.	40,000	$425,000
Paper Airplane Corporation	25,000	265,000
Amber Company	100,000	983,000
Total (proceeds: $1,555,000)		$1,673,000

The accompanying notes are an integral part of these financial statements.

7.220

XYZ Investment Company
Statement of Net Assets
December 31, 20X8

> *Note*: *Securities may be arranged by industry or other groupings (showing percentage of total portfolio or net assets invested in each grouping) that the company believes will be most meaningful to users.*

	Shares or Principal Amount	Fair Value
Assets		
Common stocks—33%		
Consumer durable goods—6%		
Allied Manufacturing Corporation[62]	25,000	$620,000
Baker Industries, Inc.[63]	15,000	150,000
Consumer Goods Company[64]	8,000	300,000
Other		16,000
		1,086,000
Consumer nondurable goods—18%		
Amalgamated Buggy Whips, Inc.	10,000	3,280,000
American Company	4,000	100,000
Other		55,000
		3,435,000
Service industries—5%		
Service Company, Inc.[65]	10,000	465,000
Cannon Sales[66]	13,000	396,000
Other		4,000
		865,000
Other industry groupings—5%		921,000
[*Additional industry groupings and details of the 50 largest holdings are not included in this illustration.*]		
Total common stocks		6,307,000
Convertible bonds—28%		
American Retailing Inc.—5.5% debenture due 20XX	$500,000	525,000
Paper Airplane Corporation—6.25% debenture due 20XX	4,500,000	4,875,000
Total convertible bonds		5,400,000

(continued)

---

[62] A portion of the security is pledged as collateral for call options written.
[63] Nonincome-producing security.
[64] Nonincome-producing security.
[65] A portion of the security is on loan.
[66] A portion of the security is on loan.

	Shares or Principal Amount	Fair Value
Indexed securities—11%		
American Trust Co. (principal linked to Euro yield curve)—10% due 20XX	2,000,000	2,100,000
Mortgage-backed securities—14%		
FNMA, 8% due 20XX	2,000,000	1,950,000
FNMA strip, principal only, zero coupon, due 20XX	1,000,000	760,000
Total mortgage-backed securities		2,710,000
Warrants—0.02%		
Banking Corp. (Expires 1/16/X9)	100	1,000
Car Motor Co. (Expires 1/01/Y3)	200	3,000
Total warrants[67]		4,000
U.S. government obligations—18%		
U.S. Treasury 6% notes due 20XX	500,000	490,000
U.S. Treasury 8% notes due 20XX	3,000,000	2,985,000
Total U.S. government obligations		3,475,000
Short term notes—6%		
Commercial Paper, Inc., 5.5% due 2/5/X9	505,000	506,000
U.S. Treasury bills, 5.2% due 1/20/X9[68][69]	720,000	719,000
Total short term notes		1,225,000
Repurchase agreements—3%		
Money Center Bank of Large City, 4%, dated 12/29/X8 due 1/3/X9, repurchase price $500,274, collateralized by U.S. Treasury 4% bonds due 20XX, par $500,000 and value $510,000	500,000	500,000
Total investments in securities (cost $19,292,000)—including $570,000 of securities loaned (note 8)[70]		21,721,000
Cash denominated in foreign currencies (cost $141,000)		139,000
Cash		60,000
Deposits with brokers for securities sold short		1,555,000
OTC swap premiums paid (note 3)		5,000
Unrealized gain on OTC swap contract (note 3)		1,000
Receivables		
Variation margin on derivative instruments (note 3)		3,000
Dividends and interest		46,000
Investment securities sold		24,000
Capital stock sold		54,000
Unrealized gain on foreign currency forward exchange contract (note 3)		419,000
Other assets		26,000
Total assets		$24,053,000

---

[67] See footnote 59.

[68] A portion of the security is purchased with the cash proceeds from securities loans. (The investment company should also footnote any restrictions associated with the investment because of the collateral arrangements.)

[69] A portion of the security is pledged as margin for centrally cleared swaps.

[70] See footnote 53.

	Shares or Principal Amount	Fair Value
Liabilities		
Call options written at fair value (premiums received: $110,000) (note 3)		230,000
Securities sold short at fair value (proceeds: $1,555,000)		1,673,000
Demand loan payable to bank (note 5)		2,000,000
Payable upon return of securities loaned (note 8)		620,000
Unrealized loss on foreign currency forward exchange contract (note 3)		108,000
Unrealized loss on swap contract (note 3)		21,000
OTC swap premiums received (note 3)		2,000
Payables		
Investment securities purchased		52,000
Variation margin on derivative instruments (note 3)		10,000
Capital stock reacquired		8,000
Other		4,000
Accrued expenses		8,000
Distribution payable		137,000
Total liabilities		4,873,000
Net assets		$19,180,000
Analysis of Net Assets:[71]		
Net capital paid in on shares of capital stock		15,184,000
Undistributed ordinary income		1,304,000
Accumulated undistributed net realized gain		1,152,000
Net unrealized appreciation		1,540,000
Net assets (equivalent to $4.55 per share based on 4,216,000 shares of capital stock outstanding) (note 6)		$19,180,000

The accompanying notes are an integral part of these financial statements.

[71] This breakout of paid in capital and distributable earnings is typically not relevant for non-registered investment companies.

7.221

XYZ Investment Company
Statement of Operations
Year Ended December 31, 20X8

Investment income

Dividends (net of foreign withholding taxes of $20,000)	$742,000	
Interest	209,000	
Income from securities loaned—net	50,000	
Total income		$1,001,000

Expenses

Investment advisory fee	135,000	
Interest	55,000	
Professional fees (note 9)	29,000	
Custodian and transfer agent fees	16,000	
Distribution expenses (note 9)	4,000	
State and local taxes other than income taxes	15,000	
Directors' fees	12,000	
Dividends on securities sold short	9,000	
Total expenses		275,000
Fees paid indirectly (note 9)		(4,000)
Fees waived (note 9)		(45,000)
Net expenses		226,000
Net investment income		775,000

Realized and unrealized gain (loss) from investments and foreign currency:

Net realized gain (loss) from—

Investments	1,105,000
Futures	73,000
Swaps	7,000
Options written	(89,000)
Foreign currency transactions[72]	(44,000)
	1,052,000

Net increase (decrease) in unrealized appreciation (depreciation) on—

Investments	(1,357,000)
Futures	(50,000)
Swaps	(120,000)
Options written	(120,000)
Translation of assets and liabilities in foreign currencies[73]	353,000
	(1,294,000)

Net realized and unrealized loss from investments and foreign currency	(249,000)
Net increase in net assets resulting from operations	$533,000

The accompanying notes are an integral part of these financial statements.

---

[72] If separate reporting is adopted, these captions would also include foreign currency effects of realized and unrealized gains and losses on investments. If separate reporting is not adopted, such foreign currency effects would be included in the investments captions.

[73] See footnote 72.

7.222

XYZ Investment Company
Statements of Changes in Net Assets
Years Ended December 31, 20X8 and 20X7

	20X8	20X7
Increase (decrease) in net assets from operations		
Investment income—net	$775,000	$492,000
Net realized gain from investments and foreign currency[74]	1,052,000	1,000,000
Unrealized appreciation (depreciation) on investments and translation of assets and liabilities in foreign currencies[75]	(1,294,000)	1,551,000
Net increase in net assets resulting from operations	533,000	3,043,000
Distributions to shareholders	(1,875,000)	(1,350,000)
Tax return of capital to shareholders	—	(66,000)
Capital share transactions (note 6)	2,730,000	1,755,000
Total increase	1,388,000	3,382,000
Net assets		
Beginning of year	17,792,000	14,410,000
End of year	$19,180,000	$17,792,000

The accompanying notes are an integral part of these financial statements.

---

[74] It is also acceptable to present each of these items as a separate line item: net realized gains from investments and net realized gains (losses) from foreign currency transactions.

[75] It is also acceptable to present each of these items as a separate line item: unrealized appreciation on investments and unrealized appreciation on the translation of assets and liabilities in foreign currencies.

7.223

XYZ Investment Company
Statement of Cash Flows
Year Ended December 31, 20X8

Increase (decrease) in cash—

Cash flows from operating activities:

Net increase in net assets from operations	$533,000
Adjustments to reconcile net increase in net assets from operations to net cash used in operating activities:	
Purchase of investment securities	(26,797,000)
Proceeds from disposition of investment securities	26,336,000
Sale of short term investment securities, net	(921,000)
Increase in deposits with brokers for short sales	(555,000)
Increase in collateral for securities loaned	(270,000)
Increase in dividends and interest receivable	(18,000)
Increase in equity on foreign currency forward contracts	(363,000)
Increase in other assets	(2,000)
Premiums from call options written	50,000
Proceeds from securities sold short	802,000
Net cash received on swap contracts	7,000
Increase in payable upon return of securities loaned	270,000
Decrease in variation margin payable	(4,000)
Decrease in accrued expenses	(8,000)
Unrealized depreciation on securities	1,597,000
Net realized gain from investments	(1,023,000)
Net cash used in operating activities	(366,000)

Cash flows from financing activities:

Decrease in loan payable	(400,000)
Proceeds from shares sold	2,143,000
Payment on shares redeemed	(450,000)
Cash distributions paid	(841,000)
Net cash provided by financing activities	452,000
Net increase in cash	86,000

Cash:

Beginning balance	113,000
Ending balance	$199,000

Supplemental disclosure of cash flow information:

Noncash financing activities not included herein consist of reinvestment of dividends and distributions of $1,000,000.

The accompanying notes are an integral part of these financial statements.

7.224

XYZ Investment Company
Notes to Financial Statements

1. Significant Accounting Policies

XYZ Investment Company (the Company) is registered under the Investment Company Act of 1940 as a diversified, open-end management investment company. The investment objective of the Company is to seek a high total return consisting of both current income and realized and unrealized gains from equity and debt securities. The Company follows the accounting and reporting guidance in FASB *Accounting Standards Codification* 946.

Security valuation. All investments in securities are recorded at their estimated fair value, as described in note 2.

Repurchase agreements. The Company may enter into repurchase agreements, under the terms of a Master Repurchase Agreement, with selected commercial banks and broker-dealers, under which the Company acquires securities as collateral (debt obligation) subject to an obligation of the counterparty to repurchase and the Company to resell the securities (obligation) at an agreed upon time and price. The Company, through the custodian or a subcustodian, receives delivery of the underlying securities collateralizing repurchase agreements. The Company requires the custodian to take possession, to have legally segregated in the Federal Reserve Book Entry System, or to have segregated within the custodian's vault, all securities held as collateral for repurchase agreements. The Company and the counterparties are permitted to sell, repledge, or use the collateral associated with the transaction. It is the Company's policy that the market value of the collateral be at least equal to 100 percent of the repurchase price in the case of a repurchase agreement of one-day duration and 102 percent of the repurchase price in the case of all other repurchase agreements. Upon an event of default under the terms of the Master Repurchase Agreement, both parties have the right to set-off. If the seller defaults or enters an insolvency proceeding, realization of the collateral by the Company may be delayed, limited or wholly denied.

At December 31, 20X8, the Company had an investments in one repurchase agreements with a gross value of $500,000, which is included as part of investments in securities at fair value on the Statement of Assets and Liabilities. The value of the related collateral that the Company received for this agreement exceeded the value of the repurchase agreements at December 31, 20X8. See note 3 for offsetting and collateral information pertaining to derivative agreements that are subject to master netting agreements.

Foreign currency. Investment securities and other assets and liabilities denominated in foreign currencies are translated into U.S. dollar amounts at the date of valuation. Purchases and sales of investment securities and income and expense items denominated in foreign currencies are translated into U.S. dollar amounts on the respective dates of such transactions.

[*The following paragraphs illustrate disclosures for a fund that chooses to report the foreign currency elements of realized and unrealized gains and losses on investments.*]

The Company does not isolate that portion of the results of operations resulting from changes in foreign exchange rates on investments from the fluctuations arising from changes in market prices of securities held. Such fluctuations are included with the net realized and unrealized gain or loss from investments.

Reported net realized foreign exchange gains or losses arise from sales of foreign currencies, currency gains or losses realized between the trade and settlement dates on securities transactions, and the difference between the amounts of dividends, interest, and foreign withholding taxes recorded on the Company's books and the U.S. dollar equivalent of the amounts actually received or paid. Net unrealized foreign exchange gains and losses arise from changes in the fair values of assets and liabilities, other than investments in securities at fiscal period-end, resulting from changes in exchange rates.

[*The following paragraphs illustrate disclosures for a fund that chooses to report the foreign currency elements of realized and unrealized gains and losses on investments.*]

The Company isolates that portion of the results of operations resulting from changes in foreign exchange rates on investments from the fluctuations arising from changes in market prices of securities held.

Reported net realized foreign exchange gains or losses arise from sales of portfolio securities; sales and maturities of short term securities; sales of foreign currencies; currency gains or losses realized between the trade and settlement dates on securities transactions; and the difference between the amounts of dividends, interest, and foreign withholding taxes recorded on the Company's books and the U.S. dollar equivalent of the amounts actually received or paid. Net unrealized foreign exchange gains and losses arise from changes in the values of assets and liabilities, including investments in securities at fiscal period-end, resulting from changes in the exchange rate.

Option writing. When the Company writes an option, an amount equal to the premium received by the Company is recorded as a liability and subsequently adjusted to the current fair value of the option written. Premiums received from writing options that expire unexercised are treated by the Company on the expiration date as realized gains from investments. The difference between the premium and amount paid on effecting a closing purchase transaction, including brokerage commissions, is also treated as a realized gain or, if the premium is less than the amount paid for the closing purchase transaction, as a realized loss. If a call option is exercised, the premium is added to the proceeds from the sale of the underlying security or currency in determining whether the Company has realized a gain or loss. If a put option is exercised, the premium reduces the cost basis of the securities purchased by the Company. The Company as writer of an option bears the market risk of an unfavorable change in the price of the security underlying the written option.

The Company's written options are entered into on an over-the-counter (OTC) basis through a bilateral agreement with the counterparty. The International Swaps and Derivatives Association, Inc. Master Agreements and Credit Support Annexes (ISDA Agreements) that govern and establish terms for the written options provide the Company with legal right of set off that is enforceable under law. The fair value of OTC derivative instruments, collateral received or pledged and net exposure by counterparty as of period end, is disclosed in note 3.

Warrants. The Company can invest in warrants and stock purchase rights of companies of any market capitalization. A warrant gives the Company the right to buy stock, typically from the issuer. The warrant specifies the amount of underlying stock, the purchase (or "exercise") price, and the date the warrant expires. Certain warrants may permit, without legal obligation, net settlement for stock or cash. The Company has no obligation to exercise the warrant and buy the stock.

Security loans. The Company may lend its portfolio securities to third party borrowers, under the terms of a Master Securities Lending Agreement, to earn additional income. The Company receives compensation in the form of fees, or it retains a portion of interest on the investment of any cash received as collateral. The Company also continues to receive interest or dividends on the securities loaned. The loans are secured by collateral at least equal, at all times, to the fair value of the securities loaned plus accrued interest. Gain or loss in the fair value of the securities loaned that may occur during the term of the loan will be for the account of the Company.

The Company has the right under the Master Securities Lending Agreement to recover the securities from the borrower on demand; if the borrower fails to deliver the securities on a timely basis, the Company could experience delays or losses on recovery. Additionally, the Company is subject to the risk of loss from investments that it makes with the cash received as collateral. The Company manages credit exposure arising from these lending transactions by, in appropriate circumstances, entering into master netting agreements and collateral agreements with third party borrowers that provide the Company, in the event of default (such as bankruptcy or a borrower's failure to pay or perform), the right to net a third party borrower's rights and obligations under such agreement and liquidate and set off collateral against the net amount owed by the counterparty.

As of December 31, 20X8, the Company loaned common stocks having a fair value of approximately $570,000 and received $620,000 of cash collateral for the loan. All individual open security loan transactions were overcollateralized. This cash was invested in U.S. Treasury bills with maturities ranging from January to April 20X9. See note 3 for offsetting and collateral information pertaining to derivative agreements that are subject to master netting agreements.

Financial futures contracts. The Company invests in financial futures contracts solely for the purpose of hedging its existing portfolio securities, or securities that the Company intends to purchase, against fluctuations in fair value caused by changes in prevailing market interest rates. Upon entering into a financial futures contract, the Company is required to pledge to the broker an amount of cash, U.S. government securities, or other assets equal to a certain percentage of the contract amount (initial margin deposit). Subsequent payments, known as *variation margin*, are made or received by the Company each day, depending on the daily fluctuations in the fair value of the underlying security. The Company recognizes a gain or loss equal to the daily variation margin. If market conditions move unexpectedly, the Company may not achieve the anticipated benefits of the financial futures contracts and may realize a loss. The use of futures transactions involves the risk of imperfect correlation in movements in the price of futures contracts, interest rates, and the underlying hedged assets. The Customer Account Agreements and related addenda governing the Company's futures transactions do not provide offsetting provisions to the Company. Cleared derivative transactions require posting of initial margin as determined by each relevant clearing agency, which and is segregated at a broker account registered with the Commodities Futures Trading Commission (CFTC), or the applicable regulator.

Short sales. The Company may sell a security that it does not own in anticipation of a decline in the fair value of that security. When the Company sells
a security short, it must borrow the security sold short and deliver it to the
broker-dealer through which it made the short sale. A gain, limited to the price
at which the Company sold the security short, or a loss, unlimited in size, will
be recognized upon the termination of a short sale. The Company is also subject to the risk that it may be unable to reacquire a security to terminate a
short position except at a price substantially in excess of the last quoted price.
The Company's borrowing agreements with broker-dealers are not subject to
master netting or similar agreements or collateral agreements.

Foreign currency forward exchange contracts. The Company may enter into foreign currency forward exchange contracts primarily to hedge against foreign
currency exchange rate risks on its non-U.S. dollar denominated investment securities. When entering into a forward currency contract, the Company agrees
to receive or deliver a fixed quantity of foreign currency for an agreed-upon
price on an agreed future date. The Company's net equity therein, representing unrealized gain or loss on the contracts, as measured by the difference
between the forward foreign exchange rates at the dates of entry into the contracts and the forward rates at the reporting date, is included in the statement
of assets and liabilities. Realized and unrealized gains and losses are included
in the statement of operations. These instruments involve market risk, credit
risk, or both kinds of risks in excess of the amount recognized in the statement
of assets and liabilities. Risks arise from the possible inability of counterparties
to meet the terms of their contracts and movement in currency and securities
values and interest rates. The ISDA Agreements that govern and establish
terms for OTC forward exchange contracts provide the Company with legal
right of set off that is enforceable under law. The fair value of OTC derivative
instruments, collateral received or pledged and net exposure by counterparty
as of period end, is disclosed in note 3.

Swap contracts. The fund may enter into swap agreements to manage exposures to interest rate, equity, foreign currency, and credit risks. Swap agreements may be centrally cleared through exchanges or entered into on an OTC
basis through a bilateral agreement with the counterparty.

For swaps that are centrally cleared, initial margins are posted, and daily
changes in fair value are recorded as a payable or receivable on the Statement
of Assets and Liabilities as "Variation Margin on Derivative Instruments" and
settled daily. Initial margin is determined by each relevant clearing agency and
is segregated at a broker account registered with the CFTC, or the applicable
regulator. The Customer Account Agreements and related addendums governing the Company's cleared swap transactions do not provide the Company with
legal right of set off and are not associated with a master netting agreement.

For OTC swaps, collateral may be posted initially by one party to the swap
with the swap counterparty, and additional collateral may be transferred periodically as the fair value of the swap becomes more favorable to one party
and less favorable to the counterparty. The ISDA Agreements that govern and
establish terms for the OTC swaps provide the Company with legal right of set
off that is enforceable under law. The fair value of OTC derivative instruments,
collateral received or pledged and net exposure by counterparty as of period
end, is disclosed in note 3.

Credit default swaps. The Company may enter into credit default swaps to
manage its exposure to the market or certain sectors of the market, to reduce

its risk exposure to defaults of corporate and sovereign issuers or to create exposure to corporate or sovereign issuers to which it is not otherwise exposed. In a credit default swap, the protection buyer makes a stream of payments based on a fixed percentage applied to the contract notional amount to the protection seller in exchange for the right to receive a specified return upon the occurrence of a defined credit event on the reference obligation that may be either a single security or a basket of securities issued by corporate or sovereign issuers. Certain OTC contracts require the protection seller or buyer to make an initial payment to the counterparty upon entering into the swap. Although contract specific, credit events are generally defined as bankruptcy, failure to pay, restructuring, obligation acceleration, obligation default, or repudiation or moratorium. Upon the occurrence of a defined credit event, the buyer of the swap may elect either to be paid in cash an amount equal to, generally, the notional value of the contract less the current fair value of the underlying instrument as determined by a facilitated auction, or to deliver the underlying instrument to the seller of the swap in exchange for cash equal to the notional value of the instrument. Periodic payments received (as a seller) or paid (as a buyer) on OTC swap agreements, and cash payments received or made in excess of the fair value of the underlying obligation in the event of a credit event, are recorded as part of "Realized gain (loss) on swap contracts" in the Statement of Operations.

Federal income taxes. The Company's policy is to continue to comply with the requirements of the Internal Revenue Code that are applicable to regulated investment companies and to distribute all its taxable income to its shareholders. The Company also intends to distribute sufficient net investment income and net capital gains, if any, so that it will not be subject to excise tax on undistributed income and gains. Therefore, no federal income tax or excise provision is required.

Distributions to shareholders. Dividends to shareholders from net investment income, if any, are paid semiannually. Distributions of capital gains, if any, are made at least annually, and as required to comply with federal excise tax requirements. Distributions to shareholders are determined in accordance with income tax regulations and recorded on the ex-dividend date.

Use of estimates. The preparation of financial statements in conformity with U.S. generally accepted accounting principles (GAAP) requires management to make estimates and assumptions that affect the reported amounts of assets and liabilities and disclosure of contingent assets and liabilities at the date of the financial statements and the reported amounts of increases and decreases in net assets from operations during the reporting period. Actual results could differ from those estimates.

Other. The Company records security transactions based on a trade date. Dividend income is recognized on the ex-dividend date, and interest income is recognized on an accrual basis. Discounts and premiums on securities purchased are accreted and amortized over the lives of the respective securities. Withholding taxes on foreign dividends have been provided for in accordance with the Company's understanding of the applicable country's tax rules and rates.

2. Securities Valuations

Processes and Structure

The Company's board of trustees has adopted methods for valuing securities and other derivative instruments including in circumstances in which market quotes are not readily available, and has delegated authority to the Company's investment adviser to apply those methods in making fair value determinations, subject to board oversight. The investment adviser has established a Joint Fair Valuation Committee (the Fair Valuation Committee) to administer, implement, and oversee the fair valuation process, and to make fair value decisions. The Fair Valuation Committee regularly reviews its own fair value decisions, as well as decisions made under its standing instructions to the investment adviser's valuation teams. The Fair Valuation Committee reviews changes in fair value measurements from period to period and may, as deemed appropriate, update the fair valuation guidelines to better reflect the results of comparisons of fair value determinations with actual trade prices and address new or evolving issues. The Fair Valuation Committee also regularly reviews pricing vendor information and market data. Pricing decisions, processes, and controls over security valuation are also subject to additional internal reviews, including an annual control self-evaluation program facilitated by the investment adviser's compliance group. The Fair Valuation Committee reports any changes to the fair valuation guidelines to the board of trustees with supplemental information to support the changes. The Company's board and audit committee also regularly review reports that describe fair value determinations and methods.

Hierarchy of Fair Value Inputs

The Company utilizes various methods to measure the fair value of most of its investments on a recurring basis. GAAP establishes a hierarchy that prioritizes inputs to valuation techniques used to measure fair value. The three levels of inputs are as follows:

- *Level 1.* Unadjusted quoted prices in active markets for identical assets or liabilities that the Company has the ability to access.

- *Level 2.* Observable inputs other than quoted prices included in level 1 that are observable for the asset or liability either directly or indirectly. These inputs may include quoted prices for the identical instrument on an inactive market, prices for similar instruments, interest rates, prepayment speeds, credit risk, yield curves, default rates, and similar data.

- *Level 3.* Unobservable inputs for the asset or liability to the extent that relevant observable inputs are not available, representing the Company's own assumptions about the assumptions that a market participant would use in valuing the asset or liability, and that would be based on the best information available.

The availability of observable inputs can vary from security to security and is affected by a wide variety of factors, including, for example, the type of security, whether the security is new and not yet established in the marketplace, the liquidity of markets, and other characteristics particular to the security. To the extent that valuation is based on models or inputs that are less observable or unobservable in the market, the determination of fair value requires more judgment. Accordingly, the degree of judgment exercised in determining fair value is greatest for instruments categorized in level 3.

The inputs used to measure fair value may fall into different levels of the fair value hierarchy. In such cases, for disclosure purposes, the level in the fair value hierarchy within which the fair value measurement falls in its entirety is determined based on the lowest level input that is significant to the fair value measurement in its entirety.

Fair Value Measurements

A description of the valuation techniques applied to the Company's major categories of assets and liabilities measured at fair value on a recurring basis follows.

Equity securities (common and preferred stock). Securities traded on a national securities exchange (or reported on the NASDAQ national market) are stated at the last reported sales price on the day of valuation. To the extent these securities are actively traded, and valuation adjustments are not applied, they are categorized in level 1 of the fair value hierarchy. Certain foreign securities may be fair valued using a pricing service that considers the correlation of the trading patterns of the foreign security to the intraday trading in the U.S. markets for investments such as American Depositary Receipts, financial futures, Exchange Traded Funds, and the movement of the certain indexes of securities based on a statistical analysis of the historical relationship and that are categorized in level 2. Preferred stock and other equities traded on inactive markets or valued by reference to similar instruments are also categorized in level 2.

Corporate bonds. The fair value of corporate bonds is estimated using various techniques, which may consider recently executed transactions in securities of the issuer or comparable issuers, market price quotations (when observable), bond spreads, fundamental data relating to the issuer, and credit default swap spreads adjusted for any basis difference between cash and derivative instruments. Although most corporate bonds are categorized in level 2 of the fair value hierarchy, in instances when lower relative weight is placed on transaction prices, quotations, or similar observable inputs, they are categorized in level 3.

Asset-backed securities. The fair value of asset-backed securities is estimated based on models that consider the estimated cash flows of each tranche of the entity, establishes a benchmark yield, and develops an estimated tranche-specific spread to the benchmark yield based on the unique attributes of the tranche. To the extent that the inputs are observable and timely, the values would be categorized in level 2 of the fair value hierarchy; otherwise, they would be categorized as level 3.

Short term notes. Short term notes are valued using amortized cost, which approximates fair value. To the extent that the inputs are observable and timely, the values would be categorized in level 2 of the fair value hierarchy.

U.S. government securities. U.S. government securities are normally valued using a model that incorporates market observable data, such as reported sales of similar securities, broker quotes, yields, bids, offers, and reference data. Certain securities are valued principally using dealer quotations. U.S. government securities are categorized in level 1 or level 2 of the fair value hierarchy, depending on the inputs used and market activity levels for specific securities.

U.S. agency securities. U.S. agency securities comprise two main categories consisting of agency-issued debt and mortgage pass-throughs. Agency-issued debt securities are generally valued in a manner similar to U.S. government securities. Mortgage pass-throughs include to-be-announced (TBA) securities and mortgage pass-through certificates. TBA securities and mortgage pass-throughs are generally valued using dealer quotations. Depending on market activity levels and whether quotations or other data are used, these securities are typically categorized in level 1 or level 2 of the fair value hierarchy.

Restricted securities (equity and debt). Restricted securities for which quotations are not readily available are valued at fair value, as determined by the board of directors. Restricted securities issued by publicly traded companies are generally valued at a discount to similar publicly traded securities. Restricted securities issued by nonpublic entities may be valued by reference to comparable public entities or fundamental data relating to the issuer, or both. Depending on the relative significance of valuation inputs, these instruments may be classified in either level 2 or level 3 of the fair value hierarchy.

Derivative instruments. Listed derivatives that are actively traded are valued based on quoted prices from the exchange and categorized in level 1 of the fair value hierarchy. Over-the-counter (OTC) derivative contracts include forward, swap, and option contracts related to interest rates; foreign currencies; credit standing of reference entities; equity prices; or commodity prices, and warrants on exchange-traded securities. Depending on the product and terms of the transaction, the fair value of the OTC derivative products can be modeled taking into account the counterparties' creditworthiness and using a series of techniques, including simulation models. Many pricing models do not entail material subjectivity because the methodologies employed do not necessitate significant judgments, and the pricing inputs are observed from actively quoted markets, as is the case of interest rate swap and option contracts. A substantial majority of OTC derivative products valued by the Company using pricing models fall into this category and are categorized within level 2 of the fair value hierarchy.

The following table summarizes the inputs used to value the Company's assets and liabilities measured at fair value as of December 31, 20X8.[76]

Financial Instruments—Assets

Categories	Level 1	Level 2	Level 3	Fair Value
Common Stocks				
Consumer durable goods	$1,086,000	$—	$—	$1,086,000
Consumer nondurable goods	155,000	—	3,280,000	3,435,000
Service industries	869,000	—	—	869,000
Other industries	921,000	—	—	921,000
Corporate bonds	—	5,400,000	—	5,400,000
Indexed securities	—	—	2,100,000	2,100,000
Mortgage-backed securities	—	2,710,000	—	2,710,000
U.S. government obligations	—	3,475,000	—	3,475,000
Short-term notes	—	1,225,000	—	1,225,000
Repurchase agreements	—	500,000	—	500,000
Total	$3,031,000	$13,310,000	$5,380,000	$21,721,000

Financial Instruments—Liabilities

Categories	Level 1	Level 2	Level 3	Fair Value
Common stocks (short sales)	$(1,673,000)	$—	$—	$(1,673,000)
Total	$(1,673,000)	$—	$—	$(1,673,000)

Derivative Instruments—Assets

Categories	Level 1	Level 2	Level 3	Fair Value
Credit contracts	$—	$3,000	$—	$3,000
Interest rate contracts	—	11,000	—	11,000
Foreign currency contracts	—	419,000	—	419,000
Total		$433,000	$—	$433,000

Derivative Instruments—Liabilities

Categories	Level 1	Level 2	Level 3	Fair Value
Credit contracts	$—	$(21,000)	$—	$(21,000)
Interest rate contracts	(50,000)	—	—	(50,000)
Equity contracts	(230,000)	—	—	(230,000)
Foreign currency contracts	—	(108,000)	—	(108,000)
Total	$(280,000)	$(129,000)	$—	$(409,000)

There were no transfers between level 1 and level 2 during the year.[77]

---

[76] The classification of various financial instruments in this table is for illustrative purposes only and should not be construed as recommended practice for any particular financial instrument or class of financial instruments.

[77] FASB ASC 820-10-50-2F provides that a nonpublic entity is not required to disclose certain information required by FASB ASC 820-10-50-2, including transfers between level 1 and level 2. See discussion of nonpublic entity disclosure requirements in paragraph 7.88 for more information.

The following is a reconciliation of assets for which level 3 inputs were used in determining value.

Financial Instruments—Assets

	Common Stock	Indexed Securities	Total
Beginning balance	$2,000,000	$—	$2,000,000
Total realized gain (loss)	(500,000)	—	(500,000)
Change in unrealized appreciation (depreciation)	780,000	(300,000)	480,000
Net purchases	—	2,400,000	2,400,000
Net sales	1,000,000	—	1,000,000
Accrued interest	—	—	—
Transfers into level 3	—	—	—
Transfers out of level 3	—	—	—
Ending balance	$3,280,000	$2,100,000	$5,380,000

Derivatives Instruments—Liabilities

	Interest Rate Contracts*	Total
Beginning balance	($313,000)	($313,000)
Total realized gain (loss)	(2,400,000)	(2,400,000)
Change in unrealized appreciation (depreciation)	313,000	313,000
Settlements	2,400,000	2,400,000
Accrued interest	—	—
Transfers into level 3	—	—
Transfers out of level 3	—	—
Ending balance	$—	$—
		$5,380,000

The total change in unrealized appreciation (depreciation) included in the statement of operations attributable to level 3 investments still held at December 31, 20X8, includes the following:

	Common Stock	Indexed Securities	Total
	$880,000	($300,000)	$580,000

*No longer held in POI

The following is quantitative information about significant unobservable inputs (level 3) for the Company as of December 31, 20X8.

Asset Categories	Fair Value	Valuation Techniques	Unobservable Input	Input Value(s)
			Broker quote	$345
Consumer nondurable goods	$3,280,000	Market comparable	Illiquidity adjustment (%)	(5)%
Indexed securities	2,100,000	Vendor pricing	Broker quote	$105

The following represents the impact on fair value measurements to changes in unobservable inputs:[78]

Unobservable Inputs*	Increase in Inputs Impact on Valuation	Decrease in Inputs Impact on Valuation
Illiquidity adjustments	Decrease	Increase

* Unobservable Inputs from the broker quote were not included because the fund does not develop the quantitative inputs and they are not readily available.

The following provides fair value information for financial assets and liabilities not measured at fair value in the statement of assets and liabilities, as of December 31, 20X8:[79]

	Carrying Amount	Fair Value	Fair Value Levels	Valuation Technique
Liabilities				
Demand loan payable to bank	$2,000,000	$2,005,000	Level 2	Quoted market prices

3. Derivatives Instruments [80]

The following contains information about the Company's use of derivative instruments, the credit-risk-related contingent features in certain derivative instruments, and how derivative instruments affect the Company's financial position, operations and cash flows.

As of December 31, 20X8, portfolio securities valued at $634,500 were held in escrow by the custodian as cover for call options written by the Company.

Transactions in options written during the year ended December 31, 20X8, were as follows:

	Number of Contracts	Premiums Received
Options outstanding at December 31, 20X7	100	$100,000
Options written	500	500,000
Options terminated in closing purchase transactions	(150)	(190,000)
Options expired	(80)	(150,000)
Options exercised	(150)	(150,000)
Options outstanding at December 31, 20X8	220	$110,000

---

[78] The illustrative disclosure of a description of sensitivity of the fair value measurement categorized within level three of three of the fair value hierarchy, as discussed in paragraph 7.87i is required for public entities only. As discussed in paragraph 7.88, this disclosure is not required for nonpublic entities.

[79] As discussed in paragraph 7.102, and pursuant to FASB ASC 825-10-50-3A, a reporting entity that is a nonpublic entity (see paragraph 7.88) is not required to disclose the level of the fair value hierarchy within which the fair value measurements are categorized in their entirety (level 1, 2, or 3) (disclosure requirement in FASB ASC 825-10-50-10(d)) for items disclosed at fair value but not measured at fair value in the statement of financial position.

[80] Practitioners should consider all the disclosure requirements of FASB ASC 815, which may not be necessarily reflected in these financial statements and notes to the financial statements.

As of December 31, 20X8, the Company held the following financial exchange traded futures contracts:

Issue	Exchange	Number of Contracts	Expiration Date	Notional Value	Unrealized Loss
10-Year U.S. Treasury Notes Futures	CME	10	March 20XX	$1,315,625	($50,000)
				$1,315,625	($50,000)

The Company has additionally recorded a liability of $10,000 as of December 31, 20X8, related to the current day's variation margin related to these contracts.

As of December 31, 20X8, the Company held the following foreign currency forward exchange contracts:

Currency Purchased		Currency Sold		Counterparty	Settlement Date	Unrealized Gain (Loss)
JPY	1,407,900,000	USD	14,588,000	ABC Bank	1/25/20XX	$419,000
Euro	14,394,000	USD	13,206,000	ABC Bank	3/7/20XX	(108,000)
						$311,000

As of December 31, 20X8, the Company held the following centrally cleared swaps:

Credit Default Swaps on Credit Indices—Buy Protection[81]

Description	Fixed Deal (Pay) Rate	Maturity Date	Notional Amount[82]	Fair Value	Unrealized Gain
CDX.HY-175-Year Index	(5.00)%	8/20/20XX	$1,500,000	$25,000	$3,000
				$25,000	$3,000

Interest Rate Swaps

Pay/Rec Floating Rate	Floating Rate Index	Fixed Rate	Maturity Date	Notional Amount	Fair Value	Unrealized Gain
Received	3-Month USD-LIBOR	2.75%	6/20/20XX	$500,000	$50,000	$10,000
					$50,000	$10,000

---

[81] When the company is a buyer or seller of protection and a credit event occurs, as defined under the terms of that particular swap agreement, the company will either receive or pay from the seller or buyer of protection an amount equal to the notional amount of the swap and deliver the referenced obligation or underlying securities comprising the referenced index, or receive a net settlement amount in the form of cash or securities equal to the notional amount of the swap less the recovery value of the referenced obligation.

[82] The maximum potential amount the company could be required to pay as seller of credit protection or receive as a buyer of credit protection, if a credit event were to occur.

As of December 31, 20X8, the Company held the following OTC swaps:

Credit Default Swaps on Corporate Issues—Sell Protection[83]

Description	Counter-party	Fixed Deal (Pay) Rate	Maturity Date	Credit Rating	Notional Amount[84]	Fair Value	Premiums Paid	Unrealized Loss
Baker Co.	ATC	1.75%	6/30/20XX	BB/Ba	$500,000	($16,000)	$5,000	($21,000)
						($16,000)	$5,000	($21,000)

Interest Rate Swaps

Pay/Rec Floating Rate	Counter-party	Floating Rate Index	Fixed Rate	Maturity Date	Notional Value	Fair Value	Premiums Received	Unrealized Gain
Pay	ATC	1-Year BRL-CDI	10.50%	9/30/20XX	$25,000	($1,000)	($2,000)	$1,000
						($1,000)	($2,000)	$1,000

The following disclosure identifies the location and fair value amounts of the Company's derivative instruments on the Statement of Assets and Liabilities and the effect on the Statement of Operations, each categorized by type of derivative contract and related risk exposure.

As of December 31, 20X8, the statement of assets and liabilities included the following financial derivative instrument fair values:

Assets	Interest Rate Contracts	Foreign Exchange Contracts	Credit Contracts	Equity Contracts	Other Contracts	Total
Variation margin receivable on derivative instruments[85]	$2,000	$—	$1,000	$—	$—	$3,000
Unrealized gain from OTC swap contract	1,000	—	—	—	—	1,000
Unrealized gain on foreign currency contract	—	419,000	—	—	—	419,000
Investments in securities[86]	—	—	—	4,000	—	4,000
	$3,000	$419,000	$1,000	$4,000	$0	$427,000
Liabilities						
Options written	$—	$—	$—	($230,000)	$—	($230,000)
Unrealized loss on foreign currency contract	—	(108,000)	—	—	—	(108,000)
Unrealized loss on OTC swap contract	—	—	(21,000)	—	—	(21,000)
Variation margin payable on derivative instruments[87]	(10,000)	—	—	—	—	(10,000)
	($10,000)	($108,000)	($21,000)	($230,000)	$0	($369,000)

---

[83] See footnote 81.

[84] See footnote 82.

[85] The Statement of Assets and Liabilities reports current day's variation margin. Variation margin reported in other tables in the footnotes to the financial statements is the cumulative unrealized gain (loss) of futures $(50,000) and of centrally cleared swaps $ 13,000.

[86] Includes the value of warrants that are considered derivatives under FASB ASC 815 guidance.

[87] See footnote 85.

For the period ended December 31, 20X8, financial derivative instruments had the following effect on the statement of operations:

Realized Gain (Loss) From:	Interest Rate Contracts	Foreign Exchange Contracts	Credit Contracts	Equity Contracts	Other Contracts	Total
Investments[88]	$—	$—	$—	$1,000	$—	$1,000
Futures	73,000	—	—	—	—	73,000
Swaps	7,000	—	—	—	—	7,000
Options written	—	—	—	(89,000)	—	(89,000)
Foreign currency transactions	—	18,000	—	—	—	18,000
	$80,000	$18,000	$15,000	($88,000)	$0	$10,000
Net Change in Unrealized Gain (Loss) From						
Investments[89]	$—	$—	$—	$4,000	$—	$4,000
Futures	($50,000)	$—	$—	$—	$—	($50,000)
Swaps	20,000	—	(140,000)	—	—	(120,000)
Options written	—	—	—	(120,000)	—	(120,000)
Foreign currency transactions	—	311,000	—	—	—	311,000
	($30,000)	$311,000	($140,000)	($116,000)	$0	$25,000

The previously disclosed derivative instruments outstanding as of December 31, 20X8, and their effect on the Statement of Operations for the period ending December 31, 20X8, serve as indicators of the volume of financial derivative activity for the Company. The following table indicates the average volume for the period:

Average notional value of:

Futures contracts	$50,000
Options written	$100,000
Swap contracts	$100,000
Foreign currency contracts	$300,000

Master Netting Agreements

The Company is subject to enforceable master netting agreements, or netting arrangements, with certain counterparties. These agreements govern the terms of certain transactions, and reduce the counterparty risk associated with relevant transactions by specifying offsetting mechanisms and collateral posting arrangements at pre-arranged exposure levels. Since different types of transactions have different mechanics and are sometimes traded out of different legal entities of a particular counterparty organization, each type of transaction may be covered by a different master netting arrangement, possibly resulting in the need for multiple agreements with a single counterparty. Master netting agreements may not be specific to each different asset type; in such instances, they would allow the Company to close out and net its total exposure to a specified counterparty in the event of a default with respect to any and all the transactions governed under a single agreement with the counterparty. Collateral or margin requirements are set by the broker or exchange clearing house for exchange traded derivatives (futures contracts and

---

[88] See footnote 86.
[89] See footnote 86.

exchange traded swaps, for example) while collateral terms are contract specific for OTC traded derivatives (forward foreign currency exchange contracts, swap agreements, and OTC options, for example). Although collateral or margin requirements may differ by type of derivative or investment, as applicable, the Company typically receives cash posted as collateral (with rights of rehypothecation) or agrees to have such collateral posted to a third party custodian under a tri-party arrangement that enables the Company to take control of such collateral in the event of a counterparty default.

ISDA Agreements govern OTC derivative transactions entered into by the Company and select counterparties. ISDA Agreements maintain provisions for general obligations, representations, agreements, collateral and events of default or termination. Under the Company's separate and distinct ISDA Agreements for OTC swaps and foreign currency forward contracts, the Company may be required to post collateral on derivatives if the Company is in a net liability position with the counterparty. Additionally, counterparties may immediately terminate derivatives contracts if the Company fails to maintain sufficient asset coverage for its contracts. An election to terminate early could be material to the financial statements. In limited circumstances, the ISDA Agreement may contain additional provisions that add additional counterparty protection beyond coverage of existing daily exposure if the counterparty has a decline in credit quality below a predefined level. These amounts, if any, may be segregated with a third party custodian. The gross fair value of OTC derivative instruments, amounts available for offset, collateral received or pledged and net exposure by instrument (Option A—Offsetting Presentation) or counterparty (Option B—Offsetting Presentation) as of period end, is disclosed below.

Disclosure Option A—Offsetting Presentation

The following tables present, as of December 31, 20X8, the gross and net derivative assets and liabilities that are netted on the statement of assets and liabilities or that are subject to a master netting agreement. The tables also present information about the related collateral amounts. See note 1 for offsetting and collateral information pertaining to repurchase and securities lending agreements that are subject to master netting agreements.

Derivative Assets As of December 31, 20X8

Financial Instrument	Gross Amounts of Recognized Assets	Gross Amounts Offset in Statement of Assets and Liabilities	Net Amounts of Assets Presented in Statement of Assets and Liabilities	Amounts Not Offset in the Statement of Assets and Liabilities		Net Amount (not less than 0)
				Financial Instruments*	Other Cash Collateral**	
Derivative Assets						
Foreign currency forward contracts	$419,000	$—	$419,000	$(108,000)	$—	$311,000
OTC interest rate swap contracts	1,000	—	1,000	(1,000)	—	—
	$420,000	$—	$420,000	$(109,000)	$—	$311,000
Derivative Liabilities						
Foreign currency forward contracts	$108,000	—	$108,000	$(108,000)	$—	$—
OTC credit swap contracts	21,000	—	21,000	(1,000)	—	20,000
Written options	230,000	—	230,000	(230,000)	—	—
	$359,000	$—	$359,000	$(339,000)	$—	$ 20,000

---

* Amounts relate to master netting agreements and collateral agreements (for example, ISDA) which have been determined by the Company to be legally enforceable in the event of default and where certain other criteria are met in accordance with applicable offsetting accounting guidance.

** Amounts relate to master netting agreements and collateral agreements which have been determined by the Company to be legally enforceable in the event of default but where certain other criteria are not met in accordance with applicable offsetting accounting guidance. The collateral amounts may exceed the related net amounts of financial assets and liabilities presented in the statement of assets and liabilities. Where this is the case, the total amount reported is limited to the net amounts of financial assets and liabilities with that counterparty.

Option B—Offsetting Presentation

The following tables present, as of December 31, 20X8, the gross and net derivative assets and liabilities that are netted on the statement of assets and liabilities or that are subject to a master netting agreement. The tables also present information about the related collateral amounts by counterparty. See note 1 for offsetting and collateral information pertaining to repurchase and securities lending agreements that are subject to master netting agreements.

Derivative Assets As of December 31, 20X8

Financial Instrument	Gross Amounts of Recognized Assets	Gross Amounts Offset in Statement of Assets and Liabilities	Net Amounts of Assets Presented in Statement of Assets and Liabilities
Foreign currency forward contracts	419,000	—	419,000
OTC interest rate swap contracts	1,000	—	1,000
	$420,000	$—	$420,000

	Net Amounts of Assets Presented in Statement of Assets	Amounts Not Offset in the Statement of Assets and Liabilities		
Counterparty	and Liabilities	Financial Instruments*	Other Cash Collateral**	Net Amount (not less than 0)
ABC Bank	419,000	(108,000)	—	311,000
ATC	1,000	(1,000)	—	—
	$420,000	$(109,000)	$—	$311,000

Derivative Liabilities As of December 31, 20X8

Financial Instrument	Gross Amounts of Recognized Liabilities	Gross Amounts Offset in Statement of Assets and Liabilities	Net Amounts of Assets Presented in Statement of Assets and Liabilities
Foreign currency contracts	108,000	—	108,000
OTC credit swap contracts	21,000	—	21,000
Written options	230,000	—	230,000
	$359,000	$—	$359,000

Counterparty	Net Amounts of Liabilities Presented in Statement of Assets and Liabilities	Financial Instruments*	Other Cash Collateral**	Net Amount (not less than 0)
		Amounts Not Offset in the Statement of Assets and Liabilities		
ABC Bank	$108,000	$(108,000)	$—	$—
ATC	21,000	(1,000)	—	20,000
AMR	230,000	(230,000)	—	—
	$359,000	$(339,000)	$—	$20,000

* Amounts relate to master netting agreements and collateral agreements (for example, ISDA) which have been determined by the Company to be legally enforceable in the event of default and where certain other criteria are met in accordance with applicable offsetting accounting guidance.

** Amounts relate to master netting agreements and collateral agreements which have been determined by the Company to be legally enforceable in the event of default but where certain other criteria are not met in accordance with applicable offsetting accounting guidance. The collateral amounts may exceed the related net amounts of financial assets and liabilities presented in the statement of assets and liabilities. Where this is the case, the total amount reported is limited to the net amounts of financial assets and liabilities with that counterparty.

4. Income Taxes

The tax character of distributions paid during 20X8 and 20X7 was as follows:

	20X8	20X7
Distributions paid from:		
Ordinary income	$755,000	$550,000
Long term capital gain	1,120,000	800,000
	1,875,000	1,350,000
Return of capital	—	66,000
	$1,875,000	$1,416,000

As of December 31, 20X8, the components of distributable earnings on a tax basis were as follows:

Undistributed ordinary income	$1,304,000
Undistributed long term gain	1,152,000
Unrealized appreciation	1,540,000
	$3,996,000

The difference between book-basis and tax-basis unrealized appreciation is attributable primarily to the tax deferral of losses on wash sales and the realization for tax purposes of unrealized gains on certain forward foreign currency contracts and investments in passive foreign investment companies.

Permanent book- and tax-basis differences, if any, result in reclassifications to paid-in capital. These reclassifications have no effect on net assets or results of operations. Permanent book- and tax-basis differences are primarily attributable to derivatives transactions.

The U.S. federal income tax basis of the Company's investments at December 31, 20X8, was $19,321,000, and net unrealized appreciation for U.S. federal income tax purposes was $1,780,000 (gross unrealized appreciation $2,380,000; gross unrealized depreciation $600,000).

The Company recognizes the tax benefits of uncertain tax positions only when the position is more likely than not to be sustained, assuming examination by tax authorities. Management has analyzed the Company's tax positions and concluded that no liability for unrecognized tax benefits should be recorded related to uncertain tax positions taken on returns filed for open tax years (20X5–X8) or expected to be taken in the Company's 20X9 tax returns. The Company identifies its major tax jurisdictions as U.S. federal, New York State, and foreign jurisdictions where the Company makes significant investments; however, the Company is not aware of any tax positions for which it is reasonably possible that the total amounts of unrecognized tax benefits will change materially in the next 12 months.

5. Bank Loans

The Company has an unsecured $3,000,000 bank line of credit; borrowings under this arrangement bear interest at 110 percent of the bank's prime rate. As of December 31, 20X8, the Company was paying weighted average interest at 8 percent per year on its outstanding borrowings. No compensating balances are required. For the year ended December 31, 20X8, the average borrowings and interest rate under the line of credit were $1,700,000 and 6.50 percent, respectively. The December 31, 20X8, balance of $2,000,000 was the maximum borrowing during the year. Please refer to note 2 for fair value information on the bank line of credit.

6. Capital Share Transactions

As of December 31, 20X8, 25,000,000 shares of $0.50 par value capital stock were authorized.

Transactions in capital stock were as follows:

	Shares		Amount	
	20X8	20X7	20X8	20X7
Shares sold	452,000	329,000	$2,186,000	$1,440,000
Shares issued in reinvestment of distributions	222,000	207,000	1,000,000	845,000
	674,000	536,000	3,186,000	2,285,000
Shares redeemed	104,000	121,000	456,000	530,000
Net increase	570,000	415,000	$2,730,000	$1,755,000

On January 3, 20X9, a distribution of $0.20 per share was declared from net investment income. The dividend was paid on January 20, 20X9, to shareholders of record on January 10, 20X9.

7. Investment Transactions

Purchases and sales of investment securities (excluding short term securities and U.S. government obligations) were $23,420,000 and $24,030,000, respectively.

8. Principal Risks

The Company in the normal course of business makes investments in financial instruments and derivatives where the risk of potential loss exists due to changes in the market (market risk), or failure or inability of the counterparty to a transaction to perform (credit and counterparty risk). See below for a detailed description of select principal risks.

Market risk. The Company's investments in financial instruments and derivatives expose it to various risks such as, but not limited to, interest rate, foreign currency, and equity.

Interest rate risk is the risk that a fixed income investment's value will change due to a change in the absolute level of interest rates, in the spread between two rates, in the shape of the yield curve or in any other interest rate relationship. Such changes usually affect securities inversely and can be reduced by diversifying (for example, investing in fixed-income securities with different durations) or hedging (for example, through an interest rate swap). The Company manages this risk through its investments in interest rate swaps.

Foreign currency risk exists if the Company invests directly in foreign currencies or in securities that trade in, and receive revenues in, foreign currencies, or in derivatives instruments that provide exposure to foreign currencies. The Company is subject to the risk that those currencies will decline in value relative to the base currency of the Company, or, in the case of hedging positions, that the Company's base currency will decline in value relative to the currency being hedged. The Company maintains foreign currency balances to settle open transactions. The Company manages foreign currency risk through its investments in foreign currency forward exchange contracts.

Equity risk is the risk that the market values of equities, such as common stocks or equity related investments such as futures and options, may decline due to general market conditions, such a political or macroeconomic factors. Additionally, equities may decline in value due to specific factors affecting a related industry or industries. Equity securities and equity related investments generally have greater market price volatility than fixed income securities. The Company manages equity risk through its investments in options and futures.

Credit and counterparty risks. The Company is exposed to credit risk to counterparties with whom it transacts with and also bears the risk of settlement default. The Company may lose money if the issuer or guarantor of a fixed income security, or the counterparty to a derivative instrument contract, repurchase agreement or securities lending is unable or unwilling to make timely principal and/or interest payments, or to otherwise honor its obligations. Securities are subject to varying degrees of credit risk, which are often reflected in credit ratings. The Company minimizes concentrations of credit risk by undertaking transactions with a diverse population of counterparties with a history of good credit quality. Further, the Company manages counterparty risk by entering into appropriate legally enforceable master netting agreements, or similar agreements which include provisions for offsetting positions, collateral, or both in the event of counterparty default or nonperformance. See note 3 for further details.

9. Investment Advisory Fees and Other Transactions With Affiliates

The Company receives investment management and advisory services under a management agreement (agreement) that provides for fees to be paid at an annual rate of 0.65 percent of the Company's average daily net assets. Certain officers and directors of the Company are also officers and directors of the investment adviser. The agreement provides for an expense reimbursement from the investment adviser if the Company's total expenses, exclusive of taxes, interest on borrowings, dividends on securities sold short, brokerage commissions, and extraordinary expenses, exceed 1.5 percent of the Company's average daily net assets for any full fiscal year. During the year ended December 31, 20X8, the investment adviser voluntarily waived $45,000 of its fee.

The investment adviser also received $5,000 in 20X8 from brokerage fees on executions of purchases and sales of the Company's portfolio investments.

During 20X8, the Company incurred legal fees of $7,000 to Brown and Smith, counsel for the Company. A partner of the firm is a director of the Company.

MNO Service Company (MNO), an affiliate of the investment adviser, is the distributor of the Company's shares and received $10,000 in 20X8 from commissions earned on sales of the Company's capital stock. The Company has entered into a distribution agreement and plan of distribution pursuant to which the Company pays MNO a fee, accrued daily and payable monthly, at an annual rate of 0.75 percent of average daily net assets of the Company. During the year ended December 31, 20X8, MNO received contingent deferred sales charges of $18,000 from redeeming shareholders. Also, the amount of distribution expenses incurred by MNO and not yet reimbursed was approximately $187,000. This amount may be recovered from future payments under the plan or contingent deferred sales charges.

Included in the statement of operations under the caption "Custodian and transfer agent fees" are expense offsets of $4,000 arising from credits on cash balances maintained on deposit.

7.225

Financial Highlights

	20X8	20X7	20X6	20X5	20X4[90]
Per Share Operating Performance (for a share of capital stock outstanding throughout the period):					
Net asset value, beginning of period	$4.88	$4.46	$4.16	$4.81	$4.53
Income from investment operations:					
Net investment income	0.21	0.15	0.19	0.17	0.15
Net realized and unrealized gain (loss) on investment transactions	(0.04)	0.76	0.52	(0.42)	0.48
Total from investment operations	0.17	0.91	0.71	(0.25)	0.63
Less distributions	(0.50)	(0.47)	(0.41)	(0.40)	(0.35)
Tax return of capital distribution	—	(0.02)	—	—	—
Total distributions	(0.50)	(0.49)	(0.41)	(0.40)	(0.35)
Net asset value, end of period	$4.55	$4.88	$4.46	$4.16	$4.81
Total Return: [91]	3.48%	20.40%	17.07%	(5.02)%	3.91%
Supplemental Data:					
Net assets, end of period (000)	$19,180	$17,792	$14,410	$15,000	$14,000
Ratio to average net assets:					
Expenses[92]	1.33%[93]	1.31%	.99%	.82%	84%
Net investment income[94, 95]	4.56%[96]	2.82%	4.22%	5.42%	5.10%
Portfolio turnover rate[97]	92%	80%	108%	75%	62%

The accompanying notes are an integral part of these financial statements.

Illustrations of Calculations and Disclosures When Reporting Expense and Net Investment Income Ratios

7.226   The following are illustrations of average net assets computations related to determining expense and net investment income ratios in which there are various capital flows, assuming a single class of investment interest. Other average net assets computation methods (for example, summing and averaging monthly net assets, including the beginning and ending net assets for the year, or a method that also weights ending net assets) are also appropriate if the result is reasonable and consistently applied.

---

[90] Period from March 1, 20X4 (inception), to December 31, 20X4.

[91] Not annualized for periods less than one year.

[92] Annualized for periods less than one year.

    Such percentages are after advisory fee waivers and expense subsidies. The adviser voluntarily waived a portion of its investment advisory fee (equal to 0.22 percent of average net assets) in 20X8 and subsidized certain operating expenses (equal to 0.21 percent of average net assets) in 20X8.

[94] Annualized for periods less than one year.

[95] The net investment income (loss) ratio excludes (includes) the effect of the incentive allocation.

[96] See footnote 93.

[97] As stated in paragraph 7.182, portfolio turnover is only required for registered investment companies.

Example 1: Computation of average net assets in a nonregistered investment partnership that allows quarterly contributions and distributions and has quarterly accounting periods (that is, capital can flow in and out only at these times).

Net assets at the beginning of the period:	$100,000,000 × 3/12 =	$25,000,000
Valuation adjustment of $10 million and capital contribution of $25 million at April 1, 20X9:	$135,000,000 × 3/12 =	$33,750,000
Valuation adjustment of $(5) million, capital contribution of $10 million, and capital withdrawals of $30 million at July 1, 20X9:	$110,000,000 × 3/12 =	$27,500,000
Valuation adjustment of $20 million, capital contribution of $15 million, and capital withdrawals of $25 million at October 1, 20X9:	$120,000,000 × 3/12 =	$30,000,000
Average net assets		$116,250,000

Example 2: Computation of average net assets in a nonregistered investment partnership that does not have predetermined accounting periods (that is, capital can be called and distributed at any time), with significant write-up in fair value during the year.

Net assets at the beginning of the period:	$100,000,000 × 2/12 =	$16,666,667
$25m capital call at February 28, 20X9:	$125,000,000 × 1/12 =	$10,416,667
$20m write-up at March 31, 20X9:	$145,000,000 × 6/12 =	$72,500,000
$55m capital call at September 30, 20X9:	$200,000,000 × 1/12 =	$16,666,667
$25m distribution at October 31, 20X9:	$175,000,000 × 2/12 =	$29,166,667
Average net assets		$145,416,668

Disclosure for Incentive and Allocation Fees

For incentive fee:	
Operating (and interest/short dividends) expense	2.25%
Incentive fee	7.35%
Total expenses	9.60%
For incentive allocations:	
Operating (and interest/short dividends) expense	2.25%
Incentive allocation	7.35%
Total expenses and incentive allocation	9.60%

The expense ratio (expense and incentive allocation ratio) is calculated for each common class taken as a whole. The computation of such ratios based on the amount of expenses and incentive fee or incentive allocation assessed to an individual investor's capital may vary from these ratios based on different management fee and incentive arrangements (as applicable) and the timing of capital transactions.

Illustration of Calculation and Disclosure When Reporting the Internal Rate of Return

7.227 The following is an illustration of how to compute IRR for nonregistered investment partnerships that meet the criteria described in paragraph

7.180c. Other nonregistered investment partnerships generally should calculate a total rate of return as described in paragraph 7.180b and illustrated in paragraph 7.228.

The following illustrates how an IRR is computed by a limited-life nonregistered investment partnership, from the perspective of the investor, at the end of its first and second years of operations. The formula used to compute the IRR is 0 = CF0 + (CF1/(1+IRR)) + (CF2/(1+IRR)2) + . . . + (CFT/(1+IRR)T).

Assume that year 1 activity includes an initial investment (capital contribution) on January 1 of $1,000,000; $50,000 of appreciation (profit) reported on March 31; an additional capital contribution of $1,000,000 on April 1; additional appreciation of $80,000 reported on June 30; a distribution of $500,000 on July 1; and depreciation (loss) of $30,000 reported on December 31, resulting in a residual value on December 31, 01, of $1,600,000. The residual value, the ending net assets at the end of the period and considered a theoretical distribution, is calculated as follows: $1,000,000 (initial capital contribution) plus $1,000,000 (additional capital contribution) minus $500,000 (cash distribution) plus the net gain of $100,000 (50,000 + 80,000 − 30,000) equals $1,600,000.

Assume that year 2 activity includes $150,000 of appreciation (profit) reported on March 31; a capital contribution of $500,000 on April 1; $350,000 of additional appreciation (profit) reported on June 30; $150,000 of additional appreciation (profit) reported on September 30; a distribution of $300,000 on December 14; and $150,000 of depreciation (loss) reported on December 31, resulting in a residual value on December 31, 02, of $2,300,000 (calculated the same way as year 01).

| | | | | | IRR Cash Flows | |
| | | Capital | Cash | Residual | Through | Through |
Date	Description	Call	Distribution	Value	12/31/01	12/31/02
1-Jan-01	Initial contribution	1,000,000			(1,000,000)	(1,000,000)
1-Apr-01	Additional capital contribution	1,000,000			(1,000,000)	(1,000,000)
1-Jul-01	Cash distribution		500,000		500,000	500,000
31-Dec-01	Residual value			1,600,000	1,600,000	N/A
1-Apr-02	Additional capital contribution	500,000				(500,000)
14-Dec-02	Distribution		300,000			300,000
31-Dec-02	Residual value			2,300,000		2,300,000
	IRR through December 31, '01				6.69%	
	IRR through December 31, '02					16.68%

The following illustrates the note disclosure of the IRR by the limited-life nonregistered investment partnership at the end of the second year of operations based on the assumptions outlined.

Note X—Financial Highlights

The internal rate of return since inception (IRR) of the limited partners, net of all fees and profit allocations (carried interest) to the manager (general partner), is 6.69 percent through December 31, year 01, and 16.68 percent through December 31, year 02.

The IRR was computed based on the actual dates of the cash inflows (capital contributions), outflows (cash and stock distributions), and the ending net assets at the end of the period (residual value) of the limited partners' capital account as of each measurement date.

Illustration of Calculation and Disclosure When Reporting the Total Return Ratio

7.228 The following are illustrations of how to compute the total return ratio for nonregistered investment partnerships, as discussed in paragraph 7.180*b*:

Example 1: The following are illustrations of how a geometrically linked cash flow is computed assuming a beginning equity of $1,000,000; a capital contribution of $1,000,000 on April 1; and a capital withdrawal of $500,000 on July 1.

Period	Cash Flows	Beginning Equity	Period Return	Ending Equity	Percent Return Period	Year to Date	Year to Date Formula
1/1–3/31		1,000,000	50,000	1,050,000	5.00%	5.00%	(1+.05)-1
4/1–6/30	1,000,000	2,050,000	80,000	2,130,000	3.90%	9.10%	[(1+0.05)*(1+0.0390)]-1
7/1–12/31	(500,000)	1,630,000	(30,000)	1,600,000	(1.84)%	7.09%	[(1+0.0910)*(1-0.0184)]-1

Example 2: The following is an illustration of a presentation of total return considering an incentive allocation or fee.

	Limited Partner or Common Class
Total return before incentive allocation/fee	7.09%
Incentive allocation/fee	(1.60%)
Total return after incentive allocation/fee	5.49%

Total return is calculated for each common class taken as a whole. An individual investor's return may vary from these returns based on participation in new issues, private investments, different management fee and incentive arrangements (as applicable), and the timing of capital transactions.

Illustration of a Condensed Schedule of Investments

7.229 The following is an illustration of a condensed schedule of investments. Net assets are assumed to be $50,000,000.

Condensed Schedule of Investments [98]
December 31, 20XX

Principal Amount, Shares, or No. of Contracts	Description	Fair Value
	COMMON STOCKS (54.9%)	
	United States (33.7%)	
	Airlines (7.2%)	
53,125	Flight Airlines, Inc.	$1,811,297
	Other (3.6%)	1,819,074
		3,630,371
	Banks (1.9%)	937,099
		(continued)

[98] This schedule does not include the disclosures relative to the investment objective and restrictions on redemption, as discussed in paragraph 7.33*g* of this guide because it is presumed that those disclosures are presented in the notes to the financial statements.

Principal Amount, Shares, or No. of Contracts	Description	Fair Value
	Financial services (2.9%)	1,433,210
	Foods (7.1%)	
106,607	Andrews Midlands Co.	2,825,078
	Other (1.4%)	702,824
		3,527,902
	Hospital supplies and services (5.6%)	
100,404	Chelsea Clinics, Inc.	2,811,297
	Technology (4.1%)	2,039,578
	Utilities (4.9%)	2,480,556
	Total United States (cost: $16,850,954)	16,860,013
	Hong Kong (5.8%)	
	Drugs (0.7%)	330,741
	Retail (4.0%)	1,984,445
	Utility telephone (1.1%)	552,235
	Total Hong Kong (cost: $2,756,959)	2,867,421
	Italy (5.6%)	
	Airlines (0.2%)	110,247
	Financial services (1.8%)	881,975
	Leisure related (3.5%)	1,763,951
	Office supplies (0.1%)	55,123
	Total Italy (cost: $2,912,465)	2,811,296
	Spain (5.4%)	
	Banks (2.4%)	1,212,716
	Oil (1.7%)	826,852
	Railroads (1.3%)	661,482
	Total Spain (cost: $2,643,197)	2,701,050
	United Kingdom (4.4%)	
	Financial services (2.3%)	1,157,593
	Technology (2.1%)	1,047,346
	Total United Kingdom (cost: $2,145,246)	2,204,939
	TOTAL COMMON STOCKS (cost: $27,308,821)	27,444,719
	DEBT SECURITIES (41.3%)	
	United States (21.4%)	
	Airlines (2.0%)	
$1,000,000	Flight Airlines Inc. 12%, 7/15/X5	1,000,000
	Government (19.4%)	
$3,000,000	U.S. Treasury bond, 4.50%, 11/15/X7	3,031,791
	U.S. Treasury bonds, 3.00%–4.75%, 1/30/X5–7/15/X7	6,686,175
		9,717,966
	Total United States (cost: $15,015,200)	10,717,966
	Mexico (19.9%)	
	Government	
$11,000,000	United Mexican States, 8.625%–9.125% 3/12/08–12/7/X9 (cost: $10,000,000)	9,922,224
	TOTAL DEBT SECURITIES (cost: $25,015,200)	20,640,190

Principal Amount, Shares, or No. of Contracts	Description	Fair Value
	LONG PUT AND CALL OPTIONS (2.4%)	
	United States	
	Telecommunications (cost: $1,225,800)	1,212,716
	INTEREST IN INVESTMENT PARTNERSHIP (10.0%)	
	(cost $4,000,000)	5,000,000
	XYZ Hedge Fund LP (35% owned) (XYZ Hedge Fund LP owns 6,000 shares valued $9,000,000 of Leisure Cruises Inc., which is a United States company in the travel industry. The partnership's share of this investment is valued at $3,150,000 as of December 31, 20XX.)	
	TOTAL INVESTMENTS (108.6%) (COST: $57,549,821)	$54,297,625
	SECURITIES SOLD SHORT (9.6%)	
	COMMON STOCKS (5.7%)	
	United States	
	Energy	
100,000	ABC Resources Co. (proceeds: $2,715,000)	$2,825,078
	DEBT SECURITIES (3.7%)	
	Canada (3.7%)	
	Telecommunication (proceeds: $1,950,000)	1,867,000
	WRITTEN OPTIONS (0.2%)	
	United States (0.2%)	
	Manufacturing (proceeds: $130,000)	127,309
	TOTAL SECURITIES SOLD SHORT	
	(proceeds: $4,795,000)	$4,819,387

Description	Fair Value	Expiration Dates	No. of Contracts
FUTURES CONTRACTS (12.5%)			
Financial (5.2%)			
Eurodollar (5.2%)	$2,611,825	Feb–Apr 20YX	122
Indexes (5.6%)			
S&P 500 (5.6%)	2,788,000	Mar–May 20YX	89
Metals (1.7%)	840,000		
TOTAL FUTURES CONTRACTS	$6,239,825		
FORWARDS (11.5%)			
Argentinian Peso (5.8%)	$2,910,000	Oct–Nov 20YX	
Other currencies (5.7%)	2,876,315		
TOTAL FORWARDS	$5,786,315		
SWAPS (13.4%)			
Interest rate swaps (5.7%)	$2,875,000		
Currency swaps (7.7%)			
Yen/U.S. dollar swaps (6.0%)	2,999,016	Jan–Feb 20YX	
Other (1.7%)	868,000		
TOTAL SWAPS	$6,742,016		

The accompanying notes are an integral part of these financial statements.

Illustrations of Nonregistered Investment Partnerships Schedule of Investments

7.230   The following are illustrative examples from Q&A section 6910.18 on how to apply the disclosure guidelines of FASB ASC 946-210-50-6 in the condensed schedule of investments for nonregistered investment partnerships. This guidance is discussed in paragraph 7.37.

Example 1:

- U.S. Treasury Bond (long)—4 percent of net assets
- U.S. Treasury Bond (short)—(1 percent) of net assets
- U.S. Treasury Bond futures contract—Appreciation equals 2 percent of net assets

In the preceding example, the investment company should present separately the long bond and the futures contract in the condensed schedule of investments because, in aggregate, the gross asset position for this issuer exceeds 5 percent of net assets. The short bond position, which represents the only liability position associated with the issuer, is not required to be disclosed separately because the gross liability position is not more than 5 percent of net assets. This assessment for derivatives is made regardless of whether the exposure to the underlying is long or short. Assessments are based solely on the value of the derivative contract (that is, either a long or short position with depreciation or a negative fair value would be considered a liability and aggregated with other liabilities for the purpose of this test). The preparer may consider whether disclosure of all positions, including those 5 percent or less, would be appropriate or meaningful to the reader in the circumstances.

Example 2:

- Various bonds of X Company (long)—4 percent of net assets
- Stock of X Company (short)—(3 percent) of net assets
- Long exposure equity swap (X Company is the underlying)—Fair value equals 2 percent of net assets
- Short exposure equity swap (X Company is the underlying)—Fair value equals (1 percent) of net assets

The guidance in paragraph 6(e)–6(f) of FASB ASC 946-210-50 relates to 5 percent disclosures for any derivative position. That guidance states, "In applying the 5-percent test, total long and total short positions in any one issuer shall be considered separately." This guidance contemplates situations such as the preceding example 2 in which an investment Company holds both a long and short exposure to the same derivative without closing out either derivative position. In such cases, the long and short exposure to the same derivative should be considered separately and should not be netted for the purpose of the 5 percent issuer exposure calculation. This is consistent with the approach for boxed security positions.

In the preceding example 2, the investment Company should present separately the various long bond positions and the long exposure equity swap contract in the condensed schedule of investments because, in aggregate, the gross asset position for this issuer exceeds 5 percent of net assets. Because none of the long bond positions is individually more than 5 percent of net assets, FASB ASC 946-210-50-6(c)(2) permits the reporting of all the long bond positions of that issuer in the aggregate (that is, naming the issuer but showing a range of maturities, interest rates, and other applicable bond disclosures as opposed to individually listing out the details of each of the long bond positions), although the preparer may consider whether disclosure of individual positions provides more meaningful information to the reader of the financial statements. The short stock position and the short exposure equity swap contract are not required to be disclosed separately because the gross liability position is, in aggregate, not more than 5 percent of net assets. Again, the investment Company is not precluded from disclosing separately the short stock position and the short exposure equity swap position if the disclosure of such positions is deemed to provide more meaningful information to the reader. The preparer should consider both the long exposure and short exposure in the equity swaps separately and should not net them for the purpose of the 5 percent exposure calculation if both equity swap contracts have not been closed out.

Example 3:

- Bond of X Company (long)—3 percent of net assets
- Stock of X Company (short)—(1 percent) of net assets
- Swap (X Company is the underlying)—Fair value equals (2 percent) of net assets

In the preceding example 3, the investment Company would not be required to present separately any of the positions in the condensed schedule of investments because the gross asset position of the issuer (represented by the bond) is not more than 5 percent of net assets, and the gross liability position (represented by the combined total values of the short stock position and the swap) is also not more than 5 percent of net assets.

Example 4:

- Bond of X Company (long)—4 percent of net assets
- Stock of X Company (short)—(2 percent) of net assets
- Swap (X Company is the underlying)—Fair value equals 2 percent of net assets
- Swap (X Company is the underlying)—Fair value equals (4 percent) of net assets

In the preceding example 4, the investment Company should present separately each of the positions in the condensed schedule of investments because the gross asset position of the issuer (represented by the combined total values of the bond and the appreciated swap) and the gross liability position of the issuer (represented by the combined total values of the short stock position and the depreciated swap) are both greater than 5 percent of net assets.

Presentation of Fully Benefit-Responsive Investment Contracts

7.231 The following is an illustration from FASB ASC 946-210-55-2 of the presentation of fully benefit-responsive investment contracts in the statement of assets and liabilities and related footnote disclosure, as discussed in paragraphs 7.32 and 7.190.

Presentation for the Statement of Assets and Liabilities

Investments (at fair value)	$8,800,000
Wrapper contracts (at fair value)	100,000
Total assets	8,900,000
Total liabilities	200,000
Net assets reflecting all investments at fair value	$8,700,000
Adjustment from fair value to contract value for fully benefit-responsive investment contracts	1,100,000
Net assets	$9,800,000

Related Footnote Disclosure

	Major Credit Ratings	Investments at Fair Value	Wrapper Contracts at Fair Value	Adjustments to Contract Value
Traditional guaranteed investment contract A	AAA/Aaa	$1,600,000	—	$400,000
Bank ABC stable value fund I	N/A	1,800,000	—	200,000
Wrapped portfolio A:				
Bond #1		850,000	—	—
Bond #2		910,000	—	—
Wrapper			40,000	—
Total wrapped portfolio A	AAA/Aa2	1,760,000	40,000	200,000
Wrapped portfolio B:				
Bond #3		850,000	—	—
Bond fund #1		860,000	—	—
Bond #4		930,000	—	—
Wrapper		—	60,000	—
Total wrapped portfolio B	AA-/Aa3	2,640,000	60,000	300,000
Short term investments	AAA/Aaa	1,000,000	—	—
Total		$8,800,000	$100,000	$1,100,000

Illustration of Deferred Fees

7.232 The following is an illustration of a deferred incentive fee presentation in the financial statements and the related disclosures, as discussed in paragraphs 7.78, 7.129, and 7.184.

Statement of Assets and Liabilities

Assets

Cash and cash equivalents	$206,000
Investments at fair value	166,585,000
Total assets	$166,791,000

Liabilities

Management fee payable	$400,000
Redemptions payable	1,000,000
Accrued expenses	100,000
Deferred incentive fees payable	4,800,000
Total liabilities	6,300,000
Net assets	$160,491,000

Statement of Operations

Investment income

Interest income	$5,576,000
Dividend income	1,766,000
Total investment income	$7,342,000

Expenses

Incentive fee	$2,680,000
Management fee	1,831,000
Change in net appreciation on deferred incentive fees	650,000
Administration fee	60,000
Professional fees and other	75,000
Total expenses	5,296,000
Net investment income	$2,046,000

Realized and unrealized gains (losses) from investment activities

Net realized gain on securities	$2,773,000
Net realized gain on swap and forward contracts	509,000
Net change in unrealized appreciation on securities	1,515,000
Net change in unrealized appreciation on swap and forward contracts	852,000
Net realized and unrealized gain from investment activities	$5,649,000
Net increase in net assets resulting from operations	$7,695,000

Notes to Financial Statements

Note X—Investment Management and Incentive Fees

Pursuant to an investment advisory agreement, the Fund pays to the adviser a quarterly management fee of of 1 percent (1 percent per annum) of the net assets of the Fund on the last day of each quarter. The adviser also is entitled to an annual incentive fee equal to 20 percent of the net profits attributable to each series of common shares, subject to a loss carryforward. If there is a net loss for the year, the incentive fee will not apply to future years until such net loss has been recovered, adjusted for redemptions.

The adviser may elect to defer receipt of all or a portion of the management or incentive fees earned for a particular fiscal year, and such amounts will be indexed to the Fund's return. In the event of liquidation of the Fund, any deferred amount, as adjusted for the appreciation or depreciation resulting from indexing, the deferred fee to the Fund's return has a priority claim over the interests of the equity holders of the Fund.

For the [*year/period*] ended December 31, 20XX, payment of 50 percent of the incentive fee incurred by the Fund was deferred for X years. Cumulative deferred incentive fees as of December 31, 20XX totaled $3,850,000, and cumulative net appreciation on such amounts totaled $950,000. The net change in appreciation or depreciation of deferred incentive fees is recorded on a separate line item under "Expenses" within the statement of operations. Distributions of 20XX and prior year deferred incentive fees are scheduled for the period from [*date range*]. During the year ended December 31, 20XX, the distribution of previously deferred incentive fees amounted to $500,000.

The following is an example disclosure of a rollforward of deferred incentive fees payable, which is a best practice disclosure.

The deferred incentive fees payable balance as of December 31, 20XX, comprises the following:

Deferred incentive fees payable at January 1, 20XX	$3,310,000
Appreciation on deferred incentive fees for the year ended December 31, 20XX	650,000
Incentive fees deferred for the year ended December 31, 20XX	1,340,000
Deferred incentive fees paid for the year ended December 31, 20XX	(500,000)
Deferred incentive fees payable at December 31, 20XX	$4,800,000

Note X—Financial Highlights

The following represents the per share information, ratios to average net assets, and other supplemental information for the year ended December 31, 20XX:

	Class A Initial Series	Class B Initial Series
Per share operating performance:		
Beginning net asset value	$1,130.35	$1,123.80
Income from investment operations:		
Net investment income	11.01	6.76
Net realized and unrealized gain from investment activities	141.50	145.64
Total income from operations	152.51	152.40
Ending net asset value	$1,282.86	$1,276.20
Ratios to average net assets:		
Expenses other than incentive fee	1.43%	1.46%
Incentive fee	1.46	1.49
Total expenses	2.89	2.95
Change in net appreciation on deferred incentive fees	(0.40)	(0.43)
Total expense excluding change in net appreciation on deferred incentive fees	2.49%	2.52%
Net investment income	1.12%	1.09%
Total return prior to incentive fee	17.07%	16.93%
Incentive fee	(3.58)	(3.37)
Total return after incentive fee	13.49%	13.56%

The per share operating performance and total return are calculated for the initial series of each share class. The ratios to average net assets are calculated for each class taken as a whole. An individual investor's per share operating performance, total return, and ratios to average net assets may vary from these per share amounts and ratios based on participation in new issues and different management fee and incentive fee arrangements and the timing and amount of capital transactions.

Disclosure—Fair Value Measurements of Investments in Certain Entities That Calculate Net Asset Value per Share (or its Equivalent)

7.233 As described in FASB ASC 820-10-50-6A and paragraph 7.94, for investments that are within the scope of paragraphs 4–5 of FASB ASC 820-10-15 measured at fair value on a recurring or nonrecurring basis during the period (regardless of whether the practical expedient has been applied), disclosure of information that enables users of its financial statements to understand the nature and risks of the investments and whether the investments are probable of being sold at amounts different from net asset value per share (or its equivalent, such as member units or an ownership interest in partners' capital to which a proportionate share of net assets is attributed) are required. FASB ASC 820-10-55-107 provides the following example of how that information may be presented (note that the classes presented are examples only and not intended to be treated as a template; the classes should be tailored to the nature and risks of the reporting entity's investments).

	Fair Value (in millions)	Unfunded Commitments	Redemption Frequency (If Currently Eligible)	Redemption Notice Period
Equity long/short hedge funds[a]	$55	—	quarterly	30–60 days
Event driven hedge funds[b]	45	—	quarterly, annually	30–60 days
Global opportunities hedge funds[c]	35	—	quarterly	30–45 days
Multistrategy hedge funds[d]	40	—	quarterly	30–60 days
Real estate funds[e]	47	$20		
Private equity funds—international[f]	43	15		
Total	$265	$35		

[a] This class includes investments in hedge funds that invest both long and short primarily in U.S. common stocks. Management of the hedge funds has the ability to shift investments from value to growth strategies, from small to large capitalization stocks, and from a net long position to a net short position. The fair values of the investments in this class have been estimated using the net asset value per share of the investments. Investments representing approximately 22 percent of the value of the investments in this class cannot be redeemed because the investments include restrictions that do not allow for redemption in the first 12–18 months after acquisition. The remaining restriction period for these investments ranged from 3 to 7 months at December 31, 20X3.

(*continued*)

^(b) This class includes investments in hedge funds that invest in approximately 60 percent equities and 40 percent bonds to profit from economic, political, and government driven events. A majority of the investments are targeted at economic policy decisions. The fair values of the investments in this class have been estimated using the net asset value per share of the investments.

^(c) This class includes investments in hedge funds that hold approximately 80 percent of the funds' investments in non-U.S. common stocks in the health care, energy, information technology, utilities, and telecommunications sectors and approximately 20 percent of the Funds' investments in diversified currencies. The fair values of the investments in this class have been estimated using the net asset value per share of the investments. For one investment, valued at $8.75 million, a gate has been imposed by the hedge fund manager and no redemptions are currently permitted. This redemption restriction has been in place for 6 months and the time at which the redemption restriction might lapse cannot be estimated.

^(d) This class invests in hedge funds that pursue multiple strategies to diversify risks and reduce volatility. The hedge funds' composite portfolio for this class includes investments in approximately 50 percent U.S. common stocks, 30 percent global real estate projects, and 20 percent arbitrage investments. The fair values of the investments in this class have been estimated using the net asset value per share of the investments. Investments representing approximately 15 percent of the value of the investments in this class cannot be redeemed because the investments include restrictions that do not allow for redemption in the first year after acquisition. The remaining restriction period for these investments ranged from 4 to 6 months at December 31, 20X3.

^(e) This class includes several real estate funds that invest primarily in U.S. commercial real estate. The fair values of the investments in this class have been estimated using the net asset value of the Company's ownership interest in the partners' capital. These investments can never be redeemed with the Funds. Distributions from each Fund will be received as the underlying investments of the Funds are liquidated. It is estimated that the underlying assets of the Fund will be liquidated over the next 7–10 years. Twenty percent of the total investments in this class is planned to be sold. However, the individual investments that will be sold have not yet been determined. Because it is not probable that an individual investment will be sold, the fair value of each individual investment has been estimated using the net asset value of the Company's ownership interest in partners' capital. Once it has been determined which investments will be sold and whether those investments will be sold individually or in a group, the investments will be sold in an auction process. The investee fund's management must approve of the buyer before the sale of the investments can be completed.

^(f) This class includes several private equity funds that invest primarily in foreign technology companies. These investments can never be redeemed with the Funds. Instead, the nature of the investments in this class is that distributions are received through the liquidation of the underlying assets of the Fund. If these investments were held, it is estimated that the underlying assets of the Fund would be liquidated over 5 to 8 years. However, as of December 31, 20X3, it is probable that all of the investments in this class will be sold at an amount different from the net asset value of the Company's ownership interest in partners' capital. Therefore, the fair values of the investments in this class have been estimated using recent observable transaction information for similar investments and nonbinding bids received from potential buyers of the investments. As of December 31, 20X3, a buyer (or buyers) for these investments has not yet been identified. Once a buyer has been identified, the investee fund's management must approve of the buyer before the sale of the investments can be completed.

Illustration of Reporting Financial Highlights, Net Asset Value Per Share, Shares Outstanding, and Share Transactions When Investors in Unitized Nonregistered Funds Are Issued Individual Classes or Series of Shares

7.234 The following is an illustration of the presentation in the financial statements and the related disclosures when investors in unitized nonregistered Funds are issued individual classes or series of shares, as discussed in paragraphs 7.150 and 7.186–.187:

> A Fund issues class A and class B nonvoting shares to investors, and within each class, a separate series of shares is issued to each individual investor. Class A shares have a 1 percent management fee and a 20 percent incentive fee; class B shares are issued to related-party investors and, therefore, are not charged a management fee or an incentive fee. Class C voting shares are management shares and do not participate in the profits or losses of the Fund. As of December 31, 20X7, there are 15,100 total shares outstanding totaling $1,517,600. The following shows such amounts outstanding as of December 31, 20X7, by class and series and the net asset values:
>
>> Class A Series 1—5,000 shares outstanding, NAV $500,000
>>
>> Class A Series 2—7,500 shares outstanding, NAV $765,000
>>
>> Class B Series 1—2,500 shares outstanding, NAV $252,500
>>
>> Class C—100 shares outstanding, NAV $100
>
> In the prior year, as of December 31, 20X6, there were 10,100 total shares outstanding, totaling $970,100. The following shows such amounts outstanding as of December 31, 20X6, by class and series and the NAVs:
>
>> Class A Series 1—6,000 shares outstanding, NAV $588,000
>>
>> Class B Series 1—3,000 shares outstanding, NAV $288,000
>>
>> Class B Series 2—1,000 shares outstanding, NAV $94,000
>>
>> Class C—100 shares outstanding, NAV $100

Investment Companies

Example Statement of Assets and Liabilities
Statement of Assets and Liabilities
December 31, 20X7

Assets

Cash and cash equivalents	$100,100
Investments at fair value	1,550,000
Total assets	$1,650,100

Liabilities

Redemptions payable	94,000
Management fees payable	4,000
Incentive fee payable	3,000
Accrued expenses	31,500
Total liabilities	132,500
Net assets (based on 12,500 class A shares; 2,500 class B shares; and 100 class C shares outstanding)	$1,517,600

Example Note Disclosures
Capital Share Transactions

As of December 31, 20X7, 5,000,000 shares of capital stock were authorized. Class A and class B shares have $0.01 par value, and class C shares have $1.00 par value. Transactions in capital stock were as follows:

Class A	Shares		Amount	
	20X7	20X6	20X7	20X6
Shares sold	7,500	6,000	$750,000	$600,000
Shares redeemed	(1,000)	—	$(99,500)	—
Net increase	6,500	6,000	$650,500	$600,000

Class B	Shares		Amount	
	20X7	20X6	20X7	20X6
Shares sold	—	4,000	—	$400,000
Shares redeemed	(1,500)	—	($148,750)	—
Net increase	(1,500)	4,000	($148,750)	$400,000

Class C	Shares		Amount	
	20X7	20X6	20X7	20X6
Shares sold	—	100	—	$100
Shares redeemed				
Net increase	—	100	—	$100

Financial Highlights

The ratios to average net assets and total return are presented in the following table for each class taken as a whole, excluding managing shareholder interests, for the year ended December 31, 20X7. The ratios and total return are not annualized. The computation of similar financial information for other participating shareholders may vary based on the timing of their respective capital transactions.

Annual ratios to average net assets and total return for the year ended December 31, 20X7, are as follows:

	Class A	Class B
Ratios to average net assets:		
Expenses other than incentive fee	2.26%	1.26%
Incentive fee	0.31%	0.00%
Total expenses	2.57%	1.26%
Net investment income	0.93%	1.93%
Total return prior to incentive fee	3.48%	5.02 %
Incentive fee	(0.40)%	(0.00)%
Total return after incentive fee	3.08%	5.02%

Illustrative Statement of Changes in Net Assets (Changes in Partners' Capital) of a Nonregistered Investment Partnership That Includes a General Partner and One or More Limited Partners

7.235 The following illustration is a statement of changes in net assets (partners' capital) for a nonregistered investment partnership (for example, a hedge fund) that includes a general partner and one or more limited partners. Pursuant to FASB ASC 946-205-45-5, a reporting entity may choose to combine the statement of changes of net assets and the statement of changes in partners' capital. The reporting entity may title the combined statement as the "Statement of Changes in Net Assets" or the "Statement of Changes in Partners' Capital." See paragraphs 7.147–.152 of this guide for further discussion of the statement of changes in net assets.

XYZ Investment Company
Statement of Changes in Net Assets [Partners' Capital]
Year Ended December 31, 20X8

	General Partner	Limited Partners	Total
Increase (decrease) in net assets [partners' capital] from operations			
Investment income—net	$7,750	$767,250	$775,000
Net realized gain from investments and foreign currency[99]	10,520	1,041,480	1,052,000
Unrealized appreciation (depreciation) on investments and translation of assets and liabilities in foreign currencies[100]	(12,940)	(1,281,060)	(1,294,000)
Net increase in net assets resulting from operations	5,330	527,670	533,000
Incentive allocation to general partner	2,665	(2,665)	—
Capital contributions	27,300	2,702,700	2,730,000
Capital distributions	(18,750)	(1,856,250)	(1,875,000)
Total increase	16,545	1,371,455	1,388,000
Net assets [partners' capital]			
Beginning of year	177,920	17,614,080	17,792,000
End of year	$194,465	$18,985,535	$19,180,000

The accompanying notes are an integral part of these financial statements.

The following illustration is an alternative presentation for the statement of changes in net assets (partners' capital). This alternative may be utilized when the reporting entity also presents a separate statement of financial condition, or when the alternative presentation is considered more meaningful to users of the financial statements.

XYZ Investment Company
Statement of Changes in Net Assets [Partners' Capital]
Year Ended December 31, 20X8

	General Partner	Limited Partners	Total
Net assets [partners' capital]—beginning of year	$177,920	$17,614,080	$17,792,000
Net increase in net assets resulting from operations	5,330	527,670	533,000
Capital contributions	27,300	2,702,700	2,730,000
Capital distributions	(18,750)	(1,856,250)	(1,875,000)
Incentive allocation to general partner	2,665	(2,665)	—
Net assets [partners' capital]—end of year	$194,465	$18,985,535	$19,180,000

The accompanying notes are an integral part of these financial statements.

---

[99] It is also acceptable to present each of these items as a separate line item: net realized gains from investments and net realized gains (losses) from foreign currency transactions.

[100] It is also acceptable to present each of these items as a separate line item: unrealized appreciation on investments and unrealized appreciation on the translation of assets and liabilities in foreign currencies.

Illustrative Disclosure for a Registered Fund Issuing Consolidated Financial Statements and Relying on CFTC Letter No. 13-51

7.236 The following illustration presents a disclosure for a registered fund issuing consolidated financial statements and relying on the CFTC's no action relief (CFTC Letter No. 13-51) that permits CPOs of registered funds to consolidate their CFCs for financial reporting purposes.

Basis of Consolidation. The Company's Consolidated Schedule of Investments includes the holdings, including any investments in derivatives, of both the Company and the Subsidiary. The Subsidiary, which is wholly owned by the Company, enables the Company to hold these commodity-related instruments and satisfy regulated investment Company tax requirements. The Company may invest up to 25 percent of its total assets in the Subsidiary. Holdings specific to the Subsidiary are footnoted on the Consolidated Schedule of Investments. The Company's Consolidated Statement of Assets and Liabilities, Consolidated Statement of Operations and Consolidated Statement of Changes in Net Assets include the account balances of both the Company and the Subsidiary. All interfund transactions have been eliminated. The net assets of the Subsidiary were $xx,xxx, which represented x.x percent of the Company's consolidated net assets. The results from operations of the Subsidiary were as follows:

Net investment income (loss)	xx,xxx
Net realized gain (loss)	xx,xxx
Net increase (decrease) in unrealized appreciation (depreciation)	xx,xxx
Net increase (decrease) in net assets resulting from operations	$xx,xxx

Chapter 8

Other Accounts and Considerations

Presentation of Pending Content in FASB ASC

Amendments to FASB *Accounting Standards Codification* (ASC) (issued in the form of Accounting Standards Updates [ASUs]) are initially incorporated into FASB ASC in "Pending Content" boxes located below the paragraphs being amended with links to the transition information. The pending content boxes are meant to provide users with information about how the guidance in a paragraph will change as a result of the new guidance.

Pending content applies to different entities at different times due to varying fiscal year-ends, and because certain guidance may be effective on different dates for public entities, as defined, and other entities. As such, FASB maintains amended guidance in pending content boxes within FASB ASC until the roll-off date. Generally, the roll-off date is six months following the latest fiscal year-end for which the original guidance being amended could still be applied.

Presentation of Pending Content in AICPA Audit and Accounting Guides

Amended FASB ASC guidance that is included in pending content boxes in FASB ASC on May 1, 2015, is referenced as "Pending Content" in this guide. Pending content referenced or discussed within this guide's chapter text is fully effective as of the date of this guide and should be considered by readers for current reporting periods. Pending content referenced or discussed within this guide's shaded "Guidance Updates" boxes or within appendix A, "Guidance Updates," is not fully effective as of the date of this guide. Readers should be aware that pending content" referenced in this guide will eventually be subjected to FASB's roll-off process and will no longer be labeled as "Pending Content" in FASB ASC (as discussed in the previous paragraph).

Investment Advisory (Management) Fee Expense

8.01   As discussed in chapter 1, "Overview of the Investment Company Industry," of this guide, an investment company usually engages an investment adviser for a fee, which is generally the largest expense incurred by the investment company. This fee is usually reflected in the periodic net asset value calculation (daily, weekly, monthly, quarterly or less frequently) at rates established by the investment advisory agreement. Certain agreements may provide for performance fee adjustments based on a comparison of the investment company's performance against an index specified in the agreement.

8.02   As stated in FASB ASC 946-20-25-10, performance fees by an investment adviser under an advisory agreement should be accrued by an investment company at interim dates based on actual performance through the accrual date. As discussed in paragraph 7.125 of this guide, Technical Questions and Answers (Q&A) section 6910.29, "Allocation of Unrealized Gain (Loss), Recognition of Carried Interest, and Clawback Obligations" (AICPA, *Technical Questions and Answers*), addresses situations in which governing documents contain provisions that do not require the payment of performance fees until a specified date or time.

8.03 However, according to the SEC's policy, interim payments to the adviser should be based on the minimum fee provided in the agreement because if performance for the year yields a fee that is lower than the interim payments, the excess may represent a loan to the adviser. Performance fees based on a rolling or moving period are discussed in Release No. 7113 of the Investment Company Act of 1940 (the 1940 Act). Investment companies should ensure that their accounting policies are in accordance with the 1940 Act, and that existing policies do not contradict what is acceptable under the 1940 Act.

Expenses

8.04 The investment company's expenses should be inspected for compliance with the provisions of the investment advisory contract, the prospectus, and other relevant agreements. The investment company estimates its other expenses for the year and the period within which it will incur them and allocates them, usually daily, in computing net asset value. Estimated annual expenses should be evaluated continually and accruals adjusted as necessary.

8.05 Asset-based fees are typically recalculated by the auditor for reasonableness, and other expense items are reviewed by analytical procedures.

8.06 Some investment company prospectuses, offering memorandums, or agreements between the adviser or other servicer (such as an administrator) and the fund may require the servicer to waive its fee and reimburse or assume certain expenses that exceed stated limitations. If so, the auditor should test the calculations for compliance with the governing document.

8.07 Expense limitation arrangements help new funds with lower asset levels maintain lower expense ratios, which results in a benefit to the shareholder. Typically, one condition attached to these arrangements is that the investment company agrees to repay the service provider (without interest) if, and to the extent that, the investment company's net assets increase sufficiently to permit such payments without exceeding the stated percentage expense limitation. Also, typically, these agreements (*a*) are terminable on short notice by either party without a penalty, (*b*) have a fixed expiration date, and (*c*) give the service provider no claim against the investment company for any amounts not reimbursed upon termination or expiration. The economic result of these agreements is to defer payment of the expenses until the investment company is financially able to bear them or, upon termination or expiration, to eliminate them entirely.

8.08 As explained in FASB ASC 946-20-05-8, some expense limitation agreements may provide that reimbursements by the fund adviser of expenses incurred by the fund in excess of the maximum permitted by the prospectus or offering document will be carried over to a future period and reimbursed to the fund adviser when, and to the extent that, the total expense ratio falls below the permitted maximum. Such agreements may also provide that reimbursement of excess expenses to the fund adviser is not required after a specified date or upon conclusion of a specified period from the time the fund initially incurred, or the adviser initially reimbursed, the expenses, such as three years.

8.09 According to FASB ASC 946-20-25-4, a liability for such excess expenses should be recognized if, and to the extent that, the expense limitation agreement's established terms for repayment of the excess expenses to the adviser by the fund and the attendant circumstances meet criteria (*a*), (*b*), and (*c*) of paragraph 36 of FASB Concepts Statement No. 6, *Elements of Financial Statements—a replacement of FASB Concepts Statement No. 3 (incorporating an amendment of FASB Concepts Statement No. 2)*, and the criteria in FASB ASC 450-20-25-2.[1] In most instances, a liability will not be recorded because it is not likely that excess expenses under such plans will meet the criteria in those paragraphs before amounts are actually due to the adviser under the reimbursement agreement. If an assessment of the specific circumstances (such as an agreement to reimburse for either an unlimited period or a period substantially greater than that necessary for the fund to demonstrate its economic viability, or an obligation to reimburse the servicer remains even after the cancellation of the fund's contract with the servicer) indicates that the preceding criteria are met, a liability should be recorded. FASB ASC 946-20-50-6 states that the existence of reimbursement agreements and the carryover of excess expenses potentially reimbursable to the adviser but not recorded as a liability should be disclosed in the notes to the financial statements.

8.10 FASB ASC 946-20-05-8 also explains that, under most excess expense plans, a fund is obligated to repay a servicer for expenses incurred previously only if, during a defined period, the fund retains the service provider and can reduce its expense ratio to a low enough level to permit payment, and the fund maintains that ratio at a sufficiently low level thereafter. Many substantive conditions could cause the fund to have no obligation to the servicer, including failure to attract assets, significant redemptions of shares by investors, market depreciation, and significant increases in other expenses, all of which could drive expenses up to or beyond the maximum under which payment would otherwise be made.

8.11 The AICPA Financial Reporting Executive Committee (FinREC) observed that even actual reimbursement of some expenses does not establish the appropriateness of accrual of additional unreimbursed amounts because these conditions must continually be met for the fund to be further obligated to the servicer.

8.12 Some advisers to nonregistered investment companies, especially those advising funds with significant private investments, will earn transaction related fees and income from investments owned by the funds they advise. In certain cases, the management fee charged to such funds will be reduced by the transaction fees and income earned by the adviser.

---

[1] Paragraph 36 of FASB Concepts Statement No. 6, *Elements of Financial Statements—a replacement of FASB Concepts Statement No. 3 (incorporating an amendment of FASB Concepts Statement No. 2)*, includes the following criteria:

    a. A present duty or responsibility to one or more other entities that entails settlement by a probable future transfer or use of assets

    b. A duty or responsibility obligat[ing] ... [the] entity, leaving it little or no discretion to avoid the future sacrifice

    c. The transaction or other event obligating the entity has already happened

FASB *Accounting Standards Codification* (ASC) 450-20-25-2 includes the following criteria:

    a. Information available before the financial statements are issued or are available to be issued (as discussed in FASB ASC 855-10-25) indicates that it is probable that an asset had been impaired or a liability had been incurred at the date of the financial statements

    b. The amount of the loss can be reasonably estimated

8.13 Auditors should examine these arrangements to ascertain that management fee reductions are calculated correctly and that the nature of transaction fees earned by the adviser are considered for presentation and disclosure in accordance with guidance covering related party transactions. See also the "Expenses" section in chapter 7, "Financial Statements of Investment Companies," of this guide.

Distribution Expenses

8.14 As discussed in FASB ASC 946-20-05-4, open-end investment companies are permitted to finance the distribution of their shares under a plan pursuant to Rule 12b-1 (Rule 12b-1 is one of the regulations implementing the 1940 Act). Under Rule 12b-1, a fund's board of directors or trustees is required to perform an annual review of the plan and determine whether to continue or terminate it. Under a traditional 12b-1 plan, a fund's distributor may be compensated or reimbursed for its distribution costs or efforts through any of the following methods:

- A 12b-1 fee, payable by the fund, based on an annual percentage of the fund's average net assets (a *compensation plan*) or based on an annual percentage of the fund's average net assets limited to actual costs incurred, after deducting contingent deferred sales loads (CDSLs) received by the distributor (a *reimbursement plan*). Therefore, a compensation plan differs from a reimbursement plan only in that the latter provides for annual or cumulative limits, or both, on fees paid. Fees for both kinds of plans are treated as expenses in a fund's statement of operations.

- A front-end load, which is assessed on purchasing shareholders at the time fund shares are sold. Such amounts are not considered an expense of the fund.

- A CDSL imposed directly on redeeming shareholders. The CDSL usually is expressed as a percentage, which declines with the passage of time, of the lesser of redemption proceeds or original cost. The CDSL normally ranges from 4 percent to 6 percent and typically is reduced by 1 percent per year (for example, from 6 percent to 5 percent) until the sales charge reaches 0 percent.

8.15 Financial Industry Regulatory Authority (FINRA) rules construe 12b-1 fees to be either *asset based sales charges* or *service fees*. These rules (section 2830 of the National Association of Securities Dealers Rules of Fair Practice, incorporated into the FINRA manual) limit the amount of asset-based sales charges that may be charged in any year to specified percentages of average net assets and provide aggregate limitations on the total amounts of sales charges received through front-end sales loads, deferred sales charges, and asset-based sales charges.

8.16 As noted in FASB ASC 946-20-05-5, Rule 12b-1 plans historically have provided that a fund's board of directors or trustees may terminate the plan with no penalty to the fund. (Termination of the plan does not necessitate termination of the fund.) Redeeming shareholders still would be subject to the CDSL, which would be paid to the distributor that sold the shares to those shareholders. However, with a traditional 12b-1 plan, the 12b-1 fees normally would be discontinued on plan termination. Some traditional reimbursement 12b-1 plans provide that, when the plan is terminated, the fund's board of directors or trustees has the option, but not the requirement, to pay the distributor for any costs incurred in excess of the cumulative CDSLs and 12b-1 fees that the distributor has received. Such a plan is referred to as a board-contingent plan. Under traditional reimbursement 12b-1 plans, including board-contingent plans, CDSL payments by shareholders continue to be remitted to the distributor until excess costs are fully recovered, after which the CDSL payments usually are remitted to the fund instead of the distributor. As stated in FASB ASC 946-20-50-4, if a 12b-1 distribution reimbursement plan provides for the carryover of unreimbursed costs to subsequent periods, the terms of reimbursement and the unreimbursed amount should be disclosed.

8.17 Reimbursement to the investment company of expenses incurred under such plan (12b-1 expense reimbursement) should be shown as a negative amount and deducted from current 12b-1 expenses. Distribution expenses paid with an investment company's assets are accounted for as operating expenses. Under 12b-1 plans, including board-contingent plans, CDSL payments by shareholders are remitted to the distributor until aggregate regulatory limitations on sales charges to be received are met. As explained in FASB ASC 946-20-05-6, with an enhanced 12b-1 plan, the fund is required to continue paying the 12b-1 fee after termination of the plan to the extent that the distributor has excess costs. CDSL payments by shareholders would continue to be remitted to the distributor to further offset excess costs. Thus, the major distinction between traditional and enhanced 12b-1 plans is the requirement for the fund to continue such payments upon plan termination.

8.18 The following table from FASB ASC 946-20-05-7 summarizes the 12b-1 plan attributes enumerated previously.

| | Traditional | | | Enhanced |
| | Compensation | Reimbursement | | |
		Nonboard-contingent	Board-contingent	
Annual review and approval of plan by board, with ability to terminate plan	X	X	X	X
Fund Payment Terms [2]				
Payment based on average net assets	X	X	X	X
Annual or cumulative limitation, or both, based on actual distribution costs		X	X	X
Upon termination of 12b-1 plan, board has option, but not obligation, to pay excess costs			X	
Upon termination of 12b-1 plan, fund is required to continue paying 12b-1 fee to the extent the distributor has excess costs				X

8.19 FASB ASC 946-20-25-3 states that a liability, with a corresponding charge to expense, should be recognized by a fund with an enhanced 12b-1 plan

---

[2] Excludes front-end and contingent deferred sales load payments, which are made by shareholders, not the fund.

for excess costs. FASB ASC 946-20-30-3 explains that the initial amount of the liability and expense should equal the cumulative distribution costs incurred by the distributor less the sum of cumulative 12b-1 fees paid; cumulative CDSL payments; and future cumulative CDSL payments by current shareholders, if reasonably estimable. Paragraphs 3–4 of FASB ASC 946-20-35 note that any future cumulative CDSL payments should be based on (a) current net asset value per share, (b) the number of shares currently outstanding and the number of years that they have been outstanding, and (c) estimated shareholder persistency based on historical fund data or, if historical fund data are not available, group or industry data for a similar class of shares. Changes in the liability should be recognized in the statement of operations as an expense or a reduction of expense.

8.20   Paragraphs 4–5 of FASB ASC 946-20-30 note that the liability and expense should be measured at its present value, calculated using an appropriate current interest rate, if both (a) the amount and timing of cash flows are reliably determinable and (b) the distribution costs are not subject to a reasonable interest charge. If these conditions are not met, the liability should be calculated without discounting to present value.

8.21   FASB ASC 946-20-25-3 states that a liability for excess costs, computed in the same way as for an enhanced 12b-1 plan, should be recorded by a fund with a board-contingent plan when the fund's board commits to pay such costs.

8.22   As explained in FASB ASC 946-20-50-3, for both board-contingent plans and enhanced 12b-1 plans, funds should disclose in their interim and annual financial statements the principal terms of such plans and any plan provisions permitting or requiring payments of excess costs after plan termination. For board-contingent and enhanced 12b-1 plans, the aggregate amount of distribution costs subject to recovery through future payments by the fund pursuant to the plan and through future CDSL payments by current shareholders should be disclosed. For enhanced 12b-1 plans, funds should disclose the methodology used to estimate future CDSL payments by current shareholders.

8.23   As stated in FASB ASC 946-20-45-2, an excess of cumulative 12b-1 fees and CDSL payments to date and future CDSL payments by current shareholders over the cumulative costs incurred by the distributor should not be reported as an asset.

Organization and Offering Costs

© **Update 8-1** *Accounting and Reporting*: **Development Stage Entities**

FASB ASU No. 2014-10, *Development Stage Entities (Topic 915): Elimination of Certain Financial Reporting Requirements, Including an Amendment to Variable Interest Entities Guidance in Topic 810*, Consolidation, was issued in June 2014. The amendments related to the elimination of inception-to-date information and the other remaining disclosure requirements of FASB ASC 915, *Development Stage Entities*, should be applied retrospectively except for the clarification to FASB ASC 275, *Risks and Uncertainties*, which shall be applied prospectively. For public business entities, those amendments are effective for annual reporting periods beginning after December 15, 2014, and interim periods therein. For other entities, the amendments are effective for annual reporting periods beginning after December 15, 2014, and interim reporting periods beginning after December 15, 2015.

For public business entities, the amendment eliminating the exception to the sufficiency-of-equity-at-risk criterion for development stage entities in FASB ASC 810-10-15-16 should be applied retrospectively for annual reporting periods beginning after December 15, 2015, and interim periods therein. For all other entities, the amendments to FASB ASC 810, *Consolidation*, should be applied retrospectively for annual reporting periods beginning after December 15, 2016, and interim reporting periods beginning after December 15, 2017.

Early application of each of the amendments is permitted for any annual reporting period or interim period for which the entity's financial statements have not yet been issued (public business entities) or made available for issuance (other entities). Upon adoption, entities will no longer present or disclose any information required by FASB ASC 915.

ASU No. 2014-10 removes all incremental financial reporting requirements from U.S. generally accepted accounting principles (GAAP) for development stage entities, thereby improving financial reporting by eliminating the cost and complexity associated with providing that information. It also eliminates an exception provided to development stage entities in FASB ASC 810 for determining whether an entity is a variable interest entity on the basis of the amount of investment equity that is at risk. The elimination of the exception may change the consolidation analysis, consolidation decision, and disclosure requirements for a reporting entity that has an interest in an entity in the development stage.

Readers are encouraged to consult the full text of this ASU on FASB's website at www.fasb.org.

Refer to section A.01 in appendix A for more information on this ASU if it is applicable to your reporting period.

8.24 The provisions of FASB ASC 915 apply to financial statements issued by investment companies in the development stage, as defined by the FASB ASC glossary. A *development stage entity* is an entity devoting substantially all its efforts to establishing a new business and for which either of the following conditions exists: (*a*) planned principal operations have not commenced, or (*b*) planned principal operations have commenced, but there has been no significant revenue therefrom.

8.25 A newly formed investment company incurs organization costs unless a sponsoring management company agrees to absorb such costs (see paragraph 8.05). Organization costs consist of costs incurred to establish the company and enable it legally to do business. A newly established series of a previously established investment company may also incur organization costs. In a master-feeder arrangement, these costs may be incurred at the master level, feeder level, or both. Organization costs for an investment company include, among other things, the following:

- Incorporation fees
- Legal services pertaining to the organization and incorporation of the business; drafting of bylaws, administration, custody and transfer agent agreements; and performing research and

consultation services in connection with the initial meeting of directors or trustees

- Audit fees relating to the initial registration statement and auditing the initial seed capital statement of assets and liabilities

8.26   In accordance with FASB ASC 720-15-25-1, organization costs should be charged to expense as they are incurred.

8.27   The following chart summarizes those costs that are, or are not, generally treated as organization and offering costs and the accounting required under FASB ASC 720-15 or other U.S. GAAP.

Cost	Accounting Treatment
Incorporation fees	Expense
Audit fees related to initial registration and seed capital audit	Expense
Legal fees related to	
• organization and incorporation of the business	Expense
• drafting bylaws	Expense
• drafting administration, custody, and transfer agent agreements	Expense
• performing research and consultation services in connection with the initial meeting of directors or trustees	Expense
• preparing the initial registration statement	Offering cost—see paragraph 8.29
Licensing fees	Amortize over term of license
Typesetting and printing prospectus	Offering cost—see paragraph 8.29
Registration fees	Offering cost—see paragraph 8.29
Tax opinion costs related to offering of shares	Offering cost—see paragraph 8.29

8.28   Once an investment company has been organized to do business, it usually engages immediately in its planned principal operations (that is, the sale of capital stock and investment of funds). Employee training, development of markets for the sale of capital stock, and similar activities are usually performed by the investment adviser or other agent, and the costs of these activities are not borne directly by the investment company. However, an investment company, particularly one not engaging an agent to manage its portfolio and perform other essential functions, may engage in such activities and bear those costs directly during its development stage.

8.29   *Offering costs*, as defined by the FASB ASC glossary, include the following:

- Legal fees pertaining to the investment company's shares offered for sale

- SEC and state registration fees

- Underwriting and other similar costs

- Costs of printing prospectuses for sales purposes

- Initial fees paid to be listed on an exchange

- Tax opinion costs related to offering of shares

- Initial agency fees of securing the rating for bonds or preferred stock issued by closed-end funds

8.30   As discussed in paragraphs 5–6 of FASB ASC 946-20-25 and 946-20-35-5, offering costs of closed-end funds and investment partnerships should be charged to paid-in capital upon sale of the shares or units. Offering costs of open-end investment companies and closed-end funds with a continuous offering period should be accounted for as a deferred charge until operations begin and thereafter be amortized to expense over 12 months on a straight-line basis.

8.31   Other kinds of offering costs, such as front-end sales charges and deferred sales charges, are deducted from the proceeds received from shareholders or redemption proceeds paid to shareholders; are not paid by the fund; and are, therefore, outside the scope of offering costs, as defined herein.

8.32   Some closed-end funds and business development companies offer stock through shelf registration statements. According to Q&A section 4110.10, "Costs Incurred in Shelf Registration" (AICPA, *Technical Questions and Answers*), legal and other fees incurred for a stock issue under a shelf registration should be capitalized as a prepaid expense. When securities are taken off the shelf and sold, a portion of the costs attributable to the securities sold should be charged against paid-in-capital. Any subsequent costs incurred to keep the filing "alive" should be charged to expense as incurred. If the filing is withdrawn, the related capitalized costs should be charged to expense.

8.33   According to Q&A section 6910.23, "Accounting Treatment of Offering Costs Incurred by Investment Partnerships" (AICPA, *Technical Questions and Answers*), an investment partnership that continually offers its interests should defer offering costs incurred prior to the commencement of operations and then amortize them to expense over the period that it continually offers its interests, up to a maximum of 12 months. The straight-line method of amortization should generally be used. If the offering period terminates earlier than expected, the remaining deferred balance should be charged to expense. Q&A section 6910.24, "Meaning of 'Continually Offer Interests'" (AICPA, *Technical Questions and Answers*), provides a definition of *continually offer interests*, which explains that an investment partnership is deemed to continually offer its interests if an eligible, new investor may enter into an agreement to purchase an interest in the partnership on any business day or on a series of specified business days over a continuous period of time. For this purpose, a new investor is one that does not already own any interest in the investment partnership at the time of purchase. Some investment partnerships may offer their interests at a single point in time and require new investors to commit to providing capital contributions over a period of time. In this scenario, because the interests are not available for purchase over a continuous period, such investment partnerships would not be deemed to have a continuous offering period.

8.34 This treatment of offering costs by closed-end funds and investment partnerships results in such costs being borne by the initial shareholders or partners of the closed-end fund or partnership. The treatment of capitalizing offering costs by open-end investment companies and certain investment partnerships that continually offer interests is consistent with their continuous issuances and redemptions of shares.

8.35 Unit investment trusts (UITs)[3] have characteristics that are similar to both open-end and closed-end investment companies. Some UITs offer shares only at a particular time, but others provide for ongoing sales over a longer offering period. FinREC recognized that requiring a UIT to charge its offering costs to paid-in capital at the commencement of its offering or immediately after its units or shares are sold to the underwriters would require the underwriters, not the shareholders, to bear those costs. The treatment of these offering costs is discussed in the following paragraph and matches those costs with the proceeds received from the sale of the units or shares. FinREC also considered whether these offering costs should be deferred until these units or shares are sold by the underwriters to the public. FinREC concluded that the capital-raising effort of the UIT is completed upon the sale of the units or shares to the underwriters; therefore, support for further deferral does not exist.

8.36 As explained in FASB ASC 946-20-35-6 and 946-20-40-1, offering costs of UITs should be treated as follows:

- Offering costs should be charged to paid-in capital on a pro rata basis as the units or shares are issued or sold by the trust (when the units are purchased by the underwriters). Units sold to underwriters on a firm basis are considered sold by the trust, and the offering costs associated with those units should be charged to paid-in capital when the units are purchased by the underwriters. Offering costs that remain unamortized at the end of the year should be reviewed for impairment.

- Offering costs that have not yet been charged to paid-in capital should be written off when it is no longer probable that the shares to which the offering costs relate will be issued in the future. It is presumed that those costs will not have a future benefit one year from the initial offering.

Unusual Income Items

8.37 Unusual income items, such as amounts recovered from the settlement of litigation, are usually recognized in the financial statements when the investment company acquires an enforceable right, in accordance with the gain contingency provisions of FASB ASC 450-30. For items considered payment in lieu of settlement to make whole for violations by an affiliate, refer to paragraph 7.138 of this guide. Before an unusual item is collected, it should be valued by the board of directors or trustees or those otherwise in charge of governance, and subsequent changes in the fair value should be recorded. Items relating to specific portfolio securities are typically recorded as an adjustment to realized

---

[3] See chapter 9, "Unit Investment Trusts" for further information.

or unrealized gains or losses. Otherwise, the item and a subsequent revaluation should be presented as other income, if any, or a separate income item. If the item is sufficiently material in relation to net investment income, it should be presented as a line item immediately before net investment income, unless the item is clearly identifiable with realized or unrealized gains or losses.

Form N-SAR

8.38   Form N-SAR is a semiannual and annual report filed with the SEC by all registered investment companies, small business investment companies, and UITs.

8.39   Form N-SAR contains numerous items and, as stated by Rule 30b1-1 of the 1940 Act, must be filed with the SEC within 60 days of the end of the semiannual or annual reporting period, as applicable. As stated by Rule 30a-1 of the 1940 Act, UITs are required to file annual reports only.

8.40   Form N-SAR requires a management investment company to provide an auditor's report on the investment company's internal controls.[4] Form N-SAR states that the report should be

> based on the review, study and evaluation of the accounting system, internal accounting controls, and procedures for safeguarding securities made during the audit of the financial statements. The report should disclose material weaknesses in the accounting system, system of internal accounting control and procedures for safeguarding securities which exist as of the end of the registrant's fiscal year. Disclosure of a material weakness should include an indication of any corrective action taken or proposed.

8.41   The auditor's report on the investment company's internal controls should be presented as an exhibit to Form N-SAR filed for the investment company's fiscal year and should be addressed to the investment company's shareholders and board of directors or trustees, dated, and signed manually. It should also indicate the city and state where issued.

8.42   The SEC has indicated that it will not regard the fact that the auditor's report is attached to Form N-SAR as acknowledgment that the auditor has reviewed the form. The auditor is not deemed to be associated with Form N-SAR and, accordingly, has no responsibility to audit, report on, or read items contained in the form.

8.43   Small business investment companies or other investment companies not required by either the 1940 Act or other federal or state laws, or rules or regulations thereunder, to have audits of their financial statements are exempt from the provisions regarding auditors' reports on internal control.

Business Combinations

8.44   According to Q&A section 6910.33, "Certain Financial Reporting, Disclosure, Regulatory, and Tax Considerations When Preparing Financial

---

[4] Paragraph 12.29 of this guide illustrates an independent registered public accounting firm's report on a registered investment company's internal control based on the results of procedures performed in obtaining an understanding of internal control over financial reporting and assessing control risks in connection with the audit of the investment company's financial statements.

Statements of Investment Companies Involved in a Business Combination" (AICPA, *Technical Questions and Answers*), most mergers of registered investment companies are structured as tax-free reorganizations in which shares of one company typically are exchanged for substantially all the shares or assets of another company (or companies). Following a business combination, portfolios of investment companies are often realigned, subject to tax limitations, to fit the objectives, strategies, and goals of the surviving company. Typically, shares of the acquiring fund are issued at an exchange ratio determined on the acquisition date, essentially equivalent to the acquiring fund's net asset value per share divided by the net asset value per share of the fund being acquired, both as calculated on the acquisition date. Adjusting the carrying amounts of assets and liabilities is usually unnecessary because virtually all assets of the combining investment companies (investments) are stated at fair value, in accordance with FASB ASC 820, *Fair Value Measurement*, and liabilities are generally short term so that their carrying values approximate their fair values.[5] However, conforming adjustments may be necessary when funds have different valuation policies (for example, valuing securities at the bid price versus the mean of the bid and asked price) in order to ensure that the exchange ratio is equitable to shareholders of both funds.

8.45   Q&A section 6910.33 also explains that only one of the combining companies can be the legal survivor. In certain instances, it may not be clear which of the two funds constitutes the acquirer for financial reporting purposes. Although the legal survivor would normally be considered the acquirer, continuity and dominance in one or more of the following areas might lead to a determination that the fund legally dissolved should be considered the acquirer for financial reporting purposes:

- Portfolio management
- Portfolio composition
- Investment objectives, policies, and restrictions
- Expense structures and expense ratios
- Asset size

8.46   As stated in Q&A section 6910.33, a registration statement on Form N-14 is often filed in connection with a merger of management investment companies registered under the 1940 Act, or of *business development companies*, as defined by Section 2(a)(48) of the 1940 Act. Form N-14 is both a proxy statement, in that it solicits a vote from the (legally) acquired fund's shareholders to approve the transaction, and a prospectus, in that it registers the (legally) acquiring fund's shares that will be issued in the transaction. Form N-14 frequently requires the inclusion of pro forma financial statements reflecting the effect of the merger.[6]

---

[5] If the carrying value of the acquired investment company's liabilities differs materially from fair value on the acquisition date, refer to FASB ASC 805-30-30-8 for guidance on the recognition of the liabilities by the surviving entity.

[6] Rule 11-02(b)(1) of Regulation S-X permits a narrative description of the pro forma effects of the transaction in lieu of condensed pro forma financial statements when there are a limited number of pro forma adjustments and those adjustments are easily understood. As discussed in paragraph .78 of the 2010/11 AICPA Audit Risk Alert *Investment Companies*, the SEC staff commented that narrative descriptions should include significant elements of the transaction, including, but not limited to

1. a general description of the merger, including the identification of the investment company whose financial performance will be carried over to financial statements prepared in future periods;

8.47   Q&A section 6910.33 also states that tax implications must be considered and monitored carefully in the planning, execution, and postmerger stages of a business combination. The tax rules that must be considered include those related to the determination that the transaction is tax-free to the funds involved and their shareholders (IRC Section 368(a) and IRS Notice 88-19), the qualification tests affecting regulated investment companies (RICs) (IRC Section 851), and the accounting for tax attributes of specific accounts such as earnings and profits (Section 1.852–12(b) of Title 26, *Internal Revenue*, of U.S. *Code of Federal Regulations*), capital loss carryforwards, and methods of tax accounting (IRC Section 381). Management may consider obtaining a private letter ruling from the IRS or an opinion of counsel on the tax-free treatment. Upon completion of the acquisition, the portfolio securities obtained from the acquiree generally should be monitored because substantial turnover of the acquiree's portfolio securities may jeopardize the tax-free status of the reorganization. There are important differences in the tax rules affecting business combinations of RICs and nonregulated investment companies.

8.48   As further stated by Q&A section 6910.33, merger-related expenses (mainly legal, audit, proxy solicitation, and mailing costs) are addressed in the plan of reorganization and often paid by the fund incurring the expense, although the adviser may waive or reimburse certain merger-related expenses. Numerous factors and circumstances should be considered in determining which entity bears merger-related expenses.

8.49   FASB ASC 805-10-25-23 notes that *acquisition-related costs* are costs that the acquirer incurs to effect a business combination. Acquisition-related costs include finder's fees; advisory, legal, accounting, valuation, and other professional or consulting fees; general administrative costs, including the costs of maintaining an internal acquisitions department; and costs of

---

Note: For transactions structured as mergers of multiple registered management investment companies, disclosure of whether the mergers are contingent upon the target companies' shareholders approving the merger.

2. disclosure of the cost of the merger to each of the participating registered management investment companies and rationale for cost allocation, whether or not the merger is consummated;

3. a general description of the tax consequences of the merger, including the capital loss carryforwards available to each investment company and whether those capital loss carryforwards are subject to expiration or limitation;

4. disclosure of information related to portfolio realignment, if any, that will take place after consummation of the merger, including

    a. the reasons for portfolio realignment,

    b. the extent and cost of portfolio realignment,

    c. the percentage of the target company's portfolio that is expected to be sold as a result of portfolio realignment and an estimate of the related realized gains expected to result from such sales, and

    d. a statement that total merger costs do not reflect commissions that would be incurred during portfolio realignment;

5. pro forma effects of the transaction (assuming all investment companies subject to merger had merged) on

    a. the significant accounting policies, including valuation policies,

    b. net assets,

    c. management fees and other expenses, and

    d. any other significant adjustments resulting from the transaction; and

6. reference to the audited financial statements of each investment company participating in the merger

registering and issuing debt and equity securities. The acquirer should account for acquisition-related costs as expenses in the periods in which the costs are incurred and the services are received. The only exception to this is for costs relating to issuance of debt or equity securities, which should be recognized in accordance with other applicable GAAP.

8.50   Q&A section 6910.33 goes on to state that if the combination is a taxable reorganization, the fair value of the assets acquired on the date of the combination becomes the assets' new cost basis. For financial reporting purposes, assets acquired in a tax-free reorganization may be accounted for in the same manner as a taxable reorganization. However, investment companies carry substantially all their assets at fair value as an ongoing reporting practice, and cost basis is principally used and presented solely for purposes of determining realized and unrealized gain and loss. Accordingly, an investment company, which is an acquirer in a business combination structured as a tax-free exchange of shares, may make an accounting policy election to carry forward the historical cost basis of the acquiree's investment securities for purposes of measuring realized and unrealized gain or loss for statement of operations presentation in order to more closely align the subsequent reporting of realized gains by the combined entity with tax-basis gains distributable to shareholders. The basis for such policy election should be disclosed in the notes to the financial statements, if material.

8.51   Q&A section 6910.33 explains that the instructions to Forms N-1A and N-2 state that, for registered investment companies, costs of purchases and proceeds from sales of portfolio securities that occurred in the effort to realign a combined fund's portfolio after a merger should be excluded in the portfolio turnover calculation. The amount of excluded purchases and sales should be disclosed in a note.[7]

8.52   FASB ASC 805-10-50-1 states that disclosures to enable users of the financial statements to evaluate the nature and effect of a business combination are required when business combinations occur during the reporting period or after the reporting date but before the financial statements are issued or available to be issued. FASB ASC 805-10-50-2 explains that disclosures for all business combinations should include the name and description of the acquiree, the acquisition date, the percentage of voting equity interests acquired, and the primary reasons for the business combination and a description of how the acquirer obtained control of the acquiree. Transactions that are recognized separately from the acquisition of assets and assumptions of liabilities in the business combination require additional disclosures. Business combinations achieved in stages also require additional disclosures.

8.53   In addition, FASB ASC 805-10-50-2 discusses that if the acquirer is a public business entity, these additional disclosures are required:

- The amounts of revenue and earnings of the acquiree since the acquisition date included in the consolidated income statement for the reporting period
- If comparative financial statements are not presented, the revenue and earnings of the combined entity for the current reporting period as though the acquisition date for all business combinations

---

[7] See instructions 4(d)(iii) of item 13 of Form N-1A and instruction 17(c) of item 4 of Form N-2.

that occurred during the year had been as of the beginning of the annual reporting period.

- If comparative financial statements are presented, the revenue and earnings of the combined entity as though the business combination(s) that occurred during the current year had occurred as of the beginning of the comparable prior annual reporting period (supplemental pro forma information). For example, for a calendar year-end entity, disclosures would be provided for a business combination that occurs in 20X2, as if it occurred on January 2, 20X1. Such disclosures would not be revised if 20X2 is presented for comparative purposes with the 20X3 financial statements (even if 20X2 is the earliest period presented).

- The nature and amount of any material, nonrecurring pro forma adjustments directly attributable to the business combination(s) included in the reported pro forma revenue and earnings (supplemental pro forma information).

If providing the public entity acquirer disclosures will not be practicable, that fact, along with an explanation of why the disclosure is impracticable, should be disclosed. In this context, *impracticable* is defined by any of the following conditions existing:

- After making every reasonable attempt to do so, the entity is unable to apply the requirement.

- Retrospective application requires assumptions about management's intent in a prior period that cannot be independently substantiated.

- Retrospective application requires significant estimates of amounts, and it is impossible to objectively distinguish information about those estimates that both

  — provides evidence of circumstances that existed on the date(s) at which those amounts would be recognized, measured, or disclosed under retrospective application and

  — would have been available when the financial statements for that prior period were issued.

8.54 Q&A section 6910.33 notes that because of the importance of investment company taxation to amounts distributable to shareholders, certain additional disclosures are recommended for combinations of investment companies, including the tax status and attributes of the merger. Additionally, if the merger is a tax-free exchange, separate disclosures of the amount of unrealized appreciation or depreciation and the amount of undistributed investment company income of the acquiree at the date of acquisition, if significant, may provide meaningful information about amounts transferred from the acquiree, which may be distributable by the combined fund in future periods. See appendix E, "Illustrative Financial Statement Presentation for Tax-Free Business Combinations of Investment Companies," of this guide for an example of the calculation of an exchange ratio in an investment company merger, as well as merger-related financial statement disclosures.

Diversification of Assets

8.55 An investment company may use a worksheet to determine and document that it has complied with the diversification requirements stated in its registration statement.

8.56 The auditor may test that worksheet to become satisfied about the fund's representations of the diversification of its assets. Those diversification requirements may differ from the requirements under IRC Subchapter M, discussed in chapter 6, "Taxes," of this guide.

Liquidation Basis of Accounting

8.57 U.S. GAAP provided minimal guidance on the application of the liquidation basis of accounting prior to the issuance of FASB ASU No. 2013-07, *Presentation of Financial Statements (Topic 205): Liquidation Basis of Accounting*. The guidance in ASU No. 2013-07, which was issued in April 2013 and is included in "Pending Content" in FASB ASC 205-30, is intended to improve the consistency of financial reporting for liquidating entities. The amendments in ASU No. 2013-07 are effective for entities that determine liquidation is imminent[8] during annual reporting periods beginning after December 15, 2013, and interim reporting periods therein. Entities should apply the requirements prospectively from the day that liquidation becomes imminent. Early adoption is permitted. Entities that were already reporting on the liquidation basis of accounting prior to the effective date of ASU No. 2013-07 need to be aware of the specific transition provisions when preparing financial statements at a date on which ASU No. 2013-07 is effective. Such financial statements should include a cumulative-effect adjustment as of the date of adoption.

8.58 The liquidation basis of accounting, as described in "Pending Content" in FASB ASC 205-30, is not applicable to investment companies regulated under the 1940 Act. Other entities should not apply this scope exception by analogy. This scope exception does not include nonregulated investment companies, such as hedge funds and private equity funds.

When to Apply the Liquidation Basis of Accounting

8.59 Entities that do not meet the previously described scope exception should consider guidance in "Pending Content" in FASB ASC 205-30-25 to determine if and when to apply the liquidation basis of accounting. "Pending Content" in FASB ASC 205-30-25-1 explains in part that the liquidation basis of accounting is required when liquidation is *imminent*. As summarized from "Pending Content" in FASB ASC 205-30-25-2, liquidation is imminent when the likelihood is remote that the entity will return from liquidation and either (*a*) a plan for liquidation is approved by the person or persons with the authority to make such a plan effective, and the likelihood is remote that the execution of the plan will be blocked by other parties, or (*b*) a plan for liquidation is being imposed by other forces (for example, involuntary bankruptcy).

8.60 "Pending Content" in FASB ASC 205-30-25-1 also provides an exception for limited life entities by explaining, in part, that the financial statements should not be prepared on the liquidation basis when the liquidation follows a

---

[8] See further discussion of the term *imminent* within paragraph 8.59.

plan that was specified in the entity's governing documents. A nonregistered investment company established as a limited life entity, such as a private equity fund, may meet this criterion and therefore may be able to apply the exception. However, readers should be aware that this exception may not be appropriate (and, therefore, the liquidation basis of accounting would be adopted) if the approved liquidation differs from a liquidation plan specified in governing documents at inception. "Pending Content" in FASB ASC 205-30-25-3 provides relevant guidance on this matter:

> An entity should presume that its plan of liquidation does not follow a plan that was specified in the entity's governing documents at its inception if the entity is forced to dispose of its assets in exchange for consideration that is not commensurate with the fair value of those assets. Other aspects of the entity's plan of liquidation also might differ from the plan that was specified in the entity's governing documents at its inception (for example, the date at which liquidation should commence). However, those factors should be considered in determining whether to apply the liquidation basis of accounting only to the extent that they affect whether the entity expects to receive consideration in exchange for its assets that is not commensurate with fair value.

8.61 "Pending Content" in FASB ASC 205-30-55-2 also provides an example fact pattern of a liquidation that does not follow a plan specified at an entity's inception. This example may be a helpful supplement when interpreting the related guidance in "Pending Content" in FASB ASC 205-30-25.

Recognition and Measurement Provisions

8.62 When an entity determines that it is appropriate to apply the liquidation basis of accounting, the entity should evaluate the following primary measurement provisions in "Pending Content" in paragraphs 4–7 of FASB ASC 205-30-25:

> *a.* Recognize other items that it previously had not recognized (for example, trademarks) but that it expects to either sell in liquidation or use to settle liabilities. These items may be recognized in the aggregate.
>
> *b.* Recognize liabilities in accordance with the recognition provisions of other relevant FASB ASC topics that otherwise would apply to those liabilities, including FASB ASC 405-20-40-1. However, the entity's liabilities should not be reduced on the basis of the assumption that the entity will be legally released from its obligation.
>
> *c.* Accrue estimated costs to dispose of assets or other items that the entity expects to sell in liquidation and present those costs in the aggregate separately from those assets or items.
>
> *d.* Accrue costs and income that are expected to be incurred or earned, respectively, through the end of the liquidation period if and when it has a reasonable basis for estimation. (See paragraphs 8.64–.65 for application considerations associated with this provision.)

8.63 When applying the provisions of item (*d*) of the preceding paragraph, an entity may encounter challenges because certain costs are dependent on how long the entity will exist under a liquidation basis of accounting. For example, regulations or a fund's governing documents may require that an annual audit be performed until the final termination of the entity, management fees and operating and legal costs will continue during the liquidation process, and administrative costs may arise to maintain books and records, communicate with stakeholders, and perform valuations of the remaining assets. A reporting entity should undertake efforts to evaluate how long it will take the entity to liquidate, and develop an estimate of future expenses to be incurred during the estimated liquidation period. Depending on facts and circumstances, there may be significant uncertainty. Therefore, determining whether the entity has a reasonable basis for estimating these costs may require significant judgment by management, such as how long it will take to liquidate the fund's illiquid investments. Such an estimate should be reevaluated at each subsequent reporting period.

8.64   When an entity measures and records an asset in its liquidation basis financial statements, it must carefully evaluate whether the measurement used implicitly includes income the entity expects to earn from the asset during the liquidation period. If such income is already included in the measurement used, the entity should not record an additional accrual for such income in accordance with the provisions of item (d) of paragraph 8.62.

8.65   "Pending Content" in FASB ASC 205-30-30-1 discusses that an entity reporting under the liquidation basis of accounting should measure assets to reflect the estimated amount of cash or other consideration that it expects to collect in settling or disposing of those assets in carrying out its plan for liquidation. As an example of when this measurement may differ from fair value, a fund may determine that the disposition of its illiquid investment during the liquidation process will not be conducted in an orderly manner such as in a distressed sale or a forced liquidation. However, although an entity should not presume this to be true for all assets, in some cases, the fair value may approximate the amount that an entity expects to collect.

8.66   "Pending Content" in FASB ASC 205-30-30-2 provides guidance for the recognition of liabilities during the liquidation period. To summarize, liabilities (excluding the accrual of estimated disposal costs as described in FASB ASC 205-30-25-6 and expected expenses as described in FASB ASC 205-30-25-7) are recorded pursuant to other applicable U.S. GAAP, with necessary adjustments for known changes in the timing of payments. FASB ASC 205-30-30-3 also explains that it is not appropriate to apply discounting provisions when measuring accruals for estimated disposal costs, expected income, or expected expenses.

Presentation and Disclosure

8.67   Practitioners should consider all financial reporting presentation and disclosure matters discussed in sections 45 and 50 of FASB ASC 205-30. "Pending Content" in FASB ASC 205-30-45-1 explains that the following two statements should be prepared, at a minimum: a statement of net assets in liquidation and a statement of changes in net assets in liquidation.[9] Paragraph

---

[9] Although "Pending Content" in FASB ASC 205-30-45-1 explicitly lists two specific statements that are required to be prepared, these two statements are the minimum requirement. Paragraph 18 of the basis of conclusions in ASU No. 2013-07, *Presentation of Financial Statements (Topic 205): Liquidation Basis of Accounting*, explains, in the context of deciding whether to prepare stub period information, that "... an entity should consider...the needs of...anticipated users of the entity's financial statements." By analogy, this same consideration may be applicable when determining which financial statements to present. As an example, for an investment company within the scope of FASB ASC 205-30, this may include preparing a schedule of investments and financial highlights.

2 of the same section explains the liquidation basis of accounting should be applied prospectively from the day that the liquidation becomes imminent. The initial statement of changes in net assets in liquidation should present only changes in net assets that occurred during the period since liquidation became imminent.

8.68 Practitioners are reminded in paragraph 18 of the basis of conclusions in ASU No. 2013-07 that the guidance in FASB ASC 205-30 requires the liquidation basis of accounting to be applied prospectively from the date that liquidation becomes imminent. However, ASC 205-30 does not provide guidance about whether an entity should present information for the period that preceded the determination that liquidation was imminent (commonly referred to as the stub period). In deciding whether to present information about the stub period, an entity should consider the requirements of its regulator and the needs of any other anticipated users of the entity's financial statements.

8.69 Entities may prepare financial statements on the liquidation basis of accounting comprising only the two required statements, as discussed in paragraph 8.67. However, although not required, entities may continue presenting a condensed schedule of investments along with statements of operations and of cash flows (if applicable) (including financial highlights) covering the period post-adoption of the liquidation basis of accounting. If stub period financial statements are prepared, all disclosures in the notes to such financial statements need to present stub period information separately from the information pertaining to the period post-adoption of liquidation basis of accounting.

8.70 FASB has indicated that when deciding whether to present stub period information, the reporting entity should consider the needs of the anticipated users of the financial statements along with any potential regulatory requirements. For example, private funds utilizing the annual audit exemption under the Custody Rule, must prepare financial statements covering the entire annual period to be in compliance with this regulation. Such financial statements would at a minimum include statements of operations, of changes in net assets and of cash flows (if applicable) for the stub period pre-adoption of the liquidation basis of accounting in addition to the two required statements discussed above. Financial highlights would then also be presented for the pre-adoption period as required under FASB ASC 946.

8.71 The following list summarizes the disclosure requirements in "Pending Content" in paragraphs 1–2 of FASB ASC 205-30-50:

- The primary purpose of an entity's disclosures is to convey the following to the users of the financial statements: information about the amount of cash or other consideration that an entity expects to collect and information about the amount of cash or other consideration that the entity is obligated or expects to be obligated to pay during the course of liquidation.

- Disclosures required by other relevant FASB ASC topics should be made to ensure understanding of the two required statements discussed in paragraph 8.67.

- All of the following information should be disclosed in financial statements prepared using the liquidation basis of accounting:

  — That the financial statements are prepared using the liquidation basis of accounting, including the facts and circumstances surrounding the adoption of the liquidation basis of accounting and the entity's determination that liquidation is imminent.

— A description of the entity's plan for liquidation, including a description of each of the following:

  • The manner by which it expects to dispose of its assets and other items it expects to sell that it had not previously recognized as assets (for example, trademarks)

  • The manner by which it expects to settle its liabilities

  • The expected date by which the entity expects to complete its liquidation.

— The methods and significant assumptions used to measure assets and liabilities, including any subsequent changes to those methods and assumptions.

— The type and amount of costs and income accrued in the statement of net assets in liquidation and the period over which those costs are expected to be paid or income earned.

———————————

Chapter 9

Unit Investment Trusts

9.01 A *unit investment trust (UIT)* is defined by Section 4(2) of the Investment Company Act of 1940 (the 1940 Act) as an investment company organized under a trust indenture, contract of custodianship or agency, or similar instrument. It has no board of directors or trustees, and it issues only redeemable securities, each representing an undivided interest in a unit of specified securities, but does not include a voting trust. Typically, a UIT will make a one-time "public offering" of only a specific, fixed number of units (similar to closed-end funds). Units remain outstanding until a unit holder tenders them to the trustee or sponsor for redemption or until the trust is terminated. The trusts typically have a limited life, ranging from 12 months to 30 years. In the case of a UIT investing in bonds, for example, the termination date may be determined by the maturity date of the bond investments. Trust agreements usually require periodic pro rata distribution to the unit holders of the trust's entire net investment income and net realized capital gains, if any, and distribution of the proceeds of redemptions, maturities, or sales of securities in the trust, unless the proceeds are used to pay for units to be redeemed. A distinguishing feature of UITs from mutual funds is that the portfolio is intended to be relatively fixed; neither the sponsor nor the trustee has power to manage the portfolio. In general, securities may be sold only for limited purposes (for example, to generate proceeds to pay a redeeming unit holder). Because a UIT does not actively trade its investment portfolio, a UIT generally buys a relatively fixed portfolio of securities (for example, five, ten, or twenty specific stocks or bonds), and holds them with little or no change for the life of the UIT. Because the investment portfolio of a UIT generally is fixed, investors know more or less what they are investing in for the duration of their investment. The portfolio securities held by the UIT are listed in its prospectus.

9.02 *Distinguishing Characteristics of UITs.* The following table presents distinguishing characteristics of UITs from mutual funds.

Characteristic	Unit Investment Trust	Mutual Fund
Portfolio Management	Static portfolio: portfolio trades only in limited circumstances	Securities or instruments may be traded every day
Structure	Must use trust format	May be structured as a corporation or a business trust
Governance	Supervised by trustee	Actively governed by board of directors or trustees
Redeemability	Units are redeemable every day at net asset value (most sponsors maintain a secondary market in units as an alternative to redemption)	Shares are redeemable every day at net asset value (minus deferred sales charge and redemption fee, if any)

(continued)

AAG-INV 9.02

Characteristic	Unit Investment Trust	Mutual Fund
Term	Generally fixed life of 1–30 years or more	Generally no term limit
Tax Treatment	Pass-through pursuant to the grantor trust provisions of Section 671 of the IRC or as a regulated investment company (RIC) under IRC Subchapter M	Flow-through distributions pursuant to its qualification as a RIC under IRC Subchapter M
Distribution	Typically sold in a single "firm commitment" offering of a fixed size through a syndicate of underwriters and dealers	Typically sold continuously through a distributor
Expenses / Fees	Generally includes a sales charge and minimal ongoing trustees' and sponsor's fees	Generally includes management fees, custody fees, transfer agency fees and other shareholder servicing fees and may include sales charges and/or ongoing distribution fees (12b-1 fees)
Registration Forms	Required Form S-6 under the 1933 Act and Form N-8B-2 under the 1940 Act	Required Form N-1A under the 1933 Act

9.03 A UIT is one of the three basic kinds of investment companies defined by the 1940 Act. The UIT structure is used primarily as an investment vehicle to hold (*a*) a portfolio of tax-exempt bonds, corporate bonds, government bonds, and/or common or preferred stocks or other kinds of securities or (*b*) the shares of a particular management investment company being accumulated under a contractual plan. (See chapter 10, "Variable Contracts—Insurance Entities," of this guide for a discussion of UITs as a funding medium for variable annuity contracts.) The form and content of financial statements of UITs are prescribed by Article 6 of Regulation S-X, and Rules 6-10(d) and 12-12 of Regulation S-X prescribe the form and content of financial schedules.

9.04 The discussion in this chapter covers two common types of UITs, fixed-income and equity UITs. The accounting and auditing procedures for UITs are similar to those for other investment companies described in this guide. (See chapter 8, "Other Accounts and Considerations," of this guide for a discussion of accounting for offering costs of UITs.)

Fixed-Income and Equity UITs

9.05 Units in UITs representing self-liquidating pools of tax-exempt or taxable bonds or other taxable fixed-income securities held in custody by a corporate trustee were first offered to the investing public in the early 1960s. Trusts investing entirely or in part in equity securities became increasingly common in the 1990s.

9.06 The principal objective of most fixed-income UITs is to generate a consistent income stream that may be taxable or tax exempt by investing in a diversified portfolio of securities. The principal objectives of most equity UITs are to generate dividend income and achieve the potential for capital appreciation through investment in a fixed portfolio of stocks.

9.07 A sponsoring organization, such as an investment banking firm or a broker-dealer, initiates a UIT by accumulating a group of securities of a kind specified in the trust indenture. Portfolios may range in fair value from a few million dollars to $100 million or more and may consist of many individual securities. However, equity portfolios are typically seeded with approximately $150,000. Trusts with fixed income portfolios are typically established based on the anticipated number of units to be sold, but they may have additional subsequent deposits. A tax-exempt bond portfolio may be diversified by economic activity (such as education, health care, and housing) or geographic area, or it may be concentrated in a particular state to provide investors with income exempt from federal, state, or local income taxes or any combination thereof. The portfolio may be accumulated by the sponsor over a period ranging from a few days to several weeks or longer. At the deposit date, the portfolio of securities or contracts to purchase securities is conveyed to a corporate trustee at prices defined in the trust agreement. For fixed-income UITs, these prices are usually based on offering prices, rather than bid prices, as determined by an independent evaluator retained by the sponsor. For equity UITs, these prices are usually based on the trustee's or evaluator's evaluation of the fair value of the securities in the portfolio as of the deposit date. Cash or an irrevocable letter of credit issued by a commercial bank is delivered to the corporate trustee to cover the cost and accrued interest to settlement dates or expected dates of delivery, if any, of portfolio securities. Securities offered on a when-issued basis, delayed deliveries, or the normal settlement process may cause delayed deposits. An audit of a UIT is usually performed as of the opening of business on the initial date of deposit. As discussed subsequently, annual update audits would also be required if the sponsor continues to offer the UITs to the public.

9.08 The sponsoring company, underwriters, and other participants sell units of undivided interest at their public offering price, which is equal to the fair value[1] of the underlying securities owned by the trust plus principal cash, divided by the number of units outstanding plus a sales charge (the "principal net asset value"). The sales charge is a percentage of principal net asset value of the trust unit, and may be reduced on a graduated scale for large purchases. The purchaser of the units also pays the undistributed net income per unit which is the net income (investment income less expense) earned since the previous distribution divided by the number of units outstanding. Upon the formation of the trust, the sponsor may realize a profit or loss on the sale of the underlying securities in the portfolio to the trust equal to the difference between the aggregate cost of the portfolio to the sponsor and the aggregate valuation on the date of deposit. A note to the initial schedule of investments should disclose the aggregate cost of the securities and the related net gain or loss to the sponsor.

---

[1] *Fair value*, as defined by the FASB *Accounting Standards Codification* (ASC) glossary, is the price that would be received to sell an asset or paid to transfer a liability in an orderly transaction between market participants at the measurement date. For further information on fair value, see FASB ASC 820, *Fair Value Measurement*, as well as chapters 1, "Overview of the Investment Company Industry," and 2, "Investment Accounts," of this guide.

9.09 A UIT may be expandable. At the initial date of deposit, a limited amount of securities is placed in the trust, and a limited number of units are issued. However, the trust agreement may provide for expanding the trust in size and number of units through additional deposits of securities in the trust, usually for a period of 90 to 180 days. According to Section 26 of the 1940 Act, any substitution of securities must be approved by the SEC. The auditor may be requested to perform certain agreed-upon procedures at the subsequent deposit dates.

9.10 A UIT generally does not offer units of participation continuously. However, the sponsor may maintain a secondary market by repurchasing units from unit holders at net asset value based on the aggregate bid price of the underlying securities and reoffering them at net asset value based on the aggregate bid or offering prices of the underlying securities plus a sales charge. If the sponsor does not maintain a secondary market or choose to purchase the units, a unit holder can redeem his or her units at net asset value that is usually based on the aggregate bid price of the underlying securities. Some UITs allow unit holders to exchange units of the trust for other kinds of UITs offered by the sponsors, based on relative net asset values, at a reduced sales charge.

9.11 After the initial deposit by the sponsoring entity, all accounting, recordkeeping, and income and principal distribution services are performed by the trustee. The trustee distributes the accumulated income to unit holders periodically, usually monthly or quarterly, but sometimes semiannually or annually. Usually, as securities are redeemed or mature, the proceeds are distributed to unit holders. Investors may have the option of reinvesting the proceeds from income or principal distributions into additional units of the trust or other investment vehicles of the sponsor.

9.12 The trustee generally reports to unit holders periodically on the fair values of the underlying securities and certain other financial information relating to the trust, as generally required by the trust agreement. The valuation policies are similar to those used by other investment companies. Audited financial statements[2] are usually not distributed to unit holders; however, unaudited calendar year-end distribution information is supplied by the sponsor or trustee. The trust agreement specifies the reporting of tax and other information.

9.13 Some or all of the debt securities owned by certain trusts are covered by insurance obtained by the issuer or trust to guarantee principal and interest payments when due. The treatment of the cost of an insurance policy on an insured portfolio is discussed in chapter 3, "Financial Instruments," of this guide.

Taxes

9.14 Most UITs elect to qualify as regulated investment companies (RICs) under IRC Subchapter M by complying with the applicable requirements (see chapter 6, "Taxes," of this guide). They usually distribute all their taxable

---

[2] On Form N-CSR, a registered investment company files its audited annual and unaudited semi-annual shareholder reports together with the certifications of principal executive and financial officers required by Rule 30a-2 of the Investment Company Act of 1940. Unit investment trusts are exempt from the requirements of Form N-CSR. Instead, the audited financial statements of a unit investment trust (UIT) are filed as part of the prospectus update (485BPOS) if the sponsor wants to maintain a secondary market for the units.

income and gains from sales of securities and are, therefore, not subject to federal income or excise taxes. Certain UITs may be organized as grantor trusts. The tax requirements for a grantor trust structure are different from a RIC. A grantor trust is formed to facilitate the direct investment of its assets, and ownership of the trust represents undivided beneficial interests in the assets of the trust. If multiple classes of ownership exist, they must be incidental to the purpose of facilitating direct ownership (for example, certain senior or subordinated rights). The trustee does not have the power to vary investments. Unlike a RIC, a grantor trust does not have income and asset qualification tests. Also, the taxable income flows through to the participant as it is earned by the trust, so income recognition to the grantor or beneficiary does not depend on distributions from the trust. UITs structured as grantor trusts pass through principal and interest payments to the grantor or beneficiary, but the cash flows may not fully correlate with the taxable income reported. Under Widely Held Fixed Investment Trust rules, a grantor trust UIT may qualify for simplified reporting on Form 1099 of income, security sales, redemption proceeds, and certain other items. To qualify, at least one interest in the grantor trust UIT must be held by a "middleman" (for example, a custodian, broker, or nominee).[3]

9.15 If a UIT is a RIC and more than 50 percent of its total assets consist of securities on which interest is exempt from federal income taxes under existing law when received by a trust, the tax-exempt character of the interest is retained when distributed (net of the trust's expenses) to unit holders. Amounts realized from capital gains and paid to unit holders by the trust are taxable to the unit holder. (Chapter 6 discusses taxes in more detail.)

Illustrative Financial Statements

9.16 The financial statements of UITs are similar to those of management investment companies. When a trust is formed, the financial statements filed with the SEC on Form S-6[4] typically include a statement of condition, schedule of investments, and related notes (see the following illustrative statements). Subsequently, if the sponsor repurchases and reoffers trust units in the secondary market, a posteffective amendment to Form S-6 must be filed during the relevant period with the SEC. The financial statements included in the posteffective amendment, which are prepared in accordance with Regulation S-X, include a statement of assets and liabilities, a schedule of investments, and statements of operations and changes in net assets (see the following illustrative statements). Audited financial statements are provided to prospective investors in the prospectus. Form S-6 requires that both the statement of operations and statement of changes in net assets cover a three-year period. Financial highlights are required to cover a five-year period.[5]

9.17 Certain disclosures required of registered investment companies for compliance with SEC rules and regulations are not presented in the illustrative financial statements that follow because they are not otherwise required by

---

[3] See Treasury Reg. 1.671-5.

[4] See paragraph 1.40 of this guide.

[5] Form S-6, the registration statement for UITs under the Securities Act of 1933, contains specific requirements for exhibits UITs must file, including financial statements, for nonregistered investees that comprise greater than 25 percent of the trust property underlying any class of securities being registered. In accordance with Rule 4-01(a)(1) of Regulation S-X, financial statements for such nonregistered investees that are filed with the Commission must be prepared in accordance with generally accepted accounting principles and must comply with Regulation S-X.

U.S. generally accepted accounting principles. Such compliance disclosures include the following:

     a.   The aggregate cost, for federal income tax purposes, of the portfolio of investments according to Rule 12-12 (note 8) of Regulation S-X

     b.   The gross unrealized appreciation or depreciation for all securities, on a tax basis, according to Rule 12-12 (note 8) of Regulation S-X

Note: The illustrative financial statements and note disclosures included in this guide have been updated to reflect FASB *Accounting Standards Codification* (ASC). However, FASB's notice to constituents suggests the use of plain English in financial statement note disclosures to describe broad FASB ASC topic references. FASB suggests a reference similar to "as required by the Derivatives and Hedging Topic of the FASB *Accounting Standards Codification.*" Entities might consider revising their financial statement references to reflect this plain English referencing, rather than the use of specific FASB ASC references. The AICPA has provided these detailed references as a resource for its users.

9.18

Anytown Income Trust
First Intermediate Series
Statement of Assets and Liabilities
August 31, 20X8

Assets

Assets

Investments in securities at fair value (cost: $14,591,035) (note 1 and schedule 1)	$13,878,788
Interest receivable	339,174
Cash	166,489
Total assets	14,384,451

Liabilities and Net Assets

Liabilities

Trustee and evaluator fees payable	47
Accrued other expenses	475
Total liabilities	522

Net assets

Balance applicable to 15,500 units of fractional undivided interest outstanding (notes 1 and 3)

Cost to original investors	15,475,560
Less gross underwriting commission	(600,000)
Less organizational costs	(19,022)
	14,856,538
Accumulated losses (note 2)	(232,610)
Principal distributions to unit holders of proceeds from investment transactions	(239,999)
Net assets	14,383,929
Total liabilities and net assets	$14,384,451
Net asset value per unit (15,500 units outstanding)	$927,995

The accompanying notes are an integral part of these financial statements.

9.19

Schedule 1
Anytown Income Trust
First Intermediate Series
Portfolio of Investments
August 31, 20X8

Name of Issuer and Title of Issue	Coupon Rate (%)	Date of Maturity or Final Sinking Fund Payment	Principal Amount or Par Value	Fair Value	
Corporate debt obligations:					
United States:					
Air transport					
Flying Tiger Lines Incorporated equipment trust certificates	9.000	10/01/Y1	$931,000	$912,380	
Total air transport (Percentage of net asset value)				912,380	(6.4%)
Banking					
Dominion Bankshares notes	9.500	4/01/Y3	1,000,000	1,022,500	
First Maryland Bancorp notes	9.750	11/01/Y3	250,000	252,500	
Southeast Banking Corporation notes	10.000	5/01/Y3	218,000	224,267	
Total banking (percentage of net asset value)				1,499,267	(10.4%)
Utilities					
Utah Power & Light Company first mortgage bonds	4.500	6/01/Y2	12,100,000	11,467,141	
Total utilities (percentage of net asset value)				11,467,141	(79.7%)
Total debt obligations (Cost $14,591,035) (percentage of net asset value)				$13,878,788	(96.5%)

The accompanying notes are an integral part of these financial statements.

9.20

**Anytown Income Trust
First Intermediate Series
Statements of Operations**

	For the Year Ended August 31, 20X8	From March 23, 20X7 (Date of Deposit) Through August 31, 20X7
Investment income		
Interest income	$1,258,975	$554,509
Expenses (note 1)		
Trustee's fee	14,063	5,411
Evaluator's fee	1,350	375
Other	1,083	351
Total expenses	16,496	6,137
Net investment income	1,242,479	548,372
Realized and unrealized gain (loss) on investments (note 1)		
Net realized losses from investment transactions	(12,738)	(12,765)
Net change in unrealized appreciation (depreciation) of investments	(738,828)	26,581
Net gain (loss) on investments	(751,566)	13,816
Net increase in net assets resulting from operations	$490,913	$562,188

The accompanying notes are an integral part of these financial statements.

Anytown Income Trust
First Intermediate Series
Statements of Changes in Net Assets

	For the Year Ended August 31, 20X8	From March 23, 20X7 (Date of Deposit) Through August 31, 20X7
Increase (decrease) in net assets resulting from operations		
Net investment income	$1,242,479	$548,372
Net realized losses from investment transactions	(12,738)	(12,765)
Net change in unrealized appreciation (depreciation) of investments	(738,828)	26,581
Net increase in net assets resulting from operations	490,913	562,188
Distributions to unit holders (note 2)		
Accrued income as of the date of deposit	5,182	360,787
Net investment income	1,231,408	54,303
Proceeds from investment transactions	129,000	110,999
Total distributions	1,365,590	526,089
Redemption of units	0	0
Total redemptions	0	0
Increase (decrease) in net assets	(874,677)	36,099
Net assets		
Beginning of period	15,258,606	15,222,507
End of period	$14,383,929	$15,258,606

The accompanying notes are an integral part of these financial statements.

9.22

**Anytown Income Trust
First Intermediate Series
Notes to Financial Statements**

1. Summary of Significant Accounting Policies

Anytown Income Trust (the Trust) was organized on March 23, 20X7, under the laws of the Commonwealth of Massachusetts by a trust indenture and agreement, and is registered as a unit investment trust under the Investment Company Act of 1940. The Trust follows the accounting and reporting guidance in FASB *Accounting Standards Codification* 946. The significant accounting policies of the Trust include the following:

Basis of presentation. The financial statements are presented on the accrual basis of accounting.

Investments in securities at fair value. Security transactions are recorded on a trade-date basis. Investments in securities owned are carried at fair value, which is the closing bid price on the last day of trading during the period. The difference between cost and fair value is reflected as unrealized appreciation (depreciation) of investments. Realized gains (losses) from securities transactions are determined for federal income tax and financial reporting purposes on the identified cost basis.

FASB ASC 820-10-35 establishes a hierarchy that prioritizes inputs to fair value measurements. The three levels of inputs are as follows:

- *Level 1.* Unadjusted quoted prices in active markets that the Trust has the ability to access for identical assets or liabilities
- *Level 2.* Inputs other than quoted prices included in level 1 that are observable for the asset or liability either directly or indirectly. These inputs may include quoted prices for the identical instrument in an inactive market, prices for similar instruments, interest rates, prepayment speeds, credit risk, yield curves, default rates, and similar data.
- *Level 3.* Unobservable inputs for the asset or liability to the extent observable inputs are not available, representing the Trust's own assumptions about the assumptions that a market participant would use in valuing the asset or liability, and that would be based on the best information available.

The following table summarizes the inputs used to value the Trust's assets and liabilities measured at fair value as of August 31, 20X8.[6]

Valuation Inputs	Corporate Debt Obligations[a]
Level 1	$—
Level 2	$13,878,888
Level 3	—
Total	$13,878,888

[a] Additional information regarding the industry classification and/or geographical location of these investments is disclosed in the portfolio of investments schedule.

[6] The classification of various financial instruments in this table is for illustrative purposes only and should not be construed as recommended practice for any particular financial instrument or class of financial instruments.

For significant movements between levels within the fair value hierarchy, the Trust has adopted a policy of recognizing the transfers into and out of all levels at the beginning of period method. There were no transfers between levels during the period.

Income taxes. No provision for federal income taxes has been made in the accompanying financial statements because the Trust has elected and intends to continue to qualify for the tax treatment applicable to regulated investment companies under the Internal Revenue Code. Under existing law, if the Trust so qualifies, it will not be subject to federal income tax on net investment income and capital gains distributed to unit holders. Distributions to unit holders of the Trust's net investment income will be taxable as ordinary income to unit holders. Capital gains distributions will be taxable as capital gains to unit holders.

Management has analyzed the Trust's tax positions and concluded that no liability for unrecognized tax benefits should be recorded related to uncertain tax positions taken on returns filed for 20X7 or expected to be taken in the Trust's 20X8 tax returns. The Trust is not aware of any tax positions for which it is reasonably possible that the total amounts of unrecognized tax benefits will change materially in the next 12 months. The Trust's federal tax returns are subject to examination by the Internal Revenue Service for a three year period. There are no examinations in progress at period end.

At August 31, 20X8, the cost of investments on a tax basis was as follows:

Cost	Gross Unrealized Appreciation	Gross Unrealized Depreciation	Net Unrealized Depreciation
$14,591,035	$8,767	$(721,014)	$(712,247)

There were no differences between book and tax basis cost of investments and net unrealized appreciation (depreciation) at August 31, 20X8.

As of August 31, 20X8, the components of distributable earnings on a tax basis were as follows:

Undistributed ordinary income		$505,140
Unrealized depreciation of investments	(712,247)	
Accumulated net realized loss from investment transactions	(25,503)	(737,750)
		$(232,610)

The differences between book and tax basis components of net assets are primarily attributable to appreciation (depreciation) of investments.

Investment expenses. The Trust pays a fee for trustee services to XYZ Bank that is based on $0.75 per $1,000 of outstanding investment principal. In addition, a fixed fee of $35 is paid to a service bureau for portfolio valuation at least weekly and more often at the discretion of the trustee.

2. Distributions of Income and Redemption of Units

The Trust agreement requires that the net investment income and net realized capital gains (if any) of the Trust and, also, the proceeds from the sale, redemption, or maturity of securities (to the extent that the proceeds are not used to redeem units) be distributed to unit holders monthly.

The agreement also requires the Trust to redeem units tendered for redemption, to the extent that such units are not purchased by the sponsor, at a price determined based on bid prices of the securities of the Trust.

3. Original Cost to Unit Holders

The original cost to investors[7] represents the aggregate initial offering price as of the date of deposit exclusive of accrued interest. The initial underwriting commission and investors' original cost of units, as shown on the statement of assets and liabilities, are based upon the assumption that the maximum sales commission was charged for each initial purchase of units. Organization costs incurred in establishing the Trust included costs of preparing documents relating to the Trust (such as the registration statement, prospectus, trust agreement and legal documents), federal and state registration fees, the initial fees and expenses of the Trustee and the initial audit.

4. Investment Transactions

Purchases and sales of investments (excluding in-kind transactions) for the period ended August 31, 20X7 were $14,856,537 and $110,999, respectively.

Purchases and sales of investments (including in-kind redemptions) for the period ended August 31, 20X8 were $0 and $129,000, respectively.

5. Financial Highlights[8]

	8/31/X8	8/31/X7[9]
Per Share Operating Performance:		
Net asset value, beginning of period	$984.43	$982.10
Income from investment operations		
Net investment income	80.16	35.38
Net realized and unrealized gain (loss) on investment transactions	(48.49)	0.89
Total from investment operations	31.67	36.27
Less distributions	(88.10)	(33.94)
Net asset value, end of period	$928.00	$984.43
Total Return:	3.22%	3.51%
Ratios as a Percentage of Average Net Assets:		
Expenses[10]	0.11%	0.09%
Net investment income[11]	8.38%	8.21%

[7] This information is required by Regulation S-X and is not otherwise required by U.S. generally accepted accounting principles.

[8] Because the Trust was organized in 20X7, only two years of financial highlights are shown versus the five years that are required.

[9] Date of deposit was March 23, 20X7.

[10] Percentages annualized for periods less than one year.

[11] See footnote 10.

Chapter 10

Variable Contracts—Insurance Entities

Separate Accounts

10.01 This chapter discusses separate accounts of life insurance entities. Separate accounts, also known as variable accounts, are used to support variable annuity contracts and variable life insurance policies (hereinafter referred to together as *variable contracts*). Separate accounts are often registered investment companies under the Investment Company Act of 1940 (the 1940 Act).[1] A variable contract is both a security registered under the Securities Act of 1933 (the 1933 Act) and an insurance policy filed with, and approved and regulated by, state insurance departments.

10.02 A *variable annuity* or *life insurance contract*[2] is a contractual arrangement that combines some features of an investment company (the contract holder assumes the risk of investment gain or loss) with certain traditional insurance features (the insurance company assumes the risk of mortality and administrative expenses). A significant difference between a traditional or fixed annuity and a variable annuity is that, in sponsoring a fixed annuity, the insurance company assumes the risk of investment gain or loss and guarantees the contract holder a specified interest rate. In a variable annuity, the contract holder assumes the risk of investment gain or loss because the value of the contract holder's account varies with the investment experience of the specific portfolio of securities (that is, the securities held in the separate account). In both fixed and variable annuities, the insurance company (rather than the separate account) assumes the mortality risk and administrative expenses for a contractually fixed fee or fees. Certain other nontraditional annuity products have emerged in recent years, such as equity indexed annuities. Equity indexed annuities represent, in effect, a combination of a fixed annuity with a derivative so that the investor is exposed to investment risk without investing in a specific portfolio of securities. Fixed and equity indexed annuities are not further discussed in this guide. Variable contracts are funded by and issued through separate accounts of insurance entities. A registered separate account is either an open-end investment company or a unit investment trust (UIT).

10.03 A *separate account*, as defined by the FASB *Accounting Standards Codification* (ASC) glossary, is a separate investment account established and maintained by an insurance entity under relevant state insurance law to which funds have been allocated for certain contracts of the insurance entity or similar accounts used for foreign-originated products. It is established solely for the purpose of investing the assets of one or more plans. Funds in a separate account are not commingled with other assets of the insurance company for investment purposes. It includes separate accounts and subaccounts or investment divisions of separate accounts.

---

[1] This chapter does not apply to separate accounts that are established as investment vehicles for pension plans, such as those described in the AICPA Audit and Accounting Guide *Employee Benefit Plans*. The financial statements of those separate accounts should be prepared in accordance with the practices discussed by chapter 7, "Financial Statements of Investment Companies," of this guide for investment companies.

[2] Hereinafter, references to variable annuity contracts also refer to variable life insurance contracts, unless otherwise indicated.

10.04 A separate account is not a legal entity but an accounting entity with accounting records for variable contract assets, liabilities, income, and expenses segregated as a discrete operation within the insurance entity. The insurance company's other separate accounts and its general account do not affect the results of a particular variable contract separate account. State insurance regulatory authorities require combined separate accounts to file an annual statement. The separate account is not taxed separately for federal and state tax purposes; it is included with the operations of the insurance entity. However, under federal regulation, variable annuity and variable life products are securities. For purposes of the 1940 Act, a separate account is an independent entity, separate from the insurance company, and it cannot rely on the act's exemption for insurance companies.

10.05 The following approaches are used to invest the underlying assets of variable contracts:

    a. Direct investment by the separate account in individual securities (the separate account is an open-end investment company)

    b. Investment in a registered investment company formed to receive proceeds from such contract holders (the separate account is a UIT)

    c. Investment in a registered investment company that sells shares to the public (the separate account is a UIT), an approach available only for tax-qualified variable annuities

10.06 Similar to an open-end investment company organized as a series fund, separate accounts are frequently structured with multiple subaccounts. Each subaccount has a unique investment strategy, and in the case of a separate account organized as a UIT, individual subaccounts will invest in different underlying investment companies. This structure allows contract holders to allocate their amount invested among various investment choices. Financial position and results of operations are maintained and reported separately for each subaccount within the separate account.

History

10.07 In 1959, the Supreme Court ruled that variable annuities constitute securities subject to registration with the SEC. In 1964, the U.S. Court of Appeals for the Third Circuit ruled that separate accounts funding variable annuities are investment funds that are separable from the insurance entity and, therefore, not exempted from the 1940 Act. Variable annuities became increasingly popular in the late 1960s after federal legislation encouraged self-employed individuals to establish pension accounts.

10.08 The insurance industry introduced investment annuities in the mid-1960s as a further variation of variable annuities. Investment annuities allowed individual contract holders to select specific investment vehicles. Custodian accounts were established with a third party, usually a bank, in which contract holders deposited cash or other assets. The insurer received an annual fee, usually based on a percentage of the invested assets. Although the account's assets were owned by the insurer, they were segregated for the benefit of contract holders, who directed their investments and could sell or exchange them at any time. Further, it was possible to fully or partially redeem investment annuities before the annuity payout period began by paying the insurer a penalty. Assets remaining in an account at the contract holder's death accrued to the insurer as a terminal premium. Investment annuities are no longer treated as annuities for federal income tax purposes.[3]

10.09   The first variable annuity wrapped using mutual fund shares as its underlying investment vehicle (a wraparound annuity) was developed in 1972. A wraparound annuity differs from other variable annuities because it is based on shares of an underlying investment vehicle, not on a pro rata share of individual stocks, bonds, and other investments owned by a separate account. The wraparound annuity separate account's assets typically are invested in a fixed income fund, an equity fund, a liquid assets fund, or some combination of these funds. The contract holder may allocate all or a portion of each payment among those investments.

10.10   Variable life insurance was first offered for sale in the United States in 1976, after having been successful for several years in the Netherlands, the United Kingdom, and Canada. Early variable life insurance policies were fixed premium contracts providing coverage for the whole of life. Death benefits and cash values varied in relation to the investment experience of a separate pool of assets. Today, most variable life insurance policies are of the variable universal life design. These newer variable life policies allow the policy owner to vary the amount of premium paid and, depending on premiums and investment experience, may expire with or without value.

Product Design

10.11   A significant objective of a variable annuity contract is to provide an investment that is responsive to changes in the cost of living and that can be used to accumulate investment funds before retirement and to pay benefits after retirement. Before retirement, the accumulated value of the individual account varies with investment performance and may be withdrawn by the contract holder in whole or part with possible surrender charges, tax liabilities, or both, including possible tax penalties. A contract holder may elect to receive the accumulated value of the individual account at retirement in a lump sum, in periodic payments that are fixed or variable, or in a combination of both (depending on the options available under the particular contract). Periodic payments also may extend for various durations (for example, over the life of the annuity holder, over a defined period, or over the combined lives of the annuity holder and a designated beneficiary, (a joint and survivor annuity).

10.12   If a lump sum is elected, the contract owner receives the account value at the payment date. If a fixed payment is chosen, the contract owner will receive (*a*) a fixed periodic payment that is based upon the account value at the date of conversion to payout and (*b*) actuarial considerations. See paragraphs 10.18–.19 for a discussion of the methodology typically used when a variable benefit option is selected. More recent innovations permit contract owners to obtain a lump-sum commutation of a portion of the contract even after payments commence, guarantees of minimum account or payment values, or periodic payments adjusted for inflation.

10.13   The provisions of a variable annuity contract may require periodic payments to the sponsoring insurance entity by contract holders. Alternatively, the contract could call for a single premium payment or provide for other

---

[3] Revenue Ruling 80-274.

methods of payment. Products typically are designed as front-end loaded or back-end loaded, as specified in the prospectus. Products with a front-end load deduct sales charges from the contract holder's purchase payments, whereas back-end loaded products reduce the surrender value by contractually specified charges, if any. The net payment is used to buy accumulation units of the separate account. The value of the separate account at any time is allocated among contract holders based on the number and value of their accumulation units representing their interest in the separate account. The concept of the accumulation unit and the unit value are analogous to fund shares and net asset value per share. The total value of the contract holder's accumulation units is the amount available to the contract holder at any time.

10.14 If a contract holder dies during the accumulation period, the death benefit varies, depending on the terms of the contract. The value of the death benefit is determined as of the valuation date and paid according to the applicable laws and regulations governing the payment of death benefits. Death benefits may be based upon the contract value at the time of death, contract value as of a stated anniversary date, or total premiums paid. If a contract holder dies after the annuity commencement date, the death benefit is the amount specified in the annuity option selected by the contract holder (under certain options, the death benefit can be zero).

10.15 Typically, the insurance entity charges the separate account a specified amount for investment management services (if the separate account is organized as an open-end investment company), an amount for administrative expenses, and fees for mortality and expense risks assumed. Certain of these charges (for example, administrative charges) may be recovered through an annual contract charge, affected through a redemption of units. The insurance entity assumes the risk that the annuitant's mortality will be less favorable (that is, he or she will live longer) than the rates assumed (mortality risk) and that administration and investment expenses will exceed the fee charged (expense risk). The mortality risk charge also covers the risk that the account value at death will be insufficient to fund the minimum benefit.

10.16 The insurance entity also assumes the mortality risk by incorporating annuity rates into the contract, which cannot be changed. Variable annuity payments are computed based on contractually specified mortality tables. The insurance entity retains the longevity risk, regardless of the method of payout that the contract holders elect, and may be obligated to continue payments, although contract holders or their beneficiaries, depending on the payment options selected, may live longer than anticipated. The insurance entity may bear additional mortality risk if it offers a guaranteed minimum death benefit under which a minimum payment is made to a beneficiary if the annuity holder dies before the payout period commences. To compensate the insurance entity for assuming this mortality risk, a *mortality risk premium*, which is an amount usually computed as a percentage of the daily net asset value of the separate account, is deducted from the separate account. If the mortality risk premium is insufficient to compensate the insurance entity for its costs, the loss is assumed by the insurance entity. Conversely, if the mortality risk premium is greater than its costs, the excess is the insurance entity's gain.

10.17 The insurance entity undertakes to pay the expenses of the separate account and may or may not charge the account a direct fee for the services rendered. Regardless of whether any fees are charged for specific services, the insurance entity charges an expense risk premium to the separate account. This charge is to compensate the insurance entity for accepting the risk that expense charges will be insufficient to cover the entity's cost of providing administrative and other services, including payments to third parties, to the separate account. The annuity contract usually provides that this expense risk charge may vary but sets a maximum.

10.18 The amount of the first annuity payment of a variable annuity is determined by applying a factor in the applicable annuity table to the contract value as of the date on which annuity payments begin, in accordance with the annuity option specified in the application. The first payment is divided by the value of an *annuity unit*, a unit of measure used to calculate variable annuity payments and establish the number of annuity units for each monthly payment. The number of annuity units for a particular annuitant, determined on the annuity commencement date, remains fixed during the annuity payment period.

10.19 Under a variable benefit option, the amounts of the second and subsequent payments are determined by multiplying the fixed number of annuity units by the annuity unit value on the date on which the payments are due. Thus, subsequent payments vary in accordance with the underlying investment performance of the separate account and the resulting annuity unit value.

10.20 Variable life insurance policies have many of the same variable features as variable annuities. The premium for a variable life policy, less an expense or sales load and mortality charge, is invested in a separate account. The policy owner may specify, within limits, where this cash value is to be invested. Several options may be available, including various kinds of money market, fixed income, and equity funds.

10.21 The policy's death benefit and cash value vary directly with the performance of the fund(s) selected. However, a guaranteed minimum death benefit is available, providing a floor of protection regardless of the investment performance of the fund(s). Investment risk in excess of any guaranteed minimum death benefit is borne by the policy owner. The insurance entity retains only expense and mortality risk, as well as the risk of paying guaranteed minimum death benefits in excess of the value of the fund(s) in which the policyholder invested.

10.22 In all other respects, a variable life insurance policy works like a traditional whole life policy, and a variable universal life policy works like a common universal life policy. All the normal riders and attachments are typically available on variable products. Further information on life insurance contracts can be found in the AICPA Audit and Accounting Guide *Life and Health Insurance Entities*.

Contracts in the Payout (Annuitization) Period

10.23 As stated previously, a variable annuity payment option provides an annuity with payment amounts that are not predetermined but vary according to the results of the underlying investment. The payout (annuitization) period begins when amounts accumulated under the contract (the contract value) are applied under the method-of-payment option selected by the contract holder. At each financial reporting date, the separate account financial statements include an aggregate amount of net assets allocated to future contract benefits for the contracts in the payout (annuitization) period.

10.24   The *net assets allocated to future contract benefits,* sometimes referred to as the annuity reserve account, is the total of an actuarial computation of the discounted amount of the expected annuity payments for each contract or group of contracts based principally on the annuity payments at the current annuity unit value multiplied by the individuals' expected mortality rates based upon an annuity table.

10.25   For variable life contracts, the insurance entity charges the separate account for the cost of fixed premium variable life insurance coverage based on traditional methodology, which can be calculated using standard techniques. The charge for variable universal life insurance policies is usually determined in accordance with the National Association of Insurance Commissioners Universal Life Insurance Model Regulation.

SEC Registration

10.26   A separate account is established by resolution of the insurance entity's board of directors or trustees in accordance with the insurance laws of the state of domicile. It is subject to policy-form approval and other requirements in each state in which the entity offers the contract. Courts have determined that variable contracts and separate accounts are subject to registration and regulation under the 1933 Act and the 1940 Act, respectively. The registrant is the separate account.

10.27   In addition to accumulation units and net assets allocated to future annuity contract benefits established at the separate account level, as described previously, certain separate accounts withhold the mortality and expense payments from the insurance entity. Instead of paying the charges to the insurance entity in cash, the separate account may apply accumulation units or net assets to the insurance entity's own account. This may occur either at the discretion of the sponsoring insurance entity to build investible assets or at the requirement of the state insurance commission. (Under insurance regulations of certain states certain separate accounts have been required to withhold payments to the insurance entity.) The purpose of this holdback is to protect contract holders against adverse mortality in the event that the insurance entity is unable to fulfill its responsibilities to insulate the separate account from mortality risk. If the holdback is maintained in the form of accumulation units or otherwise participates in the investment experience of the separate account, it should be reported in net assets by the separate account under the caption "Retained in variable account by insurance entity." If the holdback does not participate in the investment experience of the separate account (that is, it is fixed in amount), it should be reported by the separate account as a liability.

10.28   Initially, variable contract issuers registered as management investment companies because they invested their assets directly in securities and, therefore, resembled typical mutual funds in their investment objectives. The 1940 Act has many technical requirements for a management investment company, including requirements for an elected board of directors or trustees and proxy statements. The requirements for a board of directors or trustees and proxy statements in certain circumstances, among others, are inconsistent with the legal status of the separate account, which is not a legal entity existing apart from the insurance entity.

10.29 Most separate accounts have registered under the 1940 Act as UITs to avoid some technical requirements for entities registered as management investment companies under that act. Further, the form of a UIT satisfies the need for separate accounting for the performance of specific pools of assets of group annuity contracts, personal contracts, and annuity contracts subject to different tax rules. The UIT form may also accommodate lower expense charges and more flexibility in adding new products and changing the features (for example, expenses) of current products. (Changes to fund-level expenses can be achieved through contract owner approval but without the need to amend the contracts.)

10.30 There are two registration forms for use by separate accounts offering variable annuity contracts that register under the 1933 Act and the 1940 Act. Form N-3 is the registration form for separate accounts registered as management investment companies. Form N-4 is the registration form for UITs.

10.31 Variable life separate accounts, as UITs, register under the 1940 Act and register their securities under the 1933 Act on Form N-6. This form is tailored directly to variable life products.

Auditing Considerations [4]

10.32 Because most features of a variable annuity and variable life contract are similar to those of a mutual fund, the auditing guidance in other chapters of this guide also applies to these variable contracts. However, major differences exist between variable annuities and mutual funds in accounting for contracts in the payout period and in the calculation of the net assets allocated to contracts in the payout period (annuity reserve account). In addition, when a separate account organizes as a UIT investing in a mutual fund, other audit issues can arise. Finally, the auditor should consider various issues arising due to unique aspects of the taxation of insurance entities.

10.33 Mortality and interest rate assumptions (based on the annuity option selected by the contract holder, the contract holder's age at issue, and the date of issue of the annuity) are the two most significant factors in determining the annuity reserve account. The auditor should become satisfied with the annuity reserve account by consulting published tables for the appropriate factors and testing that those factors have been appropriately applied to the master file containing all outstanding contracts in the payout period. Similarly, the auditor should become satisfied with the determination of amounts receivable from or payable to the insurance entity based on its mortality experience on contracts in the payout period (see paragraph 10.35). A broad outline of procedures to be followed in auditing actuarial computations is described in the AICPA Audit and Accounting Guide *Life and Health Insurance Entities*.

---

[4] The auditing content in this guide focuses primarily on generally accepted auditing standards issued by the Auditing Standards Board and is applicable to audits of nonissuers. See the section "Applicability of Generally Accepted Auditing Standards and PCAOB Standards" of the preface to this guide for a discussion of the definitions of issuer and nonissuer as used throughout this guide. Appendix B, "Clarified Auditing Standards and PCAOB Standards," of this guide is included to assist auditors in comparing the clarified standards, many of which are referenced throughout this guide, to the PCAOB standards. Further, considerations for audits of issuers in accordance with PCAOB standards may be discussed within this guide's chapter text. When such discussion is provided, the related paragraphs are designated with the following title: *Considerations for Audits Performed in Accordance With PCAOB Standards*.

10.34   For variable life contracts, the net assets maintained by the separate account (excluding any amounts held for the account of the insurance entity) are analogous to the cash value of the underlying insurance policies. The liability for death benefits is held by the insurance entity.

10.35   As stated previously, the insurance entity assumes certain risks in issuing variable annuities and variable life contracts. If mortality experience on annuity contracts in the payout period runs favorably or unfavorably to the insurer's estimate (see paragraphs 10.23–.25), it does not affect the separate account but creates an amount payable to or receivable from the insurance entity, respectively. Among the factors that may be evaluated in examining the financial statements of a separate account funding a variable annuity is the insurance entity's ability to perform if the variable annuity's assets are insufficient to meet the variable annuity's obligations.

10.36   When the separate account is organized as a UIT, certain considerations can arise due to the relationship between the separate account and underlying investment company. If the auditor of the separate account is not the auditor of the fund, the separate account auditor should consider the effect, if any, that this has on the audit. The fiscal year-ends of the separate account and underlying investment company are often the same. In most cases, the underlying investment company is registered under the 1940 Act such that the audited financial statements of the fund will usually be available to the separate account auditor from public sources as audit evidence with respect to the fund's value. If the underlying investment company is not registered under the 1940 Act, the separate account auditor might consider what communications with the fund auditor are appropriate and, in general, may consider what other steps are appropriate, including those steps described in paragraphs 5.91–.96 of this guide, to rely on the work of another auditor or perform other procedures.

10.37   If the underlying fund and separate account have different year-ends, questions may arise regarding auditing investment valuation. As noted in the preceding paragraph, the auditor of the separate account usually has available audited financial statements to provide audit evidence with respect to the value of the investment in the fund. When the fund is not audited at the separate account year-end date, the auditor should consider what other audit procedures might be appropriate to substantiate the separate account's valuation, including, for investments in investment companies not registered under the 1940 Act, the procedures discussed in paragraphs 5.91–.96 of this guide. Audit procedures for investments in investment companies registered under the 1940 Act might include confirmation of shares outstanding and period-end net asset values with the investment company's transfer agent and review of the most recent interim (quarterly or semiannual) filing of the investment company containing portfolio information.

10.38   The auditor's report is typically addressed to the board of directors or trustees of the sponsoring insurance entity and the contract holders of the separate account.

Taxation of Variable Contracts

10.39   Variable annuity contracts are designed for use primarily by individuals for personal savings or retirement plans, which, under the provisions of the IRC, may be qualified or nonqualified plans. Variable life contracts are designed for individuals to provide market-sensitive cash surrender values and death benefits. The ultimate effect of federal income taxes on the contract value, annuity payments, cash values, death benefits, and economic benefit to the contract owner, annuitant, or beneficiary depends on the separate account's tax status, the purpose for which the contract is purchased, and the individual's tax and employment status. The discussion in this section is general and not intended to be an all-inclusive and comprehensive treatise on the current tax status of variable annuities.

10.40 If an annuity contract qualifies as such under the IRC, a contract holder is generally not taxed on increases in the value of the contract until he or she receives payment in a lump sum or as an annuity under the settlement option elected, nor is he or she taxed upon the investment buildup in cash values. Although the assets and liabilities of the separate account are segregated from the sponsoring life insurance entity's regular business, it is not considered a separate taxable entity. The tax treatment of the separate account depends upon the character of the contracts held by the separate account. If the contracts qualify as variable contracts that are adequately diversified (see paragraphs 10.50–.52), then IRC Section 817 dictates the taxation of the separate account. If the contracts do not qualify as variable or are not adequately diversified, then the activity of the separate account will be governed by the tax rules applicable to life insurance entities under IRC Subchapter L. The separate account is not subject to the tax rules applicable to regulated investment companies (RICs) under IRC Subchapter M.

10.41 Under IRC Section 817, reinvested investment income is applied to increase insurance entity reserves under the contracts, and the increase in reserves is deductible from income. Usually a provision for federal income taxes on investment income or gains is not necessary; therefore, a provision is not made in the variable annuity separate account financial statements.

10.42 IRC Section 817(g) provides that a variable annuity contract will be taxed in the same manner as a traditional or fixed annuity if the payments under the variable contract are computed based on recognized mortality tables and the investment return of the individual segregated account.

10.43 When the UIT approach was developed using mutual funds as the underlying investment, insurers relied on several tax rulings as the basis for treating mutual fund wraparounds similarly to traditional variable annuities.

10.44 In Revenue Ruling 80-274, the IRS concluded that the position of a contract holder of an annuity wrapped around a savings account is as if the investment had been maintained or established directly with a savings and loan association. Thus, the contract holder is taxed on a current basis on the separate account income.

10.45 Revenue Ruling 81-225 states that, for federal income tax purposes, the insurance entity, not the contract holder, will be considered the owner of mutual fund shares underlying investments for an annuity contract, provided that such shares are unavailable to the public. Accordingly, under that ruling, if the mutual fund shares are not available to the public, the contract holder is not treated as the owner of the shares, and dividends applicable to such shares are not currently includable in the contract holder's gross income.

10.46 On August 18, 2003, the IRS published Revenue Rulings 2003-91 and 2003-92. The IRS described Revenue Ruling 2003-91 as a safe harbor from which taxpayers may operate and referred to Revenue Ruling 2003-92 as having clarified and amplified Revenue Ruling 81-225.

10.47   Revenue Ruling 2003-91 described a situation in which a separate account used for funding variable contracts was divided into various subaccounts. The contracts and subaccounts were issued under the following conditions:

- The contract holder could not select or direct a particular investment to be made by the separate account or subaccounts; all investment decisions are made by the insurance entity or separate account in their absolute discretion.

- Investment strategies of the subaccounts are sufficiently broad to prevent a contract holder from making particular investment decisions through investing in a subaccount.

- Only the insurance entity could add or substitute subaccounts or investment strategies and the insurance entity does not communicate or consult with any contract holder regarding investment selection or strategy.

- Investments in the subaccounts are only available through the purchase of variable contracts and are not otherwise publicly available.

10.48   The IRS concluded that such an account did not provide the contract holder direct or indirect control over the separate account or any subaccount asset; thus, the holder would not be considered the tax owner of the underlying assets. The IRS also observed that the ability to allocate premiums or transfer funds between subaccounts did not indicate sufficient control for the contract holder to be treated as the owner, for tax purposes, of the underlying assets.

10.49   Conversely, Revenue Ruling 2003-92 addressed a situation in which an insurance entity proposed to offer deferred variable contracts under which certain qualified purchasers could invest in a limited number of subaccounts, each of which represented an interest in a specific investment partnership that is not publicly traded. If interests in the partnership were also available for purchase by the general public (that is, outside the variable contract structure), the IRS held that the qualified purchaser contract holder, not the insurance entity, would be the owner, for tax purposes, of the partnership interest. However, if interests in the partnership were only available for purchase within variable contract structures, the insurance entity would be considered the owner of the partnership interest.

10.50   IRC Section 817(h) and the regulations thereunder require the investments of a separate account (or the underlying mutual fund, if the separate account is a UIT) to be adequately diversified to qualify as an annuity contract under IRC Section 72 (qualification under IRC Section 72 is necessary to avoid current taxation of both current and built-up earnings of the contract). In order for the separate account to be adequately diversified, the fair value of the largest holding may not exceed 55 percent of the fair value of total assets, the 2 largest holdings may not exceed 70 percent, the 3 largest holdings may not exceed 80 percent, and the 4 largest holdings may not exceed 90 percent (measured on a quarterly basis). Regulation 1.817-5(b)(1) describes what assets must be included in the calculation and what assets may be excluded.

10.51 U.S. government securities are subject to IRC Section 817(h) diversification rules. The treatment of U.S. government securities for purposes of determining separate account diversification is different from that applied to RICs. Under IRC Section 817(h), each government agency or instrumentality is treated as a separate issuer for purposes of diversification testing.

10.52 As an alternative to the general diversification standards described previously, IRC Section 817(h)(2) provides safe harbor diversification standards that are similar to those for RICs and often easier to administer. However, the safe harbor diversification rules differ from those of RICs in that the total assets of the separate account represented by cash, cash items (including receivables), U.S. government securities, or securities of other RICs may not exceed 55 percent of the value of total assets in the account. Regulation 1.817-5(b)(3) provides special rules that apply to a segregated asset account with respect to variable life insurance contracts.

10.53 IRC Section 72(s) provides that a contract should not be treated as an annuity for tax purposes unless it provides for certain required distributions in the event of the contract holder's death.

10.54 IRC Section 72(q) imposes certain penalties on early withdrawals from annuity contracts.

10.55 The federal excise tax rules governing the timing and amounts of distributions do not apply to insurance-related mutual funds if no taxable investors are present. Further, in organizing the separate account, the sponsoring insurance entity may invest taxable seed money of up to $250,000 without subjecting the fund to the excise tax rules (IRC Section 4982).

10.56 Dividends and distributions from the fund to the separate account are usually reinvested. As a result, some insurance funds do not actually pay any dividends or distributions. Rather, they satisfy their fund-level tax qualification tests by using a procedure known as consent dividends (IRC Section 565). Under this procedure, with annual written consent from each investor (that is, the separate accounts), distributions are deemed to be passed through from the fund to the investors. This is manageable operationally because, in practice, the number of separate accounts invested in a single fund is limited.

Illustrative Financial Statements

10.57 The financial statements illustrated in this chapter are for variable annuity separate accounts registered as UITs. For separate accounts with multiple subaccounts, the financial position and results of operations generally should be presented separately for each subaccount. This kind of arrangement is presented with individual columns for each subaccount. The total information for the separate account as a whole is not meaningful. Accordingly, a subaccount that is similar to a series mutual fund is the reporting entity, and the auditor's report could be modified to cover the individual subaccounts (see paragraph 12.24 of this guide). The financial statements of a subaccount may also be presented as if the subaccount were a separate entity. Variable annuity separate accounts registered as management investment companies would prepare financial statements that conform to those presented in chapter 7, "Financial Statements of Investment Companies," of this guide, although certain financial statement notes that follow would also apply. Under the requirements of SEC Form N-4, variable annuity separate accounts registered

as UITs present a period-end statement of assets and liabilities, a statement of operations for the most recent year, and a statement of changes in net assets for the most recent two years in the same manner as a registered investment company. This format is illustrated in the exhibit. Variable life separate accounts registered as UITs on Form N-6 also would follow the form of the exhibit. Certain contract charges (for example, cost of insurance) would be shown on the statement of changes in net assets, which is similar to the presentation of annuity contract charges.

10.58   Certain disclosures required of registered investment companies for compliance with SEC rules and regulations are not presented in the following illustrative financial statements because they are not otherwise required by U.S. generally accepted accounting principles. In addition, certain disclosures are impractical due to the characteristics of the separate account. These disclosures include the following:

- The total cost, for federal income tax purposes, of the portfolio of investments according to Rules 12-12 and 12-12C[5] of Regulation S-X.

- The components of net assets presented as a separate schedule or in the notes to the financial statements according to Rule 6-05.5 of Regulation S-X. However, the net asset value per unit at the beginning and end of each period and the total net assets at the end of the period are to be provided for the most recent five years.

10.59   As stated in FASB ASC 946-205-50-31, separate accounts with more than two levels of contract charges or net unit values per subaccount may elect to present the required financial highlights for contract expense levels that had units issued or outstanding during the reporting period (including number of units, unit fair value, net assets, expense ratio, investment income ratio, and total return) for either

a. each contract expense level that results in a distinct net unit value and for which units were issued or outstanding during each reporting period or

b. the range of the lowest and highest level of expense ratio and the related total return and unit fair values during each reporting period.

The calculation of the ranges for the total return and unit fair values should correspond to the groupings that produced the lowest and highest expense ratios.

10.60   Paragraphs 32–34 of FASB ASC 946-205-50 explain that the financial highlights table in the separate account's financial statements should state clearly that the expense ratio considers only the expenses borne directly by the separate account and excludes expenses incurred directly by the underlying funds or charged through the redemption of units. If the ranges of expense ratios, total returns, and unit fair values are presented, the insurance enterprise should disclose instances in which individual contract values do not fall within the ranges presented (for example, if a new product is introduced

---

[5] Amendments to Article 12 of Regulation S-X permit a registered investment company to include a summary portfolio schedule in its reports to shareholders. Refer to chapter 7 of this guide for further discussion of U.S. generally accepted accounting principles applicable for the preparation of financial statements of investment companies.

late in a reporting period and the total return does not fall within the range). The expense disclosure should also include ranges of all fees that are charged by the separate account and a description of those fees, including whether they are assessed as direct reductions in unit values or through the redemption of units for all policies contained within the separate account.

> ***Note:*** The illustrative financial statements and note disclosures included in this guide have been updated to reflect FASB ASC. However, in FASB's notice to constituents, it suggests the use of plain English in financial statement note disclosures to describe broad FASB ASC topic references. FASB suggests a reference similar to "as required by the Derivatives and Hedging Topic of the FASB *Accounting Standards Codification*." Entities might consider revising their financial statement references to reflect this plain English referencing, rather than the use of specific FASB ASC references. The AICPA has provided these detailed references as a resource for its users.

10.61

**ABC Variable Annuity Separate Account I
of ABC Life Insurance Company
Statement of Assets and Liabilities
December 31, 20X8**

	Money Market	*Equity Index*
Assets:		
ABC Investment Fund		
Investments at fair value:		
Money Market Portfolio, 57,231,590 shares (cost: $57,231,590)	$57,231,590	$—
Equity Index Portfolio, 23,961,595 shares (cost: $325,054,036)	—	350,797,752
Total assets	57,231,590	350,797,752
Liabilities:		
Payable to ABC Life Insurance Company	—	46,109
	$57,231,590	$350,751,643
Net assets:		
Accumulation units	$57,231,590	$349,750,644
Contracts in payout (annuitization) period	—	610,108
Retained in Separate Account I by ABC Life Insurance Company	—	390,891
Total net assets	$57,231,590	$350,751,643
Units outstanding	4,136,795	19,674,291
Unit value (accumulation)	$13.83	$17.83

The accompanying notes are an integral part of these financial statements.

10.62

ABC Variable Annuity Separate Account I
of ABC Life Insurance Company
Statement of Operations
for the Year Ended December 31, 20X8

	Money Market	*Equity Index*
Income:		
Dividends	$4,602,399	$6,450,878
Expenses:		
Mortality and expense risk	548,224	1,753,874
Administrative charges[6]	182,741	584,624
Net investment income	3,871,434	4,112,380
Realized gains (losses) on investments		
Realized gain on sale of fund shares	—	4,050,008
Realized gain distributions	—	400,900
Realized gain	—	4,450,908
Change in unrealized appreciation during the year	—	20,728,111
Net increase in net assets from operations	$3,871,434	$29,291,399

The accompanying notes are an integral part of these financial statements.

---

[6] If, under the annuity contract, the administrative charge is levied as a direct charge to the contract holders' accounts, rather than against the separate account, this would be included as an item separate from contract transactions in the statement of changes in net assets. In such cases, the exclusion of the direct charges from the expense ratios appearing in the financial highlights should be noted. If the charge is applied uniformly to all accounts based on the value of the contract holder's account, consideration should be given to indicating the effect of the charge on contract holder costs (expressed as a percentage of net assets) in the note.

10.63

ABC Variable Annuity Separate Account I
of ABC Life Insurance Company
Statement of Changes in Net Assets
for the Years Ended December 31, 20X8 and 20X7

	Money Market		Equity Index	
	20X8	*20X7*	*20X8*	*20X7*
Increase in net assets from operations:				
Net investment income	$3,871,434	$3,534,624	$4,112,380	$1,100,710
Realized gains	—	—	4,450,908	462,877
Unrealized appreciation during the year	—	—	20,728,111	22,480,579
Net increase in net assets from operations	3,871,434	3,534,624	29,291,399	24,044,166
Contract transactions:				
Payments received from contract owners	14,367,366	17,444,822	37,527,318	11,075,691
Transfers between subaccounts (including fixed account), net	(15,063,795)	(18,267,246)	155,175,016	59,808,957
Transfers for contract benefits and terminations	(11,945,485)	(10,017,075)	(4,238,812)	(1,639,933)
Contract maintenance charges	(40,061)	(51,366)	(210,505)	(65,202)
Adjustments to net assets allocated to contracts in payout period	—	—	6,500	—
Net increase (decrease) in net assets from contract transactions	(12,681,975)	(10,890,865)	188,259,517	69,179,513
Increase (decrease) in amounts retained in Variable Annuity Account I, net	—	—	90,967	(122,904)
Total increase (decrease) in net assets	(8,810,541)	(7,356,241)	217,641,883	93,100,775
Net assets at beginning of period	66,042,131	73,398,372	133,109,760	40,008,985
Net assets at end of period	$57,231,590	$66,042,131	$350,751,643	$133,109,760

The accompanying notes are an integral part of these financial statements.

10.64

ABC Variable Annuity Separate Account I
of ABC Life Insurance Company
Notes to Financial Statements

1. Organization

The ABC Variable Annuity Separate Account I (Separate Account I), a unit investment trust registered under the Investment Company Act of 1940, as amended, was established by ABC Life Insurance Company (ABC) on April 1, 20XX, and exists in accordance with the regulations of the New York Insurance Department. Separate Account I is a funding vehicle for individual variable annuity contracts. Separate Account I currently consists of two investment divisions: Money Market and Equity Index, each of which is treated as an individual separate account. Each investment division invests all its investible assets in the corresponding portfolio of ABC Investment Fund, Inc.

Under applicable insurance law, the assets and liabilities of Separate Account I are clearly identified and distinguished from ABC's other assets and liabilities. The portion of Separate Account I's assets applicable to the variable annuity contracts is not chargeable with liabilities arising out of any other business ABC may conduct.

2. Significant Accounting Policies

Investments are made in the portfolios of ABC Investment Fund and valued at fair value based on the reported net asset values of such portfolios, which in turn value their investment securities at fair value. Transactions are recorded on a trade date basis. Dividend income and realized gain distributions are recorded on the ex-distribution date.

Realized gains and losses on the sales of investments are computed on the basis of the identified cost of the investment sold.

Net assets allocated to contracts in the payout period are computed according to the 1983a Individual Annuitant Mortality Table. The assumed investment return is 3.5 percent unless the annuitant elects otherwise, in which case the rate may vary from 3.5 percent to 7 percent, as regulated by the laws of the respective states. The mortality risk is fully borne by ABC and may result in additional amounts being transferred into the variable annuity account by ABC to cover greater longevity of annuitants than expected. Conversely, if amounts allocated exceed amounts required, transfers may be made to the insurance entity.

The operations of Separate Account I are included in the federal income tax return of ABC, which is taxed as a life insurance entity under the provisions of the IRC. Under the current provisions of the IRC, ABC does not expect to incur federal income taxes on the earnings of Separate Account I to the extent that the earnings are credited under the contracts. Based on this, no charge is being made currently to Separate Account I for federal income taxes. ABC will review periodically the status of this policy in the event of changes in the tax law. A charge may be made in future years for any federal income taxes that would be attributable to the contracts.

Separate Account I follows the accounting and reporting guidance in FASB *Accounting Standards Codification* 946. The preparation of financial statements in accordance with U.S. generally accepted accounting principles (GAAP) requires management to make estimates and assumptions that affect amounts reported therein. Actual results could differ from these estimates.

3. Investments

As described in note 2, Separate Account I measures the fair value of its investment in ABC Investment Fund on a recurring basis. GAAP establishes a hierarchy that prioritizes inputs to valuation methods. The three levels of inputs are as follows:

- *Level 1.* Unadjusted quoted prices in active markets for identical assets or liabilities that Separate Account I has the ability to access.

- *Level 2.* Observable inputs other than quoted prices included in level 1 that are observable for the asset or liability either directly or indirectly. These inputs may include quoted prices for the identical instrument on an inactive market, prices for similar instruments, interest rates, prepayment speeds, credit risk, yield curves, default rates, and similar data.

- *Level 3.* Unobservable inputs for the asset or liability, to the extent observable inputs are not available, representing Separate Account I's own assumptions about the assumptions that a market participant would use in valuing the asset or liability, and that would be based on the best information available.

The following table summarizes the inputs used to value Separate Account I's assets measured at fair value as of December 31, 20X8.[7]

Valuation Inputs	Money Market	Equity Index
Level 1	$57,231,590	$350,797,752
Level 2	—	—
Level 3	—	—
Total	$57,231,590	$350,797,752

There were no transfers between level 1 and level 2 during the year.

The cost of purchases and proceeds from sales of investments for the year ended December 31, 20X8 were as follows:

	Purchases	Sales
Money Market Subaccount	$13,855,466	$22,666,007
Equity Index Subaccount	245,503,854	37,232,105

4. Expenses and Related-Party Transactions

ABC deducts a daily charge from the net assets of Separate Account I equivalent to an effective annual rate of 0.25 percent for administrative expenses and 0.75 percent for the assumption of mortality and expense risks. ABC also deducts an annual maintenance charge of $35 for each contract from the ABC Retirement Reserves Contract value. The maintenance charge, which is recorded as a redemption in the accompanying statement of changes in net assets, is waived on certain contracts.

---

[7] The classification of various financial instruments in this table is for illustrative purposes only and should not be construed as recommended practice for any particular financial instrument or class of financial instruments.

Additionally, during the year ended December 31, 20X8, management fees were paid indirectly to ABC Management Company, an affiliate of ABC in its capacity as adviser to ABC Investment Fund. The fund's advisory agreement provides for a fee at the annual rate of 0.15 percent of the average net assets of the Money Market Fund and 0.45 percent of the average net assets of the Equity Index Fund.

[Other: Consider disclosures of other fees to affiliates not otherwise disclosed, such as sales load charges retained by the insurance entity.]

5. Changes in Units Outstanding

The changes in units outstanding for the years ended December 31, 20X8 and 20X7 were as follows:

	Money Market		Equity Index	
	20X8	*20X7*	*20X8*	*20X7*
Units issued	1,075,828	1,346,281	11,530,377	5,387,478
Units redeemed	(1,967,393)	(2,191,438)	(268,220)	(115,368)
Net increase (decrease)	(891,565)	(845,157)	11,262,157	5,272,110

6. Unit Values

A summary of unit values and units outstanding for variable annuity contracts, net investment income ratios, and expense ratios, excluding expenses of the underlying funds, for each of the five years in the period ended December 31, 20X8, follows:

a. The following format should be presented if the insurance enterprise chooses to disclose each contract expense level that results in a distinct net unit value and for which units were issued or outstanding during each of the five years ended December 31, 20X8.

Units	Net Assets		Investment Income Ratio [8]	Expense Ratio[9]	Total Return[10]
	Unit Value	(000s)			
Money Market Investment Division					
December 31					
20X8					
4,136,795	$13.83	$57,232	5.25%	1.00%	5.30%
20X7					
5,028,360	13.13	66,042	5.02	1.00	5.07
20X6					
5,873,517	12.50	73,398	8.46	1.00	8.54
20X5					
2,058,353	11.52	23,705	8.23	1.00	8.31
20X4					
967,550	10.63	10,291	6.24	1.00	6.30
7/1/X3					
500,000	10.00	5,000			

[8] These amounts represent the dividends, excluding distributions of capital gains (both long-term and short-term), received by the subaccount from the underlying mutual fund, net of management fees assessed by the fund investment adviser, divided by the average net assets. These ratios exclude those expenses, such as mortality and expense charges, that are assessed against contract owner accounts either through reductions in the unit values or the redemption of units. The recognition of investment income by the subaccount is affected by the timing of the declaration of dividends by the underlying fund in which the subaccount invests.

[9] These amounts represent the annualized contract expenses of the separate account, consisting primarily of mortality and expense charges, for each period indicated. These ratios include only those expenses that result in a direct reduction to unit values. Charges made directly to contract owner accounts through the redemption of units and expenses of the underlying fund have been excluded.

[10] These amounts represent the total return for the periods indicated, including changes in the value of the underlying fund, and expenses assessed through the reduction of unit values. These ratios do not include any expenses assessed through the redemption of units. Investment options with a date notation indicate the effective date of that investment option in the variable account. The total return is calculated for each period indicated or from the effective date through the end of the reporting period.

Units	Net Assets Unit Value	Net Assets (000s)	Investment Income Ratio[11]	Expense Ratio[12]	Total Return[13]
Equity Index Division					
December 31					
20X8					
19,674,291	$17.83	$350,752	2.23%	1.00%	12.68%
20X7					
8,412,134	15.82	133,110	2.35	1.00	24.16
20X6					
3,140,024	12.74	40,009	3.12	1.00	(9.50)
20X5					
3,879,972	14.08	54,630	3.24	1.00	11.94
20X4					
2,162,080	12.58	27,195	3.98	1.00	6.20

b. The following format should be presented if the insurance enterprise chooses to present the range of the lowest to highest level of expense ratio and the related total return and unit fair values during each of the five years ended December 31, 20X8. Certain of the information is presented as a range of minimum to maximum values based on the product grouping representing the minimum and maximum expense ratio amounts.

	At December 31			For the Year Ended December 31		
	Units (000s)	Unit Fair Value Lowest to Highest	Net Assets (000s)	Investment[14] Income Ratio	Expense Ratio[15] Lowest to Highest	Total Return[16] Lowest to Highest
Money Market Investment Division						
20X8	4,137	$10.51–$14.06	$57,232	5.25%	1.00%–2.65%	4.10%–5.30%
20X7	5,028	10.00–13.20	66,042	5.02	1.00–2.60	4.01–5.07
20X6	5,874	9.37–13.21	73,398	8.46	1.00–2.60	7.45–8.54
20X5	2,058	8.72–12.23	23,705	8.23	1.00–2.55	5.65–8.31
20X4	968	8.25–12.50	10,291	6.24	1.00–2.45	5.25–6.30

(continued)

---

[11] See footnote 8.
[12] See footnote 9.
[13] See footnote 10.
[14] See footnote 8.
[15] See footnote 9.
[16] These amounts represent the total return for the periods indicated, including changes in the value of the underlying fund, and expenses assessed through the reduction of unit values. These ratios do not include any expenses assessed through the redemption of units. Investment options with a date notation indicate the effective date of that investment option in the variable account. The total return is calculated for each period indicated or from the effective date through the end of the reporting period. Because the total return is presented as a range of minimum to maximum values, based on the product grouping representing the minimum and maximum expense ratio amounts, some individual contract total returns are not within the ranges presented.

	At December 31			For the Year Ended December 31		
Units (000s)	Unit Fair Value Lowest to Highest	Net Assets (000s)	Investment Income Ratio	Expense Ratio Lowest to Highest	Total Return Lowest to Highest	

Equity Index Division

Year	Units (000s)	Unit Fair Value	Net Assets (000s)	Investment Income Ratio	Expense Ratio	Total Return
20X8	19,674	$10.51–$19.06	$350,752	2.23%	1.00%–2.65%	5.10%–12.18%
20X7	8,412	10.00–20.20	133,110	2.35	1.00–2.60	6.80–24.16
20X6	3,140	9.37–14.21	40,009	3.12	1.00–2.60	(9.50)–9.10
20X5	3,880	8.72–15.23	54,630	3.24	1.00–2.55	5.65–11.94
20X4	2,162	8.25–13.50	27,195	3.98	1.00–2.45	5.25–6.20

c. An insurance enterprise may choose to present all expenses that are charged by the separate account in either a table or narrative format. The disclosure should list all fees that are charged by the separate account and a description of those fees, including whether they are assessed as direct reductions in unit values or through the redemption of units for all policies contained within the separate account. For this example, expenses disclosed are based on the ranges of all products within the separate account; the expenses may also be listed in more detail (for example, individual charges broken out by products within the separate account) in either table or narrative format.

ABC Variable Annuity Separate Account I

Mortality and Expense Charge
Basic charges are assessed through reduction of unit values.   1.00%–1.70%

Death Benefit Options
The options are assessed through reduction in unit values:

- Ratchet Option—Equal to the highest account balance among prior specified anniversary dates adjusted for deposits less partial withdrawals since the specified anniversary date   0.15%–0.20%

- Roll-Up Option—Equal to the total of deposits made to the contract less an adjustment for partial withdrawals, accumulated at a specified interest rate   0.20%–0.40%

Guaranteed Minimum Income Benefits
These benefits are assessed through a reduction in unit values and provide that the periodic annuity benefits will

- not fall below a contractually specified level.   0.20%–0.55%

- be based on the higher of actual account values at the date that the policy owner elects to annuitize or a contractually specified amount.   0.30%–0.40%

Administrative Charge

Years 1–5: $30
This charge is assessed through the redemption of units.   Years 6+: $10

Alternatively, the expense ratio represents the annualized contract expenses of ABC Variable Annuity Separate Account I for the period indicated and includes only those expenses that are charged through a reduction of the unit value. Included in this category are mortality and expense charges and the cost of any riders that the policyholder has elected. These fees range between 1.00 percent and 2.65 percent, depending on the product and options selected. Expenses of the underlying fund portfolios and charges made directly to contract owner accounts through the redemption of units are excluded. For this separate account, charges made through the redemption of units ranged from $10 to $30 per policy annually.

Chapter 11

General Auditing Considerations[1, 2]

Chapter Overview

11.01 This chapter provides selected general auditing considerations on the application of generally accepted auditing standards (GAAS) during an investment company audit. The chapter begins with general audit planning considerations that focus on the audit risk assessment process and the design of audit procedures that respond to identified risks. Audit planning considerations are followed by other general considerations for audits of investment companies. After other general considerations are discussed, the chapter turns to focus on auditing procedures specific to the investment portfolio accounts of an investment company. A variety of relevant subtopics are discussed in this section, including: the custody of securities, tests of portfolio transactions (including transactions with affiliates), income from securities, testing net asset value per share, and testing the valuation of portfolio investments. The chapter concludes with three appendixes that provide detailed considerations pertaining to (*a*) the auditor's responsibility for other information in documents containing audited financial statements, (*b*) reports on controls at outside service organizations, and (*c*) fraud risk assessment and audit responses.

11.02 Although this chapter is dedicated to general and investment portfolio auditing considerations, other chapters throughout this guide also contain auditing considerations directly related to those respective chapter topics. The following table may be helpful for readers interested in auditing considerations specific to the following topics.

Topic	Reference
Capital accounts	Chapter 4
Master-feeder structures	Chapter 5
Funds of funds structures	Chapter 5
Interim financial statements	Chapter 7
Other accounts and considerations	Chapter 8
Separate accounts of life insurance entities	Chapter 10
Auditor's reports and management representations	Chapter 12

---

[1] The auditing content in this guide focuses primarily on generally accepted auditing standards issued by the Auditing Standards Board and is applicable to audits of nonissuers. See the section "Applicability of Generally Accepted Auditing Standards and PCAOB Standards" of the preface to this guide for a discussion of the definitions of issuer and nonissuer as used throughout this guide. Appendix B, "Clarified Auditing Standards and PCAOB Standards," of this guide is included to assist auditors in comparing the clarified standards, many of which are referenced throughout this guide, to the PCAOB standards. Further, considerations for audits of issuers in accordance with PCAOB standards may be discussed within this guide's chapter text. When such discussion is provided, the related paragraphs are designated with the following title: *Considerations for Audits Performed in Accordance With PCAOB Standards*.

[2] For additional nonauthoritative guidance pertaining to internal control and risk assessment, refer to Technical Questions and Answers (Q&A) sections 8200.05–.16 (AICPA, *Questions and Answers*).

11.03 AU-C section 200, *Overall Objectives of the Independent Auditor and the Conduct of an Audit in Accordance With Generally Accepted Auditing Standards* (AICPA, *Professional Standards*), addresses the independent auditor's overall responsibilities when conducting an audit of financial statements in accordance with GAAS. Specifically, it sets out the overall objectives of the independent auditor (the auditor) and explains the nature and scope of an audit designed to enable the auditor to meet those objectives. It also explains the scope, authority, and structure of GAAS and includes requirements establishing the general responsibilities of the auditor applicable in all audits, including the obligation to comply with GAAS.

General Audit Planning Considerations

Audit Risk

11.04 Paragraph .A36 of AU-C section 200 explains that audit risk is a function of the risks of material misstatement and detection risk. The assessment of risks is based on audit procedures to obtain information necessary for that purpose and evidence obtained throughout the audit. The assessment of risks is a matter of professional judgment, rather than a matter capable of precise measurement.

11.05 Paragraphs .A38–.A40 of AU-C section 200 provide further explanation on the two levels of the risks of material misstatement. The risks of material misstatement exist at the overall financial statement level and the assertion level for classes of transactions, account balances, and disclosures. Risks of material misstatement at the overall financial statement level refer to risks of material misstatement that relate pervasively to the financial statements as a whole and potentially affect many assertions. Risks of material misstatement at the assertion level are assessed in order to determine the nature, timing, and extent of further audit procedures necessary to obtain sufficient appropriate audit evidence. This evidence enables the auditor to express an opinion on the financial statements at an acceptably low level of audit risk.

11.06 Paragraph .A44 of AU-C section 200 explains that the assessment of the risks of material misstatement may be expressed in quantitative terms, such as percentages, or in nonquantitative terms. This could be expressed, for example, as high, medium, or low.

Risk Assessment Procedures

11.07 AU-C section 315, *Understanding the Entity and Its Environment and Assessing the Risks of Material Misstatement* (AICPA, *Professional Standards*), addresses the auditor's responsibility to identify and assess the risks of material misstatement in the financial statements through understanding the entity and its environment, including the entity's internal control.

11.08 Obtaining an understanding of the entity and its environment, including the entity's internal control (referred to hereafter as an understanding of the entity), is a continuous, dynamic process of gathering, updating, and analyzing information throughout the audit. As stated in paragraph .A1 of AU-C section 315, the understanding of the entity establishes a frame of reference within which the auditor plans the audit and exercises professional judgment throughout the audit when, for example

- assessing risks of material misstatement of the financial statements;

- determining materiality in accordance with AU-C section 320, *Materiality in Planning and Performing an Audit* (AICPA, *Professional Standards*);

- considering the appropriateness of the selection and application of accounting policies and the adequacy of financial statement disclosures;

- identifying areas for which special audit consideration may be necessary (for example, related party transactions,[3] the appropriateness of management's use of the going concern assumption,[4] considering the business purpose of transactions, or the existence of complex and unusual transactions);

- developing expectations for use when performing analytical procedures;

- responding to the assessed risks of material misstatement, including designing and performing further audit procedures to obtain sufficient appropriate audit evidence; and

- evaluating the sufficiency and appropriateness of audit evidence obtained, such as the appropriateness of assumptions and management's oral and written representations.

Risk Assessment Procedures and Related Activities

11.09 It is not acceptable to simply deem risk to be at the maximum. In accordance with paragraph .05 of AU-C section 315, the auditor should perform risk assessment procedures to provide a basis for the identification and assessment of risks of material misstatement at the financial statement and relevant assertion levels. Risk assessment procedures by themselves, however, do not provide sufficient appropriate audit evidence on which to base the audit opinion. For purposes of GAAS, *risk assessment procedures* are defined in AU-C section 315 as audit procedures performed to obtain an understanding of the entity and its environment, including the entity's internal control, to identify and assess the risks of material misstatement, whether due to fraud or error, at the financial statement and relevant assertion levels.

11.10 The auditor is required to exercise professional judgment[5] to determine the extent of the required understanding of the entity. Paragraph .A3

---

[3] The PCAOB released Auditing Standard No. 18, *Related Parties* (AICPA, *PCAOB Standards and Related Rules*, Auditing Standards), in June 2014 and is effective for audits of fiscal years beginning on or after December 15, 2014. Auditing Standard No. 18 establishes requirements regarding the auditor's evaluation of a company's identification of, accounting for, and disclosure of relationships and transactions between the company and its related parties. The auditor's objective is to obtain sufficient appropriate audit evidence to determine whether related parties and relationships and transactions with related parties have been properly identified, accounted for, and disclosed in the financial statements.

[4] The PCAOB released Staff Audit Practice Alert No. 13, *Matters Related to the Auditor's Consideration of a Company's Ability to Continue as a Going Concern* (AICPA, *PCAOB Standards and Related Rules*, PCAOB Staff Guidance, sec. 400.13), in September 2014 to discuss the professional standards applicable to the auditor's evaluation of a company's ability to continue as a going concern. Readers are encouraged to read the full text of the alert, available at www.pcaobus.org/Standards/QandA/09222014 SAPA 13.pdf.

[5] Paragraph .18 of AU-C section 200, *Overall Objectives of the Independent Auditor and the Conduct of an Audit in Accordance With Generally Accepted Auditing Standards* (AICPA, *Professional Standards*), requires the auditor to exercise professional judgment in planning and performing an audit of financial statements.

of AU-C section 315 states that the auditor's primary consideration is whether the understanding of the entity that has been obtained is sufficient to meet the objectives of AU-C section 315. The depth of the overall understanding that is required by the auditor is less than that possessed by management in managing the entity.

11.11 Paragraph .06 of AU-C section 315 states that the risk assessment procedures should include the following:

- Inquiries of management, appropriate individuals within the internal audit function (if such function exists), and others within the entity who, in the auditor's professional judgment, may have information that is likely to assist in identifying risks of material misstatement due to fraud or error
- Analytical procedures
- Observation and inspection

Understanding the Entity and Its Environment, Including the Entity's Internal Control[6]

11.12 Paragraph .12 of AU-C section 315 states that the auditor should obtain an understanding of the following:

a. Relevant industry, regulatory, and other external factors, including the applicable financial reporting framework.

b. The nature of the entity, including

     i. its operations;

     ii. its ownership and governance structures;

     iii. the types of investments that the entity is making and plans to make, including investments in entities formed to accomplish specific objectives; and

     iv. the way that the entity is structured and how it is financed,

to enable the auditor to understand the classes of transactions, account balances, and disclosures to be expected in the financial statements.

c. The entity's selection and application of accounting policies, including the reasons for changes thereto. The auditor should evaluate whether the entity's accounting policies are appropriate for its business and consistent with the applicable financial reporting framework and accounting policies used in the relevant industry.

d. The entity's objectives and strategies and those related business risks that may result in risks of material misstatement.

e. The measurement and review of the entity's financial performance.

Appendix A, "Understanding the Entity and Its Environment," of AU-C section 315 contains examples of matters that the auditor may consider in obtaining an understanding of the entity and its environment.

---

[6] In May 2013, the Committee of Sponsoring Organizations of the Treadway Commission (COSO) published the updated *Internal Control—Integrated Framework* (2013 COSO framework). Although the auditing standards do not require a specific internal control framework, the COSO framework is widely used by entities for designing, implementing, and conducting internal control. The 2013 COSO framework provides guidance useful to auditors in understanding and evaluating internal control.

Paragraphs .13–.14 of AU-C section 315 state that the auditor should obtain an understanding of internal control relevant to the audit and, in doing so, should evaluate the design of those controls and determine whether they have been implemented by performing procedures in addition to inquiry of the entity's personnel. Further audit requirements and application guidance regarding the components of internal control can be found in paragraphs .15–.25 and .A78–.A107, respectively, of AU-C section 315. Appendix B, "Internal Control Components," of AU-C section 315 contains additional detailed explanation of the internal control components.

Risk Assessment and the Design of Further Audit Procedures

11.13 To provide a basis for designing and performing further audit procedures, paragraphs .26–.27 of AU-C section 315 state that the auditor should identify and assess the risks of material misstatement at the financial statement level and the relevant assertion level for classes of transactions, account balances, and disclosures. For this purpose, the auditor should

   a. identify risks throughout the process of obtaining an understanding of the entity and its environment, including relevant controls that relate to the risks, by considering the classes of transactions, account balances, and disclosures in the financial statements;

   b. assess the identified risks and evaluate whether they relate more pervasively to the financial statements as a whole and potentially affect many assertions;

   c. relate the identified risks to what can go wrong at the relevant assertion level, taking account of relevant controls that the auditor intends to test; and

   d. consider the likelihood of misstatement, including the possibility of multiple misstatements, and whether the potential misstatement is of a magnitude that could result in a material misstatement.

11.14 AU-C section 330, *Performing Audit Procedures in Response to Assessed Risks and Evaluating the Audit Evidence Obtained* (AICPA, *Professional Standards*), addresses the auditor's responsibility to design and implement responses to risks of material misstatement identified and assessed by the auditor in accordance with AU-C section 315 and to evaluate the audit evidence obtained in an audit of financial statements.

11.15 See appendix C, "Consideration of Fraud in a Financial Statement Audit," of this chapter for further consideration on how AU-C sections 315 and 330 are to be applied regarding risks of material misstatement due to fraud.

11.16

Considerations for Audits Performed in Accordance With PCAOB Standards

The PCAOB's suite of risk assessment standards (Auditing Standard Nos. 8–15 [AICPA, *PCAOB Standards and Related Rules*, Auditing Standards]) set forth requirements that are intended to enhance the effectiveness of the auditor's assessment of, and response to, the risks of material misstatement in the financial statements. The risk assessment standards address audit procedures performed throughout the audit, from the initial planning stages to the evaluation of the audit results. Appendix 11, "Comparison of the Objectives and Requirements of the Accompanying PCAOB Auditing Standards with the Analogous

Standards of the International Auditing and Assurance Standards Board and the Auditing Standards Board of the American Institute of Certified Public Accountants," of PCAOB Release No. 2010-004, *Auditing Standards Related to the Auditor's Assessment of and Response to Risk and Related Amendments to PCAOB Standards*, discusses certain differences between the objectives and requirements of the PCAOB risk assessment standards and the analogous standards of the International Auditing and Assurance Standards Board and the Auditing Standards Board. For example, Auditing Standard No. 12, *Identifying and Assessing Risks of Material Misstatement* (AICPA, *PCAOB Standards and Related Rules*, Auditing Standards), includes a requirement to evaluate, while obtaining an understanding of the company, whether significant changes in the company from prior periods, including changes in its internal control over financial reporting, affect the risks of material misstatement. As another example, the auditor is also required to consider performing certain procedures as part of obtaining an understanding of the company, including observing or reading transcripts of earnings calls, obtaining an understanding of compensation arrangements with senior management, and obtaining information about trading activity in the company's securities and holdings in the company's securities by significant holders. Please note, however, that appendix 11 of the release is not a comprehensive list of all differences between the sets of standards.

Other General Considerations for Audits of Investment Companies

11.17   AU-C section 501, *Audit Evidence—Specific Considerations for Selected Items* (AICPA, *Professional Standards*),[7] addresses specific considerations by the auditor in obtaining sufficient appropriate audit evidence, in accordance with AU-C section 330; AU-C section 500, *Audit Evidence* (AICPA, *Professional Standards*); and other relevant AU-C sections, regarding, among other things, certain aspects of investments in securities and derivative instruments. AU-C section 540, *Auditing Accounting Estimates, Including Fair Value Accounting Estimates, and Related Disclosures* (AICPA, *Professional Standards*), addresses the auditor's responsibilities relating to accounting estimates, including fair value accounting estimates and related disclosures, in an audit of financial statements. Specifically, it expands on how AU-C sections 315 and 330 and other relevant AU-C sections are to be applied with regard to accounting estimates. It also includes requirements and guidance related to misstatements of individual accounting estimates and indicators of possible management bias. See paragraphs 11.60–.76 for further discussion on the guidance contained in AU-C section 540. The audit of an investment company's investment accounts is a significant portion of the overall audit because of the relative significance of those accounts and the related income accounts. In auditing the investment accounts, the auditor could test various aspects of the investment company's transactions with brokers, custodians, and pricing services. See the "Auditing Procedures for the Investment Portfolio Accounts" section of this chapter for more information.

---

[7] For guidance on implementing the audit requirements regarding securities and derivative instruments, the reader should refer to the AICPA Audit Guide *Special Considerations in Auditing Financial Instruments*.

11.18   Economic conditions in the jurisdictions in which funds invest may affect the auditor's assessment of inherent risks for relevant assertions in investment companies' financial statements. Factors that the auditor could evaluate include local rates of inflation, government stability, and local tax rules. An auditor could consider whether such indicators create, intensify, or mitigate inherent risk.

11.19   An auditor ordinarily does not have a sufficient basis for recognizing possible violations of security regulations or laws concerning compliance with investment restrictions because they relate more to the entity's operating aspects than its financial and accounting aspects. Even when violations of such laws can have consequences material to the financial statements, the auditor may not become aware of the existence of these acts of noncompliance unless the auditor is informed by the client, or there is evidence of a governmental agency investigation or enforcement proceeding in the records, documents, or other information inspected in an audit of financial statements. When an auditor becomes aware of the possibility of noncompliance, he or she should refer to AU-C section 250, *Consideration of Laws and Regulations in an Audit of Financial Statements* (AICPA, *Professional Standards*).

11.20   The auditor may review such relevant investment company documents as the latest private placement memorandum, offering memorandum, prospectus, statement of additional information, certificate of incorporation, bylaws, and minutes of the board of directors' or trustees' and shareholders' meetings to gain an understanding of the investment company's investment restrictions and consider whether management has a program to prevent, deter, or detect noncompliance with the investment company's investment restrictions. As part of that consideration, the auditor could also obtain the written compliance policies and procedures designed to prevent the violation of federal securities laws (the "compliance program") and could meet with the designated chief compliance officer responsible for administering those policies and procedures (see paragraph 2.52 and paragraph C.34 in appendix C of this chapter). The auditor could also consider whether the compliance program has identified noncompliance with the stated investment restrictions and test the operation of the program to the extent considered necessary. An investment company's failure to comply with its stated investment restrictions may be considered a possible act of noncompliance that may have an indirect effect on the financial statements of the fund. Auditors of registered investment companies may also be required, under certain circumstances, pursuant to the Private Securities Litigation Reform Act of 1995 (codified in section 10A[b]1 of the Securities Exchange Act of 1934) to make a report to the SEC relating to an illegal act that has a material effect on the financial statements.

11.21   In reading the board of directors' or trustees' minutes, the auditor should note such significant items as dividend declarations, capital changes, and amendments to and continuation of contracts and agreements with such entities as the adviser, distributor, transfer agent, custodian, and underwriter. The auditor should note changes in fee structures or expense limitations for reference in auditing expenses.

11.22   As part of the certification of financial statements required by the Sarbanes-Oxley Act of 2002, the principal executive officer and principal financial officer of an investment company filing financial statements on Form N-CSR are required to disclose to the investment company's audit committee and independent auditors all significant deficiencies and material weaknesses in the design or operation of internal control over financial reporting that are reasonably likely to adversely affect the investment company's ability to record, process, summarize, and report financial information. Further, they are to disclose to the audit committee and auditors any fraud, regardless of whether it is material, that involves management or other employees who have a significant role in the investment company's internal control over financial reporting.

11.23 AU-C section 230, *Audit Documentation* (AICPA, *Professional Standards*), addresses the auditor's responsibility to prepare audit documentation for an audit of financial statements. The exhibit, "Audit Documentation Requirements in Other AU-C Sections" (see paragraph .A30 of AU-C section 230), lists other AU-C sections that contain specific documentation requirements and guidance. The specific documentation requirements of other AU-C sections do not limit the application of AU-C section 230. Law, regulation, or other standards may establish additional documentation requirements.

11.24 AU-C section 260, *The Auditor's Communication With Those Charged With Governance* (AICPA, *Professional Standards*), addresses the auditor's responsibility to communicate with those charged with governance in an audit of financial statements. Although this section applies regardless of an entity's governance structure or size, particular considerations apply when all those charged with governance are involved in managing an entity. This section does not establish requirements regarding the auditor's communication with an entity's management or owners unless they are also charged with a governance role.

11.25

Considerations for Audits Performed in Accordance With PCAOB Standards

Auditing Standard No. 16, *Communications with Audit Committees* (AICPA, *PCAOB Standards and Related Rules*, Auditing Standards), establishes certain required communications between the auditor and the audit committee regarding the conduct of the audit. The standard also establishes requirements that the auditor obtain certain information from the audit committee relevant to the audit. The timing, form, and documentation of the established communications are also discussed in the standard. As it relates to the timing of communications between the auditor and the audit committee, paragraph 26 of Auditing Standard No. 16 states

> All audit committee communications required by this standard should be made in a timely manner and prior to the issuance of the auditor's report. The appropriate timing of a particular communication to the audit committee depends on factors such as the significance of the matters to be communicated and corrective or follow-up action needed, unless other timing requirements are specified by PCAOB rules or standards or the securities laws.

> [Note: An auditor may communicate to only the audit committee chair if done in order to communicate matters in a timely manner during the audit. The auditor, however, should communicate such matters to the audit committee prior to the issuance of the auditor's report.]

Footnote 43 of Auditing Standard No. 16 specifically expands on this requirement for registered investment companies:

> Consistent with Rule 2-07 of SEC Regulation S-X, in the case of a registered investment company, audit committee communication should occur annually, and if the annual communication is not within 90 days prior to the filing of the auditor's report, the auditor should provide an update in the 90-day period prior to the filing of the auditor's report, of any changes to the previously reported information.

11.26 AU-C section 265, *Communicating Internal Control Related Matters Identified in an Audit* (AICPA, *Professional Standards*), addresses the auditor's responsibility to appropriately communicate to those charged with governance and management deficiencies in internal control that the auditor has identified in an audit of financial statements.

Internal Control Considerations

11.27 Establishing and maintaining internal control over financial reporting is an important management responsibility. In establishing specific controls that will enable an investment company to record, process, summarize, and report financial data that is consistent with management's assertions in the financial statements, management may wish to consider the following specific objectives:

- Transactions are executed in accordance with management's general or specific authorization.

- Transactions are recorded as necessary to permit the preparation of financial statements in accordance with U.S. generally accepted accounting principles (GAAP) or other criteria applicable to such statements and to maintain accountability for assets.

- Transactions are valued in a manner that permits recording their proper monetary value in the financial statements.

- Access to assets is permitted only in accordance with management's authorization.

- The recorded accountability for assets is compared with the existing assets at reasonable intervals, and appropriate action is taken with respect to any differences.

11.28 Form N-SAR requires auditors of registered investment companies to report any material weakness in an investment company's internal control over financial reporting, including those controls exercised on behalf of the company by agents. The report, which is filed with the fiscal year-end Form N-SAR, is based solely on the procedures performed as part of the financial statement audit. See paragraph 12.29 of this guide for an example of that report.

11.29 The auditor may decide to obtain information about controls maintained by a custodian acting as a service organization to an investment company. This information may include whether and to what extent management and the board of directors or trustees have evaluated the investment company's relationship with the securities' custodian in terms of significant recordkeeping responsibilities, financial stability, operational capabilities, and other matters pertaining to the relationship. A custodian's controls that may be relevant to an audit of an investment company's financial statements could include, among others, the following:

- Controls covering the receipt of, and payment for, securities, the delivery of securities, and control over cash received

- Controls for physically segregating and satisfactorily safeguarding the company's securities in the custodian's vaults

- Physical counts of securities and other procedures performed by the custodian's internal audit function

- Controls over securities held in central depositories

- Controls over receipts of cash, including dividend and interest payments

11.30   If the custodian has engaged a service auditor to examine the custodian's description of controls over custodial functions, the fund's auditor should consider obtaining a copy of the service auditor's report. The auditor's use of service auditors' reports is discussed in appendix B, "Reports on Controls at Outside Service Organizations," of this chapter. Further guidance for user auditors is provided in AU-C section 402, *Audit Considerations Relating to an Entity Using a Service Organization* (AICPA, *Professional Standards*), and for service auditors in AT section 801, *Reporting on Controls at a Service Organization* (AICPA, *Professional Standards*).[8]

11.31   An investment company may enter into subcustodial arrangements for investments in securities with institutions both inside and outside the United States.[9] The auditor should obtain an understanding of the extent of intercustodial responsibilities and rights under subcustodial agreements. For arrangements with foreign subcustodians, the auditor could consider inquiring about the procedures undertaken by the fund's directors or trustees in evaluating the subcustodial arrangement. Additionally, the principal custodian may perform oversight procedures, particularly over foreign subcustodians, that are relevant to the auditor when determining the extent of audit procedures to be applied to subcustodians. The auditor may apply audit procedures to each subcustodial arrangement that is similar to those for principal custodians if the existence assertion is not supported satisfactorily through the other procedures listed previously.

11.32   If an investment company enters into repurchase or securities lending agreements, the auditor may obtain an understanding of whether the investment company's controls include the following:

- A review of the creditworthiness of the issuers of repurchase agreements or counterparties for stock-lending arrangements

- A requirement that actual or constructive possession of the collateral be taken by the investment company, its custodian, or a custodian qualified under the Investment Advisers Act of 1940

---

[8] The AICPA Guide *Service Organizations: Reporting on Controls at a Service Organization Relevant to User Entities' Internal Control Over Financial Reporting* contains information for CPAs reporting on controls at a service organization that affect user entities' internal control over financial reporting. Also, the AICPA Guide *Reporting on Controls at a Service Organization: Relevant to Security, Availability, Processing Integrity, Confidentiality, or Privacy (SOC 2[SM])* summarizes the three new SOC engagements and provides detailed guidance on planning, performing, and reporting on SOC 2 engagements.

[9] SEC Final Rule Release No. 12354 under the 1940 Act.

(the 1940 Act) who verifies that the collateral is being held for the investment company

- A requirement to mark the collateral to market daily during the entire period of the agreement
- A requirement that such agreements provide that additional collateral be deposited by the issuer if the fair value of the collateral falls below the repurchase price or stock loan value[10]

The auditor could inspect the terms of the agreements and assess the related accounting and disclosure, in accordance with the criteria of FASB *Accounting Standards Codification* (ASC) 860, *Transfers and Servicing*.

Going Concern

Update 11-1 *Accounting and Reporting*: Going Concern

FASB Accounting Standards Update (ASU) No. 2014-15, *Presentation of Financial Statements—Going Concern (Subtopic 205-40): Disclosure of Uncertainties about an Entity's Ability to Continue as a Going Concern*, was issued in August 2014. The amendments in this ASU are effective for the annual period ending after December 15, 2016, and for annual periods and interim periods thereafter. Early application is permitted.

The amendments in ASU No. 2014-15 provide guidance in GAAP about management's responsibility to evaluate whether there is substantial doubt about an entity's ability to continue as a going concern and to provide related footnote disclosures. In doing so, the amendments should reduce diversity in the timing and content of footnote disclosures.

Readers are encouraged to consult the full text of this ASU on FASB's website at www.fasb.org.

11.33 AU-C section 570, *The Auditor's Consideration of an Entity's Ability to Continue as a Going Concern* (AICPA, *Professional Standards*), provides guidance on the auditors responsibilities in an audit of financial statements with respect to the evaluation whether there is substantial doubt about the entity's ability to continue as a going concern. AU-C section 9570, *The Auditor's Consideration of an Entity's Ability to Continue as a Going Concern: Auditing Interpretation of AU-C Section 570* (AICPA, *Professional Standards* AU-C sec. 9570.01–.10), provides definitions for the terms *substantial doubt about an entity's ability to continue as a going concern* and *reasonable period of time*, which are both used in AU-C section 570. AU-C section 9570 also provides interpretations regarding interim financial information and the possible effects on the financial statements and the adequacy of the related disclosure in situations when the auditor concludes there is a substantial doubt about an entity's ability to continue as a going concern.

Auditing Procedures for the Investment Portfolio Accounts

Principal Audit Objectives

11.34 The principal objectives in auditing the investment accounts are to obtain reasonable assurance of the following:

---

[10] SEC Final Rule Release No. 13005 under the 1940 Act.

- The investment company has ownership of, and accounting control over, all its portfolio investments.

- All transactions are authorized and recorded in the accounting records in the proper account, amount, and period.

- Portfolio investments are valued properly, and their costs are recorded properly.

- Income from investments and realized gains and losses from securities transactions are accounted for properly.

- Investments are free of liens, pledges, or other security interests, or if not, such matters are identified properly and disclosed in the financial statements.

Examination of Transactions and Detail Records[11]

Custody of Securities

11.35 For a registered investment company, the auditor should confirm all securities with the custodian, including securities held by the custodian on behalf of the investment company in a central securities system or similar omnibus account, or physically examine the securities, as applicable under the circumstances. Additionally, the SEC requires the auditor to confirm all unsettled securities purchased with the party responsible for delivery.[12] For those confirmations not received, the auditor should perform alternative procedures deemed appropriate in the circumstances.[13] For nonregistered investment companies, the timing and extent of testing custody is a matter of the auditor's professional judgment.

11.36 Other procedures typically performed by the auditor include the following:

- Confirmation of when-issued transactions with the underwriter, including the value of such transactions as of the valuation date.

- Confirmation of commodity futures contracts, put or call options, financial futures contracts, swaps, and similar exchange-traded or directly-negotiated (OTC) derivative contracts with the clearing broker or counterparty.

- Confirmation of forward contracts, standby commitment contracts, and repurchase agreements (with the counterparty). For forward contracts, standby commitments, and reverse repurchase

---

[11] Paragraphs .05–.06 of AU-C section 330, *Performing Audit Procedures in Response to Assessed Risks and Evaluating the Audit Evidence Obtained* (AICPA, *Professional Standards*), states that the auditor should (*a*) design and implement overall responses to address the assessed risks of material misstatement at the financial statement level and (*b*) design and perform further audit procedures whose nature, timing, and extent are based on, and responsive, to the assessed risks of material misstatement at the relevant assertion level. Paragraph .A8 of AU-C section 330 explains that the auditor requirements regarding the nature, timing, and extent of further audit procedures provide a clear linkage between the auditor's further audit procedures and the risk assessment. Refer to AU-C section 330 for additional guidance.

[12] Refer to the SEC Division of Investment Management Staff Issues of Interest Release titled "Business Development Companies—Auditor Verification of Securities Owned" at www.sec.gov. The SEC staff believes that it is a best practice for an auditor of a business development company (BDC) to verify all of the securities owned by the BDC, either by actual examination or by receipt of a certificate from the custodian, and affirmatively state in the audit opinion whether the auditor has confirmed the existence of all such securities.

[13] Section 404.03 of the SEC's *Codification of Financial Reporting Policies*.

agreements, the auditor may review the contracts or agreements and consult with the investment company's legal counsel to determine if a *senior security*, as defined in Section 18(g) of the 1940 Act, exists.

- Confirmation of short securities positions and related collateral with the broker, counterparty, or custodian.

- Confirmation of borrowed or loaned securities and related collateral with the broker, counterparty, or custodian.

Also refer to the AICPA Audit Guide *Special Considerations in Auditing Financial Instruments* for more detailed guidance and examples of substantive procedures related to planning and performing auditing procedures for assertions (including existence and occurrence assertions) about derivative instruments and investments in securities.

11.37 Paragraph .A32 of AU-C section 500 states that the reliability of information to be used as audit evidence and, therefore, of the audit evidence itself is influenced by its source and nature and the circumstances under which it is obtained, including the controls over its preparation and maintenance, when relevant. Paragraph .A32 indicates that even when information to be used as audit evidence is obtained from sources external to the entity, circumstances may exist that affect its reliability. For example, regardless of whether a response is obtained in paper form or by electronic or other medium, paragraphs .A12–.A13 of AU-C section 505, *External Confirmations* (AICPA, *Professional Standards*), explain that all responses carry some risk of interception, alteration, or fraud. The auditor's consideration of the reliability of information obtained through the confirmation process to be used as audit evidence includes consideration of the risks that (a) the information obtained may not be from an authentic source, (b) a respondent may not be knowledgeable about the information to be confirmed, and (c) the integrity of the information may have been compromised. When the auditor utilizes an electronic confirmation process or system, the auditor's consideration of the risks described in the preceding sentence includes the consideration of risks that the electronic confirmation process is not secure or is improperly controlled. Refer to AU-C section 330 for requirements and application guidance on when to use external confirmations and refer to AU-C section 505 for further requirements and application guidance on the auditor's use of external confirmation procedures to obtain audit evidence.

11.38 Under certain conditions, Section 17 of the 1940 Act and rules promulgated thereunder, principally Rules 17f-1 and 17f-2, require additional examinations of securities. When possible, in carrying out the examination, the auditor is to make a physical examination of the securities themselves. The auditor is also required to confirm securities not held in physical form or in transit at the examination date.[14],[15] In all cases, the auditor is also required to reconcile the physical count or confirmation with the fund's accounting records.

---

[14] Section 404.01.a of the SEC's *Codification of Financial Reporting Policies*.

[15] Because custodians no longer hold most securities in physical form, and custody relationships may extend through two or more levels of subcustodians (especially when funds invest in non-U.S. markets), the confirmation requirements of Rule 17f-2 are fulfilled when the auditor confirms security holdings with the highest-level unaffiliated subcustodian.

11.39   The exact requirements for the frequency and timing of examinations depend on the kind of custodial arrangement.[16] The kind of custodial arrangements and requirements include the following:

- An investment company maintaining a custodial relationship with a member of a national securities exchange should follow Rule 17f-1 of the 1940 Act. That rule requires the investment company's auditor to examine all securities at the end of each annual and semiannual fiscal period and at least one additional time during the fiscal year chosen by the auditor, without advance notification to the custodian.

- An investment company that retains possession of its securities or maintains its securities in the custody of an affiliated bank should follow Rule 17f-2 of the 1940 Act. That rule requires the company's auditor to examine the securities at least three times in each fiscal year, at least two of which should be chosen by the auditor without prior notice to such company.

After each examination, the auditor should address a report to the investment company's board of directors or trustees. The auditor is required to submit promptly a copy of that report, attached to a completed Form N-17f-1 or N-17f-2, as applicable, to the SEC stating that such an examination was performed and describing the nature and extent of work done and the results. An illustration of such a report is provided in chapter 12, "Independent Auditor's Reports and Client Representations," of this guide.

11.40   Under Rule 206(4)-2 of the 1940 Act, all registered investment advisers (or an investment adviser required to register) who have custody of client funds or securities, as defined, must have an independent public accountant conduct an examination on a surprise basis once every calendar year. Advisers to pooled investment vehicles may be deemed to comply with the surprise examination requirements of the rule by obtaining an audit of the pool and delivering the audited financial statements to pool investors within 120 days of the pool's fiscal year-end.[17] That audit must be conducted by an accounting firm registered with, and subject to regular inspection by, the PCAOB. See paragraphs 12.31–.39 of this guide for further information.

Tests of Portfolio Transactions

11.41   The auditor rarely examines all transactions during the period under audit, unless specifically requested to do so, and selects a sample of portfolio transactions for testing. Brokers' advice or other documents may be

---

[16] See footnote 13.

[17] In 2006, the SEC issued a letter indicating that it would not recommend enforcement action under this rule against an adviser of a fund of funds relying on the annual audit provision of Rule 206(4)-2 if the audited financial statements of the fund of funds are distributed to investors in the fund of funds within 180 days of the end of its fiscal year. See the August 10, 2006, SEC Staff Letter *ABA Committee on Private Investment Entities*. The amendments to the custody rule in 2009 do not affect the views of the staff expressed in that letter. In 2011, the SEC issued an FAQ that provided a scenario in which an adviser's client is a "top tier" pooled investment vehicle that invests in one or more funds of funds, and such top tier pool invests 10 percent or more of its total assets in one or more funds of funds, as defined in the ABA Letter, that are not, and are not advised by, a related person of the top tier pool, its general partner, or its adviser. In this scenario, the division would not recommend enforcement action to the SEC under Rule 206(4)-2 if the audited financial statements of the top tier pool are distributed to pool investors within 260 days of the end of the top tier pool's fiscal year.

examined to ascertain that they agree with the entries recorded in the purchase, sales, or general journals or other books of original entry. The auditor may test for proper authorizations, extensions, trade dates, and reasonableness of the transaction prices. The auditor may test whether sales have been properly accounted for during the period and that an acceptable method of costing sales (specific identification or average cost) has been applied consistently and that gains or losses have been calculated properly.

11.42 The auditor may test the classification of gains and losses for tax purposes and the adjustments to the bases of investments resulting from stock dividends, splits, rights, recapitalizations, and liquidating dividends.

Portfolio Transactions With Affiliates

11.43 Section 17 of the 1940 Act and related rules impose significant restrictions and, in some cases, prohibitions on transactions with affiliates. The terms *affiliate* and *control* in the 1940 Act have different meanings from their definitions in the FASB ASC glossary. Specifically, the term *affiliate* means an affiliated person, as defined in Section 2(a)(3) of the 1940 Act, and the term *control* has the meaning given in Section 2(a)(9) of the 1940 Act. The term *affiliated person*, as defined in Section 2(a)(3) of the 1940 Act, encompasses control relationships and the direct or indirect ownership of 5 percent or more of the outstanding voting securities of any issuer. An *affiliated person*, as defined in that section, includes officers, directors, partners, employees, investment advisers, and members of the investment adviser's advisory board.

11.44 Regulation S-X requires disclosure of more information about transactions with affiliates in prospectuses and annual reports to the SEC than is required under GAAP. Various rules of Regulation S-X require the financial statements of an investment company to state separately investments in affiliates, investment income from affiliates, gain or loss on sales of securities of affiliates, and management fees or other service fees payable to controlled entities and other affiliates.

11.45

Considerations for Audits Performed in Accordance With PCAOB Standards

In auditing a registered investment company, the auditor should be familiar with Section 17 of the 1940 Act and related rules. The guidance for auditing related party transactions in Auditing Standard No. 18, *Related Parties* (AICPA, *PCAOB Standards and Related Rules*, Auditing Standards), may be applied equally in ascertaining the existence of the 1940 Act *affiliates*, as defined under the 1940 Act, and auditing transactions with them. Further, for audits of registered investment companies, paragraph .06*l*[18] of AU section 333, *Management Representations* (AICPA, *PCAOB Standards and Related Rules*, Interim Standards), explains that information concerning related-party transactions and amounts receivable from or payable to related parties, including support for any assertion that a transaction with a related party was conducted on terms equivalent to those prevailing in an

---

[18] As amended by PCAOB Release No. 2014-002, *Related Parties, Amendments to Certain PCAOB Auditing Standards Regarding Significant Unusual Transactions and Other Amendments to PCAOB Auditing Standards* (AICPA, *PCAOB Standards and Related Rules*, Select PCAOB Releases).

arm's-length transaction should be obtained as a specific written representation. The auditor may also obtain written representations from management that, except to the extent indicated, the company

- does not own any securities either of directly affiliated or, to the best information and belief of management, indirectly affiliated entities.
- has not received income from, or realized gain or loss on sales of, investments in, or indebtedness of, such affiliated entities.
- has not incurred expenses for management or other service fees payable to such affiliated entities.
- has not otherwise engaged in transactions with such affiliated entities.

Paragraph 12.48 of this guide presents an illustrative management representation letter. If a question arises regarding whether a relationship represents an affiliation, the auditor may request that the investment company's management obtain a written opinion from legal counsel.

11.46   If affiliated entities exist, such as an underwriter or investment adviser, such auditing procedures as confirmation of transactions, examination of supporting documents, and written representations from the management of affiliated entities may be required. These procedures are necessary because the fund is required, by rules under the 1940 Act, to disclose amounts paid to affiliates in connection with their services to the investment company, such as commissions for sales of its shares and brokerage commissions for its portfolio transactions.

Income From Securities

11.47   The auditor could test investment income, which may include testing a sample of dividends and interest earned during the period, applying analytical procedures, or a combination of both. For example, in the auditor's tests of purchases and sales, the auditor may test the income for the entire year from the securities selected or, in conjunction with other procedures, may select an interim period and test the income earned during that period from a representative sample of securities. In testing a sample of dividends for publicly traded securities, the auditor may consult with independent financial reporting services to determine the ex-dividend and payable dates and the rates for the securities selected for testing. Interest payment dates and rates are also available from such services.

11.48   In connection with detailed testing, the auditor could consider unusual amounts of dividends (such as dividends in arrears) or interest (such as defaulted interest) received during the period under audit that may necessitate special disclosure. The auditor should be satisfied that the accounting is proper for material income from noncash dividends, and that the investment company's determination of the tax status of dividend income (as investment income, capital gain, or return of capital) is appropriate.

11.49   Consistent with the application guidance in paragraph .A16 of AU-C section 330, the materiality, assessed risk, and degree of assurance the auditor plans to obtain over investment income from sources other than dividends or interest determine the extent of necessary auditing procedures.

Net Asset Value

11.50   The auditor may include among the tests of net asset value per share at the financial statement date and on selected interim dates tests that

- compare the quantities and descriptions of portfolio securities owned with the investment ledger.

- agree the fair value of investments to independent sources and supporting documentation for investments stated at fair value, as determined in good faith by the board of directors or trustees (or by management under procedures approved by the board of directors or trustees). See the "Valuation of Investments" section of this chapter for further discussion.

- test the clerical accuracy of valuation extensions and totals.

- reconcile amounts of assets and liabilities to the general ledger accounts. (If it is impractical to post daily in the general ledger, a company may use worksheets instead and, accordingly, should reconcile the worksheets to the general ledger at the nearest month end or other closing date.)

- review the reasonableness of income and expense accruals.

- reconcile the number of shares outstanding to the capital stock accounts in the general ledger or substitute worksheet.

- calculate the net asset value per share by dividing the difference between total assets and total liabilities by the number of shares outstanding.

11.51   The extent of the auditor's tests of net asset value per share computations depends on, among other factors, the auditor's assessment of control risk.

Valuation of Investments[19]

11.52   For registered investment companies, the auditor could test all portfolio valuations as of the date of the financial statements. (For nonregistered investment companies, the timing and extent of testing portfolio valuations is a matter of the auditor's judgment.) In addition, because periodic computations of net asset value are based on the fair value of investments, the auditor may wish to evaluate the systems and procedures used by the fund during the period under audit in determining the fair value of investments. The auditor could test transactions on dates selected from the period under audit for agreement with the values computed by the investment company. Paragraph .A16 of AU-C section 330 explains that the extent of an audit procedure judged necessary is determined after considering the materiality, assessed risk, and degree of assurance the auditor plans to obtain.

---

[19] AU-C section 540, *Auditing Accounting Estimates, Including Fair Value Accounting Estimates, and Related Disclosures* (AICPA, *Professional Standards*), addresses the auditor's responsibilities relating to accounting estimates, including fair value accounting estimates and related disclosures, in an audit of financial statements. Portions of AU-C section 540 have been incorporated into the guidance contained in paragraphs 11.60–.76.

11.53 The fund's board of directors or trustees is responsible for approving and overseeing policies that ensure that its investments are calculated at fair value. The methods used to value investment securities are usually approved by action of the board of directors or trustees or, in some instances, stated in the bylaws, or applicable governing document of the fund (for example, limited partnership agreement for a nonregistered fund). The methods used by registered investment companies should conform with the 1940 Act. The auditor should determine whether the valuation method used conforms to the company's stated policy and, if applicable, with the rules of regulatory authorities.

11.54 As explained in paragraphs .A13–.A15 of AU-C section 501, quoted market prices for investments listed on national exchanges or OTC markets are available from sources such as financial publications, the exchanges, NASDAQ, or pricing services based on sources such as those. Quoted market prices obtained from those sources generally provide sufficient evidence of the fair value of the investments.

11.55 For certain other investments, quoted market prices may be obtained from broker-dealers who are market makers in them or though OTC Markets Group, Inc. However, using such a price quote to test valuation assertions may require special knowledge to understand the circumstances in which the quote was developed. For example, quotations published by the OTC Markets Group, Inc. may not be based on recent trades and may be only an indication of interest and not an actual price for which a counterparty will purchase or sell the underlying investments.

11.56 If quoted market prices are not available for the investments, estimates of fair value frequently may be obtained from broker-dealers or other third-party sources, based on proprietary valuation models, or from the investment company, based on internally or externally developed valuation models (for example, the Black-Scholes option pricing model). In some situations, the auditor may determine that it is necessary to obtain an estimate of fair value from more than one pricing source. For example, this may be appropriate if either a pricing source has a relationship with an entity that might impair its objectivity or the valuation is based on assumptions that are highly subjective or particularly sensitive to changes in underlying circumstances. The auditor should consider the guidance provided in AU-C sections 501 and 540[20] when auditing the fair value of investments.

11.57 For estimates of fair value obtained from broker-dealers and other third-party sources, the auditor could consider the applicability of the guidance in AU-C section 402 or AU-C section 620, *Using the Work of an Auditor's Specialist* (AICPA, *Professional Standards*). The auditor's decisions about whether such guidance is applicable and which guidance is applicable will depend on the circumstances. The guidance in AU-C section 620 may be applicable if the third-party source derives the fair value of a security by using modeling or similar techniques. If an entity uses a pricing service to obtain prices of listed securities in the entity's portfolio, the guidance in AU-C section 402 may be appropriate. Note, all assertions regarding investments may not be covered by a service provider's type 2 SOC 1 report. For example, valuation estimates are

---

[20] For guidance on implementing the audit requirements regarding securities and derivative instruments, the reader should refer to the AICPA Audit Guide *Special Considerations in Auditing Financial Instruments*.

typically not covered by the type 2 SOC 1 report. Consequently, to obtain sufficient appropriate audit evidence to support the valuation assertion, in many cases, the other substantive procedures in AU-C section 540 apply when testing the methods and assumptions used to estimate fair value for those investments not based on quoted market prices from active markets.

11.58 An entity may have an investment in a hedge fund that is reported at fair value but for which a readily determinable fair value does not exist. Further, the hedge fund may own interests in investments in limited partnership interests or other private equity securities for which a readily determinable fair value does not exist. As part of the auditor's procedures, an auditor typically would satisfy the existence assertion through confirmation with the hedge fund, examination of legal documents, or other means. In confirming existence, the auditor may request the hedge fund to indicate or confirm the fair value of the entity's investment in the hedge fund, including the fair value of investments held by the hedge fund. In some circumstances, the hedge fund will not provide detailed information about the basis and method for measuring the entity's investment in the hedge fund nor will it provide information about specific investments held by the hedge fund. In circumstances in which the auditor determines that the nature and extent of auditing procedures should include testing the measurement of investments in securities, simply receiving a confirmation from a third party, either in aggregate or on a security-by-security basis, does not in and of itself constitute sufficient appropriate audit evidence in addressing the valuation assertion. Receiving confirmation from a third party on a security-by-security basis, however, may provide support of the data used by the investor's management in its valuation process. The AICPA Audit Guide *Special Considerations in Auditing Financial Instruments* provides further guidance on testing management's fair value estimates. (See also the discussion of funds of funds in paragraphs 5.91–.96 of this guide.)

11.59 Most fixed income funds use bond dealers or other pricing services to value their portfolios. If such agents are used, the auditor should evaluate whether controls maintained by the fund or pricing service provide reasonable assurance that material pricing errors would be prevented or detected. Such controls may include the following:

- Testing methods used by the pricing service to obtain daily quotations
- Verifying daily changes of each security's fair value in excess of a stipulated percentage
- Verifying dealer quotations with other dealers on a test basis
- Maintaining a comparison of actual sales prices with the fair value assigned for the preceding day
- Consideration of fair value that has not changed for a stipulated period
- Periodic review of pricing information by portfolio managers and other knowledgeable officials

11.60 When investments are valued by the investment company using a valuation model (including an internally developed matrix pricing model), the auditor should obtain an understanding of the following, in accordance with paragraph .08 of AU-C section 540, in order to provide a basis for the identification and assessment of the risk of material misstatement for the accounting estimate:

a. The requirements of the applicable financial reporting framework relevant to the accounting estimate, including related disclosures

b. How management identifies those transactions, events, and conditions that may give rise to the need for the accounting estimate to be recognized or disclosed in the financial statements. In obtaining this understanding, the auditor should make inquiries of management about changes in circumstances that may give rise to new, or the need to revise existing, accounting estimates.

c. How management makes the accounting estimates and the data on which they are based, including

    i. the method(s), including, when applicable, the model, used in making the accounting estimate;

    ii. relevant controls;

    iii. whether management has used a specialist;

    iv. the assumptions underlying the accounting estimates;

    v. whether there has been or ought to have been a change from the prior period in the method(s) or assumption(s) for making the accounting estimate and, if so, why; and

    vi. whether and, if so, how management has assessed the effect of estimation uncertainty.

11.61 Paragraph .A26 of AU-C section 540 further explains that matters that the auditor may consider in obtaining an understanding of relevant controls include, for example, the experience and competence of those who make the accounting estimates and controls related to

- how management determines the completeness, relevance, and accuracy of the data used to develop accounting estimates.

- the review and approval of accounting estimates, including the assumptions or inputs used in their development, by appropriate levels of management and, when appropriate, those charged with governance.

- the segregation of duties between those committing the entity to the underlying transactions and those responsible for making the accounting estimates, including whether the assignment of responsibilities appropriately takes account of the nature of the entity and its products or services.

- services provided by a service organization, if any, to provide fair value or other accounting estimates measurements or the data that supports the measurement. When an entity uses a service organization, AU-C section 402 applies.

11.62 Paragraph .A27 of AU-C section 540 states that other controls may be relevant to making the accounting estimates, depending on the circumstances. For example, if the entity uses specific models for making accounting estimates, management may put into place specific policies and procedures around such models. These may include, for example, those established over

- the design and development or selection of a particular model for a particular purpose.

- the use of the model.

- the maintenance and periodic validation of the integrity of the model.

- security, such as controls that prevent changes to the model or data without authorization.

11.63 It may be possible to test the validity of the model by comparing fair values with values obtained from a second pricing matrix or quotations obtained from market makers. However, as noted in paragraph 2.36, the use of model valuations may not be necessary when market quotations are available. For example, paragraph .A5 of AU-C section 540 explains that this may be the case for some financial statement items when an active and open market exists that provides readily available and reliable information on the prices at which actual exchanges occur, in which case the existence of published price quotations ordinarily is the best audit evidence of fair value.

11.64 Based on the assessed risks of material misstatement, paragraph .12 of AU-C section 540 states that the auditor should determine

- whether management has appropriately applied the requirements of the applicable financial reporting framework relevant to the accounting estimate[21] and

- whether the methods for making the accounting estimates are appropriate and have been applied consistently and whether changes from the prior period, if any, in accounting estimates or the method for making them are appropriate in the circumstances.

11.65 Paragraph .A57 of AU-C section 540 explains that the application of the requirements of the applicable financial reporting framework requires management to consider changes in the environment or circumstances that affect the entity. For example, the introduction of an active market for a particular class of asset or liability may indicate that the use of discounted cash flows to estimate the fair value of such asset or liability is no longer appropriate. Paragraph .A58 of AU-C section 540 further explains that the auditor's consideration of a change in an accounting estimate or in the method for making it from the prior period is important because a change that is not based on a change in circumstances or new information is considered arbitrary. Arbitrary changes in an accounting estimate result in inconsistent financial statements over time and may give rise to a financial statement misstatement or be an indicator of possible management bias.

11.66 In responding to the assessed risks of material misstatement, paragraph .13 of AU-C section 540 states that the auditor should undertake one or more of the following, taking into account the nature of the accounting estimate:

a. Determine whether events occurring up to the date of the auditor's report provide audit evidence regarding the accounting estimate.

b. Test how management made the accounting estimate and the data on which it is based. In doing so, the auditor should evaluate whether

---

[21] Paragraph .A52 of AU-C section 540 further explains that, based on the assessed risk of material misstatement, the auditor is required to exercise professional judgment (in accordance with the requirements of AU-C section 200) in determining the nature, timing, and extent of the procedures necessary to conclude whether management appropriately applied the requirements of the financial reporting framework, including that the methods used for making the estimates are appropriate.

    i. the method of measurement used is appropriate in the circumstances,

    ii. the assumptions used by management are reasonable in light of the measurement objectives of the applicable financial reporting framework, and

    iii. the data on which the estimate is based is sufficiently reliable for the auditor's purposes.

c. Test the operating effectiveness of the controls over how management made the accounting estimate, together with appropriate substantive procedures.

d. Develop a point estimate or range to evaluate management's point estimate. For this purpose

    i. if the auditor uses assumptions or methods that differ from management's, the auditor should obtain an understanding of management's assumptions or methods sufficient to establish that the auditor's point estimate or range takes into account relevant variables and to evaluate any significant differences from management's point estimate.

    ii. if the auditor concludes that it is appropriate to use a range, the auditor should narrow the range, based on audit evidence available, until all outcomes within the range are considered reasonable.

11.67   Paragraphs .A63–.A67 of AU-C section 540 provide further explanation on events occurring up to the date of the auditor's report. Determining whether such events provide audit evidence regarding the accounting estimate may be an appropriate response when such events are expected to occur and provide audit evidence that confirms or contradicts the accounting estimate. Events occurring up to the date of the auditor's report may sometimes provide sufficient appropriate audit evidence about an accounting estimate. In such cases, there may be no need to perform additional audit procedures on the accounting estimate, provided that sufficient appropriate evidence about the event is obtained. However, for some accounting estimates, events occurring up to the date of the auditor's report are unlikely to provide audit evidence regarding the accounting estimate. For example, the conditions or events relating to some accounting estimates develop only over an extended period. Also, because of the measurement objective of fair value accounting estimates, information after the period-end may not reflect the events or conditions existing at the balance sheet date and, therefore, may not be relevant to the measurement of the fair value accounting estimate.

11.68   Paragraph .A69 of AU-C section 540 provides the auditor examples on testing how management made the accounting estimate and the data on which the estimate is based. For example, testing may involve the following:

- Testing the extent to which data on which the accounting estimate is based is accurate, complete, and relevant and whether the accounting estimate has been properly determined using such data and management's assumptions

- Considering the source, relevance, and reliability of external data or information, including that received from management's specialists, to assist in making an accounting estimate

- Determining how management has taken into account the effect of events, transactions, and changes in circumstances occurring between the date that the estimate or inputs to the estimate were determined and the reporting date, if the estimate was not made as of a date that coincides with the reporting date

- Recalculating the accounting estimate and reviewing, for internal consistency, information used to determine the estimate

- Considering management's review and approval processes

11.69 When the applicable financial reporting framework does not prescribe the method of measurement, paragraphs .A72–.A73 of AU-C section 540 explain that evaluating whether the method used (including any applicable model) is appropriate in the circumstances is a matter of professional judgment. For this purpose, matters that the auditor may consider include whether

- management's rationale for the method selected is reasonable.

- management sufficiently and appropriately has evaluated and applied the criteria, if any, provided in the applicable financial reporting framework to support the selected method.

- the method is appropriate and sufficient data is available in the circumstances, given the nature of the asset or liability being estimated and the requirements of the applicable financial reporting framework relevant to accounting estimates.

- the method is appropriate with regard to the business, industry, and environment in which the entity operates.

11.70 Paragraphs .A78–.A89 of AU-C section 540 provide further application and explanatory guidance on the auditor's evaluation of the assumptions used by management. The auditor's evaluation of the assumptions used by management is based only on information available at the time of the audit. Audit procedures dealing with management's assumptions, including those used as inputs to valuation models, are performed in the context of the audit of the entity's financial statements and not for the purpose of providing an opinion on the assumptions themselves.

11.71 Matters that the auditor may consider in evaluating the reasonableness of assumptions used by management underlying fair value accounting estimates, in addition to those discussed previously, when applicable, may include, for example

- when relevant, whether and, if so, how management has incorporated market-specific inputs into the development of assumptions.

- whether the assumptions are consistent with observable market conditions and the characteristics of the asset or liability being measured at fair value.

- whether the sources of market-participant assumptions are relevant and reliable and how management has selected the assumptions to use when a number of different market participant assumptions exist.

- when appropriate, whether and, if so, how management considered assumptions used in, or information about, comparable transactions, assets, or liabilities.

11.72   If unobservable inputs are used by management, the auditor's evaluation of those assumptions could be combined with other responses to assessed risks, as described in paragraph .13 of AU-C section 540, to obtain sufficient appropriate audit evidence. In such cases, it may be necessary for the auditor to perform other audit procedures (for example, examining documentation supporting the review and approval of the accounting estimate by appropriate levels of management and, when appropriate, those charged with governance).

11.73   Further, fair value accounting estimates may comprise observable inputs, as well as unobservable inputs. When fair value accounting estimates are based on unobservable inputs, matters that the auditor may consider include, for example, how management supports

- the identification of the characteristics of market participants relevant to the accounting estimate.
- modifications it has made to its own assumptions to reflect its view of assumptions market participants would use.
- whether it has incorporated appropriate information.
- when applicable, how its assumptions take account of comparable transactions, assets, or liabilities.

11.74   For accounting estimates that give rise to significant risks, in addition to other substantive procedures performed to meet the requirements of AU-C section 330, paragraph .15 of AU-C section 540 states that the auditor should evaluate the following:

- How management has considered alternative assumption or outcomes and why it has rejected them or how management has otherwise addressed estimation uncertainty in making the accounting estimate
- Whether the significant assumptions used by management are reasonable
- When relevant to the reasonableness of the significant assumptions used by management or the appropriate application of the applicable financial reporting framework, management's intent to carry out specific courses of action and its ability to do so (however, paragraph .A82 of AU-C section 540 states, in part, that certain financial reporting frameworks, however, may not permit management's intentions or plans to be taken into account when making an accounting estimate. This is often the case for fair value accounting estimates because their measurement objective requires that assumptions reflect those used by market participants.)

Paragraph .A113 of AU-C section 540 further explains that an assumption used in making an accounting estimate may be deemed to be significant if a reasonable variation in the assumption would materially affect the measurement of the accounting estimate.

11.75   Paragraph .19 of AU-C section 540 requires the auditor to obtain sufficient appropriate audit evidence about whether the disclosures in the financial statements related to accounting estimates are in accordance with the requirements of the applicable financial reporting framework. As further explained in paragraph .A125 of AU-C section 540, evaluating the reasonableness of the accounting estimate and related disclosures included in the notes to the financial statements, whether required by the applicable financial reporting framework or disclosed voluntarily, involves essentially the same types of considerations applied when auditing an accounting estimate recognized in the financial statements. For registered investment companies, the auditor should also become familiar with the provisions of the SEC's financial reporting releases on this subject, with emphasis on Section 404.03 of the SEC's *Codification of Financial Reporting Policies*.

11.76 Paragraph .A56 of AU-C section 540 explains that collateral often is assigned for certain types of investments in debt instruments that either are required to be measured at fair value or are evaluated for possible impairment. If the collateral is an important factor in measuring the fair value of the investment or evaluating its carrying amount, it may be necessary for the auditor—in determining whether management has appropriately applied the requirements of the applicable financial reporting framework—to obtain sufficient appropriate audit evidence regarding the existence; value; rights; and access to, or transferability of, such collateral (including consideration of whether all appropriate liens have been filed and appropriate disclosures have been made).

Money Market Funds

Update 11-2 *Regulatory*: Money Market Fund Reform

On July 23, 2014, the SEC issued Final Rule Release No. 33-9616, *Money Market Fund Reform; Amendments to Form PF*. The release includes varying compliance dates for the different changes within the new rule. Compliance dates begin in 2015, and extend through 2016. Readers are encouraged to consult the full text of the release for specific compliance dates.

One of the key structural changes of the new Money Market Reform Rule is that institutional prime and municipal money market funds will be required to transact at a floating net asset value. Retail funds and government funds are not required to transact at a floating net asset value. This will require those funds that transact at a floating net asset value to transact shares, rounded to the fourth decimal place (for example, $1.0000), based on the most recently determined market value of the securities in the underlying portfolios. Separately, new tax regulations and guidance have been issued as a result of this change; readers are encouraged to review this new IRS guidance. The release further provides guidance on how to determine whether a fund is considered to be an institutional money market fund, a retail money market fund, or a government money market fund.

Those money market funds adopting a floating net asset value as a result of the new rules are expected to determine the values of their investments using market-based values, as opposed to using the amortized cost of such investments as an approximation of market value. In addition to this accounting change, the new rules may result in other changes to the financial reporting of all money market funds. Readers should keep abreast of future developments as they emerge.

Additionally, the amendments in Final Rule Release No. 33-9616 give the boards of directors of money market funds new tools to stem heavy redemptions. Those tools include allowing them discretion to impose liquidity fees

in the event a fund's weekly liquidity level falls below the required regulatory threshold, and also provides them the discretion to suspend redemptions
temporarily (that is, impose a "gate"), under similar circumstances. The new
requirements dictate that all nongovernment money market funds impose a
liquidity fee if the fund's weekly liquidity level falls below the rule-established
threshold, unless the fund's board determines that imposing such a fee is not
in the best interests of the fund.

Final Rule Release No. 33-9616 also contains additional amendments. These
include enhanced disclosure requirements on fund websites, sales and marketing materials, prospectuses and SAIs; changes to Form N-MFP; an additional new Form N-CR; and various clarifying amendments under Rule 2a-7,
including stress testing and diversification provisions.

The amendments also require investment advisers of certain large unregistered liquidity funds to provide additional information about those funds to
the SEC.

Readers should consult the full text of SEC Final Rule Release No. 33-9616,
which can be accessed on the Final Rules page at www.sec.gov.

11.77   For investment companies registered as *money market funds*, as
defined in Rule 2a-7 of the 1940 Act, the auditor should consider reviewing and
performing tests of the following:

- The fund's procedures under Rule 2a-7 and the monitoring of those
  procedures
- Monitoring of the extent of deviation between net asset value per
  share calculated using amortized cost and net asset value per
  share calculated using fair value
- Monitoring the portfolio maturity, credit quality, and diversification requirements of Rule 2a-7
- Compliance with the recordkeeping requirements of Rule 2a-7

11.78

Appendix A—Auditor's Responsibility for Other Information in Documents Containing Audited Financial Statements [1]

Readers are encouraged to review the preface of this guide for the authoritative status of this appendix.

A.01 An entity may publish various documents that contain information in addition to audited financial statements (for example, annual reports and proxies). Other information in a document may be relevant to an audit performed by an independent auditor or the continuing propriety of the auditor's report.

A.02 AU-C section 720, *Other Information in Documents Containing Audited Financial Statements* (AICPA, *Professional Standards*), addresses the auditor's responsibility with respect to other information in documents containing audited financial statements and the auditor's report thereon. Paragraph .02 of AU-C section 720 explains that, among other matters, the phrase *documents containing audited financial statements* refers to annual reports (or similar documents) that are issued to owners (or similar stakeholders). Paragraph .01 of AU-C section 720 states that in the absence of any separate requirement in the particular circumstances of the engagement, the auditor's opinion on the financial statements does not cover other information, and the auditor has no responsibility for determining whether such information is properly stated. AU-C section 720 requires the auditor to read the other information of which the auditor is aware because the credibility of the audited financial statements may be undermined by material inconsistencies between the audited financial statements and other information. If the auditor identifies a material inconsistency, the auditor should determine whether the audited financial statements or the other information needs to be revised in accordance with paragraph .09 of AU-C section 720. Paragraph .10 of AU-C section 720 states that if a material inconsistency identified prior to the report release date requires revision to the audited financial statements, and management refuses to make the revision, the auditor should modify the auditor's opinion. If a material inconsistency identified prior to the report release date requires revision of the other information and management refuses to make the revision, the auditor should communicate this matter to those charged with governance and: include in the auditor's report an other-matter paragraph describing the material inconsistency in accordance with AU-C section 706, *Emphasis-of-Matter Paragraphs and Other-Matter Paragraphs in the Independent Auditor's Report* (AICPA, *Professional Standards*); withhold the auditor's report; or withdraw from the engagement (if possible under applicable law or regulation) in accordance with paragraph .12 of AU-C section 720.

---

[1] The auditing content in this guide focuses primarily on generally accepted auditing standards issued by the Auditing Standards Board and is applicable to audits of nonissuers. See the section "Applicability of Generally Accepted Auditing Standards and PCAOB Standards" of the preface to this guide for a discussion of the definitions of issuer and nonissuer as used throughout this guide. Appendix B, "Clarified Auditing Standards and PCAOB Standards," of this guide is included to assist auditors in comparing the clarified standards, many of which are referenced throughout this guide, to the PCAOB standards. Further, considerations for audits of issuers in accordance with PCAOB standards may be discussed within this guide's chapter text. When such discussion is provided, the related paragraphs are designated with the following title: *Considerations for Audits Performed in Accordance With PCAOB Standards*.

A.03 Paragraph .A3 of AU-C section 720 explains that other information may comprise the following: a report by management or those charged with governance on operations, financial summaries or highlights, employment data, planned capital expenditures, financial ratios, names of officers and directors, and selected quarterly data. Paragraph .A4 of AU-C section 720 further explains that, for purposes of generally accepted auditing standards (GAAS), other information does not encompass, for example, the following: a press release or similar memorandum, information contained in analyst briefings, and information contained on the entity's website.

A.04 Paragraph .03 of AU-C section 725, *Supplementary Information in Relation to the Financial Statements as a Whole* (AICPA, *Professional Standards*), states that the objective of the auditor, when engaged to report on supplementary information in relation to the financial statements as a whole, is to evaluate the presentation of the supplementary information in relation to the financial statements as a whole, and to report on whether the supplementary information is fairly stated, in all material respects, in relation to the financial statements as whole. *Supplementary information* (for purposes of GAAS) is defined as information presented outside the basic financial statements, excluding required supplementary information that is not considered necessary for the financial statements to be fairly presented in accordance with the applicable financial reporting framework. Such information may be presented in a document containing audited financial statements or separate from the financial statements. Paragraphs .A7–.A8 of AU-C section 725 explain that supplementary information includes additional details or explanations of items in or related to the basic financial statements, consolidating information, historical summaries of items extracted from the basic financial statements, statistical data, and other material, some of which may be from sources outside the accounting system or outside the entity. Supplementary information may be prepared in accordance with an applicable financial reporting framework, by regulatory or contractual requirements, in accordance with management's criteria, or in accordance with other requirements. The auditor may report on such information using the guidance in paragraphs .09–.13 of AU-C section 725 and the related interpretative guidance in AU-C section 9725, *Supplementary Information in Relation to the Financial Statements as a Whole: Auditing Interpretations of Section 725* (AICPA, *Professional Standards*).

A.05

Considerations for Audits Performed in Accordance With PCAOB Standards

PCAOB Auditing Standard No. 17, *Auditing Supplemental Information Accompanying Audited Financial Statements* (AICPA, *PCAOB Standards and Related Rules*, Auditing Standards), sets forth the auditor's responsibilities when the auditor of the financial statements is engaged to perform audit procedures and report on supplemental information that accompanies financial statements audited pursuant to PCAOB standards. The objective of the auditor is to obtain sufficient appropriate audit evidence to express an opinion on whether the supplemental information is fairly stated, in all material respects, in relation to the financial statements as a whole. Supplemental information, for purposes of Auditing Standard No. 17, includes

- supporting schedules that brokers and dealers are required to file pursuant to SEC Rule 17a-5;

- supplemental information (*a*) required to be presented pursuant to the rules and regulations of a regulatory authority and (*b*) covered by an independent public accountant's report on that information in relation to financial statements that are audited in accordance with PCAOB standards; or

- information that is (*a*) ancillary to the audited financial statements, (*b*) derived from the company's accounting books and records, and (*c*) covered by an independent public accountant's report on that information in relation to the financial statements that are audited in accordance with PCAOB standards.

Paragraph 4 of Auditing Standard No. 17 includes auditor performance requirements to

- obtain an understanding of the purpose of the supplemental information and the criteria management used to prepare the supplemental information, including relevant regulatory requirements;

- obtain an understanding of the methods of preparing the supplemental information, evaluate the appropriateness of those methods, and determine whether those methods have changed from methods used in the prior period and, if the methods have changed, determine the reasons for and evaluate the appropriateness of such changes;

- inquire of management about any significant assumptions or interpretations underlying the measurement or presentation of the supplemental information;

- determine that the supplemental information reconciles to the underlying accounting and other records or to the financial statements, as applicable;

- test the completeness and accuracy of the supplemental information, to the extent that it was not tested as part of the audit of the financial statements; and

- evaluate whether the supplemental information, including its form and content, complies with relevant regulatory requirements or other applicable criteria, if any.

Practitioners should review and consider all of the auditor's performance and reporting requirements contained in Auditing Standard No. 17.

11.79

Appendix B—Reports on Controls at Outside Service Organizations [1]

Readers are encouraged to review the preface of this guide for the authoritative status of this appendix.

B.01 AU-C section 402, *Audit Considerations Relating to an Entity Using a Service Organization* (AICPA, *Professional Standards*), addresses a user auditor's responsibility for obtaining sufficient appropriate audit evidence in an audit of the financial statements of a user entity that uses one or more service organizations. AT section 801, *Reporting on Controls at a Service Organization* (AICPA, *Professional Standards*), addresses examination engagements undertaken by service auditors to report on controls at organizations that provide services to user entities when those controls are likely to be relevant to user entities' internal control over financial reporting (for example, bank trust departments, plan recordkeepers, and payroll processing service organizations). Reports issued under AT section 801 will herein after be referred to as SOC 1 reports.

B.02 Paragraph .03 of AU-C section 402 states that services provided by a service organization are relevant to the audit of a user entity's financial statements when those services and the controls over them affect the user entity's information system, including related business processes, relevant to financial reporting. Although most controls at the service organization are likely to relate to financial reporting, other controls also may be relevant to the audit, such as controls over the safeguarding of assets. A service organization's services are part of the user entity's information system, including related business processes, relevant to financial reporting if these services affect any of the following:

    a. The classes of transactions in the user entity's operations that are significant to the user entity's financial statements.

    b. The procedures within both IT and manual systems by which the user entity's transactions are initiated, authorized, recorded, processed, corrected as necessary, transferred to the general ledger (or equivalent such as a trust statement), and reported in the financial statements.

    c. The related accounting records, supporting information, and specific accounts in the user entity's financial statements that are used to initiate, authorize, record, process, and report the user

---

[1] Paragraph .42 of AT section 801, *Reporting on Controls at a Service Organization* (AICPA, *Professional Standards*), states that a service auditor should inquire whether management is aware of any events subsequent to the period covered by management's description of the service organization's system up to the date of the service auditor's report that could have a significant effect on management's assertion.

The AICPA Guide *Service Organizations: Reporting on Controls at a Service Organization Relevant to User Entities' Internal Control Over Financial Reporting* contains information for practitioners reporting on controls at a service organization that affect user entities' internal control over financial reporting. Also, the AICPA Guide *Reporting on Controls at a Service Organization: Relevant to Security, Availability, Processing Integrity, Confidentiality, or Privacy (SOC 2[SM])* summarizes the three new SOC engagements and provides detailed guidance on planning, performing, and reporting on SOC 2 engagements.

entity's transactions. This includes the correction of incorrect information and how information is transferred to the general ledger; the records may be in either manual or electronic form.

d. How the user entity's information system captures events and conditions, other than transactions, that are significant to the financial statements.

e. The financial reporting process used to prepare the user entity's financial statements, including significant accounting estimates and disclosures.

f. Controls surrounding journal entries, including nonstandard journal entries used to record nonrecurring, unusual transactions, or adjustments.

B.03 If a fund uses a service organization, certain controls and records of the service organization may be relevant to the fund's ability to records, process, summarize, and report financial data in a manner consistent with the assertions in the fund's financial statements. Consistent with paragraph .07 of AU-C section 402, the objectives of the user auditor, when the user entity uses the services of a service organization, are to

a. obtain an understanding of the nature and significance of the services provided by the service organizations and their effect on the user entity's internal control relevant to the audit, sufficient to identify and assess the risks of material misstatement.

b. design and perform audit procedures responsive to those risks.

B.04 Paragraph .A1 of AU-C section 402 states that information about the nature of the services provided by a service organization may be available from a wide variety of sources, such as user manuals; system overviews; technical manuals; the contract or service level agreement between the user entity and the service organization; reports by service organization, the internal audit function, or regulatory authorities on controls at the service organization; and reports by the service auditor, if available. When obtaining an understanding of the user entity in accordance with AU-C section 315, *Understanding the Entity and Its Environment and Assessing the Risks of Material Misstatement* (AICPA, *Professional Standards*), paragraph .09 of AU-C section 402 states that the user auditor should obtain an understanding of how the user entity uses the service of a service organization in the user entity's operations, including the following:

a. The nature of the services provided by the service organization and the significance of those services to the user entity, including their effect on the user entity's internal control

b. The nature and materiality of the transactions processed or accounts or financial reporting processes affected by the service organization

c. The degree of interaction between the activities of the service organization and those of the user entity

d. The nature of the relationship between the user entity and the service organization, including the relevant contractual terms for the activities undertaken by the service organization

B.05 Nature of services provided by the service organization. As explained in paragraphs .A3–.A4 of AU-C section 402, a user entity may use a service organization, such as one that processes transactions and maintains the related accountability for the user entity or records transactions and processes related data. Examples of services provided by service organization that may be relevant to the audit include maintenance of the user entity's accounting records; management of the user entity's assets; and initiating, authorizing, recording, or processing transactions as an agent of the user entity.

B.06 Nature and materiality of transactions processed by the service organization. As explained in paragraph .A6 of AU-C section 402, a service organization may establish policies and procedures (controls) that affect the user entity's internal control. These controls are at least in part physically and operationally separate from the user entity. The significance of the controls of the service organization to the user entity's internal control depends on the nature of the services provided by the service organization, including the nature and materiality of the transactions it processes for the user entity. In certain circumstances, the transactions processed and the accounts affected by the service organization may not appear to be material to the user entity's financial statements, but the nature of the transactions processed may be significant and the user auditor may determine that an understanding of controls over the processing of those transactions is necessary in the circumstances.

B.07 The degree of interaction between the activities of the service organization and the user entity. As explained in paragraph .A7 of AU-C section 402, the significance of the controls at the service organization to the user entity's internal control also depends on the degree of interaction between the service organization's activities and those of the user entity. The degree of interaction refers to the extent to which a user entity is able to and elects to implement effective controls over the processing performed by the service organization. For example, a high degree of interaction exists between the activities of the user entity and those at the service organization when the user entity authorizes transactions and the service organization processes and accounts for those transactions. In these circumstances, it may be practicable for the user entity to implement effective controls over those transactions. On the other hand, when the service organization initiates or initially records, processes, and accounts for the user entity's transactions, a lower degree of interaction exists between the two organizations. In these circumstances, the user entity may be unable to, or may elect not to, implement effective controls over these transactions at the user entity and may rely on controls at the service organization.

B.08 In accordance with paragraphs .11–.12 of AU-C section 402, the user auditor should determine whether a sufficient understanding of the nature and significance of the services provided by the service organization and their effect on the user entity's internal control relevant to the audit has been obtained to provide a basis for the identification and assessment of risks of material misstatement. If the user auditor is unable to obtain sufficient understanding from the user entity, the user auditor should obtain that understanding from one or more of the following procedures:

a. Obtaining and reading a type 1 or type 2 SOC 1 report, if available

b. Contacting the service organization, through the user entity, to obtain specific information

c. Visiting the service organization and performing procedures that will provide the necessary information about the relevant controls at the service organization

d. Using another auditor to perform procedures that will provide the necessary information about the relevant controls at the service organization

B.09 A type 1 SOC 1 report is a report on the fairness of the presentation of management's description of the service organization's system and the suitability of the design of the controls to achieve the related control objectives included in the description as of a specified date. A type 2 SOC 1 report is a report that also includes (*a*) the service auditor's opinion on the operating effectiveness of the controls and (*b*) a detailed description of the service auditor's tests of the operating effectiveness of the controls and the results of those tests throughout a specified period.

B.10 Type 1 SOC 1 reports are designed to provide information about the flow of transactions within and controls over relevant applications at the service organization, and whether such controls were suitably designed and had been placed in operation. Such a report, either alone or in conjunction with controls at the user entity, does not provide any evidence of the operating effectiveness of the relevant controls.

B.11 Type 2 SOC 1 reports provide additional information about the nature, timing, extent, and results of the service auditor's tests of specified controls at the service organization that may be useful if the user auditor intends to place reliance on controls at the service organization to reduce the extent of their substantive procedures. Although a type 2 SOC 1 report may provide a basis for assessing control risk below the maximum, it does not permit the auditor to assess the level of control risk so low to eliminate the need to perform substantive tests for the fund's accounts and transactions.

B.12 Paragraphs .13–.14 of AU-C section 402 provide audit requirements on using a type 1 or type 2 SOC 1 report to support the user auditor's understanding of the service organization.

B.13 Paragraph .21 of AU-C section 402 states that the user auditor should not refer to the work of a service auditor in the user auditor's report containing an unmodified opinion. However, as stated in paragraph .A44 of AU-C section 402, when the user auditor expresses a modified opinion because of a modified opinion in a service auditor's report, the user auditor is not precluded from referring to the service auditor's report if such reference assists in explaining the reason for the user auditor's modified opinion. In such circumstances, the user auditor need not identify the service auditor by name and may need the consent of the service auditor before making such a reference.

Appendix C—Consideration of Fraud in a Financial Statement Audit

Readers are encouraged to review the preface of this guide for the authoritative status of this appendix.

C.01 AU-C section 240, *Consideration of Fraud in a Financial Statement Audit* (AICPA, *Professional Standards*), addresses the auditor's responsibilities relating to fraud in an audit of financial statements. Specifically, it expands on how AU-C sections 315, *Understanding the Entity and Its Environment and Assessing the Risks of Material Misstatement*, and 330, *Performing Audit Procedures in Response to Assessed Risks and Evaluating the Audit Evidence Obtained* (AICPA, *Professional Standards*), are to be applied regarding risks of material misstatement due to fraud.

C.02 Paragraph .03 of AU-C section 240 states, although fraud is a broad legal concept, for the purposes of generally accepted auditing standards (GAAS), the auditor is primarily concerned with fraud that causes a material misstatement in the financial statements. The two types of intentional misstatements relevant to the auditor are misstatements resulting from fraudulent financial reporting and misstatements resulting from misappropriation of assets. Although the auditor may suspect or, in rare cases, identify the occurrence of fraud, the auditor does not make legal determinations of whether fraud has actually occurred.

C.03 Paragraph .A1 of AU-C section 240 explains that fraud, whether fraudulent financial reporting or misappropriation of assets, involves incentive or pressure to commit fraud, a perceived opportunity to do so, and some rationalization of the act.

Professional Skepticism

C.04 In accordance with AU-C section 200, *Overall Objectives of the Independent Auditor and the Conduct of an Audit in Accordance With Generally Accepted Auditing Standards* (AICPA, *Professional Standards*), paragraph .12 of AU-C section 240 states that the auditor should maintain professional skepticism throughout the audit, recognizing the possibility that a material misstatement due to fraud could exist, notwithstanding the auditor's past experience of the honesty and integrity of the entity's management and those charged with governance.

C.05 Paragraphs .A9–.A10 of AU-C section 240 further explain that maintaining professional skepticism requires an ongoing questioning of whether the information and audit evidence obtained suggests that a material misstatement due to fraud may exist. It includes considering the reliability of the information to be used as audit evidence and the controls over its preparation and maintenance when relevant. Although the auditor cannot be expected to disregard past experience of the honesty and integrity of the entity's management and those charged with governance, the auditor's professional skepticism is particularly important in considering the risks of material misstatement due to fraud because there may have been changes in circumstances.

C.06 When responses to inquiries of management, those charged with governance, or others are inconsistent or otherwise unsatisfactory (for example, vague or implausible), paragraph .14 of AU-C section 240 requires the auditor to further investigate the inconsistencies or unsatisfactory responses.

Discussion Among the Engagement Team

C.07 AU-C section 315 requires a discussion among the key engagement team members, including the engagement partner, and a determination by the engagement partner of which matters are to be communicated to those team members not involved in the discussion. Paragraph .15 of AU-C section 240 states this discussion should include an exchange of ideas or brainstorming among the engagement team members about how and where the entity's financial statements might be susceptible to material misstatement due to fraud, how management could perpetrate and conceal fraudulent financial reporting, and how assets of the entity could be misappropriated. The discussion should occur setting aside beliefs that the engagement team members may have that management and those charged with governance are honest and have integrity, and should, in particular, also address

　　a. known external and internal factors affecting the entity that may create an incentive or pressure for management or others to commit fraud, provide the opportunity for fraud to be perpetrated, and indicate a culture or environment that enables management or others to rationalize committing fraud;

　　b. the risk of management override of controls;

　　c. consideration of circumstances that might be indicative of earnings management or manipulation of other financial measures and the practices that might be followed by management to manage earnings or other financial measures that could lead to fraudulent financial reporting;

　　d. the importance of maintaining professional skepticism throughout the audit regarding the potential for material misstatement due to fraud; and

　　e. how the auditor might respond to the susceptibility of the entity's financial statements to material misstatement due to fraud.

Communication among the engagement team members about the risks of material misstatement due to fraud should continue throughout the audit, particularly upon discovery of new facts during the audit.

C.08 Exhibit 11-1, "Fraud Risk Factors," which appears at the end of this appendix, contains a list of fraud risk factors that auditors may consider as part of their planning and audit procedures.

C.09

　　Considerations for Audits Performed in Accordance With PCAOB Standards

　　Auditing Standard No. 12, *Identifying and Assessing Risks of Material Misstatement* (AICPA, *PCAOB Standards and Related Rules,* Auditing Standards), requires a discussion among the key engagement team members of specified matters regarding fraud, including how and where the company's financial statements might be susceptible to material misstatement due to fraud, known fraud risk factors, the risk of management override of controls, and possible responses to fraud risks. Certain matters are also required to be emphasized to all engagement team members, including the need to maintain a questioning mind throughout the audit and to exercise professional skepticism in gathering and evaluating evidence, to be alert for information or other conditions that might affect the assessment of fraud risks, and actions to be taken if information or other conditions indicate that a material misstatement due to fraud might have occurred.

Risk Assessment Procedures and Related Activities

C.10 When performing risk assessment procedures and related activities to obtain an understanding of the entity and its environment, including the entity's internal control, required by AU-C section 315, paragraph .16 of AU-C section 240 states that the auditor should perform the procedures in paragraphs .17–.24 of AU-C section 240 to obtain information for use in identifying the risk of material misstatement due to fraud. As part of this work, the auditor should perform the following procedures:

a. Hold fraud discussions with management, others within the entity, and those charged with governance (unless all those charged with governance are involved in managing the entity). See specific inquiries the auditor should make in paragraphs .17–.19 and .21 of AU-C section 240.

b. Obtain an understanding of how those charged with governance exercise oversight of management's process for identifying and responding to the risks of fraud in the entity and the internal control that management has established to mitigate these risks, unless all those charged with governance are involved in managing the entity (see paragraphs .20 and .A21–.A23 of AU-C section 240).

c. Evaluate whether unusual or unexpected relationships that have been identified (based on analytical procedures performed as part of risk assessment procedures) indicate risks of material misstatement due to fraud (see paragraphs .22, .A24–.A26, and .A46 of AU-C section 240).

d. Consider whether other information obtained by the auditor indicates risks of material misstatement due to fraud (see paragraphs .23 and .A27 of AU-C section 240).

e. Evaluate whether the information obtained from the risk assessment procedures and related activities performed indicates that one or more fraud risk factors are present (see paragraphs .24 and .A28–.A32 of AU-C section 240 and paragraphs C.13–.15 of this appendix).

C.11

Considerations for Audits Performed in Accordance With PCAOB Standards

Auditing Standard No. 12 requires the auditor to make specific inquiries of management and the audit committee, among other matters, regarding tips or complaints about the company's financial reporting. The auditor is required to use his or her knowledge of the company and its environment, as well as information from other risk assessment procedures, to determine the nature of inquiries about risks of material misstatement. The auditor must take into account the fact that management is often in the best position to commit fraud when evaluating management's responses to inquiries about fraud risks.

C.12 Based on analytical procedures performed as part of risk assessment procedures, paragraph .22 of AU-C section 240 states that the auditor should evaluate whether unusual or unexpected relationships that have been identified indicate risks of material misstatement due to fraud. To the extent not already included, the analytical procedures, and evaluation thereof, should include procedures relating to revenue accounts.[1] For example, in the investment company industry, the following unusual or unexpected relationships may indicate a material misstatement due to fraud:

  a. Investment performance substantially higher (or lower) when compared with industry peers or other relevant benchmarks, which cannot be readily attributed to the performance of specific securities when prices are readily available in an active market. Particular considerations include the following:

    i. Significant gains (or losses) from securities held for extremely short periods of time

    ii. Significant gains (or losses) from instruments not typically acquired by the fund

  b. Unusually high levels of investment purchases and sales in relation to total fund net assets without apparent economic purpose.

  c. A net investment income ratio substantially higher than the industry peers or other relevant benchmarks, particularly in a fund marketed with the objective of making current income distributions.

  d. Expense ratios that change significantly from year to year with inadequate explanation.

  e. Expense ratios and transaction costs exceed industry norms.

  f. Significant differences between the prices at which securities are sold to third parties from the values reflected in the fund's net asset value in the days prior to the sale.

  g. Unusually high volumes of gross fund share sales and redemptions in relation to total shares outstanding.

Evaluation of Fraud Risk Factors

C.13 The auditor may identify events or conditions that indicate an incentive or pressure to perpetrate fraud, provide an opportunity to commit fraud, or indicate attitudes or rationalizations to justify a fraudulent action. For purposes of GAAS, such events or conditions are defined as *fraud risk factors*. Although fraud risk factors may not necessarily indicate the existence of fraud, paragraph .24 of AU-C section 240 states that they have often been present in circumstances in which frauds have occurred and, therefore may indicate risks of material misstatement due to fraud.

C.14 Paragraph .A31 of AU-C section 240 states that the size, complexity, and ownership characteristics of the entity have a significant influence on the consideration of relevant fraud risk factors. Additional fraud risk factor

---

[1] The PCAOB released Staff Audit Practice Alert No. 12, *Matters Related to Auditing Revenue in an Audit of Financial Statements* (AICPA, *PCAOB Standards and Related Rules*, PCAOB Staff Guidance , sec. 400.12) in September 2014 to highlight certain requirements of PCAOB standards related to aspects of auditing revenue. Readers are encouraged to read the full text of the alert, available at www.pcaobus.org/Standards/QandA/9-9-14˙SAPA˙12.pdf.

considerations on large and smaller, less complex entities can be found in paragraphs .A31–.A32 of AU-C section 240.

C.15 Appendix A, "Examples of Fraud Risk Factors," of AU-C section 240 identifies examples of fraud risk factors that may be faced by auditors in a broad range of situations. Exhibit 11-1 at the end of this appendix contains a list of fraud risk factors specific to the investment company industry. Remember that fraud risk factors are only one of several sources of information that an auditor considers when identifying and assessing risks of material misstatement due to fraud.

Identification and Assessment of the Risks of Material Misstatement Due to Fraud

C.16 In accordance with AU-C section 315, paragraph .25 of AU-C section 240 states that the auditor should identify and assess the risks of material misstatement due to fraud at the financial statement level, and at the assertion level for classes of transactions, account balances, and disclosures.[2] The auditor's risk assessment should be ongoing throughout the audit, following the initial assessment.

C.17

> *Considerations for Audits Performed in Accordance With PCAOB Standards*
>
> Paragraph 59 of Auditing Standard No. 12 states that the auditor should identify the risks of material misstatement at the financial statement level and the assertion level, and describes the steps the auditor should take during the identification process. Among others, the identification of fraud risks is one of the identified steps in this process. The factors relevant to identifying fraud risks are discussed in paragraphs 65–69 of Auditing Standard No. 12.

C.18 The fact that significant amounts of investments are valued by management, either judgmentally or through valuation models, presents a number of risks that the auditor should address. The following are illustrative risk factors related to the fair valuation of investments that the auditor could consider:

a. Lack of approval or oversight, or both, of a fair valuation policy by the board of directors or trustees

b. Lack of specificity in a fair valuation policy and procedures

c. Lack of consistency in the application of valuation procedures

d. Inordinate influence of portfolio management personnel over fair valuation decisions

e. Fair valuation by management when market values appear to be reasonably available

f. Lack of monitoring or follow up, or both, of fair valuation actions taken

g. Lack of evidence for fair valuation decisions made

h. Significant amounts of investments traded in "thin" markets, particularly through one market maker (either exclusively or primarily)

---

[2] This requirement provides a link between the auditor's consideration of fraud and assessment of risk and the auditor's procedures in response to those assessed risks.

    i. For securities not traded in organized markets (in particular, private placements) a determination of whether a purchase of investments has occurred, requiring the initiation of valuation procedures, or whether a sale has occurred for recognition of realized gain or loss, or both

    j. Increases in the value of investments valued by management shortly after their acquisition without adequate explanation of the circumstances

C.19 In addition to fair valuation, risks are present in daily market valuation, as well. Risks that the auditor could consider include the following:

    a. Use of a pricing service with inadequate capabilities or controls

    b. Ability of portfolio management or other unauthorized individuals to override prices

    c. Lack of consideration or availability of secondary or comparative, or both, pricing sources

    d. Significant levels of pricing from brokers

    e. Manual entry or override of prices

C.20 Derivative instruments are another class of transactions characterized by high inherent risk. The auditor could consider the following risk factors associated with derivatives:

    a. Lack of a policy governing derivative investments, including a clear definition of derivatives

    b. Lack of oversight over the use of derivative investments, including an ongoing risk assessment of derivative instruments

    c. Lack of adequate procedures to value derivatives

    d. Lack of an awareness or understanding of derivative transactions on the part of senior management or the board of directors or trustees

C.21 Trading of investment securities also poses some risks that could include the following factors:

    a. Lack of segregation of duties between portfolio management and trading functions

    b. Lack of a developed and consistently applied and enforced trade allocation policy

    c. Trading through unapproved counterparties

    d. Lack of enforcement of a personal trading (code of ethics) policy

    e. Lack of monitoring of commission levels and volume of trading by a broker

C.22 The auditor could consider the following factors for transfer agency or capital stock activity, or both:

    a. High volume of cancel, rebook, or "as-of" activity

    b. Credible shareholder complaints

    c. Activity on dormant accounts

    d. Inadequate segregation of duties among mail processing, transaction processing, and reconciliation functions *e.* Inadequate segregation of duties within transaction processing, such as allowing processors to change an address or banking instructions and initiate a redemption

C.23 Other areas that the auditor could consider because they involve a high degree of management judgment and subjectivity and are susceptible to manipulation by management include the following:

    a. Income recognition on high-yield debt instruments when collectability is in question or on asset-backed securities requiring significant estimates regarding the timing of expected cash flows

    b. Major judgments made in determining that a regulated investment company (RIC) has qualified for "pass-through" status under IRC Subchapter M, which may include determining issuers for diversification status, major determinations of classification of revenue items as ordinary income or (long-term) realized gain, and satisfaction of the minimum distribution requirement

    c. Significant elements of incentive fee computations (including the computation of any benchmarks against which performance is to be measured)

Risks of Fraud in Revenue Recognition

C.24 Paragraph .26 of AU-C section 240 states that when identifying and assessing the risks of material misstatements due to fraud, the auditor should, based on a presumption that risks of fraud exist in revenue recognition, evaluate which types of revenue, revenue transactions, or assertions give rise to such risks. Paragraph .46 of AU-C section 240 specifies the documentation required when the auditor concludes that the presumption is not applicable in the circumstances of the engagement and, accordingly, has not identified revenue recognition as a risk of material misstatement due to fraud. (See paragraphs .A33–.A35 of AU-C section 240 for application guidance on revenue recognition fraud risks).[3]

C.25 The risks of material misstatement of an investment company's financial statements due to improper revenue recognition will generally be considered inherently low. Valuations can be readily established for securities traded on active markets; interest on fixed-income securities can be readily computed as the product of coupon rate and par value, and dividend income can be readily determined through the use of widely-available reporting sources. The more that a particular fund departs from this model, the greater the risks of material misstatement due to fraud relating to revenue recognition. For example, as discussed previously, revenue recognition on certain asset-backed securities depends heavily on management's estimation of future cash flows, and management must estimate the collectability of interest (including unamortized discount) on high-yield securities when the underlying issuer is experiencing financial difficulty.

C.26 Various risks exist to the extent that securities cannot be valued on the basis of prices determined in an active market. To the extent that management is estimating the value of portfolio investments, the risk of fraudulent

---

[3] For a discussion of indicators of improper revenue recognition and common techniques for overstating revenue and illustrative audit procedures, see the AICPA Audit Guide *Auditing Revenue in Certain Industries.*

misstatement from systematic bias ordinarily exists, even when using generally recognized models. If an investment is valued through a single market maker (often the counterparty that sold the investment to the investment company), there is a risk that collusion occurred between that market maker and management in establishing a valuation for the investment. In many cases, independent valuation services provide estimates of value for fixed-income securities based on observable market transactions and financial information (including security ratings) available publicly. In some cases, however, the independent valuation service estimates value for securities that are not traded in the market, and for which the investment company may be the predominant or sole holder of the securities, based predominantly or solely on information that is provided by the investment company. In these infrequent cases, there is a risk that the information provided by management to the service is incomplete or otherwise biased. If the market for a security is "thin," there is a risk that the investment company (or related investment companies) may be able to manipulate the quoted price by systematic purchases of the security in the market. An auditor would not ordinarily be expected to identify price manipulation but may be able to identify a "thin" market in which trades are typically sporadic, so that small changes in supply or demand can have a significant effect on quoted prices. Usually, such securities only have an extremely small "float" (that is, freely tradable amounts owned by the public).

C.27 The auditor could consider the following factors related to the recognition of interest and dividend revenues:

- Cash receipts for interest or dividend payments are significantly different from accrued amounts.
- Receivable balances include potentially uncollectible interest or dividends, such as significantly overdue amounts.
- Interest or dividend accrual policies do not comply with U.S. generally accepted accounting principles or are not enforced.
- Daily interest income is erratic, rather than reasonably consistent.
- Procedures in place to identify dividends earned are lax.
- Interest or dividends receivable may be written off without independent approval.

C.28 Factors that the auditor could consider with respect to revenue recognition for realized and unrealized gains include the following:

- The stated policy for purchase lot selection on security sales is not followed.
- Realized gains are not properly calculated on sales.

C.29 The auditor also should determine that an investment company does not record capital contributions from affiliates as revenues (see paragraphs 7.137–.143 of this guide for guidance on accounting for payments by affiliates and corrections of investment restriction violations).

Identifying and Assessing the Risks of Material Misstatement Due to Fraud and Understanding the Entity's Related Controls

C.30 Paragraph .27 of AU-C section 240 states that the auditor should treat those assessed risks of material misstatement due to fraud as significant risks and, accordingly, to the extent not already done so, the auditor should obtain an understanding of the entity's related controls, including control activities, relevant to such risks, such as the evaluation of whether such controls have been suitably designed and implemented to mitigate such fraud risks. (See paragraphs .A36–.A37 of AU-C section 240 for application guidance on identifying and assessing the risks of material misstatement due to fraud and understanding the entity's related controls.)

C.31 Most investment advisers maintain extensive portfolio management controls, including the following:

- Separation of portfolio management and trading functions
- *Attribution analysis*, which is an explanation of portfolio performance against a stated benchmark, identifying industry or security exposures that caused the performance difference, to assist management in identifying abnormal items for their own follow up
- *Dispersion analysis*, which is comparing the performance of similar portfolios managed by the same individual or group with an analysis of any outlying performance, to assist management in identifying abnormal items for their own follow up
- Frequent reconciliation of cash and portfolio holdings to custodian records
- Comparison of trade terms to broker confirmation prior to recording the transaction
- Extra level of approval for nonstandard wire transfers
- Monitoring of activity on dormant shareholder accounts
- Review of nonstandard journal entries

C.32 Many investment companies also maintain extensive controls over the valuation of securities not traded on active markets, including the following:

- Written valuation policies and procedures.
- Valuation committees comprising accounting, portfolio management, and administrative or legal personnel to assess valuation procedures and significant valuation estimates. Some registered investment companies place such committees under the oversight of the board of directors or trustees, or both, and occasionally, board members will participate in committee deliberations on significant matters.
- Tracking of actual sale prices against valuations as determined by management or market makers.
- Use of secondary pricing services for comparison with the primary source.
- "Stale price" and "large price change" reports to identify securities for which prices may not have been updated on a timely basis or that have experienced unusual or abnormal changes.
- Segregation of portfolio management from valuation functions.

C.33 Examples of broader programs designed to prevent, deter, and detect fraud include the following:

- Code of conduct regarding ethical behavior, compliance with which is typically documented

- Code of ethics regarding personal trading, compliance with which is typically documented

- Compliance programs

- Periodic documentation of compliance of an investment company with its investment objectives and restrictions

- Systems controls, such as security access

- Channels available for employees to report any fraud concerns

C.34 The SEC requires both registered investment companies and registered investment advisers to adopt and implement written policies and procedures reasonably designed to prevent the violation of federal securities laws.[4] Both funds and advisers are required to appoint chief compliance officers responsible for administering these policies and procedures and to review the policies and procedures annually for adequacy and effectiveness of implementation. Among other things, the designation of a chief compliance officer of a registered investment company is required to be approved by the investment company's board of directors or trustees, and the chief compliance officer is to report directly to the board of directors or trustees and meet in an executive session with independent directors or trustees at least annually.

Responses to the Assessed Risks of Material Misstatement Due to Fraud

Overall Responses

C.35 In accordance with AU-C section 330, paragraphs .28–.29 of AU-C section 240 state that the auditor should determine overall responses to address the assessed risks of material misstatement due to fraud at the financial statement level. Accordingly, the auditor should

    a. assign and supervise personnel, taking into account the knowledge, skill and ability of the individuals to be given significant engagement responsibilities and the auditor's assessment of the risks of material misstatement due to fraud for the engagement;

    b. evaluate whether the selection and application of accounting policies by the entity, particularly those related to subjective measurements and complex transactions, may be indicative of fraudulent financial reporting resulting from management's effort to manage earnings, or a bias that may create a material misstatement; and

    c. incorporate an element of unpredictability in the selection of the nature, timing, and extent of audit procedures.

See paragraphs .A38–.A42 of AU-C section 240 for additional application guidance on overall responses to the assessed risks of material misstatement due to fraud.

---

[4] Rule 38a-1 under the 1940 Act and Rule 206(4)-7 under the Investment Advisers Act of 1940. See SEC Final Rule Release No. IC-26299 under the 1940 Act (Release No. IA-2204 under the Investment Advisers Act of 1940). The adopting release discusses issues that the SEC expects to see addressed in an adviser's or fund's policies and procedures, to the extent that they are relevant, and reviews the application of certain other critical areas that policies and procedures of investment companies should address, including the pricing of portfolio securities and fund shares, as discussed in the "Valuing Investments" section of chapter 2, "Investment Accounts."

Audit Procedures Responsive to Assessed Risks of Material Misstatement Due to Fraud at the Assertion Level

C.36 In accordance with AU-C section 330, paragraph .30 of AU-C section 240 states that the auditor should design and perform further audit procedures whose nature, timing, and extent are responsive to the assessed risks of material misstatement due to fraud at the assertion level (see paragraphs .A43–.A46 for further application guidance).

C.37 Investment company audit procedures that may be considered include the following:

    a. Analytical procedures, such as comparing fund performance to benchmark indexes and net investment income ratios to yield indexes for comparable securities or investment funds

    b. Reading compliance summaries for individual funds and testing compliance determinations contained therein

    c. Comparisons of valuations of securities determined by management or a single market maker during the year with prices received on actual sales

    d. Attempting to obtain market quotations for certain securities from broker-dealers or recognized pricing sources other than the primary pricing source (however, this may not always be possible, and even when received, the quotations may be of lesser quality because the secondary source may not have the same access to information about the security as the primary source)

    e. Testing inputs to valuation models for reasonableness in relation to published data or financial information services

    f. Reviewing minutes of board valuation committee meetings and considering whether the minutes adequately support the valuations determined or the procedures used to reach them

    g. Testing management's assumptions regarding the collectability of interest or projected cash flows for asset-backed securities by reference to issuer data available from public sources or financial information services

C.38

Considerations for Audits Performed in Accordance With PCAOB Standards

Auditing Standard No. 13, *The Auditor's Responses to the Risks of Material Misstatement* (AICPA, *PCAOB Standards and Related Rules*, Auditing Standards), requires the auditor to design and implement audit responses that address the risks of material misstatement that are identified and assessed in accordance with Auditing Standard No. 12. These audit responses include those that have an overall effect on how the audit is conducted; and those involving the nature, timing, and extent of the audit procedures to be performed. The auditor is required to determine whether it is necessary to make pervasive changes to the nature, timing, or extent of audit procedures to adequately address the assessed risk of material misstatement.

Audit Procedures Responsive to Risks Related to Management Override of Controls

C.39 Even if the auditor does not identify specific risks of material misstatement due to fraud, paragraph .32 of AU-C section 240 states that a possibility exists that management override of controls could occur. Accordingly, the auditor should address the risk of management override of controls apart from any conclusions regarding the existence of more specifically identifiable risks by designing and performing audit procedures to

a. test the appropriateness of journal entries recorded in the general ledger and other adjustments made in preparation of the financial statements, including entries posted directly to financial statement drafts;

b. review accounting estimates for biases and evaluate whether the circumstances producing the bias, if any, represent a risk of material misstatement due to fraud; and

c. evaluate, for significant transactions that are outside the normal course of business for the entity or that otherwise appear to be unusual given the auditor's understanding of the entity and its environment and other information obtained during the audit, whether the business rationale (or lack thereof) of the transactions suggests that they may have been entered into to engage in fraudulent financial reporting or to conceal misappropriation of assets.

Key Estimates

C.40 The financial statements of investment companies are typically less complicated than those of other entities and have relatively few estimates. Most key estimates relate to revenue recognition, including portfolio valuation, as well as interest recognition on high-yield and asset-backed securities, which are discussed in paragraphs C.24–.25 of this appendix. Material expense accruals (in particular, performance fees) and the effect of shareholder activity not yet fully processed by the transfer agent on shares outstanding ordinarily require significant estimation procedures.

C.41 Often, nonaccounting estimates are integral to measuring a portfolio's compliance with its investment restrictions and characteristics (for example, the duration of a fixed-income portfolio often is a key characteristic, and estimates are required to measure the duration of asset-backed and other securities subject to prepayment). Although these nonaccounting measures typically are not explicitly tested in an audit of financial statements, the auditor could become aware of their existence and consider how management controls their use. However, the auditor is not responsible for assessing whether the fund is meeting its investment objectives, its investment strategies, or complying with its investment restrictions, laws, and regulations.

Evaluation of Audit Evidence

C.42 Paragraphs .34–.37 and .A56–.A62 of AU-C section 240 provide requirements and application guidance for evaluating audit evidence. The auditor should evaluate, at or near the end of the audit, whether the accumulated results of auditing procedures, including analytical procedures, that were performed as substantive tests or when forming an overall conclusion, affect the assessment of the risks of material misstatement due to fraud made earlier in the audit or indicate a previously unrecognized risk of material misstatement due to fraud.

Consideration of Identified Misstatements

C.43 If the auditor identifies a misstatement, the auditor should evaluate whether such a misstatement is indicative of fraud. If such an indication exists, the auditor should evaluate the implications of the misstatement with regard to other aspects of the audit, particularly the auditor's evaluation of materiality, management and employee integrity, and the reliability of management representations, recognizing that an instance of fraud is unlikely to be an isolated occurrence. Furthermore, if the auditor identifies a misstatement, whether material or not, and the auditor has reason to believe that it is, or may be, the result of fraud and that management (in particular, senior management) is involved, the auditor should reevaluate the assessment of the risks of material misstatement due to fraud and its resulting effect on the nature, timing, and extent of audit procedures to respond to the assessed risks. The auditor should also consider whether circumstances or conditions indicate possible collusion involving employees, management, or third parties when reconsidering the reliability of evidence previously obtained.

C.44 If the auditor concludes that, or is unable to conclude whether, the financial statements are materially misstated as a result of fraud, the auditor should evaluate the implications for the audit. AU-C sections 450, *Evaluation of Misstatements Identified During the Audit*, and 700, *Forming an Opinion and Reporting on Financial Statements* (AICPA, *Professional Standards*), address the evaluation and disposition of misstatements and the effect on the auditor's opinion in the auditor's report.

Auditor Unable to Continue the Engagement

C.45 Paragraph .38 of AU-C section 240 states that, if, as a result of identified fraud or suspected fraud, the auditor encounters circumstances that bring into question the auditor's ability to continue performing the audit, the auditor should

   a. determine the professional and legal responsibilities applicable in the circumstances, including whether a requirement exists for the auditor to report to the person or persons who engaged the auditor or, in some cases, to regulatory authorities;

   b. consider whether it is appropriate to withdraw from the engagement, when withdrawal is possible under applicable law or regulation; and

   c. if the auditor withdraws

       i. discuss with the appropriate level of management and those charged with governance the auditor's withdrawal from the engagement and the reasons for the withdrawal, and

       ii. determine whether a professional or legal requirement exists to report to the person or persons who engaged the auditor or, in some cases, to regulatory authorities, the auditor's withdrawal from the engagement and the reasons for the withdrawal.

Given the nature of the circumstances and the need to consider the legal requirements, paragraph .A65 states that the auditor may consider it appropriate to seek legal advice when deciding whether to withdraw from an engagement and in determining an appropriate course of action, including the possibility of reporting to regulators or others.[5] For additional application guidance, including examples of circumstances that may arise and bring into question the auditor's ability to continue performing the audit, see paragraphs .A63–.A65 of AU-C section 240.

C.46

Considerations for Audits Performed in Accordance With PCAOB Standards

Auditing Standard No. 14, *Evaluating Audit Results* (AICPA, *PCAOB Standards and Related Rules*, Auditing Standards), requires the auditor to perform procedures to obtain additional audit evidence to determine whether fraud has occurred or is likely to have occurred, and, if so, its effect on the financial statements and the auditor's report if the auditor believes that a misstatement is or might be intentional, and if the effect on the financial statement cannot be readily determined.

Communications to Management and With Those Charged With Governance

C.47 Paragraph .39 of AU-C section 240 addresses the auditor's requirements regarding communications to management and with those charged with governance. If the auditor has identified a fraud or has obtained information that indicates that a fraud may exist, the auditor should communicate these matters on a timely basis to the appropriate level of management in order to inform those with primary responsibility for the prevention and detection of fraud of matters relevant to their responsibilities. Paragraph .A67 of AU-C section 240 explains that this is true even if the matter might be considered inconsequential (for example, a minor defalcation by an employee at a low level in the entity's organization). Paragraph .40 of AU-C section 240 states that unless all of those charged with governance are involved in managing the entity, if the auditor has identified or suspects fraud involving (*a*) management, (*b*) employees who have significant roles in internal control, or (*c*) others, when the fraud results in a material misstatement in the financial statements, the auditor should communicate these matters to those charged with governance on a timely basis. If the auditor suspects fraud involving management, the auditor should communicate these suspicions to those charged with governance and discuss with them the nature, timing, and extent of audit procedures necessary to complete the audit. In addition, paragraph .41 of AU-C section 240 states that the auditor should communicate with those charged with governance any other matters related to fraud that are, in the auditor's professional judgment, relevant to their responsibilities. See paragraphs .A68–.A71 of AU-C section 240 for further application guidance concerning communications with those charged with governance.

---

[5] AU-C section 510, *Opening Balances—Initial Audit Engagements, Including Reaudit Engagements* (AICPA, *Professional Standards*), provides guidance on communications with an auditor replacing the existing auditor.

C.48

Considerations for Audits Performed in Accordance With PCAOB Standards

Auditing Standard No. 16, *Communications with Audit Committees* (AICPA, *PCAOB Standards and Related Rules*, Auditing Standards), establishes certain required communications related to the communication of fraud. The requirements of the standard are substantially consistent with those established by the AICPA Auditing Standards Board (as discussed throughout this chapter). Auditing Standard No. 16 specifically discusses the following requirements associated with fraud procedures and communication of fraud-related matters:

- Paragraph 8 of Auditing Standard No. 16 requires the auditor to inquire of the audit committee about whether it is aware of matters relevant to the audit, including, but not limited to, violations or possible violations of laws or regulations. In addition to this inquiry, paragraphs 5(f) and 54–57 of Auditing Standard No. 12[6] describe the auditor's inquiries of the audit committee, or equivalent (or its chair) regarding the audit committee's knowledge of the risks of material misstatement, including fraud risks. These inquiries include, among other things, whether the audit committee is aware of tips or complaints regarding the company's financial reporting.

- Paragraph 13[7] of Auditing Standard No. 16 discusses various matters that the auditor should communicate to the audit committee, including the auditor's understanding of the business purpose (of lack thereof) for significant unusual transactions. As discussed further in paragraph C.39c of this appendix, while gaining an understanding of the business rationale for such transactions, the auditor should assess the risk of management override of controls to achieve fraudulent financial reporting or to conceal misappropriation of assets.

- Paragraph 24 of Auditing Standard No. 16 discusses the auditor's requirements for communicating other matters to the audit committee. The standard refers to guidance in paragraphs .79–.81 of AU section 316, *Consideration of Fraud in a Financial Statement Audit* (AICPA, *PCAOB Standards and Related Rules*, Interim Standards), for specific communication requirements relating to fraud. These paragraphs of AU section 316 are substantially consistent with paragraphs .39–.41 of AU-C section 240 and related application paragraphs .A67, .A69, and .A71 of AU-C section 240. See the previous paragraph of this appendix for discussion of paragraph .39 of AU-C section 240.

---

[6] As amended by PCAOB Release No. 2014-002, *Related Parties, Amendments to Certain PCAOB Auditing Standards Regarding Significant Unusual Transactions and Other Amendments to PCAOB Auditing Standards* (AICPA, *PCAOB Standards and Related Rules*, Select PCAOB Releases).

[7] See footnote 6.

Documentation

C.49 Paragraphs .43–.46 of AU-C section 240 address requirements to document certain matters related to the auditor's consideration of fraud in a financial statement audit.

Exhibit 11-1

Fraud Risk Factors

Two types of fraud are relevant to the auditor's consideration, namely, fraudulent financial reporting and the misappropriation of assets. For each of these types of fraud, the risk factors are further classified based on the three conditions generally present when material misstatements due to fraud occur, which are incentives and pressures, opportunities, and attitudes and rationalizations. The following are examples of conditions that may indicate the presence of fraud in investment companies. Although the risk factors cover a broad range of situations, they are only examples; accordingly, the auditor may identify additional or different risk factors. The order of the examples of risk factors provided is not intended to reflect any relative importance or frequency of occurrence.

Paragraph .03 of AU-C section 240 states that the auditor is primarily concerned with fraud that causes a material misstatement in the financial statements. Some of the following factors and conditions are present in entities in which specific circumstances *do not present a risk of material misstatement*. Also, specific controls may exist that mitigate the risk of material misstatement due to fraud, even though risk factors or conditions are present. When identifying risk factors and other conditions, the auditors might assess whether those risk factors and conditions, individually and in combination, present a risk of material misstatement of the financial statements.

Part 1: Fraudulent Financial Reporting

A. *Incentives and Pressures*

1. Financial stability or profitability is threatened by economic, industry, or entity operating conditions, such as (or as indicated by) the following:

    a. High degree of competition or market saturation, accompanied by declining margins

    b. High vulnerability to rapid changes, such as changes in technology, product obsolescence, or interest rates

    c. Significant declines in customer demand and increasing business failures in either the industry or overall economy

    d. Operating losses making the threat of bankruptcy, foreclosure, or hostile takeover imminent

    e. Recurring negative cash flows from operations or an inability to generate cash flows from operations while reporting earnings and earnings growth

    f. Rapid growth or unusual profitability especially compared to that of other companies in the same industry

    g. New accounting, statutory, or regulatory requirements

2. Excessive pressure exists for management to meet the requirements or expectations of third parties due to the following:

    a. Profitability or trend level expectations of investment analysts, institutional investors, significant creditors, or other external parties (particularly expectations that are unduly aggressive or unrealistic), including expectations created by management in, for example, overly optimistic press releases or annual report messages

b. Need to obtain additional debt or equity financing to stay competitive—including financing of major research and development or capital expenditures

c. Marginal ability to meet exchange listing requirements or debt repayment or other debt covenant requirements

d. Perceived or real adverse effects of reporting poor financial results on significant pending transactions, such as business combinations or contract awards

e. A need to achieve financial targets required in bond covenants

f. Pressure for management to meet the expectations of legislative or oversight bodies or to achieve political outcomes, or both

3. Information available indicates that the personal financial situation of management or those charged with governance is threatened by the entity's financial performance arising from the following:

a. Significant financial interests in the entity

b. Significant portions of their compensation (for example, bonuses, stock options, and earn-out arrangements) being contingent upon achieving aggressive targets for stock price, operating results, financial position, or cash flow[8]

c. Personal guarantees of debts of the entity

4. Management or operating personnel are under excessive pressure to meet financial targets established by those charged with governance, including sales or profitability incentive goals.

B. *Opportunities*

1. The nature of the industry or the entity's operations provides opportunities to engage in fraudulent financial reporting that can arise from the following:

a. Significant related party transactions not in the ordinary course of business or with related entities not audited or audited by another firm, such as

   i. significant transactions with affiliates that are not approved by the board of directors or trustees, in accordance with Section 17 of the 1940 Act, and

   ii. transactions involving affiliates that are not readily apparent in the circumstances or are apparent but not properly disclosed.

b. Significant investments for which readily available market quotes are not available and inadequate procedures have been performed for estimating these values

c. Significant investments in derivative financial instruments for which value is very difficult to estimate

---

[8] Management incentive plans may be contingent upon achieving targets relating only to certain accounts or selected activities of the entity, even though the related accounts or activities may not be material to the entity as a whole.

2. Components of internal control may be deficient as a result of the following:

    a. Management's failure to display and communicate an appropriate attitude regarding internal control and the financial reporting process

    b. Unusual and considerable influence of the portfolio manager over the pricing sources, fair valuation methodology, or inputs used to value securities

    c. Lack of board of directors' or trustees' involvement in the establishment of the fair valuation policies and procedures or lack of oversight over those policies and procedures

    d. Management's ability to unilaterally override internal controls, particularly security valuations

    e. Lack of adviser's supervisory or oversight procedures over its own employees or the subadviser, or both

    f. Inadequate controls around the calculation of the daily net asset value

    g. Reconciliation of security holdings with the custodian that is infrequent or incomplete

    h. Inadequate monitoring of the fund's tax status as a RIC

    i. Inadequate monitoring of the fund's compliance with its prospectus requirements

    j. Ineffective transfer agency controls or ineffective implementation of user controls

    k. Lack of an appropriate policy regarding corrections of net asset value errors or failure to comply with the policy

    l. Board of directors' or trustees' limited or lack of understanding of how portfolio management intends to implement the fund's investment restrictions, thereby creating a situation in which management can aggressively interpret or disregard adopted policies

    m. Board of directors' or trustees' limited or lack of understanding of derivatives used by portfolio managers and involvement in approving or disapproving the use of specific strategies, such as embedded leverage, thereby creating a situation in which management can aggressively interpret or disregard adopted policies

    n. Incomplete or insufficient description of portfolio positions in accounting records to permit adequate monitoring of prospectus requirements

    o. Inadequate segregation of duties between operating (for example, portfolio management, fund distribution) and compliance monitoring functions

    p. Inadequate monitoring of compliance by subservicing agents and intermediaries with prospectus requirements regarding transactions in fund shares

C. *Attitudes and Rationalizations*

1. Nonfinancial management's excessive participation in, or preoccupation with, the selection of accounting principles or the determination of significant estimates, such as the following:

    a. An excessive focus on maintaining a high rate of dividend payments, regardless of the fund's actual investment income

    b. A significant number of investments are valued by management, either judgmentally or through valuation models

2. Known history of violations of securities laws or other laws or regulation, or claims against the entity, its senior management, or members of the board of directors or trustees alleging fraud or violations of laws and regulations, such as the following:

    a. Past suspensions of the ability to act as an investment adviser or a requirement that the adviser be supervised by others

    b. Significant deficiencies cited in inspection letters by the SEC or other regulatory bodies, with a heightened emphasis on deficiencies cited in prior inspections that management has not remedied

3. The practice by management of committing to analysts, creditors, and other third parties to achieve aggressive or unrealistic forecasts, such as the following:

    a. Commitment to preserve principal or maintain a certain income or distribution yield

    b. Commitment to achieve a targeted level of assets under management by a specified date

    c. Commitment to achieve a targeted level of gross or net fund share sales during a defined period

4. Adviser's fee revenues (including performance incentives) directly related to either the value of fund assets or performance, if the adviser has substantial discretion in valuing portfolio investments, and changes in fee revenues may be significant to the adviser

5. Undisclosed use of soft-dollar credits and other items (for example, to reduce a gross ratio below a cap, so the adviser does not have to reimburse the fund for excess expenses)

Part 2: Misappropriation of Assets

Risk factors that relate to misstatements arising from misappropriation of assets are also classified according to the three conditions generally present when fraud exists: incentives and pressures, opportunities, and attitudes and rationalization. Some of the risk factors related to misstatements arising from fraudulent financial reporting also may be present when misstatements arising from misappropriation of assets occur. For example, ineffective monitoring of management and other deficiencies in internal control that are not effective may be present when misstatements due to either fraudulent financial reporting or misappropriation of assets exist. The following are examples of risk factors related to misstatements arising from misappropriation of assets.

A. *Incentives and Pressures*

1. Personal financial obligations may create pressure on management or employees with access to cash or other assets susceptible to theft to misappropriate those assets.

2. Adverse relationships between the entity and employees with access to cash or other assets susceptible to theft may motivate those employees to misappropriate those assets. For example, adverse relationships may be created by the following:

   a. Known or anticipated future employee layoffs

   b. Recent or anticipated changes to employee compensation or benefit plans

   c. Promotions, compensation, or other rewards inconsistent with expectations

B. *Opportunities*

1. Certain characteristics or circumstances may increase the susceptibility of assets to misappropriation. For example, opportunities to misappropriate assets increase with the use of soft dollar arrangements for the benefit of the adviser without client consent (including the existence of undocumented or ill-defined arrangements).

2. Inadequate internal control over assets may increase the susceptibility of misappropriation of those assets. For example, misappropriation of assets may occur because of the following:

   a. Access to funds and securities, and accounting for them is directly controlled by the adviser, with inadequate segregation of duties (or no direct communication between the custodian and accounting personnel)

   b. Lack of any periodic review of a transfer agency's control design and operation by an independent auditor knowledgeable in the area (such as a SOC 1 report)

   c. Infrequent and incomplete reconciliation of security holdings with the custodian

   d. Lack of a clearly defined policy with respect to personal investing activities (for example, front-running fund trades or taking investment opportunities for personal use)

   e. Ineffective transfer agency controls or ineffective implementation of user controls in a service center environment, particularly inadequate controls over uncashed dividend or redemption check listings that are returned by the post office and other inactive shareholder accounts; and reconciliations of transfer agency bank accounts

   f. Lack of segregation of duties between portfolio management and trading or an absence of an independent review of trading executions (for example, unexpected concentrations of trading with counterparties, poor trade executions, or higher-than-normal commissions that may indicate the existence of collusion between portfolio personnel and counterparties)

C. *Attitudes and Rationalizations*

1. Disregard for the need for monitoring or reducing risks related to misappropriations of assets

2. Disregard for internal control over misappropriation of assets by overriding existing controls or by failing to take appropriate remedial action on known deficiencies in internal control

3. Behavior indicating displeasure or dissatisfaction with the entity or its treatment of the employee

4. Changes in behavior or lifestyle that may indicate assets have been misappropriated

5. The belief by some government or other officials that their level of authority justifies a certain level of compensation and personal privileges

6. Tolerance of petty theft

Chapter 12

Independent Auditor's Reports and Client Representations[1]

Introduction

12.01   This chapter applies the reporting guidance found in AU-C sections 700, *Forming an Opinion and Reporting on Financial Statements*; 705, *Modifications to the Opinion in the Independent Auditor's Report*; and 706, *Emphasis-of-Matter Paragraphs and Other-Matter Paragraphs in the Independent Auditor's Report* (AICPA, *Professional Standards*), to audit reports on the financial statements of investment companies. Such reports may contain an unmodified opinion, an unmodified opinion with emphasis-of-matter or other-matter paragraphs, a qualified opinion, an adverse opinion, or a disclaimer of opinion. This chapter also provides illustrative management representation letters for nonregistered and registered investment companies, based primarily on guidance in AU-C section 580, *Written Representations* (AICPA, *Professional Standards*), and AU section 333, *Management Representations* (AICPA, *PCAOB Standards and Related Rules*, Interim Standards), respectively.

12.02   The auditor's reports on financial statements in this chapter illustrate pertinent items discussed in this guide, but they do not cover all the diverse circumstances that may occur in practice. It is essential, therefore, that the auditor's report reflects the requirements of the particular circumstances. Financial reporting for publicly registered investment companies is governed by the rules of the SEC (for example, Regulation S-X), and there may be differences between this guide and SEC rules.

> *Considerations for Audits Performed in Accordance With PCAOB Standards*
>
> In April 2003, the PCAOB adopted as interim standards certain preexisting auditing and related standards. Although the PCAOB has subsequently issued standards that supersede or amend those interim standards, the reporting guidance that was adopted by the PCAOB remains largely consistent with the reporting guidance applicable to audits conducted in accordance with GAAS as they existed prior to adoption of the clarified Statements on Auditing Standards (SASs). As a consequence, significant differences will exist between audit reports for audits conducted in accordance with generally accepted auditing standards (GAAS) as compared to those conducted in accordance with PCAOB standards. The PCAOB has its own project to consider changes to the auditor's reporting model.

---

[1] The auditing content in this guide focuses primarily on generally accepted auditing standards (GAAS) issued by the Auditing Standards Board and is applicable to audits of nonissuers. See the section "Applicability of Generally Accepted Auditing Standards and PCAOB Standards" of the preface to this guide for a discussion of the definitions of issuer and nonissuer as used throughout this guide. Appendix B, "Clarified Auditing Standards and PCAOB Standards," of this guide is included to assist auditors in comparing the clarified standards, many of which are referenced throughout this guide, to the PCAOB standards. Further, considerations for audits of issuers in accordance with PCAOB standards may be discussed within this guide's chapter text. When such discussion is provided, the related paragraphs are designated with the following title: *Considerations for Audits Performed in Accordance With PCAOB Standards*.

Auditing Standard No. 1, *References in Auditors' Reports to the Standards of the Public Company Accounting Oversight Board* (AICPA, *PCAOB Standards and Related Rules*, Auditing Standards), as approved by the SEC and among other matters, requires registered public accounting firms to include in their reports on engagements performed pursuant to the PCAOB's auditing and related professional practice standards a reference to the standards of the PCAOB (United States).

Forming an Opinion on the Financial Statements

12.03   Paragraphs .13–.18 of AU-C section 700 address the auditor's responsibility to form an opinion on the financial statements. The auditor should form an opinion on whether the financial statements are presented fairly, in all material respects, in accordance with the applicable financial reporting framework. In order to form that opinion, the auditor should conclude whether the auditor has obtained reasonable assurance about whether the financial statements as a whole are free from material misstatement, whether due to fraud or error. That conclusion should take into account the following:

    a. The auditor's conclusion, in accordance with AU-C section 330, *Performing Audit Procedures in Response to Assessed Risks and Evaluating the Audit Evidence Obtained* (AICPA, *Professional Standards*), about whether sufficient appropriate audit evidence has been obtained

    b. The auditor's conclusion, in accordance with AU-C section 450, *Evaluation of Misstatements Identified During the Audit* (AICPA, *Professional Standards*), about whether uncorrected misstatements are material, individually or in aggregate

    c. The evaluations required by paragraphs .15–.18 of AU-C section 700 (as discussed in the following paragraphs)

12.04   The auditor should evaluate whether the financial statements are prepared, in all material respects, in accordance with the requirements of the applicable financial reporting framework. This evaluation should include consideration of the qualitative aspects of the entity's accounting practices, including indicators of possible bias in management's judgments. In particular, the auditor should evaluate whether, in view of the requirements of the applicable financial reporting framework

    a. the financial statements adequately disclose the significant accounting policies selected and applied;

    b. the accounting policies selected and applied are consistent with the applicable financial reporting framework and are appropriate;

    c. the accounting estimates made by management are reasonable;

    d. the information presented in the financial statements is relevant, reliable, comparable, and understandable;

    e. the financial statements provide adequate disclosures to enable the intended users to understand the effect of material transactions and events on the information conveyed in the financial statements; and

    f. the terminology used in the financial statements, including the title of each financial statement, is appropriate.

12.05 The auditor's evaluation about whether the financial statements achieve fair presentation should also include consideration of the overall presentation, structure, and content of the financial statements and whether the financial statements, including the related notes, represent the underlying transactions and events in a manner that achieves fair presentation. Finally, the auditor should evaluate whether the financial statements adequately refer to or describe the applicable financial reporting framework.

Reports on Financial Statements of Nonregistered Investment Companies

Unmodified Opinion

12.06 The auditor should express an unmodified opinion when the auditor concludes that the financial statements are presented fairly, in all material respects, in accordance with the applicable financial reporting framework. The following form of the auditor's report may be used to express an unmodified opinion on the financial statements of a nonregistered investment company.

Independent Auditor's Report

To the Shareholders and
Board of Directors/Trustees of
XYZ Investment Company

Report on the Financial Statements[2]

We have audited the accompanying financial statements of XYZ Investment Company, which comprise the statement of assets and liabilities, including the schedule of investments in securities, as of December 31, 20X2, and the related statements of operations, changes in net assets, and cash flows[3] for the year then ended[4] and the related notes to the financial statements.[5]

Management's Responsibility for the Financial Statements

Management is responsible for the preparation and fair presentation of these financial statements in accordance with accounting principles generally accepted in the United States of America; this includes the design, implementation, and maintenance of internal control relevant to the preparation and fair presentation of financial statements that are free from material misstatement, whether due to fraud or error.

---

[2] The subtitle "Report on the Financial Statements" is unnecessary in circumstances when the second subtitle, "Report on Other Legal and Regulatory Requirements," is not applicable.

[3] FASB *Accounting Standards Codification* (ASC) 230-10-15-4 exempts certain companies that meet specified conditions from the requirements to provide a statement of cash flows. See chapter 7, "Financial Statements of Investment Companies," of this guide for further discussion.

[4] If the financial highlights are presented in a separate schedule (as opposed to in a footnote), the schedule of financial highlights should be mentioned, along with the financial statements, throughout the independent auditor's report.

[5] Although paragraph .25 of AU-C section 700, *Forming an Opinion and Reporting on Financial Statements* (AICPA, *Professional Standards*), does not specifically include the phrase "and the related notes to the financial statements" as a required component of the introductory paragraph of the auditor's report, the phrase is included in each of the illustrative auditor's reports in the AU-C section 700 exhibit beginning at paragraph .A58.

Auditor's Responsibility

Our responsibility is to express an opinion on these financial statements based on our audit. We conducted our audit in accordance with auditing standards generally accepted in the United States of America.[6] Those standards require that we plan and perform the audit to obtain reasonable assurance about whether the financial statements are free from material misstatement.

An audit involves performing procedures to obtain audit evidence about the amounts and disclosures in the financial statements. The procedures selected depend on the auditor's judgment, including the assessment of the risks of material misstatement of the financial statements, whether due to fraud or error. In making those risk assessments, the auditor considers internal control relevant to the entity's preparation and fair presentation of the financial statements in order to design audit procedures that are appropriate in the circumstances, but not for the purpose of expressing an opinion on the effectiveness of the entity's internal control.[7] Accordingly, we express no such opinion. An audit also includes evaluating the appropriateness of the accounting policies used and the reasonableness of significant accounting estimates made by management, as well as evaluating the overall presentation of the financial statements.

We believe that the audit evidence we have obtained is sufficient and appropriate to provide a basis for our audit opinion.

Opinion

In our opinion, the financial statements referred to above present fairly, in all material respects, the financial position of XYZ Investment Company as of December 31, 20X2, and the results of its operations, changes in net assets, and its cash flows[8] for the year then ended in accordance with accounting principles generally accepted in the United States of America.[9]

---

[6] Paragraph .31 of AU-C section 700 requires that the auditor's report state that the audit was conducted in accordance with generally accepted auditing standards and identify the United States of America as the country of origin of those standards. However, paragraphs .42–.43 of AU-C section 700 state that an auditor may indicate that the audit was also conducted in accordance with another set of auditing standards (for example, International Standards on Auditing, the standards of the PCAOB, or *Government Auditing Standards*). The auditor should not refer to having conducted an audit in accordance with another set of auditing standards in addition to GAAS unless the audit was conducted in accordance with both sets of standards in their entirety. When the auditor's report refers to both GAAS and another set of auditing standards, the auditor's report should identify the other set of auditing standards, as well as their origin. This can be done by modifying this sentence as follows (new language is shown in italics):

We conducted our audit in accordance with auditing standards generally accepted in the United States of America *and in accordance with International Standards on Auditing*.

[7] In circumstances when the auditor also has responsibility to express an opinion on the effectiveness of internal control in conjunction with the audit of the financial statements, this sentence would be worded as follows:

In making those risk assessments, the auditor considers internal control relevant to the entity's preparation and fair presentation of the financial statements in order to design audit procedures that are appropriate in the circumstances.

In addition, the next sentence, "Accordingly, we express no such opinion." would not be included.

[8] See footnote 3.

[9] In accordance with Paragraph .A31 of AU-C section 700, the identification of the applicable financial reporting framework in the auditor's opinion is intended to advise users of the auditor's

(continued)

Report on Other Legal and Regulatory Requirements

[*Form and content of this section of the auditor's report will vary depending on the nature of the auditor's other reporting responsibilities,*]

[Independent Auditor (signed)]
[Anytown, USA][10]
[February 21, 20X3]

12.07   In accordance with paragraphs .37–.38 of AU-C section 700, if the auditor addresses other reporting responsibilities in the auditor's report on the financial statements that are in addition to the auditor's responsibility under GAAS to report on the financial statements, these other reporting responsibilities should be addressed in a separate section in the auditor's report that follows the section titled "Report on the Financial Statements" (in a new section below the "Opinion" subsection) and that should be subtitled "Report on Other Legal and Regulatory Requirements" or otherwise, as appropriate to the content of the section.

Modified Opinions

12.08   AU-C section 705 addresses the auditor's responsibility to issue an appropriate report in circumstances when, in forming an opinion in accordance with AU-C section 700, the auditor concludes that a modification to the auditor's opinion on the financial statements is necessary. Paragraph .07 of AU-C section 705 states that the auditor should modify the opinion in the auditor's report when

   a.   the auditor concludes that, based on the audit evidence obtained, the financial statements as a whole are materially misstated or

   b.   the auditor is unable to obtain sufficient appropriate audit evidence to conclude that the financial statements as a whole are free from material misstatement.

12.09   AU-C section 705 establishes three types of modified opinions: namely, a qualified opinion, an adverse opinion, and a disclaimer of opinion.

(footnote continued)

report of the context in which the auditor's opinion is expressed. For example, the applicable financial reporting framework may be identified as accounting principles generally accepted in the United States of America or U.S. generally accepted accounting principles or International Financial Reporting Standards (IFRSs) promulgated by the International Accounting Standards Board (IASB) or *International Financial Reporting Standard for Small and Medium-Sized Entities* promulgated by the IASB. In that scenario, in the auditor's report, the auditor would refer to IFRSs, rather than U.S. generally accepted accounting principles. An example opinion paragraph would be as follows (new language is shown in italics):

> In our opinion, the financial statements referred to above present fairly, in all material respects, the financial position of XYZ Investment Company as of December 31, 20X2, and the results of its operations, changes in its net assets, and its cash flows for the year then ended, in accordance with *International Financial Reporting Standards [or International Financial Reporting Standard for Small and Medium Sized Entities] as issued by the International Accounting Standards Board.*

[10] According to paragraph .40 of AU-C section 700, the auditor's report should name the city and state where the auditor practices. Technical Questions and Answers (Q&A) section 9100.08, "Audit Firm With Multiple Offices on Their Company Letterhead and Effect on Report" (AICPA, *Technical Questions and Answers*), explains that an auditor's letterhead denoting multiple office locations does not meet this requirement. Q&A Section 9100.08 continues by explaining that if the firm's letterhead includes multiple office locations, it will not be clear which location is the issuing office, and, therefore, the auditor would need to indicate the city and state where the auditor practices in the auditor's report.

The decision regarding which type of modified opinion is appropriate depends upon the following:

a. The nature of the matter giving rise to the modification (that is, whether the financial statements are materially misstated or, in the case of an inability to obtain sufficient appropriate audit evidence, may be materially misstated)

b. The auditor's professional judgment about the pervasiveness of the effects or possible effects of the matter on the financial statements

It also provides guidance on the circumstances when a modification to the auditor's opinion is required as well as guidance on determining the type of modification to the auditor's opinion (for example, guidance illustrating how the auditor's professional judgment about the nature of the matter giving rise to the modification and the pervasiveness of its effects or possible effects on the financial statement opinion affects the type of opinion to be expressed).

12.10   When the auditor modifies the opinion on the financial statements, paragraph .17 of AU-C section 705 states that the auditor should, in addition to the specific elements required by AU-C section 700, include a paragraph in the auditor's report that provides a description of the matter giving rise to the modification. The auditor should place this paragraph immediately before the opinion paragraph in the auditor's report and use a heading that includes "Basis for Qualified Opinion," "Basis for Adverse Opinion," or "Basis for Disclaimer of Opinion," as appropriate. Paragraphs .18–.22 of AU-C section 705 provide further discussion on information that should be included within the basis for modification paragraph. In addition, paragraph .23 of AU-C section 705 states that the auditor should use a heading that includes "Qualified Opinion," "Adverse Opinion," or "Disclaimer of Opinion," as appropriate, for the opinion paragraph.

12.11   Consistent with paragraph .20 of AU-C section 705, if financial statements of an investment partnership that is exempt from SEC registration do not include the U.S. generally accepted accounting principles (GAAP) required schedule of investments[11] disclosures that are discussed in paragraph 7.33 of this guide, the auditor should (a) discuss the omission of such information with those charged with governance; (b) describe in the basis for modification paragraph the nature of the omitted information; and (c) include the omitted information, provided that it is practicable to do so and the auditor has obtained sufficient appropriate audit evidence about the omitted information.

12.12   Paragraph .A24 of AU-C section 705 defines *practicable* as information that is reasonably obtainable from management's accounts and records and that providing the information in the report does not require the auditor to assume the position of a preparer of financial information. Ordinarily, it would be practicable for the auditor to obtain and present the information about investments constituting more than 5 percent of net assets called for by the disclosure requirement described in paragraph 7.33c(i) of this guide. In situations where the information available to the auditor is limited as to attributes, such as industry or geographic classification, the auditor could consider disclosing the entire schedule.

---

[11] Additional financial statement presentation and disclosure requirements, of which exclusion may also result in a modified opinion, for investment partnerships that are exempt from SEC registration under the Investment Company Act of 1940 (the 1940 Act) can be found in FASB ASC 946, *Financial Services–Investment Companies.*

Qualified Opinion

12.13 In accordance with paragraph .08 of AU-C section 705, the auditor should express a qualified opinion when

    a. the auditor, having obtained sufficient appropriate audit evidence, concludes that misstatements, individually or in the aggregate, are material but not pervasive to the financial statements or

    b. the auditor is unable to obtain sufficient appropriate audit evidence on which to base the opinion, but the auditor concludes that the possible effects on the financial statements of undetected misstatements, if any, could be material but not pervasive.

12.14 For purposes of GAAS, AU-C section 705 defines *pervasive* as a term used in the context of misstatements to describe the effects on the financial statements of misstatements or the possible effects on the financial statements of misstatements, if any, that are undetected due to an inability to obtain sufficient appropriate audit evidence. Pervasive effects on the financial statements are those that, in the auditor's professional judgment

- are not confined to specific elements, accounts, or items of the financial statements;

- if so confined, represent or could represent a substantial proportion of the financial statements; or

- with regard to disclosures, are fundamental to users' understanding of the financial statements.

12.15 Consistent with illustration 2 of AU-C section 705, the following is an illustration of a report that expresses a qualified opinion because the schedule of investments in securities fails to disclose investments constituting more than 5 percent of net assets but, in all other respects, conforms to the requirements of FASB *Accounting Standards Codification* (ASC) 946, *Financial Services—Investment Companies.*

Independent Auditor's Report

To the Shareholders and
Board of Directors/Trustees of
XYZ Investment Company

Report on the Financial Statements[12]

We have audited the accompanying financial statements of XYZ Investment Company (the Company), which comprise the statement of assets and liabilities, including the schedule of investments in securities, as of December 31, 20X2, and the related statements of operations, changes in net assets, and cash flows[13] for the year then ended[14] and the related notes to the financial statements.[15]

---

[12] The subtitle "Report on the Financial Statements" is unnecessary in circumstances when the second subtitle, "Report on Other Legal and Regulatory Requirements," is not applicable.

[13] See footnote 3.

[14] If the financial highlights are presented in a separate schedule (as opposed to in a footnote), the schedule of financial highlights should be mentioned, along with the financial statements, throughout the independent auditor's report.

[15] See footnote 5.

Management's Responsibility for the Financial Statements

[Same second paragraph as the unmodified report illustrated in paragraph 12.06.]

Auditor's Responsibility

[Same third and fourth paragraphs as the unmodified report illustrated in paragraph 12.06.]

We believe that the audit evidence we have obtained is sufficient and appropriate to provide a basis for our qualified audit opinion.

Basis for Qualified Opinion

The Schedule of Investments in Securities included in the Company's financial statements does not disclose required information about the following investments, each constituting more than 5 percent of the Company's total net assets, at December 31, 20X2:

- Amalgamated Buggy Whips, Inc., 10,000 shares of common stock-fair value $3,280,000 (Consumer nondurable goods)
- Paper Airplane Corp., 6.25 percent Cv. Deb. due 20YX, $4.5 million par value-fair value $4,875,000 (Aviation)

In our opinion, disclosure of this information is required by accounting principles generally accepted in the United States of America.

Qualified Opinion

In our opinion, except for the omission of the information described in the Basis for Qualified Opinion paragraph, the financial statements referred to above present fairly, in all material respects, the financial position of XYZ Investment Company as of December 31, 20X2, and the results of its operations, changes in its net assets, and its cash flows[16] for the year then ended in accordance with accounting principles generally accepted in the United States of America.[17]

Report on Other Legal and Regulatory Requirements

[Form and content of this section of the auditor's report will vary depending on the nature of the auditor's other reporting responsibilities,]

[Independent Auditor (signed)]
[Anytown, USA][18]
[February 21, 20X3]

12.16   When the financial statements contain securities whose fair values were estimated under procedures established by those responsible for governance,[19] and the auditor is unable to obtain sufficient appropriate audit evidence on which to base the opinion (for example, the valuation procedures are inadequate or unreasonable or the underlying documentation does not support the valuation), but the auditor concludes that the possible effects on the financial statements of undetected misstatements, if any, could be material

---

[16] See footnote 3.

[17] See footnote 9.

[18] See footnote 10.

[19] AU-C section 540, *Auditing Accounting Estimates, Including Fair Value Accounting Estimates, and Related Disclosures* (AICPA, *Professional Standards*), addresses the auditor's responsibilities relating to accounting estimates, including fair value accounting estimates and related disclosures, in an audit of financial statements.

but not pervasive, the auditor should express a qualified opinion in a manner similar to the following. See also Illustration 4, "An Auditor's Report Containing a Qualified Opinion Due to the Auditor's Inability to Obtain Sufficient Appropriate Audit Evidence," of AU-C section 705.

Independent Auditor's Report

To the Shareholders and
Board of Directors/Trustees of
XYZ Investment Company

[Same first and second paragraphs as the unmodified report illustrated in paragraph 12.06.]

Auditor's Responsibility

[Same third and fourth paragraphs as the unmodified report illustrated in paragraph 12.06.]

We believe that the audit evidence we have obtained is sufficient and appropriate to provide a basis for our qualified audit opinion.

Basis for Qualified Opinion

As explained in note 2, the financial statements include securities valued at $_____ (_____ percent of net assets), whose fair values have been estimated under procedures established by the Board of Directors/Trustees. We have evaluated the procedures established by the Board of Directors/Trustees to estimate the fair values and have inspected the underlying documentation. In our opinion, those procedures are not reasonable, and the documentation is not sufficient and appropriate to determine the securities' estimated fair values. The effect on the financial statements of not applying adequate valuation procedures is not readily determinable.

Qualified Opinion

In our opinion, except for the possible effects of the matter described in the Basis for Qualified Opinion paragraph, the financial statements referred to above present fairly, in all material respects, the financial position of XYZ Investment Company as of December 31, 20X2, and the results of its operations, changes in its net assets, and cash flows[20] for the year then ended, in accordance with accounting principles generally accepted in the United States of America.

[Independent Auditor (signed)]
[Anytown, USA][21]
[February 21, 20X3]

Adverse Opinion

12.17   In accordance with paragraph .09 of AU-C section 705, the auditor should express an adverse opinion when the auditor, having obtained sufficient appropriate audit evidence, concludes that misstatements, individually or in the aggregate, are both material and pervasive to the financial statements. When the auditor expresses an adverse opinion, paragraph .25 of AU-C section 705 states that the auditor should state in the opinion paragraph that, in the auditor's opinion, because of the significance of the matter(s) described in

---

[20] See footnote 3.

[21] See footnote 10.

the basis for adverse opinion paragraph, the financial statements are not presented fairly in accordance with the applicable financial reporting framework. Furthermore, paragraph .27 of AU-C section 705 states that the auditor should also amend the description of the auditor's responsibility to state that the auditor believes that the audit evidence the auditor has obtained is sufficient and appropriate to provide a basis for the auditor's modified audit opinion.

12.18   The following is an illustration of an adverse opinion relating to failure to present the entire schedule of investments in securities and all the related required information. In the following illustration, the auditor, having obtained sufficient appropriate audit evidence, concluded that an adverse opinion is necessary because the inadequate disclosure individually or in the aggregate is both material and pervasive to the financial statements. See also Illustration 3, "An Auditor's Report Containing an Adverse Opinion Due to a Material Misstatement of the Financial Statements," of AU-C section 705.

Independent Auditor's Report

To the Shareholders and
Board of Directors/Trustees of
XYZ Investment Company

Report on the Financial Statements[22]

We have audited the accompanying financial statements of XYZ Investment Company (the Company), which comprise the statement of assets and liabilities, including the schedule of investments in securities, as of December 31, 20X2, and the related statements of operations, changes in net assets, and cash flows[23] for the year then ended[24] and the related notes to the financial statements.[25]

Management's Responsibility for the Financial Statements

[*Same second paragraph as the unmodified report illustrated in paragraph 12.06.*]

Auditor's Responsibility

[*Same third and fourth paragraphs as the unmodified report illustrated in paragraph 12.06.*]

We believe that the audit evidence we have obtained is sufficient and appropriate to provide a basis for our adverse opinion.

Basis for Adverse Opinion

The Company has declined to prepare and present a Schedule of Investments in Securities and the related information as of December 31, 20X2. Accounting principles generally accepted in the United States of America require presentation of this Schedule and the related information. Presentation of this Schedule would have disclosed required information about the following investments, each constituting more than 5 percent of the Company's total net assets, at December 31, 20X2:

---

[22] The subtitle "Report on the Financial Statements" is unnecessary in circumstances when the second subtitle, "Report on Other Legal and Regulatory Requirements," is not applicable.

[23] See footnote 3.

[24] If the financial highlights are presented in a separate schedule (as opposed to in a footnote), the schedule of financial highlights should be mentioned, along with the financial statements, throughout the independent auditor's report.

[25] See footnote 2.

- Amalgamated Buggy Whips, Inc., 10,000 shares of common stock-fair value $3,280,000 (Consumer nondurable goods)[26]
- Paper Airplane Corp., 6.25 percent Cv. Deb. due 20YX, $4.5 million par value-fair value $4,875,000 (Aviation)

In addition, presentation of the Schedule of Investments in Securities would have disclosed [*describe the nature of the information that it is not practicable to present in the auditor's report*].

Adverse Opinion

In our opinion, because of the significance of the matter discussed in the Basis for Adverse Opinion paragraph, the financial statements referred to above do not present fairly the financial position of XYZ Investment Company as of December 31, 20X2, and the results of its operations, changes in its net assets, and its cash flows[27] for the year then ended in accordance with accounting principles generally accepted in the United States of America.[28]

Report on Other Legal and Regulatory Requirements

[*Form and content of this section of the auditor's report will vary depending on the nature of the auditor's other reporting responsibilities,*]

[Independent Auditor (signed)]
[Anytown, USA][29]
[February 21, 20X3]

Review Report on Interim Financial Information[30]

12.19 The following form of report is used in connection with a review of semiannual financial statements of a nonregistered investment company.

Independent Auditor's Review Report

To the Shareholders and
Board of Directors/Trustees of
XYZ Investment Company

Report on the Financial Statements

We have reviewed the accompanying statement of assets and liabilities of XYZ Investment Company (the Company), including the schedule

---

[26] In the absence of a schedule of investments containing categorizations by type, country or geographic region, and industry, such categorizations should be provided only if readily ascertainable from management's accounts and records. The auditor should not assign such categorizations if management has not done so.

[27] See footnote 3.

[28] See footnote 9.

[29] See footnote 10.

[30] AU-C section 930, *Interim Financial Information* (AICPA, *Professional Standards*), addresses the auditor's responsibilities when engaged to review interim financial information under the conditions specified in AU-C section 930. For purposes of AU-C section 930, the term *interim financial information* means financial information prepared and presented in accordance with an applicable financial reporting framework that comprises either a complete or condensed set of financial statements covering a period or periods less than 1 full year or a 12-month period ending on a date other than the entity's fiscal year-end. Further, readers of this guide should consult illustration 2 of exhibit B, "Illustrations of Auditor's Review Reports on Interim Financial Information," of AU-C section 930 for report modifications if comparative financial information is presented. Finally, as applicable, readers of this guide should consult exhibit C, "Illustrations of Example Modifications to the Auditor's Review Report Due to Departures From the Applicable Financial Reporting Framework," of AU-C section 930 for illustrative examples of various other report modifications.

of investments in securities, as of June 30, 20X3, and the related statements of operations, changes in net assets, and cash flows[31] for the six-month period ended June 30, 20X3.

Management's Responsibilities

The Company's management is responsible for the preparation and fair presentation of the interim financial information in accordance with accounting principles generally accepted in the United States of America; this responsibility includes the design, implementation, and maintenance of internal control sufficient to provide a reasonable basis for the preparation and fair presentation of interim financial information in accordance with accounting principles generally accepted in the United States of America.

Auditor's Responsibility

Our responsibility is to conduct our review in accordance with auditing standards generally accepted in the United States of America applicable to reviews of interim financial information. A review of interim financial information consists principally of applying analytical procedures and making inquiries of persons responsible for financial and accounting matters. It is substantially less in scope than an audit conducted in accordance with auditing standards generally accepted in the United States of America, the objective of which is the expression of an opinion regarding the financial information. Accordingly, we do not express such an opinion.

Conclusion

Based on our review, we are not aware of any material modifications that should be made to the accompanying interim financial information for it to be in accordance with accounting principles generally accepted in the United States of America.

[Independent Accountant (signed)]
[Anytown, USA]
[August 7, 20X3]

Reports on Financial Statements of Registered Investment Companies

12.20   Under the Investment Company Act of 1940 (the 1940 Act), the auditor's report on the audit of a registered investment company's financial statements must state specifically that securities have been confirmed or physically examined to substantiate their existence.[32] Auditors must address their reports on financial statements of a registered investment company to the company's shareholders and board of directors.[33,34]

---

[31] See footnote 3 and footnote 24.

[32] Section 30(g) of the 1940 Act and Section 404.03a of the SEC's *Codification of Financial Reporting Policies*.

[33] Section 32(a) of the 1940 Act.

[34] Refer to SEC Guidance for Business Development Companies (BDC) Auditors at www.sec.gov/divisions/investment/issues-of-interest.shtml. Under Section 30(g) of the 1940 Act and the Commission's Accounting Series Release No. 118 (Dec. 23, 1970), the certificate of independent public accountants ("auditor") contained in the financial statements of investment companies

(continued)

12.21   The following form of auditor's report may be used to express an unqualified opinion on the financial statements of a registered investment company.[35]

The following illustrative auditor's report is prepared for informational and reference purposes only and is not authoritative. It has not been reviewed, approved, disapproved, or otherwise acted on by the PCAOB or SEC.

Report of Independent Registered Public Accounting Firm

To the Shareholders and
Board of Directors of
XYZ Investment Company

We have audited the accompanying statement of assets and liabilities of XYZ Investment Company (the Company), including the schedule of investments in securities, as of December 31, 20X8, and the related statements of operations and cash flows[36] for the year then ended, the statements of changes in net assets for each of the two years in the period then ended, and the financial highlights for each of the five years in the period then ended.[37] These financial statements and financial highlights are the responsibility of the Company's management. Our responsibility is to express an opinion on these financial statements and financial highlights based on our audits.

We conducted our audits in accordance with the standards of the Public Company Accounting Oversight Board (United States). Those standards require that we plan and perform the audit to obtain reasonable assurance about whether the financial statements and financial highlights are free of material misstatement. An audit includes examining, on a test basis, evidence supporting the amounts and disclosures in the financial statements. Our procedures included confirmation of securities owned as of December 31, 20X8, by correspondence with the custodian and brokers. An audit also includes assessing the accounting principles used and significant estimates made by management, as well as evaluating the overall financial statement

---

(footnote continued)

registered under the 1940 Act must include a statement "that such independent public accountants have verified securities owned, either by actual examination, or by receipt of a certificate from the custodian." Although Section 59 of the 1940 Act does not make Section 30(g) applicable to business development companies (BDCs), a BDC's auditor plays an important role under the 1940 Act in preventing a BDC's assets from being lost, misused or misappropriated. Therefore, the staff believes that it is a best practice for a BDC to have its auditor verify all of the securities owned by the BDC, either by actual examination or by receipt of a certificate from the custodian, and affirmatively state in the audit opinion whether the auditor has confirmed the existence of all such securities.

[35] Registered public accounting firms must comply with the standards of the PCAOB in connection with the preparation or issuance of any audit report on the financial statements of an issuer, as discussed in paragraph 12.02. Readers should understand the provisions of the Sarbanes Oxley Act of 2002, the SEC regulations implementing the Sarbanes Oxley Act of 2002, and the rules and standards of the PCAOB, as applicable to their circumstances, to determine if the standards of the PCAOB should be applied. Readers should consult the standards of the PCAOB and related interpretive guidance when preparing or issuing any audit report in accordance with the standards of the PCAOB.

[36] See footnote 3.

[37] In accordance with Item 13 of Form N1-A, in an open-end fund's registration statement, an auditor must opine on all five years of financial highlights required to be presented in the open-end fund's prospectus or, if shorter, the period of the fund's operations.

presentation. We believe that our audits provide a reasonable basis for our opinion.

In our opinion, the financial statements and financial highlights referred to above present fairly, in all material respects, the financial position of XYZ Investment Company as of December 31, 20X8, the results of its operations and its cash flows[38] for the year then ended, the changes in its net assets for each of the two years in the period then ended, and the financial highlights for each of the five years in the period then ended, in conformity with accounting principles generally accepted in the United States of America.

[Independent Auditor (signed)]
[Anytown, USA]
[January 21, 20X9]

12.22   The reference to *and brokers* in the fourth sentence of the scope paragraph is not normally necessary if the investment company's financial statements do not show an amount payable for securities purchased. When broker confirmations are not received, and alternative procedures are performed, the sentence may be modified to read "and brokers or by other appropriate auditing procedures where replies from brokers were not received." Also, if securities were physically inspected or subject to other extended procedures for purposes of the audit, the report should be modified to state that those procedures were performed.

12.23   Auditors may expand their audit reports to explain that they considered internal control over financial reporting as a basis for designing audit procedures but not for the purpose of expressing an opinion on the effectiveness of internal control over financial reporting. The following is an illustration of a report that may be used to make this clarification. The audit report is similar to the illustration in paragraph 12.21, but it also includes additional language that clarifies that the auditor is not required to audit the registered investment company's internal control over financial reporting.

Considerations for Audits Performed in Accordance With PCAOB Standards

The additional language is pertinent because, although the auditor is required to follow the standards of the PCAOB in conducting the financial statement audit of a registered investment company that is an issuer, the auditor is not required to conduct an audit of internal control over financial reporting for an investment company registered under Section 8 of the 1940 Act. Business development companies, however, are required to include a report of management on the company's internal control over financial reporting. Auditing Standard No. 5, *An Audit of Internal Control Over Financial Reporting That Is Integrated with An Audit of Financial Statements* (AICPA, *PCAOB Standards and Related Rules*, Auditing Standards), provides guidance that applies when an auditor is engaged to perform an audit of management's assessment of the effectiveness of internal control over financial reporting that is integrated with an audit of the financial statements.

---

[38] See footnote 3.

The following illustrative auditor's report is prepared for informational and reference purposes only and is not authoritative. It has not been reviewed, approved, disapproved, or otherwise acted on by the PCAOB or SEC.

Report of Independent Registered Public Accounting Firm

To the Shareholders and
Board of Directors of
XYZ Investment Company

[Same first paragraph as in the report illustrated in paragraph 12.21.]

We conducted our audits in accordance with the standards of the Public Company Accounting Oversight Board (United States). Those standards require that we plan and perform the audit to obtain reasonable assurance about whether the financial statements and financial highlights are free of material misstatement. The Company is not required to have, nor were we engaged to perform, an audit of its internal control over financial reporting. Our audits included consideration of internal control over financial reporting as a basis for designing audit procedures that are appropriate in the circumstances, but not for the purpose of expressing an opinion on the effectiveness of the Company's internal control over financial reporting. Accordingly, we express no such opinion. An audit also includes examining, on a test basis, evidence supporting the amounts and disclosures in the financial statements, assessing the accounting principles used and significant estimates made by management, as well as evaluating the overall financial statement presentation. Our procedures included confirmation of securities owned as of December 31, 20X8, by correspondence with the custodian and brokers. We believe that our audits provide a reasonable basis for our opinion.

[Same third paragraph as in the report illustrated in paragraph 12.21.]

[Independent Auditor (signed)]
[Anytown, USA]
[January 21, 20X9]

12.24   The auditor's report needs to be modified for a fund referred to as a series fund because of the uniqueness of the financial statements that have evolved to present its financial position, results of operations, and cash flows. The financial position, results of operations, and cash flows of some or all the portfolios or other entities constituting the series are frequently presented in separate columns. The financial statements of the series may also be presented as if the series were a separate entity. In both cases, the scope of the audit must be sufficient to enable the auditor to report on the individual financial statements of each series constituting the fund.

12.25   The following illustration is for a multicolumnar presentation of all the portfolios constituting the series.[39]

The following illustrative auditor's report is prepared for informational and reference purposes only and is not authoritative. It has not been reviewed, approved, disapproved, or otherwise acted on by the PCAOB or SEC.

---

[39] See footnote 35.

Report of Independent Registered Public Accounting Firm

To the Shareholders and
Board of Directors of
XYZ Series Investment Company

We have audited the accompanying statements of assets and liabilities, including the schedules of investments in securities, of XYZ Series Investment Company (the Company) comprising the Foreign, Domestic Common Stock, Long-Term Bond, and Convertible Preferred Portfolios as of December 31, 20X8, and the related statements of operations and cash flows,[40] for the year then ended, the statements of changes in net assets for each of the two years in the period then ended, and the financial highlights for each of the five years in the period then ended. These financial statements and financial highlights are the responsibility of the Company's management. Our responsibility is to express an opinion on these financial statements and financial highlights based on our audits.

[*Same second paragraph as in the report illustrated in paragraph 12.21.*]

In our opinion, the financial statements and financial highlights referred to above present fairly, in all material respects, the financial position of each of the portfolios constituting the XYZ Series Investment Company, as of December 31, 20X8, the results of their operations and cash flows[41] for the year then ended, the changes in their net assets for each of the two years in the period then ended, and their financial highlights for each of the five years in the period then ended, in conformity with accounting principles generally accepted in the United States of America.

[Independent Auditor (signed)]
[Anytown, USA]
[January 21, 20X9]

12.26   The following illustration is for a presentation of one of the portfolios or entities constituting the series.[42]

The following illustrative auditor's report is prepared for informational and reference purposes only and is not authoritative. It has not been reviewed, approved, disapproved, or otherwise acted on by the PCAOB or SEC.

Report of Independent Registered Public Accounting Firm

To the Board of Directors of
XYZ Series Investment Company and the
Shareholders of XYZ Investment Company

We have audited the accompanying statement of assets and liabilities, including the schedule of investments in securities, of the Convertible Preferred Portfolio (one of the portfolios constituting the XYZ Series Investment Company [the Company]) as of December 31, 20X8, and the related statements of operations and cash flows[43] for the year then

---

[40] See footnote 3.
[41] See footnote 3.
[42] See footnote 35.
[43] See footnote 3.

ended, the statement of changes in net assets for each of the two years in the period then ended, and the financial highlights for each of the five years in the period then ended. These financial statements and financial highlights are the responsibility of the Company's management. Our responsibility is to express an opinion on these financial statements and financial highlights based on our audits.

[*Same second paragraph as in the report illustrated in paragraph 12.21.*]

In our opinion, the financial statements and financial highlights referred to above present fairly, in all material respects, the financial position of the Convertible Preferred Portfolio of the XYZ Series Investment Company as of December 31, 20X8, and the results of its operations and its cash flows[44] for the year then ended, the changes in its net assets for each of the two years in the period then ended, and the financial highlights for each of the five years in the period then ended, in conformity with accounting principles generally accepted in the United States of America.

[Independent Auditor (signed)]
[Anytown, USA]
[January 21, 20X9]

Report for a Registered Investment Company That Includes a Summary Schedule of Investments in the Financial Statements Provided to Shareholders

12.27   The SEC permits a registered investment company to include a summary schedule of investments in securities of unaffiliated issuers in its reports to shareholders in the form prescribed by Rule 12-12C of Regulation S-X. If this presentation is elected, the more extensive schedule of investments in securities of unaffiliated issuers in the form prescribed by Rule 12-12 of Regulation S-X is filed with the SEC on Form N-CSR, Item 6 (see further discussion about these amendments in footnote 2 to paragraph 7.01 of this guide). According to SEC regulations, the more extensive schedule must be audited and accompanied by an independent auditor's report for the year-end date only. The following form of report in example 1-A may be used for an annual audit of the financial statements of a registered investment company that presents a summary schedule of investments in securities of unaffiliated issuers in its report to shareholders and files the more extensive schedule of investments in securities of unaffiliated issuers at year-end on Form N-CSR, Item 6.[45]

Example 1: Auditor's Report on Financial Statements of a Registered Investment Company for Inclusion in Form N-CSR—Stand-Alone Fund—(Shareholder Report Includes a Summary Schedule of Investments and a More Extensive Schedule of Investments Is Included in the Form N-CSR Filing)

The following illustrative auditor's report is prepared for informational and reference purposes only and is not authoritative. It has not been reviewed, approved, disapproved, or otherwise acted on by the PCAOB or SEC.

---

[44] See footnote 3.
[45] See footnote 35.

Report of Independent Registered Public Accounting Firm

To the Shareholders and
Board of Directors of
XYZ Investment Company

We have audited the accompanying statement of assets and liabilities of XYZ Investment Company, including the summary schedule of investments, as of December 31, 20X8, and the related statements of operations and cash flows[46] for the year then ended, the statements of changes in net assets for each of the two years in the period then ended (collectively, the "financial statements"), the financial highlights for each of the five years in the period then ended (the financial statements and financial highlights are included in Item 1 of this Form N-CSR), and the schedule of investments in securities as of December 31, 20X8 (included in Item 6 of this Form N-CSR). These financial statements, financial highlights, and schedule of investments in securities are the responsibility of the Company's management. Our responsibility is to express an opinion on these financial statements, financial highlights, and schedule of investments in securities based on our audits.

We conducted our audits in accordance with the standards of the Public Company Accounting Oversight Board (United States). Those standards require that we plan and perform the audit to obtain reasonable assurance about whether the financial statements, financial highlights, and schedule of investments in securities are free of material misstatement. An audit includes examining, on a test basis, evidence supporting the amounts and disclosures in the financial statements and schedule of investments in securities. Our procedures included confirmation of securities owned as of December 31, 20X8, by correspondence with the custodian and brokers.[47] An audit also includes assessing the accounting principles used and significant estimates made by management, as well as evaluating the overall financial statement presentation. We believe that our audits provide a reasonable basis for our opinion.

In our opinion, the financial statements, financial highlights, and schedule of investments in securities referred to above present fairly, in all material respects, the financial position of XYZ Investment Company as of December 31, 20X8, and the results of its operations and its cash flows[48] for the year then ended, the changes in its net assets for each of the two years in the period then ended, and the financial highlights for each of the five years in the period then ended, in conformity with accounting principles generally accepted in the United States of America.

[Independent Auditor (signed)]
[Anytown, USA]
[January 21, 20X9]

12.28 The following form of report is used in connection with a review of semiannual financial statements of a registered investment company.

---

[46] See footnote 3.
[47] See paragraph 12.22.
[48] See footnote 3.

Report Prepared in Accordance With PCAOB Standards[49]

The following illustrative auditor's report is prepared for informational and reference purposes only and is not authoritative. It has not been reviewed, approved, disapproved, or otherwise acted on by the PCAOB or SEC.

Report of Independent Registered Public Accounting Firm

To the Shareholders and
Board of Directors of
XYZ Investment Company

We have reviewed the accompanying statement of assets and liabilities of XYZ Investment Company (the Company), including the schedule of investments in securities, as of June 30, 20X8, and the related statements of operations, changes in net assets, and financial highlights for the six-month period ended June 30, 20X8. These financial statements and financial highlights are the responsibility of the Company's management.

We conducted our review in accordance with the standards of the Public Company Accounting Oversight Board (United States). A review of interim financial information consists principally of applying analytical procedures and making inquiries of persons responsible for financial and accounting matters. It is substantially less in scope than an audit conducted in accordance with the standards of the Public Company Accounting Oversight Board (United States), the objective of which is the expression of an opinion regarding the financial statements taken as a whole. Accordingly, we do not express such an opinion.

Based on our review, we are not aware of any material modifications that should be made to the accompanying financial statements and financial highlights for them to be in conformity with accounting principles generally accepted in the United States of America.

We have previously audited, in accordance with the standards of the Public Company Accounting Oversight Board (United States), the statement of changes in net assets for the year ended December 31, 20X7, and financial highlights for each of the five years in the period ended December 31, 20X7; and in our report dated January 21, 20X8, we expressed an unqualified opinion on such statement of changes in net assets and financial highlights.

[Independent Accountant (signed)]
[Anytown, USA]
[August 7, 20X8]

---

[49] AU section 722, *Interim Financial Information* (AICPA, *PCAOB Standards and Related Rules,* Interim Standards), provides additional guidance on performing reviews of interim financial information in accordance with PCAOB standards. The term *interim financial information* means financial information or statements covering a period less than 1 full year or a 12-month period ending on a date other than the entity's fiscal year-end. Registered public accounting firms must comply with the standards of the PCAOB in connection with the preparation or issuance of any report on reviews of interim financial information of an issuer, as discussed in paragraph 12.02. Readers should understand the provisions of the Sarbanes-Oxley Act of 2002, the SEC regulations implementing the Sarbanes-Oxley Act of 2002, and the rules and standards of the PCAOB, as applicable to their circumstances, to determine if the standards of the PCAOB should be applied. Readers should consult the standards of the PCAOB and related interpretive guidance when preparing or issuing any report on reviews of interim financial information in accordance with the standards of the PCAOB.

Report on Internal Control Required by the SEC Under Form N-SAR

12.29 The following is an illustration of the independent registered public accounting firm's report on a registered investment company's internal control based on the results of procedures performed in obtaining an understanding of internal control over financial reporting and assessing control risk in connection with the audit of the investment company's financial statements. Under PCAOB standards, the auditor should obtain an understanding of internal control sufficient to plan the audit by performing procedures to understand the design of controls relevant to an audit of financial statements and determining whether they have been placed in operation.[50] The instructions to Form N-SAR further note that the internal control report is to be based on review, study, and evaluation of the financial reporting information system and internal control over financial reporting, including control activities for safeguarding securities. This report should reflect any material weaknesses identified as of the fiscal year-end date.

The following illustrative auditor's report is prepared for informational and reference purposes only and is not authoritative. It has not been reviewed, approved, disapproved, or otherwise acted on by the PCAOB or SEC.

Report of Independent Registered Public Accounting Firm

To the Shareholders and
Board of Directors of
XYZ Investment Company

In planning and performing our audit of the financial statements of XYZ Investment Company (the Company) as of and for the year ended December 31, 20X8, in accordance with the standards of the Public Company Accounting Oversight Board (United States), we considered the Company's internal control over financial reporting, including controls over safeguarding securities, as a basis for designing our auditing procedures for the purpose of expressing our opinion on the financial statements and to comply with the requirements of Form N-SAR, but not for the purpose of expressing an opinion on the effectiveness of the Company's internal control over financial reporting. Accordingly, we express no such opinion.

The management of the Company is responsible for establishing and maintaining effective internal control over financial reporting. In fulfilling this responsibility, estimates and judgments by management are required to assess the expected benefits and related costs of controls. A company's internal control over financial reporting is a process designed to provide reasonable assurance regarding the reliability of financial reporting and the preparation of financial statements for external purposes in accordance with generally accepted accounting principles (GAAP). A company's internal control over financial reporting includes those policies and procedures that (1) pertain to the maintenance of records that, in reasonable detail, accurately and fairly reflect the transactions and dispositions of the assets of the company; (2) provide reasonable assurance that transactions are recorded as necessary to permit preparation of financial statements in accordance

[50] See footnote 35.

with GAAP, and that receipts and expenditures of the company are being made only in accordance with authorizations of management and directors of the company; and (3) provide reasonable assurance regarding prevention or timely detection of unauthorized acquisition, use or disposition of a company's assets that could have a material effect on the financial statements.

Because of its inherent limitations, internal control over financial reporting may not prevent or detect misstatements. Also, projections of any evaluation of effectiveness to future periods are subject to the risk that controls may become inadequate because of changes in conditions, or that the degree of compliance with the policies or procedures may deteriorate.

A deficiency in internal control over financial reporting exists when the design or operation of a control does not allow management or employees, in the normal course of performing their assigned functions, to prevent or detect misstatements on a timely basis. A material weakness is a deficiency, or combination of deficiencies, in internal control over financial reporting, such that there is a reasonable possibility that a material misstatement of the Company's annual or interim financial statements will not be prevented or detected on a timely basis.

Our consideration of the Company's internal control over financial reporting was for the limited purpose described in the first paragraph and would not necessarily disclose all deficiencies in internal control that might be material weaknesses under standards established by the Public Company Accounting Oversight Board (United States). However, we noted no deficiencies in the Company's internal control over financial reporting and its operation, including controls over safeguarding securities, that we consider to be a material weakness as defined above as of December 31, 20X8.

This report is intended solely for the information and use of management and the Board of Directors of XYZ Investment Company and the Securities and Exchange Commission and is not intended to be and should not be used by anyone other than these specified parties.

[Independent Registered Public Accounting Firm (signed)]
[Anytown, USA]
[February 14, 20X9]

Report on Examinations of Securities Pursuant to Rules 17f-1 and 17f-2 Under the 1940 Act

12.30 The following form of report is used for examinations of securities conducted pursuant to Rules 17f-1 and 17f-2 of the 1940 Act.[51] Paragraph (b)(4) of Rule 17f-1 requires that all registered investment companies whose securities are maintained in the custody of a member of a national securities exchange have an independent public accountant conduct an examination of such securities three times per year (at each of the annual and semiannual period-ends and at one other date, chosen by the accountant, during the fiscal year). Rule 17f-2(f) requires that all registered investment companies that maintain

---

[51] Section 404.01a of the SEC's *Codification of Financial Reporting Policies* describes the nature of the examination to be made and the content of the auditor's report.

custody of their own securities, as defined in the rule, have an independent public accountant conduct an examination of such securities three times per fiscal year, at least two of which shall be chosen by the accountant without prior notice to the investment company. The SEC staff requires that the examination be conducted to the first level of nonaffiliation (that is, confirmations of security holdings may be relied upon to verify existence and ownership only if they are received from a nonaffiliate, such as the Depository Trust Company or the Federal Reserve's book entry system). If a portion of an investment company's portfolio is not maintained in the custody of a member of a national securities exchange or held by the investment company, the provisions of Rules 17f-1 and 17f-2 do not apply to those securities. This report follows the examination engagement provisions of AT section 601, *Compliance Attestation* (AICPA, *Professional Standards*), and PCAOB standards and is illustrated in the following paragraph for an examination pursuant to Rule 17f-2.

This illustrative report should be used when a practitioner expresses an opinion on management's assertion about compliance with the requirements of Rule 17f-2(b)–(c) under the 1940 Act. AT section 601 enables true direct reporting on subject matter.[52]

The following illustrative auditor's report is prepared for informational and reference purposes only and is not authoritative. It has not been reviewed, approved, disapproved, or otherwise acted on by the PCAOB or SEC.

Report of Independent Registered Public Accounting Firm

To the Board of Directors XYZ Investment Company

We have examined management's assertion, included in the accompanying Management Statement Regarding Compliance With Certain Provisions of the Investment Company Act of 1940, that XYZ Investment Company (the Company) complied with the requirements of subsections (b) and (c) of Rule 17f-2[53] under the Investment Company Act of 1940 as of August 31, 20X8. Management is responsible for the Company's compliance with those requirements. Our responsibility is to express an opinion on management's assertion about the Company's compliance based on our examination.

Our examination was conducted in accordance with the standards of the Public Company Accounting Oversight Board (United States) and, accordingly, included examining, on a test basis, evidence about the Company's compliance with those requirements and performing such other procedures as we considered necessary in the circumstances. Included among our procedures were the following tests performed as of August 31, 20X8, and with respect to agreement of security purchases and sales, for the period from April 30, 20X8 (the date of our last examination), through August 31, 20X8 [*itemize all that apply*]:

- Count and inspection of all securities located in the vault of [*Custodian*] in [*location*] without prior notice to management[54]

---

[52] See footnote 35.

[53] Subsections (b)(1) and (b)(6) of Rule 17f-1.

[54] The phrase *without prior notice to management* should be deleted if the procedures were not performed on a surprise basis.

- Confirmation of all securities held by institutions in book entry form [*specify each institution, that is, the Federal Reserve Bank of (City), The Depository Trust Company, and so on*]

- Confirmation of all securities hypothecated, pledged, placed in escrow, or out for transfer with brokers, pledgees, or transfer agents

- Reconciliation of all such securities to the books and records of the Company and the Custodian

- Confirmation of all repurchase agreements with brokers/banks and agreement of underlying collateral with [*Custodian*] records

- Agreement of [*insert number*] security purchases and [*insert number*] security sales or maturities since our last report from the books and records of the Company to broker confirmations

We believe that our examination provides a reasonable basis for our opinion. Our examination does not provide a legal determination on the Company's compliance with specified requirements.

In our opinion, management's assertion that XYZ Investment Company complied with the requirements of subsections (b) and (c) of Rule 17f-2 of the Investment Company Act of 1940 as of August 31, 20X8, with respect to securities reflected in the investment account of the Company is fairly stated, in all material respects.

This report is intended solely for the information and use of management and the Board of Directors of XYZ Investment Company and the Securities and Exchange Commission and is not intended to be and should not be used by anyone other than these specified parties.

[Independent Accountant (signed)]
[Anytown, USA]
[October 21, 20X8]

Management Statement Regarding Compliance With Certain Provisions of the Investment Company Act of 1940[55]

We, as members of management of XYZ Investment Company (the Company), are responsible for complying with the requirements of subsections (b) and (c) of Rule 17f-2, "Custody of Investments by Registered Management Investment Companies," of the Investment Company Act of 1940. We are also responsible for establishing and maintaining effective internal controls over compliance with those requirements. We have performed an evaluation of the Company's compliance with the requirements of subsections (b) and (c) of Rule 17f-2 as of August 31, 20X8, and from [*last examination date*] through August 31, 20X8.

Based on this evaluation, we assert that the Company was in compliance with the requirements of subsections (b) and (c) of Rule 17f-2

---

[55] Alternatively, management's assertion may be included in a representation letter. Accordingly, the auditor's report should be modified to reflect this alternative, in accordance with AT section 601, *Compliance Attestation* (AICPA, *Professional Standards*). AT section 601 enables true direct reporting on the subject matter.

of the Investment Company Act of 1940 as of August 31, 20X8, and from [*last examination date*], through August 31, 20X8, with respect to securities reflected in the investment account of the Company.

XYZ Investment Company

By:

[*Signature*]

[*Name and title of appropriate operating official—CEO/COO*]

Report on Examinations of Securities Pursuant to Rule 206(4)-2 Under the Investment Advisers Act of 1940[56]

12.31   In December 2009, the SEC adopted rules designed to substantially increase the protections for investor funds and securities of which an investment adviser registered with the SEC has custody. Depending on the investment adviser's custody arrangement, the rules would require the adviser to be subject to a surprise examination and, in some cases, a custody controls examination, which were generally not required under the previous rules. Readers are encouraged to review the full text of Rule Release No. IA-2968, *Custody of Funds or Securities of Clients by Investment Advisers*. Additionally, both the SEC and the AICPA have released frequently asked questions that are periodically updated about the custody rule and can be accessed from the Division of Investment Management page of the SEC's website and from the Investment Companies Expert Panel page under the Financial Reporting Center on the AICPA's website, respectively.[57]

12.32   An examination of funds and securities must be conducted pursuant to Rule 206(4)-2(a)(4) under the Investment Advisers Act of 1940. This rule requires that all registered investment advisers (or an investment adviser required to register) who have custody of client funds or securities, as defined, have an independent public accountant conduct an examination on a surprise basis once every calendar year. The independent public accountant must also file a certificate on Form ADV-E with the SEC within 120 days of the time chosen by the independent public accountant stating that he or she has examined the funds and securities and describing the nature and extent of the examination.[58] This surprise examination report follows the provisions of AT

---

[56] In November 2014, the AICPA and the Center for Audit Quality jointly issued a Member Alert which summarizes the SEC's and PCAOB's independence rules for audit firms that perform audit and attestation engagements for certain nonissuers, including (1) SEC-registered broker-dealers and (2) SEC- or state-registered private funds, investment advisers, or related-party custodians for whom an engagement is subject to the requirements of the Custody Rule. The Member Alert is available at www.thecaq.org/docs/alerts/independence-alert-caqalert-201411.pdf?sfvrsn=2.

[57] On March 4, 2013, the SEC issued a Risk Alert on compliance with its custody rule for investment advisers and it also issued an Investor Bulletin about the rule, which is designed to protect advisory clients from theft or misuse of their funds and securities. The alert issued by the SEC's Office of Compliance Inspections and Examinations shares observations from a review of recent examinations where significant deficiencies were identified and showed custody-related issues in about one-third of the firms examined. The full text of this Risk Alert can be accessed on the SEC's website at www.sec.gov/about/offices/ocie/custody-risk-alert.pdf.

[58] Frequently asked questions (FAQs) on Form ADV-E can be accessed through the Division of Investment Management page, "IARD: Electronic Filing for Advisers" on the SEC's website at www.sec.gov. The independent accountant, upon finding any material discrepancies during the course of the examination, should notify the SEC within one business day of the finding by means of a

(continued)

section 601. AT section 601 enables true direct reporting on the subject matter. The rule also requires that a qualified custodian maintain client funds and securities in a separate account for each client under that client's name or in accounts that contain only the clients' funds and securities under the adviser's name as agent or trustee for the clients. Notice to clients must be provided when an account is opened (and following any changes) with a qualified custodian on their behalf, which details the qualified custodian's name and address and the manner in which the funds or securities are maintained. The investment adviser must also have a reasonable basis, after due inquiry, for believing that the qualified custodian sends an account statement, at least quarterly, to each of the investment advisers' clients for which it maintains funds or securities.[59]

12.33 Advisers to pooled investment vehicles may be deemed to comply with the surprise examination requirements of the rule by obtaining an audit of the pool and delivering the audited financial statements to pool investors within 120 days of the pool's fiscal year-end.[60] That audit must be conducted by an accounting firm registered with, and subject to regular inspection by, the PCAOB. Lastly, the advisers to pools complying with the rule by distributing audited financial statements to investors must obtain an audit upon liquidation of the pool when the liquidation occurs prior to the pool's fiscal year-end. If the pooled investment vehicle does not distribute audited financial statements to its investors, the adviser must obtain an annual surprise examination and have a reasonable basis, after due inquiry, for believing that the qualified custodian sends an account statement of the pooled investment vehicle to its investors in order to comply with the custody rule. For a pool that is not relying on the audit provision to satisfy the custody rule, the rule requires privately offered securities held by the pool to be placed with a qualified custodian (as defined in a subsequent paragraph), and it requires the accounting firm performing the surprise examination to verify these privately offered securities, along with other funds and securities.

12.34 If the investment adviser or its related person maintains client funds or securities as a qualified custodian in connection with advisory services provided to clients, additional requirements exist, in accordance with

---

(footnote continued)

facsimile transmission or e-mail, followed by first class mail, directed to the attention of the Director of the Office of Compliance Inspections and Examinations. See Rule 206(4)-2(a)(4)(ii) under the 1940 Act. For purposes of the examination, a *material discrepancy* is material noncompliance with the provisions of either Rule 206(4)-2 or Rule 204-2(b) under the Investment Advisers Act of 1940. Instructions from the SEC for sending independent accountant notification of material discrepancies found during annual surprise examination can be found within those FAQs.

[59] See Rule 206(4)-2(b) under the 1940 Act for exceptions to these requirements for shares of mutual funds, certain privately offered securities, fee deductions, limited partnerships subject to annual audit, registered investment companies, and certain related persons.

[60] In 2006, the SEC issued a letter indicating that it would not recommend enforcement action under this rule against an adviser of a fund of funds relying on the annual audit provision of Rule 206(4)-2 if the audited financial statements of the fund of funds are distributed to investors in the fund of funds within 180 days of the end of its fiscal year. See the August 10, 2006, SEC staff letter *ABA Committee on Private Investment Entities*. The amendments to the custody rule do not affect the views of the staff expressed in that letter. In 2011, the SEC issued an FAQ indicating that when an adviser's client is a "top tier" pooled investment vehicle that invests in one or more funds of funds, and such top tier pool invests 10 percent or more of its total assets in one or more funds of funds, as defined in the ABA Letter, that are not, and are not advised by, a related person of the top tier pool, its general partner, or its adviser, the division would not recommend enforcement action to the SEC under Rule 206(4)-2 if the audited financial statements of the top tier pool are distributed to pool investors within 260 days of the end of the top tier pool's fiscal year.

Rule 206(4)-2(a)(6). Such investment adviser must at least once each calendar year obtain or receive from its related person a written internal control report related to its or its affiliates' custodial services, including the safeguarding of funds and securities, which includes an opinion from an independent public accountant that is registered with, and subject to, regular inspection by the PCAOB. Regardless of whether an adviser to a pooled investment vehicle obtains a surprise examination or satisfies that requirement by obtaining an audit and distributing the audited financial statements to pool investors within 120 days of the end of the pooled investment vehicle's fiscal year,[61] if the pooled investment vehicle's assets are maintained with a qualified custodian that is either the adviser to the pool or a related person of the adviser, the adviser to the pool would have to obtain or receive from the related person an internal control report. This requirement could be satisfied with a type 2 SOC 1 report (formerly known as a type 2 SAS No. 70 report) or an examination on internal control conducted in accordance with AT section 601. As explained in question XIII.3 of the SEC's *Staff Responses to Questions About the Custody Rule*, in addition to the two types of reports mentioned previously and Release IA-2969, all of which satisfy the requirements for an internal control report, a report under AT section 101, *Attest Engagements* (AICPA, *Professional Standards*), would also be acceptable. This internal control report must include an opinion about whether controls have been placed in operation as of a specific date and are suitably designed and operating effectively to meet control objectives relating to custodial services, including the safeguarding of funds and securities held by either the investment adviser or its related person on behalf of the advisory clients during the year. The accountant must also verify that the funds and securities are reconciled to a custodian other than the investment adviser or its related person (for example, the Depository Trust Corporation). The accountant's tests of the custodian's reconciliation should include either direct confirmation, on a test basis, with unaffiliated custodians or other procedures designed to verify that the data used in the reconciliations performed by the qualified custodian is obtained from unaffiliated custodians and unaltered.

12.35 A *qualified custodian* is defined by the rule as (*a*) a bank, as defined in Section 202(a)(2) of the Investment Advisers Act of 1940, or a savings association, as defined in Section 3(b)(1) of the Federal Deposit Insurance Act of 1950, that has deposits insured by the Federal Deposit Insurance Corporation under the Federal Deposit Insurance Act of 1950; (*b*) a broker-dealer registered under Section 15(b)(1) of the Securities Exchange Act of 1934 (the 1934 Act) holding the client assets in customer accounts; (*c*) a futures commission merchant registered under Section 4f(a) of the Commodity Exchange Act holding the client assets in customer accounts, but only with respect to clients' funds and security futures, or other securities incidental to transactions in contracts for the purchase or sale of a commodity for future delivery and options thereon; and (*d*) a foreign financial institution that customarily holds financial assets for its customers, provided that the foreign financial institution keeps the advisory clients' assets in customer accounts segregated from its proprietary assets. Additionally, *related person* is defined in the rule as any person, directly or indirectly, controlling or controlled by the investment adviser and any person who is under common control with the investment adviser.

---

[61] See footnote 60.

12.36 The rule defines *custody* to mean an investment adviser or its related person holding, directly or indirectly, client funds or securities or having any authority to obtain possession of them. Custody includes the following:

- Possession of client funds or securities (but not checks drawn by clients and made payable to third parties) unless the investment adviser receives them inadvertently and returns them to the sender promptly but in any case within three business days of receiving them

- Any arrangement (including a general power of attorney) under which the investment adviser is authorized or permitted to withdraw client funds or securities maintained with a custodian upon the investment adviser's instruction to the custodian

- Any capacity (such as general partner of a limited partnership, managing member of a limited liability company or a comparable position for another type of pooled investment vehicle, or trustee of a trust) that gives the investment adviser or his or her supervised person legal ownership of, or access to, client funds or securities

Therefore, custody does not equate to serving as a qualified custodian under the rule.

12.37 When the investment adviser or its related person maintains the client funds and securities as a qualified custodian in connection with advisory services provided to clients, the independent public accountant engaged to perform the surprise examination must be registered with, and subject to regular inspection by, the PCAOB.

12.38 These illustrative reports should be used when a practitioner expresses an opinion on management's assertion about compliance with Rule 204-2(b) and certain provisions of Rule 206(4)-2 of the Investment Advisers Act of 1940 and when the practitioner expresses an opinion on the company's compliance with Rule 204-2(b) and certain provisions of Rule 206(4)-2 of the Investment Advisers Act of 1940, respectively. Paragraph .54 of AT section 601 states that the practitioner may examine and report directly on an entity's compliance, or he or she may examine and report on the responsible party's written assertion, except when the examination discloses noncompliance with the applicable requirements that the practitioner believes have a material effect on the entity's compliance (in that case, the practitioner should opine on the entity's specified compliance requirements, not the responsible party's assertion).

Illustrative Report of Independent Accountant on Examinations of Securities Pursuant to Rule 206(4)-2 (Report on Management's Assertion) and Management's Assertion

Report of Independent Accountant

[To the Board of Directors[62] of
XYZ Investment Advisers, Inc.]

We have examined management's assertion, included in the accompanying Management Statement Regarding Compliance with Certain Provisions of the Investment Advisers Act of 1940, that [*XYZ Investment Advisers, Inc.*] (the Company) complied with paragraph (a)(1) of

---

[62] If no board of directors exists, identify the equivalent body with oversight responsibility.

Rule 206(4)-2 of the Investment Advisers Act of 1940 (the Act) as of [*examination date*] and complied with Rule 204-2(b) of the Act during the period from [*prior examination date*][63] to [*examination date*].[64] Management is responsible for the Company's compliance with those requirements. Our responsibility is to express an opinion on management's assertion about the Company's compliance based on our examination.

Our examination was conducted in accordance with attestation standards established by the American Institute of Certified Public Accountants and, accordingly, included examining, on a test basis, evidence about the Company's compliance with those requirements and performing such other procedures as we considered necessary in the circumstances. Included among our procedures were the following tests which were performed for a sample of client accounts as of [*examination date*], which is a date we selected without prior notice to management: [*provide a brief description and itemize all that apply*]

- Reading contract provisions with qualified custodians;[65]
- Count and inspection of securities located in the vault of the Company in [*location*] or in [*location*] of [*persons associated with the Company*];
- Confirmation of cash and securities held by qualified custodians either under the client's name or in the name of the Company as agent or trustee for clients;
- [*Where a qualified custodian is either the adviser or a person related to the adviser*] For those client funds and securities maintained by the Company [*or a related person*] as a qualified custodian, obtaining and considering the most recent internal control report required to be obtained by the Company under Rule 206(4)-2(a)(6);
- Confirmation of privately offered securities, as defined in Rule 206(4)-2(b)(2), held directly by the Company with the issuer of or counterparty to the security [*or, where replies were not received, alternative procedures*];
- Reconciliation of cash and securities counted or confirmed to the books and records of client accounts maintained by the Company;
- Confirmation with clients[66] of the detail of cash and securities held as of the date of examination by the Company on behalf of such clients and contributions and

---

[63] In accordance with Question IV.5 of *Staff Responses to Questions About the Custody Rule*, when the investment adviser becomes subject to the surprise examination requirement for the first time, the accountant should report on the investment adviser's compliance with Rule 204-2(b) for a period beginning no later than the date that the adviser became subject to the surprise examination requirement through the examination date.

[64] This date should be the same as-of date as in the accompanying Management Statement Regarding Compliance.

[65] The practitioner should assess the need for this procedure based on the extent of the relationship between the investment adviser and qualified custodian or whether other procedures provide sufficient evidence to express an opinion on management's assertion about compliance with paragraph (a)(1) of Rule 206(4)-2.

[66] When performing a surprise examination for an adviser to a pooled investment vehicle or vehicles, the practitioner should add *and investors in pooled investment vehicles*.

> withdrawals of cash and securities to and from the account [*or for those confirmations not received, alternative procedures*],[67] and reconciliation of confirmations received [*and other evidence obtained*] to the Company's books and records;

- Confirmation with clients of accounts that were closed or for which funds were returned to the clients;
- Confirmation with clients of accounts having a zero balance as of the date of the examination.

We believe that our examination provides a reasonable basis for our opinion. Our examination does not provide a legal determination on the Company's compliance with specified requirements, including the Company's identification of "securities" as defined by Section 202(a)(18) of the Act and its determination of "custody" as defined by Rule 206(4)-2(d)(2) under the Act. It is the responsibility of [*XYZ Investment Advisers, Inc.*] to determine its investment advisory clients under the Act.

In our opinion, management's assertion that [*XYZ Investment Advisers, Inc.*] was in compliance with the requirements of paragraph (a)(1) of Rule 206(4)-2 of the Investment Advisers Act of 1940 as of [*examination date*], and has complied with Rule 204-2(b) of the Act for the period from [*prior examination date*] through [*examination date*], is fairly stated, in all material respects.

This report is intended solely for the information and use of management and the Board of Directors of [*XYZ Investment Advisers, Inc.*] and the Securities and Exchange Commission and is not intended to be and should not be used by anyone other than these specified parties.

[Independent Accountant (signed)]
[Anytown, USA]
[Date]

Management Statement Regarding Compliance With Certain Provisions of the Investment Advisers Act of 1940[68]

We, as members of management of [*XYZ Investment Advisers, Inc.*] (the Company) are responsible for complying with the requirements of Rule 204-2(b), "Books and Records to be Maintained by Investment Advisers," and Rule 206(4)-2, "Custody of Funds or Securities of Clients by Investment Advisers," of the Investment Advisers Act of 1940 (the Act). We are also responsible for establishing and maintaining effective internal controls over compliance with the requirements of Rule 204-2(b) and Rule 206(4)-2. We have performed an evaluation of the Company's compliance with paragraph (a)(1) of Rule 206(4)-2 of the Act as of [*examination date*] and compliance with Rule 204-2(b) of the Act during the period from [*prior examination date*] to [*examination*

---

[67] The report should delineate procedures performed for (*a*) confirmation replies received with exception and (*b*) confirmation requests for which replies were not received. The presentation of procedures performed should be sufficiently specific for the reader to understand the nature and extent of the procedures performed.

[68] Alternatively, management's assertion may be included in a representation letter. Accordingly, the auditor's report should be modified to reflect this alternative, in accordance with AT section 601.

date]. Based on this evaluation, we assert that the Company was in compliance with the Act as described below:

Rule 204-2(b) under the Act requires that an investment adviser who has custody or possession of funds and/or securities of any client must record all transactions for such clients in a journal and in separate ledger accounts for each client and must maintain copies of confirmations of all transactions in such accounts and a position record for each security in which a client has an interest. In addition, paragraph (1) of Rule 206(4)-2(a) provides, in general, that it shall constitute a fraudulent, deceptive, or manipulative act or practice for any investment adviser to have custody of client funds or securities unless a qualified custodian maintains those funds and securities (i) in a separate account for each client under that client's name; or (ii) in accounts that contain only clients' funds and securities, under the investment adviser's name as agent or trustee for the clients.

[*If applicable: Paragraph (a)(6) of Rule 206(4)-2 provides, in general, that an investment adviser that maintains, or has custody because a related person maintains, client funds or securities pursuant to Rule 206(4)-2 as a qualified custodian in connection with advisory services provided to clients must obtain, or receive from its related person, no less frequently than once each calendar year, a written internal control report prepared by an independent public accountant. The internal control report must include an opinion of an independent public accountant as to whether controls have been placed in operation as of a specific date, and are suitably designed and are operating effectively to meet control objectives relating to custodial services, including the safeguarding of funds and securities held by either the adviser or a related person on behalf of the advisory clients, during the year. Also, as part of the internal control report, the independent public accountant must verify that the funds and securities are reconciled to a custodian other than the adviser or the adviser's related person.*]

For purposes of this assertion, "security" has the meaning ascribed to it by Section 202(a)(18) of the Act, and "custody" has the meaning ascribed by Rule 206(4)-2(d)(2) under the Act. It is our responsibility to determine our investment advisory clients under the Act. The clients, and client funds and securities, to which this assertion applies, have been determined in a manner consistent with the manner in which we report clients for which custody of funds and securities exists under Items 9A(2) and 9B(2) of Form ADV, if the responses to those Items were prepared as of the date of this assertion.

[XYZ Investment Advisers, Inc.]

By:

_____

[*Name*]

Chief Financial Officer

_____

[Date]

Illustrative Report of Independent Accountant on Examinations of Securities Pursuant to Rule 206(4)-2 (Direct Report on Management's Compliance)

Report of Independent Accountant

[To the Board of Directors[69] of
XYZ Investment Advisers, Inc.]

We have examined the compliance of [*XYZ Investment Advisers, Inc.*] (the Company) with paragraph (a)(1) of Rule 206(4)-2 of the Investment Advisers Act of 1940 (the Act) as of [*examination date*] and with Rule 204-2(b) of the Act during the period from [*prior examination date*][70] to [*examination date*]. Management is responsible for the Company's compliance with those requirements. Our responsibility is to express an opinion on the Company's compliance based on our examination.

Our examination was conducted in accordance with attestation standards established by the American Institute of Certified Public Accountants and, accordingly, included examining, on a test basis, evidence about the Company's compliance with those requirements and performing such other procedures as we considered necessary in the circumstances. Included among our procedures were the following tests which were performed for a sample of client accounts as of [*examination date*], which is a date we selected without prior notice to management: [*provide a brief description and itemize all that apply*]

- Reading contract provisions with qualified custodians;[71]
- Count and inspection of securities located in the vault of the Company in [*location*], or in [*location*] of [*persons associated with the Company*];
- Confirmation of cash and securities held by qualified custodians either under the client's name or in the name of the Company as agent or trustee for clients;
- [*Where a qualified custodian is either the adviser or a person related to the adviser*] For those client funds and securities maintained by the Company [*or a related person*] as a qualified custodian, obtaining and considering the most recent internal control report required to be obtained by the Company under Rule 206(4)-2(a)(6);
- Confirmation of privately offered securities, as defined in Rule 206(4)-2(b)(2), held directly by the Company with the issuer of or counterparty to the security [*or, where replies were not received, alternative procedures*];

---

[69] If no board of directors exists, identify the equivalent body with oversight responsibility.

[70] In accordance with Question IV.5 of *Staff Responses to Questions About the Custody Rule*, when the investment adviser becomes subject to the surprise examination requirement for the first time, the accountant should report on the investment adviser's compliance with Rule 204-2(b) for a period beginning no later than the date that the adviser became subject to the surprise examination requirement through the examination date.

[71] The practitioner should assess the need for this procedure based on the extent of the relationship between the investment adviser and qualified custodian or whether other procedures provide sufficient evidence to express an opinion on compliance with paragraph (a)(1) of Rule 206(4)-2.

Illustrative Report of Independent Registered Public Accounting Firm on Management's Assertion Regarding Controls at a Custodian Pursuant to Rule 206(4)-2 and Release No. IA-2969 Under the Investment Advisers Act of 1940

Report of Independent Registered Public Accounting Firm

To the Board of Directors of
XYZ Custodian, Inc.[75]

[Introductory paragraph]

We have examined the assertion made by the management of XYZ Custodian, Inc. (XYZ Custodian), pertaining to its controls over the custody of client funds and securities for registered investment advisers that are related persons, as that term is defined in Rule 206(4)-2 under the Investment Advisers Act of 1940 (related persons). Management's assertion is presented in the accompanying document titled, "Management's Assertion Regarding XYZ Custodian's Controls Over Custody Pursuant to Rule 206(4)-2 Under the Investment Advisers Act of 1940 (the Act)." Management has established certain control objectives (specified control objectives) and related controls pertaining to custody services, including the safeguarding of client funds and securities, pursuant to Rule 206(4)-2 and Release No. IA-2969 under the Act. XYZ Custodian's specified control objectives and the related controls are included in the accompanying document, "Description of XYZ Custodian's Controls and Control Objectives Pursuant to Rule 206(4)-2 and Release No. IA-2969 under the Act" (management's description), which is incorporated by reference in management's assertion.

[The following paragraph should be added to the report if certain control objectives, or parts thereof, are addressed in a report on a subservice provider's controls or in another (other) report(s) on the custodian's controls and are excluded from management's assertion and description.]

As indicated in management's assertion and description, XYZ Custodian uses *[name or type of subservice provider(s)]* to perform *[function performed by the subservice provider]*. Management's description indicates that the specified control objective(s)[76] related to *[specify the subject matter of the control objective(s), or parts thereof, addressed in the report on the subservice provider's controls]* are addressed in an examination report on the subservice provider's controls issued by an independent registered public accounting firm.[77] In addition, management's description indicates that XYZ Custodian's specified control objectives[78] related to *[specify the subject matter of the control objective(s), or parts thereof, addressed in a another report on the custodian's controls]* are addressed in another examination report issued by an independent registered public accounting firm. Because [parts of] these control objectives are excluded from management's assertion and description, the scope of our work did not include examining

---

[75] If no board of directors exists, identify the equivalent body with oversight responsibility.

[76] If only certain controls within a control objective are addressed in the examination report, state "certain controls to meet the specified control objective(s)."

[77] The report on controls would cover the suitability of the design, implementation, and operating effectiveness of the controls.

[78] If only certain controls within a control objective are addressed in the examination report, state "certain controls to meet XYZ Custodian's specified control objective(s)."

the design, implementation, or operating effectiveness of controls to achieve [those parts of] the control objectives and we do not express an opinion thereon.

Management's assertion states that

- the controls described in management's description were suitably designed and implemented throughout the period January 1, 20X1, to December 31, 20X1, to provide reasonable assurance that the specified control objectives set forth therein would be achieved, if those controls were complied with satisfactorily [*and related persons applied the complementary user entity controls contemplated in the design of XYZ Custodian's controls throughout the period January 1, 20X1, to December 31, 20X1*] and

- the controls set forth in management's description were operating with sufficient effectiveness to provide reasonable assurance that the specified control objectives included in the description were achieved throughout the period January 1, 20X1, to December 31, 20X1 [*if related persons applied the complementary user entity controls contemplated in the design of XYZ Custodian's controls throughout the period January 1, 20X1, to December 31, 20X1*].

Management of XYZ Custodian is responsible for its assertion. Our responsibility is to express an opinion on management's assertion based on our examination.

[*Scope paragraph*]

Our examination was conducted in accordance with attestation standards established by the American Institute of Certified Public Accountants. Those standards require that we plan and perform the examination to obtain reasonable assurance about whether management's assertion is fairly stated in all material respects. Our examination included obtaining an understanding of and evaluating the suitability of the design, implementation, and operating effectiveness of the controls intended to achieve the specified control objectives and examining, on a test basis, evidence supporting management's assertion and performing such other procedures as we considered necessary in the circumstances. Included among our procedures were [*provide a brief description of the procedures performed, including the nature, timing, extent, and results thereof, to verify that funds and securities are reconciled to depositories and unaffiliated custodians, such as confirming and reconciling a sample of security positions with unaffiliated custodians and depositories and/or alternative procedures used to verify that the data used in reconciliations is unaltered*] as of [*identify date(s) selected for testing*]. We believe that our examination provides a reasonable basis for our opinion.

Our examination was limited to examining, for the purposes described above, management's assertion about the specified control objectives and related controls included in management's description and did not consider any other control objectives or controls that may be relevant to XYZ Custodian's or the related persons' internal control over the custody of securities and funds for any specific client or clients of

XYZ Custodian. Further, the relative effectiveness and significance of specific controls at XYZ Custodian, and their effect on related persons' internal control over custody of securities and funds, are dependent on their interaction with the controls and other factors present at individual related persons. We have performed no procedures to evaluate the effectiveness of such controls or such other factors at individual related persons.

The control objectives and related controls set forth in management's description have been provided to assist the related persons that use XYZ Custodian's services with their compliance with the requirements of SEC Rule 206(4)-2 under the Investment Advisers Act of 1940.

[Inherent limitations paragraph]

Management's description covers the period January 1, 20X1, to December 31, 20X1. Any projection of such information to the future is subject to the risk that, because of change, the description may no longer portray the controls in existence. The potential effectiveness of controls to achieve the specified control objectives is subject to inherent limitations and, accordingly, errors or fraud may occur and not be detected. Furthermore, the projection of any evaluations, based on our findings, to future periods is subject to the risk that controls may become inadequate because of changes in conditions; that the degree of compliance with such controls may deteriorate; or that changes made to the system or controls, or the failure to make needed changes to the system or controls, may alter the validity of such evaluations.

[Opinion paragraph]

In our opinion, management's assertion referred to above is fairly stated, in all material respects, based on the specified control objectives set forth in management's description.

[Restricted use paragraph]

This report is intended solely for the information and use of XYZ Custodian; related persons that used XYZ Custodian's services during some or all of the period [January 1, 20X1, to December 31, 20X1]; the independent registered public accounting firms of such related persons; and the SEC and is not intended to be and should not be used by anyone other than these specified parties.

[Signature of Independent Registered Public Accountant]
[Date]

Illustrative Management Assertion[79] Regarding XYZ Custodian's Controls Over Custody Pursuant to Rule 206(4)-2 Under the Investment Advisers Act of 1940

XYZ Custodian provides custody services to registered investment advisers that are related persons, as that term is defined in Rule 206(4)-2 under the Investment Advisers Act of 1940 (related persons). Management has established certain control objectives (specified control

---

[79] In the event that management identifies a material misstatement or deviation from the criteria, the practitioner should follow the guidance in paragraph .66 of AT section 101, *Attest Engagements* (AICPA *Professional Standards*), and report directly on the subject matter, not the assertion.

objectives) and related controls pertaining to its custody services, including the safeguarding of client funds and securities, pursuant to Rule 206(4)-2 and Release No. IA-2969 under the Act. These specified control objectives and related controls are the responsibility of XYZ Custodian and are presented in the accompanying document, "Description of XYZ Custodian's Controls and Control Objectives Pursuant to Rule 206(4)-2 and Release No. IA-2969 Under the Act" (description), which is incorporated by reference in this assertion. We, as members of management of XYZ Custodian, are responsible for the description;[80] for establishing the specified control objectives and related controls; and for the suitability of the design, implementation, and operating effectiveness of the controls.

The description is provided to enable related persons, when performing their annual evaluation of compliance with Rule 206(4)-2 under the Act, to consider such information, along with information about their own controls over the custody of client funds and securities.

[*The following paragraph should be added to the assertion if certain control objectives, or parts thereof, are excluded from the description and are addressed in a report on the subservice provider's controls or in another report on the custodian's controls. Management's description should include an appendix that identifies the control objectives that are excluded from the description and identifies the internal control report(s) in which those controls are addressed.*]

The appendix to the description identifies the control objectives, or parts thereof, that are excluded from the description and addressed in reports on the subservice provider's controls or in another report on XYZ Custodian's controls.

We have evaluated whether XYZ Custodian's controls were suitably designed, implemented, and operating effectively to achieve the specified control objectives throughout the period January 1, 20X1, to December 31, 20X1. The criteria against which the controls were evaluated are the specified control objectives included in the description. Based on our evaluation, we assert that

- the controls included in the description were suitably designed and implemented throughout the period January 1, 20X1, to December 31, 20X1, to provide reasonable assurance that the specified control objectives[81] would be

---

[80] The description should identify the nature of any subservice providers used, the functions they perform, and whether the relevant control objectives and related controls of the subservice provider are excluded from the description. If the subservice provider's controls are excluded from the description, the description would, however, include relevant user entity controls and monitoring controls over the subservice provider. Control objectives and related controls that are excluded from the description should be the subject of an examination of design, implementation, and operating effectiveness by a registered public accounting firm.

[81] The control objectives and related controls included in the description (unless covered in another report on the service organization's controls or a report on controls at a subservice provider) address the areas of client account setup and maintenance, authorization and processing of client transactions, security maintenance and setup, processing of income and corporate action transactions, reconciliation of funds and securities to depositories and other unaffiliated custodians, and client reporting. Relevant general computer controls should also be included in the description when automated controls or reliance on computer-generated information are material elements of addressing control objectives.

achieved, if those controls were complied with satisfactorily [*and related persons applied the complementary user entity controls contemplated in the design of XYZ Custodian's controls throughout the period from January 1, 20X1, to December 31, 20X1*][82] and

- the controls set forth in the description were operating with sufficient effectiveness to provide reasonable assurance that the specified control objectives included in our description were achieved throughout the period January 1, 20X1, to December 31, 20X1 [*if related persons applied the complementary user entity controls contemplated in the design of XYZ Custodian's controls throughout the period from January 1, 20X1, to December 31, 20X1*].

By:

_____

[*Signature, name, and title of appropriate official*]

By:

_____

[*Signature, name, and title of appropriate official*]

Illustrative Description of XYZ Custodian's Controls and Control Objectives Pursuant to Rule 206(4)-2 and Release No. IA-2969 Under the Act

[*In instances where the service organization uses any subservice providers, include in this section a description of the nature and functions they perform, and whether the relevant control objectives and related controls of the subservice provider are excluded from the description. If control objectives and / or related controls are so excluded from the description, include the relevant service organization controls, including monitoring controls over the subservice provider, under "Control Activities" in the control matrix below.*]

---

[82] Refer to complementary user entity controls only in situations in which the application of controls by the registered investment adviser is necessary to achieve the specified control objectives. Otherwise, omit the reference.

XYZ Custodian's Control Objectives Pursuant to Rule 206(4)-2 and Release No. IA-2969 Under the Act[83]	Control Activities[84]	Related-Person Investment Adviser Considerations, if Necessary[85]
Controls provide reasonable assurance that documentation for the opening and modification of client accounts is received, authenticated, and established completely, accurately, and timely on the applicable system.	• A new account setup specialist compares the details of new accounts in the system with the source documentation and evidences this procedure with a signature after the review is complete. Any discrepancies are forwarded to the individual who set up the account for reprocessing.	• The related-person investment adviser is responsible for submitting accurate, complete, and authorized account in-formation in a timely manner. • The related-person investment adviser is responsible for coordinating the account funding and providing instructions for the delivery of assets.
Controls provide reasonable assurance that client transactions, including contributions and withdrawals, are authorized and processed in a complete, accurate, and timely manner.		
Controls provide reasonable assurance that trades are properly authorized, settled, and recorded completely, accurately, and timely in the client account.		

---

[83] If there are substantive differences between XYZ Custodian's control objectives and those in Interpretive Release No. IA-2969, *Commission Guidance Regarding Independent Public Accountant Engagements Performed Pursuant to Rule 206(4)-2 Under the Investment Advisers Act of 1940*, of Rule 206(4)-2 of the Investment Advisers Act of 1940, those differences should be explained in the appendix.

[84] The control activities and related person considerations shown for the initial objective are intended to be illustrative and should be tailored to the circumstances of the entity that is the subject of the report. They are not intended to represent required or recommended controls.

[85] See footnote 60.

XYZ Custodian's Control Objectives Pursuant to Rule 206(4)-2 and Release No. IA-2969 Under the Act	Control Activities	Related-Person Investment Adviser Considerations, if Necessary
Controls provide reasonable assurance that new securities and changes to securities are authorized and established in a complete, accurate, and timely manner.		
Controls provide reasonable assurance that securities income and corporate action transactions are processed to client accounts in a complete, accurate, and timely manner.		
Controls provide reasonable assurance that physical securities are safeguarded from loss or misappropriation.		
Controls provide reasonable assurance that cash and security positions are reconciled completely, accurately, and on a timely basis between the custodian and depositories.		
Controls provide reasonable assurance that account statements reflecting cash and security positions are provided to clients in a complete, accurate, and timely manner.		

Relevant General Computer Control Objectives[86]	Control Activities	Related-Person Investment Adviser Considerations, if Necessary
Controls provide reasonable assurance that logical access to programs, data, and computer resources is restricted to authorized and appropriate users.		
Controls provide reasonable assurance that physical access to computer and other resources is restricted to authorized and appropriate personnel.		
Controls provide reasonable assurance that changes to application programs and related data management systems are authorized, tested, documented, approved, and implemented to result in the complete, accurate, and timely processing and reporting of transactions and balances.		
Controls provide reasonable assurance that network infrastructure is configured as authorized to support the effective functioning of application controls to result in valid, complete, accurate, and timely processing and reporting of transactions and balances and protect data from unauthorized changes.		

---

[86] These relevant general computer control objectives are included for illustrative purposes only. They are consistent with the illustrative general computer control objectives in the AICPA Guide *Service Organizations: Reporting on Controls at a Service Organization Relevant to User Entities' Internal Control Over Financial Reporting*. They may be included in the description when automated controls or reliance on computer-generated information is important to the achievement of the control objectives.

XYZ Custodian's Control Objectives Pursuant to Rule 206(4)-2 and Release No. IA-2969 Under the Act	Control Activities	Related-Person Investment Adviser Considerations, if Necessary
Controls provide reasonable assurance that application and system processing are authorized and executed in a complete, accurate, and timely manner and deviations, problems, and errors are identified, tracked, recorded, and resolved in a complete, accurate, and timely manner.		
Controls provide reasonable assurance that data transmissions between the service organization and its user entities and other outside entities are from authorized sources and are complete, accurate, secure, and timely.		

Appendix[87]

Illustrative Mapping of Control Objectives Pursuant to Rule 206(4)-2 and Release No. IA-2969 Under the Act to Independent Registered Public Accounting Reports on Controls

Control Objectives Pursuant to Rule 206(4)-2 and Release No. IA-2969 Under the Act	Report on XYZ Custodian's Controls Over Custody Pursuant to Rule 206(4)-2 Under the Investment Advisers Act of 1940	Service Auditor's Type 2 Report on ABC Trust Services for the Period January 1, 201X, to June 30, 201X	Service Auditor's Type 2 Report on DEF Subservice Organization's Controls Over Its Subcustodian's Services for the Period January 1, 201X, to June 30, 201X
Controls provide reasonable assurance that documentation for the opening and modification of client accounts is received, authenticated, and established completely, accurately, and timely on the applicable system.			
Controls provide reasonable assurance that client transactions, including contributions and withdrawals, are authorized and processed in a complete, accurate, and timely manner.			
Controls provide reasonable assurance that trades are properly authorized, settled, and recorded completely, accurately, and timely in the client account.			

---

[87] When control objectives or parts thereof are excluded from the description and covered in another report on the service organization's controls or a report on a subservice provider's controls, this mapping should be included as an appendix to management's description. The appendix should include a column for each report identifying the control objective(s) from Release No. IA-2969 covered by that report. When all the control objectives are fully covered in the description, this mapping is not necessary. In completing the mapping, checkmarks, explanations of particular facts and circumstances, or a combination of both, may be used to indicate the applicability of the report to the specific control objective(s).

Control Objectives Pursuant to Rule 206(4)-2 and Release No. IA-2969 Under the Act	Report on XYZ Custodian's Controls Over Custody Pursuant to Rule 206(4)-2 Under the Investment Advisers Act of 1940	Service Auditor's Type 2 Report on ABC Trust Services for the Period January 1, 201X, to June 30, 201X	Service Auditor's Type 2 Report on DEF Subservice Organization's Controls Over Its Subcustodian's Services for the Period January 1, 201X, to June 30, 201X
Controls provide reasonable assurance that new securities and changes to securities are authorized and established in a complete, accurate, and timely manner.			
Controls provide reasonable assurance that securities income and corporate action transactions are processed to client accounts in a complete, accurate, and timely manner.			
Controls provide reasonable assurance that physical securities are safeguarded from loss or misappropriation.			
Controls provide reasonable assurance that cash and security positions are reconciled completely, accurately, and on a timely basis between the custodian and depositories.			
Controls provide reasonable assurance that account statements reflecting cash and security positions are provided to clients in a complete, accurate, and timely manner.			

Reports on Processing of Transactions by a Transfer Agent[88]

12.40 The following illustrates a report to be issued on a description of a transfer agent's system and the suitability of the design and operating effectiveness of controls. This form of report is prescribed by paragraph .A68 of AT section 801, *Reporting on Controls at a Service Organization* (AICPA, *Professional Standards*).[89]

Independent Accountant's Report

To ABC Service Corp.

Scope

We have examined ABC Service Corp.'s description of its transfer agent controls throughout the period July 1, 20X7, to June 30, 20X8, and the suitability of the design and operating effectiveness of controls to achieve the related control objectives stated in the description. The description indicates that certain control objectives specified in the description can be achieved only if complementary user entity controls contemplated in the design of ABC Service Corp.'s controls are suitably designed and operating effectively, along with related controls at the transfer agent. We have not evaluated the suitability of the design or operating effectiveness of such complementary user entity controls.[90]

Service organization's responsibilities

On page [XX] of the description, ABC Service Corp. has provided an assertion about the fairness of the presentation and the suitability of the design and operating effectiveness of the controls to achieve the related control objectives stated in the description. ABC Service Corp. is responsible for preparing the description and for the assertion, including the completeness, accuracy, and method of presentation of the description and the assertion, providing the services covered by the description, specifying the control objectives and stating them in the description, identifying the risks that threaten the achievement of the control objectives, selecting the criteria, and designing, implementing,

---

[88] Pursuant to the New York Stock Exchange requirement under Rule 906.02, "Transfer Agent Registrar Agreement—Type A," when a transfer agent also acts as registrar for a single security issue (such as the case for closed-end funds), the transfer agent's independent public accountant is required to issue a report regarding the segregation of duties between the transfer agent and registrar functions. Such a report typically covers a period of time, rather than being stated as of a specific date.

[89] Paragraph .42 of AT section 801, *Reporting on Controls at a Service Organization* (AICPA, *Professional Standards*), requires a service auditor to inquire whether management is aware of any events subsequent to the period covered by management's description of the service organization's system up to the date of the service auditor's report that could have a significant effect on management's assertion. The AICPA Guide *Service Organizations: Reporting on Controls at a Service Organization Relevant to User Entities' Internal Control Over Financial Reporting* contains information for CPAs reporting on controls at a service organization that affect user entities' internal control over financial reporting. Also, the AICPA Guide *Reporting on Controls at a Service Organization: Relevant to Security, Availability, Processing Integrity, Confidentiality, or Privacy (SOC 2*[SM]*)* summarizes the three new SOC engagements and provides detailed guidance on planning, performing, and reporting on SOC 2 engagements.

[90] This illustrative report, in accordance with paragraph .A68 of AT section 801, includes modifications in the scope and opinion paragraphs because the application of complementary user entity controls is necessary to achieve the related control objectives stated in the description of the transfer agent's controls.

and documenting controls to achieve the related control objectives stated in the description.

Service auditor's responsibilities

Our responsibility is to express an opinion on the fairness of the presentation of the description and on the suitability of the design and operating effectiveness of the controls to achieve the related control objectives stated in the description, based on our examination. We conducted our examination in accordance with attestation standards established by the American Institute of Certified Public Accountants. Those standards require that we plan and perform our examination to obtain reasonable assurance about whether, in all material respects, the description is fairly presented and the controls were suitably designed and operating effectively to achieve the related control objectives stated in the description throughout the period July 1, 20X7, to June 30, 20X8.

An examination of a description of a transfer agent's system and the suitability of the design and operating effectiveness of the transfer agent's controls to achieve the related control objectives stated in the description involves performing procedures to obtain evidence about the fairness of the presentation of the description and the suitability of the design and operating effectiveness of those controls to achieve the related control objectives stated in the description. Our procedures included assessing the risks that the description is not fairly presented and that the controls were not suitably designed or operating effectively to achieve the related control objectives stated in the description. Our procedures also included testing the operating effectiveness of those controls that we consider necessary to provide reasonable assurance that the related control objectives stated in the description were achieved. An examination engagement of this type also includes evaluating the overall presentation of the description and the suitability of the control objectives stated therein, and the suitability of the criteria specified by the transfer agent and described at page [aa]. We believe that the evidence we obtained is sufficient and appropriate to provide a reasonable basis for our opinion.

Inherent limitations

Because of their nature, controls at a transfer agent may not prevent, or detect and correct, all errors or omissions. Also, the projection to the future of any evaluation of the fairness of the presentation of the description, or conclusions about the suitability of the design or operating effectiveness of the controls to achieve the related control objectives is subject to the risk that controls at a transfer agent may become inadequate or fail.

Opinion

In our opinion, in all material respects, based on the criteria described in ABC Service Corp.'s assertion on page [aa],

    a. the description fairly presents the transfer agent controls that were designed and implemented throughout the period July 1, 20X7, to June 30, 20X8.

    b. the controls related to the control objectives stated in the description were suitably designed to provide reasonable assurance that the control objectives would be achieved if the controls operated effectively throughout the period July 1, 20X7, to June 30, 20X8 and user entities applied the complementary user entity controls contemplated in the design of ABC Service Corp.'s controls throughout the period July 1, 20X7, to June 30, 20X8.

   c. the controls tested, which together with the complementary user entity controls referred to in the scope paragraph of this report, if operating effectively, were those necessary to provide reasonable assurance that the control objectives stated in the description were achieved, operated effectively throughout the period July 1, 20X7, to June 30, 20X8.

Description of tests of controls

The specific controls tested and the nature, timing, and results of those tests are listed on pages [yy–zz].

Restricted use

This report, including the description of tests of controls and results thereof on pages [yy–zz], is intended solely for the information and use of ABC Service Corp., user entities of ABC Service Corp.'s transfer agent controls during some or all of the period July 1, 20X7, to June 30, 20X8, and the independent auditors of such user entities, who have a sufficient understanding to consider it, along with other information including information about controls implemented by user entities themselves, when assessing the risks of material misstatements of user entities' financial statements. This report is not intended to be and should not be used by anyone other than these specified parties.

Independent Auditor (signed)]
[Anytown, USA]
[July 31, 20X8]

12.41   The following is an example of a report to be issued on the annual study and evaluation of a transfer agent's internal control, as required to be filed with the SEC pursuant to Rule 17Ad-13 of the 1934 Act. Such engagements are performed in accordance with AT section 101.

This illustrative report (example 2 in appendix A, "Examination Reports," of AT section 101, with additional language related to the restriction on the use of the report) should be used when a practitioner expresses an opinion on management's assertion about the effectiveness of an entity's internal control. If a practitioner examines and reports directly on an entity's effectiveness of internal control (versus the responsible party's written assertion), the practitioner must consider example 3 in appendix A of AT section 101 for an example of the report to be used.

Independent Accountant's Report

To the Board of Directors of
ABC Service Corp.

We have examined management's assertion, included in its representation letter dated December 15, 20X8, that ABC Service Corp. maintained effective internal control, including the appropriate segregation of responsibilities and duties, over the transfer agent and registrar[91] functions, as of October 31, 20X8, and that no material inadequacies as defined by Rule 17Ad-13(a)(3) of the Securities Exchange Act of 1934 existed at such date. ABC Service Corp.'s management is responsible for maintaining effective internal control over transfer agent and registrar functions. Our responsibility is to express an opinion on management's assertion based on our examination.

Our examination was conducted in accordance with the attestation standards established by the American Institute of Certified Public Accountants and, accordingly, included examining, on a test basis, evidence supporting management's assertion and performing such other procedures as we considered necessary in the circumstances to evaluate internal control over the transfer agent and registrar functions, using the objectives set forth in Rule 17Ad-13(a)(3) of the Securities Exchange Act of 1934. We believe that our examination provides a reasonable basis for our opinion.

[*The following optional inherent limitations paragraph may be added to reports*]

Because of inherent limitations in any internal control, material inadequacies, as defined in Rule 17Ad-13(a)(3), due to error or fraud may occur and not be detected. Also, projections of any evaluation of the internal control over the transfer agent and registrar functions to future periods are subject to the risk that the internal control may become inadequate because of changes in conditions, or that the degree of compliance with the policies or procedures may deteriorate.

In our opinion, management's assertion that ABC Service Corp. maintained effective internal control, including the appropriate segregation of responsibilities and duties, over the transfer agent and registrar functions, and that no material inadequacies existed as defined by Rule 17Ad-13(a)(3) of the Securities Exchange Act of 1934 as of October 31, 20X8, is fairly stated, in all material respects, based on the criteria established by Rule 17Ad-13(a)(3) of the Securities Exchange Act of 1934.

This report is intended solely for the information and use of management and the Board of Directors of ABC Service Corp. and the Securities and Exchange Commission and is not intended to be and should not be used by anyone other than these specified parties.

[Independent Accountant (signed)]
[Anytown, USA]
[December 15, 20X8]

12.42 Interpretation No. 8, "Including a Description of Tests of Controls or Other Procedures, and the Results Thereof, in an Examination Report," of AT section 101 (AICPA, *Professional Standards*, AT sec. 9101 par. .70–.72), discusses whether, during an examination engagement under AT section 101, a practitioner's examination report may include in a separate section a description of tests of controls or other procedures performed in support of the practitioner's opinion. Although AT section 101 does not preclude a practitioner from including a separate section of the report that contains a description of

---

[91] The words *and registrar* should be omitted throughout this report if the function does not exist within the transfer agent's operations.

tests of controls or other procedures performed and the results thereof, consideration should be given to whether this description may overshadow the overall opinion or would cause report users to misunderstand the opinion. Therefore, this determination requires judgment based on the circumstances of the particular engagement. The addition of a description of tests of controls or other procedures performed and the results thereof in a separate section of an examination report may increase the need for the use of the report to be restricted to specified parties. In determining whether to include such a description, the following conditions are relevant:

- Whether there has been a request for such information and whether the specified parties making the request have an appropriate business need or reasonable basis for requesting the information
- Whether the specified parties have an understanding of the nature and subject matter of the engagement and experience in using the information in such reports
- Whether including such a description in the examination report is likely to cause report users to misunderstand the opinion
- Whether the practitioner's tests of controls or other procedures performed directly relate to the subject matter of the engagement

Reporting Pursuant to the Global Investment Performance Standards

Note: The guidance presented in this section of the guide, including the example reports, reflects the guidance in Statement of Position (SOP) 12-1, *Reporting Pursuant to the Global Investment Performance Standards* (AICPA, *Professional Standards*, AUD sec. 45).

12.43 To promote fair representation, full disclosure, and greater comparability of investment performance, the CFA Institute developed the Global Investment Performance Standards (GIPS).[92] Although compliance with the GIPS standards is voluntary, an investment management firm's claim of compliance with the GIPS standards gives current and potential clients more confidence in the integrity of the performance presentations and the general practices of a compliant firm. SOP 12-1 provides guidance to practitioners for engagements to examine and report on aspects of a firm's claim of compliance with the GIPS standards (a third-party verification) and engagements to examine and report on any of the firm's composites and their associated compliant presentations (a performance examination). Such engagements should be performed pursuant to AT section 101. AT section 101 permits the practitioner to report either on the assertions or directly on the subject matter to which the assertions relate.

12.44 All references to the GIPS standards in SOP 12-1 refer to the 2010 edition of the GIPS standards. The GIPS standards specify that they include any updates, guidance statements, interpretations, questions and answers,

[92] For information on the appropriate use of the Global Investment Performance Standards registered trademark, see the CFA Institute website at www.cfainstitute.org.

and clarifications published by the CFA Institute and the GIPS Executive Committee, all of which are available at www.gipsstandards.org/, as well as in the *GIPS Handbook*.

12.45 The following is an example of an illustrative attest report for a verification. This report is presented in appendix C, "Illustrative Attest Report: Verification (Reporting Directly on the Subject Matter)," of SOP 12-1. The reports also illustrate how the reference to a verification may be incorporated into the attest report.

Independent Accountant's Verification Report

Investment Firm
10 Main Street
Anytown, USA

We have examined whether (1) Investment Firm (the Firm) has complied with all the composite construction requirements of the Global Investment Performance Standards (GIPS® standards) on a firmwide basis for the periods from January 1, 20X1, to December 31, 20Y0, and (2) the Firm's policies and procedures are designed to calculate and present performance in compliance with the GIPS standards as of December 31, 20Y0. The Firm's management is responsible for compliance with the GIPS standards and the design of its policies and procedures. Our responsibility is to express an opinion based on our examination.

Our examination was conducted in accordance with attestation standards established by the American Institute of Certified Public Accountants and, accordingly, included examining, on a test basis, evidence about the Firm's compliance with the previously mentioned requirements; evaluating the design of the Firm's policies and procedures previously referred to; and performing the procedures for a verification required by the GIPS standards and such other procedures as we considered necessary in the circumstances. We believe that our examination provides a reasonable basis for our opinion.

In our opinion, in all material respects

- the Firm has complied with all the composite construction requirements of the GIPS standards on a firmwide basis for the periods from January 1, 20X1, to December 31, 20Y0; and
- the Firm's policies and procedures are designed to calculate and present performance in compliance with the GIPS standards as of December 31, 20Y0.

We have not been engaged to examine and did not examine the presentations of the Firm's composites for any period, including any presentations that may accompany this report and, accordingly, we express no opinion on any such performance.[93]

[*Signature*]

[September 1, 20Y1]

---

[93] If the verifier has issued a separate performance examination report concurrently, it may insert the following instead: "This report does not relate to any composite presentation of the Firm that may accompany this report, and accordingly, we express no opinion on any such performance."

12.46   The following are examples of illustrative attest reports for a verification and performance examination. These reports are presented in appendix D, "Illustrative Attest Reports: Verification and Performance Examination (Reporting Directly on the Subject Matter)," of SOP 12-1. The reports also illustrate how the reference to a verification or performance examination may be incorporated into the attest report.

Example 1: Verification and Performance Examination Report

Independent Accountant's Verification and Performance Examination Report

Investment Firm
10 Main Street
Anytown, USA

We have examined whether (1) Investment Firm (the Firm) has complied with all the composite construction requirements of the Global Investment Performance Standards (GIPS® standards) on a firmwide basis for the periods from January 1, 20X1, to December 31, 20Y0, and (2) the Firm's policies and procedures are designed to calculate and present performance in compliance with the GIPS standards as of December 31, 20Y0. We have also examined the accompanying [*refer to accompanying composite performance presentation*] of the Firm's XYZ Composite for the periods from January 1, 20X1, to December 31, 20Y0. The Firm's management is responsible for compliance with the GIPS standards and the design of its policies and procedures and for the [*refer to accompanying composite compliant presentation*]. Our responsibility is to express an opinion based on our examination.

Our examination was conducted in accordance with attestation standards established by the American Institute of Certified Public Accountants and, accordingly, included examining, on a test basis, evidence about the Firm's compliance with the previously mentioned requirements; evaluating the design of the Firm's policies and procedures previously referred to; examining, on a test basis, evidence supporting the accompanying composite compliant presentation; and performing the procedures for a verification and a performance examination required by the GIPS standards and such other procedures as we considered necessary in the circumstances. We believe that our examination provides a reasonable basis for our opinion.

In our opinion, in all material respects,

- the Firm has complied with all the composite construction requirements of the GIPS standards on a firmwide basis for the periods from January 1, 20X1, to December 31, 20Y0; and

- the Firm's policies and procedures are designed to calculate and present performance in compliance with the GIPS standards as of December 31, 20Y0.

Also, in our opinion, in all material respects, the Firm has

- constructed the XYZ Composite and calculated the XYZ Composite performance for the periods from January 1, 20X1, to December 31, 20Y0, in compliance with the GIPS standards; and

- prepared and presented the [*refer to accompanying composite compliant presentation*] of the Firm's XYZ Composite for the periods from January 1, 20X1 to December 31, 20Y0, in compliance with the GIPS standards.

This report does not contain an opinion on accuracy of any composite presentation of the Firm other than the [*refer to accompanying composite compliant presentations*] of the Firm's XYZ Composite for the periods from January 1, 20X1, to December 31, 20Y0.

[*Signature*]

[September 1, 20Y1]

Example 1A: Illustrative GIPS—Compliant Presentation for Report Example 1

Investment Firm XYZ Composite January 1, 20X1
to December 31, 20Y0

Year	Composite Gross Return (%)	Composite Net Return (%)	Custom Benchmark Return (%)	Composite 3-Yr St Dev (%)	Benchmark 3-Yr St Dev (%)	Number of Portfolios	Internal Dispersion (%)	Composite Assets ($ M)	Firm Assets ($)
20X1	− 10.5	− 11.4	− 11.8			31	4.5	165	236
20X2	16.3	15.1	13.2			34	2.0	235	346
20X3	7.5	6.4	8.9			38	5.7	344	529
20X4	1.8	0.8	0.3			45	2.8	445	695
20X5	11.2	10.1	12.2			48	3.1	520	839
20X6	6.1	5.0	7.1			49	2.8	505	1,014
20X7	− 21.3	− 22.1	− 24.9			44	2.9	475	964
20X8	16.5	15.3	14.7			47	3.1	493	983
20X9	10.6	9.5	13.0			51	3.5	549	1,114
20Y0	2.7	1.7	0.4	7.1	7.4	54	2.5	575	1,236

Investment Firm (the Firm) claims compliance with the Global Investment Performance Standards (GIPS® standards) and has prepared and presented this report in compliance with the GIPS standards. The Firm has been independently verified for the periods from January 1, 20X1, to December 31, 20Y0. The verification report is available upon request. Verification assesses whether (1) the Firm has complied with all the composite construction requirements of the GIPS standards on a firmwide basis, and (2) the Firm's policies and procedures are designed to calculate and present performance in compliance with the GIPS standards. Verification does not ensure the accuracy of any specific composite presentation.

Notes:

1. The Firm is a balanced portfolio investment manager that invests solely in U.S. securities. The Firm is defined as an independent investment management firm that is not affiliated with any parent organization. Firm policies for valuing portfolios, calculating performance, and preparing compliant presentations are available upon request.

2. The composite includes all institutional balanced portfolios that invest in large-cap U.S. equities and investment-
grade bonds with the goal of providing long-term capital
growth and steady income from a well-diversified strategy.
Although the strategy allows for equity exposure ranging
between 50 percent and 70 percent, the typical allocation
is between 55 percent and 65 percent. The account minimum for the composite is $5 million.

3. The custom benchmark is 60 percent YYY U.S. Equity
Index and 40 percent ZZZ U.S. Aggregate Bond Index.
The benchmark is rebalanced monthly.

4. Valuations are computed and performance reported in
U.S. dollars.

5. Gross-of-fees returns are presented before management
and custodial fees but after all trading expenses. Composite and benchmark returns are presented net of nonre-
claimable withholding taxes. Net-of-fees returns are calculated by deducting the highest fee of 0.083 percent from
the monthly gross composite return. The management fee
schedule is as follows: 1 percent on the first $25 million
and 0.60 percent thereafter.

6. This composite was created in February 20X1. A complete
list of composite descriptions is available upon request.

7. Internal dispersion is calculated using the equal-weighted
standard deviation of annual gross returns of those portfolios that were included in the composite for the entire
year.

8. The 3-year annualized standard deviation measures the
variability of the composite and the benchmark returns
over the preceding 36-month period. The standard deviation is not presented for 20X1 to 20X9 because monthly
composite and benchmark returns were not available and
is not required for periods prior to 20Y0.

**Example 2: Performance Examination Report With a Reference to a
Separate Verification Report**

Independent Accountant's Performance Examination Report

Investment Firm
10 Main Street
Anytown, USA

We have examined the accompanying[94] [*refer to accompanying composite compliant presentations*] of Investment Firm's (the Firm's) ABC
and XYZ Composites for the periods from January 1, 20X1, to December 31, 20Y0. The Firm's management is responsible for these
compliant presentations. Our responsibility is to express an opinion
based on our examination. We previously conducted an examination
(also referred to as a verification) of whether (1) the Firm has complied with all the composite construction requirements of the Global

---

[94] See example 1A for an illustrative composite compliant presentation that would accompany
the report.

Investment Performance Standards (GIPS® standards) on a firmwide basis for the periods from January 1, 20X1, to December 31, 20Y0, and (2) the Firm's policies and procedures are designed to calculate and present performance in compliance with the GIPS standards as of December 31, 20Y0; our report dated August 7, 20Y1, with respect thereto is attached.

Our examination was conducted in accordance with attestation standards established by the American Institute of Certified Public Accountants and, accordingly, included examining, on a test basis, evidence supporting the accompanying composite compliant presentations, and performing the procedures for a performance examination required by the GIPS standards and such other procedures as we considered necessary in the circumstances. We believe that our examination provides a reasonable basis for our opinion.

In our opinion, in all material respects, the Firm has

- constructed the Firm's ABC and XYZ Composites and calculated the composite performance for the periods from January 1, 20X1, to December 31, 20Y0, in compliance with the GIPS standards; and
- prepared and presented the [*refer to accompanying composite compliant presentations*] of the Firm's ABC and XYZ Composites for the periods from January 1, 20X1, to December 31, 20Y0, in compliance with the GIPS standards.

This report does not attest to the accuracy of any composite presentation of the Firm other than the Firm's ABC and XYZ Composites.

[*Signature*]

[September 1, 20Y1]

Illustrative Representation Letter—XYZ Investment Company

Nonregistered Investment Company Written Representation

12.47   AU-C section 580 addresses the auditor's responsibility to obtain written representations from management, and, when appropriate, those charged with governance in an audit of financial statements. Following is an illustrative management representation letter for an audit of a nonregistered investment company's financial statements. The auditor should consider obtaining representation on additional items, including, when applicable, an investment adviser's intentions to continue waiving fees and the amount and terms of unreimbursed distribution costs carried forward.

(Entity Letterhead)

To [*Auditor*]

January 21, 20X3

This representation letter is provided in connection with your audit of the financial statements of XYZ Investment Company (the Company), which comprise the statement of assets and liabilities, including the schedule of investments in securities (or statement of net assets) as of December 31, 20X2, and the related statements of operations (and cash flows, if applicable), changes in net assets, and financial highlights for the year then ended, and the related notes to the financial statements, for the purpose of expressing an opinion on whether the financial statements are presented fairly, in all material respects, in accordance with accounting principles generally accepted in the United States (U.S. GAAP).

Certain representations in this letter are described as being limited to matters that are material. Items are considered material, regardless of size, if they involve an omission or misstatement of accounting information that, in light of surrounding circumstances, makes it probable that the judgment of a reasonable person relying on the information would be changed or influenced by the omission or misstatement.

Except where otherwise stated below, immaterial matters less than $[insert amount] collectively are not considered to be exceptions that require disclosure for the purpose of the following representations. This amount is not necessarily indicative of amounts that would require adjustment to or disclosure in the financial statements.

We confirm that, [to the best of our knowledge and belief, having made such inquiries as we considered necessary for the purpose of appropriately informing ourselves] [as of (date of auditor's report):

Financial Statements

- We have fulfilled our responsibilities, as set out in the terms of the audit engagement dated [insert date], for the preparation and fair presentation of the financial statements in accordance with U.S. GAAP.

- We acknowledge our responsibility for the design, implementation, and maintenance of internal control relevant to the preparation and fair presentation of financial statements that are free from material misstatement, whether due to fraud or error.

- We acknowledge our responsibility for the design, implementation, and maintenance of internal control to prevent and detect fraud.

- Significant assumptions used by us in making accounting estimates, including those measured at fair value, are reasonable.

- Related party relationships and transactions have been appropriately accounted for and disclosed in accordance with the requirements of U.S. GAAP.

- All events subsequent to the date of the financial statements and for which U.S. GAAP requires adjustment or disclosure have been adjusted or disclosed.

- The effects of uncorrected misstatements are immaterial, both individually and in the aggregate, to the financial statements as a whole. A list of the uncorrected misstatements is attached to the representation letter.

- The effects of all known actual or possible litigation and claims have been accounted for and disclosed in accordance with U.S. GAAP.

- The Company has no plans or intentions that may materially affect the carrying amounts or classification of assets and liabilities.

- The following have been properly recorded or disclosed in the financial statements:

  — Guarantees, whether written or oral, under which the Company is contingently liable

  — Arrangements with financial institutions involving compensating balances or other arrangements involving restrictions on cash balances, line of credit, or similar arrangements have been properly disclosed.

  — Capital stock repurchase options or agreements or capital stock reserved for options, warrants, conversions, or other requirements have been properly disclosed.

- The following information about financial instruments with off-balance-sheet risk and financial instruments with concentrations of credit risk has been properly disclosed in the financial statements:

  — The extent, nature, and terms of financial instruments with off-balance-sheet risk

  — The amount of credit risk of financial instruments with off-balance-sheet risk and information about the collateral supporting such financial instruments

  — Significant concentrations of credit risk arising from all financial instruments and information about the collateral supporting such financial instruments

- Portfolio securities are stated at fair value as determined in accordance with the valuation methods set forth in the current prospectus. All Company investments during the period were made in accordance with the investment policies stated in the current prospectus. [(*For those funds that have significant investments stated at fair value as determined by management or the board of directors or trustees to address the appropriateness of the valuation methodology and fair values assigned, the following sentence should be added: "For securities whose fair values have been estimated by management [the Board of Directors or trustees], the valuation principles and significant assumptions used result in a measure of fair value appropriate for financial statement measurement and disclosure purposes.*)]

Information Provided

- We have provided you with:

  - Access to all information of which we are aware that is relevant to the preparation and fair presentation of the financial statements such as records, documentation and other matters;

  - Additional information that you have requested from us for the purpose of the audit; and

  - Unrestricted access to persons within the entity from whom you determined it necessary to obtain audit evidence.

- All transactions have been recorded in the accounting records and are reflected in the financial statements. The financial statements include all assets and liabilities of which we are aware as of December 31, 20X2. The Company has satisfactory title to all owned assets, and there are no liens or encumbrances on such assets nor has any asset been pledged as collateral. All portfolio securities are marketable, except as disclosed in the financial statements.

- We have disclosed to you the results of our assessment of the risk that the financial statements may be materially misstated as a result of fraud.

- We have [*no knowledge of any*] [*disclosed to you all information that we are aware of regarding*] fraud or suspected fraud that affects the Company and involves:

  - Management,

  - Employees who have significant roles in internal control, or

  - Others when the fraud could have a material effect on the financial statements.

- We have [*no knowledge of any*] [*disclosed to you all information that we are aware of regarding*] allegations of fraud, or suspected fraud, affecting the Company's financial statements communicated by employees, former employees, analysts, regulators, or others.

- We have disclosed to you all known instances of noncompliance or suspected noncompliance with laws and regulations whose effects should be considered when preparing financial statements.

- We [*have disclosed to you all known actual or possible*] [*are not aware of any pending or threatened*] litigation and claims, including unasserted claims, whose effects should be considered when preparing the financial statements [*and we have not consulted legal counsel concerning litigation or claims*].

- We [*have disclosed to you all known actual or possible*] [*are not aware of*] other liabilities or gain or loss contingencies that are required to be accrued or disclosed by FASB ASC 450, *Contingencies.*

- We have disclosed to you the identity of the entity's related parties and all the related party relationships and transactions of which we are aware.
- We also advise you that, to the best of our knowledge and belief—

   a. Interests in the Company have been offered for sale in accordance with its offering document and by no other means. No offer or solicitation of the Company's interests has been made in any jurisdiction in which such offer or solicitation would be unlawful.

   b. The Company's shares have been issued and redeemed during the period in accordance with its offering document and applicable regulation. The daily net asset value has been properly computed throughout the year and was correctly applied in the computation of sales and redemption transactions.

   c. For U. S. federal income tax purposes, the Company is taxed as a [*describe*] and has incurred no material tax liabilities under the provisions of FASB ASC 740, *Income Taxes.* The Company has filed all required tax forms in the jurisdictions in which it invests or does business by the applicable deadlines in which noncompliance or failure to file would have a material effect on the Company's financial statements, and, for required tax filings not yet completed, we plan to file, and to make timely payment for any unpaid taxes due and payable, by the applicable deadlines. We have provided you with all information and our assessment related to uncertain tax positions that we have taken, or expect to take, of which we are aware. We have made you aware of and have disclosed any significant tax positions for which it is reasonably possible the amount of unrecognized tax benefit will either increase or decrease within the next 12 months.

   d. The Company has complied with the provisions of its code of ethics.

[*Name of President or Chief Executive Officer and Title*]

[*Name of Treasurer or Chief Financial Officer and Title*]

Registered Investment Company Written Representation

12.48   AU section 333 establishes a requirement that the independent auditor obtain written representations from management as part of an audit of financial statements and provides guidance concerning the representations to be obtained. Following is an illustrative management representation letter for an audit of a registered investment company's financial statements. The auditor should consider obtaining representation on additional items, including, when applicable, an investment adviser's intentions to continue waiving fees and the amount and terms of unreimbursed distribution costs carried forward.[95]

The following illustration is prepared for informational and reference purposes only and is not authoritative. It has not been reviewed, approved, disapproved, or otherwise acted on by the PCAOB or SEC.

January 21, 20X9

To [*Independent Auditor*]

We are providing this letter in connection with your audit of the statement of assets and liabilities, including the schedule of investments in securities (or statement of net assets), of XYZ Investment Company (the Company) as of December 31, 20X8, and the related statements of operations (and cash flows, if applicable), for the year then ended, changes in net assets for the two years then ended, and the financial highlights for the five years then ended, for the purpose of expressing an opinion as to whether the financial statements present fairly, in all material respects, the financial position, results of operations (and cash flows, if applicable), changes in net assets, and financial highlights of XYZ Investment Company in conformity with accounting principles generally accepted in the United States of America. We confirm that we are responsible for the fair presentation in the financial statements of financial position, results of operations, changes in net assets, (cash flows, if applicable), and financial highlights in conformity with generally accepted accounting principles.

Certain representations in this letter are described as being limited to matters that are material. Items are considered material, regardless of size, if they involve an omission or misstatement of accounting information that, in light of surrounding circumstances, makes it probable that the judgment of a reasonable person relying on the information would be changed or influenced by the omission or misstatement.

We confirm, to the best of our knowledge and belief as of [*date of auditor's report*], the following representations made to you during your audit:

1. The financial statements referred to above are fairly presented in conformity with accounting principles generally accepted in the United States of America.

2. We have made available to you all—

   a. Financial records and related data.

   b. Minutes of the meetings of stockholders, directors or trustees, and committees of directors or

---

[95] See paragraphs 75–77 of Auditing Standard No. 5 for additional written representations required from management when performing an integrated audit of financial statements and internal control over financial reporting or an audit of the financial statements in accordance with PCAOB standards. Readers should also be aware of additional written representations that may be necessary as a result of the issuance of Auditing Standard No. 18, *Related Partites* (AICPA, *PCAOB Standards and Related Rules*, Auditing Standards).

trustees, or summaries of actions of recent meetings for which minutes have not yet been prepared.

    c. Information relating to all statutes, laws, or regulations that have a direct effect on our financial statements.

    d. Information relating to contracts with and results of work by specialists, including those engaged to review investments (including investment valuations), systems, processes, operations, or compliance programs having a material effect on the financial statements or internal control over financial reporting of the Company.

3. There have been no communications from regulatory agencies, such as the SEC or the Internal Revenue Service, concerning noncompliance with or deficiencies in financial reporting practices.

4. There are no material transactions that have not been properly recorded in the accounting records underlying the financial statements.

5. We acknowledge our responsibility for the design and implementation of programs and controls to prevent and detect fraud.

6. We have no knowledge of any fraud or suspected fraud affecting the Company involving—

    a. Management,

    b. Employees who have significant roles in internal control, or

    c. Others where the fraud could have a material effect on the financial statements.

7. We have no knowledge of any allegations of fraud or suspected fraud affecting the Company received in communications from employees, former employees, analysts, regulators, short sellers, or others.

8. There are no significant deficiencies, including material weaknesses, in the design or operation of internal control over financial reporting that are reasonably likely to adversely affect the Company's ability to record, process, summarize and report financial information.

    a. (If applicable) The effects of the uncorrected financial statement misstatements summarized in the accompanying schedule are immaterial, both individually and in the aggregate, to the financial statements taken as a whole.

9. The Company has no plans or intentions that may materially affect the carrying amounts or classification of assets and liabilities.

10. The following have been properly recorded or disclosed in the financial statements:

a. Related-party transactions and other transactions with affiliates, including fees, commissions, purchases, sales, transfers, loans, leasing arrangements, and guarantees, and amounts receivable from or payable to related parties.

b. Guarantees, whether written or oral, under which the Company is contingently liable

c. Significant estimates and material concentrations known to management that are required to be disclosed in accordance with the FASB *Accounting Standards Codification* (ASC) 275-10 [*Significant estimates are estimates at the balance sheet date that could change materially within the next year. Concentrations refer to volumes of business, revenues, available sources of supply, or markets or geographic areas for which events could occur that would significantly disrupt normal finances within the next year.*]

d. Arrangements with financial institutions involving compensating balances, or other arrangements involving restrictions on cash balances and lines of credit or similar arrangements [*Note: If this is not applicable, refer to item 9.*]

e. Capital stock repurchase options or agreements, or capital stock reserved for options, warrants, or other requirements (possibly applicable to closed-end companies)

f. All financial instruments, including those with off-balance-sheet risk (such as swaps, forwards, and futures), as required under accounting principles generally accepted in the United States of America.

g. Each significant concentration of credit risk arising from all financial instruments whether from an individual counterparty or group of counterparties in accordance with FASB ASC 825-10-50.

11. There are no—

a. Violations or possible violations of laws or regulations whose effects should be considered for disclosure in the financial statements or as a basis for recording a loss contingency.

b. Unasserted claims or assessments that our lawyer has advised us are probable of assertion and must be disclosed in accordance FASB ASC 450, *Contingencies*.[96]

---

[96] If the client has not consulted a lawyer, the auditor normally would rely on the review of internally available information, and this representation might be worded as follows:

(continued)

        c. Other liabilities or gain or loss contingencies that are required to be accrued or disclosed by FASB ASC 450.

12. The financial statements include all assets and liabilities of which we are aware as of December 31, 20X8. The Company has satisfactory title to all owned assets, and there are no liens or encumbrances on such assets nor has any asset been pledged as collateral. All portfolio securities are marketable, except as disclosed in the financial statements.

13. The Company has complied with all aspects of contractual agreements that would have a material effect on the financial statements in the event of noncompliance.

14. We also advise you that, to the best of our knowledge and belief—

        a. Portfolio securities are stated at fair value as determined in accordance with the valuation methods set forth in the current prospectus. All Company investments during the period were made in accordance with the investment policies stated in the current prospectus. [(*For those funds that have significant investments stated at fair value as determined by management or the board of directors or trustees to address the appropriateness of the valuation methodology and fair values assigned, the following sentence should be added:* "For securities whose fair values have been estimated by management [the Board of Directors or trustees], the valuation principles used are appropriate and have been consistently applied and the fair values are reasonable and supported by the documentation.)][97]

(footnote continued)

    We are not aware of any pending or threatened litigation, claims, or assessments or unasserted claims or assessments that are required to be accrued or disclosed in the financial statements, in accordance with FASB ASC 450, *Contingencies*, and we have not consulted a lawyer concerning litigation, claims, or assessments.

[97] AU section 328, *Auditing Fair Value Measurements and Disclosures* (AICPA, *PCAOB Standards and Related Rules*, Interim Standards), contains expanded guidance on the audit procedures for fair value measurements and disclosures. Among other things, AU section 328 lists several representations about fair value measurements and disclosures contained in the financial statements that the auditor may consider obtaining from management. Paragraph .49 of AU section 328 provides that, depending on the nature, materiality, and complexity of fair values, management representations about fair value measurements and disclosures contained in the financial statements also may include representations about:

- The appropriateness of the measurement methods, including related assumptions, used by management in determining fair value and the consistency in the application of the methods.
- The completeness and adequacy of disclosures related to fair values.
- Whether subsequent events require adjustment to the fair value measurements and disclosures included in the financial statements.

b. The Company complied with the provisions of the Investment Company Act of 1940, as amended, and the rules and regulations thereunder, and with the provisions of its prospectus and the requirements of the various Blue Sky laws under which the Company operates.

c. The Company's shares have been issued and redeemed during the period in accordance with its registration statement and applicable regulation. The daily net asset value has been properly computed throughout the year ([*for open-end funds in accordance with Rule 2a-4 of the act*] or [*Rule 2a-7 for money market funds*]) and was correctly applied in the computation of sales and redemption transactions.

d. The Company did not make any commitments during the year as underwriter, nor did it engage in any transactions made on margin, in joint trading or in a joint investment account.

e. The Company has complied with the requirements of subchapter M of the Internal Revenue Code of 1986, as amended, through the date of this letter, and intends to continue to so comply. The Company intends to distribute substantially all of its net investment income and capital gains to shareholders; accordingly, no federal income tax liability has been recorded in the financial statements. The Company has filed all required tax forms in the jurisdictions in which it invests or does business by the applicable deadlines in which noncompliance or failure to file would have a material effect on the Company's financial statements, and, for required tax filings not yet completed, we plan to file, and to make timely payment for any unpaid taxes due and payable, by the applicable deadlines. We have provided you with all information and our assessment related to uncertain tax positions that we have taken, or expect to take, of which we are aware. We have made you aware of and have disclosed any significant tax positions for which it is reasonably possible the amount of unrecognized tax benefit will either increase or decrease within the next 12 months.

f. The Company, except to the extent indicated in its financial statements, does not own any securities of persons who are directly affiliated as defined in Section 2(a)(3) of the act.

g. The Company has complied with the provisions of its code of ethics.

To the best of our knowledge and belief, no events or transactions have occurred subsequent to the balance sheet date and through the date of this letter that would require adjustment to or disclosure in the aforementioned financial statements.

[*Name of President or Chief Executive Officer and Title*]

[*Name of Treasurer or Chief Financial Officer and Title*]

12.49 For registered investment companies that include certifications of the principal executive officer and principal financial officer in filings on Form N-CSR, the individuals certifying in those capacities should also sign the representation letter in order to directly confirm and document the communications to auditors described in their certifications (see paragraph 11.22 of this guide). Other officers who provide material representations during the audit should also be considered for inclusion as signers.

Appendix A

Guidance Updates

This appendix is nonauthoritative and is included for informational purposes only.

This appendix includes information on guidance issued through the "as of" date of this guide that is not yet effective, but that will be effective for the next edition of this guide. References to this guidance, where applicable, are included throughout the chapters of this guide in shaded text. The references use a guidance update number that consists of the chapter number followed by the sequentially numbered guidance update number within any given chapter (for example, Update 3-1 would be the first guidance update in chapter 3). The guidance in this appendix is cross-referenced using the same guidance update numbers found throughout the chapters of this guide, as applicable. Readers should consider this information for the reporting period to which it applies.

Accounting and Reporting Updates

A.01 ASU No. 2014-10

FASB Accounting Standards Update (ASU) No. 2014-10, *Development Stage Entities (Topic 915): Elimination of Certain Financial Reporting Requirements, Including an Amendment to Variable Interest Entities Guidance in Topic 810, Consolidation*, was issued in June 2014. The amendments related to the elimination of inception-to-date information and the other remaining disclosure requirements of FASB *Accounting Standards Codification* (ASC) 915, *Development Stage Entities*, should be applied retrospectively except for the clarification to FASB ASC 275, *Risks and Uncertainties*, which shall be applied prospectively. For public business entities, those amendments are effective for annual reporting periods beginning after December 15, 2014, and interim periods therein. For other entities, the amendments are effective for annual reporting periods beginning after December 15, 2014, and interim reporting periods beginning after December 15, 2015.

For public business entities, the amendment eliminating the exception to the sufficiency-of-equity-at-risk criterion for development stage entities in FASB ASC 810-10-15-16 should be applied retrospectively for annual reporting periods beginning after December 15, 2015, and interim periods therein. For all other entities, the amendments to FASB ASC 810, *Consolidation*, should be applied retrospectively for annual reporting periods beginning after December 15, 2016, and interim reporting periods beginning after December 15, 2017.

Early application of each of the amendments is permitted for any annual reporting period or interim period for which the entity's financial statements have not yet been issued (public business entities) or made available for issuance (other entities). Upon adoption, entities will no longer present or disclose any information required by FASB ASC 915.

ASU No. 2014-10 removes all incremental financial reporting requirements from U.S. GAAP for development stage entities, thereby improving financial reporting by eliminating the cost and complexity associated with providing that information. It also eliminates an exception provided to development stage entities in FASB ASC 810 for determining whether an entity is a variable interest entity on the basis of the amount of investment equity that is at risk. The elimination of the exception may change the consolidation analysis, consolidation decision, and disclosure requirements for a reporting entity that has an interest in an entity in the development stage.

Accounting and Reporting: Development Stage Entities [Update 8-1]

The following paragraph, 8.24 in chapter 8, will be deleted upon the effective date of FASB ASU No. 2014-10:

> The provisions of FASB ASC 915, *Development Stage Entities*, apply to financial statements issued by investment companies in the development stage, as defined by the FASB ASC glossary. A *development stage entity* is an entity devoting substantially all its efforts to establishing a new business and for which either of the following conditions exists: (*a*) planned principal operations have not commenced, or (*b*) planned principal operations have commenced, but there has been no significant revenue therefrom.

The following paragraph will replace paragraph 8.28 in chapter 8 upon the effective date of FASB ASU No. 2014-10:

> Once an investment company has been organized to do business, it usually engages immediately in its planned principal operations (that is, the sale of capital stock and investment of funds). Employee training, development of markets for the sale of capital stock, and similar activities are usually performed by the investment adviser or other agent, and the costs of these activities are not borne directly by the investment company. However, an investment company, particularly one not engaging an agent to manage its portfolio and perform other essential functions, may engage in such activities and bear those costs directly from inception.

A.02 ASU No. 2014-11[1]

FASB ASU No. 2014-11, *Transfers and Servicing (Topic 860): Repurchase-to-Maturity Transactions, Repurchase Financings, and Disclosures*, was issued in June 2014.

The accounting amendments are effective, for public business entities, for the first interim or annual period beginning after December 15, 2014. For all other entities, the accounting amendments in the ASU are effective for annual periods beginning after December 15, 2014 and interim periods beginning after December 15, 2015. Early adoption is prohibited for public business entities; however, all other entities may elect to adopt the accounting guidance for interim periods beginning after December 15, 2014. An entity is required to present changes related to adopting the new accounting guidance for transactions outstanding on the effective date as a cumulative-effect adjustment to retained earnings as of the beginning of the period of adoption.

---

[1] Note that banks and broker-dealers refer to a sale of securities with an agreement to repurchase as a repurchase agreement (repo) whereas an investment company refers to this transaction as a reverse repurchase agreement (reverse repo).

For public business entities, the disclosure for certain transactions accounted for as a sale is required to be presented for interim and annual periods beginning after December 15, 2014. Such entities would apply the disclosure requirement related to repurchase agreements, securities lending transactions, and repurchase-to-maturity transactions accounted for as secured borrowings, in annual periods beginning after December 15, 2014, and interim periods beginning after March 15, 2015.

For all other entities, both new disclosures are required to be presented for annual periods beginning after December 15, 2014, and interim periods beginning after December 15, 2015. The disclosures are not required to be presented for comparative periods before the effective date.

Accounting and Reporting: Transfers and Servicing [Update 2-3, 3-1, 7-3, Glossary]

The following definition will replace the existing definition of a repurchase agreement *in the glossary upon the effective date of FASB ASU No. 2014-11:*

> **repurchase agreement (repo agreement).** An agreement under which the transferor (repo party) transfers a financial asset to a transferee (repo counterparty or reverse party) in exchange for cash and concurrently agrees to reacquire that financial asset at a future date for an amount equal to the cash exchanged plus or minus a stipulated interest factor. Instead of cash, other securities or letters of credit sometimes are exchanged. Some repurchase agreements call for repurchase of financial assets that need not be identical to the financial assets transferred.

The following definition will be added in the glossary upon the effective date of FASB ASU No. 2014-11:

> **repurchase-to-maturity transaction**. A repurchase agreement in which the settlement date of the agreement to repurchase a transferred financial asset is at the maturity date of that financial asset and the agreement would not require the transferor to reacquire the financial asset.

The following paragraphs will replace the section titled "Lending of Portfolio Securities and Repurchase Financing" in chapter 2, beginning at paragraph 2.136 upon the effective date of FASB ASU No. 2014-11:

Lending of Portfolio Securities and Secured Borrowings

Investment companies may lend securities (principally to broker-dealers). Such transactions are documented as loans of securities in which the borrower of securities generally is required to provide collateral to the lender, commonly cash but sometimes other securities or standby letters of credit, with a value slightly higher than that of the securities borrowed. If the asset received as collateral is cash, the lender of securities normally earns a return by investing that cash, typically in short-term, high-quality debt instruments, at rates higher than the rate paid or rebated to the borrower. Investment of cash collateral is subject to the investment company's investment restrictions. If the asset received as collateral is other than cash, the lender of securities typically receives a fee. The investment company, as lender of securities, receives amounts from the borrower equivalent to dividends and interest on the securities loaned. As with other extensions of credit, there are risks of delay in recovery or even loss of rights in the collateral should the borrower of the securities fail financially.

The "Pending Content" in paragraphs 5A and 24A of FASB ASC 860-10-40 state that a repo-to-maturity transaction, referring to a repurchase of the same (or substantially the same) financial asset, should be accounted for as a secured borrowing as if the transferor maintains effective control, notwithstanding the characteristics discussed in the "Pending Content" in paragraphs 24–24A of FASB ASC 860-10-40.

An agreement that both entitles and obligates the transferor to repurchase or redeem transferred financial assets from the transferee before the maturity date of the transferred assets maintains the transferor's effective control over those assets under the "Pending Content" in FASB ASC 860-10-40-5(c)(1), provided that all the conditions in the "Pending Content" in FASB ASC 860-10-40-24[3] are met. Those transactions should be accounted for as secured borrowings in which either cash or securities received as collateral that the holder is permitted, by contract or by custom, to sell or repledge is considered the amount borrowed. In a securities lending transaction, the securities loaned are considered pledged as collateral against the cash borrowed and therefore reclassified as pledged, separately from other assets not so encumbered, as set forth in FASB ASC 860-30-25-5(a).

The "Pending Content" in FASB ASC 860-10-55-51A states that under certain agreements to repurchase transferred financial assets before their maturity date, the transferor maintains effective control over the transferred financial assets. If effective control is maintained or the transaction qualifies for the repurchase-to-maturity transaction exception, the agreement is accounted for as a secured borrowing. If effective control is not maintained or the repurchase-to-maturity transaction exception is not met, the transaction would be assessed under the other derecognition conditions in FASB ASC 860-10-40-5 to determine if the transferred financial asset should be derecognized and accounted for as a sale. The "Pending Content" in FASB ASC 860-10-55-51B illustrates the application of the derecognition guidance in the "Pending Content" in paragraphs 24–24A of FASB ASC 860-10-40.

Repurchase agreements and securities lending transactions are required to be evaluated under each of the conditions for derecognition in accordance with FASB ASC 860-10-40-5. The "Pending Content" in FASB ASC 860-10-55-51 states that repurchase agreements and securities lending transactions that do not meet all the conditions in FASB ASC 860-10-40-5 should be treated as secured borrowings.

FASB ASC 860-30 provides guidance related to transfers of financial assets[4] that are accounted for as secured borrowings with a transfer of collateral. This guidance applies to transactions in which cash is obtained in exchange for financial assets with an obligation to enter into an opposite exchange at a later date, including repurchase agreements, dollar rolls, and securities lending transactions. FASB ASC

---

[3] See paragraph 5.77.

[4] Some of the items subject to this guidance are financial instruments. For guidance on matters related broadly to all financial instruments, including the fair value option, see FASB ASC 825.

860-30-25-2 notes that the transferor and transferee should account for a transfer as a secured borrowing with a pledge of collateral in either of the following circumstances:

- If a transfer of an entire financial asset, a group of entire financial assets, or a participating interest in an entire financial asset does not meet the conditions for a sale in the "Pending Content" in FASB ASC 860-10-40-5
- If a transfer of a portion of an entire financial asset does not meet the definition of a *participating interest*

In either of these circumstances, the transferor should continue to report the transferred financial asset on its statement of financial condition with no change in the asset's measurement (for example, its basis of accounting).

FASB ASC 860-30-25-5 states that the accounting for noncash collateral by the obligor (or debtor) and the secured party depends on whether the secured party has the right to sell or repledge the collateral and whether the debtor has defaulted. As noted in FASB ASC 860-30-25-4, in certain cases, cash collateral should be derecognized by the payer (obligor) and recognized by the recipient (secured party) as proceeds of either a sale or borrowing, rather than as collateral. FASB ASC 860-30 provides additional guidance on accounting for collateral.

FASB ASC 860-30-25-8 states that the transferor of securities being loaned accounts for cash received in the same way whether the transfer is accounted for as a sale or secured borrowing. Cash collateral or securities received as collateral that a securities lender is permitted to sell or repledge are the proceeds of a borrowing secured by them. The cash received should be recognized as the transferor's asset—as should investments made with that cash, even if made by agents or in pools with other securities lenders—along with the obligation to return the cash. If securities that may be sold or repledged are received, the transferor of the securities being loaned accounts for those securities in the same way as it would account for cash received.

Balances arising from securities lending transactions that are accounted for as secured borrowings are reported gross on the statement of financial condition. Balances arising from repo transactions accounted for as collateralize borrowings should also be reported gross in the statement of financial condition, unless all the provisions of FASB ASC 210-20-45-11 are met. FASB ASC 210-20-45-11 may be applied only to repo and reverse repo transactions.

The following paragraphs will replace the sections titled "Repurchase Agreements" and "Reverse Repurchase Agreements" in chapter 3, beginning at paragraph 3.04 and 3.06, respectively, upon the effective date of FASB ASU No. 2014-11:

Repurchase Agreements

A *repurchase agreement accounted for as a collateralized borrowing* (repo) refers to a transaction in which a seller-borrower of securities sells those securities to a buyer-lender with an agreement to repurchase them at a stated price plus interest at a specified date or in specified circumstances. A repurchase agreement accounted for as a collateralized borrowing is a repo that does not qualify for sale accounting under FASB ASC 860. The payable under a repurchase agreement accounted for as a collateralized borrowing refers to the amount of the seller-borrower's obligation recognized for the future repurchase of the securities from the buyer-lender.

Because a repo between the two specific parties involved is not transferable, a repo has no ready market. The repo's settlement date is usually specified in the agreement. When the repo's settlement date (or maturity date) is equal to the settlement date (or maturity date) of the underlying security, the repurchase agreement is commonly referred to as a *repurchase-to-maturity transactions* (repo-to-maturity).

Repos are usually entered into with banks, brokers, or dealers. According to SEC Release No. 10666 under the Investment Company Act of 1940 (the 1940 Act), the investment company should always be sure that the repo, including accrued interest, is fully secured by the fair value of the collateral that it has received.[1] Rule 5b-3 under the 1940 Act states that for purposes of Sections 5 and 12(d)(3) of the 1940 Act, the acquisition of a repo may be deemed to be an acquisition of the underlying securities, provided that the obligation of the seller to repurchase the securities from the investment company is fully collateralized at all times by cash items, U.S. government securities, or other securities When the collateral is other than cash or U.S. government securities, such securities are required to consist of securities that the fund's board of directors (or its delegate) determines at the time the repurchase agreement is entered into are (*a*) issued by an issuer that has an exceptionally strong capacity to meet its financial obligations on the securities collateralizing the repurchase agreement and (*b*) sufficiently liquid that they can be sold at approximately their carrying value in the ordinary course of business within seven calendar days.

Reverse Repurchase Agreements

A *reverse repurchase agreement accounted for as a collateralized borrowing* (reverse repo or resale) refers to a transaction that is accounted for as a collateralized lending in which a buyer-lender buys securities with an agreement to resell them to the seller-borrower at a stated price plus interest at a specified date or in specified circumstances. The receivable under a reverse repurchase agreement accounted for as a collateralized borrowing refers to the amount due from the seller-borrower for the repurchase of the securities from the buyer-lender. In certain industries, the terminology is reversed; that is, entities in those industries refer to this type of agreement as a repo.[2]

The following paragraphs will replace paragraph 7.81 in chapter 7, upon the effective date of FASB ASU No. 2014-11:

FASB ASC 860-30-25-5 describes the accounting for noncash collateral by the debtor (obligor) and secured party, which depends on whether the secured party has the right to sell or repledge the collateral and

---

[1] SEC Release No. 10666 under the Investment Company Act of 1940 (the 1940 Act) sets forth the SEC's position that repurchase agreements should be fully collateralized (that is, "the value of the transferred security ... is at least equal to the amount of the loan including accrued interest earned thereon").

[2] For guidance on accounting for reverse repurchase agreements (reverse repos), see paragraph 7.77 of this guide.

whether the debtor has defaulted. FASB ASC 860-30-25-4 explains that cash collateral used in securities lending transactions should be derecognized by the debtor and recognized by the secured party, not as collateral, but, rather, as proceeds of either a sale or borrowing. FASB ASC 860-30-25-7 explains that many securities lending transactions (including those of many investment companies) often both entitle and obligate the transferor to repurchase or redeem the transferred financial assets before their maturity. In such a transaction, the transferor maintains effective control over those assets when all the following conditions in "Pending Content" in FASB ASC 860-10-40-24 are met:

- The financial assets to be repurchased or redeemed are the same or substantially the same as those transferred. To be substantially the same, the financial asset that was transferred and the financial asset that is to be repurchased or redeemed need to have all of the following characteristics:

  — The same primary obligor (except for debt guaranteed by a sovereign government, central bank, government-sponsored enterprise or agency thereof, in which circumstance the guarantor and the terms of the guarantee must be the same)

  — Identical form and type so as to provide the same risks and rights

  — The same maturity (or in the circumstance of mortgage-backed pass-through and pay-through securities, similar remaining weighted-average maturities that result in approximately the same market yield)

  — Identical contractual interest rates

  — Similar assets as collateral

  — The same aggregate unpaid principal amount or principal amounts within accepted good delivery standards for the type of security involved. Participants in the mortgage-backed securities market have established parameters for what is considered acceptable delivery. These specific standards are defined by the Securities Industry and Financial Markets Association and can be found in Uniform Practices for the Clearance and Settlement of Mortgage-Backed Securities and Other Related Securities, which is published by the Securities Industry and Financial Markets Association.

- The agreement is to repurchase or redeem them before maturity at a fixed or determinable price.
- The agreement is entered into contemporaneously with, or in contemplation of, the transfer.

[Note that neither the transferor's ability to repurchase or redeem the financial assets at substantially the same agreed terms, nor the transferor's maintenance of sufficient collateral, are considered during the assessment of effective control.]

FASB ASC 860-30-25-7 continues to explain that those transactions should be accounted for as secured borrowings, in which (*a*) cash (or other securities that the holder is permitted by contract or custom to sell or repledge) received as collateral is considered the amount borrowed, (*b*) the securities loaned are considered pledged as collateral against the cash borrowed and reclassified as set forth in FASB ASC 860-30-25-5(a), and (*c*) any rebate paid to the transferee of securities is interest on the cash that the transferor is considered to have borrowed.

The following paragraphs will be added following paragraph 7.83 in chapter 7, upon the effective date of FASB ASU No. 2014-11:

Disclosures Related to Transfers of Financial Assets, Including Repurchase Agreements

FASB ASC 860-20-50 discusses the disclosures required for transfers of financial assets. To provide an understanding of the nature of the transactions, the transferor's continuing exposure to the transferred financial assets, and the presentation of the components of the transaction in the financial statements, the "Pending Content" in FASB ASC 860-20-50-4D states that an entity should disclose the following for outstanding transactions at the reporting date that meet the scope guidance in the "Pending Content" in paragraphs 4A–4B of FASB ASC 860-20-50 by type of transaction (for example, repurchase agreements, securities lending transactions, and other transactions economically similar to these), with the exception of those transactions excluded from the scope, as described in the "Pending Content" in FASB ASC 860-20-50-4C:

    a. The carrying amount of assets derecognized as of the date of derecognition:

        i. If the amounts that have been derecognized have changed significantly from the amounts that have been derecognized in prior periods or are not representative of the activity throughout the period, a discussion of the reasons for the change should be disclosed.

    b. The amount of gross cash proceeds received by the transferor for the assets derecognized as of the date of derecognition.

    c. Information about the transferor's ongoing exposure to the economic return on the transferred financial assets:

        ii. As of the reporting date, the fair value of assets derecognized by the transferor.

        iii. Amounts reported in the statement of financial position arising from the transaction (for example, the carrying value or fair value of forward repurchase agreements or swap contracts). To the extent that those amounts are captured in the derivative disclosures presented in accordance with FASB ASC 815-10-50-4B, an entity should provide a cross-reference to the appropriate line item in that disclosure.

iv. A description of the arrangements that result in the transferor retaining substantially all of the exposure to the economic return on the transferred financial assets and the risks related to those arrangements.

The "Pending Content" in FASB ASC 860-20-55-108 provides an illustration of one approach for satisfying the quantitative disclosure requirements discussed in the preceding paragraph.

To provide transparency about the types of collateral pledged in agreements and the associated liabilities, the "Pending Content" in FASB ASC 860-30-50-7 requires the following disclosures for repurchase agreements, securities lending transactions, and repurchase-to-maturity transactions that are accounted for as secured borrowings:

a. A disaggregation of the gross obligation by the class of collateral pledged, which shall be determined by the reporting entity based on the nature, characteristics, and risks of the collateral pledged.

b. The remaining contractual tenor of the agreements, which shall be disclosed in maturity intervals determined by the reporting entity to convey an understanding of the overall maturity profile of the entity's financing agreements.

c. A discussion of the potential risks associated with the agreements and the related collateral pledged, including obligations arising from a decline in the fair value of the collateral pledged and how those risks are managed.

Appendix B

Clarified Auditing Standards and PCAOB Standards

This appendix is nonauthoritative and is included for informational purposes only. It has not been reviewed, approved, disapproved, or otherwise acted on by the PCAOB or any senior committee of the AICPA and does not represent official positions or pronouncements of the PCAOB or the AICPA.

The auditing content in this guide focuses primarily on generally accepted auditing standards issued by the Auditing Standards Board (referred to as the clarified standards herein), and is applicable to audits of nonissuers. Audits of issuers are performed in accordance with PCAOB standards. This appendix was developed to assist in comparing the clarified standards, many of which are referenced throughout this guide, to the PCAOB standards.

This appendix identifies PCAOB standards, or sections of PCAOB standards, that broadly correspond with the clarified standards. However, the underlying content within the clarified standards and PCAOB standards may not be analogous. Readers should review the full text of the corresponding PCAOB standards, review the related releases (available in the AICPA's publication *PCAOB Standards and Related Rules* or at www.pcaobus.org) and use professional judgment to identify all guidance applicable to their engagements.

Clarified Standards*		PCAOB Standards**		
AU-C Section	*Title*	*Section or No.***, †*	*Title*	*Applicable Paragraph(s)†† *
200	Overall Objectives of the Independent Auditor and the Conduct of an Audit in Accordance With Generally Accepted Auditing Standards	AU 110	Responsibilities and Functions of the Independent Auditor	All
		AU 150	Generally Accepted Auditing Standards	All
		AU 201	Nature of the General Standards	All
		AU 210	Training and Proficiency of the Independent Auditor	All
		AU 220	Independence	All
		AU 230	Due Professional Care in the Performance of Work	All
		AS 8	Audit Risk	All
210	Terms of Engagement	AU 315	Communications Between Predecessor and Successor Auditors [1]	Paragraphs .03–.10 and .14
		AS 16	Communications with Audit Committees [2]	Paragraphs 5–7
220	Quality Control for an Engagement Conducted in Accordance With Generally Accepted Auditing Standards	AU 161	The Relationship of Generally Accepted Auditing Standards to Quality Control Standards	All
		AS 7	Engagement Quality Review	All
		AS 10	Supervision of the Audit Engagement	All
230	Audit Documentation	AS 3	Audit Documentation	All

Clarified Standards*		PCAOB Standards**		
AU-C Section	Title	Section or No.***, †	Title	Applicable Paragraph(s)††
240	Consideration of Fraud in a Financial Statement Audit	AU 316	Consideration of Fraud in a Financial Statement Audit	All
		AS 5	An Audit of Internal Control Over Financial Reporting That Is Integrated with An Audit of Financial Statements [4]	Paragraphs 14–15
		AS 12	Identifying and Assessing Risks of Material Misstatement [5]	Paragraphs 52–53, 56–58, and 65–69
		AS 13	The Auditor's Responses to the Risks of Material Misstatement [6]	Paragraphs 7 and 12–15
		AS 14	Evaluating Audit Results [7]	Paragraphs 4d, 9, 20–23, and 28–29
250	Consideration of Laws and Regulations in an Audit of Financial Statements	AU 317	Illegal Acts by Clients	All
260	The Auditor's Communication With Those Charged With Governance	AS 16	Communications with Audit Committees [2]	All except paragraphs 5–7
265	Communicating Internal Control Related Matters Identified in an Audit	AU 325	Communications About Control Deficiencies in an Audit of Financial Statements	All
		AS 5	An Audit of Internal Control Over Financial Reporting That Is Integrated with An Audit of Financial Statements [4]	Paragraphs 62–70 and 78–84

(continued)

Clarified Standards*		PCAOB Standards**		
AU-C Section	*Title*	*Section or No.***, †*	*Title*	*Applicable Paragraph(s)††*
300	Planning an Audit	AS 9	Audit Planning [8]	All except paragraphs 11–14
315	Understanding the Entity and Its Environment and Assessing the Risks of Material Misstatement	AS 12	Identifying and Assessing Risks of Material Misstatement [5]	All except paragraphs 52–53, 56–58, and 65–69
		AS 15	Audit Evidence [9]	Paragraphs 11–12
320	Materiality in Planning and Performing an Audit	AS 5	An Audit of Internal Control Over Financial Reporting That Is Integrated with An Audit of Financial Statements [4]	Paragraph 20
		AS 11	Consideration of Materiality in Planning and Performing an Audit [10]	All except paragraph 10
330	Performing Audit Procedures in Response to Assessed Risks and Evaluating the Audit Evidence Obtained	AU 330	The Confirmation Process [12]	Paragraphs .34–.35
		AS 13	The Auditor's Response to the Risks of Material Misstatement [6]	All except paragraphs 7 and 12–15
		AS 14	Evaluating Audit Results [7]	Paragraphs 3, 4e–f, 19, and 30–36
		AS 15	Audit Evidence [9]	Paragraphs 22–28
402	Audit Considerations Relating to an Entity Using a Service Organization	AU 324	Service Organizations	All
450	Evaluation of Misstatements Identified During the Audit	AS 14	Evaluating Audit Results [7]	Paragraphs 4b, 10–12, and 14–18
500	Audit Evidence	AS 15	Audit Evidence [9]	All except paragraphs 11–12 and 22–28

Clarified Standards*		PCAOB Standards**		
AU-C Section	Title	Section or No.***,†	Title	Applicable Paragraph(s)††
501	Audit Evidence—Specific Considerations for Selected Items	AU 331	Inventories	All
		AU 332	Auditing Derivative Instruments, Hedging Activities, and Investments in Securities	All
		AU 337	Inquiry of a Client's Lawyer Concerning Litigation, Claims, and Assessments	All
		AU 901	Public Warehouses—Controls and Auditing Procedures for Goods Held	All
505	External Confirmations	AU 330	The Confirmation Process [12]	All except paragraphs .34–.35
510	Opening Balances—Initial Audit Engagements, Including Reaudit Engagements	AU 315	Communication Between Predecessor and Successor Auditors [1]	All except paragraphs .03–.10 and .14
520	Analytical Procedures	AU 329	Substantive Analytical Procedures	All
		AS 14	Evaluating Audit Results [7]	Paragraphs 4a and 5–8
530	Audit Sampling	AU 350	Audit Sampling	All
540	Auditing Accounting Estimates, Including Fair Value Accounting Estimates, and Related Disclosures	AU 328	Auditing Fair Value Measurements and Disclosures [13]	All except paragraphs .48–.49
		AU 342	Auditing Accounting Estimates	All
		AS 14	Evaluating Audit Results [7]	Paragraphs 13 and 27

(continued)

494   Investment Companies

AU-C Section	Title	Section or No.***, †	Title	Applicable Paragraph(s)††
550	Related Parties	AU 334	Related Parties†††	All
560	Subsequent Events and Subsequently Discovered Facts	AU 508	Reports on Audited Financial Statements [14]	Paragraphs .71–.73
		AU 530	Dating of the Independent Auditor's Report [15]	Paragraphs .03–.08
		AU 560	Subsequent Events [16]	All except paragraph .12e
		AU 561	Subsequent Discovery of Facts Existing at the Date of the Auditor's Report	All
		AS 5	An Audit of Internal Control Over Financial Reporting That Is Integrated with An Audit of Financial Statements [4]	Paragraphs 93–98
570	The Auditor's Consideration of an Entity's Ability to Continue as a Going Concern	AU 341	The Auditor's Consideration of an Entity's Ability to Continue as a Going Concern	All
580	Written Representations	AU 328	Auditing Fair Value Measurements and Disclosures [12]	Paragraphs .48–.49
		AU 333	Management Representations	All
		AU 560	Subsequent Events [16]	Paragraph .12e
		AS 5	An Audit of Internal Control Over Financial Reporting That Is Integrated with An Audit of Financial Statements [4]	Paragraphs 75–77

Header: Clarified Standards* | PCAOB Standards**

Clarified Standards*		PCAOB Standards**		
AU-C Section	Title	Section or No.***,†	Title	Applicable Paragraph(s)††
585	Consideration of Omitted Procedures After the Report Release Date	AU 390	Consideration of Omitted Procedures After the Report Date	All
600	Special Considerations—Audits of Group Financial Statements (Including the Work of Component Auditors)	AU 508	Reports on Audited Financial Statements [14]	Paragraphs .12–.13
		AU 543	Part of Audit Performed by Other Independent Auditors	All
		AS 9	Audit Planning [8]	Paragraphs 11–14
		AS 11	Consideration of Materiality in Planning and Performing an Audit [10]	Paragraph 10
		AS 12	Identifying and Assessing Risks of Material Misstatement [5]	Paragraph 64
610	The Auditor's Consideration of the Internal Audit Function in an Audit of Financial Statements	AU 322	The Auditor's Consideration of the Internal Audit Function in an Audit of Financial Statements	All
		AS 5	An Audit of Internal Control Over Financial Reporting That Is Integrated with An Audit of Financial Statements [4]	Paragraphs 16–19
620	Using the Work of an Auditor's Specialist	AU 336	Using the Work of a Specialist	All

(continued)

Clarified Standards*		PCAOB Standards**		
AU-C Section	Title	Section or No.***, †	Title	Applicable Paragraph(s)††
700	Forming an Opinion and Reporting on Financial Statements	AU 410	Adherence to Generally Accepted Accounting Principles	All
		AU 411	The Meaning of *Present Fairly in Conformity With Generally Accepted Accounting Principles*	All
		AU 508	Reports on Audited Financial Statements [14]	Paragraphs .01–.09, .27–.28, .65–.66, .68, .70, and .74–.75
		AU 530	Dating of the Independent Auditor's Report [15]	Paragraphs .01–.02
		AS 5	An Audit of Internal Control Over Financial Reporting That Is Integrated with An Audit of Financial Statements [4]	Paragraphs 71–74 and 85–89
		AS 14	Evaluating Audit Results [7]	Paragraphs 1–3, 4c, and 24–26
705	Modifications to the Opinion in the Independent Auditor's Report	AU 508	Reports on Audited Financial Statements [14]	Paragraphs .10, .20–.26, .29–.32, .35–.52, .58–.64, .67, and .75
		AS 5	An Audit of Internal Control Over Financial Reporting That Is Integrated with An Audit of Financial Statements [4]	Paragraphs 90–92
706	Emphasis-of-Matter Paragraphs and Other Matter Paragraphs in the Independent Auditor's Report	AU 508	Reports on Audited Financial Statements [14]	Paragraphs .10–.11, .19, .69, and .75–.76

Clarified Standards*		PCAOB Standards**		
AU-C Section	Title	Section or No.***, †	Title	Applicable Paragraph(s)††
708	Consistency of Financial Statements	AU 508	Reports on Audited Financial Statements [14]	Paragraphs .16–.18 and .53–.57
		AS 6	Evaluating Consistency of Financial Statements	All
720	Other Information in Documents Containing Audited Financial Statements	AU 550	Other Information in Documents Containing Audited Financial Statements	All
725	Supplementary Information in Relation to the Financial Statements as a Whole	AS 17	Auditing Supplemental Information Accompanying Audited Financial Statements	All
730	Required Supplementary Information	AU 558	Required Supplementary Information	All
800	Special Considerations— Audits of Financial Statements Prepared in Accordance With Special Purpose Frameworks	AU 544	Lack of Conformity With Generally Accepted Accounting Principles	All
		AU 623	Special Reports [17]	Paragraphs .01–.10 and .22–.34

(continued)

Clarified Standards*		PCAOB Standards**		
AU-C Section	Title	Section or No.***, †	Title	Applicable Paragraph(s)††
805	Special Considerations—Audits of Single Financial Statements and Specific Elements, Accounts, or Items of a Financial Statement	AU 508	Reports on Audited Financial Statements [14]	Paragraphs .33–.34
		AU 623	Special Reports [17]	Paragraphs .11–.18
806	Reporting on Compliance With Aspects of Contractual Agreements or Regulatory Requirements in Connection With Audited Financial Statements	AU 623	Special Reports [17]	Paragraphs .19–.21
810	Engagements to Report on Summary Financial Statements	AU 552	Reporting on Condensed Financial Statements and Selected Financial Data	All
905	Alert That Restricts the Use of the Auditor's Written Communication	AU 532	Restricting the Use of an Auditor's Report	All
910	Financial Statements Prepared in Accordance With a Financial Reporting Framework Generally Accepted in Another Country	AU 534	Reporting on Financial Statements Prepared for Use in Other Countries	All
915	Reports on Application of Requirements of an Applicable Financial Reporting Framework	AU 625	Reports on the Application of Accounting Principles	All

Clarified Standards*		PCAOB Standards**		
AU-C Section	Title	Section or No.***, †	Title	Applicable Paragraph(s)††
920	Letters for Underwriters and Certain Other Requesting Parties	AU 634	Letters for Underwriters and Certain Other Requesting Parties	All
925	Filings With the U.S. Securities and Exchange Commission Under the Securities Act of 1933	AU 711	Filings Under Federal Securities Statutes	All
930	Interim Financial Information	AU 722	Interim Financial Information	All
935	Compliance Audits	AU 801	Compliance Auditing Considerations in Audits of Governmental Entities and Recipients of Governmental Financial Assistance	All

Legend:

[n] Bracketed number indicates a PCAOB standard that broadly corresponds to more than one clarity standard.

Footnotes:

* These standards are codified in AICPA *Professional Standards* and referenced by "AU-C" section numbers within the codification.

** In April 2003, the PCAOB issued Rule 3200T, Interim Auditing Standards (AICPA, *PCAOB Standards and Related Rules*, Select Rules of the Board), which adopted, on an interim transitional basis, generally accepted auditing standards of the AICPA Auditing Standards Board (ASB) that were in existence on April 16, 2003. These adopted standards are referred to as "interim auditing standards." Since the adoption of the interim auditing standards, the PCAOB has issued new standards that, collectively, have superseded certain interim standards and amended the majority of the remaining interim auditing standards to varying degrees. Consequently, the PCAOB's existing auditing standards consist of new standards issued by the PCAOB and the remaining interim standards that the PCAOB has not superseded.

(continued)

In March 2015, the PCAOB adopted a final rule to reorganize the PCAOB's existing auditing standards. The reorganization will put the existing standards into a topical structure with a single integrated numbering system, and amends certain of the PCAOB's auditing standards as well as withdraws certain other interim auditing standards. The final rule will be effective, subject to SEC approval, as of December 31, 2016. If the amendments are approved by the SEC, early implementation of the reorganized standards will be permitted. Readers can access the final rule through the PCAOB website at www.pcaobus.org.

*** This column utilizes the designation "AS" for each PCAOB auditing standard and "AU" for each PCAOB interim standard.

† Section 404 of the Sarbanes-Oxley Act requires a public entity's independent auditor, registered with the PCAOB, to attest to management's disclosures regarding the effectiveness of its internal control. PCAOB Auditing Standard No. 5, *An Audit of Internal Control Over Financial Reporting That Is Integrated with An Audit of Financial Statements* (AICPA, *PCAOB Standards and Related Rules*, Auditing Standards), establishes requirements and provides direction that applies when an auditor is engaged to perform an audit of management's assessment of the effectiveness of internal control over financial reporting that is integrated with an audit of the financial statements. When an auditor is engaged to perform similar attestation procedures for a nonpublic entity, the auditor would follow the requirements and guidance found in AT section 501, *An Examination of an Entity's Internal Control Over Financial Reporting That Is Integrated With an Audit of Its Financial Statements* (AICPA, *Professional Standards*).

Although no direct correlation exists between PCAOB Auditing Standard No. 5 and the clarified standards because Auditing Standard No. 5 is associated with integrated audits and clarified standards are associated with financial statement audits (nonintegrated), Auditing Standard No. 5 does contain certain requirements that generally correspond to concepts addressed in certain clarified standards. A reader conducting an integrated audit in accordance with PCAOB standards may be interested in these generally corresponding concepts and topics and, therefore, they are included within this appendix.

†† The term *all*, as utilized within this column, indicates that the majority of the content within the referenced PCAOB standard broadly corresponds with the related clarified standard. However, the same PCAOB standard may also contain certain specific topics, sections or paragraphs that do not correspond with the related clarified standard, despite the use of the term *all*.

††† In October 2014, the SEC approved Auditing Standard No. 18, *Related Parties*, and related amendments to PCAOB standards. Auditing Standard No. 18, which supersedes PCAOB interim auditing standard AU section 334, *Related Parties* (AICPA, *PCAOB Standards and Related Rules*, Interim Standards), establishes requirements regarding the auditor's evaluation of a company's identification of accounting for, and disclosure of relationships and transactions between a company and its related parties. Auditing Standard No. 18 is effective for audits of financial statements for fiscal years beginning on or after December 15, 2014, including reviews of interim financial information within these fiscal years. Auditors should continue to follow PCAOB interim auditing standard AU section 334 for audits for which Auditing Standard No. 18 is not yet effective.

PCAOB Standards With No Corresponding Clarified Standard

PCAOB Standards		
Section or No.	*Title*	*Discussion*
AU 504	Association With Financial Statements	This PCAOB interim standard provides guidance to an accountant associated with the financial statements of a public entity's financial statements that the auditor has been engaged to audit in accordance with generally accepted auditing standards. Although maintained by the PCAOB, the ASB withdrew this standard during clarification of the standards and addressed its content related to audits of nonissuers through amendments to the Statements on Standards for Accounting and Review Services (to the extent needed) and AU-C sections 200, 230, 260, 705, and 915.
AS 1	References in Auditor's Reports to the Standards of the Public Company Accounting Oversight Board	This PCAOB auditing standard requires registered public accounting firms to include in their reports on engagements performed pursuant to the PCAOB's auditing and related professional practice standards a reference to the standards of the PCAOB.
AS 4	Reporting on Whether a Previously Reported Material Weakness Continues to Exist	This PCAOB auditing standard establishes requirements and provides direction that applies when an auditor is engaged to report on whether a previously reported material weakness in internal control over financial reporting continues to exist as of a date specified by management. This standard establishes a stand-alone engagement that is entirely voluntary, performed only at the company's request.

Appendix C

Venture Capital, Business Development Companies, and Small Business Investment Companies

This appendix is nonauthoritative and is included for informational purposes only.

As described in "Pending Content" in FASB *Accounting Standards Codification* (ASC) 946-20-05-1E, venture capital investment companies, including most small business investment companies (SBICs), and private equity investment companies, differ from other types of investment companies. The typical open-end or closed-end investment company is a more passive investor, whereas a venture capital investment company is more actively involved with its investees. In addition to providing funds, whether in the form of loans or equity, a venture capital investment company often provides technical and management assistance to its investees as needed and requested. That assistance is provided for maximizing the overall value of the investment rather than for other benefits. The portfolio of a venture capital investment company may be illiquid by the very nature of the investments, which are usually securities with no public market. Often, gains on those investments are realized over a relatively long holding period. The nature of the investments therefore requires valuation procedures that may differ from those used by the typical investment company primarily addressed by FASB ASC 946, *Financial Services—Investment Companies*.

Venture capital investment companies may also incur liabilities not generally found in other investment companies, such as certain debts or loans and might be able to use leverage more extensively.

Leverage opportunities available to the owners of SBICs are not available to other investment companies. SBICs, by statute, may borrow from the Small Business Administration (SBA), often at advantageous rates, up to two or three times their paid-in capital.

As stated by FASB ASC 946-20-45-7, although all venture capital investment companies should prepare their financial statements in conformity with U.S. generally accepted accounting principles (GAAP), the statement presentation of some venture capital investment companies may need to be tailored to present the information in a manner most meaningful to their particular group of investors. For example, if debt is a significant item, a conventional balance sheet might be more appropriate than a statement of net assets. Further, see paragraphs 1.55–.57 of this guide for discussion of the Jumpstart Our Business Startups Act of 2012, which explains that certain business development companies (BDCs) may be exempt from certain financial reporting disclosures and regulatory requirements.

Also, different regulatory requirements may apply to these entities. Publicly owned SBICs are subject to the provisions of Article 5 of Regulation S-X, whereas other closed-end funds that are similar to SBICs in their holdings of private securities and that are publicly owned (for example, BDCs) are subject to Article 6.

As noted by FASB ASC 946-20-45-6, the unique features (primarily the existence of significant debt) of SBICs often make it desirable that their financial statements be presented in a conventional balance sheet format.

SBICs are regulated by the SBA and, accordingly, are required to comply with Part 107 of the SBA rules and regulations. Part 107 deals with specific aspects of SBA regulation, such as the relevant audit procedures and reporting requirements (for example, on Form 468) of the SBA for SBICs; the system of account classification; and guidance on proper techniques and standards to be followed in valuing portfolios. SBA guidelines on valuing portfolio investments may not be in accordance with FASB ASC 820, *Fair Value Measurement.*

The auditor of an SBIC should be familiar with the relevant publications and aware of changes in SBA regulations.[1]

The format for reporting the results of SBIC operations varies from that presented in this guide for other types of investment companies because the financial statements for SBICs are presented based on regulations promulgated by the SBA, which is a comprehensive basis of accounting other than GAAP. SBICs may consider maintaining separate accounting records for GAAP and SBA reporting purposes.

---

[1] This guide primarily discusses auditing guidance issued by the Auditing Standards Board that applies to nonissuers. Issuers are defined by Section 3 of the Securities Exchange Act of 1934 and include registered investment companies. Audits of issuers are required to be performed under PCAOB standards. Users should evaluate their audit engagements to determine which auditing standards are applicable.

Appendix D

Computation of Tax Amortization of Original Issue Discount, Market Discount, and Premium

This appendix is nonauthoritative and is included for informational purposes only.

Table 1
Amortization of Original Issue Discount

	Method of Amortization	Reporting of Amortization		Characterization of Amortization	
		On a Daily Basis	At Disposition	Capital Gain	Interest Income
Taxable obligations:					
Short term corporate obligations [1]	SL [2]	X			X
Long term corporate obligations					
Issued before 5/28/69	SL		X		X
Issued 5/28/69–7/1/82	SL	X			X
Issued after 7/1/82	YTM	X [3]			X
Short term government obligations [1]	SL [2]	X			X
Long term government obligations					
Issued before 7/2/82	SL		X		X
Issued after 7/1/82	YTM	X [3]			X
Tax-exempt obligations:					
Short term obligations [1]	SL [2]	X			X [4]
Long term obligations					
Issued prior to 9/4/82 and acquired prior to 3/2/84	SL	X			X [4]
All other acquisitions	YTM	X			X [4]

SL = Straight line (ratable)

YTM = Yield to maturity

[1] *Short term* is defined as having a maturity of not more than one year after the date of issue.

[2] An election may be made to use the yield-to-maturity method.

[3] The accrual period with respect to which the original issue discount is computed and compounded is a one-year period for obligations issued before January 1, 1985, and is a six month period for obligations issued after December 31, 1984.

[4] The amortization is characterized as tax-exempt interest.

Table 2
Amortization of Market Discount

	Method of Amortization	Reporting of Amortization		Characterization of Amortization	
		On a Daily Basis	At Disposition	Capital Gain	Interest Income
Taxable obligations:					
Short term obligations[1]					
Government obligations	SL[2]	X			X
Corporate obligations	YTM[3]	X			X
Long term obligations					
Issued after 7/18/84	SL[2]	[4]	X		X[5]
Issued before 7/19/84	N/A		X	X	
Tax-exempt obligations:					
Acquired on or before 4/30/93					
Long term	N/A				
Short term	N/A				
Acquired after 4/30/93					
Long term	SL[2]	[4]	X[6]		X[6]
Short term	N/A				

SL = Straight line (ratable)

YTM = Yield to maturity

N/A = Not applicable

[1] *Short term* is defined as having a maturity of not more than one year after the date of issue.

[2] An election may be made to use the yield-to-maturity method.

[3] An election may be made to use the straight-line method.

[4] An election may be made to report amortization currently as interest. The election would apply to all market discount bonds acquired on or after the first day of the taxable year in which the election is made.

[5] The amortization of the accrued discount is treated as interest income to the extent of the realized gain on disposition.

[6] Market discount amortization represents taxable income.

Table 3
Amortization of Premium

		Reporting of Amortization		Characterization of Amortization	
	Method of Amortization	On a Daily Basis	At Disposition	Nondeductible Expense	Offset to Interest Income
Taxable obligations:					
Obligations issued after 9/27/85					
If election is made to amortize	YTM	[1]			
If no election is made to amortize	N/A[5]				
Obligations issued before 9/28/85	[3]	[1]	X		X[2]
Tax-exempt obligations:					
Obligations issued after 9/27/85	YTM[4]	X			X
Obligations issued before 9/28/85	[3]	X		X	

YTM = Yield to maturity

N/A = Not applicable; no amortization needed

[1] An election is made to report amortization currently. Such will apply to all bonds held by the taxpayer at the beginning of the taxable year and to all bonds thereafter acquired by the taxpayer.

[2] For bonds acquired between October 23, 1986, and January 1, 1988, premium amortization is treated as interest expense.

[3] Any reasonable method of amortization may be used.

[4] The amortization should be computed by taking into account call dates and call prices.

[5] Premium is part of the tax basis of security and affects tax gain or loss on the disposition or maturity of the obligation.

Appendix E

Illustrative Financial Statement Presentation for Tax-Free Business Combinations of Investment Companies

This appendix is nonauthoritative and is included for informational purposes only.

The following financial statements and disclosures illustrate a tax-free business combination of investment companies (discussed in chapter 8, "Other Accounts and Considerations," of this guide), as illustrated in Technical Questions and Answers section 6910.33, "Certain Financial Reporting, Disclosure, Regulatory, and Tax Considerations When Preparing Financial Statements of Investment Companies Involved in a Business Combination" (AICPA, *Technical Questions and Answers*). The illustrative notes are unique to a business combination. The exhibits assume that Fund B merges into Fund A as of the close of business on December 31, 20X4, and that both Fund A and Fund B have a January 31 fiscal year-end. Exhibit 1 presents the financial position of each fund immediately before the acquisition and the combined fund immediately after the acquisition. Exhibit 2 presents the results of operations and changes in net assets of each fund for the 11 month fiscal period immediately before the acquisition and the results of operations and summary changes in net assets information for the combined fund for the 1 month period subsequent to the acquisition. Exhibit 3 presents the statement of operations, statement of changes in net assets, and appropriate notes of the combined entity immediately after the acquisition. (The January 31, 20X5, statement of net assets of the combined entity is not presented because it will be identical in form to the December 31, 20X4, statement.)

> **Note:** The illustrative financial statements and note disclosures included in this guide have been updated to reflect FASB *Accounting Standards Codification* (ASC). However, in FASB's notice to constituents, it suggests the use of plain English in financial statement note disclosures to describe broad FASB ASC topic references. FASB suggests a reference similar to "as required by the Derivatives and Hedging Topic of the FASB *Accounting Standards Codification*." Entities might consider revising their financial statement references to reflect this plain English referencing, rather than the use of specific FASB ASC references. We have provided these detailed references as a resource for our users.

Exhibit 1

Financial Position of Each Fund Immediately Before Acquisition

Statement of Net Assets
December 31, 20X4

	Fund A	Fund B
Investments in securities at fair value (Cost: Fund A—$18,000,000 Fund B—$9,000,000)	$20,000,000	$10,000,000
Other assets	1,000,000	500,000
	21,000,000	10,500,000
Liabilities	1,000,000	500,000
Net assets	$20,000,000	$10,000,000
Shares outstanding	2,000,000	1,000,000
Net asset value per share	$10.00	$10.00

Calculation of Exchange Ratio

Net assets of Fund B	$10,000,000
Divided by Fund A net asset value per share	10.00
Fund A shares issuable	**1,000,000**
Fund B shares outstanding	1,000,000
Exchange ratio (Fund A shares issuable/Fund B shares outstanding)	**1 for 1**

Financial Position of Combined Entity Immediately After Acquisition

Statement of Net Assets
December 31, 20X4

Investments in securities at fair value (Cost—$27,000,000)	$30,000,000
Other assets	1,500,000
	31,500,000
Liabilities	1,500,000
Net assets	$30,000,000
Shares outstanding	3,000,000
Net asset value per share	$10.00

Note: The individual components of net assets (paid-in capital, undistributed income and capital gains, and unrealized appreciation and depreciation) are not presented in this example but are similarly combined.

Exhibit 2

Statement of Operations
Eleven Months Ended December 31, 20X4

	Fund A	Fund B
Dividend and interest income	$3,200,000	$1,600,000
Management fee	100,000	50,000
Transfer agent fee	50,000	25,000
Other expenses	50,000	25,000
	200,000	100,000
Investment income—net	3,000,000	1,500,000
Realized and unrealized gain on investments		
Net realized gain on investments	1,000,000	500,000
Change in unrealized appreciation	1,000,000	500,000
Net realized and unrealized gain on investments	2,000,000	1,000,000
Net increase in net assets resulting from operations	$5,000,000	$2,500,000

Statement of Changes in Net Assets
Eleven Months Ended December 31, 20X4

	Fund A	Fund B
Increase (decrease) in net assets		
Operations		
Investment income—net	$3,000,000	$1,500,000
Net realized gain on investments	1,000,000	500,000
Change in unrealized appreciation	1,000,000	500,000
	5,000,000	2,500,000
Dividends to shareholders from		
Investment income—net	(3,000,000)	(1,500,000)
Net realized gain on investments	(1,000,000)	(500,000)
Capital share transactions	2,000,000	250,000
Total increase	3,000,000	750,000
Net assets		
Beginning of year	17,000,000	9,250,000
End of year	$20,000,000	$10,000,000

Exhibit 2—(continued)

Statement of Operations of Combined Entity
Month Ended January 31, 20X5

Dividend and interest income	$400,000
Management fee	15,000
Transfer agent fee	5,000
Other expenses	5,000
	25,000
Investment income—net	$375,000
Realized and unrealized gain on investments	
Net realized gain on investments	100,000
Change in unrealized appreciation	100,000
Net gain on investments	200,000
Net increase in net assets resulting from operations	$575,000

Other Changes in Net Assets Information
Month Ended January 31, 20X5

a. No dividends were paid during the month.

b. Capital shares transactions were as follows:

	Shares	Amount
Shares sold	20,000	$200,000
Shares redeemed	(10,000)	($100,000)
	10,000	$100,000

Exhibit 3

**Statements of Operations and Changes in
Net Assets of the Combined Entity Immediately After Acquisition**

**Fund A
Statement of Operations
Year Ended January 31, 20X5**

Dividend and interest income ($3,200,000 + $400,000)		$3,600,000
Management fee ($100,000 + $15,000)	$115,000	
Transfer agent fee ($50,000 + $5,000)	55,000	
Other expenses ($50,000 + $5,000)	55,000	
		225,000
Investment income—net		3,375,000
Realized and unrealized gain on investments		
Net realized gain on investments ($1,000,000 + $100,000)	1,100,000	
Change in unrealized appreciation ($1,000,000 + $100,000)	1,100,000	
Net gain on investments		2,200,000
Net increase in net assets resulting from operations		$5,575,000

**Fund A
Statement of Changes in Net Assets
Year Ended January 31, 20X5**

	20X5	20X4
Increase (decrease) in net assets		
Operations		
Investment income—net	$ 3,375,000	$ 2,400,000
Net realized gain on investments	1,100,000	700,000
Change in unrealized appreciation	1,100,000	300,000
	5,575,000	3,400,000
Dividends to shareholders from		
Investment income—net	(3,000,000)	(2,400,000)
Net realized gain on investments	(1,000,000)	(700,000)
Capital share transactions (notes 6–7)	12,100,000	1,100,000
Total increase	13,675,000	1,400,000
Net assets		
Beginning of year	17,000,000	15,600,000
End of year	$30,675,000	$17,000,000

Notes to Financial Statements of the Combined Entity Immediately After Acquisition

Note 6—Acquisition of Fund B[1]

On December 31, 20X4, Fund A acquired all the net assets of Fund B, an open-end investment company, pursuant to a plan of reorganization approved by Fund B shareholders on December 26, 20X4. The purpose of the transaction was to combine two funds managed by Investment Adviser C with comparable investment objectives and strategies. The acquisition was accomplished by a tax-free exchange of 1 million shares of Fund A, valued at $10 million, for 1 million shares of Fund B outstanding on December 31, 20X4. The investment portfolio of Fund B, with a fair value of $10 million and identified cost of $9 million at December 31, 20X4, was the principal asset acquired by Fund A. For financial reporting purposes, assets received and shares issued by Fund A were recorded at fair value; however, the cost basis of the investments received from Fund B was carried forward to align ongoing reporting of Fund A's realized and unrealized gains and losses with amounts distributable to shareholders for tax purposes.[2] Immediately prior to the merger, the net assets of Fund A were $20 million.

Note: The following paragraph is only required for *public business entities*, as defined in the FASB ASC glossary. For purposes of this disclosure and consistent with FASB ASC 805-10-50-2(h), assume that, had the acquisition occurred on February 1, 20X4—the beginning of Fund A's fiscal year—$10,000 of the transfer agent fee and $15,000 of other expenses—a total of $25,000—would have been eliminated.

---

[1] FASB *Accounting Standards Codification* (ASC) 805-10-50-2(h)(4) states that if the acquirer is a public business entity, the nature and amount of any material, nonrecurring pro forma adjustments directly attributable to the business combination(s) included in the reported pro forma revenue and earnings (supplemental pro forma information) should be disclosed. The illustration provided does not include any material, nonrecurring pro forma adjustments; and thus, the additional disclosure is not required herein. However, readers should be aware such a disclosure would be necessary if a business combination did have material, nonrecurring pro forma adjustments.

[2] If material amounts of undistributed net investment income or undistributed realized gains are transferred to the acquirer, which the acquirer will be required to distribute, those amounts should also be disclosed. Material acquired loss carryovers should also be disclosed or cross referenced to related income tax disclosures.

Assuming the acquisition had been completed on February 1, 20X4, the beginning of the annual reporting period of Fund A, Fund A's pro forma results of operations for the year ended January 31, 20X5,[3] are as follows:

Net investment income	$4,900,000[4]
Net gain (loss) on investments	$3,200,000[5]
Net increase (decrease) in net assets resulting from operations	$8,100,000

Because the combined investment portfolios have been managed as a single integrated portfolio since the acquisition was completed, it is not practicable to separate the amounts of revenue and earnings of Fund B that have been included in Fund A's statement of operations since December 31, 20X4.

Note 7—Capital Share Transactions

As of January 31, 20X5, 100 million shares of $1 par value capital stock were authorized. Transactions in capital stock were as follows:

	Shares		Amount	
	20X5	20X4	20X5	20X4
Shares sold	520,000	300,000	$5,000,000	$3,000,000
Shares issued in connection with the acquisition of Fund B	1,000,000	—	10,000,000	—
Shares issued in the reinvestment of dividends	300,000	250,000	3,000,000	2,400,000
	1,820,000	550,000	18,000,000	5,400,000
Shares redeemed	610,000	450,000	5,900,000	4,300,000
Net increase	1,210,000	100,000	$12,100,000	$1,100,000

[3] FASB ASC 805-10-50-2 states that if the acquirer is a public business entity, and comparative financial statements are presented, supplemental pro forma information should be presented as if the business combination that occurred during the current year had occurred as of the beginning of the comparable prior annual reporting period. Investment companies should base the application of this provision on whether they are required to present comparative statements of operations in their financial statements. Typically, business development companies (BDCs) registered with the SEC are required to present comparative statements of operations, but other registered open-end and closed-end investment companies are not required to do so.

[4] As reported, $3,375,000 plus $1,500,000 Fund B premerger plus $25,000 of pro-forma eliminated expenses.

[5] As reported, $2,200,000 plus $1,000,000 Fund B premerger.

Appendix F

Illustrations for Separately Calculating and Disclosing the Foreign Currency Element of Realized and Unrealized Gains and Losses

This appendix is nonauthoritative and is included for informational purposes only.

As discussed in paragraphs 1–2 of FASB *Accounting Standards Codification* (ASC) 946-830-45 each transaction denominated in a foreign currency can initially be measured only in that currency. The ongoing revaluation of investments and receivables or payables representing unsettled foreign currency transactions should be classified as unrealized foreign currency gain or loss. On settlement (when there is actual cash flow), a realized foreign currency gain or loss should be recorded. Any differences between originally recorded amounts and currently consummated or measured amounts in the reporting currency are a function of both of the following factors: (*a*) foreign exchange rate changes and (*b*) changes in market prices.

Illustrations A and B apply if separate disclosures of the foreign currency elements of unrealized and realized gains and losses on investments are chosen by the reporting entity.

A. Securities Purchases and Sales

As discussed in FASB ASC 946-830-45-20, if separate reporting of foreign currency gains and losses on sales of securities is chosen by the reporting entity, the realized fair value gain or loss on the sale of the security should be measured as the difference between the sale proceeds in foreign currency and the original cost in foreign currency translated at the spot rate on the sale trade date. The realized foreign currency gain or loss should be measured as the difference between the original cost in foreign currency translated at the spot rate on the sale trade date and the historical functional currency cost. Illustration A shows the calculation of the market and currency components of realized gains and losses on the sale of an investment.

ABC Fund uses US$ as its functional currency.

ABC buys 1,000 shares of XYZ @ £15.00 with a spot exchange rate of $1.75 = £1.00.

Foreign currency (FC) cost basis = £15.00 × 1,000 = £15,000

Functional currency cost basis = £15,000 × 1.75 = $26,250

Market gain/loss = (FC sale proceeds – FC cost) × foreign exchange (FX) rate on day of sale

Currency gain/loss = FC cost × (FX rate day of sale – FX rate day of purchase)

Assume a sale of 1,000 shares of XYZ @ £12.00 and $1.50 = £1.00:

FC proceeds	=	£12.00 × 1,000	=	£12,000
Functional currency proceeds	=	£12,000 × 1.50	=	$18,000
Market loss	=	(£12,000 – £15,000) × 1.50	=	$(4,500)
Currency loss	=	£15,000 × (1.50 – 1.75)	=	$(3,750)
Total loss				$(8,250)

Proof

Functional currency proceeds	$18,000
Functional currency cost	$(26,250)
	$(8,250)

As stated in FASB ASC 946-83-45-21, the sale of a security results in a receivable for the security sold. See Illustration F for the calculation of realized gain/loss related to the change in a foreign currency denominated receivable for securities sold from the trade date to the settlement date.

B. Securities—Subsequent Measurement at Fair Value

As discussed in paragraphs 16–17 of FASB ASC 946-830-45, the fair value of securities should initially be determined in the foreign currency and translated at the spot rate on the purchase trade date. The unrealized gain or loss between the original cost (translated on the trade date) and the fair value (translated on the valuation date) comprises both of the following elements: (*a*) changes in the fair value of securities before translation and (*b*) movement in foreign currency rate. If separate disclosure of the foreign currency gain and losses is chosen, the changes in the fair value of securities before translation should be measured as the difference between the fair value in foreign currency and the original cost in foreign currency translated at the spot rate on the valuation date. The effect of the movement in the foreign exchange rate should be measured as the difference between the original cost in foreign currency translated at the current spot rate and the historical functional currency cost. Illustration B shows the calculation of the market and currency components of unrealized gains and losses on an investment.

Day 1: *1,000 shares of XYZ subsequently measured at fair value @ £16.00; spot rate: $1.85 = £1.00.*

Market gain/loss	=	(FC current fair value – FC cost) × current FX rate		
Currency gain/loss	=	FC cost × (current FX rate – FX rate on day of purchase)		
Market gain	=	(£16,000 – £15,000) × 1.85	=	$1,850
Currency gain	=	£15,000 × (1.85 – 1.75)	=	$1,500
Total gain in functional currency				$ 3,350

Total gain – (£16,000 × 1.85) – (£15,000 × 1.75) = $29,600 – $26,250 = $3,350

Journal Entries—Subsequent Measurement at Fair Value

[Average rates may be used if fluctuations in exchange rates aren't significant]

Day 2: *1,000 shares of XYZ marked to market @ £17.00; spot rate: $1.80 = £1.00.*

Market gain	=	(£17,000 – £15,000) × 1.80	=	$3,600
Currency gain	=	£15,000 × (1.80 – 1.75)	=	$ 750
Total functional currency gain				$4,350

Daily Journal Entries

Market gain/loss	=	$3,600 – $1,850	=	$1,750
Currency gain/loss	=	$750 – $1,500	=	($750)
Day 2 gain ($4,350 – $3,350)			=	$1,000

C. Other Assets/Liabilities—FX Subsequent Measurement at Fair Value

As discussed in FASB ASC 946-830-45-23 all receivables and payables that are denominated in a foreign currency and that may relate to income or expense, or to securities sold or purchased, should be recorded on the trade date at the spot rate and should be translated into the functional currency each valuation date at the spot rate on that date. The difference between that amount and the functional currency amount that was recorded at the trade date spot rate for receivables for securities sold (or payables for securities purchased) is unrealized foreign currency gain or loss. Illustration C shows the subsequent remeasurement of a receivable for securities sold between trade date and settlement date.

Sale of 1,000 shares of XYZ @ £ 12.00 = £12,000 receivable @ $1.50 = £1.00 = $18,000

Day 1: *Spot rate moves to $1.55 = £1.00.*

Currency gain	=	£12,000 × (1.55 – 1.50)	=	$600

Day 2: *Spot rate moves to $1.58 = £1.00.*

Currency gain	=	£12,000 × (1.58 – 1.50)	=	$960

	Day 1	Day 2
Currency gain		
Daily Journal Entry	$600	$360

D. Changes Between Trade and Settlement Dates[1]

As stated in paragraphs 21 and 23 of FASB ASC 946-830-45, all receivables and payables that are denominated in a foreign currency and that may relate to income or expense, or to securities sold or purchased, should be recorded on the trade date at the spot rate. On the settlement date, the difference between

---

[1] The payable should be valued between the trade and settlement date such that the balance at the settlement date would equal the amount due at the foreign exchange price. There would also be unrealized gain or loss that would be converted to realized gain or loss upon settlement. It should not be assumed, based on this example, that the calculation of foreign currency gain or loss is only recognized on the settlement date.

the recorded receivable (or payable) amount and the actual foreign currency received (or paid) converted into the functional currency at the spot rate should be recognized as a realized foreign currency gain or loss. Illustrations D and F show the calculation of realized gain or loss related to the change in a foreign currency denominated payable for securities purchased and receivable for securities sold, respectively, from the trade date to the settlement date.

Trade Date

Purchase 1,000 shares of XYZ @ £15.00; exchange rate: $1.75 = £1.00.

Cost basis:	$26,250 or	£15,000
DR: sterling securities at cost	$26,250	
CR: payables for securities purchased		$26,250

Settlement Date

Spot rate: $1.80 = £1.00; £15,000 is purchased at the spot rate for $27,000.

DR: payables for securities purchased	$26,250	
DR realized currency gain/loss	$750	
CR: cash		$27,000

E. Settlement Against Foreign Currency Cash Balances

As discussed in FASB ASC 946-830-45-8 the disbursement of a foreign currency should result in a realized foreign currency gain or loss that is the difference between the functional currency equivalent of the foreign currency when it was acquired and the foreign currency disbursement translated at the spot rate on the disbursement date. Illustration E shows the calculation of realized foreign currency gains and losses in the settlement against foreign currency cash balances.

£20,000 balance is available in London.

Lot a:	£10,000 purchased @ $1.65 per £1.00	
	$US cost basis: $16,500	
Lot b:	£10,000 purchased @ $1.85 per £1.00	
	$US cost basis: $18,500	

Assume lot b will be liquidated first at $1.80 per £1.00.

Lot b:

DR: cash	$18,000	
DR: realized currency gain/loss	$ 500	
CR: sterling cash at cost		$18,500

Assume one half of lot a will be liquidated at $1.80 per £1.00.

Lot a:

DR: cash	$9,000	
CR: sterling cash at cost		$8,250
CR: realized currency gain/loss		$750

Realized FX gain on payable remains the same.

Between Purchase Settlement and Sale Trade Dates

Subsequently measure the holding at fair value, based on both local market price and daily spot rate.

F. Sale of XYZ—Trade Date

Illustration F shows the calculation of realized gain/loss related to the change in a foreign currency denominated receivable for securities sold from the trade date to the settlement date.

Sell 1,000 shares of XYZ @ £18.00; exchange rate: $1.90   =   £1.00

Total proceeds: $34,200 or £18,000

FX gain is recognized on the sale trade date based on the holding period.

Receivable is booked at the spot rate on sale trade date.

DR: receivable for securities sold	$34,200	
CR: sterling securities at cost (£15,000 × £1.75)		= $26,250
CR: realized market gain/loss (£18,000 – £15,000) × 1.90		= $5,700[2]
CR: realized currency gain/loss (15,000 × 1.90) – 26,250		= $2,250[3]

Maintain local currency basis (£18,000) on the receivable record.

Between Sale Trade Date and Settlement Date

Subsequently measure the receivable at fair value based on the prevailing spot rate.

Sale Settlement Date

Spot rate: $1.85 = £1.00

£18,000 is converted at the spot rate to $33,300.

FX loss is recognized upon the receipt (settlement) of the receivable.

DR: cash	$33,300	
DR: realized currency gain/loss[4]	$ 900	
CR: receivables from securities sold		$34,200

If foreign currency cash received is to be kept as local currency:

Purchase:	£18,000 @ $1.85 = £1.00	
Cost basis:		$33,300
DR: sterling cash at cost	$33,300	
CR: cash		$33,300

---

[2] If separate disclosures of the foreign currency elements of unrealized and realized gains and losses on investments are chosen by the entity.

[3] See footnote 2.

[4] As discussed in FASB *Accounting Standards Codification* 946-830-45-21, on settlement date, the difference between the recorded receivable amount and the actual foreign currency received converted into the functional currency at the spot rate should be recognized as a realized foreign currency gain or loss.

Appendix G

References to AICPA Technical Questions and Answers

This appendix is nonauthoritative and is included for informational purposes only.

The following nonauthoritative questions and answers, commonly referred to as Technical Questions and Answers (Q&As), may be useful and relevant for users of this guide. Other Q&As may also be useful and relevant to users of this guide, depending on the facts and circumstances.

Q&A Section No.	Title
6910.16	Presentation of Boxed Investment Positions in the Condensed Schedule of Investments of Nonregistered Investment Partnerships
6910.17	Disclosure of Long and Short Positions
6910.18	Disclosure of an Investment in an Issuer When One or More Securities or One or More Derivative Contracts are Held—Nonregistered Investment Partnerships
6910.19	Information Required to Be Disclosed in Financial Statements When Comparative Financial Statements of Nonregistered Investment Partnerships Are Presented
6910.20	Presentation of Purchases and Sales/Maturities of Investments in the Statement of Cash Flows
6910.21	Recognition of Premium/Discount on Short Positions in Fixed-Income Securities
6910.22	Presentation of Reverse Repurchase Agreements
6910.23	Accounting Treatment of Offering Costs Incurred by Investment Partnerships
6910.24	Meaning of "Continually Offer Interests"
6910.25	Considerations in Evaluating Whether Certain Liabilities Constitute "Debt" for Purposes of Assessing Whether an Investment Company Must Present a Statement of Cash Flows
6910.26	Additional Guidance on Determinants of Net Versus Gross Presentation of Security Purchases and Sales/Maturities in the Statement of Cash Flows of a Nonregistered Investment Company
6910.27	Treatment of Deferred Fees

(continued)

Q&A Section No.	Title
6910.28	Reporting Financial Highlights, Net Asset Value (NAV) Per Share, Shares Outstanding, and Share Transactions When Investors in Unitized Nonregistered Funds Are Issued Individual Classes or Series of Shares
6910.29	Allocation of Unrealized Gain (Loss), Recognition of Carried Interest, and Clawback Obligations
6910.30	Disclosure Requirements of Investments for Nonregistered Investment Partnerships When Their Interest in an Investee Fund Constitutes Less Than 5 Percent of the Nonregistered Investment Partnership's Net Assets
6910.31	The Nonregistered Investment Partnership's Method for Calculating Its Proportional Share of Any Investments Owned by an Investee Fund in Applying the "5 Percent Test" Described in Section 6910.30
6910.32	Additional Financial Statement Disclosures for Nonregistered Investment Partnerships When the Partnership Has Provided Guarantees Related to the Investee Fund's Debt
6910.33	Certain Financial Reporting, Disclosure, Regulatory, and Tax Considerations When Preparing Financial Statements of Investment Companies Involved in a Business Combination
6910.34	Application of the Notion of Value Maximization for Measuring Fair Value of Debt and Controlling Equity Positions
6910.35	Assessing Control When Measuring Fair Value
2220.18	Applicability of Practical Expedient
2220.19	Unit of Account
2220.20	Determining Whether NAV Is Calculated Consistent With FASB ASC 946, *Financial Services—Investment Companies*
2220.21	Determining Whether an Adjustment to NAV Is Necessary
2220.22	Adjusting NAV When It Is Not as of the Reporting Entity's Measurement Date
2220.23	Adjusting NAV When It Is Not Calculated Consistent With FASB ASC 946
2220.24	Disclosures—Ability to Redeem Versus Actual Redemption Request

Q&A Section No.	Title
2220.25	Impact of "Near Term" on Classification Within Fair Value Hierarchy
2220.26	Categorization of Investments for Disclosure Purposes
2220.27	Determining Fair Value of Investments When the Practical Expedient Is Not Used or Is Not Available

Appendix H

Overview of Statements on Quality Control Standards

This appendix is nonauthoritative and is included for informational purposes only.

This appendix is a partial reproduction of chapter 1 of the AICPA practice aid *Establishing and Maintaining a System of Quality Control for a CPA Firm's Accounting and Auditing Practice,* available at www.aicpa.org/interestareas/frc/pages/enhancingauditqualitypracticeaid.aspx.

1.01 The objectives of a system of quality control are to provide a CPA firm with reasonable assurance[1] that the firm and its personnel comply with professional standards and applicable regulatory and legal requirements, and that the firm or engagement partners issue reports that are appropriate in the circumstances. QC section 10, *A Firm's System of Quality Control* (AICPA, *Professional Standards*), addresses a CPA firm's responsibilities for its system of quality control for its accounting and auditing practice. That section is to be read in conjunction with the AICPA Code of Professional Conduct and other relevant ethical requirements.

1.02 A system of quality control consists of policies designed to achieve the objectives of the system and the procedures necessary to implement and monitor compliance with those policies. The nature, extent, and formality of a firm's quality control policies and procedures will depend on various factors such as the firm's size; the number and operating characteristics of its offices; the degree of authority allowed to, and the knowledge and experience possessed by, firm personnel; and the nature and complexity of the firm's practice.

Communication of Quality Control Policies and Procedures

1.03 The firm should communicate its quality control policies and procedures to its personnel. Most firms will find it appropriate to communicate their policies and procedures in writing and distribute them, or make them available electronically, to all professional personnel. Effective communication includes the following:

- A description of quality control policies and procedures and the objectives they are designed to achieve
- The message that each individual has a personal responsibility for quality
- A requirement for each individual to be familiar with and to comply with these policies and procedures

Effective communication also includes procedures for personnel to communicate their views or concerns on quality control matters to the firm's management.

---

[1] The term *reasonable assurance*, which is defined as a high, but not absolute, level of assurance, is used because absolute assurance cannot be attained. Paragraph .53 of QC section 10, *A Firm's System of Quality Control* (AICPA, *Professional Standards*), states, "Any system of quality control has inherent limitations that can reduce its effectiveness."

Elements of a System of Quality Control

1.04   A firm must establish and maintain a system of quality control. The firm's system of quality control should include policies and procedures that address each of the following elements of quality control identified in paragraph .17 of QC section 10:

- Leadership responsibilities for quality within the firm (the "tone at the top")
- Relevant ethical requirements
- Acceptance and continuance of client relationships and specific engagements
- Human resources
- Engagement performance
- Monitoring

1.05   The elements of quality control are interrelated. For example, a firm continually assesses client relationships to comply with relevant ethical requirements, including independence, integrity, and objectivity, and policies and procedures related to the acceptance and continuance of client relationships and specific engagements. Similarly, the human resources element of quality control encompasses criteria related to professional development, hiring, advancement, and assignment of firm personnel to engagements, all of which affect policies and procedures related to engagement performance. In addition, policies and procedures related to the monitoring element of quality control enable a firm to evaluate whether its policies and procedures for each of the other five elements of quality control are suitably designed and effectively applied.

1.06   Policies and procedures established by the firm related to each element are designed to achieve reasonable assurance with respect to the purpose of that element. Deficiencies in policies and procedures for an element may result in not achieving reasonable assurance with respect to the purpose of that element; however, the system of quality control, as a whole, may still be effective in providing the firm with reasonable assurance that the firm and its personnel comply with professional standards and applicable regulatory and legal requirements and that the firm or engagement partners issue reports that are appropriate in the circumstances.

1.07   If a firm merges, acquires, sells, or otherwise changes a portion of its practice, the surviving firm evaluates and, as necessary, revises, implements, and maintains firm-wide quality control policies and procedures that are appropriate for the changed circumstances.

Leadership Responsibilities for Quality Within the Firm (the "Tone at the Top")

1.08   The purpose of the leadership responsibilities element of a system of quality control is to promote an internal culture based on the recognition that quality is essential in performing engagements. The firm should establish and maintain the following policies and procedures to achieve this purpose:

- Require the firm's leadership (managing partner, board of managing partners, CEO, or equivalent) to assume ultimate responsibility for the firm's system of quality control.

- Provide the firm with reasonable assurance that personnel assigned operational responsibility for the firm's quality control system have sufficient and appropriate experience and ability to identify and understand quality control issues and develop appropriate policies and procedures, as well as the necessary authority to implement those policies and procedures.

1.09 Establishing and maintaining the following policies and procedures assists firms in recognizing that the firm's business strategy is subject to the overarching requirement for the firm to achieve the objectives of the system of quality control in all the engagements that the firm performs:

- Assign management responsibilities so that commercial considerations do not override the quality of the work performed.

- Design policies and procedures addressing performance evaluation, compensation, and advancement (including incentive systems) with regard to personnel to demonstrate the firm's overarching commitment to the objectives of the system of quality control.

- Devote sufficient and appropriate resources for the development, communication, and support of its quality control policies and procedures.

Relevant Ethical Requirements

1.10 The purpose of the relevant ethical requirements element of a system of quality control is to provide the firm with reasonable assurance that the firm and its personnel comply with relevant ethical requirements when discharging professional responsibilities. Relevant ethical requirements include independence, integrity, and objectivity. Establishing and maintaining policies such as the following assist the firm in obtaining this assurance:

- Require that personnel adhere to relevant ethical requirements such as those in regulations, interpretations, and rules of the AICPA, state CPA societies, state boards of accountancy, state statutes, the U.S. Government Accountability Office, and any other applicable regulators.

- Establish procedures to communicate independence requirements to firm personnel and, where applicable, others subject to them.

- Establish procedures to identify and evaluate possible threats to independence and objectivity, including the familiarity threat that may be created by using the same senior personnel on an audit or attest engagement over a long period of time, and to take appropriate action to eliminate those threats or reduce them to an acceptable level by applying safeguards.

- Require that the firm withdraw from the engagement if effective safeguards to reduce threats to independence to an acceptable level cannot be applied.

- Require written confirmation, at least annually, of compliance with the firm's policies and procedures on independence from all firm personnel required to be independent by relevant requirements.

- Establish procedures for confirming the independence of another firm or firm personnel in associated member firms who perform part of the engagement. This would apply to national firm personnel, foreign firm personnel, and foreign-associated firms.[2]

- Require the rotation of personnel for audit or attest engagements where regulatory or other authorities require such rotation after a specified period.

Acceptance and Continuance of Client Relationships and Specific Engagements

1.11 The purpose of the quality control element that addresses acceptance and continuance of client relationships and specific engagements is to establish criteria for deciding whether to accept or continue a client relationship and whether to perform a specific engagement for a client. A firm's client acceptance and continuance policies represent a key element in mitigating litigation and business risk. Accordingly, it is important that a firm be aware that the integrity and reputation of a client's management could reflect the reliability of the client's accounting records and financial representations and, therefore, affect the firm's reputation or involvement in litigation. A firm's policies and procedures related to the acceptance and continuance of client relationships and specific engagements should provide the firm with reasonable assurance that it will undertake or continue relationships and engagements only where it

- is competent to perform the engagement and has the capabilities, including the time and resources, to do so;

- can comply with legal and relevant ethical requirements;

- has considered the client's integrity and does not have information that would lead it to conclude that the client lacks integrity; and

- has reached an understanding with the client regarding the services to be performed.

1.12 This assurance should be obtained before accepting an engagement with a new client, when deciding whether to continue an existing engagement, and when considering acceptance of a new engagement with an existing client. Establishing and maintaining policies such as the following assist the firm in obtaining this assurance:

---

[2] A *foreign-associated firm* is a firm domiciled outside of the United States and its territories that is a member of, correspondent with, or similarly associated with an international firm or international association of firms.

- Evaluate factors that have a bearing on management's integrity and consider the risk associated with providing professional services in particular circumstances.[3]

- Evaluate whether the engagement can be completed with professional competence; undertake only those engagements for which the firm has the capabilities, resources, and professional competence to complete; and evaluate, at the end of specific periods or upon occurrence of certain events, whether the relationship should be continued.

- Obtain an understanding, preferably in writing, with the client regarding the services to be performed.

- Establish procedures on continuing an engagement and the client relationship, including procedures for dealing with information that would have caused the firm to decline an engagement if the information had been available earlier.

- Require documentation of how issues relating to acceptance or continuance of client relationships and specific engagements were resolved.

Human Resources

1.13 The purpose of the human resources element of a system of quality control is to provide the firm with reasonable assurance that it has sufficient personnel with the capabilities, competence, and commitment to ethical principles necessary (*a*) to perform its engagements in accordance with professional standards and regulatory and legal requirements, and (*b*) to enable the firm to issue reports that are appropriate in the circumstances. Establishing and maintaining policies such as the following assist the firm in obtaining this assurance:

- Recruit and hire personnel of integrity who possess the characteristics that enable them to perform competently.

- Determine capabilities and competencies required for an engagement, especially for the engagement partner, based on the characteristics of the particular client, industry, and kind of service being performed. Specific competencies necessary for an engagement partner are discussed in paragraph .A27 of QC section 10.

- Determine the capabilities and competencies possessed by personnel.

- Assign the responsibility for each engagement to an engagement partner.

---

[3] Such considerations would include the risk of providing professional services to significant clients or to other clients for which the practitioner's objectivity or the appearance of independence may be impaired. In broad terms, the significance of a client to a member or a firm refers to relationships that could diminish a practitioner's objectivity and independence in performing attest services. Examples of factors to consider in determining the significance of a client to an engagement partner, office, or practice unit include (*a*) the amount of time the partner, office, or practice unit devotes to the engagement, (*b*) the effect on the partner's stature within the firm as a result of his or her service to the client, (*c*) the manner in which the partner, office, or practice unit is compensated, or (*d*) the effect that losing the client would have on the partner, office, or practice unit.

- Assign personnel based on the knowledge, skills, and abilities required in the circumstances and the nature and extent of supervision needed.

- Have personnel participate in general and industry-specific continuing professional education and professional development activities that enable them to accomplish assigned responsibilities and satisfy applicable continuing professional education requirements of the AICPA, state boards of accountancy, and other regulators.

- Select for advancement only those individuals who have the qualifications necessary to fulfill the responsibilities they will be called on to assume.

Engagement Performance

1.14 The purpose of the engagement performance element of quality control is to provide the firm with reasonable assurance (*a*) that engagements are consistently performed in accordance with applicable professional standards and regulatory and legal requirements, and (*b*) that the firm or the engagement partner issues reports that are appropriate in the circumstances. Policies and procedures for engagement performance should address all phases of the design and execution of the engagement, including engagement performance, supervision responsibilities, and review responsibilities. Policies and procedures also should require that consultation takes place when appropriate. In addition, a policy should establish criteria against which all engagements are to be evaluated to determine whether an engagement quality control review should be performed.

1.15 Establishing and maintaining policies such as the following assist the firm in obtaining the assurance required relating to the engagement performance element of quality control:

- Plan all engagements to meet professional, regulatory, and the firm's requirements.

- Perform work and issue reports and other communications that meet professional, regulatory, and the firm's requirements.

- Require that work performed by other team members be reviewed by qualified engagement team members, which may include the engagement partner, on a timely basis.

- Require the engagement team to complete the assembly of final engagement files on a timely basis.

- Establish procedures to maintain the confidentiality, safe custody, integrity, accessibility, and retrievability of engagement documentation.

- Require the retention of engagement documentation for a period of time sufficient to meet the needs of the firm, professional standards, laws, and regulations.

- Require that

  — consultation take place when appropriate (for example, when dealing with complex, unusual, unfamiliar, difficult, or contentious issues);

- — sufficient and appropriate resources be available to enable appropriate consultation to take place;

- — all the relevant facts known to the engagement team be provided to those consulted;

- — the nature, scope, and conclusions of such consultations be documented; and

- — the conclusions resulting from such consultations be implemented.

- Require that

  - — differences of opinion be dealt with and resolved;

  - — conclusions reached are documented and implemented; and

  - — the report not be released until the matter is resolved.

- Require that

  - — all engagements be evaluated against the criteria for determining whether an engagement quality control review should be performed;

  - — an engagement quality control review be performed for all engagements that meet the criteria; and

  - — the review be completed before the report is released.

- Establish procedures addressing the nature, timing, extent, and documentation of the engagement quality control review.

- Establish criteria for the eligibility of engagement quality control reviewers.

Monitoring

1.16   The purpose of the monitoring element of a system of quality control is to provide the firm and its engagement partners with reasonable assurance that the policies and procedures related to the system of quality control are relevant, adequate, operating effectively, and complied with in practice. Monitoring involves an ongoing consideration and evaluation of the appropriateness of the design, the effectiveness of the operation of a firm's quality control system, and a firm's compliance with its quality control policies and procedures. The purpose of monitoring compliance with quality control policies and procedures is to provide an evaluation of the following:

- Adherence to professional standards and regulatory and legal requirements

- Whether the quality control system has been appropriately designed and effectively implemented

- Whether the firm's quality control policies and procedures have been operating effectively so that reports issued by the firm are appropriate in the circumstances

1.17   Establishing and maintaining policies such as the following assist the firm in obtaining the assurance required relating to the monitoring element of quality control:

- Assign responsibility for the monitoring process to a partner or partners or other persons with sufficient and appropriate experience and authority in the firm to assume that responsibility.

- Assign performance of the monitoring process to competent individuals.

- Require the performance of monitoring procedures that are sufficiently comprehensive to enable the firm to assess compliance with all applicable professional standards and the firm's quality control policies and procedures. Monitoring procedures consist of the following:

  — Review of selected administrative and personnel records pertaining to the quality control elements.

  — Review of engagement documentation, reports, and clients' financial statements.

  — Summarization of the findings from the monitoring procedures, at least annually, and consideration of the systemic causes of findings that indicate that improvements are needed.

  — Determination of any corrective actions to be taken or improvements to be made with respect to the specific engagements reviewed or the firm's quality control policies and procedures.

  — Communication of the identified findings to appropriate firm management personnel.

  — Consideration of findings by appropriate firm management personnel who should also determine that any actions necessary, including necessary modifications to the quality control system, are taken on a timely basis.

  — Assessment of

    - the appropriateness of the firm's guidance materials and any practice aids;

    - new developments in professional standards and regulatory and legal requirements and how they are reflected in the firm's policies and procedures where appropriate;

    - compliance with policies and procedures on independence;

    - the effectiveness of continuing professional development, including training;

    - decisions related to acceptance and continuance of client relationships and specific engagements; and

    - firm personnel's understanding of the firm's quality control policies and procedures and implementation thereof.

- Communicate at least annually, to relevant engagement partners and other appropriate personnel, deficiencies noted as a result of the monitoring process and recommendations for appropriate remedial action.

- Communicate the results of the monitoring of its quality control system process to relevant firm personnel at least annually.
- Establish procedures designed to provide the firm with reasonable assurance that it deals appropriately with the following:
  - Complaints and allegations that the work performed by the firm fails to comply with professional standards and regulatory and legal requirements.
  - Allegations of noncompliance with the firm's system of quality control.
  - Deficiencies in the design or operation of the firm's quality control policies and procedures, or noncompliance with the firm's system of quality control by an individual or individuals, as identified during the investigations into complaints and allegations.

  This includes establishing clearly defined channels for firm personnel to raise any concerns in a manner that enables them to come forward without fear of reprisal and documenting complaints and allegations and the responses to them.

- Require appropriate documentation to provide evidence of the operation of each element of its system of quality control. The form and content of documentation evidencing the operation of each of the elements of the system of quality control is a matter of judgment and depends on a number of factors, including the following, for example:
  - The size of the firm and the number of offices.
  - The nature and complexity of the firm's practice and organization.

- Require retention of documentation providing evidence of the operation of the system of quality control for a period of time sufficient to permit those performing monitoring procedures and peer review to evaluate the firm's compliance with its system of quality control, or for a longer period if required by law or regulation.

1.18 Some of the monitoring procedures discussed in the previous list may be accomplished through the performance of the following:

- Engagement quality control review
- Review of engagement documentation, reports, and clients' financial statements for selected engagements after the report release date
- Inspection[4] procedures

---

[4] *Inspection* is a retrospective evaluation of the adequacy of the firm's quality control policies and procedures, its personnel's understanding of those policies and procedures, and the extent of the firm's compliance with them. Although monitoring procedures are meant to be ongoing, they may include inspection procedures performed at a fixed point in time. Monitoring is a broad concept; inspection is one specific type of monitoring procedure.

Documentation of Quality Control Policies and Procedures

1.19 The firm should document each element of its system of quality control. The extent of the documentation will depend on the size, structure, and nature of the firm's practice. Documentation may be as simple as a checklist of the firm's policies and procedures or as extensive as practice manuals.

Appendix I

The New Revenue Recognition Standard: FASB ASU No. 2014-09

This appendix is nonauthoritative and is included for informational purposes only.

Overview

On May 28, 2014, the International Accounting Standards Board (IASB) and FASB issued a joint accounting standard on revenue recognition to address a number of concerns regarding the complexity and lack of consistency surrounding the accounting for revenue transactions. Consistent with each board's policy, the FASB issued FASB Accounting Standards Update (ASU) No. 2014-09, *Revenue from Contracts with Customers (Topic 606)*, and the IASB issued International Financial Reporting Standard (IFRS) 15, *Revenue from Contracts with Customers*. FASB ASU No. 2014-09 will amend the FASB *Accounting Standards Codification* (ASC) by creating a new Topic 606, *Revenue from Contracts with Customers*, and a new Subtopic 340-40, *Other Assets and Deferred Costs—Contracts with Customers*. The guidance in FASB ASU No. 2014-09 provides what FASB describes as a framework for revenue recognition and supersedes or amends several of the revenue recognition requirements in FASB ASC 605, *Revenue Recognition*, as well as guidance within the 900 series of industry-specific topics.

As part of the boards' efforts to converge U.S. generally accepted accounting principles (GAAP) and IFRSs, the standard eliminates the transaction- and industry-specific revenue recognition guidance under current GAAP and replaces it with a principles-based approach for revenue recognition. The intent is to avoid inconsistencies of accounting treatment across different geographies and industries. In addition to improving comparability of revenue recognition practices, the new guidance provides more useful information to financial statement users through enhanced disclosure requirements. FASB and the IASB have essentially achieved convergence with these standards, with some minor differences related to the collectibility threshold, interim disclosure requirements, early application and effective date, impairment loss reversal, and nonpublic entity requirements.

The standard applies to any entity that either enters into contracts with customers to transfer goods or services or enters into contracts for the transfer of nonfinancial assets unless those contracts are within the scope of other standards (for example, insurance or lease contracts).

Effective/Applicability Date

The guidance in FASB ASU No. 2014-09 is effective for annual reporting periods of public entities beginning after December 15, 2016 (equates to January 1, 2017, for calendar year-end entities), including interim periods within that reporting period. Early application is not permitted.

For nonpublic entities, the amendments in the new guidance are effective for annual reporting periods beginning after December 15, 2017, and interim periods within annual periods beginning after December 15, 2018. Non-public entities may elect to adopt the standard earlier, however, only as of the following:

- An annual reporting period beginning after December 15, 2016, including interim periods within that reporting period (public entity effective date)

- An annual reporting period beginning after December 15, 2016, and interim periods within annual periods beginning after December 15, 2017

- An annual reporting period beginning after December 15, 2017, including interim periods within that reporting period

As of the publication of this appendix, FASB is currently discussing a proposal to defer the effective date of ASU No. 2014-09. Refer to the "Latest Developments" section of this appendix for more information.

Overview of the New Guidance

The core principle of the revised revenue recognition standard is that an entity should recognize revenue to depict the transfer of goods or services to customers in an amount that reflects the consideration to which the entity expects to be entitled in exchange for those good or services.

To apply the proposed revenue recognition standard, FASB ASU No. 2014-09 states that an entity should follow these five steps:

1. Identify the contract(s) with a customer.
2. Identify the performance obligations in the contract.
3. Determine the transaction price.
4. Allocate the transaction price to the performance obligations in the contract.
5. Recognize revenue when (or as) the entity satisfies a performance obligation.

Under the new standard, revenue is recognized when a company satisfies a performance obligation by transferring a promised good or service to a customer (which is when the customer obtains control of that good or service). See the following discussion of the five steps involved when recognizing revenue under the new guidance.

Understanding the Five-Step Process

Step 1: Identify the Contract(s) With a Customer

FASB ASU No. 2014-09 defines a contract as "an agreement between two or more parties that creates enforceable rights and obligations." The new standard affects contracts with a customer that meet the following criteria:

- Approval (in writing, orally, or in accordance with other customary business practices) and commitment of the parties

- Identification of the rights of the parties
- Identification of the payment terms
- Contract has commercial substance
- Probable that the entity will collect the consideration to which it will be entitled in exchange for the goods or services that will be transferred to the customer

A contract does not exist if each party to the contract has the unilateral enforceable right to terminate a wholly unperformed contract without compensating the other party (parties).

Step 2: Identify the Performance Obligations in the Contract

A *performance obligation* is a promise in a contract with a customer to transfer a good or service to the customer.

At contract inception, an entity should assess the goods or services promised in a contract with a customer and should identify as a performance obligation (possibly multiple performance obligations) each promise to transfer to the customer either

- a good or service (or bundle of goods or services) that is distinct, or
- a series of distinct goods or services that are substantially the same and that have the same pattern of transfer to the customer.

A good or service that is not distinct should be combined with other promised goods or services until the entity identifies a bundle of goods or services that is distinct. In some cases, that would result in the entity accounting for all the goods or services promised in a contract as a single performance obligation.

Step 3: Determine the Transaction Price

The transaction price is the amount of consideration (fixed or variable) the entity expects to receive in exchange for transferring promised goods or services to a customer, excluding amounts collected on behalf of third parties. To determine the transaction price, an entity should consider the effects of

- variable consideration,
- constraining estimates of variable consideration,
- the existence of a significant financing component,
- noncash considerations, and
- consideration payable to the customer.

If the consideration promised in a contract includes a variable amount, then an entity should estimate the amount of consideration to which the entity will be entitled in exchange for transferring the promised goods or services to a customer. An entity would then include in the transaction price some or all of an amount of variable consideration only to the extent that it is probable that a significant reversal in the amount of cumulative revenue recognized will not occur when the uncertainty associated with the variable consideration is subsequently resolved.

An entity should consider the terms of the contract and its customary business practices to determine the transaction price.

Step 4: Allocate the Transaction Price to the Performance Obligations in the Contract

The transaction price is allocated to separate performance obligations in proportion to the standalone selling price of the promised goods or services. If a standalone selling price is not directly observable, then an entity should estimate it. Reallocation of the transaction price for changes in the standalone selling price is not permitted. When estimating the standalone selling price, entities can use various methods including the adjusted market assessment approach, expected cost plus a margin approach, and residual approach (only if the selling price is highly variable and uncertain).

Sometimes, the transaction price includes a discount or a variable amount of consideration that relates entirely to one of the performance obligations in a contract. Guidance under the new standard specifies when an entity should allocate the discount or variable consideration to one (or some) performance obligation(s) rather than to all of the performance obligations in the contract.

Step 5: Recognize Revenue When (or as) the Entity Satisfies a Performance Obligation

The amount of revenue recognized when transferring the promised good or service to a customer is equal to the amount allocated to the satisfied performance obligation, which may be satisfied at a point in time or over time. Control of an asset refers to the ability to direct the use of, and obtain substantially all of the remaining benefits from, the asset. Control also includes the ability to prevent *other entities* from directing the use of, and obtaining the benefits from, an asset.

When performance obligations are satisfied over time, the entity should select an appropriate method for measuring its progress toward complete satisfaction of that performance obligation. The standard discusses methods of measuring progress including input and output methods, and how to determine which method is appropriate.

Additional Guidance Under the New Standard

In addition to the five-step process for recognizing revenue, FASB ASU No. 2014-09 also addresses the following areas:

- Accounting for incremental costs of obtaining a contract, as well as costs incurred to fulfill a contract.
- Licenses
- Warranties

Lastly, the new guidance enhances disclosure requirements to include more information about specific revenue contracts entered into by the entity, including performance obligations and the transaction price.

Transition Resource Group

Due to the potential for significant changes that may result from the issuance of the new standard, FASB and the IASB have received an abundance of implementation questions from interested parties. To address these questions, the boards have formed a joint Transition Resource Group (TRG) for revenue recognition to promote effective implementation and transition to the converged standard.

Since the issuance of the standard, the TRG has met several times to discuss implementation issues raised by concerned parties and actions to take to address these issues. Refer to FASB's TRG website for more information on this group and the status of their efforts including meeting materials and meeting summaries.

Latest Developments

After receiving requests for additional time to implement the requirements of FASB ASU No. 2014-09, the board issued a proposed ASU on April 29, 2015, to defer the effective date of the new standard on revenue recognition by one year. Under this proposal, public companies would apply the new requirements to annual reporting periods beginning after December 15, 2017. Nonpublic companies would apply the new requirements to annual reporting periods beginning after December 15, 2018. Both public and nonpublic companies would be permitted to adopt the new standard early, but not before the original public company effective date of December 15, 2016. The proposed ASU to defer the effective date of the new standard is exposed for comments until May 29, 2015.

In addition, based on discussions held thus far on individual areas affected by the new standard, the TRG has informed the boards that technical corrections are needed to further articulate the guidance in the standard. As a result, FASB has added several research projects to its agenda and may expose proposals on the following areas of guidance within FASB ASU No. 2014-09:

- Identifying performance obligations
- Licenses
- Principal versus agent (reporting revenue gross vs net)

Refer to each board's website for more information on the status of their efforts.

Conclusion

Upon implementation of the new standard, consistency of revenue recognition principles across geography and industry will be enhanced and financial statement users will be provided better insight through improved disclosure requirements. To provide CPAs with guidance during this time of transition, the AICPA's Financial Reporting Center (FRC) offers invaluable resources on the topic, including a roadmap to ensure that companies take the necessary steps to prepare themselves for the new standard. In addition, the FRC includes a list of conferences, webcasts, and other products to keep you informed on upcoming changes in revenue recognition. Refer to www.aicpa.org/INTERESTAREAS/ FRC/ACCOUNTINGFINANCIALREPORTING/REVENUERECOGNITION/ Pages/RevenueRecognition.aspx to stay updated on the latest information available on revenue recognition.

Appendix J

Schedule of Changes Made to the Text From the Previous Edition

This appendix is nonauthoritative and is included for informational purposes only.

As of May 1, 2015

This schedule of changes identifies areas in the text and footnotes of this guide that have that have changed since the previous edition. Entries in the table of this appendix reflect current numbering, lettering (including that in appendix names), and character designations that resulted from the renumbering or reordering that occurred in the updating of this guide.

Reference	Change
General	Information related to standards issued but not yet effective on or before the "as of" date of this guide has been placed in shaded "Guidance Update" boxes, with a reference to appendix A, "Guidance Updates." See appendix A for more information.
General	"Guidance Update" boxes found in the prior year edition of the guide containing information on guidance now fully effective have been removed. Information and guidance related to these topics have been incorporated into the text of the guide.
General	Editorial changes, including rephrasing, have been made in this guide to improve readability where necessary.
General	The abbreviation for Technical Questions and Answers recently changed from TIS to Q&A. All references in this guide have been updated to reflect this change.
Preface	Updated.
Paragraph 1.04	Revised for changes in industry practice or developments that are not related to an issuance of authoritative guidance.
Special Notice before paragraph 1.05	Deleted due to passage of time.
Paragraphs 1.05, 1.08, and 1.11	Revised due to passage of time.
Former footnote 3 to paragraph 1.11	Deleted due to passage of time.

(continued)

Reference	Change
Paragraph 1.24	Added for changes in industry practice or developments that are not related to an issuance of authoritative guidance.
Former footnote 6 to the heading preceding paragraph 1.30	Deleted due to passage of time.
Paragraph 1.40 and footnotes 10, 11, and 13 to paragraph 1.40	Added for changes in industry practice or developments that are not related to an issuance of authoritative guidance.
Paragraph 1.58	Revised due to passage of time.
Former appendix A to chapter 1	Deleted due to passage of time.
Former footnote 17 to paragraph 2.29 and former footnote 18 to paragraph 2.31	Deleted due to passage of time.
Paragraph 2.31	Revised for changes in industry practice or developments that are not related to an issuance of authoritative guidance.
Paragraph 2.37	Revised to reflect the issuance of FASB Accounting Standards Update (ASU) No. 2011-04, *Fair Value Measurement (Topic 820): Amendments to Achieve Common Fair Value Measurement and Disclosure Requirements in U.S. GAAP and IFRSs.*
Former footnote 27 to paragraph 2.55	Deleted.
Paragraph 2.96	Revised due to passage of time.
Former footnote 37 to paragraph 2.100 and former footnote 42 to paragraph 2.137	Deleted due to passage of time.
Former footnote 43 to paragraph 2.139	Incorporated into paragraph 2.139.
Former footnote 44 to paragraph 1.11	Deleted due to passage of time.
Paragraph 2.149	Revised for changes in industry practice or developments that are not related to an issuance of authoritative guidance.
Paragraphs 2.151, 2.156–.157, and 2.159	Revised due to passage of time.
Footnote 1 to paragraph 3.03	Added for issuance of SEC Release No. 33-9616, *Money Market Fund Reform; Amendments to Form PF.*

Reference	Change
Former footnote 2 to paragraph 3.06	Deleted.
Paragraphs 3.14–.15	Revised for changes in industry practice or developments that are not related to an issuance of authoritative guidance.
Paragraph 3.18	Added for changes in industry practice or developments that are not related to an issuance of authoritative guidance.
Paragraphs 3.25, 3.33, 3.36, 3.39, and 3.56	Revised for changes in industry practice or developments that are not related to an issuance of authoritative guidance.
Footnote 7 to paragraph 3.58	Updated for issuance of SEC Final Rule No. 34-72472, *Application of "Security-Based Swap Dealer" and "Major Security-Based Swap Participant" Definitions to Cross-Border Security-Based Swap Activities.*
Paragraph 3.65	Revised for changes in industry practice or developments that are not related to an issuance of authoritative guidance.
Paragraphs 4.31–.32 and 4.45–.46	Revised for changes in industry practice or developments that are not related to an issuance of authoritative guidance.
Footnote 13 to paragraph 4.46	Added for changes in industry practice or developments that are not related to an issuance of authoritative guidance.
Paragraph 5.25	Revised for changes in industry practice or developments that are not related to an issuance of authoritative guidance.
Paragraph 5.30	Added for issuance of SEC Investment Management Guidance Update 2014-11, *Guidance Regarding Investment Company Consolidation.*
Footnote 1 to the heading preceding paragraph 5.40	Deleted.
Footnote 3 to paragraph 5.40 and footnote 4 to paragraph 5.44	Added for issuance of SEC Investment Management Guidance Update 2014-11.
Paragraphs 5.45 and 5.54	Added for changes in industry practice or developments that are not related to an issuance of authoritative guidance.
Footnote 5 to the heading preceding paragraph 5.55	Added for issuance of SEC Investment Management Guidance Update 2014-11.

(continued)

Reference	Change
Paragraph 5.60	Revised due to passage of time.
Paragraph 5.67	Revised for changes in industry practice or developments that are not related to an issuance of authoritative guidance.
Paragraph 5.71	Revised due to passage of time.
Paragraph 5.72	Revised for issuance of Statement on Auditing Standards No. 128, *Using the Work of Internal Auditors* (AICPA, *Professional Standards*, AU-C sec. 610).
Exhibits 5-3–5-6 to chapter 5	Updated.
Footnotes to chapter 6	Footnotes within chapter 6, where possible, have been incorporated into the chapter text.
Paragraph 6.09	Added from appendix A in prior edition of the guide.
Former paragraph 6.09	Deleted in conjunction with the overall deletion of Technical Questions and Answers section 5250.15, "Application of Certain FASB Interpretation No. 48 (codified in FASB ASC 740-10) Disclosure Requirements to Nonpublic Entities That Do Not Have Uncertain Tax Positions" (AICPA, *Technical Questions and Answers*).
Paragraphs 6.20, 6.24–.25, 6.27, 6.31, and 6.44	Revised for changes in industry practice or developments that are not related to an issuance of authoritative guidance.
Footnotes 4 and 5 to paragraph 6.44	Added for changes in industry practice or developments that are not related to an issuance of authoritative guidance.
Paragraphs 6.45, 6.50–.52, 6.55, and 6.73	Revised for changes in industry practice or developments that are not related to an issuance of authoritative guidance.
Paragraphs 6.80–.81	Revised for issuance of the Tax Increase Prevention Act of 2014.
Paragraph 6.82	Added for issuance of the Tax Increase Prevention Act of 2014.
Paragraphs 6.87, 6.94, 6.106, and 6.121	Revised for changes in industry practice or developments that are not related to an issuance of authoritative guidance.
Footnote 17 to the heading preceding paragraph 7.08	Added for issuance of SEC Investment Management Guidance Update 2014-11.

Reference	*Change*
Paragraph 7.17	Added for changes in industry practice or developments that are not related to an issuance of authoritative guidance.
Footnote 34 to paragraph 7.77	Revised for issuance of FASB ASU No. 2014-11, *Transfers and Servicing (Topic 860): Repurchase-to-Maturity Transactions, Repurchase Financings, and Disclosures.*
Former footnote 36 to paragraph 7.81	Deleted due to passage of time.
Paragraphs 7.101–.102 and 7.124	Revised due to passage of time.
Paragraph 7.160	Revised for issuance of FASB ASU No. 2013-08, *Financial Services—Investment Companies (Topic 946): Amendments to the Scope, Measurement, and Disclosure Requirements.*
Former footnote 46 to paragraph 7.160	Deleted due to passage of time.
Paragraphs 7.191 and 7.196	Revised due to passage of time.
Paragraphs 7.204–.205 and footnote 50 to the heading preceding paragraph 7.204	Added for issuance of SEC Investment Management Guidance Update No. 2013-07, *Business Development Companies–Separate Financial Statements or Summarized Financial Information of Certain Subsidiaries.*
Former footnote 53 to paragraph 7.215	Deleted due to passage of time.
Paragraph 7.224	Revised for changes in industry practice or developments that are not related to an issuance of authoritative guidance.
Paragraph 7.236	Added for issuance of the Commodity Futures Trading Commission Letter No. 13-51.
Footnotes to chapter 8	Footnotes within chapter 8, where possible, have been incorporated into the chapter text.
Former paragraph 8.09	Relocated to paragraphs 8.12–.13.
Paragraph 8.22	Revised due to passage of time.
Former footnote 3 to paragraph 8.24	Deleted due to passage of time.

(continued)

Reference	Change
Paragraph 8.37	Revised for changes in industry practice or developments that are not related to an issuance of authoritative guidance.
Footnote 6 to paragraph 8.46	Added for changes in industry practice or developments that are not related to an issuance of authoritative guidance.
Paragraphs 8.57, 8.64–.66, and 8.68	Revised for issuance of FASB ASU No. 2013-07, *Presentation of Financial Statements (Topic 205): Liquidation Basis of Accounting*.
Paragraphs 8.69–.70	Added for issuance of FASB ASU No. 2013-07.
Paragraph 9.01	Revised for changes in industry practice or developments that are not related to an issuance of authoritative guidance.
Paragraphs 9.18–.19 and 9.21–.22	Updated.
Paragraph 10.36	Revised for changes in industry practice or developments that are not related to an issuance of authoritative guidance.
Paragraphs 10.60 and 10.64 and footnote 2 to the heading preceding paragraph 11.01	Revised due to passage of time.
Footnote 3 to paragraph 11.08	Added for issuance of PCAOB Auditing Standard No. 18, *Related Parties* (AICPA, *PCAOB Standards and Related Rules*, Auditing Standards).
Footnote 4 to paragraph 11.08	Added for issuance of PCAOB Staff Audit Practice Alert No. 13, *Matters Related to the Auditor's Consideration of a Company's Ability to Continue as a Going Concern* (AICPA, *PCAOB Standards and Related Rules*, PCAOB Staff Guidance, sec. 400.13).
Footnote 6 to the heading preceding paragraph 11.12	Added for changes in industry practice or developments that are not related to an issuance of authoritative guidance.
Paragraphs 11.20 and 11.30	Revised for changes in industry practice or developments that are not related to an issuance of authoritative guidance.

Reference	Change
Paragraph 11.33	Added for issuance of AU-C section 9570, *The Auditor's Consideration of an Entity's Ability to Continue as a Going Concern: Auditing Interpretation of AU-C Section 570* (AICPA, *Professional Standards*, AU-C sec. 9570.01–.10).
Paragraph 11.39	Revised for changes in industry practice or developments that are not related to an issuance of authoritative guidance.
Paragraph 11.45	Revised for issuance of PCAOB Auditing Standard No. 18.
Footnote 18 to paragraph 11.45	Added for issuance of PCAOB Release No. 2014-002, *Auditing Standard No. 18, Related Parties, Amendments to Certain PCAOB Auditing Standards Regarding Significant Unusual Transactions, and Other Amendments to PCAOB Auditing Standards* (AICPA, *PCAOB Standards and Related Rules*, Select PCAOB Releases).
Paragraphs 11.53, 11.57, and 11.70	Revised for changes in industry practice or developments that are not related to an issuance of authoritative guidance.
Paragraph 11.72	Added for changes in industry practice or developments that are not related to an issuance of authoritative guidance.
Paragraph 11.74	Revised for changes in industry practice or developments that are not related to an issuance of authoritative guidance.
Former footnote 4 to paragraph 11.44	Incorporated into paragraph 11.44.
Paragraph A.02 in appendix A in chapter 11	Revised for changes in industry practice or developments that are not related to an issuance of authoritative guidance.
Paragraph A.05 in appendix A in chapter 11	Revised due to passage of time.
Former footnote 2 to paragraph A.05 in appendix A in chapter 11 and former footnote 2 to paragraph B.01 in appendix B in chapter 11	Deleted due to passage of time.

(continued)

Reference	Change
Footnote 1 to paragraph C.12 in appendix C in chapter 11	Added for issuance of PCAOB Staff Audit Practice Alert No. 12, *Matters Related to Auditing Revenue in an Audit of Financial Statements* (AICPA, *PCAOB Standards and Related Rules*, PCAOB Staff Guidance, sec. 400.12).
Footnotes 6 and 7 to paragraph C.48 in appendix C in chapter 11	Added for issuance of PCAOB Release No. 2014-002.
Paragraphs 12.02 and 12.12	Revised for changes in industry practice or developments that are not related to an issuance of authoritative guidance.
Former footnote 2 to paragraph 12.02	Deleted due to passage of time.
Former paragraph 12.18 and former footnotes 29–30 to former paragraph 12.18	Relocated to paragraph 12.16.
Footnote 56 to the heading preceding paragraph 12.31	Added for issuance of AICPA and the Center for Audit Quality joint Member Alert.
Paragraph 12.32	Revised for changes in industry practice or developments that are not related to an issuance of authoritative guidance.
Former footnote 68 to paragraph 12.38	Deleted.
Appendixes A–C and F–G	Updated.
Appendixes H–I	Added.
Glossary	Updated.
Index of Pronouncements and Other Technical Guidance	Updated.
Subject Index	Updated.

Glossary

The following terms can be found in the FASB *Accounting Standards Codification* (ASC) glossary:

actual-income-available method. A method to calculate distributions to shareholders from net investment income in which actual net investment income that has been allocated to each class (as recorded on the books) is divided by the record date shares for each class to derive the dividend payable per share.

affiliated entity. An entity that directly or indirectly controls, is controlled by, or is under common control with another entity; also, a party with which the entity may deal if one party has the ability to exercise significant influence over the other's operating and financial policies (further industry specific information provided in the second section of this glossary).

amortization. The process of reducing a recognized liability systematically by recognizing revenues or reducing a recognized asset systematically by recognizing expenses or costs.

amortized cost. The sum of the initial investment less cash collected less write-downs plus yield accreted to date.

annuity contract. A contract in which an insurance entity unconditionally undertakes a legal obligation to provide specified pension benefits to specific individuals in return for a fixed consideration or premium. An annuity contract is irrevocable and involves the transfer of significant risk from the employer to the insurance entity. Annuity contracts are also called allocated contracts.

board-contingent plan. A reimbursement 12b-1 plan that provides that, on the plan's termination, a fund's board of directors or trustees has the option, but not the requirement, to pay the distributor for any excess costs incurred by the distributor.

callable obligation. An obligation is callable at a given date if the creditor has the right at that date to demand, or to give notice of its intention to demand, repayment of the obligation owed to it by the debtor [further industry-specific information is provided in the second section of this glossary under the term **callable**].

call option. A contract that allows the holder to buy a specified quantity of stock from the writer of the contract at a fixed price for a given period [further industry-specific information is provided in the second section of this glossary].

capital infusions. Expenditures made directly to the issuer to ensure that operations are completed, thereby allowing the issuer to generate cash flows to service the debt. Such expenditures are usually nonrecurring. In certain cases, bondholders may receive additional promissory notes, or the original bond instrument may be amended to provide for repayment of the capital infusions.

compensation plan. A plan that provides for a 12b-1 fee, payable by the fund, based on a percentage of the fund's average net assets. The 12b-1 fee may be more or less than the costs incurred by the distributor.

conduit debt securities. Certain limited-obligation revenue bonds, certificates of participation, or similar debt instruments issued by a state or local governmental entity for the express purpose of providing financing for a specific third party (the conduit bond obligor) that is not a part of the state or local government's financial reporting entity. Although conduit debt securities bear the name of the governmental entity that issues them, the governmental entity often has no obligation for such debt beyond the resources provided by a lease or loan agreement with the third party on whose behalf the securities are issued. Further, the conduit bond obligor is responsible for any future financial reporting requirements.

control. The direct or indirect ability to determine the direction of management and policies through ownership, contract, or otherwise [further industry-specific information is provided in the second section of this glossary].

convertible security. A security that is convertible into another security based on a conversion rate. For example, convertible preferred stock that is convertible into common stock on a two-for-one basis (two shares of common for each share of preferred).

distributor. Usually the principal underwriter that sells the fund's capital shares by acting as an agent (intermediary between the fund and an independent dealer or the public) or as a principal, buying capital shares from the fund at net asset value and selling shares through dealers or to the public (see definition of *underwriter* in Section 2(a)(40) of the Investment Company Act of 1940 [the 1940 Act]).

dividends. Dividends paid or payable in cash, other assets, or another class of stock and does not include stock dividends or stock splits (further industry specific information provided in the second section of this glossary).

enhanced 12b-1 plan. A reimbursement 12b-1 plan that provides that, on termination of the plan, the fund is required to continue paying the 12b-1 fee to the extent the distributor has excess costs.

equity security. Any security representing an ownership interest in an entity (for example, common, preferred, or other capital stock) or the right to acquire (for example, warrants, rights, and call options) or dispose of (for example, put options) an ownership interest in an entity at fixed or determinable prices. However, the term does not include convertible debt or preferred stock that by its terms either must be redeemed by the issuing entity or is redeemable at the option of the investor.

exchange market. A market in which closing prices are both readily available and generally representative of fair value. An example of such a market is the New York Stock Exchange. [Further industry-specific information is provided in the second section of this glossary under the term **exchange**].

fail-to-deliver. A fail-to-deliver is a securities sale to another broker-dealer that has not been delivered to the buying broker-dealer by the close of business on the settlement date.

fail-to-receive. A fail-to-receive is a securities purchase from another broker-dealer not received from the selling broker-dealer by the close of business on the settlement date.

fair value. The price that would be received to sell an asset or paid to transfer a liability in an orderly transaction between market participants at the measurement date.

Fed Funds effective swap rate (or overnight index swap rate). The fixed rate on a U.S. dollar, constant-notional interest rate swap that has its variable-rate leg referenced to the Fed Funds effective rate with no additional spread over the Fed Funds effective rate on that variable-rate leg. That fixed rate is the derived rate that would result in the swap having a zero fair value at inception because the present value of fixed cash flows, based on that rate, equates to the present value of the variable cash flows.

forward exchange contract. A forward exchange contract is an agreement between two parties to exchange different currencies at a specified exchange rate at an agreed-upon future date.

front-end load. A sales commission or charge payable at the time of purchase of mutual fund shares.

futures contract. A standard and transferable form of contract that binds the seller to deliver to the bearer a standard amount and grade of a commodity to a specific location at a specified time. It usually includes a schedule of premiums and discounts for quality variation.

high-yield debt securities. Corporate and municipal debt securities having a lower-than-investment-grade credit rating (BB+ or lower by Standard & Poor's, or Ba or lower by Moody's). Because high-yield debt securities typically are used when lower-cost capital is not available, they have interest rates several percentage points higher than investment-grade debt and often have shorter maturities. These high-yielding corporate and municipal debt obligations are frequently referred to as junk bonds [further industry-specific information is provided in the second section of this glossary under the term **junk bonds**].

interest method. The method used to arrive at a periodic interest cost (including amortization) that will represent a level effective rate on the sum of the face amount of the debt and (plus or minus) the unamortized premium or discount and expense at the beginning of each period.

liquidity. An asset's or liability's nearness to cash [further industry specific information is provided in the second section of this glossary].

mortgage-backed securities. Securities issued by a governmental agency or corporation (for example, Government National Mortgage Association [GNMA] or Federal Home Loan Mortgage Corporation [FHLMC]) or by private issuers (for example, Federal National Mortgage Association [FNMA], banks, and mortgage banking entities). Mortgage-backed securities generally are referred to as mortgage participation certificates or pass-through certificates. A participation certificate represents an undivided interest in a pool of specific mortgage loans. Periodic payments on GNMA participation certificates are backed by the U.S. government. Periodic payments on FHLMC and FNMA certificates are guaranteed by those corporations, but are not backed by the U.S. government.

most advantageous market. The market that maximizes the amount that would be received to sell the asset or minimizes the amount that would be paid to transfer the liability, after taking into account transaction costs and transportation costs.

net asset value per share. Net asset value per share is the amount of net assets attributable to each share of capital stock (other than senior equity securities, that is, preferred stock) outstanding at the close of the period. It excludes the effects of assuming conversion of outstanding convertible securities, whether or not their conversion would have a diluting effect [further industry-specific information is provided in the second section of this glossary].

nonregistered investment partnerships—financial highlights. Nonregistered investment partnerships, when disclosing financial highlights, shall interpret the terms classes, units, and theoretical investments as follows:

    a.   Classes. Nonregistered investment funds typically have one of the following two classes of ownership interest, with one class being the management interest in the fund and the other being the investment interest:

        1. For unitized funds (that is, funds with units specifically called for in the governing underlying legal or offering documents), the management interest usually is a voting class and the investment interest is a nonvoting class. Temporary series of shares (that is, shares that are intended at the time of issuance to be consolidated at a later date with another specified series of shares that remains outstanding indefinitely) are not considered separate classes. Permanent series of a class of share shall be the basis for which that share's financial highlights are determined and presented.

        2. For nonunitized funds, the management interest usually is the general partner class and the investment interest usually is the limited partner class. Generally, a class has certain rights as governed by underlying legal documents or offering documents and local law. Rights to certain investments that do not otherwise affect the rights available under the underlying legal documents and local law do not ordinarily represent a separate share class. For example, rights to income and gains from a specific investment attributed solely to investors at the date the investment is made (side-pocket investments) are not considered to give rise to a share class. Similarly, a temporary series of shares is not considered a share class.

    b.   Units. Only funds with units specifically called for in the governing underlying legal or offering documents shall be considered unitized. Some funds may employ units for convenience in making allocations to investors for internal accounting or bookkeeping purposes, but the units are not required or specified by legal or offering documents, and for all other purposes operate like nonunitized investment partnerships. For per-share operating performance, those funds are not considered unitized.

    c.   Theoretical investment. The term theoretical investment in FASB ASC 946-205–50-20 shall be considered as the actual aggregate amount of capital invested by each reporting class of investor as of the beginning of the fiscal reporting period, adjusted for cash flows related to capital contributions or withdrawals during the period.

offering costs. Offering costs include all of the following:

a. Legal fees pertaining to the investment company's shares offered for sale

b. Securities and Exchange Commission (SEC) and state registration fees

c. Underwriting and other similar costs

d. Costs of printing prospectuses for sales purposes

e. Initial fees paid to be listed on an exchange

f. Tax opinion costs related to offering of shares

g. Initial agency fees of securing the rating for bonds or preferred stock issued by closed-end funds.

payment-in-kind bonds. Bonds in which the issuer has the option at each interest payment date of making interest payments in cash or in additional debt securities. Those additional debt securities are referred to as baby or bunny bonds. Baby bonds generally have the same terms, including maturity dates and interest rates, as the original bonds (parent payment-in-kind bonds). Interest on baby bonds may also be paid in cash or in additional like-kind debt securities at the option of the issuer.

public business entity. A public business entity is a business entity meeting any one of the criteria below. Neither a not-for-profit entity nor an employee benefit plan is a business entity.

a. It is required by the U.S. Securities and Exchange Commission (SEC) to file or furnish financial statements, or does file or furnish financial statements (including voluntary filers), with the SEC (including other entities whose financial statements or financial information are required to be or are included in a filing).

b. It is required by the Securities Exchange Act of 1934 (the Act), as amended, or rules or regulations promulgated under the Act, to file or furnish financial statements with a regulatory agency other than the SEC.

c. It is required to file or furnish financial statements with a foreign or domestic regulatory agency in preparation for the sale of or for purposes of issuing securities that are not subject to contractual restrictions on transfer.

d. It has issued, or is a conduit bond obligor for, securities that are traded, listed, or quoted on an exchange or an over-the-counter market.

e. It has one or more securities that are not subject to contractual restrictions on transfer, and it is required by law, contract, or regulation to prepare U.S. GAAP financial statements (including footnotes) and make them publicly available on a periodic basis (for example, interim or annual periods). An entity must meet both of these conditions to meet this criterion.

An entity may meet the definition of a public business entity solely because its financial statements or financial information is included in another entity's filing with the SEC. In that case, the entity is only a public business entity for purposes of financial statements that are filed or furnished with the SEC.

put option. A contract that allows the holder to sell a specified quantity of stock to the writer of the contract at a fixed price during a given period [further industry-specific information is provided in the second section of this glossary].

record-share method. A method to calculate distributions to shareholders from net investment income in which the sum of net investment income available for all classes after deducting allocated expenses, but before consideration of class-specific expenses, is divided by the total outstanding shares on the dividend record date for all classes to arrive at a gross dividend rate for all shares. From this gross rate, an amount per share for each class (the amount of incremental expenses accrued during the period divided by the record date shares outstanding for the class) is subtracted. The result is the per-share dividend available for each class.

reimbursement plan. A plan that provides for a 12b-1 fee, payable by the fund, that may not exceed the lesser of an annual percentage of the fund's average net assets or actual costs incurred by the distributor net of CDSL received by the distributor.

repurchase agreement (repo agreement).[1] An agreement under which the transferor (repo party) transfers a security to a transferee (repo counterparty or reverse party) in exchange for cash and concurrently agrees to reacquire that security at a future date for an amount equal to the cash exchanged plus a stipulated interest factor. Instead of cash, other securities or letters of credit sometimes are exchanged. Some repurchase agreements call for repurchase of securities that need not be identical to the securities transferred.

repurchase agreement accounted for as a collateralized borrowing (repo agreement). A transaction in which a seller-borrower of securities sells those securities to a buyer-lender with an agreement to repurchase them at a stated price plus interest at a specified date or in specified circumstances. A repurchase agreement accounted for as a collateralized borrowing is a repo that does not qualify for sale accounting under FASB ASC 860, *Transfers and Servicing*. The payable under a repurchase agreement accounted for as a collateralized borrowing refers to the amount of the seller-borrower's obligation recognized for the future repurchase of the securities from the buyer-lender. In certain industries, the terminology is reversed; that is, entities in those industries refer to this type of agreement as a reverse repo (see reverse repurchase agreement accounted for as a collateralized borrowing).

reverse repurchase agreement accounted for as a collateralized borrowing (reverse repo or resale agreement). A transaction that is accounted for as a collateralized lending in which a buyer-lender buys securities with an agreement to resell them to the seller-borrower at a stated

---

[1] FASB Accounting Standards Update No. 2014-11, *Transfers and Servicing (Topic 860): Repurchase-to-Maturity Transactions, Repurchase Financings, and Disclosures,* was issued in June 2014. The amendments in ASU No. 2014-11 change the definition of a *repurchase agreement.* Refer to section A.02 in appendix A, "Guidance Updates," for more information.

price plus interest at a specified date or in specified circumstances. The receivable under a reverse repurchase agreement accounted for as a collateralized borrowing refers to the amount due from the seller-borrower for the repurchase of the securities from the buyer-lender. In certain industries, the terminology is reversed; that is, entities in those industries refer to this type of agreement as a repo (see **repurchase agreement accounted for as a collateralized borrowing**).

return of capital. Distributions by investment companies in excess of tax-basis earnings and profits.

separate account. A special account established by an insurance entity solely for the purpose of investing the assets of one or more plans. Funds in a separate account are not commingled with other assets of the insurance entity for investment purposes [further industry-specific information is provided in the second section of this glossary].

simultaneous-equations method. A method to calculate distributions to shareholders from net investment income that seeks to ensure, by using simultaneous equations, that the distribution rates will differ among the classes by the anticipated differential in expense ratios.

step bonds. Bonds that involve a combination of deferred-interest payment dates and increasing interest payment amounts over the bond lives and, thus, bear some similarity to zero-coupon bonds and to traditional debentures.

stock dividend. An issuance by a corporation of its own common shares to its common shareholders without consideration and under conditions indicating that such action is prompted mainly by a desire to give the recipient shareholders some ostensibly separate evidence of a part of their respective interests in accumulated corporate earnings without distribution of cash or other property that the board of directors or trustees deems necessary or desirable to retain in the business. A stock dividend takes nothing from the property of the corporation and adds nothing to the interests of the stockholders; that is, the corporation's property is not diminished and the interests of the stockholders are not increased. The proportional interest of each shareholder remains the same.

stock split. An issuance by a corporation of its own common shares to its common shareholders without consideration and under conditions indicating that such action is prompted mainly by a desire to increase the number of outstanding shares for the purpose of effecting a reduction in their unit market price and, thereby, of obtaining wider distribution and improved marketability of the shares. Sometimes called a stock split-up.

structured note. A debt instrument whose cash flows are linked to the movement in one or more indexes, interest rates, foreign exchange rates, commodities prices, prepayment rates, or other market variables. Structured notes are issued by U.S. government-sponsored enterprises, multilateral development banks, municipalities, and private entities. The notes typically contain embedded (but not separable or detachable) forward components or option components such as caps, calls, and floors. Contractual cash flows for principal, interest, or both can vary in amount and timing throughout the life of the note based on nontraditional indexes or nontraditional uses of traditional interest rates or indexes.

traditional 12b-1 plan. A compensation or reimbursement plan pursuant to Rule 12b-1 that permits the use of a fund's assets to pay distribution-related expenses under certain conditions. The 12b-1 fees under traditional 12b-1 plans are normally discontinued upon plan termination, but may continue to be paid after plan termination under a board-contingent plan.

transfer. The conveyance of a noncash financial asset by and to someone other than the issuer of that financial asset. A transfer includes the following

    a. Selling a receivable

    b. Putting a receivable into a securitization trust

    c. Posting a receivable as collateral.

    A transfer excludes the following

    a. The origination of a receivable

    b. Settlement of a receivable

    c. The restructuring of a receivable into a security in a troubled debt restructuring [further industry-specific information is provided in the second section of this glossary].

variable annuity contract. An annuity in which the amount of payments to be made are specified in units, rather than in dollars. When payment is due, the amount is determined based on the value of the investments in the annuity fund [further industry-specific information is provided in the second section of this glossary under the term **variable annuity**].

warrant. A security that gives the holder the right to purchase shares of common stock in accordance with the terms of the instrument, usually upon payment of a specified amount [further industry-specific information is provided in the second section of this glossary].

workout expenditures. Professional fees (legal, accounting, appraisal) paid to entities unaffiliated with the investment company's advisor or sponsor in connection with any of the following:

    a. Capital infusions

    b. Restructurings or plans of reorganization

    c. Ongoing efforts to protect or enhance an investment

    d. The pursuit of other claims or legal actions.

The following is a list of additional terms that have been used in this guide and further information on select terms defined in the FASB ASC glossary:

401(k) plan. A plan by which an employee may elect, as an alternative to receiving taxable cash as compensation or a bonus, to contribute pretax dollars to a qualified tax-deferred retirement plan.

accumulation unit. The basic valuation unit of a deferred variable annuity. Such units are valued daily to reflect investment performance and the prorated daily deduction for expenses.

adjustable rate mortgage. A mortgage loan whose interest is reset periodically to reflect market rate changes.

adviser. See **investment adviser**.

advisory and service fee (contract). The fee charged to an investment company by its investment adviser under a contract approved by vote of a majority of the company's shares. The fee is usually computed as a percentage of the average net assets and may also provide for an additional bonus or penalty based on performance (see **incentive fee**).

affiliated company (person). Under Sections 2(a)(2) and 2(a)(3) of the 1940 Act, an *affiliated company* means a company that is an affiliated person. An *affiliated person of another person* means (*a*) any person directly or indirectly owning, controlling, or holding, with power to vote, 5 percent or more of the outstanding voting securities of such other person; (*b*) any person 5 percent or more of whose outstanding voting securities are directly or indirectly owned, controlled, or held, with power to vote, by such other person; (*c*) any person directly or indirectly controlling, controlled by, or under common control with such other person; (*d*) any officer, director, partner, copartner, or employees of such other person; (*e*) if such other person is an investment company, any investment adviser thereof or any member of an advisory board thereof; and (*f*) if such other person is an unincorporated investment company not having a board of directors, the depositor thereof (see **control** and **controlled company**).

against the box. Short sale by the holder of a long position in the same stock.

American depository receipt (ADR). A certificate issued by an American bank to evidence ownership of original foreign shares. The certificate is transferable and can be traded. The original foreign stock certificate is deposited with a foreign branch or correspondent bank of the issuing American bank.

as-of transaction. A transaction recorded on the books of an investment company after the date on which the transactions should have been recorded. This term relates to shareholder purchases and redemptions and also portfolio security purchases and sales.

asked price. The lowest price that a dealer is willing to accept to sell a security at a particular time (also known as the offer price).

asset allocation. Apportioning of investment funds among categories of assets, such as cash equivalents, stocks, and fixed income instruments.

baby bond. A bond having a par value of less than $1,000, usually $25–$500. Also refers to the distribution of additional bonds instead of cash payments in connection with interest payable on a payment-in-kind bond or similar security (also known as bunny bonds).

banker's acceptance. A time or sight draft drawn on a commercial bank by a borrower, usually in connection with a commercial transaction. The borrower is liable as is the bank, which is the primary obligor, to pay the draft at its face amount on the maturity date.

basis point. A measurement of changes in price or yields for fixed-income securities. One basis point equals 0.01 percent, or 10 cents per $1,000 per annum.

bid price. The highest price that a dealer is willing to pay to purchase a security at a particular time.

bifurcation. When applied to securities traded in foreign currencies, the separation of underlying factors relating to a transaction initially measured in one currency and reported in a second currency. Any difference between originally recorded amounts and currently consummated or measured amounts can be split into changes in the foreign exchange rate and changes in foreign currency-denominated fair value.

Blue Sky laws. State laws governing the sale of securities, including mutual fund shares, and activities of brokers and dealers within the particular state and applicable also in interstate transactions having some substantial connection with the state.

bond discount. The difference between the face amount of a bond and the lower price paid by a buyer.

bond premium. The difference between the face amount of a bond and the higher price paid by a buyer.

book entry shares. Share ownership evidenced by records maintained by a transfer agent, rather than by physical stock certificates.

break point. A quantity of securities purchased at which a lower sales charge takes effect. Also, an aggregate amount of investment company assets in excess of which a lower rate of investment advisory fee is chargeable.

broker. Any person engaged in the business of effecting transactions in securities for the account of others (with certain exceptions). This does not include any person solely by reason of the fact that such person is an underwriter for one or more investment companies (see Section 2[a][6] of the 1940 Act).

business development company (BDC). A company defined in Section 2(a)(48) of the 1940 Act as a closed-end investment company that chooses to be treated as a BDC under the act and is operated to make investments in eligible portfolio companies, follow-on investments in former eligible portfolio companies acquired by the company when the investee was an eligible portfolio company, and investments in certain bankrupt or insolvent companies.

CBOE. Abbreviation for the Chicago Board Options Exchange, a national securities exchange based in Chicago that provides a continuous market for trading in put and call options.

CFTC. Abbreviation for the Commodity Futures Trading Commission, an agency established by Congress to regulate U.S. commodity futures markets and futures commission merchants. Among other things, this agency establishes rules governing the minimum financial, reporting, and audit requirements of its members. Its function is similar to that performed by the SEC in regulating broker-dealers in securities and various securities markets.

CUSIP (number). A means of uniformly describing and identifying specific security issues in numeric form. Developed by the Committee on Uniform Security Identification Procedure.

callable. Redeemable by the issuer before the scheduled maturity. The issuer may pay the holders a premium price if such a security is retired early. Such securities are usually called when interest rates fall so significantly that the issuer can save money by floating new bonds at lower rates (defined in the FASB ASC glossary, as presented in the first section of this glossary under the term **callable obligation**).

call option. A contract that entitles the holder to buy (call), at his or her option, a specified number of underlying units of a particular security at a specified price (strike price) either on (European style) or at any time until (American style) the stated expiration date of the contract. The option, which may be transferable, is bought in the expectation of a price rise above the strike price. If the price rises, the buyer exercises or sells the option. If the price does not rise, the buyer lets the option expire and loses only the cost of the option. There is a listed and also an over-the-counter (OTC) market in options. During the existence of an option, the exercise price and number of underlying units are adjusted on the ex-dividend date for cash dividends, rights, and stock dividends or splits. (Defined in the FASB ASC glossary, as presented in the first section of this glossary.)

capital gain dividend. Under IRC Section 852 (and as used in chapter 6, "Taxes," of this guide), any dividend or part thereof that is reported by the company as a capital gain dividend in written statements furnished to its shareholders, except in the case of excess reported amounts. If the aggregate reported amount with respect to the company for any taxable year exceeds the net capital gain of the company for such taxable year, a capital gain dividend is the excess of the reported capital gain dividend amount over the excess reported amount that is allocable to such reported capital gain dividend amount. In nontax contexts, however, this term is used interchangeably with capital gains distribution.

capital gain or loss. A profit or loss realized from the sale of capital assets, such as *portfolio securities*, as defined in IRC Section 1221.

capital gains distribution. A dividend paid to investment company shareholders from net capital gains realized by a regulated investment company on the disposition of portfolio securities (see Section 19[b] and Rules 19a-1 and 19b-1 of the 1940 Act).

certificates of deposit. Short-term, interest-bearing certificates issued by commercial banks or savings and loan associations against funds deposited in the issuing institution.

classes of shares. Securities offered by an investment company with different shareholder requirements and commitments. For example, class A shares may be sold with a front-end load, but class B shares may be sold with a 12b-1 asset-based charge and a contingent deferred sales charge.

clearing agency. A central location at which security transactions of members are matched to determine the quantities to be received or delivered.

closed-end fund. An investment company having a fixed number of shares outstanding, which it does not stand ready to redeem. Its shares are traded similarly to those of other public corporations. See Section 5(a) of the 1940 Act.

collateralized mortgage obligation (CMO). A mortgage-backed bond that separates mortgage pools into different maturity classes called tranches. Each tranche is then sold separately.

commercial paper. Short-term, unsecured promissory notes issued by corporations. Commercial paper is usually sold on a discount basis (see Section 3[a][3] of the Securities Act of 1933 [the 1933 Act] and Section 3[a][10] of the Securities Exchange Act of 1934 [the 1934 Act]).

common (collective) trust fund. An account maintained by the trust department of a bank or trust company for the pooling of investment funds of its own trust account customers. It is exempt from the 1940 Act under Section 3(c)(3) or 3(c)(11).

contingent deferred sales charge (CDSC). A charge related to an issuer's payments for distribution pursuant to a Rule 12b-1 plan. It is imposed only on redemption and may be reduced or eliminated as the duration of ownership continues. Also known as a contingent deferred sales load (CDSL) or a back-end load.

contractual plan. A type of accumulation plan under which the total intended investment is specified with provisions for periodic payments over a stated period. Such plans are sometimes called front-end load plans because a substantial portion of the sales charge applicable to the total investment is usually deducted from early payments (see Sections 2[a][27] and 27 of the 1940 Act concerning periodic purchase plans).

control. Defined by Section 2(a)(9) of the 1940 Act as the power to exercise (regardless of whether exercised) a controlling influence over the management or policies of a company, unless that power results solely from an official position with the company (defined in the FASB ASC glossary, as presented in the first section of this glossary). Any person who owns beneficially, either directly or through one or more controlled companies, more than 25 percent of the voting securities of a company shall be presumed to control such company. Any person who does not so own more than 25 percent of the voting securities of any company shall be presumed not to control such company. A natural person shall be presumed not to be a controlled person within the meaning of this title. Any such presumption may be rebutted by evidence.

controlled company. Defined by the 1940 Act as a direct or an indirect ownership of more than 25 percent of the outstanding voting securities of a company (see **control** and **affiliated company**).

corporate actions. An action by a company's board of directors or trustees, including dividend declarations, reorganizations, mergers, and acquisitions.

corporate bonds. Debt instruments issued by private corporations as distinct from those issued by government agencies or municipalities. Corporate bonds have three distinguishing features: they are taxable; they normally have a par value of $1,000; and they normally have a term maturity.

custodian. A bank; trust company; or, less frequently, a member of a national securities exchange responsible for receiving delivery and the safekeeping of an investment company's cash and securities (see Section 17[f] of the 1940 Act).

DTC. Acronym for the Depository Trust Company. A depository for eligible securities that facilitates clearance between member organizations and banks without the necessity of receiving or delivering actual certificates.

DVP. Abbreviation for delivery versus payment, under which physical possession and ownership are transferred only upon cash payment.

daily limits. Limits established by exchanges on fluctuations in prices of futures contracts (other than the current month's delivery contracts) during a trading session.

dealer. Any person engaged in the business of buying and selling securities for such person's own account through a broker or otherwise (does not include an insurance or investment company). Mutual fund shares are frequently sold through dealers (see Section 3[a][5] of the 1934 Act and Section 2[a][11] of the 1940 Act).

declaration date. The day on which the board of directors or trustees or, if so authorized, a committee of the board announces a distribution of cash or other specified assets to be paid at a specified future time to shareholders of record on a specified record date. The amount of distribution is usually specified on a per share basis, although investment company distributions are occasionally specified in an aggregate amount to assure the desired federal income tax consequence.

deemed dividend. A dividend not paid in cash or other consideration. For a regulated investment company, the term is used in connection with net realized long-term capital gains that are retained undistributed, in whole or part, by the regulated investment company and on which it pays the federal income tax on behalf of shareholders as a whole. Each shareholder reports his or her share of the deemed dividend as a long-term capital gain and receives (*a*) a credit against his or her federal income tax liability for his or her share of the tax paid by the regulated investment company and also (*b*) an increase in basis of those shares. (See **designated capital gain**.)

deficiency dividend. A special dividend attributable to the underdistribution of taxable income paid by a regulated investment company to protect its special tax status.

delayed delivery contract. A transaction involving deferral of the settlement date beyond normal terms to some point further in the future, as agreed upon by both buyer and seller.

depositor. A person other than the trustee or custodian who is primarily responsible for the organization of a unit investment trust (UIT) that deposits the portfolio with (that is, sells the portfolio to) the trustee and who has certain continuing responsibilities in administering the affairs of that trust (see Sections 17(a)(1)(C) and 26 of the 1940 Act).

designated capital gain. A term used by a regulated investment company to refer to its election to retain long-term capital gains realized during the year (see **deemed dividend**).

distributions. Dividends paid from net investment income and realized capital gains (see **capital gains distribution**).

diversification. Investment of a portfolio in securities that have different kinds of investment risk in order to moderate the portfolio's overall risk of loss. Most commonly refers to diversification by a securities issuer but can also be used in reference to industry exposure; creditworthiness or quality of security issuers taken as a whole; or, in international portfolios, exposure to national (or regional) economies. Sometimes, the term may be used in reference to security kinds (for example, fixed income versus equity securities).

diversified investment company. A management investment company having at least 75 percent of its total assets in cash and cash items (including receivables), government securities, securities of other investment companies, and other securities limited to not more than 5 percent of its total assets in any one issuer and not more than 10 percent of the voting securities of any one issuer, in accordance with Section 5(b)(1) of the 1940 Act.

dividends. Pro rata payments to shareholders, typically from earnings. In the context of investment companies, applied to payments derived from net investment income and realized capital gains (see **distributions**). (Defined in the FASB ASC glossary, as presented in the first section of this glossary.)

dollar roll. A series of securities transactions in which an investment company purchases a mortgage-backed security (such as terms to be announced) and concurrently sells that security for settlement at a future date.

eligible portfolio company. Defined by Section 2(a)(46) of the 1940 Act of 1940 as any issuer that (*a*) is organized under the laws of, and has its principal place of business in, any state or states; (*b*) is neither an investment company (other than a small business investment company [SBIC] that is licensed by the Small Business Administration [SBA] to operate under the Small Business Investment Act of 1958 and that is a wholly-owned subsidiary of the BDC) nor a company that would be an investment company, except for the exclusion from the definition of *investment company* in Section 3(c); and (*c*) satisfies one of the following: (i) does not have a class of securities registered on a national securities exchange or eligible for margin purchase under Federal Reserve Board rules; (ii) is actively controlled by a BDC, either alone or as part of a group acting together, and has an affiliate of the BDC on its board of directors; (iii) has total assets of not more than $4 million and capital and surplus (shareholders' equity less retained earnings) of not less than $2 million; (iv) meets such other criteria as the SEC may, by rule, establish as consistent with the public interest, the protection of investors, and the purposes fairly intended by the policy and provisions of the 1940 Act. In most instances, it must be a company to which the BDC extends significant managerial assistance, either through the exercise of control or through an arrangement whereby the BDC, acting through its directors, officers, and employees, provides significant guidance and counsel concerning the management, operations, or business objectives and policies of the company.

equalization. An accounting method used to prevent a dilution of the continuing shareholders' per share equity in undistributed net investment income caused by the continuous sales and redemptions of capital shares.

eurodollars. U.S. dollars deposited in banks outside the United States.

evaluator. One who determines the daily or periodic value per unit for UITs.

exchange. An organized forum for the trading of securities or commodities by members for their own accounts or the accounts of their customers. The most active U. S. securities exchange is the New York Stock Exchange (NYSE); the most active domestic commodities exchanges are the CBOE and the Chicago Mercantile Exchange. (Defined in the FASB ASC glossary, as presented in the first section of this glossary, under the term **exchange market**.)

exchange privilege. The ability of a shareholder to redeem shares of an open-end fund and simultaneously purchase shares of another open-end fund within the same family of investment companies, often at no or reduced fees. When applied to variable annuities and variable life insurance contracts, refers to the ability of an investor to exchange shares of one fund owned indirectly through the contract for another fund offered as an investment option within that contract.

exchange traded fund (ETF). A form of open-end investment company (or, less frequently, a UIT), the shares of which are traded on a stock exchange. An ETF also permits subscriptions or redemptions daily but only through the in-kind receipt or delivery of specified quantities of specific securities in exchange for a minimum number of ETF shares (referred to as a creation unit).

excise tax. A 4 percent tax imposed if a regulated investment company (RIC) fails to make minimum distributions to shareholders each calendar year. The required distribution is the sum of 98 percent of net investment income for the calendar year and 98.2 percent of capital gain net income for the 12 months ended October 31. The difference between actual distributions and the required distribution is subject to the tax. If the RIC distributed less than 100 percent of income in a prior year, the shortfall increases the current-year required distribution.

ex-dividend or ex-distribution date. Synonym for shares being traded without dividend or capital gains distribution. The buyer of a stock selling ex-dividend does not acquire a right to receive a previously declared but not-yet-paid dividend. Dividends are payable on a fixed date to shareholders recorded on the stock transfer books of the disbursing company as of a previous date of record (see **record date**). For example, a dividend may be declared as payable to holders of record on the books of the disbursing company on a given Friday. Because three business days are allowed for delivery of the security in regular-way transactions, the stock is declared ex-dividend as of the opening of the market on the preceding Wednesday (or on one business day earlier for each intervening nontrading day). Therefore, anyone buying the stock on and after Wednesday is not entitled to the dividend. For nontraded shares of mutual funds, the ex-dividend date is the same as the record date.

expense limitation. An agreement between an investment company and its investment adviser in which the adviser agrees to limit its advisory fee or the total expenses of the company to an amount that is usually based on a stipulated relationship between total expenses and average net assets. Limitations may be either contractual or voluntary.

ex-rights. Similar to ex-dividend. The buyer of a stock selling ex-rights is not entitled to a rights distribution.

ex-warrants. Stocks or bonds trading without attached warrants, entitling holders to subscribe to additional shares within specified periods and at specified prices.

FINRA. Financial Industry Regulatory Authority, formed by the combination of the regulatory functions of the National Association of Securities Dealers, Inc. (NASD) and the NYSE.

face amount certificate company. As defined by Section 28 of the 1940 Act, an investment company that issues *installment-type certificates*, as defined by Section 2(a)(15) of the act.

fixed income security. A preferred stock or debt security with a stated percentage or dollar income return.

flat. A method of trading in certain kinds of bonds, usually income bonds that do not pay interest unless it has been earned and declared payable, or bonds on which the issuer has defaulted in paying interest. The seller of a bond trading flat is not entitled to receive the interest that has accrued since the date of the last interest payment and delivers the bond with all unpaid coupons attached or a due bill authorizing the buyer to collect interest, if any, which may be paid by the issuer in the future.

forward placement commitment contract. An OTC contract for delayed delivery of securities in which the buyer agrees to buy, and the seller agrees to deliver, a specified security at a specified price at a specified future date.

forward pricing. The pricing of mutual fund shares for sale, repurchase, or redemption at a price next computed after an order has been received. Mutual fund shares are usually priced once or twice per day.

guaranteed investment contract. Nontradeable contract that guarantees the return of principal and a specific minimum rate of return on invested capital over the life of the contract. Many contracts also provide for withdrawals of principal at par at specified dates or upon specified conditions before maturity, or both. Most frequently used by pension and retirement plans in which withdrawals are permitted to fund retirement benefits, payments to employees leaving the company, or transfers of benefits among investment options (see also FASB ASC 946-210-45 and 946-210-50).

hedge fund. A general, nonlegal term used to describe private, unregistered investment pools that are not widely available to the public and have traditionally been limited to accredited investors and large institutions. Hedge funds likely originated as private investment funds that combined long and short equity positions within a single leveraged investment portfolio. Currently, hedge funds employ a wide variety of trading strategies and techniques to generate financial returns, and may or may not utilize complex derivative instruments or leverage in the investment portfolio. Hedge funds are not mutual funds and, as such, are not subject to certain regulations that apply to mutual funds for the protection of its investors.

hedging. A means of risk protection against loss, typically reducing market price risk, market interest rate risk, foreign exchange risk, or credit risk.

hypothecate. To pledge securities to brokers as collateral for loans made to purchase securities or cover short sales.

illiquid. Not readily convertible into cash, such as a stock, bond, or commodity that is not actively traded and would be difficult to sell in a current sale. Not more than 15 percent of the net assets of an open-end investment company registered under the 1940 Act (5 percent for money market funds) may be invested in illiquid securities.

inadvertent investment company. An industrial or service company deemed to be an investment company because it inadvertently meets the criteria of Section 3(a) of the 1940 Act and must register under that act and comply with its provisions. Under the 1940 Act, also known as a transient investment company.

incentive allocation. A partnership allocation based upon the fund's performance reallocating profits from the capital account of a limited partner to the capital account of a general partner. The incentive may be an absolute percentage of the fund's performance or a percentage of performance in excess of a specified benchmark.

incentive fee. A fee paid to an investment adviser based upon the fund's performance for the period. The incentive may be an absolute share of the fund's performance or a share of performance in excess of a specified benchmark. For registered investment companies offered to the general public, any performance fee must be based on a comparison of performance to a specified index and must provide for an equivalent penalty if the performance fails to match the index return.

index. A statistical composite that measures changes in the economy or financial markets.

index option. Calls or puts on indexes of stock, or less frequently, other securities.

indexed security. A security whose value is based on the absolute or relative value, over a period of time or at a point in time, of a financial indicator, such as a measure of interest rates, exchange rates, commodity prices, or stock prices.

indexing. Constructing a portfolio to match the composition or performance of a broad-based index.

initial margin deposit. A commodity transaction term meaning the amount of money or its equivalent specified by the commodity exchange under which the contract is traded, held as a good faith deposit to make sure that the customer meets the variation margin requirement. Maintenance margin refers to additional deposits. (See **margin**, a securities transaction term.)

interested person. Under Section 2(a)(19) of the 1940 Act, a person affiliated with an investment company, a member of his or her *immediate family* (as defined), a person affiliated with the company's investment adviser or principal underwriter, an investment company's legal counsel, any broker or dealer or its affiliated persons, and any other person as so determined administratively by the SEC based on relationships.

interval fund. A form of closed-end fund registered using Form N-2 under the 1933 Act and the 1940 Act, which may sell shares to investors on a regular basis (as frequently as daily) but only repurchases shares at specified intervals (for example, monthly or quarterly).

inverse floater. A floating rate note in which the rate paid increases (decreases) at a multiple of declines (rises) in the floating market rate.

investment adviser (manager). Under Section 2(a)(20) of the 1940 Act, any person who, pursuant to contract with an investment company, regularly furnishes advice with respect to the desirability of investing in, purchasing or selling securities or other property, or is empowered to determine what securities or other property shall be purchased or sold.

Investment Advisers Act of 1940. Provides for the registration and regulation of most persons who render investment advice to individuals or institutions, including investment companies, for compensation.

investment advisory agreement. An agreement between an investment company and investment manager engaging the investment manager to provide investment advice to the investment company for a fee (see Sections 15[a], 15[c], and 36[b] of the 1940 Act).

investment company. An entity that pools shareholders' funds to provide the shareholders with professional investment management.

Investment Company Act of 1940. Provides for the registration and regulation of investment companies.

investment company trade associations. Such associations as the Investment Company Institute, the National Investment Company Service Association, the Mutual Fund Education Alliance, the National Association of Small Business Investment Companies, the Mutual Fund Directors Forum, the Independent Directors Council, and the Closed-End Fund Association.

investment grade bonds. Bonds rated by a rating service in one of its top four categories (AAA to BBB/Baa).

investment partnership. A partnership, usually a limited partnership, organized under state law to invest and trade in securities.

junk bonds. Bonds with a rating of BB+/Ba or lower issued by a company without a long record of sales and earnings or with questionable credit strength, which often include step-interest and payment-in-kind bonds. (Also known as high-yield bonds and defined in the FASB ASC glossary, as presented in the first section of this glossary, under the term **high-yield debt securities**.)

LIBOR (London Interbank Offered Rate). The rate of interest that the most creditworthy international banks dealing in eurodollars charge each other for large loans. Various instruments' rates are tied to LIBOR.

letter of intent. An agreement by which a shareholder agrees to buy a specified dollar amount of mutual fund shares, usually over 13 months, in return for a reduction in the sales charge applicable to a comparable lump-sum purchase.

leverage. Borrowing to enhance return. Buying securities on margin is an example of leverage.

liquidity. A measure of the ease with which a security trades in large blocks without a substantial drop in price (defined in the FASB ASC glossary, as presented in the first section of this glossary).

listed security. A security listed and traded on a stock exchange.

long. Denotes ownership or right to possession of securities.

management fee. An amount charged by an investment adviser under a contract approved by the holders of a majority of a registered investment company's outstanding shares. The fee may gradually decline as a fixed or reducing percentage of the average net assets and may also provide for an additional bonus (or penalty) based on performance. (See **incentive fee**.)

management investment company. Under Section 4(3) of the 1940 Act, a management company (often referred to as a management investment company) is defined as any investment company other than a face amount certificate company (as defined in Section 4[1]) or a UIT (as defined in Section 4[2]). The term *management company* is sometimes used to refer to the investment adviser of an investment company.

margin. A securities transaction term meaning the amount of money or its equivalent, specified by the Board of Governors of the Federal Reserve System, that a customer must deposit with a broker in a securities transaction on margin (see **initial margin deposit**, a commodity transaction term).

margin account. A means of leveraging offered by security brokers or dealers to permit their customers to buy securities, in part, with borrowed funds. The difference between the price of a security and funds provided by the customer is loaned by the broker or dealer to the customer.

market price. Usually the last reported price at which a security has been sold or, if the security was not traded or trading prices are not reported, a price arrived at based on recent bid and asked prices.

mark-to-market. A procedure to adjust the carrying value of a security, an option, or a futures contract to fair value. (This term is synonymous with *subsequent measurement at fair value* or *changes in fair value*, which are terms used throughout FASB ASC.)

matrix pricing. A mathematical technique used to value normal institutional-sized trading units of debt securities without relying exclusively on quoted prices of the specific security. Factors such as the issue's coupon or stated interest rate, maturity, rating, and quoted prices of similar issues are considered in developing the issue's current market yield.

money market fund. A mutual fund whose investments are primarily or exclusively in short-term debt securities designed to maximize current income with liquidity and capital preservation, usually maintaining per share net asset value at a constant amount, such as $1.

money market investments. Short-term government obligations, commercial paper, bankers' acceptances, and certificates of deposit, of high credit standing and typically with remaining terms to maturity of one year or less.

municipal bond fund. An investment company whose shares represent holdings solely or largely of securities on which interest is exempt from federal income taxes.

municipal notes and bonds. Securities that are issued by states, cities, and other local government authorities to fund public projects. The interest on these bonds is often exempt from federal taxes and, under certain conditions, is exempt from state and local taxes. Municipal notes usually mature in less than three years.

mutual fund. The popular name for an open-end management investment company (see **open-end investment company**).

NASDAQ. Abbreviation for the NASDAQ Stock Market, an electronic stock market (formerly known as the National Association of Securities Dealers Automated Quotation System).

NASD. Acronym for the National Association of Securities Dealers, Inc. Formerly an association of broker-dealers doing business in the OTC market. Prior to its incorporation into FINRA, NASD supervised and regulated the trading conduct and sales practices of its members.

NSCC. Abbreviation of the National Securities Clearing Corporation, a subsidiary of the Depository Trust & Clearing Corporation that provides trade processing, clearance, delivery, and settlement services to its members. It deals with brokers, dealers, and banks in the United States and Canada.

NYSE. Acronym for the New York Stock Exchange. It is the largest securities exchange in the United States. The NYSE also furnishes facilities for its members, allied members, member firms, and member corporations to aid them in conducting securities business.

net assets. The term used by an investment company to designate the excess of the fair value of securities owned, cash, receivables, and other assets over the liabilities of the company.

net asset value per share. The value per share of outstanding capital stock of an investment company computed (usually daily by mutual funds) by dividing net assets by the total number of shares outstanding. (See Rule 2a-4 of the 1940 Act; defined in the FASB ASC glossary, as presented in the first section of this glossary).

no-action letter. A letter issued to an investment adviser or investment company (registrant) by the staff of the SEC in response to a request filed by the registrant describing a proposed business activity that may or may not conform to SEC rules and regulations. In a no-action letter, the SEC staff indicates whether, based on the facts presented by the registrant, the SEC staff will recommend no action be taken against the registrant for engaging in the proposed activity. A no-action letter does not have the force of law; however, it represents an interpretation of the SEC staff that may be applied in a situation in which the registrant is engaging in an activity not addressed by existing SEC rules and regulations.

no-load fund. A mutual fund selling and redeeming its shares at net asset value without adding sales charges, although some such funds have Rule 12b-1 plans permitting payment of distribution expenses with fund assets. A mutual fund may not call itself no load if a 12b-1 fee is levied exceeding 0.25 percent of fund assets per year. Investors deal directly with the fund, not through an investment dealer or broker.

nondiversified investment company. A management investment company other than a *diversified company*, as defined in Section 5(b) of the 1940 Act.

offering price. The price at which mutual fund shares or investment trust units can be bought, often equaling net asset value plus a sales load.

offset. A closing transaction involving the purchase or sale of an option or futures contract having the same features as one already held. This could be a hedge, such as a short sale of a stock, to protect capital gain or the purchase of a futures contract to protect a commodity price or a straddle representing the purchase of offsetting put and call options on a security.

offshore fund. An investment company organized outside the United States.

open contract. An unperformed or unsettled contract. May be used in referring to new issues traded when, as, and if issued or in referring to commodity futures trading. The term is used to designate contracts bought or sold and still outstanding.

open-end investment company. A mutual fund that is ready to redeem its shares at any time and that usually offers its shares for sale to the public continuously (see Section 5[a][1] of the 1940 Act).

original issue discount. A federal income tax term for interest to the holder of a bond that represents the difference between the face amount of a bond and its original sales price.

over-the-counter (OTC). A securities trading market made up of broker-dealers that may or may not be members of a securities exchange. Securities are traded in the OTC market between broker-dealers acting either as principals (dealers) or agents for customers (brokers). The OTC market is the principal market for U.S. government bonds, corporate bonds, and municipal securities, and a substantial number of U.S. equity securities are traded on an OTC basis.

passive foreign investment company (PFIC). A foreign corporation is a PFIC if either 75 percent of its gross income is passive, or 50 percent or more of the average value of its assets, computed quarterly, produce or could produce *passive income*, as defined in the IRC.

payable date. The date on which a dividend is payable to holders of record on some previous record date.

penny-rounding method. A method permitted by Rule 2a-7 of the 1940 Act under which the net asset value per share of a money market fund is computed based on the fair values of all investments and then rounded to the nearest 1 percent.

performance fee. See **incentive fee**.

periodic payment plan. See **accumulation unit** and Sections 2(a)(27) and 27 of the 1940 Act.

personal holding company. An income tax term defined as a corporation of which 60 percent of adjusted ordinary gross income is *personal holding company income*, as defined in the IRC, and 5 or fewer individuals own more than 50 percent in value of its outstanding stock during the last half of the taxable year.

point. A rise or decline of $1 per share used to refer to the purchase or sale of stocks. If used for the purchase or sale of bonds, the term means a rise or decline of $10 per $1,000 principal amount.

portfolio. Securities owned by an investment company or other investor in securities.

portfolio turnover rate. A measure of portfolio activity calculated for an investment company by dividing the lesser of purchases or sales of securities, excluding securities having maturity dates at acquisition of one year or less, by the average value of the portfolio securities held during the period (see Form N-SAR instructions to item 71, Form N-1A Item 13 Instruction 4(d), and Form N-2 Item 4 Instruction 17).

premium on redemptions (repurchases). See **redemption (repurchase) fee (or charge)**.

price make-up sheet. A detailed computation of the net asset value of a mutual fund.

principal. A person, especially a dealer, who buys or sells securities for his or her own account. Also refers to the face amount of a security without accrued interest.

principal underwriter. See **distributor**, defined in the FASB ASC glossary, as presented in the first section of this glossary, and the definition of *underwriter* in Section 2(a)(40) of the 1940 Act.

private equity fund. A general, nonlegal term used to describe private, unregistered pools that are not widely available to the public and have traditionally been limited to accredited investors and large institutions. Private equity funds typically seek to generate returns through longer term appreciation from investments in privately held and nonlisted publicly traded companies. Private equity funds often obtain majority controlling interests or significant minority interests that allow for active involvement in investee operations, restructuring, and merger and acquisition activity, through board oversight positions.

private placement. The direct sale of a block of securities of a new or secondary issue to a single investor or group of investors. The sale or placement is usually made through an investment banker, and the securities' public resale is restricted if they are not registered under the 1933 Act. (See **restricted security**.)

prospectus. A circular required by the 1933 Act describing securities being offered for sale to the public (see Section 2[a][31] of the 1940 Act).

proxy. A person authorized to vote the shares of an absent shareholder at a meeting of shareholders. Also refers to the written authorization given to that person. (See Section 20[a] of the 1940 Act.)

proxy statement. A publication sent to stockholders by a board of directors or trustees or its adversaries or others usually containing financial reports (for merger and other financial proposals), stockholders' meeting notices, and voting information on certain matters to solicit proxies from the holders (see Rule 20a-1 under the 1940 Act and Regulation 14A under the 1934 Act).

put option. A contract that entitles the holder to sell (put), at his or her option, a specified number of underlying units of a particular security at a specified price (strike price) either on (European-style) or at any time until (American-style) the contract's stated expiration date. The option, which may be transferable, is bought in the expectation that the price will decline below the strike price. If the price declines below the strike price, the buyer exercises or sells the option. If the price does not decline below the strike price, the buyer lets the option expire and loses only the cost of the option. There are both listed and OTC markets in options. During the existence of an option, the exercise price and number of underlying units are adjusted on the ex-dividend date for cash dividends, rights, and stock dividends or splits (defined in the FASB ASC glossary, as presented in the first section of this glossary).

real estate mortgage investment conduit (REMIC). An investment vehicle created to hold pools of mortgages and to issue two classes of interest in the REMIC: regular interest and residual interests. The vehicle is not subject to taxation and may be used to protect investors in mortgage-related instruments from double taxation.

realized gain or loss. See **capital gain or loss**.

record date. The date on which an owner of a share of stock must be registered on the books of a company as a shareholder to receive a declared dividend or, among other things, to vote on company affairs.

recordkeeping agent. An outside service bureau, bank, or other agency engaged by an investment company to maintain records of purchases and sales of investments, sales and redemptions of fund shares, and shareholders' account statements.

redemption. A stockholder's tender of investment company shares to the company or person designated by the company, requiring liquidation of such shares in exchange for proceeds, usually in cash, representing the net asset value of the shares tendered, occasionally less a redemption fee (see Section 2[a][32] of the 1940 Act).

redemption in kind. Redemption of investment company shares by payment in portfolio securities, not cash. Permissible in certain circumstances for many mutual funds and tax-free exchange funds. (see Rule 18f-1 under the 1940 Act).

redemption or repurchase price. The price, net asset value less a redemption fee, at which a share of a mutual fund is redeemed or repurchased (see Section 2[a][32] of the 1940 Act).

redemption (repurchase) fee (or charge.) A percentage of net asset value that may be charged to the investor on redemptions or repurchases of an open-end investment company's shares (see Section 10[d][4] of the 1940 Act).

registered investment company. An investment company that has filed a registration statement with the SEC as an investment company, in accordance with the requirements of the 1940 Act. The *investment company*, as defined in Section 3(a) of the act, primarily invests, reinvests, or trades in securities; issues face-amount certificates; or engages in investing and owning investment securities, other than government securities, that have a value exceeding 40 percent of the company's total assets (Section 3[a][1]), with some exceptions to the latter (stated in Section 3[b]).

registrar. Usually a trust company or bank responsible for preventing the issuance of more stock than authorized by the issuing company (see **transfer agent**).

regulated investment company (RIC). An investment company that qualifies for the special tax treatment provided for by IRC subchapter M.

Regulation S-X. Accounting rules for the form and content of financial statements and schedules required under the 1933 Act, the 1934 Act, and the Energy Policy and Conservation Act of 1975. Article 6 applies to financial statements for, and specified rules in article 12 apply to financial schedules of, registered investment companies.

reinvestment. The automatic purchase of additional shares using the proceeds of dividends and capital gain distributions.

repurchase. Liquidation of investment company shares through a principal underwriter or a broker-dealer on behalf of shareholders, sometimes for a purchase or service charge or brokerage commission.

repurchase agreement. An agreement under which an investment company pays for and receives (purchases) securities from a seller who agrees to repurchase them within a specified time at a specified price. A repurchase agreement is known on the side of a selling broker-dealer or other seller as a reverse repurchase agreement.

restricted security. A portfolio security that may be sold privately but that is required to be registered with the SEC or exempted from such registration before it may be sold in a public distribution. A private placement stock is frequently referred to as letter stock.

return. See **yield**.

reverse repurchase agreement. An agreement under which the investment company transfers (sells) securities for cash to another party (purchaser), usually a broker, and agrees to repurchase them within a specified time at a specified price. A reverse repurchase agreement is known in the broker-dealer industry as a repurchase agreement.

right. A privilege offered by a corporation to its shareholders pro rata to subscribe to a certain security at a specified price, often for a short period. Rights may or may not be transferable.

right of accumulation. A method permitting aggregation of mutual fund shares being acquired with shares previously acquired and currently owned to qualify for a quantity discount that reduces the sales charge on a single purchase.

Rule 2a-7. A rule under the 1940 Act that permits money market funds to value investments at amortized cost or through the use of the penny-rounding method.

Rule 12b-1. A rule under Section 12 of the 1940 Act that permits the use of a fund's assets to pay distribution-related expenses under conditions prescribed therein (see **board-contingent plan** and **enhanced 12b-1 plan** defined in the FASB ASC glossary, as presented in the first section of this glossary).

Rule 144A. A rule under the 1933 Act that provides a safe harbor exemption from the registration requirements for resales of restricted securities to qualified institutional buyers.

SBA. Acronym for the Small Business Administration, an agency established by Congress to administer the Small Business Investment Company Act of 1958.

SBIC. Acronym for a small business investment company, an investment company registered under the Small Business Investment Company Act of 1958 and established to provide capital to small business enterprises.

SEC. Acronym for the Securities and Exchange Commission, an agency established by Congress to administer federal securities laws.

sale against the box. Similar to a short sale, except that the seller already owns the stock being sold but keeps possession of it and, therefore, has to borrow the equivalent stock to deliver to the purchaser.

sales charge. An amount providing for the underwriter's and dealer's commission that is added to the net asset value of an open-end investment company's shares in computing the offering price and stated as a percentage of the offering price. A sales charge can also be imposed on redemption.

Section 4(2). A section of the 1933 Act that exempts transactions by an issuer not involving a public offering from registration under that act.

Securities Act of 1933 (1933 Act). Principal federal law regulating the public offering of corporate securities. Among other things, it regulates the contents of prospectuses and similar documents and is intended to ensure that potential investors receive adequate information to make reasonably informed investment decisions.

Securities Exchange Act of 1934 (1934 Act). Regulates securities brokers and dealers, stock exchanges, transfer agents, and the trading of securities in the securities markets. Also, among other things, establishes requirements for periodic reporting by registrants.

Securities Investor Protection Corporation (SIPC). A federal corporation established for the purpose of protecting customers of broker-dealers in financial difficulty.

securities lending. The practice of lending portfolio securities, usually for delivery against a short sale. The loan is usually collateralized by cash or government securities.

seed money. An initial amount of capital contributed to a company at its inception (see Section 14[a] of the 1940 Act).

senior security. Under Section 18 of the 1940 Act, any obligation constituting a security (as defined) and evidencing indebtedness and any class of equity security having priority over any other class with respect to distribution of assets and payment of dividends.

separate account. An account established and maintained by an insurance company that holds particular assets allocated to that account and is credited or charged with income, gains, or losses from these assets separately from income, gains, or losses of the insurance company's general accounts. Sometimes referred to as a variable account, a separate account funds variable annuities or variable life insurance policies. Although it is not an entity but is only an account within the insurance company, it may be an *investment company* within the meaning of the 1940 Act. (See Section 2[a][37] of the act; defined in the FASB ASC glossary, as presented in the first section of this glossary.)

series fund. An investment company that offers multiple segregated portfolios of common stock (see Rule 6-03[j] of Regulation S-X).

settlement date. The date on which security transactions are settled by delivering or receiving securities and receiving or paying cash pursuant to an earlier agreement of purchase and sale called a trade (see **trade date**).

short. A stock record position representing the physical location of a security (such as box, transfer, and so forth) or meaning that the security is due from others (such as failed to receive or owed to the brokerage concern by a customer due to a short sale).

short sale. A sale of securities that requires borrowing equivalent securities to make delivery to the purchaser.

Small Business Investment Incentive Act of 1980. Amended the 1940 Act by, among other things, allowing closed-end companies to elect to be regulated as BDCs under Section 2(a)(48) and Sections 54–65 of the 1940 Act (see **business development company [BDC]**).

Small Business Investment Company Act of 1958. Authorizes the SBA to provide government funds to small business investment companies licensed under that act.

spread. A combination of put and call options at different prices—one below and the other above the current market price—for the same quantity of a security. Also refers to the difference between the bid and asked prices of a security and to the dealer's commission on a security offering.

standby commitment contract. An agreement to accept future delivery of a security at a guaranteed price or fixed yield on exercise of an option held by the other party to the agreement.

straddle. A combination of one put and one call option, identical with respect to the security issue, number of shares, exercise price, and expiration date.

stripping. The brokerage practice of separating a fixed income security into its corpus and coupons, which are then sold separately.

synthetic floaters. A structured instrument that uses the principal of, and a portion of the interest payments from, long-term municipal bonds, (in some cases combined with interest rate swaps), to create an investment that pays a floating short-term interest rate. Often issued in tandem with inverse floaters. Many synthetic floaters are known as "tender option bonds", as they include the right to put the instruments to the issuer or a third party at regular intervals, or upon the occurrence of certain events, at a stated price (usually par).

TBA. Abbreviation for to be announced future government-sponsored enterprises' pools that are bought and sold for future settlement. TBA refers to the announcement of the specific pools to be delivered or received.

tender offer. A public offer to buy from all current holders not less than a specified amount of an issuer's securities at a fixed price.

total return. A periodic measure of a fund's overall change in value that assumes the reinvestment of dividends and capital gain distributions. (Total return is a standardized method prescribed by the SEC, as described in item 26 of Form N-1A.)

trade. An agreement of purchase and sale in a securities market to be settled or performed by payment and delivery on a later settlement date.

trade date. The date that a security transaction is actually entered into to be settled on a later settlement date.

transfer. A change of ownership of registered securities on the books of the issuer (defined in the FASB ASC glossary, as presented in the first section of this glossary).

transfer agent. An agent for a securities issuer who keeps records of the names of the issuer's registered shareholders, their addresses, and the number of shares that they own. The agent must be sure that certificates presented to the office for transfer are canceled and that new certificates are issued in the name of the transferee. (See **registrar.**)

turnover. The frequency at which securities are purchased and sold by an investment company.

undertaking. An agreement between a registrant and the SEC staff in connection with the filing of a registration statement whereby the registrant agrees to take a future action requested by the staff but not otherwise necessarily or expressly required by the securities' statutes but (in a federal registration) that may be required by SEC rules or SEC forms that have the same legal status as the rules by which they were adopted.

underwriting. The act of distributing a new issue of securities (primary offering) or a large block of previously issued securities (secondary offering). A firm-commitment underwriting obligates the underwriter to purchase the underwritten securities, regardless of whether they can be resold. A best-efforts underwriting only obligates the underwriter to buy from the issuer only those securities that it is able to sell to purchasers.

unit investment trust (UIT). An investment company organized under a trust indenture that issues only redeemable securities, each of which represents an undivided interest in a unit of specified (usually unmanaged) securities (see Section 26 of the 1940 Act).

unlisted security. A security that is not listed on a securities exchange (see **over-the-counter [OTC]**).

unrealized appreciation or depreciation. The excess (appreciation) or deficiency (depreciation) of the fair value of securities over (under) their cost.

unregistered securities. Securities that are not registered under the 1933 Act.

variable annuity. An annuity having a provision for the accumulation of an account value, benefit payments, or both that vary according to the investment experience of the separate account to which the amounts paid for the annuity are allocated (defined in the FASB ASC glossary, as presented in the first section of this glossary, under the term **variable annuity contract**).

variation margin. A term used in commodity operations. Refers to last-day point fluctuation—a difference between the settling price of the day before and the last day's settling price—on net positions long and short.

venture capital investment company. A closed-end investment company whose primary investment objective is capital growth and whose capital is usually invested wholly or largely in restricted securities in negotiated transactions to form or develop companies with new ideas, products, or processes.

warrant. A type of option to purchase additional securities from the issuer. Commonly affixed to the certificates for other securities at the time when the combined securities units are originally issued and usually separable, sometimes, on and after a subsequent date. Also, a document evidencing options to purchase shares. (Defined in the FASB ASC glossary, as presented in the first section of this glossary.)

wash sale. A sale of stock or other securities in which a taxpayer has acquired or entered a contract or option to acquire substantially identical stock or other securities within a period beginning 30 days before and ending 30 days after the date of the sale (a 61-day period). A loss resulting from such a sale is not deductible for federal income tax purposes, but a gain is taxable. (See IRC Section 1091.)

when-issued. A short form designation for when, as, and if issued. The term indicates a conditional transaction in a security authorized for issuance but not yet actually issued. All such transactions are settled if and when the actual security is issued.

yield. The return on investment that an investor receives from dividends or interest expressed as a percentage of the current market price of the security or, if the investor already owns the security, the price paid. Yield also may refer to the SEC yield, a standardized yield calculation method prescribed by the SEC based upon interest and dividend income of the fund (see item 26 of the instructions to Form N-1A).

yield to maturity. The rate of return on a debt security held to maturity, giving effect to the stated interest rate, accrual of discount, and amortization of premium.

zero coupon bond. A type of debt instrument that makes no periodic interest payment but is issued at a deep discount from its face value. The holder derives his or her return from the gradual appreciation in the value of the security, which redeems at face value at a specified maturity date.

Index of Pronouncements and Other Technical Guidance

A

Title	Paragraphs
AT Section	
101, *Attest Engagement*	12.34, 12.41–.43
Interpretation No. 8, "Including a Description of Tests of Controls or Other Procedures, and the Results Thereof, in an Examination Report"	12.42
601, *Compliance Attestation*	12.30, 12.32, 12.34, 12.38
801, *Reporting on Controls at a Service Organization*	11.30, 12.40
AU Section	
333, *Management Representations*	11.45, 12.01, 12.48
722, *Interim Financial Information*	7.211
AU-C Section	
200, *Overall Objectives of the Independent Auditor and the Conduct of an Audit in Accordance With Generally Accepted Auditing Standards*	11.04–.15
230, *Audit Documentation*	11.23
240, *Consideration of Fraud in a Financial Statement Audit*	5.71
250, *Consideration of Laws and Regulations in an Audit of Financial Statements*	11.19
260, *The Auditor's Communication With Those Charged With Governance*	11.24
265, *Communicating Internal Control Related Matters Identified in an Audit*	11.26
315, *Understanding the Entity and Its Environment and Assessing the Risks of Material Misstatement*	4.32, 4.36, 5.71–.72
320, *Materiality in Planning and Performance of an Audit*	11.08

Title	Paragraphs
330, *Performing Audit Procedures in Response to Assessed Risks and Evaluation the Audit Evidence Obtained*	4.36–.37, 11.14–.15, 11.17, 11.37, 11.49, 11.52, 12.03
402, *Audit Considerations Relating to an Entity Using a Service Organization*	4.21, 11.30, 11.57, 11.61
450, *Evaluation of Misstatements Identified During the Audit*	12.03
500, *Audit Evidence*	11.17, 11.37
501, *Audit Evidence—Specific Considerations for Selected Items*	11.17, 11.54, 11.56
Interpretation No. 1, "The Effect of an Inability of Obtain Audit Evidence Relating to Income Tax Accruals"	5.85
505, *External Confirmations*	11.37
540, *Auditing Accounting Estimates, Including Fair Value Accounting Estimates and Related Disclosures*	11.17, 11.56, 11.60–.70, 11.72, 11.74–.76
570, *The Auditor's Consideration of an Entity's Ability to Continue as a Going Concern*	11.33
9570, *The Auditor's Consideration of an Entity's Ability to Continue as a Going Concern: Auditing Interpretation of AU-C Section 570*	11.33
580, *Written Representations*	5.83, 5.88, 12.01, 12.47
620, *Using the Work of an Auditor's Specialist*	11.57
700, *Forming an Opinion and Reporting on Financial Statements*	12.01, 12.03, 12.07–.08, 12.10
705, *Modifications to the Opinion in the Independent Auditor's Report*	12.01, 12.08–.18
706, *Emphasis-of-Matter Paragraphs and Other-Matter Paragraphs in the Independent Auditor's Report*	12.01
930, *Interim Financial Information*	7.209–.212
Accounting Guide *Brokers and Dealers in Securities*	1.52
Audit and Accounting Guide *Life and Health Insurance Entities*	10.22, 10.33
Audit Guide *Special Consideration in Auditing Financial Instruments*	11.36, 11.58

C

Title	Paragraphs
CFR Regulation	
1.817-5(B)(1)	10.50
1.817-5(B)(3)	10.52
Title 26, *Internal Revenue*	8.47
CFTC	
Letter No. 13-51	7.236
Regulation 4.22(C)	7.17
Commodity Exchange Act of 1974, Section 4F(a)	12.35

F

Title	Paragraphs
FASB ASC	
205, *Presentation of Financial Statements*	
205-10	7.05, 7.07
205-30	8.57–.62, 8.65–.68, 8.71
210, *Balance Sheet*	
210-20	7.37, 7.67–.68, 7.191–.192, 7.194–.197, 7.199–.201
225, *Income Statement*	
225-20	7.140
230, *Statement of Cash Flows*	7.159, 7.161, 7.164, 7.166
230-10	1.47, 7.01, 7.159–.160, 7.162, 7.164–.165, 7.168
250, *Accounting Changes and Error Corrections*	2.60, 2.123
250-10	2.60
270, *Interim Reporting*	7.210
275, *Risks and Uncertainties*	7.188, Update 8-1 at 8.24

Title	Paragraphs
275-10	7.29
310, *Receivables*	
310-10	7.127, 7.165, 7.168
310-20	2.118
320, *Investments—Debt and Equity Securities*	7.166, 7.168
325, *Investments—Other*	
325-40	2.121–.124
350, *Intangibles—Goodwill and Other*	2.44
360, *Property, Plant and Equipment*	7.87
405, *Liabilities*	
405-20	8.62
450, *Contingencies*	2.103
450-20	2.129, 3.39, 8.09, 8.37
460, *Guarantees*	3.01
460-10	3.39, 7.40–.41
480, *Distinguishing Liabilities From Equity*	7.83
480-10	4.23, 7.83, 7.107–.110
505, *Equity*	
505-10	4.22
606, *Revenue Recognition*	1.01, Appendix I
720, *Other Expenses*	
720-15	8.26–.27
740, *Income Taxes*	6.06, 6.15, 7.188
740-10	6.05, 6.07–.11
805, *Business Combinations*	
805-10	8.49, 8.52–.53
810, *Consolidation*	Update 7-2 at 7.08, Update 8-1 at 8.24
810-10	7.14–.16, Update 8-1 at 8.24
815, *Derivatives and Hedging*	2.143, 3.01, 3.39, 3.41, 3.43, 7.58, 7.78, 7.102, 7.188, 7.192

Title	Paragraphs
815-10	2.143, 3.41, 7.37, 7.58–.64, 7.66–.70, 7.78, 7.93, 7.191–.192, 7.194, 7.196
815-15	3.67, 7.78
815-20	7.62
820, *Fair Value Measurement*	1.01, Update 2-1 at 2.01, 2.34, 2.78–.84, 2.87, 2.93, 2.99, 2.151, 3.01, 7.89–.90, 7.160, 7.188, 8.44
820-10	1.01, Update 2-1 at 2.01, 2.31, 2.33–.34, 2.37–.38, 2.40, 2.43, 2.46, 2.48–.51, 2.58–.77, 2.80, 2.84–.99, Update 7-1 at 7.01, 7.84–.97, 7.233
825, *Financial Instruments*	2.77, 7.75–.77, 7.97, 7.188
825-10	7.28, 7.75, 7.99–.102, 7.188
830, *Foreign Currency Matters*	
830-230	7.171
835, *Interest*	
835-30	2.118
850, *Related Party Disclosures*	7.113, 7.118, 7.129
850-10	7.72, 7.138
855, *Subsequent Events*	
855-10	7.154–.158
860, *Transfers and Servicing*	2.30, 3.01, 3.23, 3.74, 7.188, 11.32
860-10	2.137, 2.139–.140, 7.81–.82
860-30	2.137–.138, 7.81
860-50	7.76, 7.82
915, *Development Stage Entities*	8.24, Update 8-1 at 8.24

Title	Paragraphs
946, *Financial Services—Investment Companies*	1.01, 1.03, 1.05–.11, 2.78–.79, 2.86, 2.89–.93, 2.96, 5.94, 7.05, 7.184
946-10	1.04–.07, 1.09, 1.11, 2.20
946-20	3.13, 4.22, 4.26, 5.02, 7.103, 7.105, 7.112, 7.119–.120, 7.122–.124, 7.137–.138, 7.141–.143, 7.148, 7.176, 7.179, 7.207, 8.08–.10, 8.14, 8.16, 8.17–.23, Table at 8.18, 8.30, 8.36
946-205	5.36, 5.38, 5.47–.48, 5.51, 5.53, 5.63, 7.01, 7.12–.13, 7.25, 7.148–.149, 7.173–.177, 7.179–.180, 7.186, 7.235, 10.59–.60
946-210	5.31, 5.33, 5.42–.43, 5.56, 7.01, 7.12, 7.18, 7.21, 7.23–.27, 7.32–.33, 7.37, 7.42–.43, 7.146, 7.151–.152, 7.190, 7.230–.231
946-225	5.35, 5.44–.45, 5.58–.59, 5.61, 6.15, 7.12, 7.111, 7.116, 7.130–.131, 7.133, 7.135–.136, 7.144–.145
946-230	7.12, 7.172
946-235	5.37, 5.49–.50, 5.62, 7.12
946-305	7.51
946-310	7.54
946-320	1.50, 2.01, 2.25, 2.27, 2.29, 2.31, 2.36, 2.101, 2.104–.105, 2.108, 2.111–.114, 2.116, 2.118, 2.130–.134, 2.150, 3.30, 3.33, 3.35, 7.08–.09, 7.50, 7.112

Title	Paragraphs
No. 2015-07, *Fair Value Measurement (Topic 820): Disclosures for Investments in Certain Entities That Calculate Net Asset Value Per Share (Or Its Equivalent)*	1.01, Update 2-1 at 2.01, Update 7-1 at 7.1
FASB EITF No. D-98, "Classification and Measurement of Redeemable Securities"	7.107
FASB FAC No. 6, *Elements of Financial Statements—A Replacement of FASB Concepts Statement No. 3*	7.78, 8.09
FASB FSP No. 157-3, "Determining the Fair Value of a Financial Asset When the Market for That Asset Is Not Active"	7.89
Federal Deposit Insurance Act of 1950, Section 3(b)(1)	12.35

I

Title	Paragraphs
IAS No. 34, *Interim Financial Reporting*	7.210
Investment Advisers Act of 1940 Rules	
202(a)(2)	12.35
204-2(b)	12.38
206(4)-2	11.40, 12.38
206(4)-2(a)(4)	12.32
206(4)-2(a)(6)	12.34
Investment Company Act of 1940 Rules and Regulations	
Section 8	12.23
Section 18	2.09
Section 26	9.09
Section 31	2.04
Investment Management Guidance Update No. 2013-07, *Business Development Companies—Separate Financial Statements or Summarized Financial Information of Certain Subsidiaries*	7.204
IRC Form	
1099	9.14

Title	Paragraphs
1099-DIV	6.26–.27
1120-RIC	6.27
2439	6.40
5452	6.27
8937	6.27
N-8A	6.45
IRC Revenue Procedure	
96-47	5.08, 6.68
99-40	5.09, 6.68
2001-36	5.21
IRC Revenue Ruling	
55-416	6.75
73-463	6.106
80-274	10.44
81-225	10.45–.46
83-69	6.55
89-81	6.69
92-56	6.51
94-70	6.106
94-71	6.93
2003-91	10.46–.47
2003-92	10.46, 10.49
2007-58	6.58
IRC Schedule K-1	6.50
IRC Section	
1(h)(11)	6.43
67(c)(2)(B)	6.68
72	10.50
72(q)	10.54
72(s)	10.53
162(k)(2)(B)	6.107
171(a)(2)	6.36
243(a)(2)	6.132

Title	Paragraphs
246(c)	6.29
265(a)(3)	6.36
301(c)	6.97
301(c)(1)	6.26
301(c)(2)	6.26
301(c)(3)	6.26
302(b)(5)	6.75
307	2.115
316(b)(4)	6.27
368(a)	8.47
542(c)(7)	6.132
561	6.25
562(c)	5.08, 6.68
565	10.56
671	9.02
704(b)	5.21
817	10.40–.41
817-5(b)	6.58
817-5(c)(1)	6.58
817-5(f)(3)	6.58
817(g)	10.42
817(h)	10.50–.51
817(h)(2)	6.60, 10.52
851	8.47
851(a)	6.45
851(b)	6.50
851(b)(1)	6.45
851(b)(2)	6.48
851(b)(2)(G)	6.52
851(b)(3)(A)	6.53
851(b)(3)(B)	6.54
851(c)(2)	6.54
851(d)(1)	6.56

Title	Paragraphs
851(d)(2)	6.56
851(d)(2)(G)	6.56
851(e)	6.53, 6.57
851(g)	6.19
852(a)(2)	6.24, 6.64
852(b)(1)	6.66
852(b)(2)(A)	6.20
852(b)(2)(B)	6.20–.21
852(b)(2)(C)	6.20
852(b)(2)(D)	6.20
852(b)(2)(G)	6.20, 6.52
852(b)(3)(A)	6.66
852(b)(3)(B)	6.39
852(b)(3)(C)	6.23, 6.39, 6.44
852(b)(3)(D)	6.40
852(b)(5)	6.34
852(b)(5)(A)	6.38, 6.44
852(b)(7)	6.70
852(c)	6.25
852(g)	6.31, 6.34
853	6.31–.33
853(c)	6.33
854	6.28, 6.30
855(a)	6.65
860(a)	6.72
860(c)	6.73
901(k)	6.32
988	6.94, 6.109–.110, 6.113–.115, 6.118
988(d)	6.117
1044	6.134
1092(c)	6.104
1202	6.26, 6.134
1202(a)(3)	6.42

Title	Paragraphs
1202(a)(4)	6.42
1202(g)	6.42
1212(a)(3)	6.21
1222(9)	6.36
1242	6.133
1244	6.134
1250	6.26
1256	6.94, 6.103, 6.118
1293(a)	6.122
1295	6.122
1296	6.94, 6.123
1297(a)	6.121
4982	10.55
4982(a)	6.83
4982(b)	6.89
4982(c)(1)	6.92
4982(c)(2)	6.91
4982(e)(1)	6.85
4982(e)(2)	6.87
4982(e)(2)(B)	6.94
4982(e)(4)	6.88
4982(e)(5)	6.85
4982(e)(6)	6.123
4982(e)(7)	6.86
4982(f)	6.95
6045B	6.27
(b)(3)(C)	6.78
(b)(8)	6.78
381–384	6.108
IRC Subchapter	
L	10.40
M	6.03, 6.13, 6.16–.17, 6.25, 6.45, 7.189, 8.56, 9.02, 10.40

N

Title	Paragraphs
NASD Rules of Fair Practice	
Rule 2830, *Investment Company Securities*	8.15
Rule 387, *COD Orders*	2.14

P

Title	Paragraphs
PCAOB AS	
No. 1, *References in Auditors' Reports to the Standards of the PCAOB*	12.02, 12.30
No. 5, *An Audit of Internal Control Over Financial Reporting That Is Integrated With an Audit of Financial Statements*	4.21, 12.23
No. 8, *Audit Risk*	11.16
No. 9, *Audit Planning*	11.16
No. 10, *Supervision of the Audit Engagement*	11.16
No. 11, *Consideration of Materiality in Planning and Performing an Audit*	11.16
No. 12, *Identifying and Assessing Risks of Material Misstatement*	11.16
No. 13, *The Auditor's Responses to the Risks of Material Misstatement*	11.16
No. 14, *Evaluating Audit Results*	11.16
No. 15, *Audit Evidence*	11.16
No. 16, *Communications With Audit Committees*	11.25
No. 18, *Related Parties*	11.45
PCAOB Release No. 2010-04, *Auditing Standards Related to the Auditor's Assessment of and Response to Risk*	11.16

Title	Paragraphs
Sarbanes-Oxley Act of 2002	
Section 404	4.21
Section 404(b)	1.57
Section 404(c)	4.21
Section 405	4.21
SAS No. 118, *Other Information in Documents Containing Audited Financial Statements*	2.32
SEC *Codification of Financial Reporting Policies*	2.28, 2.32, 2.35, 2.53, 2.57, 11.75
Section 404	7.215
Section 404.03	2.32, 2.35, 11.75
Section 404.03.a	2.28, 2.55
Section 404.04	2.55
SEC Final Rule Release	
No. 1C-28617, *Interactive Data for Mutual Fund Risk Return Summary*	1.45
No. 33-6753, *Strengthening the Commission's Requirements Regarding Auditor Independence*	3.31
No. 33-9002, *Interactive Data to Improve Financial Reporting*	1.44
No. 33-9616, *Money Market Fund Reform Amendments to Form Pf*	1.50, Update 2-2 at 2.100, Update 5-1 at 5.01, 11.77
No. 7113	8.03
No. 10666	2.09, 3.05
No. IA-2968, *Custody of Funds or Securities of Clients by Investment Advisers* and the Related Interpretive Release No. IA-2969	12.31
No. IA-2968, *Custody of Funds or Securities of Clients by Investment Advisers* and The Related Interpretive Release No. IA-2969 (Custody Rule)	8.70

Title	Paragraphs
No. IA-2969, *Commission Guidance Regarding Independent Public Accountant Engagements Performed Pursuant to Rule 206(4)-2 Under the Investment Advisers Act of 1940*	12.39
SEC FORM	
13F	1.40
ADV-E	12.32
N-1	1.40
N-1A	1.40–.42, 2.52, 5.52, 7.178, 7.181–.183, 8.51, 9.02
N-2	1.40, 1.42, 7.178, 7.181–.183, 8.51
N-3	1.40, 2.52, 10.30
N-4	1.40, 10.30, 10.57
N-5	1.40
N-6	1.40, 10.31, 10.57
N-8A	1.40, 6.45
N-8B-2	1.40, 9.02
N-14	1.40, 8.46
N-17F-1	11.39
N-17F-2	11.39
N-CR	1.50, Update 2-2 at 2.100
N-CSR	1.40, 1.43, 1.46, 11.22, 12.27, 12.49
N-MFP	1.40, 1.50, Update 2-2 at 2.100
N-PX	1.40
N-Q	1.40
N-SAR	1.40, 1.43, 7.183, 8.39–.43, 11.28, 12.29
PF	1.40
S-6	1.40, 9.02, 9.16

Title	*Paragraphs*
SEC Regulation S-X	1.43, 1.46, 4.30, 5.57, 7.01, 7.08, 7.19, 7.22, 7.30, 7.44, 7.49, 7.56, 7.80, 7.113, 7.115, 7.117, 7.132, 7.204, 7.210, 7.215, 9.03, 9.16, 9.17, 10.58, 11.44
Article 6	9.03
SEC Rules and Regulations	
1-02(w)	7.205
2a-2	2.102
2a-4	1.51, 4.01
2a-4(a)	2.21
2a-7	1.50, 2.100, Update 2-2 at 2.100, 11.77
2(a)(3)	11.43
2(a)(9)	11.43
2(a)(41)	2.32
2(a)(48)	8.46
3-09	7.204–.205
4	1.40
4-08(g)	7.204–.205
4(2)	9.01
5	3.05
5b-3	3.05
6-10(d)	9.03
6.09.2	4.30
12-12	5.57, 7.215, 9.03, 9.17
12-12C	5.57
12-14	5.57
12b-1	4.01, 4.06, 8.14–.23, Table at 8.18
12(d)	5.22
12(d)-(1)(E)(ii)	5.22
12(d)(1)	5.23
12d1-1	5.23

Title	Paragraphs
12d1-2	5.23
12d1-3	5.23
12(d)(3)	3.05
15(b)(1)	12.35
17	4.32, 11.38, 11.43, 11.45
17A	1.36
17(A)(c)	1.39
17Ad-13	12.41
17f-1	11.38–.39, 12.30
17f-2	11.38–.39, 12.30
17f-5	2.179
17f-7	2.179
18f-3	2.24, 4.01, 4.07, 4.55, 5.06–.10, 5.65
18(g)	11.36
19	1.53
19a	1.53
19b-1(e)	4.46
22c-1(b)	2.19
22d-1	1.33
24e	4.19
24f	4.19
26	1.40
30a-1	8.39
30a-2	1.40
30b1-1	8.39
30d-1	7.206
30(e)(5)	7.121
31	1.48
31a-1	2.13
32(a)	1.54
38a-1	2.52
206(4)-2	12.31–.39

Title	Paragraphs
SEC SAB	
No. 105, *Application of Accounting Principles to Loan Commitments*	7.76
No. 109, *Written Loan Commitments Recorded at Fair Value Through Earnings*	7.76
Topic 5T, *Codification of Staff Accounting Bulletins* "Accounting for Expenses or Liabilities Paid by Principal Stockholders"	7.139
SEC Schedule	
13D	1.40
13G	1.40
SEC *Staff Responses to Questions About the Custody Rule*	12.34
SOP 12-1, *Reporting Pursuant to the Global Investment Performance Standards*	12.43–.46

Q

Title	Paragraphs
Q&A	
1100.15, "Liquidity Restrictions"	7.53
2220.18, "Applicability of Practical Expedient"	2.88, 5.29
2220.19, "Unit of Account"	2.88, 5.29
2220.20, "Determining Whether NAV Is Calculated Consistent With FASB ASC 946, *Financial Services—Investment Companies*"	2.90–.91, 5.29
2220.21, "Determining Whether an Adjustment to NAV Is Necessary"	5.29
2220.22, "Adjusting NAV When It Is Not as of the Reporting Entity's Measurement Date"	2.92, 5.29
2220.23, "Adjusting NAV When It Is Not Calculated Consistent With FASB ASC 946"	2.93, 5.29
2220.24, "Disclosures—Ability to Redeem Versus Actual Redemption Request"	2.99, 5.29
2220.25, "Impact of 'Near Term' on Classification Within Fair Value Hierarchy"	2.99, 5.29
2220.26, "Categorization of Investments for Disclosure Purposes"	5.29, 7.98

Title	Paragraphs
2220.27, "Determining Fair Value of Investments When the Practical Expedient Is Not Used or Is Not Available"	2.96, 5.29
4110.10, "Costs Incurred in Shelf Registration"	8.32
6910.16, "Presentation of Boxed Investment Positions in the Condensed Schedule of Investments of Nonregistered Investment Partnerships"	7.31, 7.35
6910.17, "Disclosure of Long and Short Positions"	7.32, 7.36
6910.18, "Disclosure of an Investment in an Issue When One or More Securities and/or One or More Derivative Contracts Are Held—Nonregistered Investment Companies"	7.33, 7.37
6910.19, "Information Required to Be Disclosed in Financial Statements When Comparative Financial Statements of Nonregistered Investment Partnerships Are Presented"	7.06–.07
6910.20, "Presentation of Purchases and Sales/Maturities of Investments in the Statement of Cash Flows"	7.150, 7.164
6910.21, "Recognition of Premium Discount on Short Positions in Fixed-Income Securities"	2.81, 2.116, 2.125
6910.22, "Presentation of Reverse Repurchase Agreements"	7.69
6910.23, "Accounting Treatment of Offering Costs Incurred by Investment Partnerships"	8.33
6910.24, "Meaning of 'Continually Offer Interests'"	8.33
6910.25, "Considerations in Evaluating Whether Certain Liabilities Constitute 'Debt' for Purposes of Assessing Whether an Investment Company Must Present a Statement of Cash Flows"	7.147, 7.161
6910.26, "Additional Guidance on Determinants of Net Versus Gross Presentation of Security Purchases and Sales/Maturities in the Statement of Cash Flows of a Nonregistered Investment Company"	7.151, 7.165

Title	Paragraphs
6910.27, "Treatment of Deferred Fees"	7.70, 7.117, 7.169, 7.184
6910.28, "Reporting Financial Highlights, Net Asset Value (NAV) Per Share, Shares Outstanding, and Share Transactions When Investors In Unitized Nonregistered Funds Are Issued Individual Classes or Series of Shares"	7.136, 7.138, 7.150, 7.170–.172
6910.29, "Allocation of Unrealized Gain (Loss), Recognition of Carried Interest, And Clawback Obligations"	7.113–.115, 7.125–.127, 8.02
6910.30, "Disclosure Requirements of Investments for Nonregistered Investment Partnerships When Their Interest in an Investee Fund Constitutes Less Than 5 Percent of the Non-Registered Investment Partnership's Net Assets"	7.34, 7.38
6910.31, "The Nonregistered Investment Partnership's Method for Calculating Its Proportional Share of Any Investments Owned by an Investee Fund in Applying The '5 Percent Test' Described in TIS Section 6910.30"	7.35, 7.39
6910.32, "Additional Financial Statement Disclosures for Nonregistered Investment Partnerships When The Partnerships Has Provided Guarantees Related to the Investee Fund's Debt"	7.36, 7.40
6910.33, "Certain Financial Reporting, Disclosure, Regulatory, and Tax Considerations When Preparing Financial Statements of Investment Companies Involved in a Business Combination"	8.43–.51, 8.53–.54
6910.34, "Application of the Notion of Value Maximization for Measuring Fair Value Of Debt And Controlling Equity Positions"	2.75
6910.35, "Assessing Control When Measuring Fair Value"	2.76
9170.02, "Supplementary Information That Accompanies Interim Financial Information"	7.212

T

Title	Paragraphs
Treasury Regulation	
1.263(a)-2(e)	6.101
1.312-6	6.25
1.337(d)-7(c)	6.24
1.337(d)-7(d)(2)	6.24
1.562-1(b)(1)	6.76
1.817-5(a)(2)	6.63
1.817-5(b)	6.58
1.817-5(b)(1)(ii)	6.59
1.817-5(b)(3)	6.61
1.817-5(c)(1)	6.58
1.817-5(c)(2)	6.62
1.817-5(d)	6.62
1.817-5(f)(3)	6.58
1.852-9	6.40
1.852-12	6.24
1.864-2	6.128
1.985-1(f)	6.111
1.988-1(b)	6.114
1.988-2(a)	6.114, 6.116
1.988-2(a)(2)	6.115
1.988-2(b)(1)	6.112
1.988-2(d)	6.117–.118
1.988-5	6.117
1.1012-1(c)(1)	6.99
1.1091-1(g)	6.100

Subject Index

